W9-BSX-087

# THE CANON LAW DIGEST FOR RELIGIOUS

# THE CANON LAW DIGEST FOR RELIGIOUS

Officially Published Documents Affecting the Code of Canon Law as Pertinent to Religious

Volume I
1917–1963

*By*

T. LINCOLN BOUSCAREN, S.J., A.M., LL.B., S.T.D.

*and*

JAMES I. O'CONNOR, S.J., A.M., S.T.L., J.C.D.

THE BRUCE PUBLISHING COMPANY
MILWAUKEE

IMPRIMI POTEST:

IOANNES R. CONNERY, S.I.
*Provincialis*
Provinciae Chicagiensis, S.I.

NIHIL OBSTAT:

JOHN A. SCHULIEN, S.T.D.
*Censor librorum*

IMPRIMATUR:

✠ WILLIAM E. COUSINS
*Archbishop of Milwaukee*
August 12, 1964



*Library of Congress Catalog Card Number: 65–16199*

# LIST OF ABBREVIATIONS

| | |
|---|---|
| AAS | *Acta Apostolicae Sedis* |
| A.E.R. | *American Ecclesiastical Review* |
| Ap. Const. | Apostolic Constitution |
| Archiv K. KR. | *Archiv für Katholisches Kirchenrecht* |
| ASS | *Acta Sanctae Sedis* |
| Cancell. | The Apostolic Chancery |
| Cod. Com. | The Pontifical Commission for the Authentic Interpretation of the Code (Code Commission) |
| *Collectanea* | *Collectanea Sacrae Congregationis de Propaganda Fide* (1907 edition, two volumes) |
| Datar. | The Apostolic Datary |
| *Fontes* | Gasparri, *Codicis Juris Canonici Fontes* |
| Homil. | *The Homiletic and Pastoral Review* |
| I.E.R. | *Irish Ecclesiastical Record* |
| Instr. | Instruction |
| J.P. | *Jus Pontificium* |
| Monit. | *Monitor Ecclesiasticus* |
| N.R.T. | *Nouvelle Revue Théologique* |
| *Periodica* | *Periodica de Re Morali, Canonica, Liturgica* |
| R.D. | *Sacrae Romanae Rotae Decisiones seu Sententiae* |
| *Resol.* | *Resolutio* |
| Rota | The Sacred Roman Rota |
| S. C. Caer. | The Sacred Congregation of Ceremonies |
| S. C. Conc. | The Sacred Congregation of the Council |
| S. C. Consist. | The Sacred Consistorial Congregation |
| S. C. Neg. Eccl. Ext. | The Sacred Congregation for Extraordinary Ecclesiastical Affairs |
| S. C. Or. | The Sacred Congregation for the Oriental Church |
| S. C. Prop. Fid. | The Sacred Congregation of Propaganda |
| S. C. Rel. | The Sacred Congregation of Religious |
| S. C. Rit. | The Sacred Congregation of Rites |
| S. C. Sacr. | The Sacred Congregation of the Sacraments |
| S. C. Sem. | The Sacred Congregation of Seminaries and Universities |
| Sec. Stat. | Office of the Papal Secretary of State |
| Signatura | The Supreme Tribunal of the Signatura |
| S. Off. | The Supreme Sacred Congregation of the Holy Office |
| S. Poen. | The Sacred Penitentiary |
| T.P. Quart. | *Theologische-Praktische Quartalschrift* |
| Zeit. K. T. | *Zeitschrift für Katholische Theologie* |

# PREFACE

The *Canon Law Digest*[1] came into existence because of the well-founded belief that all pronouncements issuing from the Holy See are worthy of study and that all priests, seminarians and others interested in canon law would be greatly helped and saved much time and energy if all such documents were available in English and in a single source.

In recent years many Sisters and Brothers have been studying the canon law pertinent to their status as religious. Consequently, they have expressed the desire to derive the same benefit of having documents pertaining to the religious life and its related apostolates in a handy form in English. While the regular edition of the *Canon Law Digest* can satisfy this desire, some religious superiors refrained from buying it or did so only somewhat reluctantly because much of the material contained in the regular edition has no relevance to the religious life and its apostolates.

Out of a wish to provide religious with those documents only which are necessary or helpful to them has been born this new specialized edition called the CANON LAW DIGEST FOR RELIGIOUS. It is a reference work which will be kept up to date according to arrangements to be announced by the publisher.

**Time Period Covered.** Although the Code of Canon Law, with very few exceptions,[2] went into effect only on Pentecost Sunday, 19 May, 1918, it was promulgated on Pentecost Sunday of the previous year, 27 May, 1917. As a result, this volume covers, in general, all available official documents from 1917 to the end of 1963.

By way of exception, a very few precode documents have been included either because of an official declaration that they still oblige even after the Code went into effect, or because they were judged useful for understanding and interpreting some special provisions of Code law.

[1] Volumes 1–3 by T. Lincoln Bouscaren, S.J.; Volumes 4–5 and supplements by T. Lincoln Bouscaren, S.J., and James I. O'Connor, S.J. All are published by The Bruce Publishing Co., Milwaukee, Wisconsin.

[2] CANON LAW DIGEST, 1, pp. 585–586.

Not reported in this work are those documents which have been rendered completely out of date by subsequent provisions, e.g., the earlier formula for the quinquennial report;[3] previous determinations of the limit-values affecting alienation and debts by religious;[4] prior faculties of the U. S. Apostolic Delegate regarding such alienations and debts;[5] etc. Anybody wishing to consult such documents will find them in the regular edition of the *Canon Law Digest*.

**Documents Found in the Acta Apostolicae Sedis.** The organ for official publication of documents issued by the Roman Pontiff, the Sacred Congregations, the Tribunals and Offices of the Holy See is the *Acta Apostolicae Sedis*. Most such documents are of pertinence to the whole Catholic Church or to a whole class of persons within it, e.g., to all religious. At times, a reply or a decision is given to a particular person or to a particular group, e.g., to a particular diocese or to a particular religious institute. A reply or decision of this kind directly binds only the party to whom it was given. Yet, the very fact that it is found in the *Acta* seems to manifest the Holy See's mind as to how the point of law at issue is to be understood and applied. For this reason all such documents are reported in this volume. All documents found in the *Acta* are identified by the letters *AAS* together with the number of the volume and page, e.g., **AAS 43–26.**

**Private Documents.** In addition to documents issued to a particular party and published in the *Acta* are many more documents which are not to be found in the Holy See's official publication but are contained in other periodicals or in books. Yet others have come to the editors of this work either directly or indirectly from the parties to whom they were given. All these documents, because they are not contained in the *Acta Apostolicae Sedis,* are designated **Private.** One exception to this general plan is the first document under canon 973; the reason for this exception is given in the note at the end of that document.

These "private" documents have no force of law in themselves and bind only those to whom they were issued (canon 17, § 3). Nevertheless, they may serve as guides to others in the understanding and application of the law.

---

[3] *Op. cit.,* 1, pp. 282–293.

[4] *Op. cit.,* 3, p. 212; 4, p. 203.

[5] *Op. cit.,* 3, p. 368; 4, p. 206.

**Arrangement of Documents.** All documents are arranged in the same order as the canons of the Code themselves and are correspondingly numbered. This work, therefore, serves as a companion to the sections of the Code of Canon Law pertinent to religious. The documents can also be found under exactly the same canon numbers in the regular edition of the *Canon Law Digest*. As a result, if one wishes to see if there are any other documents on the same canon, even though not pertaining to religious as such, or if pertinent, outdated by later documents, he or she can simply look up the canon number in the various volumes and supplements of the regular edition.

Under a given canon all documents which are reported in whole or in part are, with almost no exceptions, lined up according to the chronological sequence of the date of issuance. On the other hand, those documents which are merely referred to are placed at the end of the fully or partially reported documents and are listed alphabetically according to the key topic of the document. See, for example, the materials reported under canon 488.

**Method of Reporting Documents.** Almost always the documents are reported in full. In some instances where only part of a document directly affects religious, only that portion is provided. Rarely, because the document is not of general importance to all religious but still may be of some interest to others besides the party to whom it was given, no more will be noted than the general topic, the source of the document and, if known, a reference to an English version.

At the end of each document is indicated the source from which the original was derived.

**Annotations.** This work contains no commentary since that is not its purpose. Nevertheless, it is realized that it would be helpful if some indication were given as to where a commentary on the precise document under consideration can be found. Hence, where possible, at the end of each document, after the source indication, reference is made to one or more such commentaries. These references do not pretend to be exhaustive but serve as mere points of departure for a more thorough study of the document.

**How to Use This Work.** There are three methods for finding a document in this work. They are: 1. the canon number;

2. the date of the document; 3. the subject matter.

1. *Canon Number.* As already explained under *Arrangement of Documents* above, if it is known what canon is affected by a certain document, that document can be located simply by turning to that canon number in this volume.

2. *Date of Document.* Often a document is referred to by its date and the authority from which it proceeded. If this information is had, the document can be found by looking up the date and authority in the **Chronological Index** near the end of the volume. If it happens that the document does not appear in the chronological index of this volume, it may be that the document was considered out of date or not directly pertinent to religious and, accordingly, was not included in this collection. It can then be looked up in the chronological index of volume 5 of the regular edition whose index lists all documents reported in all five volumes.

3. *Subject Matter.* At the very end of this volume is a **General Index** arranged alphabetically according to the principal subjects treated in the various documents. Hence, the subject being investigated can be looked up in this index which will refer the reader to pages where that subject is principally taken up. This index parallels that in the regular edition of the *Canon Law Digest* so as to make it easy, if need be, for the user to pass from this specialized edition to the regular edition. As a result, for documents on many subjects as they affect religious, the general subject-heading *Religious* with its numerous subdivisions will often be the most useful starting point.

**Conclusion.** It is our hope that this time-saving and up-to-date tool will help all religious, subjects as well as superiors, to an easier and wider knowledge and understanding of canon law as it pertains to them and, as a further consequence, will enable them to be even better religious in whatever role they have to play in the apostolates of the sanctification of themselves and others, the good of their own Community and the Church, and the glory of God.

T. LINCOLN BOUSCAREN, S.J.
JAMES I. O'CONNOR, S.J.

Bellarmine School of Theology
North Aurora, Ill. 60542

# CONTENTS

# BOOK I
## GENERAL NORMS
### Canons 1–86

# BOOK I
## GENERAL NORMS
## Canons 1–86

### CANON 1

**Latin Church Bound by Certain Canons of the Oriental Code on Rites** (Pius XII, *Motu proprio,* 2 June, 1957) **AAS 49–433.**

In virtue of canon 15 of the Oriental Code on Rites and Persons, which was promulgated by a *Motu proprio* of Pope Pius XII on 2 June, 1957,[1] and went into effect on 25 March, 1958, the following canons or sections thereof are obligatory on both the clergy and the faithful of all rites, including those of the Latin rite.

Can. 5. When clerics and religious, even those who are exempt, labor in places where a rite differing from their own is the only rite or is so prevalent among the faithful that in the common opinion it is considered the only rite, they are dependent upon the local Hierarch of the said rite in what pertains to the sacred ministry and are fully subject to him.

AAS 49–433; Pius XII, Apostolic Letter, *Motu proprio,* 2 June, 1957. *Amer. Eccles. Review,* 139 (1958)–249 (Lover).

### CANON 2

**Biblico-Liturgical Vigils, Not a Strictly Liturgical Function** (S. C. Rit., 1 Apr., 1958) **Private.**

The following question was presented to the S. C. of Rites by His Excellency Bishop Francisco Miranda, President of the National Association of the Liturgical Apostolate in Spain:

---

[1] CANON LAW DIGEST, 4, p. 20.

**Question:** Can the local Ordinary permit this kind of Biblico-Liturgical or Paraliturgical Vigil to be performed in the church, and if not, can he permit it at least outside the church?

**Reply:** Since there is question of a paraliturgical function, its use is left to the prudent judgment of the Ordinary.

This function must always close with the Eucharistic Benediction.

It can never take the place of Vespers, and hence Vespers may never be replaced by these Biblico-Liturgical Vigils.

**(Private)**; S. C. Rit., 1 Apr., 1958. Private reply in Spanish by Monsignor Dante in *Ilustracion del Clero,* 51 (1958)–242, with annotations by G. Martinez de Antoñana, C.M.F.

**Declaration Regarding Particular Calendars** (S. C. Rit., 26 July, 1960) **AAS 52–730.**

Since His Holiness John XXIII, by his *motu proprio* Apostolic Letter, *Rubricarum instructum,*[1] of the 25th of July of the present year, decreed that "all whose business it is to do so shall as soon as possible see to it that diocesan and religious Calendars and *Propria* be conformed to the rule and spirit of the new revision of the rubrics and Calendar, and be approved by the Sacred Congregation of Rites," this Sacred Congregation of Rites will issue appropriate instructions for the revision of particular Calendars and the *Propria* of Offices and Masses. But in the meantime it has decided to announce the things that will have to be observed in particular calendars from the beginning of the year 1961:

1. All the provisions that are made under the title "*Variationes in Breviario et Missali Romano ad Normam Novi Codicis Rubricarum,*" are to be observed also in particular calendars.

2. In both diocesan and religious calendars, all particular feasts which are now inscribed in them are to be retained for the present.

3. The grade of those feasts should be indicated according to the norms given in the *Variationes,* nn. 1–4.

4. As regards *proper* feasts and their grade, nn. 42–46 of the new code of rubrics must be strictly observed.

---

[1] Canon Law Digest, 5, p. 24.

5. As for feasts which are to be celebrated by Religious together with the diocesan clergy in various dioceses, the prescription of n. 57 of the new code of rubrics is to be observed.

6. The *universal* feasts which, according to nn. 5 and 8 of the *Variationes,* are either reduced to a commemoration or expunged from the calendar, let them for the present be retained in the particular calendar, if they are inscribed there as feasts of the I or II class.

7. If feasts of the III class have not the proper lesson which is commonly called *"contracta,"* the indications given in n. *221 b* of the new rubrical code are to be followed.

8. The Bishop of the diocese should determine the day on which, according to nn. 362 and 364 of the new code of rubrics, the Mass for the anniversary of the election of the Bishop and the prayer for the Bishop in all the churches of the diocese shall be said.

**AAS 52–730**; S. C. Rit., 26 July, 1960. Annotations in *The Clergy Review,* 45 (1960)–641–650 (O'Connell).

## Instruction for the Revision of Particular Calendars and the Propers of Offices and Masses According to the Code of Rubrics (S. C. Rit., 14 Feb., 1961) AAS 53–168.

In order to put the Code of rubrics into practice, the Supreme Pontiff in the *Motu proprio, Rubricarum instructum,* of 25 July, 1960, decreed that "all whose business it is to do so shall as soon as possible see to it that diocesan and religious calendars and *Propria* be conformed to the rule and spirit of the new revision of the rubrics and calendar, and be approved by the Sacred Congregation of Rites."[1]

By way of a first adjustment, some norms were given in the *Declaration* of this Sacred Congregation, to be observed since 1961.[2] It remains to provide appropriate instructions for the revision of particular calendars and the *Propria* of Offices and Masses *according to the rule and spirit* of the new rubrics, as stated in the said *Declaration.*

---

[1] *Motu proprio,* n. 6; AAS 52–595; reported in *Canon Law Digest,* V. 5, p. 26.

[2] 26 July, 1960; AAS 52–730; reported in this volume, p. 4.

## CHAPTER I — General Norms

1. In the Code of rubrics certain general principles stand out, which are to be observed also in the calendars and *Propria* of Offices and Masses, both diocesan and religious, namely:

*a*) the *Proprium de Tempore,* which celebrates the entire mystery of the Redemption, has preeminence over all other Offices and Masses;

*b*) the principal feasts of the Blessed Virgin Mary and of the Saints for the universal Church, are to be preferred to particular feasts;

*c*) particular feasts should be arranged and celebrated according to the importance of each;

*d*) the requirements of simplicity, right order, and pastoral care should be considered.

2. Although it is proper that every diocese have its calendar and *Proprium* of Offices and Masses, yet it is sometimes advisable to have calendars and *Propria* for a whole province, region, or nation, or even for a large territory, prepared by collaboration of those concerned. Similarly, this principle may be applied to religious calendars for several provinces of the same civil territory.

3. The work of revision, as prescribed by the *Motu proprio* (n. 6), should be done "as soon as possible."

4. For the revision of the calendars and *Propria* the Ordinaries should choose men who are familiar with liturgy, history, and hagiography, so as to do the work in a competent manner.

5. Particular calendars and the *Propria* of Offices and Masses are to be sent to this Sacred Congregation in three neat copies, with one copy also of the preceding calendar and *Proprium* of Offices and Masses. Moreover when the whole work is sent:

*a*) there should be a brief but clear statement of the reasons for each of the changes that have been made, especially if they are at variance with the norms of this Instruction;

*b*) also, if there are new Offices and Masses, there should be an indication of which parts are taken from Offices and Masses already approved, and which are newly composed.

## CHAPTER II — Number and Extension of Feasts

6. The particular feasts which are to be inscribed in the calendars and which are called *ipso iure proper,* are listed in the Code of rubrics, nn. 41–46.

The number of feasts designated as *by indult* (Codex n. 47) should be reasonably limited; for keeping old ones or introducing new ones, there should be some special reason.

7. In preparing or revising a diocesan or religious calendar, the provisions of numbers 43 *d* and 46 *e* of the rubrical Code concerning the insertion of feasts of Saints or Blessed in particular calendars should be observed. Only those feasts of Saints or Blessed should be adopted or retained which have some *special* relation to the diocese or Institute, and the liturgical grade assigned to them should correspond to that peculiar relationship (cf. nn. 16–20 below).

8. Feasts which were introduced in earlier times because of some political regime or particular devotion, but which now have only a very slight relation or none at all to the diocese or Institute, should be expunged.

9. There may be other feasts which, because of changed boundaries, are now strictly proper to only a part of a certain diocese or nation or territory; such feasts should be celebrated only in the places where they are strictly proper.

10. Feasts which are celebrated in honor of some Saint or Blessed because of their relics, according to n. 45 *c* and *d* of the Code of rubrics, are to be kept with their corresponding grade only in that church or oratory where the body (and not merely a relic, even a distinguished one) of that Saint or Blessed is kept; but such feasts are not to be retained in the calendar of the entire diocese or Institute, except on some other title.

11. Let it be a general principle that a Saint or Mystery is to have but *one* feast. Exceptions, however, are admitted, and are even allowed in the universal calendar, namely when there is question of celebrating a truly singular fact or relation concerning the same Mystery or the same Saint: this can occur in feasts of the Translation, or Finding, or Patronage, and the like.

But hereafter only the principal Patron, Titular, and Founder can be honored with more than one feast. Feasts of this sort which are secondary, if they be not suppressed, are to have merely a commemoration.

12. Periodic remembrances of the same Saint or Mystery by an Office and Mass, or by way of commemoration, if there are any such, are to be suppressed.

13. There is no objection to two Saints or Blessed other than Martyrs, or several Martyrs, being celebrated with one feast, if there are special reasons for it; in which case also the Common of several Confessors, Pontiffs or non-Pontiffs, or of several Virgins or non-Virgins, may be used.

14. In diocesan calendars which have several Saints or Blessed from among Martyrs or Bishops of earlier times, about whom little is historically known except their names, it would be well to expunge these feasts; but a feast of all the Martyrs or Bishops of the diocese should be established, and a separate particular feast should be celebrated only for the more illustrious Martyrs and Bishops who are historically certain.

15. In religious calendars the Saints or Blessed of that Institute should receive appropriate worship. But when an Institute has many Saints and Blessed, care should be taken not to burden excessively the calendar of the Institute as a whole. Hence:

*a*) there may be in the first place a feast of all the Saints and Blessed of the Institute;

*b*) only those Saints or Blessed who are of special importance to the whole Institute should be celebrated with a special feast;

*c*) for other Saints and Blessed, according to their importance in the history of the Institute, there may be either a feast in their respective province, with a commemoration in the whole Institute; or, in the case of Blessed of minor importance, a feast in the place where their relics are preserved, with a commemoration only in their province.

## CHAPTER III — The Grade of Feasts

16. The feasts which are to be inscribed as of I or II class in particular calendars are expressly mentioned in the rubrical Code, nn. 42–46.

17. Besides the feasts of the I or II class in the universal Church, and proper feasts which are entitled to that grade ac-

cording to the rubrics, only very few feasts of those classes are to be admitted in the various calendars.

In order that this be allowed, there must be *altogether special* reasons, liturgical, historical, or pastoral.

18. From the text and spirit of the Code of rubrics it is clearly seen that the III class is the ordinary grade which is perfectly suitable for Saints and Blessed or Mysteries and Titles which have no right to a higher grade according to n. 17 above, or for which a simple commemoration, as provided in nn. 19 and 20 is not sufficient.

19. The commemoration is not to be entirely neglected; indeed it is of great importance in the make-up of the calendar. The commemoration is designed to afford some relief to the universal or particular calendars which are so crowded with liturgical celebrations that sometimes it becomes impossible to celebrate some of the feasts of the universal Church. Hence a reasonable and appropriate use of the commemoration is recommended.

20. Often enough, for an *entire* diocese, region, province (ecclesiastical, religious or civil), nation, or Institute, a commemoration or a feast of the III class is quite sufficient, whereas for a *specific* place, diocese, province, or region, a higher grade seems more appropriate. A judicious use of this distinction will somewhat alleviate the burden of particular celebrations and will adapt the calendars better to particular needs and niceties.

## CHAPTER IV — The Date of Feasts

21. On this matter the provisions of the rubrical Code, nn. 59–62 are to be followed. However, when possible:

*a*) proper feasts which are observed also in the universal Church should be celebrated on the same day on which they occur in the universal calendar;

*b*) proper feasts of the Saints, which are not in the universal calendar, should be celebrated on their natal day.

22. Dates which usually occur during Lent or within the octave of Easter, and also the days from the 17th to the 23rd of December, should be kept free from new particular feasts; as for particular feasts which are already assigned to these days, let them generally be observed by way of a commemoration, as is done for universal feasts, unless in the case of some feast

of special importance it be thought proper to transfer it to another time.

23. As regards feasts which formerly were permanently assigned to some Sunday:

*a*) if they are feasts of our Lord of the I Class, assigned to a Sunday of the II class, nothing is to be changed (Code, n 17 *e*);

*b*) if they are in the universal calendar, they are to be celebrated on the day to which they are assigned there;

*c*) if they are not in the universal calendar, any other suitable day may be chosen.

24. Particular feasts of the Blessed Virgin Mary which were formerly assigned to the 31st of May should now be assigned to the 8th of that same month.

25. According to n. 100 of the rubrical Code, feasts of the universal Church of the III class in occurrence with a particular feast are permanently either commemorated or omitted. However:

*a*) a universal feast of the III class in honor of a Saint who was of great importance for the whole Church, should be celebrated on the proper day also in particular calendars; and a particular feast of the III class occurring on the same day should be displaced to the nearest day that is free;

*b*) if a feast of the universal Church of the III class, which is of great importance, occurs with a particular feast of a higher class, the universal feast should be transferred;

*c*) if a particular feast of the I class, outside its proper day, was assigned to a day on which the universal calendar afterward admitted a feast of the II class, the particular feast should be transferred to another day.

26. In sending in the *Propria,* the natal day of the Saints should always be indicated, as well as the day on which each feast has hitherto been celebrated, and the reasons why that day has been retained or changed.

## CHAPTER V — Certain Specific Particular Feasts

### A) *Feasts of Patrons*

27. A principal Patron or a secondary or nonprincipal one "duly constituted" refers only to a Patron *in the proper sense,* that is, a Saint (never a Blessed) who has been *formally* chosen

and declared a Patron according to the ancient practice of the Sacred Congregation of Rites, or who has been accepted according to an immemorial tradition: only such a Patron is entitled to the special liturgical celebration prescribed by the rubrics.

28. The *principal* Patron of any place or diocese, etc., should regularly be only one; sometimes another Saint can be added as *equally principal* Patron, with the same rights and observances as the principal Patron. Similarly not more than two *secondary* Patrons are admitted for any place, diocese, etc.

29. Patrons, principal or secondary, who were formerly constituted for some regime or kingdom which no longer exists, and Patrons formerly chosen because of some extraordinary circumstances, such as pestilence, war, or other calamity, or by reason of some special devotion which is now abandoned, are henceforth not to be liturgically celebrated as such.

30. Only the Sacred Congregation of Rites can grant that Patrons of a religious Institute or province have the liturgical rights of Patrons, unless they have been thus liturgically honored from time immemorial. But for Patrons of individual religious houses, if there are any such, this sort of celebration is not allowed.

31. Patrons of any other kind, besides those mentioned in the preceding numbers, are to be considered Patrons *in a wide sense,* that is, presented merely out of devotion, without any liturgical privileges.

### B) *Feasts which Are Known as "Feasts of Devotion"*

32. Such feasts, which since the Middle Ages have passed from private devotion into the public worship of the Church, have grown too numerous in particular calendars.

Consequently, let feasts of this sort be retained in the calendars only if really special reasons require it.

33. Of these feasts the following, which for the most part are already alluded to in other feasts or at other times of the year, or are related only to some particular place, should be expunged from the calendars:

The translation of the Holy House of the Blessed Virgin Mary (10 December);

The expectancy of the Blessed Virgin Mary (18 December);

The betrothal of the Blessed Virgin Mary to Saint Joseph (23 January);

The flight of Our Lord Jesus Christ into Egypt (17 February);

The prayer of Our Lord Jesus Christ (Tuesday after Septuagesima Sunday);

The Commemoration of the Passion of Our Lord Jesus Christ (Tuesday after Sexagesima Sunday);

The Crown of Thorns of Our Lord Jesus Christ (Friday after Ash Wednesday);

The sacred Spear and Nails of Our Lord Jesus Christ (Friday after the I Sunday of Lent);

The Holy Shroud of Our Lord Jesus Christ (Friday after the II Sunday of Lent);

The Five Wounds of Our Lord Jesus Christ (Friday after the III Sunday of Lent);

The Precious Blood of Our Lord Jesus Christ (Friday after the IV Sunday of Lent);

The Eucharistic Heart of Jesus (Thursday after the octave of Corpus Christi);

The Humility of the Blessed Virgin Mary (17 July);

The Purity of the Blessed Virgin Mary (16 October).

These feasts may be retained if they have a special relationship to some particular place.

The feast of Saint Philomena, Virgin and Martyr, is to be expunged from all calendars.

### C) *Feasts which Are Expunged from the Universal Calendar*

34. As regards feasts which in virtue of n. 8 of the *Changes in the Roman Breviary and Missal* in accordance with the rubrical Code have been expunged from the universal calendar, the following more specific provisions are made for particular calendars:

*a*) the feast of Saint Anacletus, on whatever ground and in whatever grade it is celebrated, is transferred to April 26th, under its right name, Saint Cletus;

*b*) the feast of Saint Vitalis is transferred to November 4th, together with Saint Agricola;

*c*) the feast of the Chair of Saint Peter is to be celebrated only on February 22nd;

*d*) it is well that the feasts mentioned in n. 8, *b, c, d, g,* and *h,* even though they be considered in some place as the principal Patron or Title of the church, be transferred to the principal feasts, namely:

the feast of the Finding of the Holy Cross, from May 3rd to September 14th;

the feast of Saint John before the Latin Gate, from May 6th to December 27th;

the feast of the Apparition of Saint Michael Archangel from May 8th to September 29th;

the feast of Saint Peter in Chains, from August 1st to June 29th;

the feast of the Finding of Saint Stephen, from August 3rd to December 26th.

These feasts may, however, be kept on the day on which they have hitherto been celebrated if *altogether special* reasons require it, and unless it be considered sufficient to assign to that day only the external solemnity, as provided in the rubrical Code, nn. 359 and 360. A special indult must be obtained to have either the feast or the external solemnity inscribed in the calendar.

## CHAPTER VI — The Text of Offices

35. In preparing or revising the historical lessons of feasts of whatever class, the following should be observed:

*a*) they should be brief and discreet; each lesson should be no longer than an ordinary lesson of the Breviary, most of which are of not more than 120 words;

*b*) the style should be improved and made easier;

*c*) commonplace should be avoided; false or inappropriate passages should be deleted or corrected; if historical data be entirely or almost entirely lacking, lessons from the Common should be assigned, or some other more appropriate text from the Fathers should be chosen.

36. Historical truth should be attended to not only in the lessons but also in the antiphons, responsories, hymns, and other parts of the Office, if there are any such proper parts; otherwise those parts should be taken from the Common.

37. In feasts of the III class:

*a*) if Matins has proper antiphons, the provisions of nn. 40

and 41 of the *Variationes* should be observed for the first and second lessons;

*b*) if Matins has no proper antiphons, the first and second lessons are to be taken from the current Scripture, unless there are *strictly proper* lessons, that is, directly concerning the Mystery or Saint: in which case the responsories also are taken from the feast, that is, either proper or *de Communi;*

*c*) if only the responsories are proper, the lessons are said from the current Scripture, with the responsories of the feast, according to n. 42 of the *Variationes.*

38. In feasts of the III class, the third lesson of the single Nocturne is always of the feast, and:

*a*) if there was only one historical lesson or a "contracted" one, that is kept;

*b*) if there were two or three historical lessons, one new one should be composed;

*c*) if there was a lesson, only the former fourth lesson, that is the first of the second Nocturne is to be kept, or some other appropriate text from the sermons of the Fathers should be chosen.

39. As regards the hymns:

*a*) if there are four different hymns, all on the life of the Saint, and the feast is not of the I class, the first (formerly assigned to I Vespers) is prefixed, without its conclusion, to the hymn of Matins; if they can be shortened one or two stanzas should be omitted; if the two cannot be joined, being of different meter or not historical, let one of them be dropped;

*b*) if there are two or three hymns, let them be suitably distributed; if the feast is of the I class, the same hymn should ordinarily be used for both Vespers.

## CHAPTER VII — Arranging the Offices and Masses

### A) *General Norms for the Offices*

40. After the title of the feast, its grade should be indicated (I, II or III class, or a Commemoration).

41. The nomenclature of the Hours should be uniformly as follows: "Ad I Vesperas," "Ad Matutinum," "Ad Laudes," "Ad

II Vesperas," etc. The Nocturnes should be indicated thus: "In I Nocturno," etc.

42. The chapter and verse of the book of Scripture should be indicated before each lesson.

43. The rubrics referring to the doxology of the hymns are to be deleted; for example, "Haec conclusio numquam mutatur." "Sic concluduntur hymni eiusdem metri," and the like.

44. In the use of capital and lower case letters, the style of the rubrical Code is to be followed.

45. In all Offices, at Lauds and Vespers, under the respective titles, there should always appear, even if they are taken from the Common, the verse, the antiphons for the *Benedictus* and the *Magnificat,* and the prayer.

Before the other Hours there should be a title, if there are proper parts or if they are repeated for convenience.

46. If a commemoration of a Saint has to be made, there should be, after the oration of the day, a rubric always in this form: "Et fit commemoratio S. ——"; and then, preferably *in extenso,* the antiphon, verse, and prayer.

To indicate a commemoration *de Tempore,* the rubrics now in the Breviary are to be retained.

### B) *Particular Norms for the Various Offices*

47. In feasts of the I class everything is to be arranged as it is now in the Breviaries and *Propria,* except what may be changed by the rubrical Code or by this Instruction.

48. In feasts of the II class, the I Vespers:

*a*) are to be given with all the proper parts for feasts of Our Lord which may occur on a Sunday of the II class, under this title: "Ad I Vesperas, quando festum occurrit in dominica vel celebratur gradu I classis";

*b*) likewise the antiphons of psalms or the hymn, if there are proper ones, should be given under this title: "Ad I Vesperas, sicubi festum celebratur gradu I classis";

*c*) the I Vespers are to be expunged from all feasts of the II class; but the verse and antiphon at the *Magnificat,* if there are proper ones, are to be placed in the II Vespers under the rubric "Ad I Vesperas, sicubi dicendae occurrunt."

49. If, *in feasts of the III class,* at Matins, the invitatory

and hymn are given in full, there should be added after the hymn the title "Ad Nocturnum."

50. In feasts which have proper antiphons at Lauds, after the first antiphon there should be the rubric "Psalmi de dominica"; if the Office is celebrated from Advent to Pentecost, the words "1° loco" should be added.

51. *In feasts of the II class,* if Lauds are given *in extenso* at least from the chapter, there should be at the end the rubric "Ad Horas minores antiphona et psalmi de feria currenti." But in feasts of Our Lord which may occur on a Sunday of the II class, the rubric at the end of Lauds should be "Ad horas minores antiphona et psalmi de currenti die." At the end of Vespers there should appear the rubric "Completorium de dominica."

52. In feasts of the III class having proper antiphons at Lauds and Vespers, the rubric at the end of Lauds should be "Ad horas minores antiphona et psalmi de feria currenti," and at the end of Vespers, "Completorium de feria."

53. On days when a commemoration of a Saint occurs in the feria, after the indication of the day and the Saint, there should be the word "Commemoratio" and the title "Ad Laudes"; and then, preferably *in extenso,* the antiphon, verse and oration.

### C) *The Arrangement of Masses*

54. In Masses which are printed in full, there should be for the sake of clearness a space of at least one line between the following parts:

*a*) between the oration (or orations) and the Epistle;

*b*) between the gradual (or tract) and the Gospel;

*c*) between the secret and the antiphon at the Communion.

55. The following terms should be used: "Antiphona ad Introitum, antiphona ad Offertorium, antiphona ad Communionem."

56. The orations which belong to a commemoration, and the parts which are used only for votive Masses, should be so placed as to be indented by the space of a letter or two with reference to the proper texts of the Mass.

57. The greatest care should be taken to avoid the necessity of turning the page in the course of an oration, secret, post-

communion, or other prayer which the celebrant must recite with hands extended.

58. On days when a commemoration of a Saint occurs in the feria, after the indication of the day and the Saint, there should be the word "Commemoratio"; and then an indication of the Mass that is to be said, either by a reference to the Common or by giving the proper Mass or the proper parts of it.

## CHAPTER VIII — Concerning Privileges and Indults in Liturgical Matters

### A) *Privileges and Indults in General*

59. Privileges and indults contrary to the rubrical Code are revoked (*Motu proprio,* n. 3). However, if any Ordinary finds it necessary to renew one or another of these privileges and indults, let him present a petition stating the reasons which seem to favor it.

60. Privileges and indults which are not contrary to the rubrical Code remain in effect; but it will be necessary to adapt these also to the rule and spirit of the Code, so that they may be followed with greater security.

61. Consequently every Ordinary should take care to send a list of such liturgical privileges together with the calendar and the *Proprium* of the Offices and Masses to this Sacred Congregation for appropriate revision and renewal, annexing a copy of the preceding grant.

62. It is further recommended that in printing the *Propria* there be added a list of the liturgical privileges, so that it be available to all who use the *Proprium.*

### B) *Privileges and Indults regarding Votive Masses*

63. Indults heretofore granted for votive Masses for external solemnities and for sanctuaries and pious places remain in effect, but they will have to be exactly accommodated to the prescriptions of the rubrical Code (nn. 358 *c,* 359, 361 and 373–377).

64. Other indults for votive Masses, in whatsoever manner or by whatsoever authority they were granted, are abrogated by n. 3 of the *Motu proprio, Rubricarum instructum.*

65. Indults for votive Masses will be granted or renewed only for special reasons of public necessity or public devotion.

Such votive Masses, if they are granted:

*a*) are ranked as of the III class;

*b*) are forbidden during the entire time of Advent, Lent, and the Passion;

*c*) only one or two may be for the same day.

His Holiness Pope John XXIII in the Audience granted to the undersigned Cardinal Prefect of the Sacred Congregation of Rites on the 8th of February 1961, deigned to approve this Instruction in all respects and decreed that it be observed by all concerned.

All things to the contrary notwithstanding.

Given at Rome from the office of the Sacred Congregation of Rites, the 14th of February 1961.

AAS 53–168; S. C. Rit., Instruction, 14 Feb., 1961. Annotations in *Ephemerides Liturgicae,* 75 (1961)–154–173 (Braga).

### Second Class Votive Mass of Our Lord Allowed on Second Class Sunday (S. C. Rit., 20 July, 1961) Private.

The Very Reverend John Humphreys, Ordo editor for the Archdiocese of Birmingham, England, requested from the Sacred Congregation of Rites, a solution to the following doubt:

In view of n. 317 of the *Code of Rubrics*[1] in conjunction with n. 355, may a second class votive Mass of our Lord (e.g., the Mass of the Blessed Sacrament on the occasion of Forty Hours) be celebrated on Sundays of the second class?

**Reply.** *In the affirmative.*

(Private); S. C. Rit., 20 July, 1961, Prot. N. B. 52/961; reported in *Ephemerides Liturgicae,* 77 (1963)–188 with annotations on p. 190.

### Female Permitted to Read Aloud the Epistle and Gospel in Vernacular at Mass (S. C. Prop. Fid., 16 Dec., 1961) Private.

On the 9th of November last, His Excellency, the Most Rev. Maximilian de Furstenberg, Apostolic Delegate to Australia, New

[1] Reported in CANON LAW DIGEST, 5, pp. 27–120.

Zealand, and Oceania, submitted the following question to this S. Congregation of Propaganda Fide on behalf of His Lordship, the Most Rev. Launcelot Goody, Bishop of Bunbury:

"Is it permitted in a community of Religious, or at a Mass when only females are present, or at a school Mass, when both boys and girls are present, for a female Religious, or a school-girl to read the Epistle or the Gospel or both in the vernacular during a Dialogue Mass?"

In reply I wish to inform Your Excellency that this Sacred Congregation, after mature deliberation, answers: "Yes."

**(Private)**; S. C. Prop. Fid., 16 Dec., 1961, Prot. No. 5338/61; transcribed from *The Australasian Catholic Record,* 39 (1962)–98.

## Nodeless Chalices Permitted (S. C. Rit., 28 Feb., 1962) Private.

**Petition.** The Reverend Romuald Bissonnette, rector of the Pontifical Canadian College, in the name of His Eminence, the Ordinary of Montreal, asked this Sacred Congregation whether chalices without a node below the cup may be consecrated.

**Reply.** The Sacred Congregation of Rites, after mature consideration of everything, replied: "It suffices that the priest can satisfactorily hold the chalice with his thumb and index finger joined."

All things to the contrary notwithstanding.

**(Private)**; S. C. Rit., 28 Feb., 1962, Prot. No. M. 21/962; copy of the original rescript kindly sent us by the Rev. John McConnell, Vice-Chancellor of Montreal.

## Holy Week: Nuns May Receive Communion on Good Friday Even if no Services in Their Church (S. C. Rit., 1 Feb., 1963) Private.

With the former order of Holy Week restored, there was reintroduced the ancient custom whereby all who desire to do so and who are properly prepared, may go to Holy Communion on Good Friday but only during the solemn liturgical action in the afternoon. Excepted are the sick who are in danger of death (cf., Instruction, 16 Nov., 1955, n. 19; Ordinances and Declarations, 1 Feb., 1957, n. 18).[1]

[1] Reported respectively in CANON LAW DIGEST, 4, pp. 59 and 66.

However, in many churches and oratories of nuns living in cloister, the said solemn liturgical action cannot be performed because of the scarcity of priests, although a priest could be had for at least the distribution of Communion to them. This situation the nuns have frequently reported to this Sacred Congregation and have besought the favor whereby they would be allowed to receive the Body of Christ on that sacred day outside of the aforesaid solemn liturgical action.

Our Holy Father, Pope John XXIII, at the suggestion of the undersigned Cardinal Prefect and having attended to the special circumstances of the case, has graciously granted that on Good Friday Holy Communion may be distributed to nuns bound by the law of cloister, outside of the solemn liturgical action whenever this action cannot be carried out in their churches or oratories. However, this distribution may be done only in the afternoon hours.

All things to the contrary notwithstanding.

**(Private)**; S. C. Rit., 1 Feb., 1963, Prot. N. R. 4/963; copy of the original rescript kindly sent us by the Rev. Richard F. Smith, S.J. Annotations in *Review for Religious,* 22 (1963)–377–380 (Frison) where it is observed that this is a general rescript, even if it is not later published in AAS.

**Constitution on the Sacred Liturgy** (Conc. Vat. II, 4 Dec., 1963) **AAS 56–97.**

From this constitution are cited the following sections which pertain directly to religious as religious. The complete text of this document is available in the regular edition of CANON LAW DIGEST.

15. Professors who teach the sacred liturgy in seminaries, religious houses of study, and theological faculties must be well trained for their work in institutes which make a specialty of this subject.

16. The sacred Liturgy in seminaries and religious houses of study is to be regarded as one of the necessary and important courses, and in theological faculties as among the principal ones; it is to be taught in its theological and historical aspect, and also from the spiritual, pastoral, and juridical standpoints. Moreover the teachers of other subjects, especially of dogmatic the-

ology, sacred Scripture, and spiritual and pastoral theology, should take care to bring out, in connection with the intrinsic exigencies of each subject, the mystery of Christ and the history of salvation in such a way that their relation to the liturgy and the unity of priestly training be made perfectly clear.

17. Clerical students in seminaries and religious houses of study should be given a liturgical formation in their spiritual life, not only through appropriate guidance which will enable them to understand sacred rites and to take part in them wholeheartedly, but also by actually celebrating the sacred mysteries and by other exercises of piety which breathe the spirit of the sacred Liturgy. They should likewise learn to observe liturgical regulations so that life in seminaries and religious institutes be deeply influenced by the liturgical spirit.

18. Priests, both secular and religious, who are already at work in the Lord's vineyard are to be helped in every appropriate way to understand ever more fully what it is that they are doing when they perform sacred rites, and to live the liturgical life and communicate it to the faithful under their care.

55. That more perfect form of participation in the Mass whereby, after the priest's Communion, the faithful receive the Body of the Lord from the same Sacrifice, is strongly recommended.

Without prejudice to the dogmatic principles laid down by the Council of Trent,[40] Communion under both species may be granted to clerics and religious and also to the laity, when the Bishops think fit, in the cases which will be defined by the Apostolic See; as for example, to the newly ordained in the Mass of their sacred ordination, to the newly professed in the Mass of their religious profession, and to the newly baptized in the Mass which follows their Baptism.

80. The rite for the Consecration of Virgins, which is in the Roman Pontifical is to be revised.

Moreover a rite for religious profession and renovation of vows shall be drawn up, which should conduce to a greater unity,

---

[40] Session XXI, 16 July, 1562. Doctrine on Communion under both Species, chap. 1–3; *Concilium Tridentinum, Diariorum, Actorum, Epistolarum, Tractatuum nova collectio,* ed. Goerresiana, t. VIII (Freiburg im Br., 1919), 698–699.

sobriety, and dignity, and which shall be used, in the absence of particular law to the contrary, by those who make their profession or renovation at Mass.

Religious profession will preferably be made within the Mass.

95. Communities which are bound to choir duty, in addition to the conventual Mass, are obliged to celebrate the Divine Office in choir every day. In particular:

a) Orders of Canons, of Monks and of Nuns, and of other Regulars, who are bound to choir duty by law or by their constitutions, must celebrate the entire Office;

b) Cathedral or collegiate Chapters are obliged to celebrate those parts of the Office which are made obligatory for them by general or particular law;

c) All members of the above Communities who are either in major Orders or solemnly professed, excepting those known as *conversi,* are bound to recite individually those canonical Hours which they did not perform in choir.

98. The members of any Institute which belongs to the states of perfection, who according to their constitutions perform any part of the Divine Office, are thereby performing the public prayer of the Church.

They likewise perform the public prayer of the Church if they recite any small Office, provided it be drawn up after the manner of the Divine Office and be duly approved.

101. § 2. For monastic nuns and for members of Institutes of the states of perfection, both men who are not clerics and women, the competent Superior can give the permission to use the vernacular in celebrating the Office, even in choir, provided the translation is one that has been approved.

115. Great importance is to be attached to the teaching and practice of music in seminaries, in the novitiates and houses of study of religious of both sexes, and in other Catholic institutions and schools. In order to secure this instruction, the masters who are to teach sacred Music must be most thoroughly prepared.

It is recommended that, where it can be done, higher institutes of sacred Music be established.

Composers of music and singers, especially boys, must also be given a genuine liturgical training.

129. During their philosophical and theological studies, clerics should be taught the history and development of sacred Art and

the sound principles which should govern its productions, so that they may appreciate and preserve the venerable monuments of the Church and be able to give proper advice to artists in the production of their works.

AAS 56–97; Conc. Vat. II, Constitution on the Sacred Liturgy, 4 Dec., 1963.

## Some Provisions of the Constitution on the Sacred Liturgy Take Effect from 16 February, 1964 (Paul VI, Apostolic Letter *Motu proprio,* 25 Jan., 1964) AAS 56–139.

From this *Motu proprio* are cited the following sections which pertain directly to religious as religious. The complete text of this document is available in the regular edition of the CANON LAW DIGEST.

I) In connection with the prescriptions of art. 15, 16 and 17, on the liturgical instruction to be given in seminaries, schools of religious Sodalities, and theological Faculties, We desire that in those same institutions the *rationes studiorum* be prepared even now, so that those prescriptions may be diligently observed from the beginning of the next scholastic year.

VI) Although the Divine Office is not yet revised and restored as provided in art. 89, We now give permission to those who are not bound to choir duty, so that from the expiration of the suspension period they may omit the Hour of Prime and choose among the other little Hours the one which corresponds most closely with the hour of the day.

In giving this permission We are quite confident that sacred ministers will be sufficiently careful not to grow remiss in their devotion, so that, if they have diligently performed the duty of one of their priestly offices for the love of God, they may be supposed to remain mentally united to Him for the entire day.

VIII) Concerning the recitation of this same Divine Office, We declare that the members of any Institute, who profess religious perfection and who according to their rules recite either some parts of the Divine Office or some little Office which is composed after the manner of the Divine Office and duly approved, are to be considered as praying publicly with the Church.[7]

---

[7] Cf. Constitution, art. 98.

IX) Because art. 101 of the Constitution, for those who are bound to recite the Divine Office, grants the faculty, in various ways for various classes of persons, to use the vernacular instead of the Latin language, We wish to make it clear that these various popular translations must be drawn up and approved by the competent ecclesiastical territorial authority, as provided in art. 36, §§ 3 and 4; and that the acts of this authority, according to art. 36, § 3, must be duly approved and confirmed by the Apostolic See. We order that this be always observed whenever any liturgical Latin text is translated by the said authority into the vernacular.

XI) Finally, We wish it to be understood that, aside from the liturgical matters which by the present Apostolic Letter We have either changed or ordered to become effective in advance, the regulation of the sacred Liturgy depends solely on the authority of the Church: that is, it depends on this Apostolic See and, as may be provided by law, on the Bishops; and therefore no other person, not even a priest, may add, remove, or change anything in the liturgy on his own authority.[8]

**AAS 56–139**; Paul VI, Apostolic Letter *Motu proprio,* 25 Jan., 1964.

---

**Little Office of the Blessed Virgin:** *Te Deum.* S. C. Rit., 2 May, 1924; (AAS 16–248), *Periodica,* 13 (1925)–118 (Pauwels).

## CANON 6

**Decree Regarding Religious in Military Service, Not Revoked** (S. C. Rel., 15 July, 1919) **AAS 11–321.**

The Decree of the Sacred Congregation of Religion, 1 Jan., 1911, *de religiosis servitio militari adstrictis,* was not revoked by the Code, since it was a particular and temporary provision.

**AAS 11–321**; S. C. Rel. 15 July, 1919.
*Irish E.R.,* 14 (1919)–172.

## CANON 10

**Vows Pronounced Before Code: Dismissal** (Cod. Com., 16 Oct., 1919) **AAS 11–476.**

Simple vows of religion, which are perpetual as far as the

[8] Cf. Constitution, art. 22, § 1 and 22, § 3.

individual pronouncing them is concerned, and which were pronounced before the promulgation of the Code, in religious societies of men or women having solemn vows, are to be governed, as regards the manner of dismissal and its effects, by the law as it stood before the Code.

AAS 11–476; Cod. Com., 16 Oct., 1919, 2.
*J.P.*, 3 (1923)–9.

## CANON 17

**Replies of Code Commission** (Cod. Com., 9 Dec., 1917) **AAS 10–77.**

The Code Commission itself, on 9 Dec., 1917, decided that replies should be given only to questions proposed by Ordinaries, or by major Superiors of religious Orders or Congregations, and not to those proposed by private individuals, unless this were done through their Ordinary.

AAS 10–77; Cod. Com., 9 Dec., 1917.
*Irish E.R.*, 11 (1918)–342.

## CANON 33

**Regional Time, Permitted Provided It Is Legal** (Cod. Com., 10 Nov., 1925) **AAS 17–582.**

The Code Commission was asked:

Whether, everywhere on earth, in the cases mentioned in c. 33, § 1, a person may follow regional time (*tempus vulgo zonarium*).

**Reply.** In the affirmative, provided that time is legal.

AAS 17–582; Cod. Com., 10 Nov., 1925, I.
*Periodica*, 14 (1926)–178; *N.R.T.*, 53 (1926)–225; *J.P.*, 6 (1926)–5; *T.P. Quart.*, 79 (1926)–165.

**Choosing Different Times for Formally Different Actions** (Code Com., 29 May, 1947) **AAS 39–373.**

The Code Commission was asked:

I. Whether, after one method of computing time has been chosen, this can be changed, in virtue of canon 33, § 1, in formally different actions.

**Reply.** In the affirmative.

II. Whether the three Masses celebrated on Christmas night are formally different actions.

**Reply.** In the negative.

**AAS 39–373**; Code Commission, 29 May, 1947.

Cf. *Periodica,* 36 (1947)–334 (Aguirre); *Commentarium pro Religiosis,* 27 (1948)–35 (Gutiérrez).

## CANON 53

**Roman Agents Can Obtain General Authorization to Notify Clients in the Name of the S. C. of Religious, That Their Rescripts Are Granted** (S. C. Rel., 2 May, 1955) **Private.**

A Rescript given by the S. C. of Religious, 2 May, 1955 (Prot. N. 8640/55), is as follows:

**The Petition.** J. S., agent in Rome for the Dioceses of Spain, prostrate at the feet of Your Holiness, humbly states the following:

It often happens that among the matters which this Petitioner presents to the Sacred Congregation of Religious, some are rather urgent and require an early reply, which the Ordinaries not infrequently request by telegraph.

In these cases the practice has arisen, as we have heard, for the agents, as soon as they receive the Rescript, to telegraph to the Ordinaries that the favor is granted; and the Ordinaries, satisfied with this notification, proceed to execute the Rescript.

Since this procedure does not seem to conform entirely to the letter at least of canon 53 of the Code of Canon Law, the Petitioner humbly prays that in cases such as these, in so far as any permission is needed, the Ordinaries may proceed to execute the Rescript, when they receive such notice from the Petitioner.

**The Rescript.** In virtue of faculties granted by His Holiness, the S. C. of Religious, in view of the facts stated in the petition, graciously grants the favor as requested, for three years, observing the provisions of law. All things to the contrary notwithstanding.

Given at Rome, 2 May, 1955.

**(Private)**; S. C. Rel., 2 May, 1955. Reported in *Commentarium pro Religiosis,* 34 (1955)–291, with annotations by Gutiérrez.

NOTE: In other words, as Gutiérrez points out, an agent or Procurator, though recognized by the Sacred Congregation as the authorized representative of his clients, is not by that very fact the authorized representative of the Sacred Congregation, so as to be entitled to send a message *"auctoritate rescribentis."* Such a Rescript as the above, however, authorizes him to do so regularly for the duration of the indult.

## CANON 66

### Quinquennial Faculties of Local Ordinaries: Formula III-B (S. C. Consist., 12 Sept., 1957) Private.

Following is the formula (III-B)[1] of faculties given to local Ordinaries in all of Europe with the exception of Belgium, France, Italy, Portugal and Spain (Suso Mayer, O.S.B.: *Neueste Kirchen Rechts Sammlung,* vol. 4, p. 48).

In accord with the *Motu proprio, Post datam,* of 20 April, 1923,[2] our Holy Father, Pius XI, by divine Providence, Pope, by this letter from the Sacred Consistorial Congregation, graciously grants that, from the date given below until the end of 1962 when the law requires that the diocesan report be made, the Ordinary may use the faculties listed by the respective Sacred Congregations and contained in this schedule.

### 4. Faculties From the S. C. for Religious

1. To dispense from illegitimate birth for entrance into religion, in as far as such dispensation is made necessary by the constitutions of the institute, at the request of Superiors of the institute, provided the case be not one of sacrilegious offspring, and that the persons dispensed be excluded from major offices in accordance with canon 504.

2. To permit the celebration of three Masses according to the ritual on Christmas night in churches of religious which are not included in canon 821, § 3, with permission to those present to receive Holy Communion, on condition, however, that the three Masses be said by the same priest.

---

[1] For Formula IV of quinquennial faculties given to Ordinaries in the United States and Canada, see below.

[2] Reported in CANON LAW DIGEST, 1, p. 76.

3. To dispense persons who are too old to enter the religious life, in as far as such dispensation is made necessary by the constitutions of any institute, on condition that in each case the consent of the Superioress General or of the Provincial, with that of their respective boards of consultors, be obtained in advance, and provided that the applicant be not over forty and have the other requisite qualifications.

4. To dispense from the want of dowry, in whole or in part, in the case of nuns or sisters, provided that the financial condition of the institute does not suffer thereby, and that the applicants have such qualifications that they give certain promise of being of great service to the institute.

5. To approve a confessor for a fourth and fifth three-year period, provided that the consent of the majority of the religious, including those who have no right to vote in other matters, expressed by secret vote in Chapter, be obtained beforehand, and that provision be made for the dissentients, if there be any and they desire such provision.

6. To allow the celebration of Mass on Holy Thursday, with permission to those who habitually live in the community to receive Holy Communion, even for the purpose of fulfilling their Easter duty.

7. To allow nuns to go to the church in order to clean or decorate it more thoroughly, on condition that all externs first leave the church, including the confessor himself and those who serve the monastery but live outside the cloister, and that the doors of the church be closed and the key be given to the Superioress. The nuns must always be two together and the inner door of the church must be closed with a double lock, and one key be kept by the Superioress and the other by a nun deputed by the Ordinary; and the door shall not be opened except in the cases specified and with the prescribed precautions.

8. To permit nuns to leave the cloister to undergo a surgical operation, even though there be no danger of death or of very great harm, for such time as may be strictly necessary, and with proper precautions.

**(Private)**; S. C. Consist., 12 Sept., 1957. Translated from the text graciously provided by the Rev. Terence P. Cunningham, of St. Patrick's College, Maynooth.

NOTE: This schedule of Formula III of quinquennial faculties *supplants* that of 1947 which is reported in the *Irish Ecclesiastical Record,* 70 (1948)–369–376.

Formula III-B, reported above, was renewed for another five years in October 1962.

## Quinquennial Faculties of Local Ordinaries: Formula IV (S. C. Consist., 1959) Private.

Formula IV is the schedule of quinquennial faculties given to Ordinaries in the United States and Canada.

## 5. Faculties From the Sacred Congregation of Religious

1. To dispense from illegitimate birth for entrance into religion, in as far as such dispensation is made necessary by the constitutions of the institute, at the request of Superiors of the institute, provided the case be not one of sacrilegious offspring, and that the persons dispensed be excluded from major offices in accordance with canon 504.

2. To permit the celebration of three Masses according to the ritual on Christmas night in churches of religious which are not included in canon 821, § 3, with permission to those present to receive Holy Communion, on condition, however, that the three Masses be said by the same priest.

3. To dispense persons who are too old to enter the religious life, in as far as such dispensation is made necessary by the constitutions of any institute, on condition that in each case the consent of the General Superioress or of the Provincial, with that of their respective boards of consultors, be obtained in advance, and provided that the applicant be not over forty and have the other requisite qualifications.

4. To dispense from the want of dowry, in whole or in part, in the case of nuns or sisters, provided that the financial condition of the institute does not suffer thereby, and that the applicants have such qualifications that they give certain promise of being of great service to the institute.

5. To approve a confessor for a fourth and fifth three-year period, provided that the consent of the majority of the religious,

including those who have no right to vote in other matters, expressed by secret vote in Chapter, be obtained beforehand, and that provision be made for the dissentients, if there be any and they desire such provision.

6. To allow the celebration of Mass on Holy Thursday, with permission to those who habitually live in the community to receive Holy Communion, even for the purpose of fulfilling their Easter duty.

7. To allow nuns to go to the church in order to clean or decorate it more thoroughly, on condition that all externs first leave the church, including the confessor himself and those who serve the monastery but live outside the cloister, that the doors of the church be closed and the key be given to the Superioress. The nuns must always be two together and the inner door of the church must be closed with a double lock, and one key be kept by the Superioress and the other by a nun deputed by the Ordinary; and the door shall not be opened except in the cases specified and with the prescribed precautions.

8. To permit nuns to leave the cloister to undergo a surgical operation, even though there be no danger of death or of very great harm, for such time as may be strictly necessary, and with proper precautions.

(**Private**); S. C. Consist., 1959. This renewal is valid in the *United States* until the end of 1964 inclusive.

**Decennial Faculties for Mission Countries** (S. C. Prop. Fid., 1960) **Private.**

The following is the Formula of the Decennial Faculties approved by the Sacred Congregation for the Propagation of the Faith, to be granted to Ordinaries for the ten-year period from 1 Jan. 1961 to 31 Dec. 1970 (Prot. N. 2150/60).

A) *Concerning Sacraments and Sacred Rites*

23. To permit that religious of either sex may do the first washing of palls, corporals, and purificators. (*May be subdelegated.*)

B) *Concerning Absolutions, Blessings, Indulgences, and Various Indults*

46. To grant a plenary Indulgence to all clerics and to religious of either sex who have been present for at least three whole days at spiritual Exercises, and, celebrating the Holy Sacrifice of the Mass or at least receiving Holy Communion, have piously prayed for the propagation of the holy faith and according to the intentions of the Supreme Pontiff.

58. To permit clerics and religious to practice medicine and surgery for the purpose of spreading the Kingdom of Christ, provided that they are truly skilled in these professions and that in caring for the sick they carefully avoid everything that is unbecoming to clerics or religious, or that might cause scandal, and that they accept nothing for their services.

(**Private**); S. C. Prop. Fid., Prot. N. 2150/60. Translated from a printed copy of the official Latin text sent to us by the Sacred Congregation. The original text also appeared in *Periodica,* 49 (1960)–341, with an extensive commentary by Buijs. For other commentaries, cf. *Commentarium pro Religiosis,* 41 (1962)–285–307, 369–373 (Ting Pong Lee); *The Clergy Monthly,* 24 (1960)–361–386 (Timmermans); *Australasian Catholic Record,* 37 (1960)–273 (Leonard); 285–308 (Madden); 317–332 (Murphy).

## CANON 81

**If Recourse to Holy See Through Apostolic Legate Is Easy, This Canon Cannot Be Applied** (Code Commission, 26 June, 1947) **AAS 39–374.**

The Code Commission was asked:

Whether the clause of canon 81, "unless recourse to the Holy See is difficult," applies when Ordinaries can easily have recourse to the Legate of the Roman Pontiff in the country, who is in communication with the Holy See.

**Reply:** In the negative.

**AAS 39–374**; Code Commission, 26 June, 1947.

Cf. *Periodica,* 36 (1947)–343 (Cappello); *Commentarium pro Religiosis,* 27 (1948)–32 (Gutiérrez).

**Dispensing Power Does Not Extend to Reserved Vows Nor to Obligation of Celibacy** (Code Commission, 26 Jan., 1949) **AAS 41–158.**

The Code Commission was asked:

I. Whether the words of canon 81, *"a generalibus Ecclesiae legibus,"* include vows reserved to the Holy See.

II. Whether, in virtue of canon 81 and under the clauses there contained, Ordinaries can dispense subdeacons and deacons from the obligation of observing sacred celibacy.

**Reply.** In the negative to both.

**AAS 41–158;** Code Com., 26 Jan., 1949. Commentary by Goyeneche in *Commentarium pro Religiosis,* 29 (1949)–25.

# BOOK II
## PERSONS
Canons 87–725

# BOOK II
## PERSONS
## Canons 87–725

### CANON 101

**Majority of Those Voting, Sufficient** (S. C. Conc., 12 Nov., 1921 and 10 June, 1922) **AAS 14–459.**

In an election, the candidate received 4 votes from the 9 members of the Chapter who were present. Of the remaining 5, one handed in a blank ballot; the other 4 abstained from voting. The Sacred Congregation of the Council, although it decided the case on another point, intimated that the election was valid under c. 101, the words *demptis suffragiis nullis* indicating that merely a majority of those *voting,* and not necessarily a majority of those *present,* is required and sufficient.

**AAS 14–459**; S. C. Conc., *Resolutio,* 12 Nov., 1921, and 10 June, 1922.

### CANON 116

**Incardination of Clerics Coming From Europe to America** (S. C. Consist., 30 Dec., 1918) **AAS 11–39.**

The following is excerpted from a Decree of the Sacred Consistorial Congregation, entitled: *De clericis in certas quasdam regiones demigrantibus.*

9. Religious may at the command of their Superior be sent across the ocean to religious houses belonging to their society, on the sole condition, which is of grave obligation on Superiors, that the religious so sent be of good character, with a sound vocation, and up in ecclesiastical studies.

10. Religious who are *exclaustrati* (cf. c. 638, 639) during the

period that they remain out of their houses, and those who have been secularized (c. 640) are subject to the same regulations as the secular clergy.

**AAS 11–39**; S. C. Consist., Decree, 30 Dec., 1918. Annotations in *Periodica*, 10 (1922)–42 (Vermeersch).

## CANON 121

Decree *De Clericis a Militia Redeuntibus* (S. C. Consist., 25 Oct., 1918) **AAS 10–481.**

The Holy Father "deeply deplores the grave wound inflicted upon ecclesiastical discipline by forcing clerics to bear arms"; the damage done is to be repaired as well as possible by the Ordinaries, acting according to the following rules:

### V. Novices and Religious Clerics

13. As for novices and clerics of various religious societies who return to their societies after military service, the same rules, with due proportion, should be observed, as have been laid down for seminarians.

14. The transfer of religious, after military service, to the secular clergy, and their admission to seminaries, remain forbidden according to the general law.

### VI. Lay Brothers of Various Religious Societies

15. Lay brothers of various religious societies who, after military service, return to their houses, shall undergo the usual examination as above provided; and if it appear that they have behaved well while they were in the service, shall, after the spiritual exercises, with the precautions and observances which have already been outlined, be admitted again as members of the community. If it appear that they have misbehaved, then, if they have not solemn vows, they should be dismissed, and they will by the very dismissal be released from all vows, even from that of perpetual chastity. If they are under solemn vows, Superiors shall refer the matter to the Sacred Congregation of Religious, and shall in the meantime make them live with their families, or in the monastery but in a place apart from the others.

## VII. Clerics in Sacred Orders, Secular or Religious, Who Have Fallen into Grave Crimes

16. As to clerics in sacred orders who may have had the misfortune of falling into any of the major crimes during their military service, Ordinaries, while they should, on their return, treat them paternally, should nevertheless, for their amendment and salvation, and for the public good of the Church, not fail to proceed in each case according to the nature of the crime, as prescribed in Book V of the Code, especially if they have incurred infamy of law or of fact.

In regard to those who by deplorable apostasy from their vows or from their religious society have gone over to the secular state, the Ordinaries must, as far as in them lies, play the part of the Good Shepherd seeking the lost sheep. Let them also take care to the best of their ability, at least to prevent their bad example from working scandal and harm to others of the faithful.

Let them also remember that it is their duty, in their report upon the state of their dioceses or religious societies, to state plainly whether there have been any such deplorable cases of apostasy, and how many.

His Holiness enjoins upon all Ordinaries exact observance of all these provisions, and doubts not that in view of the singular importance of the matter, all will employ the greatest care to fulfill them entirely and minutely.

**AAS 10-481**; S. C. Consist., Decree, 25 Oct., 1918. Annotations in *Periodica,* 9 (1921)-128 (Vermeersch).

## Religious After Military Service Unfitted for Religious Life (Reply, S. C. Rel., 23 Dec., 1918) AAS 10-18.

Petitions have been presented to His Holiness, Benedict XV, on behalf of those religious who, having been forced to do military service, upon their return therefrom feel incapable of taking up the religious life.

His Holiness refers these petitions to the Sacred Congregation of Religious with instructions that this Sacred Congregation, with due regard to the peculiar circumstances of such religious, make due provision in particular cases, with paternal solicitude.

**AAS 10-18**: S. C. Rel., Reply, 23 Dec., 1918. Annotations in *Periodica,* 10 (1922)-66.

## Further Declaration Regarding the Decree *Redeuntibus* (S. C. Consist., 20 Jan., 1919) AAS 11–43.

In the Decree *Redeuntibus,* the term "Ordinaries" includes the Superiors General of the Congregations of the Priests of the Sacred Heart, of Betharram, and of the Missionaries of La Salette, respectively, as regards the specification of religious exercises, absolution from irregularities, and the other effects of the aforesaid Decree.

AAS 11–43; S. C. Consist., *Declaratio,* 20 Jan., 1919. Annotations in *Periodica,* 10 (1922)–46.

## Religious Who Are Obliged to Military Service (S. C. Rel., Decree, 30 July, 1957) AAS 49–871.

A Decree of the Sacred Congregation of Religious "concerning religious who are bound to military service" is as follows:

Experience has shown that military service, which is imposed by the civil authority on religious and members of Societies of common life in disregard of the privilege of clerical immunity, may easily jeopardize a divine vocation and the religious spirit. To meet so serious a danger the Holy See has deemed it appropriate and necessary to establish definite regulations.

To this end the Sacred Congregation of Religious, on January 11, 1911, issued the Decree "*Inter reliquas,*"[1] which had been confirmed by the special approval of Saint Pius X, and interpreted and applied it through repeated declarations, as for example those of 1 Feb., 1912,[2] 15 July[3] and 30 Nov., 1919,[4] and 16 March, 1922.[5]

Since, however, the actual conditions of military service have greatly changed in these most recent times and since more effective means of preservation are now available, it has been decided to reconsider the entire subject.

Accordingly, after having carefully considered the matter in the Plenary Meeting of the Most Eminent Fathers and with the approval of His Holiness Pius XII given in the Audience of

---

1 AAS 3–37; CANON LAW DIGEST, 1, p. 106.
2 AAS 4–246.
3 AAS 11–321; CANON LAW DIGEST, 1, p. 105.
4 AAS 12–73; CANON LAW DIGEST, 1, p. 109.
5 AAS 14–196; CANON LAW DIGEST, 1, p. 311.

30 July, 1957, this Sacred Congregation has decided to decree as follows.

### Art. 1 — *The Notion of Military Service*

Military service in this Decree means the ordinary service which young religious, when first received in some branch of the service and placed under military authority and discipline, are by civil law obliged to render for at least six months, continuously or intermittently, either by bearing arms or by serving in an auxiliary capacity, even in that pertaining to sanitation and health.

### Art. 2 — *Perpetual Vows and Military Service*

No one can be validly admitted to perpetual profession before he has performed his military service or has been absolutely declared unfit for it, or has for any reason become legitimately and permanently free from the obligation to serve.

### Art. 3 — *Temporary Vows and Military Service*

§ 1. The temporary vows of a religious who has been called to the service are suspended when he comes under military discipline, without prejudice to the prescription of § 2.

§ 2. However, the major Superior with the advice of his Consultors can, according to his conscience and prudence, permit a religious called to military service, who asks for the favor and is certainly worthy of it, to remain under temporary vows during such service, for a definite time or *ad nutum.*

§ 3. During the period of military discipline the same Superior for just and serious cause can, by a notice in writing, suspend the vows which were allowed to a religious according to paragraph 2; and he can likewise grant the restoration of the same vows, which were suspended either at the beginning of military service or afterward.

### Art. 4 — *The Juridical Condition of a Religious during Military Service*

§ 1. During military service the religious is legitimately absent from the religious house, and consequently remains bound by those obligations of the religious life which, in the judgment of the major Superior, are reconcilable with his military status.

§ 2. The time which one has spent in military service while bound by religious vows according to Art. 3, §§ 2 and 3, can be counted for the purpose of canon 574 § 1, without prejudice to Art. 6.

§ 3. A religious, although he be not bound by vows during military service, continues to be a member of his Institute and under the authority of his Superiors.

§ 4. A religious who is not bound by vows can, in accordance with canon 637, freely leave the Institute, having previously as a condition for the validity of his action, given notice thereof to his Superiors by a declaration in writing, or by an oral declaration made in the presence of witnesses. An oral declaration is effective immediately; a written one becomes effective when the religious is informed that the Superior has received it.

Similarly, and observing the same formalities, the Institute can declare the religious dismissed for just and reasonable causes according to the same canon 637.

### Art. 5 — *Poverty*

As regards property which religious may acquire during their military service or which may afterward come to them from such service, whether they were during their service bound by their vows or freed from them, the following are to be observed:

§ 1. 1) Whatever the religious acquires through his own industry or because he is a religious, is the property of the Institute.

2) He acquires by his own industry his military pay and in general whatever comes to him because he is in the service.

§ 2. 1) A gratuity which is given to a professed of simple vows and which can accrue to his patrimony, shall be considered like a dowry, to be converted into capital whose income shall be received by the Institute as long as the individual remains in it. At his death the capital becomes the property of the Institute. If the religious for any reason leaves the Institute, it is to be restored to him in its entirety, without the interest that has already accrued. In the case of regulars canons 581 and 582 are to be observed.

2) Pensions which come to a religious because of outstanding merit or by reason of wounds received or disease contracted in military service, are turned over to the Institute and belong to it as long as he remains in it; the individual acquires them for himself if he leaves.

3) Gratuities, gifts, or any such largesses given on account of the death of a religious in military service, go to the Institute if he was a member thereof at the time of death.

### Art. 6 — *The Probation after Military Service*

Without prejudice to canon 574, a religious after finishing his military service, is to remain for some time under the regime of the common life and in temporary vows. As a rule this time should not be less than three months. The major Superior with the advice of his Council can for a grave reason shorten this period, or according to his prudent judgment extend it to a year before admitting the religious to perpetual profession.

### Art. 7 — *Extension of this Decree*

§ 1. The prescriptions of the above Articles, with appropriate adjustments, are binding also on Societies of common life without vows.

§ 2. Without prejudice to canon 556, § 1, novices who are called to military service, unless they have been legitimately dismissed or have left of their own accord, continue to belong to the Institute and enjoy the privileges of novices.

### Art. 8 — *Relation to the Previous Law*

All religious professions which have hitherto been made contrary to the prescriptions of the Decree *"Inter reliquas"* or of the succeeding declarations, are healed as to all canonical effects by the present Decree.

All things to the contrary notwithstanding; and all privileges and concessions hitherto given in this matter are revoked.

Given at Rome, the 30th of July, 1957.

**AAS 49–871**; S. C. Rel., Decree, 30 July, 1957. Annotations, *Commentarium pro Religiosis,* 36 (1957)–337; 37 (1958)–163, 296, 358 (Gutiérrez).

# CANON 129

**Clerics: Attending Secular Universities** (Decree, S. C. Consist., 30 April, 1918) **AAS 10–237.**

A summary of the Decree is as follows:

No cleric may attend a secular university except at the request or with the approval of his Bishop. This is clearly deducible from the prescriptions of the Code; but it is not new legislation, since it was already contained in the Instruction of the Sacred Congregations of Bishops and Regulars, under Leo XIII (21 July, 1896); in the Encyclical of Pius X, *Pascendi* (7 Sept., 1907); and in the *Motu proprio* of Pius X, *Sacrorum antistitum* (1 Sept., 1910). These ordinances are now confirmed, and it is further decreed:

1. No cleric is to be sent to a secular university unless he is already ordained to the priesthood, and unless he be one who gives promise of being a credit to the ecclesiastical order both by the force and perspicacity of his mind and by his holiness of life.

2. In sending any of his priests to secular universities, a Bishop should have no other purpose than the need or advantage of his diocese, namely to provide suitable teachers for its schools.

3. Priests so attending secular universities are not thereby exempt from the examinations which are prescribed in canons 130 and 590; on the contrary, they should be the more strictly required to undergo them, lest through interest in profane sciences they neglect ecclesiastical studies, contrary to the prescriptions of c. 129.

4. After finishing their studies in any secular university, the priests remain subject to their Ordinary in exactly the same way as before, and they remain bound to the service of the diocese. Hence, no one of them has the right to accept at will a professorship or other office, especially against the wishes of his Ordinary. If anyone does so, let him be punished by suitable penalties, not excluding suspension.

5. All of this applies, in as far as it can be applied, to religious, and even to regulars.

**AAS 10–237**; S. C. Consist., 30 Apr., 1918. Annotations in *Periodica,* 9 (1921)–120 (Creusen).

**Psychoanalysis** (Holy Office, *Monitum,* 15 July, 1961) **AAS 53–571.**

This Supreme Sacred Congregation, knowing that many dangerous opinions concerning sins against the VI Commandment and the imputability of human acts have become current and are still being spread abroad, has decided to publish the following regulations:

1. Bishops, Presidents of Theological Faculties, and the Superiors of Seminaries and schools of Religious, must strictly require of all persons engaged in teaching moral theology or a similar subject, that they conform entirely to the teaching of the Church.[1]

2. Ecclesiastical censors should use great caution in reviewing and passing judgment on books and periodicals which treat of the sixth Commandment of the Decalogue.

3. Clerics and Religious are forbidden to practice psychoanalysis, according to canon 139, § 2.

4. To be condemned is the opinion of those who hold that a previous training in psychoanalysis is altogether necessary for receiving Sacred Orders, or that candidates for the priesthood and for religious profession should undergo an examination and tests of a strictly psychoanalytic character. This applies also where there is question of ascertaining the fitness required of candidates for the priesthood or for the religious profession. Likewise, priests and Religious of either sex should not consult psychoanalysts unless their Ordinary for grave reason gives permission.

Given at Rome from the Holy Office, the 15th of July, 1961.

**AAS 53–571;** Holy Office, *Monitum,* 15 July, 1961. Annotations in the *Clergy Review,* 46 (1961)–755 (McReavy); *Etudes,* 311 (1961)–116–119 (Beirnaert); *L'Ami du Clerge,* 71 (1961)–736; *Nouvelle Revue Théologique,* 83 (1961)–856–861 (Carpentier); *Theological Studies,* 23 (1962)–233–239 (Lynch); *Commentarium pro Religiosis,* 41 (1962)–82 (Frison); *Periodica,* 51 (1962)–207–246.

## CANON 130

**Religious: When Exempt from Examination** (Cod. Com., 14 July, 1922) **AAS 14–526.**

[1] Cf. canon 129.

The Code Commission was asked:

1. Whether religious who are pastors or vicars with the care of souls, are obliged to undergo the examination mentioned in c. 130, § 1, before the Ordinary or his delegate, if they have undergone the examination mentioned in c. 590 before their religious Superior or his delegates. And, if *not,* then:

2. Whether in the case of negligence of the religious Superior in regard to the examination mentioned in c. 590, the Ordinary of the place can compel those religious to undergo the examination according to c. 130, § 1, before him or his delegates.

**Reply.** To 1: In the negative.

To 2: Recourse should be had in such case to the Sacred Congregation of Religious.

**AAS 14–526;** Cod. Com., 14 July, 1922, II. Annotations in *Periodica,* 11 (1923)–166 (Vermeersch); *Jus P.,* 2 (1922)–84.

## CANON 131

**Diocesan Conferences: When to Be Attended by Religious** (Cod. Com., 12 Feb., 1935) **AAS 27–92.**

The Code Commission was asked:

Whether among those "having the care of souls" mentioned in canon 131, § 3, are to be included religious priests who are acting as catechists, or as assistants in parishes, or as chaplains dependent upon the pastor in hospitals and other pious houses.

**Reply.** In the negative as regards religious catechists; in the affirmative as regards religious assistants or chaplains, if, according to canon 476, § 6, of the Code of Canon Law, they are taking the place of the pastor and helping him in the entire parochial ministry.

**AAS 27–92;** Cod. Com., 12 Feb., 1935.
*Periodica,* 24 (1935)–95; *Irish Ecclesiastical Record,* 45 (1935)–532 (Browne); *Jus Pontificium,* 15 (1935)–82; *Clergy Review,* 9 (1935)–528 (Bentley); *Amer. Eccles. Review,* 92 (1935)–506.

## CANON 135

**Indulgence Extended to Nuns and Pious Women Living in Community** (Decree, S. Poen., 5 Dec., 1930) **AAS 23–23.**

His Holiness, Pius XI, in the audience of 21 Nov., 1930, extended the plenary indulgence, just as it was granted to clerics in the Decree of 23 Oct., 1930,[1] "to nuns and all other pious women living in community, who, according to the constitutions of their own institute, are bound to the daily recitation of the divine office."

AAS 23–23; S. Poen., Decree, 5 Dec., 1930.
*Periodica,* 20 (1931) 146 (Vermeersch).

---

**Divine Office Recited by Religious.** See c. 2, AAS 56–97. Constitution on the Sacred Liturgy, nn. 95, 98, 101, § 2; reported in this volume, p. 22.

## CANON 139

### Instruction to Superiors of Orders and Congregations of Religious of Both Sexes on the Promotion of Catholic Action (Cardinal Secretary of State, 15 Mar., 1936) Private.

On the 15th of March, 1936, a very important letter was addressed by His Eminence, Cardinal Pacelli, in the name of the Holy Father, to the Superiors General of all religious institutes of either sex, on the promotion of Catholic Action. It was published in Italian in *L'Osservatore Romano,* 4 June, 1936, and in Latin in *Periodica,* 25–209. We give the full text of the letter.

Your Reverence is well aware that the Supreme Pontiff reposes a lively confidence for the restoration of a Christian social order in Catholic Action, and receives great consolation from the reports which come in from all sides, even from Mission countries, of its uninterrupted development and the precious fruits which our Lord is producing by means of it.

One of the principal sources of this consolation has been the generous constancy with which certain religious Orders and Congregations of men and women have devoted their members to the service of Catholic Action, with the result that they have contributed to its growth and fertility by their writings, their sermons, and their intelligent co-operation. The Holy Father himself has often praised and commended them; and in the letter which he addressed last October to the Bishops of Brazil, he even expressed the hope that the aid furnished to Catholic Action by religious institutes would be "more effective and far-reaching than any other."

---

[1] AAS 22–493; reported in CANON LAW DIGEST I, p. 121.

This will actually be the case if, as is recommended in that same very important document, special courses of study are arranged, to prepare religious for this new work, so that through their preaching and their manifold apostolic activities the faithful may be inspired and trained for the apostolate of Catholic Action. Moreover, since one of the great services rendered by religious is to give spiritual instruction to the clergy, especially by means of spiritual exercises, it is to be hoped that, with this better preparation, they will be able more readily and with greater authority to recommend to priests, together with the discharge of their other priestly duties, this duty of Catholic Action in particular, which the Supreme Pontiff, even in his first Encyclical, declared to be "among the most important duties of a pastor of souls." No less valuable surely will be the aid supplied by religious in the education of youth, which is very commonly intrusted to their care, and is thus placed in circumstances of time and place which are the best that could be desired.

The August Pontiff has often, and in various connections, come back to this thought: the training of youth to the spirit of the apostolate, which is the peculiar province of Catholic Action, is a most necessary element of education in these modern days; it is a safeguard of Christian living, and a peculiarly precious gift by which they are called to an apostolate which is closely connected with that of the priesthood. A wise educator cannot be unmindful of this: for by so doing he would narrow the horizon of well-doing which should lie open before the generous soul of youth, he would deprive the Church of a precious resource, and would find it difficult to attain the objectives of a truly Christian education.

Moreover, this apostolic training of youth makes for the welfare of the school itself. For no one will question the incalculable good it does by way of mutual example among the better disposed of the students; the power it gives them to bring their less exemplary fellow students to better ways; the impulse it gives them to draw from their daily life at school or college a true preparation for the work which they expect to undertake, either during the vacation or at the end of their studies, in the ranks of Catholic Action. This very training will, therefore, make them more hardy soldiers to overcome the many grave dangers which are incident to the social life of our day, and which, as we know too well from experience, are very common even among young people who have been educated in Catholic schools.

For these grave reasons, His Holiness had already recommended that *Internal Associations* be established, such as are already active in a number of institutes, and that the Pious Associations which are under the care of religious be encouraged to "offer their providential aid to Catholic Action, either by their prayers, or by making the need and advantages of Catholic Action better known, or by urging their own members to take it up; and this is especially applicable to those institutes and Congregations who bring together young people in order to preserve in them the fruits of a Catholic education" (Letter of His Eminence, Cardinal Pacelli, Secretary of State, to Augustus Ciriaci, General President of Italian Catholic Action, 30 Mar., 1930).

If then, all good religious will not only direct their prayers toward this high goal, but also by their persuasion and exhortation induce those who are under their spiritual care to pray for Catholic Action and to enlist under its standard, then truly will their co-operation be perfect, and it will result in copious blessings for Catholic Action and for the whole Church. If religious will conform their conduct to these instructions, they will be following their glorious tradition of generous alacrity in ministering to the spiritual needs of the people and in complying with the wishes of the Vicar of Christ, especially in these times when many difficulties attend the care of young people, beset as they are by so many enemies and harassed on all sides by the falsehoods of Communism. It will, therefore, be an exquisite form of charity to co-operate wholeheartedly with the secular clergy for the spread of the Kingdom of Christ, which is the constant desire of the August Pontiff.

With a sure confidence that these high hopes will be fulfilled, the Holy Father, as a sign of benevolence and as a pledge of heavenly graces, imparts to all Superiors and members of your religious family his Apostolic Blessing.

For my part, with the most earnest good wishes for the success of your collaboration in so holy a cause, I remain,

Devotedly yours in Christ,

E. Cardinal Pacelli

(Private); Sec. State, 15 Mar., 1936.
*Periodica,* 25 (1936)–214 (Tromp).

## CANON 142

**Business and Trading Forbidden to Clerics and Religious: New Penalty for Violation of This Canon** (S. C. Conc., 22 March, 1950) **AAS 42–330.**

A Decree of the Sacred Congregation of the Council:

It is clear from many documents that secular businesses, especially business and trading, have at all times in the Church been forbidden under severe penalties and censures to clerics who are called to the inheritance of the Lord.

Indeed the Apostle himself in the Second Epistle to Timothy (Chapter II, verse 4) already sounded the warning: "No man, being a soldier to God, entangleth himself with secular businesses." It is no wonder then that the Council of Trent (Sess. XXII, Chapter I, *de reformatione*), treating of these crimes, did not hesitate to decree, "that the copious and useful provisions which have already been enacted by the Supreme Pontiffs and the Sacred Councils to the effect that clerics are to abstain from secular businesses, are in future to be observed under the same or greater penalties, to be imposed at the discretion of the Ordinary."

Accordingly the Code of Canon Law, adhering completely to this tradition, provided, in canon 142, regarding this matter: "Clerics are forbidden to conduct business or trade, either personally or through agents, either for their own benefit or that of other persons." And this prohibition applies also to religious according to canon 592. Moreover, the Code armed this prescription of law with special sanctions in canon 2380, where it is further provided: "Clerics or religious who, personally or through others, conduct commerce or trading in violation of the provision of canon 142, are to be visited with appropriate penalties by the Ordinary according to the gravity of the case."

To the end that a firmer and more uniform ecclesiastical discipline may be had in that matter and that abuses may be forestalled, His Holiness Pius XII has deigned to provide that all clerics and religious of the Latin rite mentioned in canons 487–681, not even excepting members of the recent secular

Institutes, who conduct trade or business of any kind, even that which consists in exchange of currencies, either in person or through others, whether for their own benefit or that of others, in violation of the provision of canon 142, shall incur, as being guilty of this crime, a *latae sententiae* excommunication specially reserved to the Holy See, and shall in a proper case be further punished by the penalty of degradation.

Superiors who shall have failed to prevent these same crimes according to their office and power, are to be deprived of their office and declared incapable of any office of government or administration.

Finally, for all persons to whose malice or negligence such crimes are attributable, there remains the obligation to make good the damages that have been caused.

All things to the contrary notwithstanding.

Given at Rome, 22 March, 1950.

**AAS 42–330**; S. C. Conc., Decree, 22 March, 1950. *Periodica,* 39 (1950)–231 (Abellán); *Commentarium pro Religiosis,* 29 (1950)–183; 30 (1951)–151, etc. (Gutiérrez); *Monitor Ecclesiasticus,* 75 (1950)–171 (***).

## CANON 175

### Acceptance of Election After Confirmation: Right to Annul (Benedict XV, 11 Feb., 1920) Private.

The Order of Preachers addressed the following petition to the Holy Father:

The Superior General of the Order of Preachers, humbly prostrate at the feet of Your Holiness, considering that from the beginning of the Order the practice has been that the decree of election is communicated to the elect only after the confirmation of the election; considering further that canon 175 and the following canons on the notification of the election do not introduce a new law, since they are entirely in agreement with the provisions of the Council of Trent and with the Decretals themselves, earnestly petitions, with the consent of his Council, that Your Holiness, by your supreme authority, deign to approve and declare:

1. That in the Order of Preachers the original practice may be preserved, according to which even to this day, the intima-

tion of the election is given to the elect by the one who confirms the election:

2. That in the Order of Preachers, according to the same original practice, the one who confirms the election has the right to annul it, even though it was conducted according to law, whenever, in his judgment, the annulment would be for the common good of the Order.

**Reply.** We grant the faculty requested, notwithstanding the provisions of the new law.

**(Private)**; Benedict XV, 11 Feb., 1920; reported by Fanfani, *De Iure Religiosorum,* ed. 1920, p. 44, note 4.

## CANON 177

**Confirmation of Election: When It Can Be Refused** (Code Com., 4 Nov., 1919) **Private.**

The Code Commission was asked:

Whether the one who confirms an election is bound according to canon 177, § 2, to grant the confirmation, if he finds the elect fit and if the election was conducted according to law, or whether he can refuse the confirmation, not at his pleasure, but for the common good according to his judgment.

**Reply.** In the affirmative to the first part; but if there is a serious reason against the elect, that is a sign that he is not fit for the office, and therefore the Superior can refuse the confirmation.

**(Private)**; Code Commission, 4 Nov., 1919. See Fanfani, *De Iure Religiosorum,* ed. 1925, n. 109, p. 126.

## CANON 180

**Election and Postulation** (Cod. Com., 1 July, 1922) **AAS 14–406.**

The Code Commission was asked:

1. Whether, according to c. 180, § 1, in a case where a postulation concurs with an election, and where, on the first three ballots, the votes are divided between the postulate and the eligible candidate, the postulate receiving less than two thirds,

and the eligible candidate only a relative, not an absolute, majority, the eligible candidate is validly elected?

**Reply.** In the affirmative, that is, the eligible candidate is validly elected on the third ballot, by a relative majority, to the exclusion of the postulate.

2. If there are several eligible candidates, whether that one of them is validly elected who receives a relative majority?

**Reply.** In the affirmative, that is, the one among the eligible candidates who receives a relative majority, is validly elected, to the exclusion, in this case also, of the postulate.

**AAS 14–406;** Cod. Com., 1 July, 1922. Annotations in *Periodica,* 11 (1923)–127 (Vermeersch); *Jus Pontificium,* 2 (1922)–83.

## CANON 181

**Postulation: to Whom to Be Addressed** (Code Com., 4 Nov., 1919) **Private.**

The Code Commission was asked:

Whether the instrument of postulation is to be sent to the Provincial, or directly to another who has the faculty to dispense, that is, to the Superior General or to the Roman Pontiff.

**Reply.** The instrument of postulation, according to canon 181, § 1, can be sent to the Superior who has the right to confirm the election, etc., through the Provincial.

**(Private);** Code Commission, 4 Nov., 1919. Cf. Fanfani, *De Iure Religiosorum,* ed. 1925, n. 115, p. 132; *Analecta Ord. Praedic.,* 1924, p. 422.

## CANON 197

**Certain Canons on Jurisdiction May Apply to Dominative Power of Religious Superiors** (Code Com., 26 March, 1952) **AAS 44–497.**

The Code Commission was asked:

Whether the prescriptions of canons 197, 199, 206–209, concerning the power of jurisdiction, are to be applied, unless the nature of the matter or the text or context of the law prevent it, to the dominative power which Superiors and Chapters have in religious Institutes and in Societies of men or women living in common without public vows.

**Reply.** In the affirmative.

Given at Rome, from Vatican City, 26 March, 1952.

AAS 44–497; Code Com., 26 March, 1952. Annotations, *Monitor Ecclesiasticus,* 77 (1952)–418 (Bidagor); *Review for Religious,* 20 (1961)–180–195 (O'Connor); other annotations in *The Jurist,* 21 (1961)–1–26 (O'Connor).

## CANON 214

### Religious Clerics Reduced to Lay State by Trial: Practice of the S. C. of Religious (S. C. Rel., 1952) Private.

When a religious cleric claims that he received sacred orders under coercion of grave fear and did not afterward ratify the ordination by exercising his orders, the following points of practice of the Sacred Congregations are outlined by Gutiérrez in a Consultation in *Commentarium pro Religiosis,* 31(1952)–214.

1. Competency for the trial or administrative decision belongs to the Sacred Congregation of the Sacraments, or in special cases to the Holy Office, according to canons 214 and 1993. The competency of the S. C. of the Sacraments was upheld by a decision of the Special Commission of Cardinals, 7 Dec., 1922.[1]

2. Formerly, by agreement between the two Congregations (Sacr. and Rel.), the practice was that the petition should be first presented to the S. C. of Religious, which decreed the secularization of the cleric in question and then sent the dossier to the S. C. of the Sacraments for their decision. If the petition was made to the S. C. of the Sacraments, it was sent to the S. C. of Religious and the cleric was first secularized before the S. C. of the Sacraments would decide the case.

3. This practice led to a number of incongruities and difficulties. Consequently it has, since 1952, been abandoned. According to present practice, no preliminary steps are to be taken before the S. C. of Religious, and the cleric is not secularized. Pending the trial or decision, the subject remains a religious, bound by all his *religious* obligations; the exercise of *orders* is suspended according to canon 1997. When the decision is made, the

---

[1] Canon Law Digest, 1, p. 159.

competency of the S. C. of the Sacraments is at an end. If the decision was for nullity of the orders or of the obligation, the subject can remain in religion as a lay brother; if he is to be secularized the petition is made to the S. C. of Religious. If the decision was unfavorable, he remains a cleric, either in the religious Institute as before, or upon finding a favorable Bishop according to canon 641, in a diocese, through secularization obtained with the recommendation of his religious Superiors, from the S. C. of Religious.

(**Private**); S. C. Rel., 1952; practice of the Sacred Congregations, outlined in *Commentarium pro Religiosis,* 31 (1952)–241 (Gutiérrez).

## CANON 218

**Catholic Teaching:** Pius XII, Allocution to the Third General Assembly of the International Office of Catholic Teaching (O.I.E.C. — Office International de l'Enseignement Catholique), Rome, 14 Sept., 1958 (AAS 50–696). English text, *The Pope Speaks,* 5 (1958–59)–337.

**Nursing:** Some moral and religious aspects. Pius XII, Allocution, 1 Oct., 1953 (AAS 45–725). *The Pope Speaks,* 1 (1954), 54.

**Nursing Sisters:** Allocution of Pius XII, 24 April, 1957 (AAS 49–291). *The Pope Speaks,* 4 (1957–58)–135–140.

**Radio and Television:** Use of, in schools and colleges, John XXIII, Allocution, 7 Dec., 1961 (AAS 53–815).

**Suffering:** Meaning of: John XXIII, Allocution, 19 Mar., 1959. English text, *The Pope Speaks,* 5 (1958–59)–331.

## CANON 222

### Prayer to the Holy Spirit, an *Oratio Imperata* During Sessions of the Council (S. C. Rit., 24 Sept., 1963) AAS 55–838.

A decree of the S. C. of Rites:

In the Apostolic Exhortation to all Bishops which His Holiness Paul VI gave on 14 September, 1963, to invoke the light and help of the Holy Spirit for the happy outcome of the II Vatican Council, His Holiness prescribed "that in all Masses of the Latin rite the *collecta imperata* of the Holy Spirit be recited."

In order to remove all doubt in the execution of this august mandate and in order also that due regard be had to the prescriptions of the Code of Rubrics, this Sacred Congregation of Rites, by order of His Holiness, declares: that the *oratio imperata de Spiritu Sancto* is to be recited in all Masses during the sessions of the Vatican Council; observing, however, the prescription of the Code of Rubrics n. 457 d, which provides: "it is forbidden on all liturgical days of the I and II class, in votive Masses of the I and II class, in sung Masses, and whenever the privileged commemorations complete the number fixed for the various liturgical days."

All things to the contrary notwithstanding.

From the Secretariate of the Sacred Congregation of Rites, 24 September, 1963.

**AAS 55–838**; S. C. Rit., 24 Sept., 1963.

## CANON 247

### *Radiaesthesia:* Ordinaries and Religious Superiors to Forbid Consultations to Clerics and Religious (Holy Office, 26 Mar., 1942) AAS 34–148.

The Supreme Sacred Congregation of the Holy Office, having maturely considered the disadvantages to religion and genuine piety which flow from consultations of *Radiaesthesia* engaged in by clerics concerning the divination of personal circumstances and events, and mindful of the provisions of canons 138 and 139, § 1, of the Code of Canon Law restraining clerics and religious from activities which are unbecoming to their office and dignity, or which might impair their authority, decrees as follows, without however intending by this Decree to touch upon scientific questions regarding *Radiaesthesia:*

The S. C. orders the Most Excellent Ordinaries of places and Superiors of Religious, that they strictly forbid their clerics and religious from ever attending those seances of *Radiaesthesia* which concern the aforesaid consultations.

If any cleric or religious becomes a *recidivus* in disobeying the said prohibition, or causes grave inconveniences or scandal, the Ordinaries or Superiors are to report the fact to this Supreme Sacred Tribunal.

Given at Rome, from the Holy Office, 26 Mar., 1942.

**AAS 34–148**; Holy Office, 26 Mar., 1942. *Periodica,* 31 (1942)–280 (Willwoll and Creusen).

## CANON 248

**Priests Going to North America From Latin America or the Philippines** (S. C. Consist., 13 Feb., 1960) **AAS 52–410.**

A Decree of the Sacred Consistorial Congregation:

For the better ecclesiastical discipline of priests who go from Latin America or the Philippine Islands to North America for any reason, including studies, whether they intend to remain temporarily or permanently, this Sacred Congregation has decided to apply to them the same laws as those established by the Apostolic Constitution *Exsul Familia,*[1] Title II, art. 3, for priests who wish to migrate from Europe or any Mediterranean country to foreign regions across the seas.

Accordingly, hereafter:

§ 1. 1) When priests desire to migrate from Latin America or the Philippines to the United States or to Canada for any space of time, short, long, indefinite, or perpetually, it belongs exclusively to the Sacred Consistorial Congregation to give them permission to go and to remain there or to extend their stay.

2) Nuncios, Internuncios, and Apostolic Delegates can grant this same permission to priests of the nation to which they are permanently assigned, provided this faculty has been given them and been reserved to them.

§ 2. 1) The priests mentioned in § 1, n. 1 must obtain this same permission in order to be incardinated in a certain diocese overseas, observing the other provisions of the law.

2) Religious also need this same permission, except those who are sent by their Superiors to other houses of their Institute; so also do excloistered religious during the time of their exclaustration; as well as secularized religious who have been accepted by a benevolent Bishop either simply and definitely or by way of trial.

§ 3. This permission, however, without prejudice to the other

---

[1] Ap. Const., 1 Aug., 1952; AAS 44–649; Canon Law Digest, 3, p. 84.

laws established in the Decree, *Magni semper negotii*,[2] shall not be granted unless there is certainty regarding:

1) the testimonials of good conduct of the petitioner;

2) a just and reasonable cause for migrating;

3) the consent both of the Bishop *a quo* or, in the case of religious, of the religious Superior, and of the Bishop *ad quem*.

4) an indult obtained from the S. C. of the Council in the case of pastors, if the absence is to be for more than two months.

§ 4. Priests, whether secular or religious, who after having obtained this permission to migrate, wish to go from one jurisdiction to another, need a new permission.

§ 5. Priests who, without observing these laws, rashly and arrogantly migrate, are *ipso facto* suspended from sacred functions; if any (which God forbid) nevertheless dare to perform such functions, they incur an irregularity; and they can be absolved from these penalties only by this Sacred Congregation.[3]

When these provisions were reported to His Holiness John XXIII by the undersigned Cardinal Secretary of this Sacred Congregation in the Audience of 13 February of this year, His Holiness approved and confirmed them and ordered that this Decree be enacted.

Given at Rome from the Sacred Consistorial Congregation, the 13th of February, 1960.

**AAS 52–410**; S. C. Consist., 13 Feb., 1960. Annotations, *Monitor Ecclesiasticus*, 85 (1960)–543 (Ferretto).

**Apostolate of the Sea: Dispensation for Seamen and Passengers From Law of Fast and Abstinence** (S. C. Conc., 1 Dec., 1961) **Private.**

**Petition.** The International General Secretariate of the Apostolate of the Sea manifests to Your Holiness that the National Directors, especially those in the United States of America, in Australia, and Asia, have presented the inherent difficulty on the part of seamen and passengers (*naviganti*) to observe the ecclesiastical law of fast and abstinence.

In fact, while fishermen can live on fish almost all year, seamen

[2] S. C. Consist., 30 Dec., 1918; AAS 11–39; Canon Law Digest, 1, p. 93.

[3] *Ibid.*, n. 16; Canon Law Digest, 1, p. 97.

and passengers (*naviganti*), on the other hand, must from the beginning of their long voyages necessarily procure provisions at various supply stores in strange countries. As a result, in such circumstances, it is difficult, if not to say impossible, to obtain meatless foods.

Moreover, the seamen (*marinai*) find themselves with fellow-laborers of different religions.

Finally, there are always present the long periods of work and their very long absences from home.

For these reasons some bishops have already granted for the seamen and passengers (*naviganti*) of their respective dioceses, a dispensation from the ecclesiastical law of fast and abstinence.

Now the International General Secretariate of the Apostolate of the Sea, in order to provide opportune peace of conscience for all seamen and passengers (*naviganti*) requests for all of them a dispensation from the ecclesiastical law of fast and abstinence.

**Reply.** The Sacred Congregation of the Council, having attended to the recitals and the recommendation of His Eminence, the Cardinal Secretary of the Sacred Consistorial Congregation, has graciously granted the requested favor of dispensation for as long as the present condition of things continues, with the exception of Friday of Holy Week, in as far as it is possible to observe this day.

(**Private**); S. C. Conc., 1 Dec., 1961, Prot. No. 67566/D; copy of the original rescript kindly given us by the Rev. Thomas A. McDonough, C.SS.R., secretary of the National Catholic Apostleship of the Sea Conference, New Orleans, La.

Note: It should be noted, as Fr. McDonough well points out, that the Holy See in its documents distinguishes between seamen alone and all seafarers, i.e., seamen and passengers, using the terms *marinai* and *maritimi* when referring to seamen alone, and *naviganti* and *navigantes* when intending both seamen and passengers.

---

**Religious as Emigrants.** On the 10th anniversary of the Apostolic Constitution, *Exsul Familia* (Canon Law Digest, 3, p. 84), a commentary on that document, especially as it concerns religious, was begun in *Commentarium pro Religiosis,* 41 (1962)–345 (Ochoa).

## CANON 249

### Competency of S. C. Sacr.: Cases Involving Obligations or Validity of Orders Where Petitioner Is a Religious

(Special Commission of Cardinals, 7 Dec., 1922) **AAS 15–39.**

The Special Commission of Cardinals provided for in c. 245 was asked:

II. Whether the decision of questions relating to the obligations annexed to sacred orders, or to the validity of sacred ordination, in the case of religious, belongs to the S. C. Sacr, or to the S. C. Rel.

**Reply.** It belongs to the Sacred Congregation of the Sacraments in accordance with c. 1993.

**AAS 15–39**; Special Commission of Cardinals, 7 Dec., 1922. Annotations in *Periodica,* 12 (1924)–44 (Vermeersch); *Jus Pontificium,* 3 (1923)–39.

## CANON 251

### Competency of S. C. Rel. (Special Commission of Cardinals, 24 Mar., 1919), AAS 11–251.

The special Commission of Cardinals provided for by c. 245 was asked the following questions:

1. Whether all questions or recourses (*instantiae*) which affect any right or interest of any religious family or of members of a religious society, belong exclusively to the S. C. Rel.

**Reply.** In the affirmative, but in the sense of c. 251.

2. Whether the granting, in the customary manner, of sanations and condonations for the past, and reductions for the future, in regard to chaplaincies and other foundations which are established, either originally or by transfer, in the churches of religious, although they are not intrusted to the religious Order or to the community as such, belongs to the S. C. Conc. or to the S. C. Rel.

**Reply.** Exclusively to the S. C. Rel., to the extent that the administration or execution of the foundation so established is intrusted to religious.

3. Which of the Congregations is competent in regard to dispensations for the receiving of sacred orders by religious, either from the impediment of age (cf. c. 975) or from irregularity (cf.

c. 983 *sq.*) or regarding the conditions required for orders, or the studies which must precede sacred orders?

**Reply.** The S. C. Rel.

4. Which of the Congregations is competent to dispense religious who, owing to sickness or other causes, are physically or morally impeded from saying Mass, for example, if they cannot stand on their feet?

**Reply.** The S. C. Rel.

**AAS 11–251**; Special Commission of Cardinals, 24 March, 1919.
*Periodica,* 10 (1922)–99 (Vermeersch).

## Dispensation of Religious from Eucharistic Fast (Special Commission of Cardinals, 7 Dec., 1922) AAS 15–39.

The Special Commission of Cardinals provided for in c. 245 was asked:

I. Whether the power of granting to religious of either sex dispensation from the law of Eucharistic fast for the receiving of Holy Communion, belongs to the S. C. Sacr. or to the S. C. Rel.

**Reply.** It belongs to the Sacred Congregation of Religious.

**AAS 15–39**; Special Commission of Cardinals, 7 Dec., 1922.
*Periodica,* 12 (1924)–44 (Vermeersch); *Jus Pontificium,* 3 (1923)–12.

## Sacred Congregation of Religious: Special Commission for Education of Aspirants, Novices, and Younger Religious (S. C. Rel., 24 Jan., 1944) AAS 36–213.

A Decree of the Sacred Congregation of Religious is as follows:

To the end that the S. C. of Religious may be able more effectively and fruitfully to perform the duty assigned to it by canon 251, His Holiness Pius XII, in the audience granted to the undersigned Secretary on 24 January, 1944, deigned to approve by his Apostolic authority the erection and establishment in this S. C. of a special Body or Commission of chosen men, which shall deal with all questions and matters pertaining in any way to the religious and clerical education and to the training in literature, science, and ministry, of aspirants, novices, and junior members of all religious institutes and societies living in common without vows.

The newly erected Commission shall have especially the following duties:

*a*) To define and outline the principal criteria and peculiar characteristics according to which the education and training of religious must always be conducted;

*b*) To watch over the ordinances which are enacted by Superiors and Chapters in matters which concern education and instruction; and to inspect and review the reports made on this matter by Superiors and Apostolic Visitors.

The Commission shall be convoked in ordinary or extraordinary sessions, plenary or partial, as the nature and importance of the business may require. The sessions shall be held under the presidency and direction of the Secretary of the Sacred Congregation. The discussions and decisions shall be duly entered in the record.

The Officials of the Sacred Congregation shall gather, arrange, and properly prepare all matters which are to be considered by the Commission and which are to be presented for study and examination to the individual members of the Commission or to experts; and they shall also preserve in the Archives the records and documents pertaining to the Commission, see to the execution of the decisions taken, under the direction of the President, and put into practice and expedite other matters pertaining to the work of the Commission.

All things to the contrary, even such as are worthy of special mention, notwithstanding.

Given at Rome, from the S. C. of Religious, January 24, 1944.

**AAS 36–213**; S. C. Rel., Decree, 24 Jan., 1944.
*Periodica,* 33 (1944)–245 (Creusen).

NOTE: In order to implement this Decree, a Letter of the S. C. of Religious, 10 June, 1944 (N. 2090/44) was sent to a certain number of religious Major Superiors, together with a list of questions to be answered. These documents are published in *Periodica,* 33 (1944)–246.

## Primary Pontifical Work for Religious Vocations Established (Pius XII, *Motu proprio,* 11 Feb., 1955) AAS 47–266.

In response to Our supreme paternal solicitude, the Sacred Congregation of Religious has declared that it would be very opportune to establish a Primary Work for Religious Vocations, having for its purpose — to be attained by all appropriate means but especially by establishing this Work in various countries — to stimulate the desire of fostering, protecting, and helping vocations to the states of Christian perfection, to spread correct notions of the dignity and usefulness of the states of perfection, and to unite the faithful of all parts of the world in a union of prayers and pious exercises for that intention.

Accordingly, *of Our own motion* and in the fulness of Our Apostolic authority, We will, ordain, and decree the establishment in that same Sacred Congregation of a Work, which We designate as Pontifical, with the faculty of affiliating to itself Works and persons when requested to do so, and to extend to all its members the indulgences that have been or shall be granted and other spiritual favors.

Let this Our will be and remain valid and firm, all things to the contrary notwithstanding, even those worthy of special mention.

Given at Rome, from Saint Peter's, the 11th day of February, 1955, the sixteenth year of Our Pontificate.

AAS 47–266; Pius XII, *Motu proprio,* 11 Feb., 1955. Annotations in *Commentarium pro Religiosis,* 34 (1955)–136 (Liévin).

## Statutes and Norms for the Pontifical Work of Religious Vocations (S. C. Rel., 11 Feb., 1955) AAS 47–298.

The Sacred Congregation of Religious issued the following Statutes and Norms for the Pontifical Work of Religious Vocations:

### I. Statutes

I. The Pontifical Work for protecting and promoting vocations to the states of perfection is a Work of primary grade and importance, established by His Holiness Pius XII by the Apostolic Letter *Cum supremae,* given of his own motion on the 11th of February, 1955.

II. This Pontifical Work has its headquarters in the Sacred Congregation of Religious.

III. To attain the end for which it is established, the Pontifical Work:

1. Attends in the first place to popularizing correct notions of the nature, usefulness, and excellence of the states of perfection, as explained in recent Pontifical documents.

2. Promotes works of piety, penance, and charity so that God may grant many and excellent vocations to the states of perfection.

3. Favors the growth of Works for religious vocations which already exist in various countries, and sees to their erection if not yet established.

IV. The following can be affiliated to the Pontifical Work:

All religious Institutes and Societies which are analogous to religious Institutes, secular Institutes of men and women, monasteries and individual religious houses, Councils of Major Superiors of men or women such as now exist in various countries, and any works which may be established to cultivate and assist religious vocations in a special way.

The following can be inscribed as members of the same: ecclesiastical colleges and Catholic associations, any of the individual faithful either of the clergy or of the laity who may wish to help in so great a work.

V. The Pontifical Work for Religious Vocations is placed under the protection of the Holy Family of Nazareth, which offers to all the states of perfection an example of the "suave and effective union of the contemplative and the active life" (Apostolic Constitution, *Sponsa Christi*).[1]

## II. Norms for Putting the Statutes Into Practice

*The Government.* At the head of the Pontifical Work of Religious Vocations is His Eminence the Cardinal Prefect of the Sacred Congregation of Religious; he is represented by His Excellency the Secretary of the same Sacred Congregation.

The Pontifical Work in no way derogates from the autonomy and legitimate freedom of other special Works, which are defined and regulated by their own laws.

*Affiliation or Ascription.* The petition for affiliation or ascription to the Pontifical Work for the states of perfection, in favor of ecclesiastical colleges, other Catholic institutions or associa-

[1] Reported in this volume, p. 336.

tions, and special Works for religious vocations, is made by their Superiors or Directors.

In the act of affiliation or ascription, the Pontifical Work gives to Societies a diploma and to persons a special certificate.

All those ascribed or affiliated shall contribute a small fee annually.

*Exercises of Piety.* To the end that Almighty God may deign to grant excellent vocations to the various states of perfection and give the graces which are necessary to bring these vocations to fruition, the following works are strongly recommended:

1. Abstinence and fasting on the vigils of the Assumption of Our Lady and the Nativity of Our Lord Jesus Christ for the special intention of the Work for Religious Vocations.

2. Prayers to be recited in turn without intermission by the various states of perfection.

3. The celebration of the *Day of Religious Vocations* with some pious exercise approved by a decree of the Sacred Congregation of Rites and enriched with special indulgences by the Sacred Apostolic Penitentiary.

4. The celebration of the *Day of Oblation* on which the sick will offer to God their sufferings and infirmities for religious vocations in union with the Most Precious Blood of Christ.

*The Activities of the Pontifical Work.* The Pontifical Work shall:

1. See to the proper publication and diffusion of writings designed to promote a wider knowledge and higher esteem of the dignity and usefulness of religious vocations.

2. Influence priests to grasp every opportunity to treat of this subject (for example, lenten sermons, spiritual exercises, novenas, classes in Christian doctrine for adults, and the like).

3. Exhort the faithful to study the documents issued by the Holy See and also the writings of the Fathers of the Church and of pious authors on the states of evangelical perfection and the religious life.

4. Cultivate in children and adolescents of both sexes, especially those who are in any way under the care of members of any of the states of perfection, an esteem for the religious life, and nourish in them a deep desire of Christian perfection.

5. Call meetings in which this subject shall be discussed, or

at least see to it that also in other meetings some consideration be given to the subject of religious vocations.

6. Keep up relations and contact with the religious Institutes, Societies, and organizations which are affiliated to it. Assist, promote, and unite among themselves special Works and other useful undertakings by suggesting more effective means to obtain the desired end. These organizations shall then in turn report briefly, clearly, and accurately to the Pontifical Work all that they have done and accomplished.

*Feast Days.* The principal feasts of the Pontifical Work shall be:

1. The feast of the Holy Family, the Sunday within the octave of the Epiphany;
2. The feasts of all holy Founders;
3. The feast of Saints Peter and Paul, June 29;
4. The name's day of the Holy Father, Supreme Superior of all states of perfection.

**AAS 47-298**; S. C. Rel., Statutes and Norms, 11 Feb., 1955. Annotations in *Commentarium pro Religiosis,* 34 (1955)-136 (Liévin).

---

**Course of Practical Study:** Established in S. C. of Religious. S. C. Rel., 23 Oct., 1951 (AAS 43-806).

**Sisters Caring for Men Patients.** See Circular Letter of S. C. Rel., 12 Sept., 1940, reported by Sartori, *Enchiridion Canonicum,* ed. 1944, p. 56; cf. *Perfice Munus,* 15 (1940)-117.

**Sisters Caring for the Sick:** Special office in S. C. Rel. See S. C. Rel., 25 July, 1932, reported by Sartori, *Enchiridion Canonicum,* ed. 1944, p. 55.

## CANON 252

### Relation Between the Pontifical Work of the Propagation of the Faith and the Missionary Religious Institutes (Declaration of Pont. Op. Prop. Fid., 9 July, 1928) AAS 20-266.

Declaration of the Pontifical Work of the Propagation of the Faith, an organ of the S. C. Prop. Fid.:

At the full meeting of the Supreme General Council of the Pontifical Work of the Propagation of the Faith which was held at Rome in the month of April of this year [1928], the following wishes were expressed regarding the mutual relations of the Pontifical Work of the Propagation of the Faith, and the missionary religious institutes:

I. That religious, just as all others, would please to favor earnestly and constantly the Pontifical Work of the Propagation of the Faith, above all other works which are designed for the help of the missions. For:

*a*) It is a pontifical work, and it has been raised to the dignity of an instrument of the Apostolic See by His Holiness, Pius XI, by *Motu proprio, Romanorum Pontificum,* of 3 May, 1922.

*b*) The missions which are intrusted to the religious institutes receive every year considerable help from this very Pontifical Work, and the Superiors of missions often ask for extra help.

II. That the same religious would please to devote their efforts to secure the success of the special feast for the missions, which is to be celebrated in the month of October.

III. That the religious would, moreover, please to abstain from beginning undertakings, or using means, or founding works, which by reason of any resemblance could be confused with the Pontifical Work of the Propagation of the Faith, and thus hinder the growth of the said work.

IV. Wherefore, for the better coöperation and fuller success of mission works, the Supreme General Council, fully realizing that the Pontifical Work of the Propagation of the Faith cannot meet the needs of all the missions, freely declares that it does not wish to prevent the missionary institutes from collecting money from their friends and benefactors for the needs of their missions; the Supreme General Council hopes, however, that the missionary institutes will commend to their friends and benefactors the Pontifical Work itself, so that they may also give their support to it, for the reasons above stated.

**AAS 20–266;** Pontifical Work of the Propagation of the Faith; *Declaratio,* 9 July, 1928.

*Periodica,* 17 (1928)–198 (Vermeersch).

---

**Religious Congregation Subject to Propaganda.** A Congregation of pontifical right was declared to be proximately under the jurisdiction of this Sacred Congregation. See S. C. Prop. Fid., 2 Dec., 1942 (AAS 35–26).

# CANON 267

## Apostolic Legates in Mission Countries: Additional Faculties (S. C. Prop. Fid., 28 Feb., 1961) Private.

A Circular Letter sent by the S. C. of Propaganda to all Apostolic Legates (Nuncios, Internuncios, Apostolic Delegates) in territories subject to that Sacred Congregation, dated 28 February, 1961 (Prot. N. 997/61) is as follows:

Your Excellency:

In order to lighten the labors of the Secretariate of this Sacred Congregation, and above all to augment the bonds of union which connect your Pontifical Legation with the Most Reverend Ordinaries who depend upon it, the S. C. of Propaganda has deemed it opportune to grant to Your Excellency the following special faculties, which you may use *durante munere:*

4. To dispense for just and reasonable cause regarding the time and place of religious profession.

Your Excellency will please direct the Most Reverend Ordinaries to apply to your Pontifical Legation when they need any of the above favors.

At the end of every year Your Excellency will please send a report to this Sacred Congregation on the use you have made of these same faculties.

Very sincerely yours in Christ,
Gregory P. Cardinal Agagianian, Prefect
Pietro Sigismondi, Secretary.

(**Private**); S. C. Prop. Fid., 28 Feb., 1961; reported in *Periodica,* 52 (1963)–50, from the *Bibliografia Missionaria,* 25 (1961), with an extended commentary by Buijs. A footnote explains that the *Bibliografia Missionaria,* a publication edited by Monsignor Paventi and Father Kowalski, O.M.I., of the S. C. of Propaganda, has since 1961 a *Supplementum* reporting documents of the S. C. which are not published in the *Acta Apostolicae Sedis.* The present document is taken from the first *Supplementum, Documenti e problemi missionarii,* p. 23.

## New Faculties for the Apostolic Nunciature of Indonesia (Ap. Nunc., Indonesia, 14 March, 1961) Private.

The following Circular (N. 3595) was sent on the 14th of

March, 1961, by the Apostolic Nunciature of Indonesia to the Most Reverend Ordinaries of the Archipelago:

Djakarta, 14 March, 1961

Your Excellency:

I have the honor to inform Your Excellency that the Sacred Congregation for the Propagation of the Faith has just granted me the following faculties:

4. To dispense, for a just and reasonable cause, as regards the time and place of religious profession.

Hence in case of need Your Excellency may make application for the desired faculty to this Apostolic Nunciature.

With kindest personal regards,

devotedly yours in Christ,
Apostolic Nuncio

(**Private**); Apostolic Nunciature of Indonesia, 14 March, 1961.

## Faculties of Apostolic Nuncios, Internuncios, and Delegates. Private.

Following is the latest publicly available list of faculties which the Holy Father has decreed to give to Apostolic Nuncios, Internuncios, and Delegates for the territories of their respective assignments. It revokes all previously granted faculties.[1] This list, originally published in this form in 1947 (Vermeersch-Creusen: *Epitome Iuris Canonici,* 1949, ed. 7, v. 1, p. 658, footnote), is still given as the current catalog of faculties in Beste: *Introductio in Codicem,* 1961, ed. 5, pp. 1095–1101. It should be remembered that this identical index of faculties is not necessarily possessed as it stands by all Apostolic Representatives. Moreover, some Apostolic Representatives enjoy more ample faculties in certain matters.

### Chapter I

*General Faculties*

10. To grant permission to clerics and religious as individuals, to anticipate, for a reasonable cause, the private recitation of

[1] Canon Law Digest, 1, pp. 175–187.

Matins and Lauds immediately after noon at any time of the year.

## Chapter IV

### *Faculties Concerning Other Sacraments and Sacred Rites*

34. To grant *as often as there is urgent necessity and lack of time for recourse to the Holy See:*

*e*) to priests who are journeying by sea or by river, the faculty to celebrate Mass aboard ship on a portable altar, provided that there is nothing indecent or unbecoming about the place where Mass is celebrated and that there is no danger of upsetting the chalice;

*f*) to priests of both ranks of clergy who are suffering from weak eyesight or from other infirmity, the faculty to celebrate on feast days and doubles a votive Mass of the Virgin Mother of God or some other votive Mass approved by the Holy See, and on ferial days, a requiem Mass, making use, as often as necessary, of the assistance of another priest and, in the case of pastors, without prejudice to their obligation to explain the gospel on the prescribed days;

*g*) to priests who are totally blind, the same faculty mentioned in *f*), on condition that they always have the assistance of another priest or a deacon and provided that as a result of actual trial, they are found free of all defects.

## Chapter V

### *Faculties Concerning Religious*

42. To take cognizance, in extraordinary cases and in urgent necessity, of matters concerning the condition of any house of any religious institute and to hold counsel with superiors and to cooperate with them to provide appropriate remedies for the abuses and to restore the religious to the perfection of their state. They should, however, inform the Holy See as soon as possible if any new regulation seems to be called for in the interest of cloistered communities.

43. To dispense, for just cause and at the request of the community, from defect of the dowry required in the institute for sisters and nuns.

44. To grant to diocesan Ordinaries in particular cases or for a time, the faculty of placing religious in charge of parishes when secular priests are not available, but always with the consent of the religious superiors and with the understanding that at least two other religious shall live with the pastor, and observing in other respects the dispositions of the sacred canons.

45. To allow nuns in case of sickness or for other just and grave reasons, to live *outside the religious house* for a time to be determined prudently, on condition, however, that they shall always have the association and assistance of those who are relatives by blood or by marriage, or of some respectable woman; that they shall live at home or elsewhere a religious life free from the society of men, as becomes virgins consecrated to God, and without prejudice to the prescriptions of canon 639.

46. To dispense religious of either sex, for the forum of conscience only, from the obligation of returning to religious life and to permit them to remain in the world, whenever the latter have invalidly obtained a declaration of nullity of their vows, provided, however, that the invalidity of the decree be occult. It is to be understood that the vow of perpetual chastity always remains, and that the substantial obligations of the other vows are to be observed until the persons concerned obtain a special dispensation from the Holy See. It is to be further understood, if the persons be priests, that they shall wear the dress of secular priests.

**(Private)**; Faculties of Apostolic Nuncios, Internuncios, and Delegates.

## CANON 296

### Use and Administration of Funds Collected by the Franciscan Missionary Union (S. C. Prop. Fid., 28 July, 1932) Private.

The Sacred Congregation of Propaganda was asked:

Whether the alms collected by the Franciscan Missionary Union are or are not subject to the vigilance and visitation of the Vicar Apostolic.

**Reply.** On 28 July, 1932, the Sacred Congregation replied:

The alms, offerings, and donations which are collected by the Franciscan Missionary Union certainly cannot be regarded as belonging of right to the Order, as though they were given to it for its own. These gifts are to be considered as given to the Order for the aid of the missions intrusted to it, as appears from the very name "Franciscan Missionary Union."

Hence the Order is bound to expend all such funds exclusively for its missions; either to educate, prepare, or send missionaries, or to relieve the necessities of the various missions. These things are all done by the Order for the good of the mission.

And, since the Vicar Apostolic has the full right to administer the property of the mission and to make disbursements for the mission, the regular Superior may no longer exercise any control over this property. (Cf. the Instruction of the Sacred Congregation of Propaganda of 8 Dec., 1929.)[1]

As regards such funds as are given by the donors for some particular mission, they are to be faithfully turned over to that mission in accordance with the donors' intention. Likewise, funds which are given for some particular work of the mission: e.g., to build a church, or a certain hospital, infirmary, orphanage, or mission station, must be used for that purpose, and may not be diverted to any other purpose or work. But all these funds are subject to the vigilance and visitation of the Vicar Apostolic, according to the dispositions of canons 296, and 533, § 1, 4°.

**(Private)**; S. C. Prop. Fid., 28 July, 1932.
*Periodica,* 22 (1933)–162.

## CANON 300

**Quinquennial Report** (Letter, S. C. Prop. Fid., 16 Apr. 1922) **AAS 14–287.**

A Letter of the S. C. Prop. Fid., addressed to the Bishops, Vicars and Prefects Apostolic, and Superiors of missions, who are subject to that Sacred Congregation, gives a new formula for the quinquennial report, to supplant the old one which had been issued 1 June, 1877. Besides the questions in detail, for which the Latin text must be consulted, the Letter gives the following general norms:

---

[1] Reported in this volume, p. 567.

I. The report is to be in Latin, neatly written, on opaque paper, signed by the Ordinary and by at least one of the canons or consultors (in dioceses), or by one of the mission Council, bearing the day, month, and year.

II. In the first report which is made after the publication of this Letter, a full and exact answer must be given to all the questions detailed in the formula.

III. The same must be done by every new Superior of a mission the first time that he sends a quinquennial report.

IV. In subsequent reports, the Ordinaries may omit those things that refer to the historical and other general information concerning the missions, if they are the same as those contained in former reports.

AAS 14–287; S. C. Prop. Fid., 16 Apr., 1922. Annotations in *Periodica,* 11 (1923)–86.

## CANON 329

### Faculties and Privileges Granted to Local Ordinaries by *Pastorale Munus* (Paul VI, Apostolic Letter *Motu proprio,* 30 Nov., 1963) AAS 56–5.

From this document are cited the following sections as being of pertinence to religious as religious.

#### *I. Faculties*

1. To extend for a just cause but not for a period exceeding a month, the lawful use of rescripts or indults which were granted by the Apostolic See and have expired without petition for their renewal having been made in due time to the same Apostolic See.

13. To grant to chaplains of any kind of hospital, infant asylum, and prison the faculty to administer the sacrament of confirmation, in the absence of the pastor, to those of the faithful who are in danger of death. To be observed are the norms set forth by the Sacred Congregation of the Sacraments in its decree, *Spiritus Sancti munera,*[2] of 14 September, 1946, for a priest administering the sacrament of confirmation.

---

[2] Reported in CANON LAW DIGEST, 3, pp. 303–311.

28. To permit minor clerics, lay religious as well as pious women to perform even the first washing of palls, corporals, and purificators.

29. To use the faculties and privileges, with due observance of their scope and tenor, which religious resident in the diocese enjoy for the welfare of the faithful.

32. To grant permission, for a legitimate reason, to alienate, pledge, mortgage, rent out, or perpetually lease[4] ecclesiastical property and to authorize ecclesiastical moral persons to contract debts to the sum of money determined by the National or Regional Conference of Bishops and approved by the Apostolic See.

33. To appoint for as many as five terms the ordinary confessor of religious women if other provision cannot be made because of a dearth of priests suitable for this office or if the majority of the religious, including even those who in other matters have no right to vote, petition by secret voting for the reappointment of the same confessor. For those who dissent, it must, however, if they so desire, be otherwise provided.

34. To enter for a just reason within the papal enclosure of nuns' monasteries which are located in his diocese and to permit, for a just and serious reason, that others may be admitted within the enclosure and that the nuns may leave it. The permission is only for the amount of time truly necessary.

35. To dispense, at the request of the competent superior, from the impediment whereby those who have adhered to a non-Catholic sect are barred from admission into religious life.

36. To dispense, at the request of the competent superior, from the impediment of illegitimacy those who are to be admitted into religious life and are destined for the priesthood; also those who are barred from admission into religious life by a prescription of the constitutions. In both cases a dispensation cannot be given to those who are adulterously or sacrilegiously illegitimate.

37. To dispense in whole or in part, at the request of the competent superior, from the dowry which should be brought

---

[4] Translator's note: *Emphyteusi redimi,* i.e., to enter a contract of emphyteusis. This type of contract is unknown in Anglo-American law. Its closest parallel in American law is a ninety-nine year lease. The redemption of the rental is almost equivalent to the exercise by the lessee of an option of purchase which, upon payment of a lump sum, transfers to him the full legal title and relieves him of the obligation of further annual payments of rental. Cf. CANON LAW DIGEST, 1, pp. 732–733.

by postulants who are to be admitted into monasteries of nuns or into another religious institute, even one of pontifical law.

38. To permit religious to transfer from one religious institute of diocesan law to another institute of diocesan law.

39. To dismiss from the diocese for an urgent, very serious reason, individual religious if the major superior, after having been notified, fails to take proper measures. However, the matter must be immediately referred to the Apostolic See.

40. To grant permission, even through other prudent and qualified men (*viros*), for individual members of the faithful subject to him to read and retain prohibited books and papers, not excepting those which professedly propagate heresy or schism or those which attempt to undermine the foundations of religion. Precautions must be taken lest these writings fall into other hands. This permission, however, can be granted to those only who need to read prohibited books and papers to refute them, or to discharge one's function adequately, or to pursue a lawful course of studies.

### *II. Privileges*

2. To hear confessions of the faithful, even of religious women, everywhere in the world unless a local Ordinary expressly disapproves.

**AAS 56–5;** Paul VI, Apostolic Letter *Motu proprio,* 30 Nov., 1963. The above translation is from the text in AAS, which differs in a number of places, most especially in Faculties 11–14 and Privileges 4 and 8, from the Italian version published in *L'Osservatore Romano,* for 4 Dec., 1963, no. 280, p. 7, and from the English version distributed to the Bishops as they left the second session of Vatican Council II, a copy of which was kindly sent us by the Rt. Rev. Msgr. Cornelius Sweeney, Chancellor of the Archdiocese of Indianapolis.

## CANON 349

**Use of Rochet Accorded to All Bishops of the Regular Orders** (Benedict XV, *Motu proprio,* 25 April, 1920) **AAS 12–149.**

All Bishops who are of the regular Orders may henceforth forever use the rochet, and shall be dressed in all respects in the same way as the secular Bishops, save as regards the usual color and quality of the vestments. Accordingly, besides the cases in which, according to the Bishops' Ceremonial and the Decrees, the mozzetta alone, or the mozzetta with the mantellatta, should or may be worn, at other times, they, as well as all other Bishops, shall in this Holy City wear the mantellatta alone over the rochet; any Apostolic Constitutions or other reasons to the contrary notwithstanding.

**AAS 12–149**; Benedict XV, *Motu proprio,* 25 Apr., 1920.
*Periodica,* 10 (1922)–142 (Pauwels).

**Resident Bishops May Grant Indulgences to Exempt Religious, or in Their Churches** (Cod. Com., 6 Dec. 1930) **AAS 23–25.**

The Code Commission was asked:

Whether the words *in suae jurisdictionis locis,* of c. 349, § 2, 2°, are to be understood in the sense that Bishops are prohibited from granting indulgences to exempt religious, or in their churches?

**Reply.** In the negative.

**AAS 23–25**; Cod. Com., 6 Dec., 1930.
*Periodica,* 20 (1931)–148 (Vermeersch).

## CANON 423

**Diocesan Consultors: Not to Be Religious Nor Ex-Religious** (Cod. Com., 29 Jan., 1931) **AAS 23–110.**

The Code Commission was asked:

Whether, in the term *sacerdotes,* as used in c. 423, are included also religious, or religious who have been secularized.

**Reply:** In the negative.

**AAS 23–110**; Cod. Com., 29 Jan., 1931. Annotations in *Periodica,* 20 (1931)–152 (Cappello); *Jus Pontificium,* 11 (1931)–107.

## CANON 451

**Religious Military Chaplains** (S. C. Rel., Instruction, 2 Feb., 1955) **AAS 47–93.**

An Instruction of the Sacred Congregation of Religious on Religious Military Chaplains:

Since priests of the secular clergy are often insufficient in number, Military Vicars must at times receive members of religious Institutes or of Societies of common life, to exercise the sacred ministry for the benefit of the armed forces.

Accordingly some Legates of the Supreme Pontiff have inquired whether this Sacred Congregation has established any special regulations and norms on this subject.

In the Instruction of the Sacred Consistorial Congregation on Military Vicars, of 23 April, 1951, n. 13,[1] issued with the previous approval of the Supreme Pontiff, the following provision was made: "Also excellent and well tried religious priests should be chosen for the office of chaplain, observing however the special norms laid down for them by the Sacred Congregation of Religious; and these men if possible should be assigned to places where there is a house of their Institute."

The Sacred Congregation of Religious, therefore, in its diligent solicitude for the perfection of religious, has decided to issue this Instruction outlining the principles according to which the office of chaplain can safely be accepted and establishing norms for fulfilling it in a holy and fruitful manner in cases where it is to be accepted.

### Art. I. *The Appointment and Removal of Religious Military Chaplains and Vigilance Over Them*

1. The office of military chaplain, which cannot be exercised by a priest while remaining in his own religious house and observing all the practices of the common life, but which on the contrary demands that nearly his whole life be continuously spent outside the religious family and in the manner of a military and secular person, should not be accepted unless there is a real necessity for it, that is, when there are not enough chaplains from the secular clergy.

2. The appointment of religious to the office of military chaplain and their removal, are canonically regulated by the same rules and norms which govern the appointment and removal of religious pastors (canons 456, 454, § 5; observing however Art. III, n. 1 of this Instruction). Vigilance over them and their correction pertain to the Military Vicar and their religious Su-

[1] AAS, 43–564; Canon Law Digest, 3, p. 116.

periors according to canon 631 and the Instruction of the Sacred Consistorial Congregation.

3. In this matter the local Ordinary means the Military Vicar.

4. In view of the peculiar circumstances in which this ministry is exercised, the religious Superior should not, without serious reflection and unusually grave reasons, impose it upon any one against his will.

### Art. II. *The Necessary Qualifications of a Military Chaplain*

It is an obligation in conscience upon those concerned to choose for the office of military chaplain, in time of peace, religious:

1) Who have reached their thirty-fifth year, or in case of real necessity, have completed at least thirty years, on condition, however, that they show real maturity of character.

2) Who are outstanding in learning, piety, and religious spirit, and do not take the office for the sake of enjoying a false liberty.

### Art. III. *The Duration of the Office*

1. Religious military chaplains can be removed from office for just cause at the discretion of the Military Vicar and of the religious Superior. The religious Superior should in due time so arrange the matter with the Military Vicar that the chaplain's removal occasion neither any difficulty with the military authorities nor any detriment to the apostolic ministry.

2. Religious military chaplains are not to be appointed for more than five years, and the consent of the religious Superiors should be renewed every two years.

3. They should not again assume the same office until they shall have submitted themselves willingly and humbly to perfect religious discipline in a religious house for at least some months. The religious Superior upon his conscientious responsibility can dispense from this obligation especially those who during their service as chaplains were not entirely deprived of the benefits of a religious community life.

### Art. IV. *The Religious Condition of the Military Chaplain*

1. The religious military chaplain is not to be numbered among excloistered religious (canon 639) but rather among

those who, as long as they retain that office, are legitimately absent to work in the sacred ministry, remaining subject to their Superiors (canon 606, § 2).

2. Military chaplains, as religious legitimately absent, enjoy the rights and privileges of their Institute and can retain or assume such offices in their Institute as do not conflict in law or in fact with the office of military chaplain.

3. The religious military chaplain is likewise bound to his vows made to God, and has the obligation ever faithfully to keep them. Nor does he cease to be bound by the rules, Constitutions, and prescriptions of the life which he has professed, when these are consistent with his state and office.

### Art. V. *The Religious and Priestly Discipline of the Military Chaplain*

1. As to the priestly discipline of the religious military chaplain, attention is called to the Instruction for Military Vicars issued by the Sacred Consistorial Congregation on 23 April, 1951.[2]

2. Major Superiors should give to those of their subjects who receive the grave charge of military chaplain, letters of obedience in which the precepts of the present Instruction are defined for particular conditions and places, and also prudently supplemented if that seems providentially desirable.

3. In the first place every religious military chaplain should be assigned to some house of his own Institute, whose Superior should have charge of such a religious both spiritually and materially.

4. If the number of religious military chaplains seems, in the judgment of Major Superiors, to demand it, an Office may be created for the Province, region, or country, which under the vigilance of Superiors shall have charge of the chaplains spiritually, intellectually, and materially, and assist local Superiors, or partly take over their duties.

5. It is also very advisable that one or two religious military chaplains be assigned to the Military Vicar to advise him and to assist the religious who are in the service.

6. *a*) Religious Superiors, personally or through the Office

[2] AAS, 43–562; Canon Law Digest, 3, p. 113.

mentioned above (n. 4), should see to it that religious chaplains be stationed if possible in places where there is a house of their own Institute; and this is also earnestly recommended to Military Vicars.

*b*) Religious chaplains shall if possible spend the night in a house of their own Institute or, if there is none, in another religious or at least pious house.

*c*) Superiors shall constantly admonish the chaplains to put diligently into practice the norms of prudence and the appropriate safeguards which are laid down in the Constitutions, rules, and statutes of their Institute for the protection of chastity.

*d*) Religious Superiors shall at appropriate times and often inquire of the Military Vicar how the chaplains who are his subjects are behaving, and in a proper case shall also confer with him about a particular religious chaplain who needs to be forbidden some dangerous association or to be effectively stimulated to do his duty diligently.

7. *a*) A religious chaplain must be well aware that he is under the authority of his Superiors in almost the same way as religious who have charge of a parish. Consequently, of course without prejudice to the rights of the Military Vicar, his whole religious and priestly life is subject to their vigilance, inspection, and judgment. He is to ask and obtain from them, as occasion offers, the dispensations and faculties which he may need concerning the religious life. He may also, according to the prudent judgment of his Superiors, follow the *Ordo* established by the Military Vicar for saying the Office and celebrating Mass (Instruction of the Sacred Consistorial Congregation, n. 7).[3]

*b*) At the times fixed by Superiors, the religious chaplain must give an account of receipts and expenses to the religious Superior to whom he is immediately subject, so that his poverty may suffer no harm.

*c*) Whatever money is left over as not needed for his necessary living expenses nor spent in the course of his office shall be turned over by the religious chaplain to his religious Superior according to canon 594, § 2, with due regard to the prescriptions, if any, of the laws of his country or of the Military Vicar regarding mutual financial assistance to be given by military chaplains to one another.

---

[3] CANON LAW DIGEST, 3, p. 115.

8. *a*) There should be regular correspondence by letter between the religious chaplain and his superiors.

*b*) Superiors whenever they can should come in person to visit the chaplains, or should send others to do so in their name.

*c*) Superiors should see to it that members especially of the house to which chaplains are assigned and of houses situated in the place where they are staying, visit the chaplains and invite them to return the visit, and treat them with unfailing fraternal charity. Superiors should willingly practice the same charity toward other religious military chaplains who are far from any house of their own Institute.

9. *a*) Religious chaplains should strive to excel among military chaplains in their spirit of brotherly love and in the ardor of their priestly zeal, and thus to present a living likeness of a good soldier of Jesus Christ.

*b*) They should faithfully perform the duty of making the spiritual exercises every year, observing the custom of retiring to a house of their own Institute for that purpose.

*c*) Once a month they should retire to the religious house for recollection, and there, apart from the world, spend the day in spiritual meditation.

*d*) Whatever time by way of furlough is regularly allowed, or granted on request, should be spent by the chaplains, not with relatives or in places of their own choice, but in religious houses or in places assigned to them by Superiors, and under obedience to them.

10. The prescriptions of Articles IV and V are to be observed even in time of war.

Rome, 2 Feb., 1955.

**AAS 47–93**; S. C. Rel., Instruction, 2 Feb., 1955. Annotations, *Commentarium pro Religiosis,* 34 (1955)–65 (Guttiérrez), and *Monitor Ecclesiasticus,* 80 (1955)–236 (Gutiérrez).

## CANON 462

**Public Processions of Exempt Religious** (Cod. Com., 10 Nov., 1925) **AAS 17–582.**

The Code Commission was asked:

Whether, according to c. 462, 7°, and the Reply of 12 Nov.,

1922,[1] the right of the pastor to conduct public processions outside the church applies also to processions of exempt religious outside their churches and cloisters.

**Reply.** In the affirmative, without prejudice, however, to cc. 1291, § 2, and 1293.

**AAS 17–582;** Cod. Com., 10 Nov., 1925, V.
*Periodica,* 14 (1926)–183 (Vermeersch); *Jus Pontificium,* 6 (1926)–9.

## CANON 469

**The Apostolate of the Cinema** (S. C. Rel., Instruction, 11 May, 1953) **Private.**

An Instruction of the Sacred Congregation of Religious on the Apostolate of the Cinema, is as follows:

"In our times," wrote Pope Pius XI in the Encyclical, *Vigilanti cura,* of 29 June, 1936, "there is need of vigilance and effort that the cinema may be no longer a school of corruption but may become a precious instrument for right education and a higher standard of morality."

This vigilance and effort, so often recommended also by the present Sovereign Pontiff, have been worthily exercised both by the Pontifical Office of the Cinema, which was established by the Holy See to study those problems of the cinema which have a relation to faith and morals, and by the Catholic Hierarchy and the secular and religious clergy, who have followed and continue to follow the grave problem of the cinema with attentive solicitude. "Among modern forms of entertainment, this one has achieved a position of universal importance" (Pius XI, *ibid.*), and it has now become a need, strongly felt not only among the people of large cities but even in small rural communities.

The concrete results of the interest which the Bishops and the clergy have taken in the problems of the cinema, are the numerous exhortations and regulations which have been issued by ecclesiastical authorities in various countries, and the many projects which have been launched to protect the spiritual interests of the faithful and to exercise a morally elevating influence in the moving picture industry. Worthy of special mention in

[1] AAS 14–661; reported in CANON LAW DIGEST, 1, p. 251.

this connection are the cinematographic theaters which are conducted, often at considerable sacrifice, by priests and religious who have the care of souls or are in charge of specialized apostolates of an educative or social nature. These halls not only afford the faithful, and especially the young people, a healthy form of amusement, but they are often an effective means of education and of progress in culture and religious spirit.

There are, however, some drawbacks, resulting chiefly from the real difficulties which the managers of Catholic movie halls must encounter, the scarcity of films which are morally sound and the financial burdens which the said managers have to bear. These difficulties, though they be keenly felt, evidently cannot justify the showing in a Catholic hall, of films which are morally objectionable.

Certainly many of these difficulties are finding and will find an adequate solution in the words of Pius XI in the Encyclical already cited: "The establishment of these Catholic theaters, which are often good customers for the movie industry, makes it possible to claim a new right, namely the right to demand that the industry itself produce films which are in full accord with our principles and which will easily get a showing not only in Catholic halls but in other movie houses as well."

To carry out these directives, national Catholic associations of practical moving picture men have been and are being organized in different countries according to the exigencies of this form of apostolate. These associations have as their definite purpose to represent the moral and material interests of the Catholic houses before the civil authorities, to defend their rights in respect to other associations, and to give them legal, administrative, and financial assistance. How appropriate it is, not to say necessary, that Catholic houses should belong to such associations — a thing which, for that matter, has often been emphasized by ecclesiastical authorities — scarcely needs further mention.

The Encyclical, *Vigilanti cura,* further provides, "that in every country the Bishops should establish a permanent national Reviewing Board which may promote good shows and classify others, and make their decisions known to priests and the faithful."

The decisions issued by the national Reviewing Boards should furnish a norm for every one; and the faithful should conform to them, both to avoid the occasions of sin and scandal and to take a stand against immoral films, thus inducing the producers to turn out better pictures.

When one considers the number of religious Institutes which profess as their proper end, according to their Constitutions approved by the Holy See, to practice the apostolate of the cinema, not only by showing and distributing morally good films but also by producing them, it is easy to see how large a part religious have, both *de iure* and *de facto,* in this apostolate which is developing in all parts of the world.

If one further considers the work being done by religious men and women who are engaged in teaching, in relief work, in youth and adult education, and in all the other forms of apostolate, it becomes evident that they come in contact more and more, though indirectly, with the world of the cinema.

The problem of the apostolate of the cinema concerns not only the parishes which are entrusted to religious but also the Associations which religious Institutes of men and women organize and control for young people everywhere.

This fact is supported by statistics: indeed this Sacred Congregation of Religious has direct information that a very important percentage of the Catholic moving picture houses in various countries are conducted by persons who depend upon this Sacred Congregation. In Italy, for example, on the basis of precise investigations, out of four thousand cinema halls which depend upon or are controlled by ecclesiastical authorities, more than half belong to religious men or women. (The industrial movie houses number about eight thousand.)

Accordingly, for the purpose of providing more adequately for the complex and urgent needs of this sector of the apostolate of religious, with a conviction of the great educational importance of the cinema, both as a positive auxiliary of the apostolate (for liberal and Christian training) and as a negative one (as a preservative), this Sacred Congregation of Religious has deemed it opportune by the present Instruction directed to the Very Reverend Superiors General and Superioresses General of the religious Institutes which directly or indirectly exercise this apostolate, to provide according to its competency as follows:

1. Since the public management of cinema halls constitutes a *commercial activity* in the sense of the Code of Canon Law

(canons 142, 592, 2380) and of the Decree, *De vetita clericis et religiosis negotiatione et mercatura,* of 22 March, 1950,[1] religious who intend to open a hall must ask the permission (*nulla osta*) of the Holy See (S. C. of Religious), which is necessary to remove the canonical impediment established by the law itself and sanctioned by canonical penalties.

2. It is considered that *public management* in the sense of the present Instruction exists when the religious — either for themselves or for others (c. 142) — conduct a moving picture theater showing films for the general public and at the same time engaging in any lucrative activity whatever.

3. No permission of the Holy See (that is, in the instance, of the S. C. of Religious, according to canon 7) is required when there is question of private showings, that is, when either the shows are not destined for the public or admission is free of charge.

4. The S. C. of Religious in granting the *nulla osta* will hear the opinion of the Pontifical Commission for the Cinema, the organ of the Holy See for the study of problems connected with the cinema which have a bearing on faith and morals.

5. When the canonical impediment mentioned in n. 1 is removed, the Institute becomes capable of exercising the activity in question, which as a consequence is legitimate.

6. Thereafter, in deciding that it is advisable in view of all the conditions of place, persons, and circumstances to open a hall to the public, the *nulla osta* of the Ordinary of the place is required, together with that of the major religious Superior.

7. It is to be noted that, according to the principles of canon law, the regulations issued by the Most Excellent diocesan Ordinaries in regard to the apostolate of the cinema in what concerns the faith, morals, or public order, are binding on religious, including exempt religious, who conduct moving picture halls that are open to the public.

8. The holder of the license for a moving picture hall operated by religious can be only the Superior of the house to which the hall is attached or on which it depends, the religious Pastor, or a delegate of either; never a lay person.

9. It will not be permitted except by way of very rare exception duly proved, to transfer the management of a (religious)

[1] AAS, 42–330; reported in this volume, p. 48.

hall temporarily or permanently to private parties. The *nulla osta* mentioned in n. 1 never includes this permission.

10. The managers are bound in conscience to keep a careful watch during the exhibitions, to forestall dangers or untoward occurrences of any kind.

11. The making up of the programs for the shows belongs exclusively to the holder of the license, and he is always responsible for it, even if he employs lay helpers.

12. The films to be shown may be selected only from among those which are classified as suitable *for all persons* by the permanent national Reviewing Board, or from among those classified as suitable *for adults,* but this by way of exception and with the proper corrections according to the regulations issued by the Ordinary.

13. In no case will the showing of films be permitted, which are classified by the competent national Reviewing Board as: *for adults with reservations,* or *not recommended,* or *excluded.*

14. The exposition of publicity material or posters on the façade or near the entrance of the church is to be avoided.[2]

Rome, 11 May, 1953 (Prot. N. 01666/53).

(**Private**); S. C. Rel., Instruction, 11 May, 1953.

NOTE: This translation is made from the Italian text published in *Commentarium pro Religiosis,* 32 (1953)–254. Strictly speaking, even the fourteen specific regulations reported above are not absolutely obligatory outside of Italy; for according to the practice of the Roman Curia, documents intended for universal application as formally binding, are issued in Latin (cf. *Commentarium pro Religiosis,* 31 (1952)–249) whereas this is in Italian only. However, the expository parts of the Instruction are evidently of universal value for religious; and its dispositive provisions are virtually universal in as much as they express the mind of the Holy See and indicate a legitimate practice which is independent of locality, and which might reasonably in the future be extended so as to become formally obligatory everywhere. Cf. Annotations in *Commentarium pro Religionis,* 32(1953)–258 (Canals), and in *Monitor Ecclesiasticus,* 79 (1954)–64 (Gutiérrez).

---

[2] Here follow six regulations for Italy only, which we omit from this report.

## CANON 470

**Parish in Russia: Notice to Be Sent to Commission** (Commission for Russia, 13 July, 1928) **AAS 20–260.**

The Russian Commission issued the following Decree:

To prevent the dispersion of ecclesiastical documents which can easily occur, not without grave loss, while the present circumstances in Russia continue, the Pontifical Commission for Russia, with the approval of His Holiness, Pius XI, decrees:

Until otherwise provided, all notices which are to be given to the pastor of baptism according to canons 470, § 2, 576, § 2, 798, 1011, and 1103, § 2, shall be sent to this Pontifical Commission by those whose duty it is, if the parish of baptism is within the limits of the Russian jurisdiction.

**AAS 20–260**; Commission for Russia, 13 July, 1928.
*Periodica,* 17 (1928)–206.

## CANON 487

**Erroneous Translations of Canons Relating to Lay Religious Societies** (S. C. Rel., 2 April, 1919) **AAS 11–179.**

It was pointed out to the Sacred Congregation of Religious that some "authorized" but unofficial translations of those canons of the Code which relate to lay religious societies (cf. c. 488, 4°) differed from the original text of the Code. Hence, the question was asked:

Whether the Code had been modified, or the translations were erroneous.

**Reply.** The original prescriptions of the Code remain unchanged, and the translations are to be amended.

**AAS 11–179**; S. C. Rel., 2 Apr., 1919.
*Periodica,* 10 (1922)–67.

**Praise and Esteem of the Religious State** (Letter, Pius XI, 19 Mar., 1924) **AAS 16–133.**

In an Apostolic Letter addressed to Superiors General of all religious Orders and societies of men, His Holiness, Pius XI, quoting c. 487, praises the religious state, the variety and holiness of religious institutes in the Church, and gives an earnest exhortation regarding the training of religious, especially those destined for the priesthood.

**AAS 16–133**; Pius XI, Apostolic Letter, 19 Mar., 1924.
*Periodica,* 13 (1925)–14 (Vermeersch).

NOTE: Some features of this Letter are summarily reported in this volume on pp. 296, 316, 582, 583.

## Consecration of Virgins Living in the World Without Vows (S. C. Rel., 25 Mar., 1927) AAS 19–138.

Some Bishops had asked the Sacred Congregation of Religious for faculties to bless and consecrate virgins living in the world without vows, according to the rites described in the Roman Pontifical. Hence, the question was proposed to the consultors and discussed in plenary session:

**Question.** Is it advisable to grant the faculty of giving to women living in the world the blessing and consecration of virgins?

**Reply.** In the negative, and let no novelties be introduced.

**AAS 19–138**; S. C. Rel., *Dubium,* 25 Mar., 1927.
*Periodica,* 16 (1927)–30 (Vermeersch); *Jus Pontificium,* 7 (1927)–11.

## The Religious Life (Pius XII, Allocution, 8 Dec., 1950) AAS 43–26.

An Address of Pius XII to the assembled delegates of all religious Orders and Congregations, Societies and Secular Institutes, after their first general Congress held in Rome near the close of the Holy Year, 1950, is as follows:

1. The Holy Year through no merit of Ours but through the favor of God's mercy has proved more bountiful in blessings than the foresight of men had anticipated. In the eventful cycle of its notable achievements, it has manifested the strong faith and richly abundant life of the Church of Christ, our Mother. Your Congress rightly takes its place among the more significantly important events and over them your fraternal gathering reflects its own characteristic luster. To you now We wish to address Our words of affectionate greeting.

2. The annals of Church History record no meeting similar to this. Here for the first time, religious organizations whose members have selected as the goal of their lives the attainment of consummate evangelical perfection have assembled in large numbers over a period of several days to discuss and weigh the problems of their common interest.

3. It was Our judgment that the circumstances of the times made it altogether necessary to do so. For the changed conditions of the world which the Church must encounter, certain points of doctrine touching upon the status and condition of moral perfection, not to mention the pressing needs of the apostolic work which you have so widely and so generously undertaken, all these have called you to devote yourselves to this systematic study and discussion.

4. Your work is at its close. It was energized by careful discussions, it has been prolific in proposals, and it will be no less fruitful, We hope, in perfecting the virtues which will realize your projects. With the resolute cooperation of your wills, the grace of God will enkindle those virtues, the grace, that is, which your prayers and religious acts of self-denial, more especially, because of their burning devotion, those of your Sisters in Christ, have already invoked upon this present undertaking.

5. You have requested the fatherly blessing of the Vicar of Christ as a pledge of divine guidance and assistance so that your Congress might be fittingly completed and terminated. But before imparting that blessing to you, We think it proper to present to you orally certain thoughts on the religious life which call for an explanation and which, once explained, may serve hereafter as a norm to direct your thoughts and actions.

## I

6. First of all, it will be useful for Us to indicate briefly the place held in the Church by the religious Orders and Congregations. You are, of course, aware that Our Redeemer founded a Church endowed with an hierarchical organization. For between the Apostles and their successors, with whom must also be grouped their assistants in the ministry, and the ordinary faithful He drew a definite line of demarcation, and by the union of these two elements the structure of the Kingdom of God on earth stands firm. Consequently the distinction between the clergy and

the laity is fixed by divine law (cfr. can. 107). Interposed between these two grades is the religious state which deriving its origin from the Church has its existence and strength from its intimate connection with the end of the Church herself, which is to lead men to the attainment of holiness. Though every Christian should scale these sacred heights under the guidance of the Church, nevertheless the religious moves toward them along a path that is peculiarly his own and by means that are of a more exalted nature.

7. Moreover, the religious state is not restricted to either of the two groups which exist in the Church by divine right, since both clerics and lay persons alike can become religious, and on the other hand, the clerical dignity lies open to religious and those who are not religious. One would therefore be mistaken in appraising the value of the foundations which Christ laid in building His Church, if he should judge that the peculiar form of the secular clerical life as such was established and sanctioned by our Divine Redeemer, and that the peculiar form of the regular clerical life, though it is to be considered good and worthy of approbation in itself, is still secondary and auxiliary in nature, since it is not derived from Christ. Wherefore, if we keep before our eyes the order established by Christ, neither of the two special forms of clerical life holds a prerogative of divine right, since that law singles our neither form, nor gives to either precedence over the other. What, then, the difference is between these two forms, what their mutual relations are, what special task in working out the salvation of mankind has been assigned to each, all these details Christ left to be decided according to the needs and conditions of succeeding ages; or rather, to express Our mind more exactly, He left them to the definitive decisions of the Church herself.

8. Undoubtedly it is according to the divine law that every priest, be he secular or regular, should fulfill his ministry in such a way as to be a subordinate assistant to his Bishop. This has always been the customary practice in the Church, and the prescriptions in the Code of Canon Law which deal with the members of religious societies as pastors and local Ordinaries make this clear (can. 626–631; 454, par. 5). And it often happens in missionary territories that all the clergy, even including the Bishop, belong to the regular militia of the Church. Let no

one think this is an extraordinary or abnormal state of affairs to be regarded as only a temporary arrangement, and that the administration should be handed over to the secular clergy as soon as possible.

9. Again, the exemption of religious Orders is not contrary to the principles of the constitution given to the Church by God, nor does it in any way contradict the law that a priest owes obedience to his Bishop. For according to Canon Law, exempt religious are subject to the authority of the local Bishop so far as the administration of the episcopal office and the well-regulated care of souls require. But even putting aside this consideration, in the discussions of the past few decades concerning the question of exemption perhaps too little attention has been paid to the fact that exempt religious even by the prescriptions of Canon Law are always and everywhere subject to the authority of the Roman Pontiff as their supreme moderator, and that they owe obedience to him precisely in virtue of their religious vow of obedience (can. 499, par. 1). Indeed the Supreme Pontiff possesses ordinary and immediate jurisdiction over each and every diocese and over the individual faithful just as he does over the universal Church. It is therefore clear that the primary law of God whereby the clergy and the laity are subject to the rule of the Bishop is more than sufficiently observed as regards exempt religious, as it is no less clear that both branches of the clergy by reason of their parallel service conform to the will and precept of Christ.

## II

10. There is another question connected with what has so far been said which We wish to explain and clarify. It concerns the way in which the cleric and the religious should strive for their due moral perfection.

11. It is a distortion of the truth to say that the clerical state as such and as divinely established demands either by its very nature or by some postulate of that nature that the evangelical counsels be observed by its members, and that for this very reason it must be called a state of achieving evangelical perfection. A cleric therefore is not bound by the divine law to observe the evangelical counsels of poverty, chastity, and obedience; above all he is not bound in the same way or for the same reason

as the one for whom such obligation arises from vows publicly pronounced upon entering the religious life. This does not, however, prevent the cleric from assuming these bonds privately and of his own accord. So too, the fact that the priests of the Latin rite are bound to observe holy celibacy does not remove or lessen the distinction between the clerical and the religious states. Moreover a member of the regular clergy professes the state and condition of evangelical perfection not inasmuch as he is a cleric, but inasmuch as he is a religious.

12. And although we have declared in Our Apostolic Constitution *Provida Mater Ecclesia* that the form of life followed by the Secular Institutes is to be considered as a state of evangelical perfection and recognized as such by the common law of the Church, since their members are in some way bound to the observance of the evangelical counsels, still this in no way contradicts what We have just affirmed. Assuredly there is no reason preventing clerics from joining together in Secular Institutes so that by their choice of this manner of life they may strive for the attainment of religious perfection; but in that case they are in a state of acquiring perfection not inasmuch as they are clerics, but inasmuch as they are members of a Secular Institute. After all such an institute adopts, in the way of life it proposes to follow, the evangelical counsels which are proper to the religious state and are there realized in their highest perfection; but the Institute so achieves that end that it is not dependent on the traditional pattern of the religious state but stands by itself in an external form of life which bears no necessary relation to the perfection just mentioned.

## III

13. We think it timely now to touch upon some of the reasons which the religious state holds out to men as motives for embracing it.

14. It is asserted by some that the religious state by its very nature and purpose, even though meriting approval, is nothing but a safe refuge offered to the fearful and timid who have not the strength to stand up to the dangers of life's storms, and lacking the knowledge, or perhaps the will, to face difficulties, are led by their indolence to bid farewell to the world and fly to the haven of cloistered peace. Wherefore we must inspire

self-confidence and reliance on God's grace in those who seek such idle tranquillity, so that they may overcome these traits of character and attain the courage to face the struggles of common life. Is this indeed true?

15. It is not Our purpose here to evaluate the various motives inducing individuals to betake themselves to the religious life. We do wish, however, to indicate the principal and indeed the valid reason that should induce one to enter the protected enclosure of the cloister. And it is certainly different from that distorted opinion stated above, which if taken as a whole, is both untrue and unjust. For not otherwise than the resolution to enter the priesthood, the resolve to embrace the religious state, together with a firm constancy in executing it, demands greatness of soul and an ardent zeal for self-consecration. The history of the Church in its record of the glorious achievements of the saints in heaven and of the religious Institutes on earth, in its account of successful missionary enterprises, in its sketching of the Church's ascetical teaching, no less than experience itself, indicates more clearly than the light of day that men and women of indomitable and whole-souled courage have flourished in the religious state as well as in the world. Again, do those religious men and women who so strenuously exert themselves to spread the Kingdom of the Gospel, who tend the sick, train the young, and toil in the classrooms, shun the society of their fellow men and shut them out from their love? Are not very many of them, no less than the secular priesthood and their lay helpers, fighting in the very front ranks of the battle for the Church's cause?

16. Here We cannot refrain from directing Our attention to another matter which completely denies the false assertion mentioned previously. If the number of candidates wishing to enter the enclosed garden of the religious life is diminishing, especially among young women, the reason very frequently is that they find it too difficult to divest themselves of their own judgment and surrender their freedom of action, as the very nature of the vow of obedience demands. Indeed some praise as the real peak of moral perfection, not the surrender of liberty for the love of Christ, but the curbing of such surrender. The norm therefore to be preferred in the formation of a just and holy person would seem to be this: restrict liberty only where necessary; otherwise, give liberty free rein as far as possible.

17. We transmit the question whether this new foundation on which some are trying to erect the edifice of sanctity will be as effective and as solid in supporting and augmenting the apostolic work of the Church as was the one which through fifteen hundred years has been provided by that ancient rule of obedience undertaken for the love of Christ. What is now of supreme importance is to examine this proposal thoroughly, to disclose what lies concealed beneath the surface. This opinion, if carefully considered, not only fails to appreciate the nature of the evangelical counsel, but it somehow twists it to a meaning in accord with its theory. No one is obliged to choose for himself the counsel of perfect obedience, which essentially is a rule of life whereby one surrenders the control of his own will; no one, We repeat, be it an individual or a group. They can if they wish conform their conduct to this new rule. But words must be understood and accepted according to their obvious meaning, and if this norm is compared with the vow of obedience, it surely does not possess the same supreme value, nor is it an adequate expression of the wonderful example recorded in Holy Scripture: "He humbled Himself becoming obedient unto death" (Phil. 2:8).

18. He therefore is himself deceived and deceives others who forgetting the propensities of the soul and the inspiration of divine grace, offers as a guide to one seeking advice about entering the religious state only that new norm. Hence if it is clear that the voice of God is calling someone to the heights of evangelical perfection, without any hesitation he should be invited for the attainment of this lofty purpose to offer freely the sacrifice of his liberty as the vow of obedience demands, that vow, We proclaim, which the Church through so many centuries has weighed, has put to the test, has properly delineated, and has approved. Let no one against his will be compelled to this self-consecration; but if he does will it, let no one counsel him against it; above all, let no one hold him back.

## IV

19. But enough on this point. At the moment, We wish to speak on external works and the interior life. Hardly any question of grave importance for the life of regulars, or for the religious life in general, has been treated at greater length. Nevertheless We wish to present Our own judgment on this matter.

20. It was not mere chance that brought about, in our day, the rise and elaboration of the philosophy known as "Existentialism." The men of our time, when confronted by events which bring up difficult metaphysical and religious problems to be solved, gladly, without a thought of higher principles, persuade themselves that it is enough to act as the exigencies of the moment demand. But the man who professes our holy faith refuses to follow such principles and to make each passing moment of time his whole concern, hurling himself headlong into the stream of life. He knows that the "things that appear not" (Heb. 11:1) are to be considered of supreme worth, are preeminently true, and so enduring in the future as to last forever. Yet — be it said with sorrow — though warnings and exhortations have not been lacking, even some ecclesiastics, not excepting religious, have been deeply infected by this contagion, and while not denying a reality that transcends the senses and the whole natural order, they esteem it of little importance.

21. Has this grave and dangerous crisis been overcome? Thanks be to God, We may hope that it has. Certain things which We have Ourselves witnessed, and which events have made known to Us, offer this assurance.

22. The most active zeal can be closely allied with the quest for the riches of the interior life. Two stars that shine in the firmament of the religious life, St. Francis Xavier and St. Teresa of Jesus, are brilliant proofs of this.

23. An eager external activity and the cultivation of the interior life demand more than a bond of fellowship; as far at least as evaluation and willed effort are concerned, they demand that they should march along together step by step. With the growth of devotion to exterior works therefore, let there shine forth a corresponding increase in faith, in the life of prayer, in zealous consecration of self and talents to God, in spotless purity of conscience, in obedience, in patient endurance of hardship, and in active charity tirelessly expended for God and one's neighbor.

24. This is true not only of the individual religious, who really is such in heart as well as in habit, but it is also the reason why communities as a whole are solidly founded in the sight of God and men, and are deserving of the most generous praise. The Church insistently demands of you that your external works correspond to your interior life, and that these two main-

tain a constant balance. Do you not, both clerical and lay religious, profess that you have embraced the state of evangelical perfection? If so, bring forth the fruits proper to your state, so that the Mystical Body of Christ, which is the Church, may draw ever-increasing vitality from your strength and fervor. This is the very reason why religious Orders totally dedicated to the contemplative life are in their own way necessary to the Church, since they are for her a perpetual ornament and a copious source of heavenly graces.

25. You know, of course, that it has often been remarked that charity to the neighbor is gradually losing its religious character and is becoming secularized. But an honorable and kind treatment of others that has no foundation in faith, and springs from some other source, is not charity nor may it be called Catholic. Charity possesses a dignity, an inspiration, and a strength that is lacking in mere philanthropy however endowed with wealth and other resources. Thus if We compare our Catholic Sisters who nurse the sick with some others who perform this same task out of mere humanitarianism or for pay, We discover in them something entirely different and of higher value. They may at times be inferior to others in technical advantages, and We take this occasion to urge them not only to keep abreast of others in this matter but even to surpass them. But where our religious women, deeply imbued with the vital spirit of their Institutes and daily prepared for the love of Christ to lay down their lives for the sick, perform their labors, a different atmosphere prevails, in which virtue works wonders which technical aids and medical skill alone are powerless to accomplish.

26. Therefore let those religious Orders and Congregations that devote themselves to the active life keep ever before their eyes and inwardly cherish all that stamps their souls with the lineaments of holiness and nourishes the fire of the Holy Spirit in the depth of their pure souls.

## V

27. Dearly Beloved, We wish also to refer briefly to the efforts of religious Institutes to adapt themselves to our changed times, and to join the new and the old in harmonious union.

28. When young people hear the statements: "We must keep

up to date" and "Our efforts must be commensurate with the times," they are fired with an extraordinary ardor of soul, and if they are serving under the standard of the religious militia, they keenly desire to direct the efforts of their future religious undertakings according to this principle. And to a certain extent, this is proper. For it often has happened that the founding fathers of religious Institutes conceived new projects in order to meet the challenge which newly emerging needs were urgently presenting to the Church and her works; and in this way they harmonized their enterprises with their age. Hence if you wish to walk in the footsteps of your predecessors, act as they acted. Examine thoroughly the beliefs, convictions, and conduct of your own contemporaries, and if you discover in them elements that are good and proper, make these worthwhile features your own; otherwise you will never be able to enlighten, assist, sustain and guide the men of your own time.

29. However the Church possesses a patrimony preserved intact from her earliest origin, which is unchanged in the course of ages, and which is in perfect accord with the needs and the aspirations of the human race. The Catholic faith is the most important part of this patrimony, and in the Encyclical Letter *Humani Generis* We recently defended it from new errors. Preserve most diligently this faith undefiled by any blemish; hold firmly to the conviction that it contains within itself exceedingly powerful forces that can mold any age.

30. A part of this patrimony is the good pursued in the state of perfection and this you must seek with the utmost zeal, so that by the use of its methods and resources you may become holy yourselves, and either directly or indirectly make your neighbors also holy. In this manner they, sharing ever more richly in divine grace, may live a holy life and die a holy death. Another factor in this patrimony is the lofty and sublime truth that self-denial for the love of Christ must be considered the only path to perfection. This truth the changing times can never change.

31. There are however circumstances, and not a few, when you can and ought to accommodate yourselves to the temper and the needs of men and the age. Indeed to a great extent this has actually been done, and now the task is being completely and perfectly accomplished by your combined counsels and plans.

As may be seen from the variety of your undertakings both as individuals and as Institutes, you have already initiated many adjustments in schools, in the training of youth, in the alleviation of human misery, and in the cultivation and promotion of learning. Hence it must be admitted, and Our affirmation admits of no denial, that a vast amount of energy is even now being expended to meet the altered conditions of our era with new and effective resources.

32. Nevertheless in striving to adapt yourselves to the exigencies of the present, it is, in Our judgment, of paramount concern that you shrewdly investigate what spiritual forces lie latent in your contemporaries, by what secret desires they are motivated, and what the true picture is of their souls. We do not, of course, mean the picture that manifests their detestable and censurable qualities and expresses the tumult of passion and the corruption of vice. But in men as men, and most of all as Christians, though entangled in error and sin, there is not a little good and even a desire for greater good. You must encourage these good impulses and foster these aspirations, being always careful, however, not to accept from the world what keeps it wretched and evil, but rather to infuse into the world what is good and holy in yourselves, and in harmony with these salutary longings. Being solicitous, therefore, for that feeble good in the hearts of others, furbish and develop it, molding from its grains of gold precious vessels and gathering its rivulets into mighty streams.

33. Some think, and perhaps rightly, that three marks are characteristic of our age: amplitude in thought and discussion, unification of plan and organization, and speed in execution. Are not these three notes also distinctive marks of the Gospel? Are they not characteristic of those who profess the Catholic faith and live according to its principles? What greater amplitude of vision can be opened to our minds than that offered in the words of the Apostle: "All things are yours and you are Christ's and Christ is God's" (1 Cor. 3:25)? What closer unity in understanding and love than the simplicity and the unity declared to you in the Sacred Scripture: "God, all in all" (1 Cor. 15:26) and "Thou shalt love the Lord thy God with thy whole heart and with thy whole soul and with thy whole mind and with thy whole strength. . . . Thou shalt love thy neighbor as thyself" (Mark 12:28–34)?

34. To enable us to be swift and spirited and unhampered by the recollection of perishable things, we are admonished: "No man putting his hand to the plow and looking back is fit for the Kingdom of God" (Luke 9:62). And if you wish to behold models of virtue in whom these three laudable qualities shine forth, recall to your minds the Apostle Paul and all those who have been engaged in wondrous exploits worthy of an immortal remembrance.

35. Moreover the ideals which light your way to contemplation and action, as well as the goal of the Church's other children, both priests and laity, are the achievement of Christian perfection and the salvation of the human race. For your part, you have at hand the most effective aids, namely the evangelical counsels through the profession of your vows of religion, and through these by unremitting warfare you can overcome the concupiscence of the flesh, the concupiscence of the eyes, and the pride of life (cfr. 1 John 2:16), and thus become ever holier and efficient servants of God for the salvation of mankind. Direct your thoughts and your actions to reach these lofty heights, "so that being rooted and grounded in love" (Eph. 3:17), steadfast in the power of faith and rich in humility, you may lose no opportunity to lead men, your brothers, to their Creator and Redeemer, as stray sheep returning to their Shepherd.

36. Faithful and true to your duty of good example, see to it that your conduct harmonizes with the name you bear, and that your whole manner of life conforms to your profession. According to the words of the Apostle of the Gentiles: "Careful to preserve the unity of the Spirit in the bond of peace" (Eph. 4:3), let peace reign within you and among you, among members of the same Institute and among members of the same community, and with those of other Institutes; between you and all who labor with you and with whom you labor to win men for Christ. Put far from you discords and disagreements which weaken and cripple undertakings begun with the highest hopes. The Church, as a field for apostolic endeavor, is spread out all over the world, and an opportunity for toil and sweat is open to all.

37. If the faith of religious is strengthened by the example of a life whose pattern is unyielding observance of the vows, if the priest regards nothing as hard or irksome in his quest for the

salvation of souls, then the expression of the Apostle when referring to the word of God will also be true of them today, "living . . . and efficient and keener than any two-edged sword" (Heb. 4:13). We recently warned the faithful that in these calamitous days, when the misfortune and grievous want of many is in sharp contrast to the immoderate luxury of others, they should be willing to live temperately and to be generous to their neighbors oppressed by poverty. Come then, excel all others by your example in this insistent work of Christian perfection, justice, and charity, and thus lead them to imitate Christ.

38. Finally, with a great hope that the efficacious grace of Our Lord Jesus Christ may bring forth from your Congress benefits of enduring value, and as a pledge of Our abiding love, We affectionately bestow upon all here present and upon religious communities everywhere in the world the Apostolic Benediction.

**AAS 43–26**; Pius XII, Allocution, 8 Dec., 1950.

NOTE: The above translation, made by the Reverend S. F. McNamee, S.J., and others of the Maryland Province of the Society of Jesus, and reproduced in the *Canon Law Digest* with due permission, is also obtainable separately (with Latin and English parallel texts) from the Maryland Province of the Society of Jesus, 720 North Calvert Street, Baltimore 2, Maryland.

## Oriental Code: Canons on Religious, Church Property, and Meaning of Terms Promulgated (Pius XII, *Motu proprio,* 9 Feb., 1952) AAS 44–65.

The *Motu proprio, Postquam Apostolicis,* of Pius XII:

By the Apostolic Letters given of Our own motion under date of 22 February, 1949, and 6 January, 1950, respectively, We provided for regulating the discipline of marriage[1] and the conduct of ecclesiastical trials[2] in the Oriental Churches. We now turn Our attention and Our thoughts to two other questions, the first concerning religious Institutes, and the second concerning ecclesiastical property.

---

[1] *Motu proprio,* 22 Feb., 1949; AAS 41–89, reported in CANON LAW DIGEST, 3, p. 399.

[2] *Motu proprio,* 6 Jan., 1950; AAS 42–5, reported in CANON LAW DIGEST, 3, p. 585.

Everyone knows with what virtues and merits monasticism has flourished through the centuries. From the earliest times of Christianity, monks, like buds bursting into flower in the garden of the Church, shone with evangelical splendor. Responsive to the call of divine grace, dominating the concupiscence of the flesh, the concupiscence of the eyes, and the pride of life, and so freed from earthly impediments, aflame with love of God and men, they devoted themselves to attaining the perfection of evangelical morality. Anchorets, cenobites, and sacred virgins, by prayers, heavenly contemplations, voluntary corporal penances, and the practice of the other virtues, scaled the mountain of God with eager steps. The active life also in all its forms was not neglected by the monks of the Oriental Churches. They regarded it as a sacred and inviolable duty to practice and defend the Catholic faith, to teach it more thoroughly to the Christian people, and to propagate it among the nations who were deprived of that highest good. History bears brilliant witness to the ardor and success with which the followers of Anthony, Pachomius, Aphraates, Ephraem, Hilarion, and Basil the Great cultivated both sacred and civil studies and the theory and practice of the liberal arts. It is true that this splendor of supernatural life and this readiness and zeal in active works gradually waned among them and in some places, owing to the well-known ills which long afflicted the Oriental Churches, disappeared entirely.

Nevertheless the provident and wise labors of certain restorers of religious discipline, such as Theodore of Studion, Josaphat Kuntsevyc, and Mekhitar, and the maternal care of the Holy See brought it about that in those districts of the Oriental Churches which followed the teaching of the Chair of Peter, the ancient vigor was born anew.

But experience soon showed that the norms of the ancient law had to be perfected and adapted to the needs of the present time, so as to be made more concordant and helpful to the life and progress both of the monks and of those who have embraced other later forms of evangelical perfection: We refer to the Orders, Congregations, and Societies of men who, although they have not publicly professed the three customary religious vows, are yet bound by the ties of religious community life. These defects will easily be discerned by anyone who reads either the laws which are still in effect regarding the form of religious

Institutes, or the prescriptions which have been enacted by recent Synods. For this reason, among other measures which the Sacred Congregation for the Oriental Church proposed to undertake, the principal one was this: to revise, amend, and improve the said statutes and decrees. The obstacle to the fulfillment of this most urgent and well-conceived plan is that there is as yet no common primary legal norm which may serve as a guide for the other changes and amendments which ought to be made. For this reason We judged it most opportune that these canons on religious should be promulgated.

Equally clear and evident is the reason which induces Us to present the canons on ecclesiastical property: Since in certain countries the effort is being made to take away or impair the inherent right of the Church to possess property, We judged it to be part of Our Apostolic duty to assert and defend all these rights and each of them. And We take this occasion to warn those persons who are in any way in control of such property, that they are bound by the strictest obligation to administer it completely, faithfully, and diligently as is required by its purpose; and that purpose is to provide for the elegance of divine worship, the decent support of sacred ministers, and the relief of the poor. Wherefore, all who are charged with the administration of such property must see to it that they clear themselves of all evil suspicion and incur not even the slightest blame for the manner in which they fulfill their offices. But it is also necessary that wise and absolute laws, by prohibitive, preceptive, and precautionary norms, stand as a potent authority to govern and control the administrators of ecclesiastical property, so that they may care for and administer it "as it were under the eyes of God"[3] and "with all solicitude and in good conscience before God who knoweth all things."[4]

Now the Commission for preparing a Code of Canon Law for the Oriental Churches has attentively considered laws concerning both of these questions, and after hearing from the Bishops of the Oriental Churches and others whose opinions it was useful to know, has proposed the canons on the aforesaid juridical institutions for Our approval, at the same time asking Us to promulgate also a chapter *on the meaning of terms*, since this is

---

[3] *Canones SS. Apostolorum,* 38.

[4] *Syn. antiochena,* can. 24.

quite necessary for the right understanding of these canons on religious.

After carefully considering all this in the presence of God with earnest prayers to the Divine Majesty, We have decided to grant without delay the petition made to Us, and to promulgate at once, if not the entire Code of Laws for the Oriental Churches, at least those canons which concern religious Institutes, ecclesiastical property, and the meaning of certain terms; and, for the reasons given, We have decided of Our own motion, from certain knowledge and in the fullness of Our authority, by this Letter presently to promulgate those canons which concern the discipline of religious Institutes, the temporal property of the Church, and the significance of certain words, which canons were prepared by the Commission for preparing the Code of Laws for the Oriental Churches.

The canons, which We approve with Our Apostolic authority, are the following:

Canons 1–231: on Religious
Canons 232–301: on Ecclesiastical Property
Canons 302–325: on the Meaning of Terms[5]

By this Apostolic Letter given of Our own motion We promulgate the above canons and endow them with the force of law for the faithful of the Oriental Churches, wherever on earth they may be and even though they be subject to a Prelate of another rite. As soon as these canons become effective by this Apostolic Letter, every statute, general, particular, or special, even though enacted by Synods which were approved in the special form, and every prescription and custom still in effect, general or particular, shall lose all force; so that the discipline of religious and of ecclesiastical property and likewise the significance of certain words will be governed exclusively by these same canons, and particular laws which are contrary to them will no longer have any effect except when and in as far as they are admitted in them.

But in order that this Our will may have time to come to the notice of all concerned, We will and ordain that this Apostolic Letter given of Our own motion shall go into effect from the twenty-first day of November, the Feast of the Presentation of

[5] For the text of the canons, cf. AAS 44, pp. 67–150.

the Blessed Virgin Mary, all things to the contrary, even those worthy of the most special mention, notwithstanding.

Given at Rome, from Saint Peter's, the ninth of February, Feast of Saint Cyril of Alexandria, Pontiff and Doctor, in the year 1952, the thirteenth of Our Pontificate.

**AAS 44–65**; Pius XII, *Motu proprio,* 9 Feb., 1952. Annotations, *Monitor Ecclesiasticus,* 77 (1952)–233 (Herman).

**Consecration of Virgins: Indult to Benedictine Sisters in the United States, With Its Interpretation** (S. C. Rel., 24 Oct., 1950, and 24 Sept., 1952) **Private.**

**Petition:** The Procurator General of the Swiss Congregation of Benedictines, humbly prostrate at the feet of Your Holiness, by the special mandate of the Illustrious and Most Reverend Abbot-Primate and at the ardent desire of the Superiors of the Benedictine Sisters of the United States of North America, present in Rome, on the occasion of a pilgrimage, petitions that an indult be granted for the reception of the Consecration of Virgins. Moreover he humbly asks that in addition to the Bishops of the United States, who often are so greatly preoccupied, also the Abbots of the Benedictine Order of the United States may be permitted to perform the Consecration.

**Rescript:** In virtue of the faculties granted by our Most Holy Father, the Sacred Congregation in Charge of the Affairs of Religious, after having considered the matter proposed by the Right Reverend Procurator General, petitioner, graciously commissions him to grant the desired favor, as petitioned, according to his judgment and conscience, observing all that has to be observed.

All things to the contrary notwithstanding.

Given at Rome, on the 24th of October, 1950.

**(Private)**; S. C. Rel., 24 Oct., 1950 (N. 8855/50).

NOTE: After the promulgation of the Apostolic Constitution, *Sponsa Christi,* 21 Nov., 1950 (*Canon Law Digest,* 3, p. 221), some doubts arose as to whether the above privilege was abrogated. This and several other points were clarified by Father Larraona, Secretary of the S. C. of Religious, on Sept. 24, 1952, as follows:

**Interpretation:** 1. Since the Indult given to the American Benedictine Sisters is a *privilege*, the *Sponsa Christi* does not abrogate the privilege. For the present, the privilege certainly may be used.

2. The privilege was granted according to the customs and the approved Constitutions of the American Benedictine Sisters; hence the obligation of solemn vows does not hold.

3. For the same reasons the Sisters are not bound to papal enclosure.

4. No obligation for the individual recitation of the divine Office is attached to the use of this privilege. The Monastic Office recited in choir suffices.

5. Regarding the inviolability of virginity as an essential qualification, we may say that all who have never been married may be admitted to the ceremony, provided they have vowed themselves to God in perpetuity. The forum of conscience is not to be infringed upon. One who has dedicated herself to God in the state of virginity in contradistinction to the state of matrimony is eligible for the privilege.

6. In the early Church, the age for this complete consecration to God was forty years. This need not be adhered to in the use of the privilege. It might be wise to defer the consecration until some years after perpetual vows, as an incentive for a deeper and more mature spirituality. Some think that *ten years* after perpetual vows would be a mature time.

**(Private)**; S. C. Rel., 24 Sept., 1952. The text of the Indult and interpretation was graciously supplied by the Superioress of St. Walburg Convent, Covington, Kentucky.

NOTE: The rite for the consecration of virgins is to be revised. See **c. 2, AAS 56–97,** Constitution on the Sacred Liturgy, n. 80; reported in this volume, p. 21.

## Norms for Congresses of Religious and Members of States of Perfection (S. C. Rel., Decree, 26 March, 1956) AAS 48–295.

A Decree of the Sacred Congregation of Religious, entitled: "Norms Regarding Congresses on the Appropriate Renovation of the States of Perfection," is as follows:

That salutary and fruitful movement for the appropriate renovation of the states of perfection, which happily took its rise from the great Congress held in Rome toward the close of the Holy Year 1950 under the paternal and distinguished leadership of His Holiness Pius XII, has during this entire five-year period (1950–1956) everywhere produced abundant results, both as to religious perfection and formation and as to the apostolic ministry and the coordination of institutes among themselves.

But in order that this beneficent renewal and adaptation may proceed in a wise and orderly manner, that it may make continual progress, grow in intensity, and spread with greater security, the Sacred Congregation of Religious, after obtaining the permission and approval of His Holiness in the Audience granted to His Eminence the Cardinal Prefect of this Sacred Congregation on the 3rd of November 1955, decided to establish the following norms which shall be especially applicable when there is question of a renewal of the discipline and internal life of the states of perfection, without prejudice, of course, to the rights of Ordinaries as provided in the sacred Canons.

1. Conventions or Congresses, diocesan, regional, or national, or courses of lectures and special classes for men or women who are members of states of perfection, in which their internal life, juridical condition, or the education and formation to be given in them are dealt with, may not be conducted or begun without consulting the Sacred Congregation of Religious. For a fundamental law and the very nature of the matter require that the Holy See, to which the supreme and effective control of the public state of perfection is reserved, should be assured both as regards the doctrine and the appropriateness of the programs and also as regards the competence and experience of those who are to preside or to teach at these sessions.

2. Therefore those who promote or preside over these conventions and courses should take care to present to this Sacred Congregation in due time a schedule of the subjects and speakers; and after the convention is over, the one who was in charge should report to the same Sacred Congregation on the matters that were treated, the discussions that were held, the conclusions that were drawn, and in general on whatever concerns the appropriate renovation of the states of perfection.

3. In places where there are already in existence federations or councils of Major Superiors with their own statutes and special commissions approved by the Holy See, it will be appropriate that they choose and present to the Sacred Congregation well qualified men to speak in these conventions and courses.

4. It would be a commendable move on the part of the Most Excellent local Ordinaries to call together members of the states of perfection who have a house in the diocese and exercise the ministry there, in order to consider and to communicate or

paternally discuss with them matters regarding their ministry, in as far as these are of legitimate concern to the diocese. Such meetings are warmly recommended because they seem decidedly well suited to manifest and to further unity with the Father and Pastor of the flock and to promote and effectively direct the works of the apostolate.

If these things are earnestly and carefully attended to, far from hindering or repressing assemblies, conventions, and any sort of project for the appropriate renovation of the states of perfection, they will help them very much to become ever more productive of good results.

All things to the contrary notwithstanding.

Given at Rome, the 26th of March, 1956.

AAS 48–295; S. C. Rel., Decree, 26 March, 1956. Annotations, *Monitor Ecclesiasticus,* 81 (1956)–368 (Canals).

## Principles and General Statutes for Those Called to States of Perfection (Pius XII, Ap. Const., 31 May, 1956) AAS 48–354.

This Apostolic Constitution, *Sedes Sapientiae,* is entitled: "Principles and General Statutes by which Should be Inspired and Governed Those Who Are Called to Embrace a State for Acquiring Religious Perfection, and Their Educators."

Pius, Bishop, Servant of the Servants of God, for a perpetual memorial:

The Seat of Wisdom, Mother of God the Lord of the Sciences,[1] and Queen of the Apostles,[2] the Most Holy Virgin Mary, to whose veneration We consecrated an entire year, is truly in a special manner the Mother and Mistress of all those who embrace a state for acquiring perfection and at the same time aim to march in the apostolic militia of Christ the Supreme High Priest. For in order to apply themselves effectively to adopting and developing properly so great and exalted a vocation, one which is both priestly and apostolic, they have great need of the guidance and assistance of her who is the Mediatrix of all the graces of sanctification and is truly called the Mother and Queen of the Catholic priesthood and apostolate. We therefore eagerly

---

1 Cf. 1 Kings 2:3.

2 From the Litany of Loretto.

implore her favor, that she who obtained for Us the light of divine grace in decreeing these norms, may by her patronage stand by to assist those whose duty it is to put them into practice.

I

It is a great blessing of Divine Providence that right down through the centuries Christ the Redeemer has constantly breathed into souls of His choice, as if by an interior and mystical speech, that invitation which His living voice once extended to the young man inquiring about eternal life: "Come, follow me."[3] A goodly number of those who by the grace of God have accepted that invitation and professed with the holy Apostles, "Behold, we have left all things and have followed thee,"[4] our Lord has likewise constantly made "fishers of men,"[5] and has chosen them as laborers,[6] sending them "into his harvest."

This is as true today as it was of old, since the conjunction of the states for acquiring perfection with the priestly dignity and the apostolic office has ever grown more frequent and more intimate. In olden days the Monks were for the most part not priests; only a few of them, compelled as it were by necessity to receive priestly orders so that the nations might be converted to Christianity, became almost separated from their proper Rule; afterward the Mendicants, although they were imbued with a wonderful apostolic spirit, were not all summoned by their Rule to the priesthood — even the saintly Father of Assisi did not receive it; the Canons Regular, on the other hand, and likewise particularly the Clerics Regular, were accustomed to receive and exercise Sacred Orders as part of their special divine vocation. Afterward a great number of Congregations and Societies of common life, likewise clerical, did the same. And now, as God always provides for the needs of successive ages, we have also some Secular Institutes which are likewise clerical.

At the present time, moreover, also in the older Orders of the Latin Church which are not formally designated as lay institutes,[7] all the members, with the exception of those who are called coadjutors or *conversi,* are destined for the priesthood,

---

[3] Mt. 19:21.
[4] Mt. 19:27.
[5] Mt. 4:19.
[6] Mt. 9:38.
[7] Cf. canon 488, 4°.

which moreover is absolutely required for those who are charged with the government of those Orders.

Accordingly in our days the Church has a great host of ministers who apply themselves at the same time to the acquirement of perfection through the evangelical counsels and to the performance of priestly functions. This multitude constitutes what is called the religious clergy, side by side with that which is called secular or diocesan, both, however, thriving and flourishing in fraternal rivalry and enjoying the fruits of mutual assistance, under one and the same supreme authority of the Roman Pontiff, without prejudice, of course, to the power of the Bishops.

Now everyone knows that that religious clergy, in order to achieve its twofold purpose fittingly and securely, must have very wise regulations to govern and promote the education and the religious as well as the clerical and apostolic training of its members.

This need has indeed hitherto been very well fulfilled by the constitutions of the various Institutes or by their statutes on the training of youth or on the arrangement of the course of study; and certainly there are also prescriptions and recommendations of the Holy See on this matter. Nevertheless the need has long been felt of some general ordinances, well coordinated and more complete, fortified by the authority of the Holy See and to be observed everywhere by all, in order that this important activity, which concerns closely the good of souls, may be assured of a successful development and completion through continuous and well-directed effort.

A work of such excellence demands the constant vigilance of the Apostolic See itself; for, just as diocesan schools for clerics, in their character of public ecclesiastical institutions, are placed under the active care and constant control of the Holy See acting through the Sacred Congregation of Seminaries and Universities,[8] so for the same reason the special schools for the states of perfection, which are recognized and sanctioned by the Church, are public and are under the authority of the Sacred Congregation of Religious.[9]

---

8 Cf. canon 256.

9 Cf. canon 251; Pius XII, Ap. Const., *Provida Mater,* art. IV, § 1, 2 Feb., 1947, AAS, Vol. 39, p. 121 (*Enchiridion de statibus perfectionis,* Rome, 1949, n. 387, p. 584); CANON LAW DIGEST, 3, p. 135.

For these several reasons, as early as the year 1944 We authorized, within the Sacred Congregation of Religious, "the erection and establishment . . . of a special Body or Commission of chosen men, which shall deal with all questions and matters pertaining in any way to the religious and clerical education and to the training in literature, science, and ministry of aspirants, novices, and junior members of all religious institutes and societies living in common without vows."[10]

This Commission, made up of learned men from various religious institutes and countries, after having examined all the extant documents on the subject and received reports in response to the Circular Letter which was sent to all Superiors General,[11] had already done a great deal of work when the general Congress of the states of perfection was convened in 1950. Thereafter the Commission, making use of various appropriate suggestions which had been presented at the Congress, reexamined and revised the plans they had already prepared and submitted them for Our approval.

Accordingly We now decree a certain number of Statutes, first, however, presenting some fundamental principles and norms concerning the religious, clerical, and apostolic training of the members, which are always to be observed by all.

## II

First, We would have everyone remember that the foundation of the religious and of the sacerdotal and apostolic life, which is called a divine vocation, consists of two essential elements, one divine, the other ecclesiastical. As to the first of these, a call from God to enter the religious or the sacerdotal state is so necessary that if this is lacking the very foundation on which the whole edifice rests is wanting.

For, whom God has not called, His grace does not move nor assist. For that matter, if a true vocation to any state of life is considered in a certain sense divine, in as much as God is the principal author of all states of life and of all dispositions and

---

[10] S. C. Rel., Decree, *Quo efficacius,* 24 Jan., 1944; AAS, Vol. 36, p. 213 (*Enchiridion,* n. 381, p. 560); English text, Canon Law Digest, 3, p. 100.

[11] S. C. Rel., Circular Letter, *Quantum conferat,* 10 June, 1944 (*Enchiridion,* n. 382, pp. 561–564); published also in *Periodica,* 33 (1944)–246. Cf. Canon Law Digest, 3, p. 101, note.

gifts, natural and supernatural, how much more is this true of a religious and priestly vocation, which is of such exalted splendor and is made up of gifts so numerous and so great that they can come down only "from the Father of lights, from Whom is every best gift and every perfect gift."[12]

Passing on now to the other element of a religious and priestly vocation, let us recall the teaching of the Roman Catechism, that "*they are said to be called by God, who are called by the lawful ministers of the Church.*"[13]

And this not only does not contradict what We said about a divine vocation, but is strictly consistent with it. For the divine call to the religious and clerical state, since it destines a man to lead publicly a life of sanctification and to exercise the hierarchical ministry in the Church, that is in a visible and hierarchical society, has to be authoritatively approved, admitted, and controlled also by hierarchical superiors, to whom the government of the Church has been divinely entrusted.

And this must be kept in mind by whoever has charge of finding and approving these vocations. Never should they in any way coerce anyone into the sacerdotal or religious state;[14] nor should they entice or admit anyone who does not show signs of a genuine call from God; nor promote anyone to the clerical ministry if he shows that he has received from God only a religious vocation; neither should they, in the case of those who have received from God also the gift of a priestly vocation, limit them to the secular clergy or try to draw them to it; finally, let them never turn away from the priestly state one who gives reliable signs of being called to it by God.[15]

For it is evident that those who aspire to the clerical ministry in a state of perfection, and for whom these norms are intended, must unite in themselves all the elements which are needed to constitute a multiple vocation of this kind, religious, priestly, and apostolic, and hence must have all the gifts and qualities which are necessary for fulfilling such exalted divine functions.

## III

It is clear that the germs of a divine vocation and the qualities

[12] Cf. James 1:17.

[13] *Catech. Rom. ad Parochos,* cura Pii V editus, pars II, cap. 7.

[14] Cf. canon 971.

[15] Cf. canon 971.

needed for it, if they are present, require education and training to develop and mature them. For there is nothing that attains perfection the moment it is born; perfection is acquired through gradual progress. In regulating this development, all the conditions of the individual who has received the divine call and all the circumstances of place and time must be considered in order effectively to attain the desired end. Consequently the education and training of young members must be altogether safe, enlightened, solid, complete, wisely and courageously adapted to both the internal and external exigencies of the present day, carefully cultivated, vigilantly tested with regard not only to the perfection of the religious life but also to that of the priestly and apostolic life.

All this, as We know from experience, can be provided only by well-chosen men, who are not only outstanding in learning, prudence, understanding of characters, wide experience of men and things, and in other human qualities, but who are also filled with the Holy Spirit and who will give the young men a shining example of holiness and of all virtue; for it is well known that in the whole matter of training they are more influenced by virtue and right conduct than by words.[16]

In fulfilling this most important duty, let educators have as their first rule the one which our Lord announced in the Gospel when He said: "I am the good shepherd. The good shepherd giveth his life for his sheep. . . . I am the good shepherd; and I know mine, and mine know me";[17] and which Saint Bernard expressed in these words: "Learn that you are to be mothers to your subjects, not masters; strive rather to be loved than to be feared";[18] and the Council of Trent itself, frequently exhorting ecclesiastical superiors, "considers that they should be urged first of all to remember that they are shepherds and not slave-drivers, and that they must so rule over their subjects as not to domineer over them but to love them as sons and younger brothers; they should endeavor by exhortation and admonition to deter them from wrongdoing lest they be obliged to administer due punishment after faults have been committed. Yet if through human frailty their subjects do wrong, they must observe the precept of the Apostle and reprove, entreat, rebuke them in all patience

[16] Cf. canon 124.

[17] Jn. 10:11, 14.

[18] *In Cantica, Sermo* 23, Migne, *P.L.*, 183, 885 B.

and doctrine; for sympathy is often more effective for correction than severity, exhortation better than threats of punishment, kindness better than insistence on authority. If in view of the seriousness of a crime there be need of punishment, then they must combine authority with leniency, judgment with mercy, severity with moderation, to the end that discipline, so salutary and essential to public order, be maintained without asperity, and that those who have been punished may amend their ways or, if they refuse to do so, that others may be deterred from wrongdoing by the salutary example of their punishment."[19]

All who are in any way responsible for the education of the members should also remember that this education and training must be imparted with an organic progression and making use, as occasion offers, of all appropriate resources and methods; it must embrace the whole man under all the aspects of his vocation, so as to make of him truly in all respects a "man perfect in Christ Jesus."[20] With regard to the resources and methods of education, those which nature itself supplies and those which are offered by the human ingenuity of the present age, if they are good, are clearly not to be neglected, but to be highly esteemed and wisely employed. However, there is no more fatal mistake than to rely exclusively or excessively on these natural means and to relegate supernatural aids and resources to a secondary place or in any way to neglect them. Because in order to attain religious and clerical perfection and apostolic results, the supernatural means, the sacraments, prayer, mortification, and the like, are not merely necessary but altogether primary and essential.

But, supposing that this order of methods and works is observed, absolutely nothing should be neglected which would conduce in any way to the cultivation of all the natural virtues and to the development of a well-rounded and virile human personality, so that the supernatural religious or priestly training may rest firmly on this solid foundation of natural goodness and human culture,[21] for people are brought to Christ the more easily and securely in proportion as they find in the person of the priest "the goodness and kindness of God our Saviour."[22]

Nevertheless, though all should make much of the human and

---

[19] Cf. canon 2214, § 2; Conc. Trid., sess. XIII, *de ref., cap.* 1.
[20] Col. 1:28. [21] Cf. Phil. 4:8. [22] Tit. 3:4.

natural training of the religious cleric, the supernatural sanctification of the soul undoubtedly has the first place in the entire course of his development. For if the warning of the Apostle, "For this is the will of God, your sanctification,"[23] applies to every Christian, how much more is he bound by it who not only has received the priesthood but has publicly professed the aim of attaining evangelical perfection, and is by his very office an instrument for the sanctification of others, so much so that the salvation of souls and the growth of the Kingdom of God depend in a considerable degree upon his holiness?

Let all, therefore who belong to the states for acquiring perfection, remember and frequently consider in the presence of God that, to fulfill the demands of their profession, it is not enough for them to avoid grave sin or even with the aid of God's grace venial sins, nor to obey in a merely material way the orders of their Superiors or even to observe their vows or other conscientious engagements, or the constitutions of their institute, according to which, says the Church herself in the sacred Canons, "all and every religious, Superiors as well as subjects, are bound . . . to order their life, and thus tend to the perfection of their state."[24] For they must do all this with their whole soul and an ardent love, not merely through necessity, "but also for conscience' sake,"[25] because to scale the heights of sanctity and to present themselves to all men as living springs of Christian charity, they have to be inflamed with an ardent love of God and neighbor and be adorned with every virtue.

## IV

Now, when this sanctification of the soul has been provided for, the intellectual and pastoral training of the religious cleric must be attended to most carefully, and on this subject, in view of the importance of the matter and the responsibility of Our supreme office, We wish to explain and recommend the principles at somewhat greater length.

How great is the need for these religious of a solid and altogether finished intellectual training and formation, is clear especially from their three-fold dignity in the Church of God, religious, sacerdotal, and apostolic.

---

[23] 1 Thess. 4:3. [24] Cf. canon 593. [25] Rom. 13:5.

Religious men, whose chief duty it is to seek God alone, to be united to Him in contemplation and to give the divine truths to others, must know that they cannot fulfill this most sacred duty well and fruitfully nor be raised to a sublime union with Christ if they lack that copious and deep knowledge of God and His mysteries which is drawn from sacred doctrines and must ever be perfected.[26]

The dignity of a priest, which makes him an ambassador of the Lord of all knowledge[27] and designates him as the *salt of the earth* and the *light of the world,*[28] demands a full and solid training especially in ecclesiastical subjects, such a formation as can nourish and sustain his spiritual life and preserve him from all error and the vagaries of novelty; one which will make him a faithful dispenser of the mysteries of God,[29] and a perfect man of God, *instructed for every good work.*[30]

Finally, the apostolic office which members of the states of perfection perform, each according to his vocation — by sacred sermons to the people, the Christian education of children and young people, the administration of the sacraments, especially that of confession, mission work among infidels, the spiritual direction of souls, or finally by the mere contacts of daily life with the people — can never produce abundant and permanent results unless they themselves are thoroughly grounded in the knowledge of sacred doctrine, and cultivate it by uninterrupted study.

In order to attain this solid and finished intellectual culture and formation concomitantly with the natural development of the young men and the arrangement of their studies, religious Superiors must first of all use every means to see to it that in the knowledge of literature and doctrine, religious students "be in no way inferior to young men of the laity who are studying the same subjects. For if this is securely provided for, it will be assured that the students receive a thorough mental training, and that they will be the more available for service each in his

---

26 Cf. Pius XI, Ap. Letter, *Unigenitus Dei Filius,* 19 March, 1924; AAS, Vol. 16, pp. 137–138 (*Enchiridion* n. 348, pp. 403–404). Cf. CANON LAW DIGEST, 1, pp. 265, 302, 312, 313, 661, 670.

27 Cf. 1 Kings 2:3.

28 Cf. Mt. 5:13–14.

29 Cf. 1 Cor. 4:1–2.

30 Cf. 2 Tim. 3:17.

own time,"[31] and also that they will be prepared and equipped to go on to higher ecclesiastical studies.

In philosophical and theological courses, which are to be taught only by qualified and well-chosen professors, all the prescriptions of the Sacred Canons and those made by Our Predecessors and Ourselves must be most faithfully observed, regarding especially the reverence which is due to the *Magisterium* of the Church and which on all occasions must be professed and instilled into the minds and hearts of the students; regarding the prudence and caution which must always accompany the careful and highly praiseworthy investigation of new questions which arise from time to time; and regarding the system, doctrine, and principles of the Angelic Doctor, which are to be faithfully held and are decidedly to be followed in the teaching of philosophy and theology to students.[32]

Following the guidance and authority of Aquinas, theology is to be taught according to a method which is both positive and scholastic, that is, in such a way that in the light of the authentic *Magisterium* the sources of Divine Revelation are very thoroughly examined, making use of all the appropriate aids to that study, and that the treasures of truth drawn therefrom be clearly explained and effectively defended. For, since the deposit of Revelation is entrusted for authentic interpretation to the *Magisterium* of the Church alone, it must be most faithfully explained according to the sense and mind of the Church herself, and not according to mere human reason and private judgment. Let professors of Christian philosophy and theology, therefore, take notice that they perform their function not in their own right and name but in the name and by the authority of the supreme *Magisterium,* and hence subject to its vigilance and control, having received from it, as it were, a canonical commission. Consequently, without restriction of freedom of opinion in those matters which are still open to discussion, "they must remember that they have received the authority to teach, not that they may communicate their own opinions to their students, but in

---

[31] Pius XII, Ap. Exhort., *Menti Nostrae,* 23 Sept., 1950; AAS, Vol. 42, p. 687.

[32] Pius XII, Encyclical, *Humani Generis,* 12 Aug., 1950; AAS, Vol. 42, pp. 573, 577–578; canon 1366.

order to teach them the established doctrines of the Church."[33]

Moreover, both masters and pupils should always remember that ecclesiastical studies are designed, not merely for intellectual training, but for a complete and thorough religious, or sacerdotal and apostolic formation; and hence they must be directed not merely to the successful passing of examinations, but to giving the students a stamp of character which shall never be effaced and from which, when need arises, they may ever draw light and strength for themselves and others.[34]

To this end, intellectual instruction must first of all be intimately united to a love of prayer and the contemplation of heavenly truth; it must also be complete, not omitting any of the prescribed subjects, coherent and so well arranged in its entirety that all the courses of study coalesce in one single well-rounded system. It must also be very wisely adapted to refute the errors and meet the needs of our time; it must take account of the recent discoveries of scholarship and at the same time be entirely in accord with venerable tradition; finally, it must be effectively designed for the fruitful performance of every kind of pastoral ministry, so that the future priests with this training may be ready and well prepared to present and defend sound doctrine in sermons and catechetical instructions to both learned and unlearned audiences, to administer the sacraments properly, to promote vigorously the good of souls and help every one by word and work.

Though all that We have said about the spiritual and intellectual formation of students is most conducive and altogether necessary to the making of truly apostolic men, it being evident that if a priest lacks holiness and learning he lacks everything; yet it is Our solemn duty to add here that, in addition to holiness and learning, if the priest is to fulfill his apostolic ministry properly, he must have a most careful and quite perfect pastoral preparation such as to awaken and develop a genuine skill and dexterity in the due performance of the manifold works of the Christian apostolate.

---

[33] St. Pius X, *Motu proprio, Doctoris Angelici,* 29 June, 1914; AAS, Vol. 6, p. 338 (*Enchiridion,* n. 284, p. 336).

[34] Cf. Pius XII, Speech to Clerical Students, 24 June, 1939; AAS, Vol. 31, p. 246 (*Enchiridion,* n. 373, p. 531); English text, CANON LAW DIGEST, 2, p. 427.

For if the practice of any craft requires some previous preparation, theoretical, technical, and practical, and this latter tested by a long apprenticeship, who can deny that a similar, nay a much more careful and profound previous preparation, is needed for that profession which is truly called the art of arts?

This pastoral training of the students, which should begin at the very inception of the course of studies, develop gradually to perfection with the growing age of the student, and finally be consummated after the completion of the theology course by a special period of trial according to the particular end of the respective religious institute, must have for its primary purpose to imbue the future ministers and apostles of Christ solidly and thoroughly, after the model of Christ Himself, with the apostolic spirit and virtues, and to give them practice in them: namely, an ardent and unmixed desire for promoting the glory of God; an active and burning charity for the Church and for defending her rights and preserving and spreading her truth; a flaming zeal for the salvation of souls; supernatural prudence in word and work, together with evangelical simplicity, humble self-denial, and obedient subjection to Superiors; an unshakable trust in God and a keen sense of duty; a virile ingenuity in starting projects and constancy in pursuing them; unceasing fidelity in the performance of duty; generosity in the greatest sufferings and labors; finally, that Christian affability and kindness which wins all hearts.

Another objective which must be aimed at in pastoral training is that the students, according to the stage and progress of their studies, be instructed in all those subjects which can contribute very much to the complete development of "a good soldier of Christ Jesus,"[35] and to providing him with suitable apostolic weapons. Hence, besides philosophical and theological studies, which, as We said, must also be appropriately adapted to pastoral work, it is altogether necessary that the future shepherds of the Lord's flock receive from learned teachers according to the norms issued by this Apostolic See, an instruction in psychology and pedagogy, didactics and catechetics, social science and pastoral practice, and other subjects, which is in step with

[35] 2 Tim. 2:3.

the progress now being made in these subjects and which will render them fit and ready to meet the many needs of the apostolate in our day.

This doctrinal instruction and preparation for the apostolate, in order that it may be confirmed by use and experience, must be accompanied also by practical exercise in well-planned progressive stages and under prudent control; then after the priesthood is received We wish this practical exercise to be continued and perfected by a special period of trial under the guidance of men who are outstanding in doctrine, counsel, and example, and to be constantly strengthened by uninterrupted sacred studies.

Now that We have prepared the way by giving these fundamental principles which must imbue and direct the work of education and both the educators and those to be taught, We proceed after mature consideration, of certain knowledge, and in the fulness of Apostolic authority, to decree and establish the following general norms on the various aspects of this very important matter, which are to be observed by all whom they concern. Moreover, we empower the Sacred Congregation of Religious to put into practice the General Statutes which We have already approved, by ordinances, instructions, declarations, and interpretations given with Our Authority, and to take all measures which may be appropriate to secure the faithful observance of this Constitution and of the Statutes and Ordinances.

All things to the contrary notwithstanding, even though worthy of special mention.

Given at Rome, from Saint Peter's this thirty-first day of May, the Feast of the Blessed Virgin Mary, Queen of the World, in the year of Our Lord 1956, the eighteenth of Our Pontificate.

**AAS 48–354**; Pius XII, Ap. Const., 31 May, 1956. Cf. *Homiletic and Pastoral Review,* 58 (1957–58) 455 (White); *Monitor Ecclesiasticus,* 81 (1956)–563 (Pugliese).

NOTE: The General Statutes, though mentioned in the title and definitely approved in the Apostolic Constitution itself, were not published in the *Acta Apostolicae Sedis,* but were issued in booklet form by the Sacred Congregation of Religious. Since this booklet is readily available also in English from the Catholic University of America Press, we have not thought it necessary to transcribe it here.

## *Sedes Sapientiae:* Decree on Execution (S. C. Rel., 7 July, 1956) Private.

The Sacred Congregation of Religious, in order to fulfill the commission given to it by His Holiness Pius XII to put into execution in a timely and orderly way the Apostolic Constitution *Sedes Sapientiae* and the General Statutes, promulgated and approved by himself, declares and provides as follows:

I. The Apostolic Constitution *Sedes Sapientiae* and the General Statutes attached to it go into effect according to the norm of canon 9 of the Code of Canon Law at the expiration of three months from the 31st of May 1956, the date of the issue of the *Acta Apostolicae Sedis* in which the said Constitution is contained, that is on the 31st of August 1956.

II. The General Statutes are to be applied to members of clerical states of perfection whom they concern, as regards rules and norms which are applicable to them, as soon as they go into effect.

III. However, as far as they concern Colleges or houses of formation (and) the various aspects of the program of studies and its several curricula and grades, in those places where the scholastic year usually begins with the last three months of the solar year, the General Statutes are to be put into practice beginning with the present scholastic year 1956–1957.

IV. If anything is found in the General Statutes which in the prudent judgment of Superiors General cannot be put into practice immediately at the start of the scholastic year, let them make regulations so that this important and wise legislation may be put fully into practice as soon as possible. If any doubt remains or if there is just cause for some slight delay, recourse should be had to the Sacred Congregation. All things to the contrary notwithstanding.

Given at Rome, from the S. C. of Religious, 7 July, 1956.

**(Private)**; S. C. Rel., 7 July, 1956; *Commentarium pro Religiosis,* 36 (1957)–110. Not published in the AAS.

## General Statutes Interpreted: Absence of a Month and a Half Invalidates the Semester (S. C. Rel., 16 Feb., 1957) Private.

The Sacred Congregation of Religious on 16 Feb., 1957, replied to a question proposed by the Superior General of the Society of Mary regarding Art. 42, § 4, 1° of the General Statutes.

The paragraph in question reads as follows: "1° In curriculis philosophico ac theologico, studiorum et scholarum intermissio etiam non culpabilis, quae una simul tres menses attigerit, annum scholarem nullum ac invalidum reddit."

The reply of the Sacred Congregation was:

**Reply:** This S. C. after having maturely weighed all the considerations which were presented by the Superior General regarding the interpretation of Art. 42, § 4, 1° of the General Statutes, and having considered all aspects of the question, decided to reply and does reply as follows:

This Sacred Congregation understands Art. 42, § 4, 1° of the General Statutes as permitting the custom or practice of dividing the scholastic year into distinct and separate semesters; consequently, as to a semester, the period of absence which invalidates the semester is a month and a half.

**(Private)**; S. C. Rel., 16 Feb., 1957, N. 2090/57. Copy kindly sent to us for the CANON LAW DIGEST, by the Very Reverend James Lambert, S.M., Assistant General of the Marist Fathers.

***Ratio Studiorum*** **and Index of Houses of Formation to Be Sent to the Sacred Congregation of Religious** (S. C. Rel., 12 March, 1957) **Private.**

A Letter sent out by the Secretary of the Sacred Congregation of Religious (12 March 1957; Prot. N. 2090/43) is as follows:

Very Reverend Father:

As the General Statutes attached to the Apostolic Constitution *Sedes Sapientiae* provide that "the various Institutes should have and observe, in addition to the common legislation, also their own *program and method ("Ratio") of formation and especially of studies,* duly adapted to the peculiar needs and circumstances of the Institute, and to be submitted as soon as possible to the Holy See" (Art. 19, § 1), this Sacred Congregation has ordered that in the course of the present year 1957, the *"Ratio Institutionis praesertim Studiorum"* of each Institute be sent to the Sacred Congregation.

And as an aid to drawing up this Ratio, fuller directions may appropriately be asked of the special Office *De Formatione Religiosorum* which has been established in the said Sacred Congregation.

Together with the *"Ratio Institutionis praesertim Studiorum"* each Institute should send a complete index of its houses of formation, which are, according to the classification in the said General Statutes (Art. 21) as follows:

1. Apostolic Schools or minor Seminaries of religious;
2. Houses of Novitiate or of equivalent probation;
3. Colleges or major Seminaries of religious:
   a) for classical studies;
   b) for philosophical studies;
   c) for theological studies;
4. Houses or Colleges for pastoral formation;
5. Houses or Colleges for special studies (Art. 21, § 2).

For each house there should be given exactly, besides the address, the duration of the studies (that is, in how many years the course is completed), and the number of professors and of students in residence there.

**(Private)**; S. C. Rel., Letter, 12 March, 1957; *Commentarium pro Religiosis,* 37 (1958)–10. The *Normae* for making out this *Ratio Studiorum* are reported below, under this same canon.

## Norms for Making Out the *Ratio Studiorum* (S. C. Rel., 12 March, 1957) Private.

As a guide for making out the required report on the *Ratio Studiorum* according to the General Statutes, Art. 19, the S. C. of Religious, together with the Letter of 12 March, 1957 (above), sent the following Norms to the Superiors General of Clerical Institutes.

*Praenotanda*

(1) These Norms are given for compiling the *Ratio Studiorum,* which concerns studies and intellectual formation, not for the *Ratio* of spiritual training or formation under its threefold aspect, religious, clerical, and apostolic, which every Institute must also have and observe according to Art. 19, § 1.

(2) The *Ratio Studiorum* should set forth the arrangement of

studies which is in effect in each Institute *according to its own traditions,* but conformed to the prescriptions of the Apostolic Constitution *Sedes Sapientiae* and the General Statutes.

(3) It can be made out in various ways but, though it may contain other things and be differently arranged, it should declare the following:

1. *General Norms.*

Origin, nature, obligation of and dispensation from this *Ratio Studiorum.*

Whether there are also particular *Rationes Studiorum* for various districts and provinces (Art. 19, §§ 3 and 4).

2. *Centers of Studies.*

Whether there are general or international, interprovincial, provincial, local seats or centers for studies; whether these are multiplied without good reason (Art. 21).

How they are established and what are the conditions for their establishment (Art. 22–23), especially in the case of the library and the means of perfecting it.

3. *The Administration of Studies.*

The General Superior and the Commission or Office of Studies in the General Curia, and their work (Art. 20).

The Provincial Superior and provincial Office of Studies (if there is one) and their work (Art. 20).

The local Superior and the management of studies in the several houses.

The Prefect of studies, his work, and how he is appointed (Art. 29).

The other officials (librarian, secretary, etc.).

Consultors on studies.

4. *Professors and the Spiritual Prefect.*

Their qualifications and function. How they are prepared, appointed, removed (Art. 30, 28, §§ 2 and 3). How many there are for the various courses, and whether they have any duties which are incompatible with their office.

5. *The Students.*

The care and direction given to them in their studies. Their offices. Their regularity in attendance at classes (Art. 42, § 4).

6. *Apostolic Schools and Minor Seminaries* (Art. 35 and 37).

Are there any of these; and what studies are required before entrance.

How many years of studies they have.

What subjects are taught.

For how many years and how many hours a week the various subjects are taught.

What examinations are prescribed and how they are conducted.

Whether these studies are recognized for civil certificates.

7. *Studies during the Noviceship* (Art. 36).

What studies are required before entering the novitiate.

What studies are pursued during the canonical year and for how many hours a week.

What studies are done during the second year of noviceship if there is one.

8. *Studies in Humanities after the Noviceship* (Art. 43).

What studies in humanities are done after the novitiate.

For how many years do these studies continue.

What subjects are taught, and how.

How many years and how many hours a week are given to each subject.

What examinations are required and how they are conducted.

Whether these studies are recognized for civil certificates.

9. *Philosophical Studies* (Art. 44).

How many years of philosophy there are after the humanities.

If scholastic philosophy is taught in the last years of humanities, for how many years and how many hours a week.

What subjects are taught in the philosophy course.

For how many years and how many hours a week each subject is taught.

What method is followed in teaching philosophy and what textbooks are used.

What repetitions, disputations, and other exercises are had.

What examinations are required and how they are conducted: written or oral, of what duration, how many examiners, how are the votes expressed.

10. *The Interruption of Studies after Philosophy* (Art. 13).

Is there an interruption and how is it arranged.

11. *The Theological Course* (Art. 45).

How many years are given to the study of theology.

What subjects are taught in the theological course.

For how many years and how many hours a week each subject is taught.

What doctrine is followed and what is the method of teaching; what texts are used.

What repetitions, disputations, and other exercises are held.

What examinations are required and how are they conducted: written or oral, of what length, how many examiners, how the votes are given.

12. *The Pastoral Course* (Art. 48).

How it is conducted and what subjects are taught.

How many hours a week are given to each subject.

What examinations are held and how are they conducted.

What practical pastoral exercises are had.

13. *Special Studies* (Art. 46).

What, if any, special studies are required of all students; when do they come and how are they conducted.

What special studies are prescribed for those students who are destined for special assignments (e.g., for teaching); when and how are these to be made, in houses of the Institute itself or in Universities.

14. *Degrees Peculiar to the Institute* (Art. 46, § 4).

Are there any degrees peculiar to the Institute (*"tituli interni"*), and what are they.

By what authority are they conferred.

What conditions are required for meriting each of them.

15. *The Scholastic Year and Vacations* (Art. 42).

For how many months does the scholastic year last. How many full days according to Art. 42, § 3.

What vacations are there in the course of the scholastic year.

What vacations are there after the scholastic year is finished, and how are these conducted (whether there are summer courses, etc.).

16. *The Continuance of Studies after the Pastoral Course is Finished* (Art. 49 and 50).

What are the regulations for the quinquennial examinations.

What are the norms for the conferences mentioned in canon 591.

What other regulations are there for promoting intellectual progress (regarding libraries, reviews, congresses of studies, etc.).

P.S. — Along with the *Ratio Studiorum* there should be sent (unless this has already been done) an index of the houses of formation, according to the Letter of the S. C. of Religious of 12 March, 1957.

**(Private)**; S. C. Rel., Norms, 12 March, 1957; *Commentarium pro Religiosis,* 37 (1958)–7.

## *Sedes Sapientiae* and Statutes Apply to Societies Without Public Vows Which Depend on the S. Consistorial C. and on the S. C. Prop. Fid. (S. C. Rel., 30 July, 1957) AAS 50–103.

Since many religious Congregations and Societies of common life without public vows, which depend on the Sacred Consistorial Congregation or on the S. C. for the Propagation of the Faith have asked "whether the entire plan of training which is contained in the Apostolic Constitution *Sedes Sapientiae* and in the General Statutes which accompany it, apply to and are binding on these Institutes also, the Supreme Pontiff, in the Audience graciously granted to the undersigned Cardinal Prefect of the Sacred Congregation of Religious on the 30th of July, 1957, deigned to declare and reply:

**Reply:** In the affirmative, without prejudice however, as regards the merely executive function (Art. 18), to the competency of the Sacred Consistorial Congregation and the S. C. for the Propagation of the Faith, over religious Institutes and Societies which are subject to these Sacred Congregations by law (c. 252, § 1) or by apostolic privilege.

**AAS 50–103**; S. C. Rel., Declaration, 30 July, 1957. Cf. *Commentarium pro Religiosis,* 36 (1957)–227.

**Second General Congress of the States of Perfection** (Pius XII, Allocution, 9 Dec., 1957) **AAS 50–34.**

On the occasion of the second General Congress of the States of Perfection, 9 December, 1957, His Holiness Pius XII delivered the following Allocution to the assembled delegates:

Under the maternal protection of Mary Immaculate, most sublime of all creatures and model of those who strive for perfection of Christian life, you have chosen, dear sons and daughters, to gather in Rome in order to study the actual problems of the states of perfection, while at the same time celebrating the fiftieth anniversary of the priestly ordination of the very worthy and zealous Cardinal Prefect of the Sacred Congregation of Religious.

In more than twenty-five nations of all the continents there are today associations of major Superiors of both men and women who, in close cooperation with the Holy See and the hierarchy of their country, are working together at the tasks of organization and adaptation which the breadth and complexity of the present-day apostolate demand. We know that many projects have been initiated during these latter years through the enlightened action of your associations; let it suffice to mention the national and regional congresses of the states of perfection, reunions for prayer and study, and especially the establishment of institutions of formation and higher religious education for members of the states of perfection.

This great Congress which has sprung, root and branch, from the desire to effect an ever more complete insertion of the states of perfection in the Church, the Mystical Body of Christ, purposes to take account of the progress that has been made everywhere in the organization of the states of perfection and their adaptation to the needs of the Church; then to present clearly the ends to be attained, the limits to be observed and the principles which should guide the action of the conferences, unions, and committees of major Superiors; and finally to work out a program of activities and projects which will render the movement of renovation effective by strengthening the bonds of union of the organizations among themselves and with the Holy See.

The reports and documents of this Congress as a whole aim to provide a commentary on the three Apostolic Constitutions,

*Provida Mater,*[1] *Sponsa Christi,*[2] and *Sedes Sapientiae,*[3] and the Decree, *Salutaris atque,* of the Sacred Congregation of Religious,[4] which gives the norms that should guide the movement of adaptation and renovation. It is not Our intention to speak of the particular questions which are to be the subject of your sessions, but rather to emphasize certain points of a general character which concern the problem of perfection and that of renovation and adaptation of the means by which individuals and communities tend toward it. We shall speak first of the perfection of Christian life in general and then of its realization in the groups called "states of perfection," considering in the first place the relation of the groups with their members and then their relation among themselves and with the Holy See.

## I. The Perfection of Christian Life

We must remember that the concept of "perfection" is not strictly identical with that of the "state of perfection," but is considerably broader. One may find heroic Christian perfection, that of the Gospel and of the Cross of Christ, outside any "state of perfection."

By the pursuit of perfection therefore, We mean a habitual disposition of the Christian in virtue of which, not content with fulfilling the duties that are binding under pain of sin, he gives himself completely to God in order to love and serve Him, and consecrates himself for the same ends to the service of the neighbor.

The perfection of any free human activity, like that of any reasonable creature, consists in voluntarily adhering to God. In part, as a consequence of the very condition of a creature, this perfection is obligatory; one must tend toward it under pain of missing one's final destiny. We need not now consider its elements in detail. We wish to speak merely of the habitual and permanent tendency which, going beyond whatever is of obligation, takes the whole man and consecrates him unreservedly to the service of God. This perfection consists primarily in union with God, which is effected through charity and hence is fulfilled

1 AAS 39–114; below, p. 143.
2 AAS 43–5; below, p. 326.
3 AAS 48–354; above, p. 105.
4 26 March, 1956; AAS 48–295; above, p. 103.

in charity. It is also called a perpetual and universal holocaust of oneself, willed for the love of God and in order deliberately to show Him this love.

The ideal of Christian perfection is contained in the teachings of Christ, particularly in the evangelical counsels, in His life, passion, and death, inexhaustible sources which supply the heroism of all the generations of Christians. It includes also Christ's work, that is, the service of the Church for the love of the Saviour, in the place and according to the function which each one has in the Mystical Body.

Toward this ideal every Christian is invited to strive with all his strength, but it is attained more completely and securely in the three states of perfection in the manner described in Canon Law and the Apostolic Constitutions already mentioned. In particular the Constitution *Provida Mater* of 2 February, 1947, on Secular Institutes, opens the way to states of perfection for the greatest possible number of those souls who today aspire ardently to a more perfect life. This Constitution, it is true, states that associations which do not meet the prescribed requirements are not "states of perfection," but it nowise claims that there is no true tending toward perfection outside these states.

We are thinking of those many men and women in every condition of life who follow professions and occupations of various kinds in the modern world and consecrate themselves and all their activities to God for His love and in order to serve Him in serving the neighbor. They bind themselves to practice the evangelical counsels by vows that are private and secret, known only to God, and they choose as guides in matters which concern the submission of obedience and poverty, persons whom the Church has judged fit for this function and to whom she has entrusted the task of directing others in the practice of perfection. These men and women lack none of the elements which constitute Christian perfection and an effective tending toward its attainment; hence they really share in it, even though they do not belong to any juridical or canonical state of perfection.

It is clear that Christian perfection in the essential elements of its definition and realization, admits of no renovation or adaptation. But since the conditions of modern life are subject to profound changes, the way in which that perfection is practiced will in turn have to be modified. These modifications will affect those who live in the states of perfection and those who do not, but especially these latter, particularly if they move in a higher social and occupational sphere. Under such circumstances, are they not forced to surround themselves with some of the comforts of life, to attend official festivities, and to use expensive means of travel — things which seem hardly in accord with that constant quest of mortification which must characterize one who seeks to follow and imitate Christ in His poverty and humility? Nevertheless, even amid material blessings these men and women depart no whit from their utter consecration to God, nor cease to offer a complete holocaust to the Saviour. Such is the power of grace which works in man according to the word of Christ: "The things that are impossible with men are possible with God" (Luke 18, 27).

## II. The States of Perfection

The problems of adaptation and renovation within the states of perfection are now to be looked at more closely. We shall consider first the persons who belong to these states and then the communities themselves in their pursuit of perfection.

### 1. *The Members of the States of Perfection*

In regard to individuals We have but one point to emphasize: what We have said in the first part of Our address, on the perfection of Christian life in general, applies to the members of all the states of perfection and constitutes their primary and essential duty, whether they be inferiors or Superiors; they must unite themselves to God by charity and offer themselves to Him as a holocaust, they must imitate and follow Christ, His life and His Cross, consecrate themselves to the service of His work, the Church, as chosen and active members of the Mystical Body. Once this essential obligation is well established, they are not forbidden to think of renovation and the adaptation of the means for fulfilling it, without failing in respect for the tradition and without detracting from those prescriptions which the Constitutions consider inviolable. Inferiors must moreover observe religious discipline, which forbids them to arrogate to themselves what belongs to the competency of Superiors or to undertake of their own motion reforms which ought not to be attempted without their authorization.

### 2. *The Communities Themselves*

The first thing to consider is the mutual relations between the community as a whole and the individuals, Superiors and inferiors, who belong to it. In this matter two elements claim our attention: first, the spirit which characterizes the mutual relations of the communities with their members, and secondly the obstacles arising from certain prejudices against religious obedience, on which the renovation of the peculiar spirit of the community essentially depends.

An organized society constitutes one body and has a typical physiognomy to the formation of which each member contributes his share. Any attempt at adaptation within the group necessarily entails some modifications of its peculiar spirit; the most intimate fibres of its make-up are affected. Now every society wishes to keep its spirit intact, as it has the right and duty to do; it wants to see its members imbued with this spirit and eager to permeate their lives with it. The Church, for her part, and the Supreme Pontiffs in approving a definite way of life, intend that it should be preserved in all its purity, and they exercise a watchful care to this end.

While it is generally admitted that major Superiors have the right to tell their subjects what is the spirit of their community, still there will always remain the question, where to find the objective expression of that spirit. Major Superiors cannot decide it according to their taste or impression, even with perfect good faith and sincerity. If the major Superior is also the Founder, and if he has received the approval of the Church for his personal views as the norm of a state of perfection, he may always make appeal to his own intentions. But if not, he must go back to the idea of the Founder as expressed in the Constitutions which have been approved by the Church. A subjective conviction, therefore, is not enough, even though it be supported by this or that passage of the Constitutions. When the Superior proposes to the members of his community the true spirit of the Founder, he is exercising his right, and the subjects are bound in conscience to obey. In this matter the rights of Superiors and the obligations of subjects are correlative. The Church and the Sovereign Pontiffs intend always to defend rights and urge obligations, but within proper limits. To avoid exasperating either party and to keep the peace, it is enough that every one recognize and live up to this norm, which has been that of the Church and the Popes for centuries and remains in effect.

Coming now to the actual difficulties in regard to religious obedience, it is to be observed that the movement of adaptation has created a certain tension in this field; not that there is any lack of sincere purpose to tend toward perfection through obedience, but because emphasis is being placed on certain features of obedience which even some religious of serious spirit and delicate conscience would like to see abandoned. In particular, obedience is accused of imperiling the human dignity of the religious, of retarding the development of his personality, of disturbing his orientation toward God alone. It seems that these objections rest on certain disillusionments which have been experienced personally or observed in others; and they claim support also from various juridical considerations.

In order to dispel the feeling of sadness which comes from a mistaken interpretation of the principles governing the religious life or from practical errors in their application, let us first recall the words of our Saviour: "Come to me, all you that labor and are burdened, and I will refresh you. . . . Learn of me, because I am meek and humble of heart, and you shall find rest to your souls."[5] If our Lord thus invites men to take up His yoke, it is to teach them that beyond legal observance, which easily becomes burdensome and hard to bear, they are to discover the meaning of true submission and Christian humility. Far from offending the dignity of the one who submits, this will give him interior liberty and show him how to accept his state of subjection, not as a constraint from without, but as a surrender of himself into the hands of God, whose will is expressed through the visible authority of those whose mission it is to command. The Superior for his part will use his powers in the same evangelical spirit: "He that is the greater among you, let him become as the younger; and he that is the leader as he that serveth."[6] Hence the needed firmness on his part will always be accompanied by the profound respect and delicacy of a father's love.

Is the religious state an obstacle to the harmonious development of the human personality? Does it, as some pretend, keep the personality in a state of "infantility"?

---

[5] Mt. 11:28–29.

[6] Lk. 22:26.

Just observe without prejudice the behavior of the men and women who belong to the states of perfection! Surely no one would have the hardihood to assert that most of them are victims of infantilism in their intellectual and affective life or in their actions. And — if the objection is urged in another form — it would be equally unreasonable to pretend that at least in the course of time communities and Superiors constrain the subjects to grow into ways of thought and action which furnish a basis for this reproach. Those who complain of this would do well to remember that Saint Paul, stating to the faithful the purpose of a life regulated by faith, urges them to progress in "the edifying of the body of Christ," until they attain "unto a perfect man, unto the measure of the age of the fulness of Christ. That henceforth," he continues, "we be no more children tossed to and fro, . . ."[7] Hence the Apostle does not permit the faithful to yield to infantilism, but he demands that they become "perfect men." Moreover, in the First Epistle to the Corinthians he explicitly rejects in adult Christians the ways of thinking and feeling which characterize infancy. "When I was a child, I spoke as a child, I understood as a child, I thought as a child. But when I became a man, I put away the things of a child."[8]

We quoted this same text in Our allocution of 18 April, 1952, on the education of the Christian conscience, to recall the truth that the purpose of a sound education is to teach man to make a judicious use of his liberty and thus to be beyond the need of a teacher. Let every member of the states of perfection, Superior or subject, apply to himself the words of the Apostle; then all danger of infantilism will vanish, without thereby impairing respect for lawful authority or sincere submission to its decisions.

Nor have We any modification to make in what We said in Our allocution of 8 December, 1950, to the First Congress of the States of Perfection, replying to objections that are advanced as to a supposed diminution of the personal and social value of the religious; if his rights undergo a certain limitation, the state to which he belongs, the offering of himself through obedience, give him a dignity which abundantly compensates for this voluntary sacrifice.

---

[7] Ephes. 4:12–14.

[8] 1 Cor. 13:11.

Another argument against obedience is drawn from the claim that man's dependence on the Superior is an obstacle to the supreme and direct dominion of God over the conscience. To insist that a man depend on another even as to his personal life and activity — is not this to confer on the Superior prerogatives which belong only to God?

The Church has never defended nor approved such a contention. She regards obedience as a means of leading man to God. Since the motive which inspires it is union with God and since the final aim of obedience is growth in charity, the Superior is by no means an obstacle standing between God and the subject and arrogating to himself the homage which is directed only to God. The Superior can command only in the name of God and in virtue of the powers entrusted to him, and the subject is bound to obey only for love of Christ, not for any motives of human advantage or convenience — and much less by mere constraint. Thus he will preserve, even in the most complete submission, the eager joy of renewing each day concretely his total consecration to the one supreme Master.

The program of your second General Congress shows that there will be an ample treatment of the relations of the communities among themselves in regard to your movement of renovation and adaptation. Here too We do not wish to enter into details. We are quite sure that the regulations established by the Sacred Congregation of Religious will be faithfully observed. We would only remind you that, while preserving the distinctions which exist and should exist between the communities, there should be a sincere and benevolent tendency toward union and collaboration. There is in fact such a thing as a "common good" of communities, which implies that each one is prepared to take account of the others, to adapt itself to the demands of a coordination which necessarily involves also some sacrifice in view of the general welfare.

There is an analogy which makes applicable to your communities, united by divine grace in the Body of the Church, what Saint Paul says in the well known passage of the First Epistle to the Corinthians[9] about the relation between the members: each one of those who belong to the body is entitled on that ground to the help and collaboration of all in view of the

[9] 1 Cor. 12:12–27.

one common good, that of Holy Church. It is easy to deduce from this passage the sentiments of esteem, benevolence, service, desire to work together, holy emulation, unselfish generosity, which should characterize the relations of the communities among themselves. Each member must of course hold fast to its own nature and peculiar function in the body, but also understand and respect the function of the others and learn how to combine with them in view of the common good.

What concerns the relations of the states of perfection to the Vicar of Christ and the Holy See scarcely needs to be recalled: the prerogatives of the Apostolic See which are based on their institution by Christ Himself and which the Church in the course of the centuries has only clarified and defined more accurately, must remain inviolable and sacred. Whereas all the faithful respect and observe them, members of the states of perfection will in this regard be an example to all. It is important, then, to seek and maintain contact with the Holy See. In the Encyclical *Humani generis* We pointed out that the tendency to avoid contact and to keep away was one important reason for the errors and deviations which it exposed; and this regrettable attitude was particularly that of some members of states of perfection. If this contact is to be fruitful it must be full of confidence, sincerity, and docility.

The Holy See would like to receive from you information which is not only truthful but frank, such as to present the actual state of each community as regards doctrine and way of living, ascetical training and observance, religious discipline, temporal administration, and so on. Only then will it be possible to promote what is good and correct what is wrong before it is too late; for it is in these favorable spiritual dispositions that the replies, regulations, and instructions of the Holy See bear fruit.

There is one thing more of which We would say a word; that is the desire of "centralization" which many reproachfully attribute to the Holy See. The word "centralization" could mean a system of government which insists on centering everything in itself, on deciding and directing everything, reducing all lesser authorities to the role of mere instruments. Centralization in this sense is absolutely foreign to the spirit of the Roman Pontiffs and of the Holy See. The Holy See cannot, however, renounce its character of being the governing center of the Church. While leaving to established Superiors the initiative which belongs to them by the Constitutions, it must still preserve its right and exercise its function of vigilance.

What might be said on the subject of the renovation and adaptation of the relations of the communities among themselves and with the Holy See is, We think, sufficiently indicated in your program. The principles which We have called to your attention provide you with direction, and We doubt not that you will derive profit from their study.

* * *

The domain of perfection, in which We have taken a few steps with you, is very vast and very beautiful, and has still some zones to be explored. We have drawn your attention to perfection in general and in the states of perfection. There are today many persons, not only among clerics and religious but also among the laity, who are interested in these questions. When they confront them with certain modern ideas and principles they discover some serious and complex problems, without however finding the answers to them notwithstanding their ardent desire to do so. It is for this reason that We have chosen to give them some light by recalling the principles that lead to their solution.

Let Us in conclusion leave with you another thought of Saint Paul from his Epistle to the Colossians:[10] "But above all these things have charity, which is the bond of perfection." Beyond all problems and discussions, seek especially union with God, and you will advance constantly toward perfection. That is the grace which We wish for you and which We implore for you of the Most High, whilst We bestow upon you most heartily Our paternal Apostolic Blessing.

**AAS 50–34**; Pius XII, Allocution, 9 Dec., 1957. Annotations, *Commentarium pro Religiosis,* 36 (1957)–278 (Peinador); *Periodica,* 49 (1960)–3 (Hürth).

**Norms for Religious Women Conducting Guest Houses in Rome** (Prefect of S. C. Rel., Letter, 31 July, 1961) **Private.**

A letter of Cardinal Valeri, Prefect of the S. C. of Religious,

[10] Col. 3:14.

31 July, 1961, to Rev. Mother Christina Estrada, President of the Central Council of the Union of Italian Major Superiors (U.S.M.I.):

Reverend Mother General:

This Sacred Congregation is informed from various sources that many religious Congregations have opened or propose to open, especially in Rome, houses destined to receive as guests, not only persons already known but often also transient boarders: women, men, and families of pilgrims and tourists.

In this connection, I desire that Your Reverence should make known, especially through the *"Revista delle Religiose di Italia"* (formerly A.L.A.) the dispositions which this Sacred Congregation has several times already issued:

1. The Holy See has always been reluctant to approve institutions destined among other purposes to offer hospitality in their own houses, especially to persons of both sexes, and above all when such activity borders on that which is proper to hotels. This was stated explicitly in the Norms of 1901, art. 16; the Norms of 1921, art. 14 excluded activity of this sort.

2. In 1950, because of the great influx of pilgrims, the competent authorities, especially in Rome, granted ample permissions for receiving guests, but on certain conditions, which perhaps have not always been completely kept in mind.

3. At the present time circumstances are rather different from those of 1950, and the hotel accommodations of the city have increased, though not to such an extent as to render a similar activity on the part of religious institutes entirely superfluous.

In any event, whenever, with due permission from the Vicariate of Rome or the proper diocesan Curia, there are houses which give hospitality to pilgrims or tourists, there is a grave obligation to observe the canonical regulations mentioned below, and also to comply with the requirements of the civil law, as set forth in the attached summary.

4. The canonical norms are especially the following:

*a*) The hospitality which is offered in the religious houses should have an apostolic character and not be assimilated to any sort of hotel service.

*b*) There should be complete separation between the places that are reserved to the community of Sisters and those that are destined for the guests; passage from one to the other should be prudently controlled and supervised by the Superiors or those in charge.

*c*) The Sisters should not be charged with services that are not becoming to religious persons: such as taking care of the rooms of men or families who are guests, serving table, and the like.

*d*) All appearance of working for profit or of competing with hotels should be avoided.

*e*) In the performance of these works the prescriptions that may be enacted by the civil authorities must be faithfully observed.

As President of the U.S.M.I. Your Reverence will please kindly see to it that this letter be not only brought to the attention of all the Reverend Superioresses General, but also that it be published at least in substance in the *Rivista* above mentioned, by agreement with the Reverend Father Director of said Review, also as regards the publication of the civil regulations attached hereto.

I take this occasion to thank Your Reverence for all you are doing for the good of religious women in Italy, and remain,

Sincerely yours in Christ,
Valerio Cardinal Valeri
Prefect

**(Private)**; S. C. Rel. Letter of the Cardinal Prefect, 31 July, 1961; published in *Rivista delle Religiose,* 10 (1961)–519; and reported in *Commentarium pro Religiosis,* 51 (1962)–12.

## **Sound Doctrine and Solid Virtue in Preparation of Religious for the Priesthood in Italy** (S. C. Rel., 6 Oct., 1961) **Private.**

This letter was sent by the S. C. of Religious to the Superiors General of male religious and secular Institutes having houses or centers in Italy:

In the light of the Apostolic Constitution, *Sedes Sapientiae,* and of the Instruction, *Religiosorum institutio,* this Sacred Congregation deems it opportune to insist on certain aspects of the disciplinary and doctrinal preparation of the young clergy in Italy.

It is in fact not altogether rare that certain attitudes are observed — such as a want of humility, a lively spirit of criticism of the acts of Superiors, a not quite correct notion of obedience, an aversion to sacrifice, a sometimes mistaken evaluation of certain doctrinal questions — which seem to indicate a view of life scarcely in accord with that which is proper in one who aspires to the priesthood.

These deficiencies, which certainly cannot be imputed to failures on the part of the organs responsible for the formation of young religious, may perhaps have their roots in the milieu from which the vocations are drawn, often impregnated with worldliness and laicism, in contrast with the spirit of mortification and respectful obedience to legitimate ecclesiastical authorities.

Accordingly, this Sacred Congregation feels it its duty to call the attention of Your Very Reverend Paternity and of all who are in charge of the government, teaching, and spiritual formation of the new groups of religious, especially of those who are candidates for the priesthood, to the following recommendations:

"The preparation of religious should be intensified so as to meet the deviations of the world of today without danger or compromise, with security in doctrine and the possession of the necessary virtues, especially humility, obedience, and the spirit of sacrifice. In particular the young levites must be well trained in *the sound social doctrine of the Church.*"

**(Private)**; S. C. Rel., Circular Letter of Cardinal Valeri, Prefect of the S. C., 6 Oct., 1961; reported in *Commentarium pro Religiosis,* 41 (1962)–226.

## The *Ratio Institutionis* (S. C. Rel., 15 Nov., 1962) Private.

A letter of the S. C. of Religious sent to the General Superiors of clerical institutes:

Very Reverend Father:

Some religious institutes and societies for acquiring evangelical perfection, which had obtained approbation of their *Ratio Studiorum* for three years, have asked this Sacred Congregation to grant them a permanent approval of the same. But in view of the circumstances of the present time this Sacred Congregation has thought it best to defer all approbations of the *Rationes Studiorum* until the Second Vatican Ecumenical Council which is now in progress comes to an end. Consequently, by the present Letter, it extends the temporary approbations already given, until the end of the Council.

Now, since the General Statutes[1] prescribe, in addition to the *Ratio Studiorum,* also a *Ratio Institutionis,* or system of training (art. 19, § 1), all Abbots General and General Superiors are instructed to present their *Ratio Institutionis* to this Sacred Congregation within the year 1963. It should contain, not merely in a descriptive but in a normative manner as laws are usually framed, the method of formation, humanistic, religious, priestly and apostolic, proper to each institute; that is, the system of training which is used in the middle-classical curriculum, in the novitiate, in the courses of philosophy and theology, in the pastoral course and in the third probation.

Religious institutes which already have a method approved and in use for all or some of the stages of formation indicated above, can satisfy this obligation by presenting to the Sacred Congregation as soon as possible two copies of the books dealing with this matter, for revision, taking account however of the documents issued by the Holy See on this subject in recent years.

I remain, Your Paternity, very sincerely yours in Christ,

Valerius Cardinal Valeri
Prefect

**(Private)**; S. C. Rel., 15 Nov., 1962; *Commentarium pro Religiosis,* 42 (1963)–3.

NOTE: Following this text (*ibid.,* pp. 5–20) are two schemes or outlines for the composition of this *Ratio Institutionis,* one in combination with the *Ratio Studiorum,* the other independently.

---

**Alphonsian Academy of Moral Theology:** The Sacred Congregation of Religious, on 25 March, 1957 (Prot. N. 1960/57), issued a Letter and a Decree approving and confirming the Alphonsian Academy newly established in Rome by the Fathers of the Congregation of the Holy Redeemer for the advanced study of moral theology in the tradition of Saint Alphonsus Liguori, Doctor of the Church and patron of confessors and

[1] Not published in the AAS but available in English from the Catholic University of America Press; see CANON LAW DIGEST, 4, p. 182, note.

moralists. The Academy is approved and established as a public internal school of higher studies according to the Apostolic Constitution *Sedes Sapientiae,* n. 8 and the General Statutes, art. 41. Both are published in *Commentarium pro Religiosis,* 36 (1957)–296 to 300, with annotations by van Biervliet.

**Consecration of Virgins:** Rite to be revised. See **c. 2,** AAS 56–97, Constitution on the Sacred Liturgy, n. 80.

**Contemplative Life:** Pius XII, Radio Address to cloistered nuns of the whole world, delivered in three installments on successive dates: 1. Knowing the Contemplative Life, 19 July, 1958; 2. Loving the Contemplative Life, 25 July, 1958; 3. Living the Contemplative Life, 2 Aug., 1958 (AAS 50–563). English text, *The Pope Speaks,* 5 (1958–59) 61; *Review for Religious,* 18 (1959) 4–12; 65–76; 133–142. Annotations, *Commentarium pro Religiosis,* 38 (1959)–149 (Peinador).

**Nursing Sisters:** Allocution of Pius XII, 24 April, 1957 (AAS 49–291). *The Pope Speaks,* 4 (1957–58)–135–140.

***Ratio Studiorum* Urged to Include Liturgical Instruction.** See **c. 2;** *Motu proprio* to implement Constitution on the Liturgy, n. I.

**States of Perfection:** Allocution of John XXIII, 16 Dec., 1961 (AAS 54–32).

## CANON 488

### Monastic Nuns: Foundation of New Monasteries (S. C. Rel., 11 Oct., 1922) AAS 14–554.

The Sacred Congregation of Religious was asked:

It sometimes happens that monasteries of monastic nuns, which by their institute have solemn vows, but in which, nevertheless, by order of the Holy See in certain places simple vows only are taken, proceed to found a new monastery of the same Order, by sending some nuns into a place where such an order of the Holy See is not in effect. Hence:

1. Are the vows which have been pronounced or will be pronounced in the new monastery, founded or to be founded as above stated, to be regarded as solemn vows according to the common law?

**Reply.** In the affirmative, provided there has been a *beneplacitum* from the Holy See (cf. c. 497).

2. Can the nuns mentioned in c. 488, 7°, found new monasteries in other places without the *beneplacitum* of the Holy See?

**Reply.** In the negative, and the Holy Father is to be asked to ratify foundations heretofore made without the permission of the Holy See.

3. Does a monastery of nuns with solemn vows and papal cloister, when it is transferred to another place, continue to be one of solemn vows and papal cloister?

**Reply.** Recourse should be had in individual cases to the Holy See.

4. What is the law when a monastery of nuns such as are mentioned in c. 488, 7° is moved to a place where the order of the Holy See referred to in that canon is not in effect?

**Reply.** Recourse should be had in individual cases to the Holy See.

AAS 14–554; S. C. Rel., 11 Oct., 1922.
*Periodica,* 11 (1923)–160 (Vermeersch); *J.P.,* 2 (1922)–134.

## Congregations of Diocesan Law: Decree Relating to Erection and Approval (S. C. Rel., 30 Nov., 1922) AAS 14–644.

It had already been provided by the Constitution, *Conditae a Christo,* of Leo XIII, and is more explicitly prescribed by the Code (c. 488) that there should be some religious Congregations of pontifical law, others of diocesan law; both kinds having the nature of religious societies with the rights pertaining thereto. Among those rights is this fundamental one, that every religious Congregation legitimately organized is invested with and enjoys moral personality according to law. Lest any doubt should arise in a matter of such grave importance, and in order that the legitimacy of this moral personality should be always capable of proof, c. 100, § 1, wisely provides that (with the exception of the Catholic Church and the Holy See) no moral person can be created without a formal decree to that effect by the competent ecclesiastical Superior.

It has happened, however, especially before the Constitution, *Conditae a Christo,* and the *Motu proprio* of Pius X, *Dei Providentia,* of 16 July, 1906, that certain religious Congregations arose, which are now regarded as tolerated or even implicitly approved by the Ordinaries, without, however, any proof that they were erected by formal decree.

Since this state of affairs may give rise to many inconveniences, and it is desirable to remove all occasions of doubt regarding the legitimacy of religious Congregations, the S. C. Rel., after mature consideration, decrees as follows:

I. Every Bishop, or prelate exercising quasi-episcopal jurisdiction in a separate territory, shall as soon as possible make inquiry regarding all religious Congregations or pious societies of persons of either sex, living as religious, even if they consist of but one house, in his diocese or territory, and which have not been approved by the Holy See at least by a *decretum laudis:*

1. Whether they were erected by a formal episcopal Decree whose tenor is known;

2. Whether they have an organic law or constitutions approved by the same authority.

II. If he finds any Congregations or pious societies for which a formal decree of erection is either certainly nonexistent or doubtful, but which were equivalently regarded by the Ordinary as approved through repeated acts in the course of several years before the promulgation of the Code, as, for example, by the reception of their vows, by episcopal visitations, ordinations, or the like, the Bishop shall, unless the circumstances make a different course advisable as provided herein under n. III, recognize them by his formal Decree, in which, after briefly reciting the conditions above referred to, he shall declare the religious Congregation or pious society erected as of diocesan law; provided that, as regards institutes which arose subsequently to the aforesaid *Motu proprio, Dei Providentia,* of 1906, the permission of the Holy See has been obtained. And this Sacred Congregation declares that the aforesaid Decree of recognition shall have the effect of curing the want of canonical erection, as far as need be, for the past.

III. If the institute has spread through several dioceses, the Ordinary of the place, mentioned in n. I, is the one in whose diocese the principal house is located. He should not, however, issue a Decree of recognition except after having consulted with the other Bishops, and only in case they at least make no objection.

IV. If, on account of the condition of the institute, or the small number of its members, or the absence of the circumstances mentioned in n. II, or for other reasons, the Ordinary shall deem it inadvisable to recognize by formal Decree some

Congregation or pious society, or if some one of the Ordinaries mentioned in n. III positively objects, he should refer the matter to this Sacred Congregation (cf. c. 493).

V. In regard to all and each of the Congregations or pious societies of diocesan law already lawfully erected or now recognized as above provided, whose principal or only house is now located in the diocese, the Ordinary shall send to this Sacred Congregation a report in which is distinctly stated: (*a*) the name of the Congregation or pious society; (*b*) its purpose; (*c*) the name of its founder and its organic law; (*d*) the Decree of erection or recognition; (*e*) the dioceses to which it has spread; (*f*) the number of its houses and members.

VI. If any Ordinary of a place learns that there is no principal house or independent house of a religious Congregation of diocesan law now located in his territory, he shall inform this Sacred Congregation of that fact by an express declaration in writing.

VII. For the future, however, whenever an Ordinary, after obtaining the required permission from the Holy See, shall desire to erect any new religious Congregation or pious society, he shall take care that it be erected by formal Decree in writing, a copy of which shall be kept both in the archives of the institute and in the archives of the diocese. He shall, moreover, notify this Sacred Congregation of his act erecting the Congregation, and shall send a copy of the Decree in which he shall take special care that the title and purpose of the particular institute be explicitly and exactly defined, having in view the prescription made in this regard in the *Normae* approved by this Sacred Congregation on 6 March, 1921.[1]

AAS 14–644; S. C. Rel., Decree, 30 Nov., 1922.
*Periodica,* 11 (1923)–173 (Vermeersch).

## Sisters of Mercy Are a Congregation of Pontifical Law
(S. C. Rel., 24 Nov., 1925) **AAS 18–14.**

The Sacred Congregation of Religious was asked:

I. Whether the Congregation of the Sisters of Mercy who, according to their constitutions, approved by Gregory XVI through the Sacred Congregation of Propaganda on 6 June, 1841,

[1] See c. 492; AAS 13–312; this volume, p. 185.

have separate houses under the respective jurisdiction and authority of the Bishop, is to be regarded as a religious institute of pontifical law or only of diocesan law. And, if it is one of pontifical law:

II. Are those several Congregations of Sisters of Mercy whose various houses in divers places have, with the approval of the Holy See, been united under one central government, likewise to be considered as of pontifical law?

**Reply.** To I: In the affirmative to the first part; in the negative to the second.

To II: In the affirmative.

Approved and confirmed by His Holiness, Pius XI, 24 Nov., 1925.

AAS 18–14; S. C. Rel., *Declaratio,* 24 Nov., 1925.
*Periodica,* 15 (1926)–52 (Vermeersch).

NOTE: The annotations in *Periodica* point out consequences of this Decree in connection with cc. 500, 506, 512, 533, 638.

## **Apostolic Constitution on Secular Institutes** (Pius XII, 2 Feb., 1947) **AAS 39–114.**

An Apostolic Constitution, *Provida Mater Ecclesia,* of 2 February, 1947, entitled: *On the Canonical States and on Secular Institutes for Acquiring Christian Perfection,* is as follows:

The care and maternal affection with which Holy Mother Church has ever solicitously striven on behalf of the children of her predilection, who have given their whole lives to Christ in order to follow Him freely on the arduous path of the counsels, that she might constantly render them worthy of their heavenly resolve and angelic vocation, and at the same time make wise provisions governing their way of life, is witnessed by a host of documents and memorials of Popes, Councils, and Fathers, and is clearly proved by the whole course of church history and by all the canonical legislation on the subject up to our own time.[1]

Certainly from the very beginnings of Christianity, the Church

[1] The original text contains a wealth of footnote references to Sacred Scripture and the Fathers, invaluable for historical study of the religious life. We reproduce only the few footnotes which refer to recent canonical sources.

in her *magisterium* earnestly developed the doctrine of Christ and the Apostles and their example inviting souls to perfection, by securely teaching how a life devoted to perfection was to be lived and properly ordered. At the same time, by her work and ministry, she so earnestly favored and propagated an entire dedication and consecration to Christ that in the early ages the Christian communities, by practicing the evangelical counsels, freely offered a good ground prepared for the seed and giving secure promise of a rich harvest; and shortly afterward, as can easily be proved from the Apostolic Fathers and the older ecclesiastical writers, the profession of the life of perfection was so flourishing in the various churches that its followers were beginning to constitute in the bosom of the Church, as it were a distinct order and social class, which was clearly recognized under various names — ascetics, continents, virgins, among others — and which was approved and held in honor by many.

In the course of the centuries, the Church, ever faithful to Christ her Spouse, and true to herself, under the guidance of the Holy Spirit, with continuous and unhesitating progress up to the establishment of the present Code of Canon Law, gradually developed the discipline of the state of perfection. With a peculiar motherly affection for those who freely, under various forms, made external and public profession of a life of perfection, she constantly gave them every encouragement in their pursuit of so holy a purpose, and that under two distinct heads. In the first place, the individual profession of the life of perfection, always, however, to be made publicly and before the Church — such as the ancient and venerable liturgical blessing and consecration of virgins — was not only admitted and recognized, but the Church herself wisely sanctioned and strongly defended it, and attached to it a number of canonical effects. But the principal favor and more diligent care of the Church, from the earliest times after the peace of Constantine, were rightly and properly directed toward and exercised in favor of that complete and more strictly public profession of the life of perfection, which was made in societies and organized groups erected with her permission or approval or by her positive authority.

It is common knowledge that the history of the holiness of the Church and of the Catholic apostolate is most closely and intimately connected with the history and records of the canonical religious life, as, under the constant vivifying grace of the Holy Spirit, it continued from day to day to exhibit a wonderful variety and at the same time to grow into a new and ever deeper and stronger unity. It is not to be wondered at that the Church, even in the field of law, faithfully following the direction which the provident Wisdom of God clearly indicated, purposely cultivated and regulated the canonical state of perfection in such wise that she rightly and properly designed to build the edifice of ecclesiastical discipline upon this as upon one of its cornerstones. Hence, in the first place, the public state of perfection was counted as one of the three principal ecclesiastical states, and in it alone the Church found the second order and grade of canonical persons (c. 107). Here is something surely worthy of attentive consideration: while the other two orders of canonical persons, namely clerics and the laity, are found in the Church by divine law, to which the ecclesiastical institution is superadded (cc. 107, 108, § 3), in as much as the Church is established and organized as a hierarchical society, this class, namely that of religious, intermediate between clerics and the laity and capable of being participated in by both clerics and the laity (c. 107), is entirely derived from the close and very special relationship which it has to the end of the Church, that is, to the efficacious pursuit of perfection by adequate means.

Nor was this all. Lest the public and solemn profession of holiness should be frustrated and come to nothing, the Church with ever increasing strictness was willing to recognize this canonical state of perfection only in societies which were erected and governed by herself, that is, in religious Institutes (c. 488, 1°), whose general form and purpose she had approved by her *magisterium* after a slow and careful examination, and whose institute and rules she had in every case not only scrutinized more than once doctrinally and in the abstract, but had also tested by actual trial. These requirements are laid down so strictly and absolutely in the Code of Canon Law, that in no case, not even by way of exception, is the canonical state of perfection recognized, unless its profession is made in a religious Institute approved by the Church. Finally, the canonical discipline of the state of perfection as a public state was so wisely regulated by the Church that, in the case of clerical religious Institutes, in all those matters in general which govern the clerical life of the religious, the Institutes took the place of dioceses, and membership in a religious society was equivalent to the incardination of a cleric in a diocese (cc. 111, §1; 115; 585).

After the Code of Pius and Benedict, in the second Part of Book II, which is devoted to religious, had diligently collected, revised, and carefully improved the legislation regarding religious, and had thus in many ways confirmed the canonical state of perfection also in its public aspect, and, wisely perfecting the work begun by Leo XIII of happy memory in his immortal Constitution, *Conditae a Christo,* had admitted Congregations of simple vows among religious Institutes in the strict sense, it seemed that nothing remained to be added in the discipline of the canonical state of perfection. Yet the Church, with her great breadth of mind and vision and with true maternal solicitude, decided to add to the legislation on religious, a brief title as an appropriate supplement. In this title (Title XVII of Book II), the Church declares as in a fairly complete sense equivalent to the canonical state of perfection, certain societies, of great value to herself and frequently also to the State, which, though they lacked some of the requirements which are necessary for the complete state of perfection, such as public vows (cc. 488, 1° and 7°; 487), yet in other respects which are regarded as essentials of the life of perfection, bear a close similarity to religious Institutes and are almost necessarily connected with them.

When all this had been wisely, prudently, and lovingly ordained, ample provision had been made for the great number of souls who wish to leave the world and to embrace a new canonical state strictly so called, exclusively and completely dedicated to the attainment of perfection. But the good Lord, who without respect of persons again and again invited all the faithful to seek and to practice perfection everywhere, in the admirable designs of His divine Providence, so disposed that even in the world, depraved by so many vices especially in our own time, there have been and are now great numbers of chosen souls who not only burn with the desire of individual perfection, but who, while by a special vocation from God they remain in the world, are able to find excellent new forms of Consociation, beautifully corresponding to the needs of the times, in which they can lead a life very well adapted to the acquirement of Christian perfection.

While We heartily commend to the prudence and zeal of spiritual directors the noble strivings of individuals toward perfection in the internal forum, We turn Our attention at this time to the Associations which, before the Church, in the so-called external forum, work and strive to lead their own subjects as it were by the hand to a life of solid perfection. Yet We are not dealing here with all Consociations which sincerely seek Christian perfection in the world, but with those only which, in their internal constitution, in the hierarchical order of their government, in the full dedication, unlimited by any other ties, which they require of their members strictly so called, in their profession of the evangelical counsels, and finally in their manner of exercising the ministry and apostolate, bear a closer essential resemblance to the canonical states of perfection, and especially to the Societies without public vows (Tit. XVII), even though they do not practice the religious life in common, but make use of other external forms.

These Consociations, which shall hereafter be called "secular Institutes," began to be founded, not without the inspiration of divine Providence, in the first half of the last century, in order faithfully "to follow the evangelical counsels in the world and to devote themselves more freely to works of charity, which, owing to the iniquity of the times, were almost or entirely forbidden to religious."[2] Since the older Institutes of this class have given a good account of themselves and have sufficiently and increasingly demonstrated, by the severe and prudent selection of their members, by their careful and sufficiently protracted training, and by an appropriate blending of firmness and flexibility in their way of life, that even in the world, with a special vocation from God and with the help of divine grace, it is certainly possible to attain a rather strict and effective self-consecration to God, which is not merely internal but also external and almost religious, and that thus a very appropriate instrument of penetration and apostolate is provided — for all these reasons, "these Societies of the faithful have more than once been commended by the Holy See in the same way as have true religious Congregations."[3]

---

[2] S. C. Ep. et Reg., 11 Aug., 1889; ASS 23–634.

[3] *Ibid.*

The prosperous growth of these Institutes has shown with increasing clarity in how many ways they can be turned to the effective service of the Church and of souls. For living seriously the life of perfection at all times and in all places; for embracing such a life in many cases where the canonical religious life was either impossible or not appropriate; for the thorough Christian renovation of families, professions, and civil society through an intimate and daily contact with a life perfectly and entirely dedicated to holiness; for exercising a varied apostolate and ministry in places, times, and circumstances forbidden or inaccessible to priests and religious — for all these purposes, these Institutes can easily be used and adapted. On the other hand, experience has shown that this free and independent living of the life of perfection — without the protection of an external religious habit, without the support of a common life, without supervision on the part of Ordinaries, who could easily remain unaware of its existence, or of Superiors, who frequently were far away — was at times, nay rather easily, attended by certain difficulties and dangers. There had also arisen some discussion about the juridical nature of these Institutes, and about the mind of the Holy See in approving them. Here We think it useful to mention the Decree, *Ecclesia Catholica,* which the Sacred Congregation of Bishops and Regulars issued, and which was confirmed on the 11th of August 1889[4] by Our Predecessor of immortal memory, Leo XIII. In this Decree the commendation and approval of such Institutes was not forbidden, but it was stated that the Sacred Congregation, when it did give commendation or approval to these Institutes, had wished to commend and approve them, not as religious Institutes of solemn vows, nor as true religious Congregations of simple vows, but only as pious sodalities, in which, not to speak of the other things which are wanting according to the present discipline of the Church, no religious profession in the proper sense is pronounced, but the vows, if there are any, are considered private, and not public in the sense of being accepted by the legitimate Superior in the name of the Church. These sodalities, moreover — said the same Sacred Congregation — are commended or approved under this essential condition, that they become fully and perfectly known to their respective

[4] *Ibid.*

Ordinaries and be entirely subject to their jurisdiction. These prescriptions and declarations of the Sacred Congregation of Bishops and Regulars made a timely contribution toward defining the nature of these Institutes, and guided without impeding their development and progress.

In this present century secular Institutes have quietly multiplied, and have taken on a considerable variety of forms, some autonomous and some united in various ways to religious Institutes or Societies. The Apostolic Constitution, *Conditae a Christo,* makes no provision for them, as it was exclusively concerned with religious Congregations. The Code of Canon Law also was intentionally silent as regards these Institutes, and, since they did not seem to be yet mature, it left it to future legislation to determine what provision should be made for them.

Having more than once considered all this in view of Our conscientious duty and Our paternal affection for the souls who so generously seek holiness in the world; and to the end that a wise and searching discrimination may be exercised in regard to these Societies, and that those only which authentically profess the full life of perfection be acknowledged as true Institutes; in order to avoid the dangers of the continual erection of new Institutes — which are sometimes founded without prudent consideration; and at the same time that those Institutes which do merit approval may have the special juridical regulation which corresponds suitably and fully to their purposes and conditions. We have considered and decided upon doing for secular Institutes what Our Predecessor of immortal memory, Leo XIII, so prudently and wisely provided for Congregations of simple vows by the Apostolic Constitution, *Conditae a Christo.* Accordingly, the general statute of secular Institutes, which had been carefully examined by the Supreme Sacred Congregation of the Holy Office in matters relating to its competency, and had been, by Our will and direction, carefully drawn up and revised by the Sacred Congregation of Religious, We now approve by this present Letter; and do by Our Apostolic authority declare, decree, and establish the following.

And for putting into execution the provisions as above established, We depute the Sacred Congregation of Religious, investing it with all necessary and appropriate faculties.

*Special Law of Secular Institutes*

Art. I

Societies, whether clerical or lay, whose members, in order to attain Christian perfection and to exercise a full apostolate, profess the evangelical counsels in the world, that they may be properly distinguished from other common Associations of the faithful (Part Three, Book II of the Code of Canon Law) are rightly called Institutes, or secular Institutes, and are subject to the norms of this Apostolic Constitution.

*Art. II*

§ 1. Secular Institutes, since they neither admit the three public vows of religion (cc. 1308, § 1, and 488, 1°), nor oblige their members to live the common life, that is, to dwell together under the same roof, according to the canons (cc. 487 sqq., and 673 sqq.):

1° By law, according to their rule, neither are nor can properly be called religious Institutes (cc. 487 and 488, 1°) nor Societies of the common life (c. 673, § 1);

2° They are not bound by the proper and special law of religious Institutes or of Societies of the common life, nor can they use the same, except in as far as some provision thereof, especially of the law governing Societies without public vows, may by way of exception have been legitimately adapted and applied to them.

§ 2. These Institutes, without prejudice to the common norms of canon law which concern them, are governed by the following prescriptions as their proper law, more closely corresponding to their peculiar nature and condition:

1° By the general norms of this Apostolic Constitution, which constitute as it were the peculiar statute of all secular Institutes;

2° By the norms which the Sacred Congregation of Religious, according as necessity shall demand and experience shall suggest, may decide to issue, either by way of interpreting this Apostolic Constitution or of perfecting and applying it for all or some of these Institutes;

3° By the particular Constitutions, approved according to the Articles which follow (Art. V–VIII), which may prudently adapt the general rules of law and the special norms set forth above (nn. 1° and 2°) to the quite different purposes, needs, and circumstances of the various Institutes.

Art. III

§ 1. In order that any pious Consociation of the faithful may be erected as a secular Institute according to the Articles which follow, it must satisfy, in addition to those of the common law, the following requisites (§§ 2–4):

§ 2. As regards the consecration of life and the profession of Christian perfection:

Persons who desire to be ascribed to the Institutes as members in the strict sense, in addition to practicing those exercises of piety and self-denial which all must practice who aspire to the perfection of Christian life, must effectively tend toward that same perfection also in the special ways which are here enumerated:

1° By making profession before God of celibacy and perfect chastity, which shall be confirmed by vow, oath, or consecration binding in conscience, according to the Constitutions;

2° By a vow or promise of obedience, so that they dedicate themselves entirely to God and to works of charity or apostleship by a stable bond, and are always in all respects morally in the hands and under the guidance of their Superiors, according to the Constitutions;

3° By a vow or promise of poverty, in virtue of which they have not the free use of temporal property, but a restricted and limited use, according to the Constitutions.

§ 3. As regards the incorporation of the members in their own Institute and the bond arising therefrom:

The bond by which the secular Institute and its members in the strict sense are to be united must be:

1° Stable, according to the Constitutions, either perpetual or temporary but to be renewed at its expiration (c. 488, 1°);

2° Mutual and complete, so that, according to the Constitutions, the member gives himself wholly to the Institute, and the Institute takes care of and is responsible for the member.

§ 4. As regards the establishments and houses of secular Institutes:

Secular Institutes, though they do not impose upon their members the common life and cohabitation under the same roof according to the common law (Art. II, § 1), yet should have one or more common houses, according to need or utility, in which:

1° Those may live who have the government of the Institute, especially the supreme or regional government;

2° Where the members may live, or to which they may come, to receive and complete their training, to make spiritual exercises, and for other such purposes;

3° Where members may be received when, because of ill health or other circumstances, they cannot provide for themselves, or when it is not advisable that they live privately, either by themselves or with others.

### Art. IV

§ 1. Secular Institutes (Art. I) are under the Sacred Congregation of Religious, without prejudice to the rights of the Sacred Congregation for the Propagation of the Faith according to canon 252, § 3, as regards Societies and Seminaries destined for the Missions.

§ 2. Consociations which have not the character or do not fully profess the purpose described in Article I, and those also which lack any of the elements mentioned in Articles I and III of this Apostolic Constitution, are governed by the law of Associations of the faithful as in canons 684 and the following canons, and are under the Sacred Congregation of the Council, except as provided in canon 252, § 3 for the territory of the Missions.

### Art. V

§ 1. Secular Institutes can be established and erected as moral persons according to canon 100, §§ 1 and 2, by Bishops, but not by Vicars Capitular or Vicars General.

§ 2. Bishops should not, however, establish them nor allow them to be established without consulting the Sacred Congregation of Religious, according to canon 492, § 1, and the following Article.

### Art. VI

§ 1. In order that the Sacred Congregation of Religious may give Bishops the permission to erect Institutes, when they consult it on the matter in advance according to Article V, § 2, the said Sacred Congregation must be informed, making due allowances according to its own judgment for the differences between the respective cases, of all those matters which are specified in the Norms issued by the same Sacred Congregation for the erection of a Congregation or Society of the common life (nn. 3–5),[5] and also of other matters which have been or shall in future be required by the practice and procedure of the same Sacred Congregation.

§ 2. When Bishops have obtained the permission of the Sacred Congregation of Religious, there will be nothing to prevent their freely using their right and erecting the Institute. They should not fail to send official notice of the erection to the same Sacred Congregation.

### Art. VII

§ 1. Secular Institutes which shall have obtained approval or a decree of praise from the Holy See, become Institutes of pontifical right (cc. 488, 3°; 673, § 2).

§ 2. In order that secular Institutes of diocesan right may be able to obtain a decree of praise or of approbation, in general, making due allowances according to the judgment of the Sacred Congregation of Religious for the differences between the respective cases, the same conditions are required which according to the Norms (nn. 6 sqq.) and according to the practice and procedure of the same Sacred Congregation, have been, or may in future be prescribed and defined for Congregations and Societies of the common life.

§ 3. The procedure in granting the first, any further provisional, and finally the definitive approval of these Institutes and their Constitutions, shall be as follows:

1° A first discussion of the case, after it has been prepared according to the usual practice and illustrated by the opinion and explanation of at least one Consultor, shall take place in the Commission of Consultors, under the leadership of the Most Excellent Secretary of the same Sacred Congregation, or of some one taking his place.

---

[5] S. C. Rel., 6 March, 1921; AAS 13–312. Not contained in CANON LAW DIGEST because the publication of translations was forbidden by the Holy See.

2° Then the entire matter is to be submitted to the examination and decision of the full *Congressus* of the Sacred Congregation, with the Eminent Cardinal Prefect of the Sacred Congregation presiding, and in the presence of learned or more learned Consultors who have been invited in order to scrutinize the case more carefully as necessity or utility may suggest.

3° The decision of the *Congressus* shall be reported by the Eminent Cardinal Prefect or the Most Excellent Secretary to His Holiness in an audience, and be thus submitted to his supreme judgment.

### Art. VIII

Secular Institutes, besides being subject to their own laws if they have any or if any be established in the future, are subject to the Ordinaries of places, according to the law which is in effect for nonexempt Congregations and Societies of common life.

### Art. IX

The internal government of secular Institutes may be arranged hierarchically after the manner of the government of religious Institutes and Societies of common life, due allowances being made in the judgment of the same Sacred Congregation for the respective differences, and taking into account the nature, ends and circumstances of the Institutes themselves.

### Art. X

As to the rights and obligations of Institutes which are already established and were approved either by the Bishops after consulting the Holy See or by the Holy See itself, this Apostolic Constitution makes no change.

Thus We decree, declare, and provide, decreeing moreover that this Apostolic Constitution is and shall always be firm, valid, and effective, and shall have its full and entire effects, all things to the contrary, even such as are worthy of most special mention, notwithstanding. Let no one therefore infringe this Constitution promulgated by Us, nor rashly dare to contravene the same.

Given at Rome, at Saint Peter's the second day of February,

Feast of the Purification of the Blessed Virgin Mary, in the year nineteen hundred and forty-seven, the eighth of Our Pontificate.

**AAS 39–114**; Pius XII, Apostolic Constitution, 2 Feb., 1947.

Cf. *Commentarium pro Religiosis,* 26 (1947)–12 (Goyeneche); *Periodica,* 36 (1947)–118 (Creusen).

## Commission for Secular Institutes Appointed (S. C. Rel., 25 March, 1947) AAS 39–131.

A Decree of the Sacred Congregation of Religious:

Now that the Apostolic Constitution, *Provida Mater Ecclesia,*[1] has been made public, whatever seems necessary or opportune for its interpretation, application, or complement should be carefully prepared. Accordingly, by authority of His Holiness in an audience granted to the undersigned Cardinal Prefect of this Sacred Congregation on the 24th of the present month of March, a special Commission of jurists is established, which shall assist the Sacred Congregation in all matters which concern legislation in any way affecting secular Institutes and the approval and development of such Institutes.

As members of this Commission, to which other members will be added as necessity or utility may suggest, the following reverend Fathers have been appointed:

The Very Reverend Emmanuel Suarez, Master General of the Order of Preachers;

The Very Reverend Joseph Grendel, Superior General of the Congregation of the Divine Word;

The Very Reverend Agatangelus a Langasco, Procurator General of the Order of Friars Minor Capuchin;

The Very Reverend Joseph Creusen, of the Society of Jesus, Professor of Canon Law in the Pontifical Gregorian University;

The Very Reverend Servus Goyeneche, of the Congregation of the Sons of the Immaculate Heart of Mary, Professor of Canon Law in the Pontifical Lateran Athenaeum *Utriusque Iuris;*

The Very Reverend Alvarus del Portillo, Procurator General of the secular Institute *"Opus Dei,"* Secretary.

Given at Rome, from the Sacred Congregation of Religious, March 25, 1947.

**AAS 39–131**; S. C. Rel., 25 March, 1947.

[1] The Apostolic Constitution on secular Institutes, 2 Feb., 1947, reported above in this volume, p. 143.

## Secular Institutes: Local Ordinaries and Other Ecclesiastical Superiors Obliged to Secrecy in Certain Cases
(S. C. Rel., 24 July, 1947) **Private.**

The Procurator General of the Secular Institute, *Opus Dei,* proposed the following question to the Holy See.

With regard to Secular Institutes which, according to their own constitutions or their approved character, must keep secret their houses, works, and members, are diocesan Ordinaries and other ecclesiastical superiors to whom, in virtue of their office, such matters must be manifested, also obliged to secrecy with reference to all persons who do not have a right to knowledge of these matters?

This S. Congregation for Religious, after mature consideration of the matter proposed, has decided to reply: *In the affirmative.* All things to the contrary notwithstanding.

Given at Rome, from the S. C. for Religious, 24 July, 1947.

(**Private**); S. C. Rel., 24 July, 1947; reported with annotations (Larraona) in *Commentarium pro Religiosis,* 28 (1949)–298–300.

## Secular Institutes: Formula Authorizing Local Ordinaries to Erect (S. C. Rel., 1 Feb., 1948) Private.

The following formula, although given to a particular Bishop for a particular Secular Institute, is said by Larraona to be typical for such cases.

1) On the part of the Sacred Congregation there is nothing to prevent Your Excellency from safely proceeding to the erection of the said Secular Institute according to Art. VI of the Apostolic constitution, *Provida Mater Ecclesia.*[1]

2) When the erection has been duly made, all the members shall renew in the Institute thus erected the consecration which they previously made in the Pious Association and in the same manner, sc., temporary or perpetual. The duration of the preceding consecration as well as the period of probation which the member completed in the Pious Association must be computed, for all canonical effects, in the Secular Institute.

3) Houses or centers founded before the erection of the Institute, if they were established with the approval of each Bishop

[1] Reported above on p. 143.

in accordance with canon 495, become, by the very fact of the erection, parts of the Institute.

4) Property which the Institute really possesses as its own, should be set up in juridically valid form as soon as possible.

5) Your Excellency should take care that, with observance of the prescriptions of the Apostolic constitution, *Provida Mater Ecclesia,* and the general norms of law, the constitutions, whose text is to be submitted to mature examination by the Sacred Congregation, be corrected and completed according to the animadversions which the same Sacred Congregation will take care to send you as soon as possible.

6) When the formal decree of the erection of the Institute has been issued, Your Excellency is not to fail to send to this Sacred Congregation a copy of said decree (*Provida Mater Ecclesia,* Art. VI, 2) together with a copy of the text of the constitutions amended as provided for in the animadversions.

Given at Rome, from the Sacred Congregation, 1 February, 1948.

(**Private**); S. C. Rel., 1 Feb., 1948; reported with annotations (Larraona) in *Commentarium pro Religiosis,* 28 (1949)–300–303.

## **Secular Institutes Commended and Confirmed** (Pius XII, *Motu proprio,* 12 March, 1948) **AAS 40–283.**

This *Motu proprio,* entitled *"De Institutorum Saecularium Laude atque Confirmatione,"* is as follows:

Now that the first year has passed since the promulgation of Our Apostolic Constitution *Provida Mater Ecclesia,*[1] having in mind the great number of souls "hidden with Christ in God,"[2] who aspire to sanctity in the world and joyfully consecrate their whole life to God "with a great heart and a willing mind"[3] in the new Secular Institutes, We cannot but give thanks to the Divine Goodness for this new division which has come to swell the army of those who profess the evangelical counsels in the world, and also for the strong arm which has come to reinforce the Catholic apostolate in these troubled and sorrowful times.

---

[1] Pius XII, 2 Feb., 1947; AAS 39–114. Cf. above in this volume, p. 143.
[2] Col. 3:3.
[3] Mach. 1:3.

The Holy Spirit, Who ceaselessly re-creates and renews the face of the earth,[4] constantly desolated and defiled as it is with so many and such great evils, has called to Himself by a great and special grace many beloved sons and daughters, whom We lovingly bless in the Lord, to the end that, being united and organized in Secular Institutes, they may be the salt of the earth — of that world of which they are not,[5] yet in which by the will of God they must remain — the unfailing salt which, ever renewed by the grace of vocation, does not lose its savor;[6] the light of the world which shines in the darkness and is not extinguished;[7] the small but potent leaven which, always and everywhere active, mingling with every class of persons from the lowest to the highest, strives by example and in every way to reach and to transfuse them individually and collectively until the whole mass is so permeated that it is all leavened in Christ.[8]

In order that, through this consoling outpouring of the Spirit of Christ,[9] the many Institutes which have arisen everywhere may be effectively governed according to the Apostolic Constitution *Provida Mater Ecclesia,* and may bring forth in abundance those excellent fruits of sanctity which We hope for; also that, drawn up in solid and well-ordered battle array,[10] they may be able to fight valiantly the battles of the Lord in the special and common works of the apostolate, We now very joyfully confirm the aforesaid Apostolic Constitution, and with mature deliberation, of Our own motion, from certain knowledge and out of the fulness of Apostolic power, We declare, decree and establish the following:

I. Societies, whether of clerics or of lay persons, which profess Christian perfection in the world, and which seem certainly and fully to possess the elements and requisites prescribed in the Apostolic Constitution *Provida Mater Ecclesia,* should not and may not arbitrarily on any pretext be left among the common Associations of the faithful (cc. 684–725), but must necessarily be brought up and advanced to the proper nature and form of

[4] Cf. Psalms 103:30.

[5] Cf. John 15:19.

[6] Cf. Matt. 5:13; Mark 9:49; Luke 14:34.

[7] Cf. John 9:5; 1:5; 8:12; Eph. 5:8.

[8] Cf. Matt. 13:33; 1 Cor. 5:6; Gal. 5:9.

[9] Cf. Rom. 8:9.

[10] Cf. Cant. 6:3.

Secular Institutes which aptly correspond to their character and needs.

II. In this elevation of Societies of the faithful to the higher form of Secular Institutes (cf. n. I), and in working out the general as well as the particular organization of all these Institutes, this must always be kept in mind, that in all of them their special and peculiar character as *secular* Institutes, which is the whole reason for their existence, be clearly expressed. Nothing is to be subtracted from the full profession of Christian perfection, solidly based on the evangelical counsels, and in substance truly religious; but this perfection is to be exercised and professed *in the world,* and therefore in all things which are licit and which can be brought into conformity with the duties and works of that same perfection, it must be adapted to the secular life.

The whole life of members of Secular Institutes, sacred to God through the profession of perfection, must be turned toward the apostolate, which ought to be so constantly and virtuously practiced through purity of intention, interior union with God, generous forgetfulness of self, strong self-denial and love of souls, that it shall bear the mark of the interior spirit which informs it and at the same time shall constantly nourish and renew that spirit. This apostolate embracing the whole of life is usually felt so constantly, deeply and sincerely in these Institutes that, by the aid and according to the plan of Divine Providence, an ardent thirst for souls seems not only to have furnished the happy occasion for a life of consecration but to have impressed upon it largely its peculiar nature and form, and in a marvelous way to have demanded and brought forth the so-called specific end of the Institute as well as its generic end. This apostolate of Secular Institutes is to be faithfully practiced not only *in the world,* but as *of the world,* and therefore with avowed aims, practices, forms, and in places and circumstances corresponding to this secular condition.

III. According to the Apostolic Constitution *Provida Mater Ecclesia,* things which pertain to the canonical discipline of the religious state do not concern Secular Institutes, and in general religious legislation neither should nor can be applied to them (Art. II, § 1). On the other hand, those elements in the various Institutes which are found to be in friendly accord with their secular character, provided they in no way detract from a full and entire self-consecration and are consistent with the Constitution *Provida Mater Ecclesia,* may be retained.

IV. An interdiocesan and universal hierarchical organization can be applied to Secular Institutes (Art. IX), and such application should without doubt give them internal vitality, a wider and more powerful influence and great stability. In this organization however, which should be adapted to each Institute, the nature of the end which the Institute professes, the greater or lesser expansion which it may expect, its degree of development and maturity, its circumstances and other such matters must all be considered. Nor should those forms of Institutes be rejected or despised which exist as federations and wish to retain and moderately to favor a local character in various nations, regions, or dioceses, provided such character be right and in due accord with the catholicity of the Church.

V. Secular Institutes, even though their members live in the world, still by reason of the full dedication to God and to souls which they profess with the approval of the Church, and by reason of the internal interdiocesan and universal hierarchical organization which they can have in varying degrees, are according to the Apostolic Constitution *Provida Mater Ecclesia* rightly and properly numbered among the states of perfection which are juridically constituted and recognized by the Church. It was therefore of set purpose that these Institutes were assigned and entrusted to the competency and care of that Sacred Congregation which has the control and charge of *public states of perfection.* Hence, always without prejudice, according to the canons and the express provision of the Apostolic Constitution *Provida Mater Ecclesia* (Art. IV, §§ 1 and 2), to the rights of the Sacred Congregation of the Council regarding common pious sodalities and pious unions of the faithful (c. 250, § 2) and of the Sacred Congregation for the Propagation of the Faith regarding societies of ecclesiastics and[11] seminaries for the foreign missions (c. 252, § 3), all societies anywhere in the world — though they have the approval of the Ordinary or even of the Holy See — as soon as they are known to have the elements and requisites proper to Secular Institutes, must immediately be conformed to this new standard according to the norms above set forth (cf. n. I), and

[11] It seems evident from the canon cited and from the context that the word *ad* of the original is a misprint for *ac.*

in order that unity of direction be preserved, We have decreed that they are rightly assigned and entrusted exclusively to the Sacred Congregation of Religious, in which a special Office for Secular Institutes has been established.

VI. To the moderators and assistants of Catholic Action and of other Associations of the faithful, in whose maternal bosom are being trained to full Christian living and introduced to the exercise of the apostolate so many chosen young people who are called by divine vocation to a higher life either in Religious Institutes and Societies of common life or in Secular Institutes, We recommend with fatherly affection that they generously promote such holy vocations, and that they lend a helping hand not only to Religious Institutes and Societies but also to these truly providential Institutes, and as far as their own internal government permits, freely make use of their services.

The faithful execution of all these provisions which We have made of Our own motion, We in virtue of Our Apostolic Authority entrust to the Sacred Congregation of Religious and the other Sacred Congregations above mentioned, to the Ordinaries of places and to the Directors of the Societies concerned.

And We order that what We have established by this Letter given of Our own motion shall be forever valid and firm, all things to the contrary notwithstanding.

Given at Rome, from Saint Peter's, the 12th of March in the year nineteen hundred and forty-eight, at the commencement of the tenth year of Our Pontificate.

**AAS 40–283**; Pius XII, *Motu proprio,* 12 March, 1948.
*Periodica,* 37 (1948)–266 (Creusen).

**Instruction on Secular Institutes** (S. C. Rel., 19 March, 1948) **AAS 40–293.**

This Instruction, entitled, *"De Institutis Saecularibus,"* is as follows:

When His Holiness Pius XII promulgated the Apostolic Constitution, *Provida Mater Ecclesia,*[1] he deigned to depute for the more effective execution of all its wise provisions the Sacred Congregation of Religious, within whose competency the Secular

[1] Apostolic Constitution, 2 Feb., 1947; AAS 39–114; cf. above in this volume, p. 143.

Institutes were placed (*Lex Peculiaris,* Art. IV, §§ 1 and 2), and for this purpose he granted to the said Sacred Congregation all necessary and appropriate faculties.

Among the functions and duties which rest upon this Sacred Congregation according to this pontifical deputation and the express provision of the Constitution itself, is this, that the Sacred Congregation can issue norms "according as necessity shall demand and experience shall suggest, either by way of interpreting this Apostolic Constitution or of perfecting and applying it," which may be deemed necessary or useful for Secular Institutes in general or for some of them in particular (Art. II, § 2, 2°).

Now, although complete and definitive norms regarding Secular Institutes had best be postponed to a more opportune time lest the present-day development of the said Institutes be dangerously restricted, yet it is expedient that some of the provisions of the Apostolic Constitution, *Provida Mater Ecclesia,* which were not clearly understood and rightly interpreted by all persons, be immediately made clearer and placed beyond danger of misunderstanding, keeping carefully the prescriptions which are laid down in the Letter, *Primo feliciter,* given by His Holiness of his own notion on the 12th of this month.[2] Hence the Sacred Congregation has decided to put together in clear arrangement and so to issue by way of an Instruction the supreme norms which may rightly be regarded as fundamental for the solid initial establishment and regulation of Secular Institutes.

1. In order that an Association, even though it be ardently dedicated to the profession of Christian perfection and to the exercise of the apostolate in the world, may have the full right to assume the name and title of a Secular Institute, not only must it possess all and each of the elements which are mentioned and explained in the Apostolic Constitution, *Provida Mater Ecclesia,* as necessary and integral in Secular Institutes (Art. I and III), but it is moreover quite necessary that the Institute be approved and erected by some Bishop after having previously consulted this Sacred Congregation (Art. V, § 2; Art. VI).

2. All Associations of the faithful in any part of the world,

---

[2] *Motu proprio,* 12 March, 1948; AAS 40–283; See this volume: p. 143.

whether in territories subject to the common law or in those of the Missions, if they have the character and features described in the Apostolic Constitution, are according to the Constitution itself dependent on this Sacred Congregation of Religious (Art. IV, §§ 1 and 2) and are governed by the *Lex Peculiaris* or Special Law of the said Constitution; nor may they on any ground or pretext, according to the *Motu proprio, Primo feliciter* (n. V), remain among common Associations of the faithful (Book II, Part III of the Code of Canon Law), without prejudice to n. 5 of this Instruction.

3. To obtain permission to erect a new Secular Institute, the Bishop of the place and none other must apply to this Sacred Congregation, informing it clearly of all the matters which are explained in the Norms for the erection and approval of Congregations, issued by this same Sacred Congregation of Religious (*Normae,* 6 March, 1921, nn. 3–8; AAS 13–312),[3] with appropriate adjustments to fit the case (Art. VII). Copies of the Constitutions must also be sent (at least six) in Latin or in one of the other languages accepted in the Roman Curia, as well as the Directory and other documents which can be of service in showing the nature and spirit of the Association. The Constitutions should contain everything which concerns the nature of the Institute, classes of members, government, form of consecration (Art. III, § 2), the bond arising from the incorporation of the members in the Institute (Art. III, § 3), common houses (Art. III, § 4), the training of the members and exercises of piety.

4. Associations which, prior to the Constitution, *Provida Mater Ecclesia,* and legitimately according to the then existing law, had been erected or approved by Bishops or had obtained some sort of pontifical approval as Associations of lay persons, in order to obtain recognition from this Sacred Congregation as Secular Institutes whether of diocesan or pontifical right, must send to this Sacred Congregation their documents of erection or approval, the Constitutions under which they have hitherto been governed, a brief account of their history, discipline and apostolate, and, especially if they be only of diocesan right, also testimonials from the Ordinaries in whose dioceses they have houses. After all this has been considered and carefully exam-

[3] See below, p. 185.

ined according to Articles VI and VII of the Constitution, *Provida Mater Ecclesia,* the permission to erect, or the Decree of praise as the case may be, can be granted.

5. Associations which have only recently been founded or are not sufficiently developed, as well as those which spring up from time to time, even though they give good ground for the hope that if things go well they may develop into solid and genuine Secular Institutes, had best not be presented immediately to this Sacred Congregation to obtain from it the permission to erect them. As a general rule, which should admit of exceptions only for grave reasons strictly proved, these new Consociations, until they shall have proved themselves sufficiently, should be retained and exercised under the paternal hand and guardianship of diocesan Authority, first as mere Associations existing in fact rather than *de iure,* and then, not in one leap but gradually and by degrees, should be developed under some of the forms of Associations of the faithful, such as Pious Unions, Sodalities, Confraternities, as may seem appropriate according to the case.

6. While these preliminary developments (n. 5) are going on to prove clearly that the Associations in question really aim at an entire consecration of life to perfection and the apostolate, and that they have all the other features which are required in a true Secular Institute, vigilant care must be exercised to see that nothing be permitted either internally or externally to these Associations, which is beyond their present condition and seems to belong specifically to Secular Institutes. Those things especially should be avoided which, in case the permission to erect the Association as a Secular Institute is later refused, could not easily be taken away or undone and would seem to exert a sort of pressure on Superiors to make them grant approval outright or too easily.

7. In order to form a safe practical judgment whether an Association has the true character of a Secular Institute, that is, whether it effectively leads its members in the secular state and condition to that full consecration and dedication which reproduces even in the external forum the figure of a complete state of perfection in substance truly religious, the following questions must be carefully considered:

*a*) whether the persons who are members of the Association in the strict sense, "in addition to practicing those exercises of piety and self-denial" without which the life of perfection must be judged illusory, profess in a practical and substantial way the three general evangelical counsels in one of the various forms admitted by the Apostolic Constitution (Art. III, § 2). It is permitted, however, to admit as members in the broad sense, ascribed to the body of the Association by a more or less firm bond or intention, persons who aspire to evangelical perfection and strive to practice it in their condition of life, even though they do not or cannot embrace all the evangelical counsels in the highest degree;

*b*) whether the bond by which the members in the strict sense are attached to the Association is stable, mutual and complete, so that, according to the Constitution, the member gives himself wholly to the Association, and the Association is already, or it is seriously foreseen that it will be, such as will and can take care of and be responsible for the member (Art. III, § 3, 2°);

*c*) whether, and how or under what aspect, the Association has or is striving to acquire the common houses which are prescribed in the Apostolic Constitution (Art. III, § 4) for the attainment of the ends for which these houses are destined;

*d*) are those things being avoided which would not be in accord with the nature and character of Secular Institutes, as for example: a habit which is inappropriate for life in the world, a common life externally ordered (Art. II, § 1; Art. III, § 4) after the manner of religious common life or in a manner equivalent to that (Book II, Title XVII of the Code of Canon Law).

8. According to Art. II, § 1, 2°, of the Apostolic Constitution, *Provida Mater Ecclesia,* and without prejudice to Art. X and Art. II, § 1, 1°, of the same Constitution, Secular Institutes are not bound by the special and peculiar law of religious Institutes or Societies of common life, nor may they live by such law. Yet the Sacred Congregation may by way of exception, according to the tenor of the Constitution (Art. II, § 1, 2°) adapt and apply to them some particular provisions of the law of religious which may be suitable also to Secular Institutes, and may even prudently borrow from the aforesaid law certain more or less general criteria which are approved by experience and are in accord with the inner nature of things.

9. In particular: *a*) Although the provisions of canon 500, § 3 do not strictly concern Secular Institutes and need not be

applied to them as they stand, yet a solid criterion and clear guidance may be purposely drawn from them for the approval and ordering of Secular Institutes.

*b*) Although according to law (c. 492, § 1) there is no objection to Secular Institutes being aggregated by special concession to religious Orders and even to other religious Institutes, and to their being helped in various ways by the latter, and even in a sense morally guided by them, yet other forms of closer dependence, which would seem to detract from the autonomy of government of Secular Institutes, or to subject that autonomy to a more or less strict tutelage, even though such relations may be desired and asked for by the Institutes themselves, especially if these be Institutes of women, can be granted only with difficulty, upon careful consideration of the good of the Institutes, after pondering their spirit and the nature and character of the apostolate to which they are dedicated, and only with appropriate precautions.

10. Secular Institutes: (*a*) by reason of the state of full perfection which they profess and of the entire dedication to the apostolate which they impose, are within that same kind of perfection and of apostolate, evidently called to higher things than those which would seem sufficient for the faithful, even the best of them, working in merely lay Associations or in Catholic Action and other pious works; (*b*) must however take up the peculiar apostolic exercises and ministries which constitute their special ends, in such a way that their members — carefully avoiding all confusion — may be able to do their best in giving to the other faithful who see and observe them an outstanding example of self-denying, humble, and constant collaboration with the Hierarchy, always without prejudice to their own internal government (cf. *Motu proprio, Primo feliciter,* n. VI).

11. *a*) The Ordinary, when after obtaining permission from the Holy See he erects a Secular Institute which formerly existed as an Association either *de facto* or in the form of a Pious Union or Sodality, may determine whether it is advisable, in connection with fixing the condition of persons and computing the requisites laid down in the Constitutions of the Institute, to take account of things that were done antecedently, for example probation, consecration, and the like.

*b*) During the first ten years of a Secular Institute, counting from the time of its erection, the Bishop of the place has the power to dispense from requirements of age, time of probation, years of consecration, and other such matters which may be prescribed for all Institutes in general or for some one in particular, as regards offices, occupations, grades and other juridical effects.

*c*) Houses or centers founded before the canonical erection of the Institute, if they were established with the permission of both Bishops as required by canon 495, § 1, *ipso facto,* become parts of the Institute upon its erection.

Given at Rome, from the Sacred Congregation of Religious, on the 19th of March, Feast of Saint Joseph, Spouse of the Blessed Virgin Mary, in the year 1948.

**AAS 40–293**; S. C. Rel., Instruction, 19 March, 1948.
*Periodica,* 37 (1948)–266 (Creusen); *Review for Religious,* 10 (1951)–296 (Korth).

## **Secular Institutes: Nature of Obligations Assumed** (S. C. Rel., 19 May, 1949) **Private.**

Some questions were proposed to the S. C. for Religious regarding the nature of the obligations set down in Article III of the papal constitution, *Provida Mater Ecclesia.*[1] The S. C. thus defined these obligations.

1. The obligations which are contracted by members in the strict sense (Art. III, §§ 2 and 3) for the full pursuit of the juridical state of perfection in Secular Institutes (Art. III, § 2), if they are to correspond to the purpose and nature of the Institutes, cannot be light in their general nature and under every respect (*ex genere suo atque ex omni parte*).

2. On the other hand, the bonds on which this state of perfections rests, are considered so to oblige in conscience that the obligations thus produced must be called grave in their general nature (*ex genere suo*).

3. In individual cases, an obligation must be considered grave only when its matter must be considered as certainly grave according to the constitutions and the common teaching regarding equal or similar bonds. Moreover, according to the well-known

[1] Reported above on p. 143.

rule of law (*Reg. 30 in VI°*), *"In obscure matters, one is obliged to follow only the least obligation,"* it cannot be affirmed in a doubtful case that an obligation is grave or more grave, for example, on the ground that an obligation arises from or is reinforced by the formal virtue of religion.

4. Just what is the nature of the bonds assumed in individual Institutes and what is the precise mode of obligation — e.g., in addition to justice and fidelity, is there also and, if so, to what degree, an obligation from the virtue of religion — must be learned from the constitutions, which should give an accurate presentation of the matter, and from the formula of consecration or incorporation in which the bonds are expressed.

5. Even when it is certain that there is a formal obligation arising from the virtue of religion, since there is question of vows or bonds which, although they are not fully private, nevertheless, in law, cannot be called public in the strict and specific sense and do not effect a public consecration of the person, the malice of sacrilege must not be attributed to their violation.

(**Private**); S. C. Rel., 19 May, 1949; reported with annotations (Fuertes) in *Commentarium pro Religiosis,* 28 (1949)–292–298.

## Secular Institutes: Documents Which Must Be Shown to Local Ordinary When Permission Sought to Open Center or Exercise the Apostolate Corporately (S. C. Rel., 1 Aug., 1949) Private.

The Procurator General of the Institute, *Opus Dei,* humbly prostrate at the feet of Your Holiness, asks whether it must be considered necessary and expedient to show the whole of the constitutions to local Ordinaries when a new center is to be opened in the diocese proper to each Ordinary or when permission is sought to carry on apostolic work corporately; and, in as much as the reply is negative, what documents of the Institute is it necessary and expedient to show to the Ordinaries?

The Sacred Congregation for Religious, having attended to the special character of the Institute, *Opus Dei,* has decided to reply:

To 1: In the negative and according to its mind. Its mind is that it is neither necessary nor can it be said to be regularly expedient to show to local Ordinaries the complete constitutions of the Institute or other documents pertinent to its internal nature.

To 2: Only these documents must necessarily be shown to Ordinaries who demand them: 1) the decree of approbation of the Institute and its constitutions; 2) the summary of the constitutions approved by the S. C.; 3) privileges, if any are had or are obtained in the future, with regard to those matters in which clerical congregations of pontifical law (among which the Institute is numbered because officially and juridically equated with them) are necessarily subject to local Ordinaries. Canon 51 is to be observed.

All things to the contrary notwithstanding.

Given at Rome, from the S. C. for Religious, 1 August, 1949.

(**Private**); S. C. Rel., 1 Aug., 1949; reported with annotations (Larraona) in *Commentarium pro Religiosis,* 28 (1949)–303–305.

**Secular Institutes: Consent of Local Ordinary Not Required for Non-Autonomous Centers Nor for Communities Not Juridically Constituted** (S. C. Rel., 8 Aug., 1949) **Private.**

The Procurator General of the Institute, *Opus Dei,* asked:

1. On analogy with the law for religious (c. 497), is the consent of the local Ordinary, which is prescribed as necessary in the constitutions (n. 290) of the Institute for the erection of an autonomous center of *"Opus Dei,"* required also so that members legitimately assigned to a center lawfully erected may live their private lives elsewhere as lay and secular persons?

2. In as much as the answer to n. 1 is negative, may the members in question freely live a life which is common actually and materially but not canonically?

3. May they likewise freely exercise the apostolate proper to the Institute, not corporately but individually and personally?

The Sacred Congregation for Religious, having maturely considered the special nature of *"Opus Dei,"* has decided to reply:

To 1. *In the negative.*

To 2. *In the affirmative,* provided there is really question of life common in fact but not by law. The formalities prescribed by law are required for all those matters which are set down in the constitutions or common law for common life juridically considered, e.g., as regards a liturgical oratory, reservation of the Blessed Sacrament, etc.

To 3. *In the affirmative,* as regards all matters which have a truly personal and not corporative character.

All things to the contrary notwithstanding.

Given at Rome, from the Sacred Congregation, 8 August, 1949.

**(Private)**; S. C. Rel., 8 Aug., 1949, Prot. N. 6388/49; reported with annotations (Larraona) in *Commentarium pro Religiosis,* 28 (1949)–305–307.

### The Vocation of Teaching in Lay Institutes of Men (Pius XII, Letter, 31 March, 1954) AAS 46–202.

A Letter of Pius XII to Cardinal Valeri, Prefect of the S. C. of Religious, entitled: *On the Better Way for the Proper Instruction of Youth by Members of Religious Brotherhoods,* is as follows:

Beloved Son, health and Apostolic Benediction.

After the annual convention for France which was held in Paris last year, the Procurators General of eight lay religious Brotherhoods, which have as the peculiar object of their Institute the proper training and education of youth, dutifully sent Us a letter in which they informed Us of the proceedings and resolutions of their meeting, and humbly and reverently asked Us to give them the benefit of Our paternal advice and point out to them the road to ever greater and more beneficial progress.

We are very happy to do so concisely and briefly in this Letter. And in the first place We take great comfort in the knowledge that these religious men are devoting themselves with earnestness and energy to the work entrusted to them, a work which can be of the greatest benefit to the Church, the family, and civil society. It is indeed a work of great importance. Youth are the budding hope of the future. Beyond a doubt the course of the coming age depends on those of them especially who are trained to a liberal culture and instructed in a variety of subjects so that they will be fitted in due time to occupy not only private positions but public offices as well. If their minds are illumined by the light of the Gospel, their souls trained in the precepts of Christianity and their wills strengthened by the grace of God, then one may hope to see a new generation of youth, which will conquer the difficulties, dangers, and troubles of our time and eventually build a better and sounder society by its learning, virtue, and example. To this end, as We know to Our great satisfaction, also lay religious Institutes are laboring faithfully, guided by the wise regulations which their Founders respectively left them as a sacred heritage. We desire that they should do so not only with the greatest skill, diligence, and earnestness, but also with that high spirit which brings human undertakings to flourishing vigor and happy fruition. Particularly it is Our wish that they strive to imbue the youth entrusted to them with doctrine which is not only sincere and free from all error, but also open to and concordant with all the practices and methods which the present day has introduced in the various subjects.

The principal thing is that they draw from the religious life, which they must live wholeheartedly, the supernatural strength to train their pupils in Christian virtue, as the Church absolutely demands of them by reason of their position. For if this virtue is neglected or abandoned, letters and culture are of no account for living a good life; they may even, especially at that pliable age which is easily turned to evil, become the crafty means of perversion and so of unhappiness.

Let them therefore watch over the characters of their charges; let them seek to know thoroughly and to direct wisely their dispositions, their secret impulses and their inner sentiments, which are at times disturbed and uneasy. Let them see to it by all means that the deceits which endanger virtue be repelled as quickly and energetically as possible, that all dangers which might besmirch the purity of the soul be removed, and that all the circumstances of their lives be so ordered that while the mind is enlightened with truth, the will also may be strongly trained to what is right and moved to the choice of all that is good.

These religious know of course that the education of youth is the art of arts and the science of sciences, but they also know that with the divine assistance they can do all things, according to that saying of the Apostle of the Gentiles, "I can do all things in him who strengtheneth me." They must therefore practice piety intensely as becomes men who, though they do not belong to a clerical religious Institute, are nevertheless lawfully enrolled in a lay religious Institute. Such an Institute, though it consists almost entirely of members who, by a special call from God, renounce the dignity of the priesthood and the consolations which are attached to it, is nevertheless highly honored in the Church and is of very great assistance to priests themselves in the Christian education of youth. For, as We said on another occasion, "the religious state is not restricted to either of the two groups which exist in the Church by divine right, since clerics and lay persons alike can become religious."[1] Now since the Church has endowed lay persons also with this dignity and function, certainly this is a patent proof that both branches of the sacred militia can work with great usefulness for their own and others' salvation, each according to the canonical system and regulations by which it is governed.

Hence let no one have less regard for the members of those Brotherhoods or for the fruitfulness of their apostolate from the fact that they are not priests. Besides, it is a fact within Our knowledge that they give the boys who are under their care such training and education that many of them who seem to be called by divine grace come to the happy reception of priestly orders. There have been some among them who are gloriously numbered among the Bishops and even among the Cardinals. And this is a further reason why these Brotherhoods, deserving as they are of Our praise and that of the whole Church, also win the good will of the Bishops and Clergy; for they give them valuable assistance not only in procuring the sound education of youth but also by encouraging, with the aid of divine grace, candidates for sacred orders.

May they therefore be ever more active and alert in following the way of life which is theirs; and together with other religious Orders and Congregations who serve the same cause, may they work concordantly and earnestly for the training and education of youth.

We earnestly implore for them the divine assistance, and in token thereof and of Our special benevolence, We lovingly impart to you, Beloved Son, and to all the Superiors, members and pupils of their Brotherhoods, the Apostolic Benediction.

Given at Rome, from Saint Peter's, the 31st day of March in the year 1954, the sixteenth of Our Pontificate.

**AAS 46–202**; Pius XII, Letter, 31 March, 1954.

---

[1] Address to the general meeting of delegates from all religious Institutes, in Rome, 8 Dec., 1950. AAS, 43–26; reported above on pp. 86–98.

**The Institute *Regina Mundi*** (Pius XII, *Motu proprio,* 11 Feb., 1956) **AAS 48–189.**

Nothing is more desired by the Church than that virgins consecrated to God, professing the evangelical counsels in states of perfection or similar institutes and firmly dedicated to the salvation of the neighbor and to many forms of well-doing, should with steady pace and equal progress both attain to the holiness which they have professed and constantly make a worthy and well-directed effort to fulfill the apostolic ministries or works of charity which the Holy See entrusts to them in the approbation of their Statutes and Institutes.

Since the love of God and of neighbor is one and the same, the Church rightly demands that the ardor for sanctity take the form of an earnest desire to perform one's own duties ever more thoroughly and perfectly, and to prepare oneself for them with careful and unsparing effort.

In order by suitable preparation to attain effectively this desired divine and human perfection in the performance of duty, the Apostolic See has tried by all appropriate means gently and firmly to stimulate religious women and other virgins consecrated to God and to the apostolate, and at the same time to lead them as it were by the hand to make use of everything which might be found suitable and helpful for their apostolic work.

Hence also all Superiors and religious, faithfully following the regulations and repeated exhortations of the Holy See, have ceaselessly urged, as they still do, that women who as part of their vocation and for apostolic reasons have to perform civil or social services, be provided among other things with diplomas, legal certificates, and such other testimonials as may be requisite for the proper and worthy performance of their offices and works. To this end special Institutes, colleges, academies, and schools have been either founded or at least advanced and helped in many ways. Moreover, by means of various lectures and exercises, frequent conventions, by establishing also Federations to carry on various forms of apostolate, by aids and encouragements of every sort, the Church has earnestly sought to bring it about that in all those who are engaged in ministries for the love of God and the neighbor, religious zeal should be inseparably accompanied by technical preparation for and skill in the performance of their work.

For in the mind of the Church it can neither be conceived nor tolerated that all who devote themselves to social or professional services in pursuance of religious profession and an apostolic vocation, should be in reality or even be considered to be inferior in the performance of those works, to all others who, inspired though they be by noble motives, follow those same activities or professions in the world.

All this is *a fortiori* especially true of those religious women and of those virgins consecrated to God who, especially in our day, apply themselves in a variety of ways to the education, training, and formation of youth. An arduous task indeed it is, not only because of the dispositions of the girls and the temper of the times, but also because of the wider knowledge of the many-sided science and practice of the art of teaching — to be acquired by a long course of studies and tested by many examinations — and other such requirements which are everywhere demanded of teachers.

Surely no one will call into question the principle that these our teachers and educators of girls, adolescents, and young people, whether they teach mostly in intermediate and high schools, or have charge of young women who are taking university courses even in extern public institutions, or finally are engaged in the more important works of their own Institute, in governing or educating its members, should have a superior technical training and especially a religious formation which is at once solid, well-ordered, and, for their condition, complete.

To the end that members of the states of perfection and other virgins who are dedicated to perfection and to the apostolate may become first class educators and teachers according to modern requirements, in many places higher schools, academies, and institutes, generally very good ones, have been opened, where they may receive a serious training in doctrine, especially in religious and moral subjects.

That fruitful movement of *appropriate renovation* which, after the solemn Congress of the Jubilee year (1950, Nov. 26 to Dec. 8), sponsored and tirelessly continues to sponsor one after another so many and such great improvements in the field of education and training, was the reason which led the Sacred

Congregation of Religious in September, 1952, to call a meeting of the Superioresses General to consider establishing in Rome a new Institute which would serve not only as an example but also in many ways as a complement and crown to all similar institutes either already in existence or later to be erected throughout the world.

Accordingly the same Sacred Congregation, at Our command and under Our patronage, in fulfilment of the wishes of the Congress and with the cooperation of the Superioresses General everywhere, *during the Marian Year,* proceeded to erect in the Eternal City an Institute of the Blessed Virgin Mary, whom We had solemnly proclaimed and crowned as Queen. Since this Institute, which received the name of *Regina Mundi,* has during these years given a good account of itself and gives Us secure assurance of the happy results which We ardently desire, with the intention that it may be strengthened and advanced by Our Pontifical approval, and may become an outstanding and auspicious model for all similar institutes which already exist or may in future be legitimately established throughout the world, We *of Our own motion* and with mature deliberation decree and prescribe the following.

I. The Institute called *"Regina Mundi,"* for imparting higher training, education, and formation in sciences and subjects of study, especially sacred ones, to virgins who are consecrated to God and dedicated to the ministry of souls, We hereby declare to be a *Pontifical* Institute, and allow it to be honored with this title.

II. This Institute shall be governed in Our name and with Our authority by the Sacred Congregation of Religious under Statutes approved by Us. In the work of organizing, governing, and perfecting this Our Institute, the Sacred Congregation of Religious will be powerfully assisted, according to the Statutes, by Delegates from the Sacred Congregation of Seminaries and Universities, the Secretariate of State, and the Vicariate of Rome.

III. We grant to the Institute the right and faculty, according to the Statutes, to confer upon the students after the due completion of their studies and the passing of the examinations, degrees in virtue of which they may teach courses in colleges for women, either secular or religious, of whatever grade, within the scope which will be accurately stated in each diploma. In order that they may teach in lay schools for men, all the provisions of law in that regard must be carefully observed.

IV. Finally, We grant to this Institute the faculty, according to the Statutes, to affiliate to itself such Schools and Institutes or Sections thereof as may seem to be of similar character.

These things We decree and establish, notwithstanding all things to the contrary, even though worthy of special mention.

Given at Rome, from Saint Peter's on the 11th day of February 1956, the seventeenth year of Our Pontificate.

**AAS 48–189;** Pius XII, *Motu proprio,* 11 Feb., 1956. Annotations, *Monitor Ecclesiasticus,* 82 (1957)–194 (Liévin).

---

**Augustinians:** Apostolic Epistle addressed to the Superiors General of various branches of the Augustinian Order on their great Patron, Saint Augustine of Hippo. Pius XII, 25 July, 1954 (AAS 46–513). *The Pope Speaks,* 1 (1954)–229.

Letter to the General of the Order of Hermits of Saint Augustine, on the 7th centenary of their union. Pius XII, 2 Feb., 1956 (AAS 48–209).

**Basilian Order of Saint Josaphat:** Constitutions approved. Pius XII, Ap. Letter, 14 June, 1954 (AAS 47–588).

**Benedictine Order:** The following documents refer to the Confederation of the Monastic Congregations of the Order of Saint Benedict:

1) Pius XII, Encyclical, *Fulgens radiatur,* on the fourteenth centenary of the death of Saint Benedict, 21 March, 1947 (AAS 39–137).

2) Pius XII, Homily delivered at St. Paul's outside the walls on the occasion of the election of an Abbot Primate, 17 Sept., 1947 (AAS 39–452).

3) Pius XII, Ap. Letter formally approving the *Lex propria* or revised Constitutions of the Confederation of Monastic Congregations of the Order of Saint Benedict, 21 March, 1952 (AAS 44–520). Annotations, *Monitor Ecclesiasticus,* 77 (1952)–549 (Oesterle).

4) The Pontifical Brief, *Pacis vinculum,* of 21 March, 1952, approving and confirming the *Lex Propria* or Constitutions of the Confederation (AAS 44–520).

5) The text of the *Lex Propria* itself, with annotations by Gambari (*Commentarium pro Religiosis,* 32 (1953–244 seq., 305 seq., and 33 (1954)–3 seq.).

6) A decree of the S. C. Rel., of 21 March, 1953, reporting the approval already given by the Sovereign Pontiff (*Commentarium pro Religiosis,* 32 (1953)–243.

7) An Allocution of Pius XII to the Abbots and Priors of the Confederation, 24 Sept., 1953 (AAS 45–621).

**Canons Regular of Saint Augustine:** Confederation of Congregations of the Order approved. John XXIII, Ap. Letter, 4 May, 1959 (AAS 51–630).

**Carmelites:** Letter of Pius XII to Cardinal Piazza commemorating the fifth centenary of the founding of the Second and Third Orders, 25 July, 1952 (AAS 44–811).

Commemoration of fourth centenary of the reform by Saint Teresa. John XXIII, Letter to Cardinal Cento, 16 July, 1962 (AAS 54–566).

**Congregation of the Immaculate Heart of Mary.** Letter of John XXIII to the Very Reverend Otmar Fegrisje, Superior General, on the first centenary of the foundation of the Congregation, 27 March, 1962 (AAS 54–385).

**Congregation of the Most Blessed Sacrament:** Pius XII, Letter to General on first centenary, 10 April, 1956 (AAS 48–268).

**Franciscan Order:** Letter of Pius XII to General of Franciscans, O.F.M. Conventuals, O.F.M.Cap., and Third Order Regular, 15 Aug., 1952 (AAS 44–814).

**Friars Minor:** Constitutions approved and confirmed. Pius XII, Ap. Letter, 14 July, 1953 (AAS 46–91).

Letter to the Minister General and Major Officialis of the Franciscan Order on the 750th anniversary of the *viva voce* approval of the Rule of Saint Francis by Innocent III. John XXIII, Letter, 4 Apr., 1959 (AAS 51–296).

Address on the 750th anniversary of papal approval of the rule of St. Francis. John XXIII, Allocution, 16 April, 1959 (AAS 51–307). *The Pope Speaks,* 6 (1959–60)–350.

Letter of Paul VI to the Very Reverend Basil Heiser, Minister General, on the third centenary of the death of Saint Joseph of Cupertino, 27 June, 1963 (AAS 55–736).

**Knights of Malta:** As a result of investigations conducted by a specially constituted Tribunal of five Cardinals as judges, the Order of the Knights of Malta (*Sovrano Militare Ordine Gerosolimitano di Malta*) was definitely decided to be not only a religious Institute but a religious Order with pontifical approval according to canons 487 and 488, 1° and 2°.—Other points of the decision concerned the nature of the sovereignty of the Order, the reciprocal relations of the sovereign Order to the religious Order, and the relations of each with the Holy See. Special Tribunal of Cardinals, 24 Jan., 1953 (AAS 45–765). Annotations, *Commentarium pro Religiosis,* 33 (1954)–34 (Ruiz).

Commission of Cardinals for revision of Constitutions and further measures of rehabilitation, appointed. Pius XII, 1 Feb., 1955 (AAS 47–59).

**Knights of the Holy Sepulchre:** Ap. Letter of John XXIII approving new statutes, 8 Dec., 1962 (AAS 55–444). These statutes are a revision of those approved by Pius XII in 1949. See Canon Law Digest, 3, p. 59.

**Mercedarians:** Letter to General, on 7th centenary of death of Saint Peter Nolasco. Pius XII, 19 Jan., 1956 (AAS 48–80).

**Missionaries of the Sacred Heart of Jesus:** Letter to the Very Reverend Patrick McCabe, Superior General, on the centenary of their foundation. Pius XII, Letter, 14 Nov., 1954 (AAS 46–760).

**Mistresses of Novices:** School established in Rome, with name *"Mater Divinae Gratiae."* S. C. Rel., Decree, 15 March, 1957 (AAS 49–749).

**Passionists:** Congregation of Discalced Clerics of the Holy Cross and Passion of Our Lord Jesus Christ; revised Rule and Constitutions approved.

John XXIII, Ap. Letter, 1 July, 1959 (AAS 51–634). Annotations, *Commentarium pro Religiosis,* 39 (1960)–36 (Thyssen).

**Pontifical Institute** ***"Iesus Magister":*** Established in Rome for higher education of teachers in lay institutes of men. S. C. Rel., Decree, 1 July, 1957 (AAS 49–751).

**Pontifical Institute** ***"Regina Mundi":*** Norms for affiliation and recognition. S. C. Rel., 12 March, 1957 (AAS 49–869).

**Redemptorists:** Allocution of John XXIII to the General Council of the Congregation of the Holy Redeemer meeting in Rome, 8 Feb., 1963 (AAS 55–229).

***Regina Mundi:*** An article by Paul Dezza, S.J., President of this Pontifical Institute, outlines its history, organization, and functioning (*Com. pro Rel.,* 39 (1960)–253). The text of the decree of erection (S. C. Rel., 31 May, 1955) and of the Statutes (approved 11 Feb., 1956), and a list of Institutes in various countries which have been granted affiliation with *Regina Mundi,* are also given (*Com. pro Rel.,* 39 (1960)–256–262). Cf. Pius XII, *Motu proprio,* 11 Feb., 1956; AAS 48–189, reported above under this same canon.

**Rosary:** Promotion by Dominican Order. Pius XII, Letter to Master General of Dominicans, 11 July, 1957 (AAS 49–726).

**Society of Jesus:** Pius XII, Address to delegates to Thirtieth General Congregation, 10 Sept., 1957 (AAS 49–806). *The Pope Speaks,* 4 (1957)–447.

Value of third year of probation. Pius XII, Allocution, 25 March, 1956 (AAS 48–269). English version: *Review for Religious,* 16 (1957)–236.

**Teaching Sisters:** Apostolic Exhortation of Pius XII to the International Convention of Teaching Sisters, 13 Sept., 1951 (AAS 43–738). English text, *The Catholic Mind,* 1952, p. 376.

**Third Order of Saint Dominic:** Pius XII, Allocution to the International Congress of the Third Order of Saint Dominic assembled in Rome, 25 Aug., 1958 (AAS 50–674).

**Trappists:** Allocution to members of the General Chapter meeting in Rome. John XXIII, 1 Sept., 1962 (AAS 54–661).

**Vincentians (Congregation of the Mission):** Revised Constitutions approved. Pius XII, Apostolic Letter, 19 July, 1953 (AAS 47–141).

Letter of John XXIII to the Very Rev. William Slattery, Superior General, 20 Feb., 1960, on the 300th anniversary of the death of Saint Vincent de Paul (AAS 52–147).

Allocution of Paul VI to the assembled delegates to the 33rd general congregation of the institute, 30 Aug., 1963 (AAS 55–744).

## CANON 489

**Religious Constitutions Which Are to Be Revised to Conform to the Code Are to Be Sent for Examination to the Sacred Congregation of Religious** (S. C. Rel., 26 June, 1918) **AAS 10–290.**

All religious institutes of pontifical law and all societies of men or women living in common without vows, must submit the amendments made in their rules and constitutions to be examined by this Sacred Congregation. This may be done when they send their report as required under c. 510. All religious societies are to send with this report some copies of their rules or constitutions.

Ordinaries of places where Superiors or Superioresses General live, are urged to notify them as soon as possible of this obligation.

**AAS 10–290**; S. C. Rel., Decree, 26 June, 1918.
*Periodica,* 9 (1921)–137 (Creusen).

## Custom Books and Books of Prayers to Be Said in Common Are to Be Revised by the Sacred Congregation of Religious (Decree, S. C. Rel., 31 Mar., 1919) AAS 11–239.

All institutes or Congregations of religious women of pontifical law, and all approved societies of pious women living in common without vows, must within one year from the date of this Decree send their custom books and books containing prayers peculiar to their institute which are recited in common, to this Sacred Congregation to be inspected and revised. Ordinaries of places where Superioresses General of any such institutes or congregations of women live, shall notify them as soon as possible of this obligation; and also inform them that in the meantime the use of such books is not prohibited.

**AAS 11–239**; S. C. Rel., Decree, 31 Mar., 1919.
*Periodica,* 10 (1922)–68.

## Declaration Regarding Submission of Constitutions for Revision (S. C. Rel., 26 Oct., 1921) AAS 13–538.

Referring to the Decree of 26 June, 1918,[1] the Sacred Congregation of Religious further declares:

I. Constitutions, *statuta,* or laws, by whatever name they are called, governing religious societies, are to be sent to this Sacred Congregation, only if it is certain that the text thereof has been approved by the Holy See.

[1] AAS 10–290; reported above.

II. The work of amending the text to conform to the Code rests upon the Order or religious society, or monastery itself; and two copies of the text so amended are to be sent to this Sacred Congregation.

III. The text is to be amended only in those things in which the constitutions are opposed to the Code; or if it is a case of deficiency, additions may be made; and as far as possible the words of the Code itself are to be used.

IV. If any religious society wishes to take advantage of this revision to make some changes in the constitutions which are not necessary, that is, not prescribed by the Code, this should not be done in the amended text submitted as herein prescribed; but there should be sent to the Sacred Congregation a separate petition for permission, containing both the text as already approved and the amended text submitted for approval, in full, together with the reasons for the change now desired.

Such a petition will not be accepted, however, by this Sacred Congregation, unless the proposed changes have been discussed and approved by the general Chapter. Although, if there is question of minor changes or mere verbal substitutions, or of abrogating practices which have fallen into desuetude through changes of times and manners, or other such things, the consent of the general Council is sufficient.

V. Lest there be differences in the text of the same constitutions as used in various independent houses or monasteries of the same Order or institute, the Sacred Congregation orders that for such constitutions a single text of the amendments be accepted by all the houses, the text to be drawn up either by the houses themselves or by this Sacred Congregation.

**AAS 13–538**; S. C. Rel., *Declaratio,* 26 Oct., 1921.
*Periodica,* 10 (1922)–361 (Vermeersch).

**Maternity Training for Missionary Sisters** (Instruction, S. C. Prop. Fid., 11 Feb., 1936) **AAS 28–208.**

An Instruction by the Sacred Congregation of Propaganda is as follows:

It has been the constant and sedulous practice of this Sacred Congregation to adapt the character of the apostolate to the varying necessities of times and places. At the present time many Ordinaries of Missions have of their own accord represented to the Holy See the necessity of providing more suitable assistance for the welfare of mothers and infants. In certain districts of Africa some tribes are daily decreasing and will be brought to extinction unless they are helped by more efficacious care of the lives of mothers and infants. In other places, children but a few days old are dying in large numbers through neglect of the elementary principles of health. The civil authorities and the non-Catholic sects in these parts are turning their minds and attention earnestly to this matter. Some governments refuse to admit Sisters to hospital service unless they are fully qualified nurses.

Societies for the care of mothers and children have already been formed in some places through private initiative, and it is necesary, as soon as possible, to co-ordinate these and give them a definite discipline.

Accordingly, this Sacred Congregation, solicitous to provide for this very urgent necessity of the Missions, after having obtained the necessary powers from the Holy Father, Pius XI, by Divine Providence, Pope, and after having consulted with the Sacred Congregation of Religious, considers it opportune to issue the following regulations and instructions.

It is earnestly desired that new Congregations of Sisters be founded to devote themselves, with the necessary precautions, to the care of mothers and infants who are in danger. These much-desired institutes should be constituted in accordance with the provisions of the common law. It will also be pleasing and acceptable to this Sacred Congregation if, in the religious institutes already existing, there be groups of Sisters who will apply themselves to the aforesaid work. If the matter demands it, opportune regulations will be added to the constitutions of the institutes dependent upon this Sacred Congregation.

This provision, however, is subject to the following conditions:

*a*) It is not necessary that all religious women should take up every kind of nursing. They may have subject to them native laywomen who are duly accredited nurses, and who are joined to the institute in a common life and spirit.

*b*) No Sister can be obliged by her Superiors to take up the work of midwife, but it shall be for those Sisters only who freely chose to accept from their Superior this special work of missionary charity.

*c*) These new duties require, not only an adequate knowledge of medicine, but also special spiritual training. It is necessary, therefore, that Sisters should obtain public diplomas either in medicine or nursing; but especially they must be strengthened and safeguarded by special helps, which spiritual helps are to be determined by the Superiors. They must realize that the care of the sick involves a holy exercise of charity, and is meritorious; for, whilst they are relieving bodily pain, they are also preparing the soul for the grace of Redemption. It is well to recall the saying of Saint Francis de Sales, that charity is the watchful guardian of chastity.

*d*) In order to obtain their diplomas, it is, of course, necessary that the Sisters attend Catholic nursing schools and universities, or, if these be wanting, then hospitals under Catholic management. If, however, they cannot attend Catholic nursing schools and universities, the Sisters may, with the permission of this Sacred Congregation, attend lay nursing schools. The candidates should frequent these hospitals in twos at least, and, as far as may be necessary, in modest lay dress; they must live in religious houses where they may have daily spiritual helps and safeguards.

*e*) In the new institutes, however, which will apply themselves *ex professo* to this care of mothers and infants, the candidates should complete these university studies before they take their perpetual vows. In institutes already existing this regulation is to be borne in mind and, as far as the constitutions allow, is to be observed.

With regard to the practice of medicine or surgery by missionaries, this is regulated by the prescriptions of canon 139 of the Code of Canon Law and the indults which this Sacred Congregation is accustomed to grant.

Given at Rome, from the Sacred Congregation of Propaganda, 11 Feb., 1936.

**AAS 28–208**; S. C. Prop. Fid., 11 Feb., 1936. *Commentarium pro Religiosis,* 17 (1936)–63; *Amer. Eccles. Review,* 95 (1936)–69; *Homiletic and Pastoral Review,* 36 (1935–36)–1092; *Clergy Review,* 11 (1936)–331; *Irish Ecclesiastical Record,* 48 (1936)–427; *Nouvelle Revue Theologique,* 63 (1936)–580; *Periodica,* 25 (1936)–47 (Creusen); cf. *Periodica,* 24 (1935)–77*.

**Order of the Blessed Virgin Mary for the Redemption of Captives: Military Insignia Abolished for the Future** (Special Commission of Cardinals, 13 July, 1936) **AAS 28–306.**

A special Commission of Cardinals was appointed by His Holiness, Pius XI, to decide the question:

Whether it is expedient that the Holy See recognize the knightly honors and insignia which are conferred by the Order of the Blessed Virgin Mary for the Redemption of Captives.

**Reply.** In the negative, *et ad mentem:*

I. Let the aforesaid Order in future abstain from conferring any such knightly honors and insignia, either by aggregation or by direct decoration.

II. Let the constitutions of the Order be conformed to the rules of the Code of Canon Law as soon as possible. The name of the Order shall be merely "The Order of the Blessed Virgin Mary for the Redemption of Captives," omitting entirely the adjectives "Celestial, Royal, Military," and any other such terms.

III. Let the aggregations of the faithful to the Order in future be purely and strictly religious and spiritual, excluding entirely any ceremony of aggregation or title for the members, which has a military flavor or knightly significance; and hence the Ceremonials of the said Order must be adapted explicitly to this purpose.

IV. The Commission, however, all things considered, declares that persons who have hitherto received honors or insignia of any kind from the said Order are not to be disturbed.

Approved and confirmed by His Holiness on the 13th of July, 1936, and declared effective from that day.

**AAS 28–306;** Special Commission of Cardinals, 13 July, 1936.
*Periodica,* 25 (1936)–195 (Creijghton).

**Substitution of Small Breviary in the Vernacular for Little Office of the Blessed Virgin in Lay Congregations of Men and Women** (S. C. Rel., 1953) **Private.**

The Practice of the Sacred Congregation of Religious as regards allowing the substitution of the small Breviary in the vernacular for the Little Office of the Blessed Virgin, is summarized as follows by Gutiérrez in *Commentarium pro Religiosis,* 32 (1953)–266:

1. Where the drawbacks and difficulties which might easily accompany such a change are not to be feared, the Sacred Congregation will readily grant permission to those Congregations who ask for it. As a matter of fact, however, it is rare that the change can be made without serious difficulties; hence it cannot be said that the Sacred Congregation favors the change.

2. In the case of diocesan Institutes, Ordinaries can change the Constitutions (c. 495, § 2). In the case of pontifical Institutes, the S. C. usually requires that the matter be voted on in the General Chapter and that there be not a bare absolute majority in favor of the change, but something approaching moral unanimity. If the Institute has few members and is not widely diffused, the S. C. sometimes allows the change on the petition of the entire General Council, but on the terms stated below.

3. The permission is not given permanently, but by way of experiment for five years.

4. The favor is granted by way of experiment, *provided* the following conditions are fulfilled:

a. That there is nothing in the traditions of the Institute which is directly opposed to the change;

b. That the Superiors and the Sisters be in agreement as regards the change, so that there will be no danger of a division;

c. That the change cause no disturbance in the horarium and domestic order.

(**Private**); S. C. Rel., 1953; summary of practice as reported by Gutiérrez in *Commentarium pro Religiosis,* 32 (1953)–266. Cf. also 33 (1954)–162.

NOTE: Cf. also Letter of Pius XII, 12 March, 1953, to the Superioress General of the Sisters Teachers of the Holy Cross of the Third Order of Saint Francis, of Menzingen, in which the Holy Father praises the Little Office of the Blessed Virgin and commends its use in a new and enlarged edition edited by Father Augustine Bea, S.J. This Letter is reported by Schmidt in *Periodica,* 43 (1954)–116. Both Gutiérrez and Schmidt speak of the advantages of the small Breviary, but also of the difficulties which may make its adoption inadvisable.

---

**Discalced Carmelite Nuns:** Text of revised Constitutions of 1926 to be used exclusively in all monasteries. S. C. Rel., 19 Sept., 1936 (AAS 28–405).

**Japan: Instruction to Superiors of Religious Institutes.** An Instruction from the Apostolic Delegate of Japan to the Superiors of all institutes and Congregations of religious in Japan, instructs them, among other things, to accommodate their common way of life as far as possible to the native ways and customs. Apostolic Delegate of Japan, 8 Dec., 1935 (*Periodica,* 25 (1936)–88).

**Pseudo-Religious Institute.** The Holy Office, July 3, 1937, declared that the so-called religious Institute started by the lawyer Giuseppe di Maggio at Partinico in the Archdiocese of Monreale in Sicily, has no approval from the Church. See *L'Osservatore Romano,* 4 July, 1937; *Documentation Catholique,* 38 (1937)–416.

## CANON 492

### Norms for the Approbation of New Congregations (S. C. Rel., 6 Mar., 1921) AAS 13–312.

Norms according to which the S. C. Rel. usually proceeds in granting approbation to new religious Congregations, were issued by the Sacred Congregation on 6 March, 1921. These norms contain full directions to Bishops as to how to proceed in the founding of new Congregations. A special prohibition of the Holy See exists against translating these norms into other languages; hence, the original text in the AAS must be consulted.

**AAS 13–312;** S. C. Rel., 6 Mar., 1921.
*Periodica,* 10 (1922)–295 (Creusen). Cf. Creusen-Garesché, *Religious Men and Women in Church Law,* n. 21 (Bruce, Milwaukee).

### Instruction on Establishing Native Religious Congregations (S. C. Prop., Fid., 19 Mar., 1937) AAS 29–275.

In missionary lands which are under the jurisdiction of this Sacred Congregation of Propaganda, it is not unusual in these days that new Congregations of religious of either sex are established, which by the good example and the labors of their members come to be of great assistance to the Ordinaries of places. Not only is such a work deserving of the highest praise, but it is to be zealously promoted in accordance with the wishes of the Supreme Pontiff, Pope Pius XI, who, in his Encyclical, *Rerum Ecclesiae,* under date of February 28, 1926,[1] exhorts the

[1] See AAS 18–65; Canon Law Digest, 1, p. 462.

Ordinaries of mission countries in these words: "It is necessary . . . that you establish native religious societies of both sexes" in which the members may "profess the evangelical counsels."

And in order to provide a safe way for Ordinaries who wish to undertake this most useful work, this Sacred Congregation, mindful of the Norms which were issued by the Sacred Congregation of Religious in the year 1922,[2] has decided to recall the following Rules to be observed by the Ordinaries who are under its jurisdiction, in the establishment of native religious Congregations.

1. Before founding a new Congregation, let the Ordinary consider whether any of the Congregations already established can adequately serve the territory which is subject to him. If so, he should not establish a new Congregation, but should call for members of those Institutes.

2. If after mature consideration he thinks that a new Congregation of natives should be erected for the benefit of his mission, let him establish it after the model of some Institute which is already flourishing in the Church.

3. The title or name of the new Congregation may be taken from the attributes of God, from the Mysteries of our Holy Faith, or from some feast of our Lord or of the Blessed Virgin, or from the Saints, or from the special purpose of the new Congregation. Canon 492, § 3, provides that new Congregations shall not assume either the name or the habit of any religious society already established.

4. Moreover, the title or name of the Congregation should not be too extraordinary, nor should it express or insinuate any form of devotion which is not approved by the Holy See.

5. If there is question of religious women, at least two sisters from some Institute already duly approved should be available to act temporarily as Superior General and Mistress of Novices in the proposed new Congregation, that is, until the latter can develop its own religious life.

6. Prudent provision must also be made as regards the necessary means of support for the new Congregation.

7. When the aforesaid conditions have been attended to, the

---

[2] The reference is certainly to the *Normae* of 6 Mar., 1921; see AAS 13–312; reported above on p. 185; though there is also a Decree dated 30 Nov., 1922; CANON LAW DIGEST, 1, p. 267.

Ordinary, before taking definite measures, shall apply to this Sacred Congregation, in accordance with canon 492, § 1, ask the required permission, and consult the Sacred Congregation on the requisites for the establishment of the Congregation, submitting a suitable report on the following points:

*a*) What is the reason for which the Ordinary wishes to establish it;

*b*) What is to be the title or name of the new Congregation;

*c*) What is to be the design, color, and material of the habit to be worn by the novices and the professed;

*d*) What works is it to undertake;

*e*) What resources will it have for its support?

8. After the permission has been obtained, nothing prevents the Ordinary from establishing the new Congregation, which shall be of diocesan law, and as long as it has not the decree of approval or the decree of praise from the Holy See, it shall remain diocesan, entirely subject to the jurisdiction of the Ordinary in accordance with the sacred canons.

9. The establishment shall be made by the Ordinary through a formal decree of erection in writing, a copy of which shall be preserved both in the archives of the new Congregation and in the archives of the Ordinary. The Ordinary shall notify this Sacred Congregation of the fact that the establishment has been made, and shall send it a copy of the decree, taking special care that both the name and the purpose of the Institute are explicitly and exactly defined therein.

10. The Constitutions of the new Congregation, in Latin and in the vernacular (at least six copies), must as soon as possible be submitted to this Sacred Congregation so that they may be duly examined, amended, and returned with suitable remarks to the Ordinary, to be approved by him.

11. The book of the Constitutions must contain everything that concerns the nature, members, vows, of the new Congregation, the manner of life of its members, and its government. The text of the Constitutions shall be divided into two parts; the parts into chapters; the chapters into articles, which shall be designated by a continuous series of numbers from the beginning to the end.

12. The following are to be excluded from the text of the Constitutions:

*a*) Prefaces, historical information, letters of exhortation, and other things of the sort;

*b*) Quotations from the texts of Sacred Scripture and from any other books or authors;

*c*) Ritual and ceremonial rules, and practices and customs which may be introduced into the Congregation;

*d*) The daily order and the calendar which are to be adopted;

*e*) Theological or juridical questions;

*f*) Ascetical instructions, spiritual exhortations, and mystical considerations;

*g*) The provisions of the common law, since these are presupposed.

13. Daily orders, exercises of piety, and other matters of the kind are to be inserted in the *Directorium.*

14. After a suitable time has elapsed from the establishment of the Congregation, if it has by God's blessing shown a notable increase and has spread to other missions, and if it is distinguished for the number of its members, for its works, and for its religious life, the Ordinary may apply to this Sacred Congregation asking that it be made a Congregation of Pontifical law, and submitting the following documents:

*a*) The petition to the Supreme Pontiff for his approval;

*b*) Testimonial letters of the Ordinaries in whose territories the Congregation has houses;

*c*) A report on the personal, disciplinary, material, and economic condition of the new Congregation;

*d*) Constitutions which have been examined and approved by the Ordinary himself.

If the request is approved by this Sacred Congregation, it will be given effect through a *decree of praise,* which will be followed in due course by a decree of approval, together with a decree by which the Constitutions are approved, by way of experiment, for at least seven years.

Given at Rome, from the office of the Sacred Congregation of Propaganda, on the Feast of St. Joseph, Spouse of the Blessed Virgin Mary, 1937.

**AAS 29–275**; S. C. Prop. Fid., 19 Mar., 1937. *Sylloge,* n. 204.
*Periodica,* 26 (1937)–484 (Ellis).

---

**Model Constitutions for Native Missionary Sisters.** The Sacred Congregation of Propaganda proposed a full draft of constitutions for native sisters in the missions (*Sylloge,* n. 205).

## CANON 493

**Suppression of Religious Order.** See Apostolic Letter, Pius XI, 20 Nov., 1935 (AAS 27–482). Cf. *Periodica,* 25 (1936)–22.

## CANON 497

### Special Faculty to Consider Mission Stations as Religious Houses (S. C. Rel., 2 Oct., 1951) Private.

The Sacred Congregation of Religious received the following petition from the Superior General of a certain religious Congregation:

**The Petition:** In Mission countries considerable difficulty is experienced in trying to define accurately the authority of religious Superiors, from the fact that religious establishments cannot generally be organized according to the Code and their Constitutions; long and extended experience has shown that this can easily impair good discipline and the religious life.

For in various Missions entrusted by the Holy See to this Congregation, although there are a great number of our religious, only a few *Religious Houses* can be established with the special permission of the S. C. for the Propagation of the Faith according to canon 497, § 1; whereas most of our missionaries engaged in the work of the Mission live and work in a number of *Mission Stations* under the sole authority of the Ecclesiastical Superior (upon whom, after all, they are entirely dependent).

The consequence is that these religious have no true religious Superior, since only the Superiors of houses which have been canonically erected by the Superior General according to the law and the Constitutions as authentic religious houses, are true religious Superiors. Neither is it possible to join these stations to some regular religious house, especially because of the great distances, which would render such a subordination vain and merely apparent. There results an uncertainty regarding the authority, not only of local Superiors, but also in turn of Major Superiors, because, as there are not enough religious houses to join together to make up a Province or Vicariate (as our Constitutions provide), there is not even an authentic Major Superior.

Hence, in order to provide a remedy for this uncertain condition of religious authority, the Petitioner earnestly asks Your Holiness to grant a special provision or faculty:

1. That in all Residences where our men live, even though not canonically erected as religious houses, the Petitioner may have power to appoint true *Superiors* or *Directors* of these Residences, who shall have the same rights and duties as the other Directors of Residences provided for in our Constitutions.

2. That, with the aforesaid Residences (together with one or other religious house which may be canonically erected in the territory) the Petitioner may have power also to establish one or more *Vicariates* with their own Major Superior or Vicar, who shall be equal to the other Vicars provided for in the Constitutions.

**The Rescript:** In virtue of faculties granted by His Holiness, this Sacred Congregation graciously grants the favor according to the petition in all respects, *et ad mentem:* The mind is that a plan be drawn up in the form of articles of the Constitutions and that it be submitted to this S. C. for approval.

**(Private)**; S. C. Rel., Rescript, 2 Oct., 1951. Annotations, *Commentarium pro Religiosis,* 32 (1953)–167 (Poza).

## *Beneplacitum* of Holy See Required Only for First House of Diocesan Law Institutes in a Given Ecclesiastical Territory Subject to S. C. Prop. Fid. (S. C. Prop. Fid., 20 Jan., 1940; 2 July, 1956) Private.

Contrary to what seems to be the meaning of canon 497, § 1, *sc.,* an apostolic *beneplacitum* is required for the opening of *any kind* (*quamlibet*) of house in territories subject to the S. C. Prop. Fid., Msgr. X. Paventi, a canonist of the S. C. Prop. Fid., in his book, *Breviarium Iuris Missionalis,* p. 150, notably limits this requirement in the case of diocesan law institutes and cites the S. C. Prop. Fid. itself for his comment which, translated, is as follows.

Religious institutes of diocesan law, if they are subject to the S. C. for the Propagation of the Faith, according to the norm established by the S. C. Prop. Fid. in its session of 20 January, 1940, do not need a *beneplacitum* of the said S. C. Prop. Fid. for opening other houses within the limits of the mission of the principal house; such a *beneplacitum* has to be sought only for the opening of the first house in another ecclesiastical jurisdiction.

Since this interpretation seemingly was not published in any other way, a question was sent in 1956 to Msgr. Paventi at S. C. Prop. Fid. to know if the statement in his book could be safely followed. He replied that "without any scruple we may follow the norm as stated by the S. Congr. of Propaganda on Jan. 20, 1940. It is a practical norm which is still adhered to today. The S. Congregation causes it to be inserted into the newly submitted constitutions of religious institutes under its jurisdiction."

**(Private)**; S. C. Prop. Fid., 20 Jan., 1940; reported in *The Clergy Monthly,* 20 (1956)–271.

— — — —

Subsequent to the above, the following rescript from S. C. Prop. Fid. on this matter was sent to the Archbishop of Ranchi, India.

According to the printed norms for opening a religious house in a given mission, the consent of the Sacred Congregation for the Propagation of the Faith is always required. This prescription is in full accord with can. 497. However, a few years ago, this Sacred Congregation somewhat modified the general prescription so that when there is question of a diocesan law institute, only for the opening of the first house in a new ecclesiastical jurisdiction is an apostolic *beneplacitum* required.

**(Private)**; S. C. Prop. Fid., 2 July, 1956, Prot. No. 2651/56; reported in *The Clergy Monthly,* 20 (1956) 422.

## Rights of and Limitations on Lay Religious and Local Ordinaries as to the Teaching of Religion in Intermediate and Higher Schools (S. C. Rel., 26 Jan., 1959) Private.

The following letter was sent to the Very Reverend Brother Guillermo Felix, Assistant General of the Brothers of the Christian Schools.

In your letter dated 15 Oct., 1958, you represented to this Sacred Congregation the feelings that have been aroused among the Brothers of the Christian Schools in some regions by the fact that they have been collectively deprived of the authority to teach religion in their legitimately established schools. Thus you are deprived of one of your most valuable prerogatives, namely, that which constitutes the very purpose of your Congregation and which is the most serious of your religious-professional duties. The fact that it happens in schools where you have been exercising your right peacefully for many years, before as well as after the promulgation of the Code of Canon Law, is a circumstance that aggravates the situation.

Leaving the authentic interpretation of the law, especially of canon 1373, § 2, to the Pontifical Commission, this Congregation, in answer to your kind letter, simply recalls for the present the common interpretation that has been followed in practice up to now in full accord with the mind of this Sacred Congregation for Religious.

According to canon 497, § 2, the permission given by the bishop to establish a religious house in his diocese includes the faculty of performing all the works which are proper to the institute, with the exception of conditions set down in the said permission of foundation. Therefore, the permission to found a house given to a religious institute of teaching includes the faculty of teaching religion. For if it is true that when the Church approves the institute and its constitutions, she entrusts to that particular religious institute the mission of teaching all disciplines, including the profane ones (c. 1375), it is also true that the teaching of religion is precisely what the Church asks and entrusts most especially, since it is this discipline which exerts a more powerful influence on the Christian training of youth. The letter of His Holiness, Pius XII, of venerable memory, addressed to His Eminence, the Cardinal Prefect of the Sacred Congregation for Religious, 31 March, 1954,[1] can be presented as good confirmation of this statement.

The Code of Canon Law subjects the exercise of this apostolate to the vigilance and control of the local Ordinary; hence it entrusts to him the approval of textbooks and teachers of religion, and the visitation of educational centers (cc. 1381; 1382). From such supervision the schools conducted by religious are not exempt (cfr. also cc. 618, § 2, 2° and 512, § 2, 3°).

However, as the bishop cannot deprive all the religious priests

[1] Reported above on p. 170.

of a formed house of jurisdiction to hear confessions (c. 880, § 3), in like manner, when dealing with schools of religious men, it is not sound to deprive all the religious of a school collectively of the mission to teach religion, even prescinding from whether these Brothers have or do not have a pontifical diploma which, as is known, authorizes its possessor to teach religion in the whole Church.

Canon 1373, § 2 recommends that the bishop provide *priests* as teachers of religion in intermediate and higher schools, but it has never been applied to schools of religious, especially of men, in which such need is, as a general rule, sufficiently provided for. Moreover, as you pointed out very well in your excellent letter, such disposition would mean that the Brothers would be deprived of the main purpose of their existence in the Church.

Even apart from the fact that what has been set forth is accepted in practice as the usual interpretation (c. 29), the sources cited for this canon do not authorize a different interpretation. For example, you can read in no. V of the dispositive part of the encyclical of St. Pius X, *Acerbo nimis,* of 15 April, 1905, a very recent source of the said canon: "In the larger cities, and especially in those where there are universities, colleges and academies, let classes in religious doctrine be established for the purpose of teaching the truths of the faith and the principles of Christian living to the youths who attend such public schools wherein no mention whatsoever is made of religion" (*Fontes,* vol. III, pp. 653–654).

Aside from this, and limiting ourselves to the case at hand, this Sacred Congregation knows the program of religious formation and the way it is carried out in practice by the Congregation of Brothers of the Christian Schools. As a result, we would not hesitate to recommend to His Excellency, the Archbishop, the Brothers who have been legitimately appointed by superiors to teach religion.

I take this occasion to declare myself

Sincerely yours in the Lord,
Valerio Card. Valeri
Prefect

(**Private**); S. C. Rel., 26 Jan., 1959, Prot. N. S.R. 1385/59; reported in *Vida Religiosa,* 16 (1959)–258; also in *Commentarium pro Religiosis,* 39 (1960)–49 with annotations (Luis).

# CANON 499

## Government of Religious: Their Place in the Church

(Pius XII, Allocution, 11 Feb., 1958) **AAS 50–153.**

An Allocution of Pius XII to the Superiors General of Religious Orders and Congregations of men, delivered in Rome on the 11th of February 1958, is as follows:

Beloved Sons, who by the suave design of God's Providence have been placed in command of your members engaged in the quest of perfection, gathered as you are in Our presence, it is with uncommon joy that We salute you in the name of the Lord, as men chosen to be associated with Us — and in no mean capacity — in Our Apostolic office. For, as We said a few years ago in speaking to your members at the first General Congress of the states of perfection, the religious state "has its existence and strength from its intimate connection with the end of the Church herself, which is to lead men to the attainment of holiness."[1] And the Church, the Spouse of Christ, would not fully correspond to His will, nor would the eyes of men be raised to her in hope as to a "standard set up unto the nations,"[2] if there were not to be found in her some who, more by example than by word, are especially resplendent with the beauty of the Gospel.

In this department of Our work therefore, beloved Sons, We have taken you as associates of Our supreme office, either directly by delegating to you through the Code of Canon Law some share of Our supreme jurisdiction, or by laying the foundations of your so-called "dominative" power by Our approval of your rules and Constitutions. And so We have it very much at heart that you should exercise this authority of yours according to Our mind and that of the Church.

What your subjects should in this age especially preserve, and what they should innovate and adapt, We explained at length in that exhortation of the Holy Year of 1950. Today it is Our purpose to set forth the way in which you, who govern those We were then addressing, should collaborate with Us to the end We have in view.

At that time We issued a warning that the members of states

---

[1] AAS 43–28; above, p. 88. [2] Isaias, 11:12.

of perfection must in no way indulge in the attitudes of that philosophy which is called "existentialism," for that would be a detriment to eternal truth.[3] It is the part of Superiors, with clear vision and turning neither to the right nor to the left, to lead their subjects securely to eternal life by the safe way of truth, with firm leadership and if necessary with a strong hand. To quote the patriarch of those who, in the Western world, strive for evangelical perfection: "the Abbot should neither teach nor establish nor command anything that is outside the teaching of the Lord; his commands and his teaching should enter the minds of his disciples permeated with the leaven of divine justice."[4] Superiors in the states of perfection must constantly derive the regulations by which they govern their subjects, not from what people are saying, nor from what is considered the latest thing in doctrine and conduct, now at last becoming popular after the older commentaries of the fathers have been abandoned, nor from what may seem more suitable for people living in the world, but from the pure font of revealed truth and the teaching of the Church. It takes strength of soul to oppose occasionally the views of the many. Unless a Superior is willing at times and in the eyes of some persons to appear old-fashioned, how will he keep intact the truth of Christ, which is ever new indeed but also ever ancient? Also in regard to the norms governing ascetical doctrine and the standard of living in the states of perfection (as We noted in connection with a more serious matter in the Encyclical *Humani generis*), there are those today who "unduly attracted to novelty, . . . try to evade the control of the Church's *Magisterium* and so fall into the danger of gradually drifting away from the very truth revealed by God, and of drawing others after them into error."[5] True, it is less serious to err in regard to morals than in regard to faith; but each in its own way is by nature fraught with disaster, and undoubtedly retards and hinders us from attaining as we ought to the Supreme Good.

Superiors must cling firmly to well-balanced and solid ascetical doctrine as handed down by the first Founders and approved by long practice in the Church, and not depart from it in favor of any novelty. For we must hold fast to the truth, not because it

---

[3] AAS 43–32; above, p. 93.

[4] Saint Benedict, *Regula Monasteriorum,* cap. II.

[5] AAS 42–564.

wins the assent of men, but because it is the truth, either implanted by God in man's nature or graciously revealed to him. What if there are some who detract from it, does it thereby cease to be the truth and the way of God? Doubtless, a prudent Superior will willingly and freely consult and listen to advice; he will thoroughly examine and ponder the opinions of wise and learned men; he will never so trust in his own judgment as though the danger of error were not ever present for all men on this earth. But when this has been done, after having heard especially those whom the Rule assigns to him as consultors, after having prayed much to the Holy Spirit and maturely considered the entire matter, he will as far as possible come to a certain and definite decision, and not be afraid to impose it properly and with paternal and humble firmness on his subjects, and to make it the norm of their actions and conduct. "Just as disciples must obey their master, so too it is his part to arrange everything with providence and justice."[6]

Therefore, whatever captious objections you may hear from those who regard religious obedience as a yoke too burdensome for men of this day and age to bear, never forget that it is the Superior's duty to lead his subjects, albeit with all the humility and charity of Christ, yet firmly; and that God, the Judge of men, will demand an accounting not only from individuals but also from those in whose charge He has placed them. "Let him hold it for certain that, whatever the number of the brethren whom he has under his care, he will have to give an account to God on the day of judgment for the souls of every one of them."[7]

As time marches on and new necessities are constantly arising, there have sprung up in the Church, under the guidance as we may hope of the Holy Spirit, one form after another for leading a life in the pursuit of perfection. These various forms of the life of perfection make different demands upon their members; the requirements for monks are not the same as those imposed on clerics regular; those for religious are not the same as those for the more recent secular Institutes. One thing, however, is and will remain common to all of them: whoever is following a life of evangelical perfection must withdraw and separate himself from this world, actually as far as the requirements of his God-

[6] Saint Benedict, *Regula Monasteriorum,* cap. III.

[7] *Ibid.,* cap. II.

given vocation demand, but as far as his affections are concerned, completely. From this world, We say, of which our Lord and Master warned His disciples: "you are not of the world";[8] and the Beloved Disciple: "the whole world is seated in wickedness";[9] and the Apostle of the Gentiles: "the world is crucified to me and I to the world."[10]

In affection, he who intends to live for God and to serve Him perfectly must be detached from the world completely; for the Lord is one who if He be not served exclusively is not served perfectly. Indeed, what created good can be in any way compared to the perfection of God — to say nothing of rivaling it? One who has not cleansed his soul and kept it free from the pride of the world and its manifold concupiscence — how can such a one rise to God as it were on the wings of unfettered love and live a life of union with Him? A life of union, consisting not only of that vital incorporation by sanctifying grace, but also of fervent charity which is the proper quality of a life of striving for perfection?

Where is the man tainted with the weakness consequent on the sin of Adam — unless he be one of exalted perfection and extraordinarily favored with grace — who can remain entirely free from earthly attractions in spirit, without also in fact detaching himself from them, even in a notable degree, and abstaining from them with courage? No one (except in consideration of an office assigned him by obedience in the Church) can enjoy all the comforts with which this world abounds, and indulge in the joys and pleasures of the senses which it offers with increasing prodigality to its votaries, without losing something of the spirit of faith and of the love of God. Nay more, one who yields to laxity for a considerable time will gradually deviate from the ideal of sanctity and incur the risk that the fervor of charity and the very light of faith may decline to such an extent that he may miserably fall from the high state to which he aspired.

Your standards of judgment for doctrines and opinions as well as for action, must be different from the standards of this world; your conduct, and also the ways in which you try to influence people, will be different. Your standards of judgment and appreciation must be drawn from the Gospel and from the teaching of the Church; for "it pleased God, by the foolishness of preach-

[8] Jn. 15:19. [9] I Jn. 5:19. [10] Gal., 6:14.

ing, to save them that believe";[11] "for the wisdom of this world is foolishness with God";[12] because "we preach Christ crucified."[13] Unless a man, far from poisoning his soul by constant immersion in the things of this world, nourish it on the contrary by assiduous reading and reflection on the things of God, by the study of sound doctrine, by familiarity with the ancient and modern writings of those who were distinguished for solid faith and tranquil piety, how will he ever come to relish what is right?[14]

Similar standards of action must be observed by your subjects. They cannot be absorbed in the pursuit of pleasure, enjoyment, or comfort, but must seek only God; and they will not find Him without the constant curbing of their senses and self-will — the will, especially by humility and the submission of obedience, the senses by austerity of life and the voluntary assumption of corporal penances. Without these helps, which are recommended by both the Old and New Testaments and by the whole tradition of the Church, it is almost futile for the Christian soul to flatter itself that it can rise to the love of God and of the neighbor for God's sake.

Are not also the means by which you will be able to influence others and bring them to God, their last end, different from those which the mind left to itself would have thought likely to prove effective? What we call the apostolate depends entirely on the necessity of antecedent grace to open the hearts and ears of the listeners, and of helping grace, without which no one can do anything toward salvation nor persevere in the right. God's ways are not our ways; the power to move souls to faith and salutary works is not always to be found "in the persuasive words of human wisdom,"[15] "but in showing of spirit and power,"[16] in that "showing," deeply mysterious, through which a marvelous effectiveness in winning souls and leading them to God springs forth from the simple sincerity, the charity, the courage of the believer. It is not by those novel and unheard-of things which human ingenuity is constantly inventing, that men are moved to a good life, but by the hidden power of grace and the Sacra-

[11] I Cor., 1:21.

[12] I Cor., 3:19.

[13] I Cor., 1:23.

[14] Cf. the Collect for the Mass of the Holy Ghost.

[15] I Cor., 2:4.

[16] *Ibid.*

ments, especially confession and Communion. And once more: unless a person is withdrawn from the world at least for a time, and even almost daily retires to a certain tranquillity to consider these things serenely and lovingly in solitary communion with the Spirit of Wisdom, will he not be infected with that restless and often fruitless fever of so-called "action," which is dazzling rather than effective?

It was to enable your sons to live in that peace and serenity of mind, so conducive to the right appreciation of things divine, that your Founders, drawing upon the ancient tradition of the Church, handed down by the Fathers of the desert according to the true wisdom of the Gospel, fortified them with the safeguard which we call discipline or observance. This, varied though it be in different Institutes according to their different ends, is enjoined to be practiced in all of them. Its necessity for the end which you profess arises from the very weakness of human nature, burdened as it is with original sin; its enduring efficacy for the attainment of Christian perfection is proved by experience both ancient and modern; its holiness is attested perennially by the Church in word and action.

There never was a time when the observance prescribed by Rule in the states of perfection was not unwelcome to human nature, inclined as it is to laxity; still more unwelcome it may easily be to the men of our time, who before their conversion to a state of perfection have been more accustomed to an easy life. But it is not for that reason to be less esteemed, and much less is it to be abandoned. As of old, now too that saying of the Book of Proverbs is true: "Take hold on instruction, leave it not: keep it because it is thy life."[17] Cannot the same thing which the inspired writer here affirms of self-imposed discipline, be truly said also of the discipline which one assumes and promises to follow in professing a more perfect life? "Those who are impelled by the desire of progress toward eternal life choose the narrow road, . . . so that, not living according to their whim nor yielding to their inclinations and pleasures but walking according to the judgment and at the behest of another, and living in monasteries, they desire to have an Abbot at their head."[18]

It is part of your official duty to help your subjects and to

[17] Prov., 4:13.

[18] Saint Benedict, *Regula Monasteriorum,* cap. V.

hold them within bounds with paternal firmness by exhortations, admonitions, reproofs, and even punishments when these are needed, holding fast to the straight road indicated by the Rules of your respective Institutes. It is not right for a Superior to evade his official duty by putting all the responsibility on the negligent or delinquent subject, saying "he is of age; let him see to it." That is not the way the Lord will look at the matter when He calls you to account for the souls entrusted to your care. "Behold, I myself come upon the shepherds, I will require my flock at their hand."[19] The shepherd who blinks his charge and leaves the sheep, however wayward and foolish, to themselves, instead of holding them firmly in line with his staff, will have to account to Him for their blood! True paternal charity shows itself not only in caresses but also in direction and punishment. That firmness must never be harsh, nor angry, nor impulsive; it must always be right and serene, meek, merciful, ready to forgive and to help a son who tries to rise from his error or his fault; but it must never relax its vigilance nor ever grow weary. Your guidance and vigilance must be applied not only to the so-called "regular" life within the religious house, but to the entire work which your men are doing in the Lord's vineyard. It is your duty to watch over the work of your subjects according to the norms given you by the ecclesiastical authorities who are competent in the matter, so that they will do nothing which will harm their own soul or cause dishonor or damage to the Church and to the people, but will rather strive for their own welfare and that of the neighbor.

This very association of Superiors General, which first came into being spontaneously some time ago, which has continued to meet spontaneously, and has been approved as a permanent institution by this Apostolic See and erected as a moral person, demands of you the utmost good will in working for all the projects for which the Church desires your services. For you know very well that you are all one army in which, though some are in the infantry, others in the cavalry, others among the archers, yet all are fighting the same good fight. You understand how fitting it is, or rather how necessary, that whilst the enemy of Christianity is uniting his forces in an ever closer solidarity which he hopes will make them invincible, you too, all who serve

[19] Ezech., 34:10.

under God, must combine your forces and, each in your proper field and with your peculiar weapons, march together to victory. This unity, which is rendered difficult by diversities of race, of mentality, of customs and other human elements, will flourish wonderfully if you have deeply implanted in your souls the true charity of Christ which the Holy Spirit infuses into that unity. Charity bestowed from above, if it finds us ready to cooperate, will easily relax the ties of that too narrow predilection which, according to human weakness, creeps into our justly loyal attachment to our own Institute. It is right that every one should love his own Institute, the one to which God in His Providence has called him, that he should train his character and form his conduct according to its norms, that he should, to a degree, choose and fulfill apostolic ministries according to its rules; but all are dedicated to harmonious service of the same Church, Spouse of the same divine Lord and Saviour.

Hence that affectionate attachment to the Chair of Peter and to the Vicar of Christ which is common to all the faithful, is to be cherished in a special way by you who strive for perfection. This Apostolic See knows that you will be the first to obey its directions; it confidently expects you to be most faithful teachers of the true doctrine which proceeds from this Chair; it firmly hopes that you will lead the way in promoting ecclesiastical discipline by word and example. And if ever, as is natural in the Kingdom of God upon earth, where the good are mingled with the bad and the wheat with the cockle, something somewhere falters, totters, goes astray or falls apart, do not fail, beloved Sons, to combat valiantly along with Us for "the Kingdom of justice, and love, and peace."[20] Not with that immoderate self-confidence with which Peter before his confirmation by the Holy Spirit exclaimed, "though all . . . yet not I,"[21] but with the same love, you can make the same profession in humble reliance on the grace of your vocation to the states of perfection. And if it come to pass that others forget their filial duty and cause anxiety to this Apostolic See, We shall certainly with God's help remember faithfully those words of our Lord: "Thou art Peter, and upon this rock I will build my Church"; "and thou, . . . confirm thy brethren."[22]

---

[20] Preface of the Mass of Christ the King.

[21] Mk., 14:29.

[22] Mt., 16:18; Lk., 22:32.

In order that your Institutes may always correspond to these wishes of the Vicar of Christ, it is your duty to admit to the ranks of your Institutes only such young men as are in every respect fit, that is, outstanding in virtue and if possible also in talent and other qualities. Away with any excessive concern to herd together a crowd of candidates who might later prove not entirely worthy of your high vocation; such men, far from being an honor and a help to the Church, will be an occasion of loss and sorrow. If on the other hand you hold to the norms which the Church has established and admit only such as are truly worthy, God will take care to raise up vocations of this type, and the high esteem in which your state will be commonly held will prepare the way for the grace of God in many souls. Put your trust in God: if you serve Him as worthily as possible He will take care of you and of preserving and advancing your Institutes.

God grant that upon this select group of His servants, to Him and to Us most dear among the other soldiers of the same army, may descend in abundance the light and warmth of the Holy Spirit. And whilst We gratefully recall those sweetly miraculous visions of the Blessed and Immaculate Virgin Mary at the grotto of Lourdes, We beg that the prayers of that same Mother of grace may obtain this most excellent gift for you her devoted sons. As a pledge of this divine favor We most heartily and lovingly impart to you, beloved Sons, to your assistants in the government of your Institutes, to all your subjects who are carrying the standard of Christ in any part of the world, and especially to those who are being persecuted by the enemies of Christ, Our Apostolic Blessing.

AAS 50–153; Pius XII, Allocution, 11 Feb., 1958. Annotations, *Commentarium pro Religiosis,* 37 (1958)–110 (Bajo).

## CANON 500

### Monastic Nuns in France and Belgium: Dependence on The Ordinary (S. C. Rel., 22 May, 1919) AAS 11–240.

The Sacred Congregation of Religious was asked on the part of several Bishops and religious communities:

Whether monasteries of nuns, in France and Belgium, whose

vows according to their institute are solemn, but are simple according to the prescriptions of the Holy See, are dependent on the Ordinaries of places in the same way as before the promulgation of the Code.

**Reply.** The Sacred Congregation, after mature consideration of the matter, replied: His Holiness is to be petitioned to decree that no change is to be made in the dependence of the aforesaid nuns upon the Ordinaries of places in France and Belgium, as it has existed since the restoration now for over a century: with this proviso, however, that the Bishops shall have no power to change the rules of ancient Orders, nor the constitutions of monastic nuns which have been approved by the Holy See.

In the audience of 13 May, 1919, His Holiness approved this reply and ordered that it be made public.

**AAS 11–240**; S. C. Rel., Reply, 22 May, 1919.
*Periodica,* 10 (1922)–69 (Creusen).

**Status of Monastic Nuns in France and Belgium** (Decree, S. C. Rel., 23 June, 1923) **AAS 15–357.**

A Decree of the Sacred Congregation of Religious is in substance as follows:

The religious families of nuns which after the changes of government in France and Belgium began once more to come together, were nevertheless in such circumstances, owing to new provisions of the civil laws, that the Holy See regarded them as neither strictly monastic nuns according to the ancient common discipline of the Church, nor as bound by solemn vows or the law of papal cloister; but permitted them to be under the jurisdiction of the Bishops, with merely simple vows.

It is with reference to this state of affairs that the response of this Sacred Congregation given in 1919 is to be understood, viz., that nothing was to be changed regarding the dependence of the aforesaid nuns on the Ordinaries of places.[1] Since, however, that response settled nothing in regard to the nature and status of those nuns, and since there are numerous grave difficulties, especially when there is question of revising according to the Code the constitutions of those nuns who follow the rules of the Orders, with the result that the peace and tranquillity of the

[1] AAS 11–240; reported above on p. 202.

monasteries can easily be disturbed, now therefore, after mature consideration, this Sacred Congregation has decided to declare solemnly:

I. In France and Belgium, monastic nuns in monasteries which profess the rules of the regular Orders, or where the vows taken are according to their institute solemn, although in fact they profess only simple vows, are true monastic nuns of pontifical law in the sense of c. 488, 7°, just as are other monastic nuns in the universal Church.

II. Those monasteries, however, in the absence of a peculiar privilege, are not subject to regular Superiors, and hence have not the privilege of exemption under c. 615; but are subject to the jurisdiction of the Ordinaries of places in those matters in which the Code gives Bishops jurisdiction over monastic nuns.

III. If any monastery asks for it, there is at present nothing to prevent the nuns of that monastery from pronouncing solemn vows and keeping the papal cloister, provided they obtain that right from the Holy See.

Approved by His Holiness, Pius XI, with ample ratification for the past, as far as needed.

**AAS 15–357**; S. C. Rel., Decree, 23 June, 1923.

*Periodica,* 12 (1924)–77 (Vermeersch); cf. *Periodica,* 13 (1925)–63; 15 (1926)–230.

---

**Congress Promoted by Religious:** The S. C. of Religious was asked what are the rights of local Ordinaries as regards controlling scientific, liturgical, and cultural Congresses which are promoted by religious in their dioceses. As to strictly internal Congresses, held in the religious house and attended only by religious, no question can arise. But the question concerned outside Congresses, held outside and attended by the public: has the Ordinary the right to approve the Congress and its program, and to be represented personally or by proxy? — The Reply: These public and external Congresses should not be held without the Ordinary's consent; this consent is not necessary for internal Congresses, even if they are attended by externes. The "Liturgical Weeks" held in Belgium are presented as an example. There, for external Congresses, not only the Ordinary's permission was obtained, but the organization of the Congress and its presidency were reserved to the Bishop; for internal Congresses, the Ordinary's permission was not asked. This case is reported under the heading, *"Ex Iurisprudentia S. C. de Religiosis,"* in *Commentarium pro Religiosis,* 32 (1953)–165.

**Dismissal of Religious from Diocese:** Power of local Ordinary. See **c. 329,** AAS 56–5, *Motu proprio, Pastorale munus,* n. 39; reported above on p. 73.

## CANON 501

### Crude or Rash Articles on the Virgin Birth Prohibited

(Holy Office, 27 July, 1960) **Private.**

The following letter was addressed to superiors general of religious institutes.

It is a matter of deep concern to this Supreme Sacred Congregation of the Holy Office to notice that several times in the recent past theological studies have been published in which the delicate subject of Mary's virginity *in partu* is treated in terms of lamentable crudity and, what is worse, in a manner which is clearly opposed to the traditional doctrine of the Church and to the devotional sentiments of the faithful.

In the plenary session on Wednesday, the 20th of this month, the most eminent Fathers of the Holy Office, in view of their very serious responsibility to watch over the sacred deposit of Catholic doctrine, have deemed it necessary to make a decision on the matter: for the future, it is forbidden to publish similar studies on this question.

You will please see to it, Very Reverend Father, that this decree of the Supreme Congregation is exactly observed by the religious of your order.

With the assurance of a good response from you, and with sentiments of religious respect, I gladly remain your reverend paternity's devoted

Raymond Verardo, O.P., Commissary

(**Private**); Holy Office, 27 July, 1960. Prot. N. 311/60/i; reported in *La Documentation Catholique,* 58 (1961)–240.

NOTE: Subsequent to the above decision, at least one superior general inquired of the Holy Office about the absoluteness of its decision and was informed that its mind was not to prohibit such writings absolutely but that authors should not write rashly, neglecting the unanimous tradition of two thousand years concerning the venerable mystery, nor with such freedom of expression as to fail in the reverence and discretion due such delicate matter.

---

**Superiors of Religious Women:** Allocution of Pius XII, 13 Sept., 1952 (AAS 44–823). English text, *Review for Religious,* 11 (1952)–305.

# CANON 502

**Founder or Foundress May Not Hold Superior-Generalship for Life Contrary to Constitutions, Unless by Apostolic Indult** (Reply, S. C. Rel., 6 Mar., 1922) **AAS 14–163.**

The Sacred Congregation of Religious was asked:

Whether founders or foundresses of religious Congregations or pious societies living as religious, who occupy the office of Superior or Superioress General in their Congregation, have the right to retain that office for life notwithstanding the provision of their constitutions limiting the duration of that office to a certain time, and forbidding the reëlection of the same person beyond a certain limit.

**Reply.** In the negative, unless they have an apostolic indult.

**AAS 14–163;** S. C. Rel., Reply, 6 Mar., 1922.
*Periodica,* 11 (1923)–31 (Vermeersch).

**Government of Religious Women** (Address of Father Arcadio Larraona, Secretary of the Sacred Congregation of Religious, September, 1952) **Private.**

At the conclusion of the International Congress of Mothers General which was held in Rome in September, 1952, for Superioresses General of Institutes of pontifical right, Father Arcadio Larraona, Secretary of the Sacred Congregation of Religious, delivered the following address:

. . .

It is not without deep emotion that I address you this morning. I behold in you the hundreds of thousands of consecrated souls for whom you are responsible before God. Your presence here shows that you feel the full force of this great responsibility. Nevertheless the thought of it should not exclude deep and trustful feelings of confidence. In your administration strive to imitate those qualities which we find in God's administration of the world, if we may so speak, that is, the qualities of understanding, far-sightedness, kindness, and patience. If you work in this spirit, then have confidence that God will work for you and in you.

## I. Revision of Constitutions

In 1922 the S. Congregation of Religious ordered all approved religious communities to send in their constitutions for revision and, if need be, correction in the light of the provisions of the recently published Code of Canon Law. But even after this general obligatory revision of some thirty years ago, the S. Congregation does not necessarily feel that all the details of all constitutions must remain forever unchanged. Rome is ready to consider the advisability of changes on certain points, provided the individual communities show good reasons for the modifications they wish to introduce. Rome wants this evolution to be without spurts or shocks — a genuinely vital evolution, imitating the growth and development of a human being. Hence the usual procedure is to require that all proposed modifications be first submitted to a general chapter, and that the changes be approved, not merely by an absolute majority, but even by the moral unanimity of the capitulars. In this connection, the following particular points may be mentioned.

*Custom-Books:* The custom-books of religious communities, sometimes called "directories," are not approved by the S. C. Congregation of Religious except in a negative sense. That is to say that the S. Congregation examines these books in order to make sure that they contain nothing theologically or canonically erroneous, but does not approve them in the strict sense of the term. In this, the custom-books differ from the constitutions.

Notwithstanding all their good qualities, it is undeniable that custom-books, because of their detailed regulating of many aspects of daily life, can and do become oppressive, or at least embarrassing. There are superiors of all types and temperaments, and some of them are unduly attached to the letter of the prescription, without considering the spirit, and without thinking sufficiently of the end at which they aim, an end which frequently can be obtained through the use of different means.

Superiors may therefore legitimately make known their wishes to the S. Congregation of Religious. They should not fear to request such changes on the ground that they will be thought to be unfaithful to their community traditions. Change in itself is not heresy, but it goes without saying that no changes should be proposed merely because they fall in line with the caprices or personal likes of an individual superior. All changes submitted to the S. Congregation must usually have the morally unanimous approval of the general chapter. In case of urgent modifications, the S. Congregation will take action even between general chapters, but with the obligation to submit the matter to the next chapter.

*The Religious Habit:* The Holy See leaves to every individual community full freedom of action regarding all the details of its specific habit. The S. Congregation is interested mainly in maintaining the peace of mind of all religious. Peace and charity are of much higher importance than the advantages to be gained through improvement in some detail of the habit. Rome's only question in such cases will be: "Are you all agreed?" The modifications will be approved, provided they are supported by the general chapter, and provided the minority, if there be one, is not unduly obstreperous in its opposition. If that should be so, Rome would counsel patient waiting.

*The Abolition of Class Distinctions:* The same principles are followed when there is question of removing from the constitutions the articles which set up different classes among the religious of one same community. Peace is the paramount consideration. Rome will approve the elimination of class distinction, but only on the three following conditions: (*a*) that the change insures absolute equality of rights and obligations; (*b*) that the superiors be fully empowered to appoint any religious to any office, due regard being given to the individual capacities of each one and the needs of the community; (*c*) that all the religious, irrespective of the class to which they may have previously belonged, contribute their share of effort in providing for the common needs of the community. Saving these principles, the abolition of the distinction between classes will be approved by Rome, but the S. Congregation will never use any pressure in order to bring this about in any particular institute.

## II. Substitution of the Divine Office for the Little Office of the Blessed Virgin

Through the constantly growing liturgical movement, there is an increasing tendency among religious communities of women to introduce the recitation of the Divine Office in the vernacular instead of the Little Office of the Blessed Virgin. Needless to say, the S. Congregation is favorable in principle to all proposals which will insure a deeper and richer participation of religious in the sacred liturgy, since such participation brings them into more living contact with the Church. Nevertheless, all innovations must be worked out in a spirit of good balance and discretion. Again, nothing is comparable to the advantages of peace in a community. The S. Congregation does not grant any general permission for substituting the Divine Office in the vernacular for the Little Office. Each individual institute must ask for it and submit its own particular reasons for so doing. Proponents of the change oftentimes forget that it is hardly possible that an entire community will react favorably to the innovation, and it is the responsibility of the S. Congregation of Religious to forestall discontent and opposition as far as possible.

Consequently, the permission for the Divine Office in the vernacular instead of the Little Office will be granted on request, with due regard to the following conditions: (1) that the request be supported by the morally unanimous agreement of the general chapter — what causes trouble is not from God; (2) that the request be not in opposition with either the constitutions or the tradition of the community involved — sometimes the recitation of the Little Office is in conformity with a vow or promise made by the founder or foundress; (3) that the apostolate of the sisters allow them time for the recitation of the Divine Office without unduly overloading their day. This does not mean that the S. Congregation always drives with its brakes on — but everyone knows that it is dangerous to drive without brakes.

## III. The Different Stages of Formation

1. *Apostolic Schools:* Apostolic schools are of comparatively recent origin, the earliest of them dating from about the middle of the last century. They were first introduced in institutes of men; but they have now become increasingly common in religious communities of women. The Holy See has issued practically no legislation on the organization of such apostolic schools. The S. Congregation is patiently awaiting the guidance of experience.

These apostolic schools are not permitted by the S. Congregation for cloistered nuns or for religious whose lives closely approximate that of cloistered nuns. This is not a real law of the Holy See, but rather a guiding norm, based on Rome's desire to avoid any semblance of pressure when there is question of a vocation calling for such special qualities as those required by the contemplative life.

The S. Congregation regards apostolic schools as internal schools of a religious community. This point is of canonical importance in determining the degree of freedom to be allowed the community in the organization and administration of these schools: (*a*) those which do not require any actual signs of vocation to the religious life; (*b*) those which demand at least the seeds of vocation to the religious life; (*c*) those which require signs of a vocation to a specific type of religious life.

In any case, the organization and rules of an apostolic school should not lose sight of the fact that the girls in them are young. The atmosphere as far as possible should be that of a family. The apostolic school should not be turned into a novitiate in miniature. There should be nothing to interfere with the full freedom of the candidates in the final determination of their vocation. The program of studies should not be so highly specialized as to make adjustment to a different type of life outside difficult. Teach the girls, first of all, to lead good Christian lives. No asceticism at the expense of the moral law. Avoid whatever might even remotely result in deformation of the natural qualities and virtues of the candidates.

2. *The Postulancy:* The postulancy is obligatory for all women religious. It must last at least six months. If the constitutions prescribe a postulancy of one year, the six months' prolongation is still permissible. The maximum length of the postulancy in any community is eighteen months. Rome does not want the decision as to admission to be delayed too long, and this is why the time limit is imposed.

3. *The Noviceship:* Rome will easily grant permission to have two years of noviceship instead of one, if the same conditions are complied with as those previously mentioned in other connections. But if such permission is granted the change becomes obligatory, and superiors have no faculty to dispense from any period of this two-year noviceship. It makes a bad impression on

the S. Congregation when a community advances good and cogent reasons for two years of noviceship, and then almost immediately begins to ask for dispensations from the change which the community itself requested.

The S. Congregation permits the employment of novices in works of the institute during the second year of novitiate. This was a courageous step, which at first seemed to some people to be in open conflict with the fundamental spiritual purpose of the novitiate. The reason is that today no formation can be regarded as complete without some concrete contact with the apostolate. During such employment the novice remains a novice. She must be given to understand that she is still on probation, even though she be outside the novitiate. She should be under the supervision and guidance of an experienced sister, since the superior of the house, unless it be a small house, will ordinarily be too absorbed with administrative details to give her the time and attention required by her special situation. The use of novices during the second year must be motivated by the welfare of the novice, not by the needs of the community. During this period she is given a chance to prove her qualities, and to learn under supervision how to use the apostolate as a means of personal sanctification. She should be protected and safeguarded without being mollycoddled. Superiors should not forget that when young religious are taken from the hothouse atmosphere of the novitiate and sent out indiscriminately into houses where, so to speak, all the windows and doors are open, they cannot fail to catch cold.

4. *The Juniorate:* In the novitiate the formation of the religious is begun. In the juniorate it is continued, though not with the detailed program of the novitiate year. The juniorate is an initiation into the apostolate, while the young nun still remains under the safeguarding influence of supervision and guidance. The juniorate is intended to forestall the catastrophes which have sometimes befallen young professed sisters who were sent into the active life without any transition period to prepare them for the special problems confronting them in that life. Sisters in the juniorate are in a kind of middle stage of formation, in which they are not subjected to the restrictions of the novitiate in all their rigor nor yet allowed all the freedom of perpetually

professed religious. At the same time they are provided with an opportunity to integrate their technical training with the demands of their religious vocation.

During the juniorate, whatever may be the special form it may take, the sisters should be under the close-range guidance of experienced and capable religious. Unless a house is specifically set up as a juniorate, the superior will ordinarily not be in a position to carry out the functions of mistress of juniors. The duration of the juniorate will depend on its intensity, the duration increasing according as the juniorate is less intense. All communities could at least provide their temporarily professed sisters with special courses and help during the summer vacation. There is no objection to the juniorate's lasting for the entire period of temporary profession. The ideal is a special house, for those communities which can provide one. The threefold aim of the juniorate is: formation, practice, probation.

## IV. Religious Profession

The S. Congregation is ready to allow up to five years of temporary profession, with the possibility of an extension of one year. No temporary profession can be extended beyond six years, according to the Code of Canon Law. The reason is that if a sister has not succeeded in satisfying her superiors as to her vocation during the period of postulancy, noviceship, and six years of temporary vows, it is hardly probable that she will be able to provide this satisfaction in an extended period of probation.

Rome views with favor the so-called "third year of probation," which can be organized either immediately prior to perpetual profession or at some later period after time spent in the apostolate. In whatever form it is organized, the third year of probation has incalculable advantages. Nevertheless, although it is highly recommended, it is not in any way imposed by the S. Congregation.

## V. The Vow of Poverty

I should like to have time to go over with you each of the vows of religion. Time does not permit, but I cannot resist the desire to say something to you about the vow of poverty, which is the bulwark and safeguard of the religious spirit. At the Congress at Notre Dame, after a splendid paper on poverty and the common life in present-day America, a sister asked whether custom could justify the keeping of personal gifts, etc. The speaker, a Dominican Father, replied immediately that neither custom nor any superior could legitimately give a permission which might run counter to the demands of the common life. No superior can allow what is against the spirit of poverty. It is important to cultivate disinterested motives for zeal in the apostolate. The ministry, in no matter what form it is exercised, should be emptied completely of all concern over personal gain. It is a fact of experience that zeal oftentimes diminishes in proportion as interest in personal aggrandizement increases.

## VI. Government

1. *Elections:* Sisters often fall into one or the other of two extremes in chapters: either they organize a real electoral compaign for or against a religious, or they go around in a state of unconcerned passivity. Canon Law forbids electioneering or anything approximating it. But good sense demands, especially in congregations with world-wide expansion, that the electors take means to assure themselves of the qualities (health, virtue, experience, etc.) of the candidates for the various offices. The line of demarcation between asking for information and organizing a campaign is not always too clear, but it can usually be made clear by the good sense and virtue of the religious themselves.

It should not be forgotten that a half-vote is sufficient to constitute the absolute majority (for instance, 17 votes out of 33 is an absolute majority). It is not required that the majority be constituted by one vote more than half.

2. *Re-elections:* Canon Law sets no limit to the terms of major superiors, but leaves this to the constitutions. The S. Congregation is not only not favorable to election beyond the terms provided in the constitutions, but is opposed to it on principle. Superiors and capitulars should remember that they, no less than their subjects, have an obligation to observe the law of the Church. Perpetuation of individuals in office tends to prevent the formation of capable superiors or makes it necessary for them to be chosen from within a closed circle. Other things being

equal, the S. Congregation definitively prefers the election of a new superior rather than the re-election of the one in office, when the term fixed by the constitutions has expired.

In case of a superior general, this re-election is called postulation, and requires a two-thirds majority of the chapter. Some constitutions forbid all postulation. The fact of having the two-thirds majority must be accompanied by sufficiently serious reasons to influence the judgment of the S. Congregation. The reasons will be judged with severity, and the confirmation of re-election after the term fixed by the constitutions will constitute a rare exception.

3. *Admission to Profession:* The freedom to refrain from perpetual profession is mutual on the part of both the institute and the subject. The sister may leave, and the community may refuse to admit her to perpetual profession. Such refusal may not be motivated by ill health, unless there is proof that the illness was fraudulently concealed or dissimulated prior to first profession. It is not necessary that this deceit or dissimulation should have come from the religious herself. A religious suffering from some hereditary disease which has been concealed from her by her parents may be refused admission to profession on this score, even though the deceit did not come from herself. The language of the Code is purely impersonal.

There are difficult cases of ineptitude coupled with ill health. If the ineptitude is in any way connected with the ill health, then the rule is the same as for a religious in poor health: she cannot be dismissed or refused admission to final vows. If it be simply ineptitude for the works of the community, then the community enjoys perfect freedom, since the period of temporary profession was intended precisely to determine whether or not the subject is able to make a contribution to the apostolate of the institute.

4. *Exclaustration:* An indult of exclaustration suspends the canonical obligation of the common life for an individual religious. It entails dispensation from the points of rule incompatible with the new status of the religious, forbids her to wear the religious habit, and deprives her of active and passive voice for the period of her stay outside the community. If there is no scandal, and especially when the reason underlying the exclaustration is not one for which the religious is responsible, Rome

may, with the recommendation of the superior, permit the religious to retain the habit. The religious, however, has no right to demand such permission. Exclaustration is a favor, not a right, and the religious has the obligation to return whenever the superiors so wish.

Superiors cannot allow subjects to remain outside the community, except for purposes of study, for more than six months. This residence outside the community is not the equivalent of exclaustration and thus does not entail any of the restrictions mentioned in the preceding paragraph. Such residence is not favored. Any situation demanding the residence of a religious outside her community for more than six months is, generally speaking, a dangerous situation.

Exclaustration *"ad nutum Sanctae Sedis"* — at the good pleasure of the Holy See — is a measure adopted to cope with those situations in which a religious shows malice enough to be impossible to live with, and yet not canonically sufficient to justify dismissal. Oftentimes these cases involve a certain degree of mental weakness: unbalanced enough to be impossible, and not unbalanced enough to be locked up. In such cases, the S. Congregation orders exclaustration, with all the above-mentioned restrictions, and the exclaustration perdures as long as Rome so wishes. The institute is obliged to assist in the maintenance of the religious.

The present practice of the S. Congregation demands, under pain of subsequent invalidity of the rescript, that all rescripts for dispensation from vows be definitely accepted or rejected within ten days of the date the subject is notified of the granting of the rescript.

**(Private)**; Secretary of the S. C. Rel., Address to Mothers General, Sept., 1952. This text is taken from the *Review for Religious,* 13 (1954)–297–305, with the kind permission of the Editors, who published it with the permission of Father Larraona himself, from the *Acta et Documenta Congressus Internationalis Superiorissarum Generalium* (Rome, 1952).

## CANON 505

**Superiors of Hospitals, Etc.: When Not to Be Appointed for More than Three Years** (Cod. Com., 2–3 June, 1918) **AAS 10–344.**

The Code Commission was asked:

Whether the prescription of c. 505: "minor local Superiors shall not be appointed for a term exceeding three years," etc. applies also to Superiors or directors of schools, hospitals, and other houses devoted to pious works.

**Reply.** In the affirmative, if these Superiors or directors are also Superiors of religious, having other religious under their authority also as regards religious discipline.

**AAS 10–344**; Cod. Com., 2–3 June, 1918, II.
*Periodica,* 9 (1921)–151 (Vermeersch); *J.P.,* 2 (1922)–22.

## Repeated Election of Same Person as Superioress General (Letter, S. C. Rel., 9 Mar., 1920) AAS 12–365.

A Letter of the Sacred Congregation of Religious to the Ordinaries of places regarding the repeated election of the same person to the place of Superioress General in religious Congregations and in monasteries of monastic nuns, is as follows:

It very often happens that Superioresses General of religious institutes, who according to the constitutions are elected for a term of years, and may again immediately be elected to the same position, are sought for the place a third or even a fourth time, and have to have recourse to this Sacred Congregation to obtain the necessary dispensation.

This frequent lengthening of the tenure of office beyond the time fixed or allowed by the constitutions seems inadvisable, especially as the term of a Superioress General usually lasts six years; and so it happens that the same person, elected a second time, is able legitimately to hold the government for twelve years in succession. But if even further reëlections be permitted, they frustrate the purpose intended by the constitutions, which prescribe that the government of an institute is to be held by the same person *for a time;* and this temporary tenure is a basic feature in the entire constitutions. Hence, it not infrequently happens that the institute suffers considerable disadvantages and even harm from this too-protracted tenure of office by the same person. Nor is it a sufficient answer to say that in the constitutions of many Congregations of religious women it is expressly stated that the Superioress General may be elected even a third time provided two thirds of the votes be in her favor and the confirmation of the Holy See be obtained. For this is to be understood in the sense that if there ever occur grave reasons requiring that the same person be chosen a third or fourth time, this cannot be done unless those two conditions are fulfilled. There exists, therefore, in the instance, a real ineligibility for the place; and whenever a real ineligibility exists on any legal ground, grave reasons are required for a dispensation. Hence, the simple will of the voters or the fitness of the person is not a sufficient reason for the dispensation. A person who is thus ineligible must not be elected, but must be canonically *postulated*.

All this, of course, holds, with due proportion, for the election of Abbesses or Superioresses of monastic nuns, who were forbidden by a Constitution of Gregory XIII to hold the government of a monastery beyond three years. For, although that provision was not confirmed by the Code, yet the practice of this Sacred Congregation, by command of the Holy Father, has been to require its observance in the constitutions of monasteries. However, since in monasteries the election is confined to the members of the community, who are often few in number, there may more easily be a reason sufficient for a dispensation, to wit, the want of any other fit candidate.

In view of all this, the Holy Father, Benedict XV, to guard against the abuses that can easily arise in this matter, has ordered that notice be given to all Ordinaries of places, whose duty it is to preside at the election of Superioresses General in Chapters of religious Congregations, or of Abbesses in monasteries of monastic nuns, in their respective dioceses, that they inform the voters of the aforesaid ineligibility; and, in case they learn that the members of the Chapter intend to vote for the same person beyond the time allowed by the constitutions, that they inquire about the special and grave reasons which seem to require a postulation, and warn the voters that the Holy See is quite averse to granting this permission. They must know, moreover, that postulation is not allowed except after the mature weighing of the causes, which consequently should be explained by the Ordinary to the Holy See itself by letter. Of course this requires some time, and involves a certain inconvenience to the members of the Chapter, since they have to wait for a reply before taking any further steps.

If, however, there are such grave reasons as to require the

election of the same person beyond the time allowed by the constitutions, the Ordinary, to obtain the dispensation, should clearly and distinctly report how many ballots were taken in the postulation, and how many votes of those belonging to the Chapter were in favor of the person elected; especially, the petition should state the reasons which seem to require such a re-election; and the Ordinary should state his own opinion on the matter.

**AAS 12–365**; S. C. Rel., Letter, 9 Mar., 1920.
*Periodica,* 10 (1922)–196 (Vermeersch).

## Superiors of Filial Houses Are Not Local Superiors, But Definite Provisions Are to Be Made Regarding Them in Revising Constitutions to Conform to the Code (Reply, S. C. Rel., 1 Feb., 1924) AAS 16–95.

Since in some religious Orders or Congregations there are strictly "filial" houses, that is, houses which do not constitute their own distinct community, nor possess their own property, but are, as it were, members of the principal house, being entirely dependent on it and being governed by a Superior delegated at will by the Superior who governs the whole community and resides in the principal house, the following question was proposed to the Sacred Congregation of Religious:

**Question.** Are the Superiors of these strictly filial houses, who are simple delegates at the will of the Superior of the mother house, included under the designation of local Superiors in the Code?

**Reply.** The Sacred Congregation, having heard the opinions of several of the Reverend Consultors, proposed the matter to their Eminences, who, in the plenary session held at the Vatican on 30 Nov., 1923, after mature consideration, replied: In the negative, *et ad mentem:* the mind of the Sacred Congregation is that in the revisions of the constitutions of the various Orders or Congregations to conform to the Code (cf. c. 489) appropriate provision be made for the application of those canons which more closely concern the relations between subjects and Superiors, as shall be judged best in the various cases.

His Holiness, Pius XI, in the audience of 5 Dec., 1923,

deigned to approve and confirm this reply, and ordered that it be made public.

**AAS 16–95;** S. C. Rel., Reply, 1 Feb., 1924.
*Periodica,* 13 (1925)–53 (Vermeersch) cf. *Periodica,* 15 (1926)–171; *J. P.,* 4 (1924)–8.

## Canon 505 Applies to Societies Without Vows and to Houses Not Exclusively Religious (Cod. Com., 25 July, 1926) AAS 18–393.

The Code Commission was asked:

Whether the prescription of canon 505 includes also the societies mentioned in canons 673–681 and those among their houses which are not truly and properly religious houses, but external, that is, not belonging to the society, those, namely, in which a few of the members are commonly employed; for example, seminaries, schools, or hospitals.

**Reply.** In the affirmative according to the Reply of 3 June, 1918.[1]

**AAS 18–393;** Cod. Com., 25 July, 1926, II.
*Periodica,* 15 (1926)–170 (Vermeersch); *J.P.,* 6 (1926)–132.

## Change in Constitutions as Affecting Tenure of Major Superior Already in Office (Practice of the S. C. Rel., 1958) Private.

Two "recent" private replies of the Sacred Congregation of Religious have appeared, indicating the practice of this S. C. regarding the expiration of the office of a major Superior when the term has been extended by a change in the Constitutions during his tenure.

1. The Minister General of the Franciscans had been elected for six years according to the Constitutions of 1921. In 1953 while he was still in office, the new Constitutions (approved 14 July, 1953) provided that the term of the Minister General should be twelve years. Nevertheless at the expiration of the six years, with the approval of the Sacred Congregation of Religious, a General Chapter was held for the election of a Minister General.

---

[1] See c. 505; AAS 10–344.

2. In the Society of Mary (of Saint Grignion de Montfort) the General Consultors were for six years; by the new Constitutions of 1953 the term was extended to twelve years. When the general election came up at the end of the six years, the S. C. of Religious *provided by a special rescript* for the extension of the term of the Consultors then in office; thus implying that according to normal practice the term would expire according to the Constitutions under which the officials had been chosen.

**(Private)**; S. C. Rel., 1958; reported by Gutiérrez in *Commentarium pro Religiosis,* 37 (1958)–161. The dates of these rescripts are not given precisely. It is pointed out that an exception to the rule stated might well arise from a provision in the Constitutions, either express or implied, that they should be retroactive in this respect (cf. c. 10).

---

**Superioress General:** Practice of the S. C. Rel., regarding the postulation of a Superioress General who has already been in office for twelve years. *Commentarium pro Religiosis,* 32 (1953)–90, *"Ex Iurisprudentia et Praxi S. C. de Religiosis."*

## CANON 506

### Right of Ordinary to Preside, Even Vicariously, at Election (Cod. Com., 24 Nov., 1920) AAS 12–575.

The Code Commission was asked:

Whether in c. 506, § 2, the words: *"secus, Superior regularis: sed etiam hoc in casu Ordinarius tempestive moneri debet de die et hora electionis, cui potest una cum Superiore regulari per se ipse vel per alium assistere, et, si assistat, praesse,"* are to be understood to mean that the Ordinary of the place may, but need not, be present in person or by another at the election of the Superioress in monasteries of nuns who are subject to regular Superiors (even exempt), and may preside, that is, govern the election, either in person or by another; or only in person?

**Reply.** In the affirmative to the first part; in the negative to the second. That is, the Ordinary may preside whether he be present in person or by another.

**AAS 12–575**; Cod. Com., 24 Nov., 1920.
*Periodica,* 10 (1922)–252; *J.P.,* 3 (1923)–117.

## Election of Superioress General of Diocesan Congregation Which Has Already Spread to Several Dioceses: What Ordinary to Preside (S. C. Rel., 2 July, 1921) AAS 13–481.

The Sacred Congregation of Religious was asked:

I. Whether the right to determine the place where the general Chapter shall be held belongs to the Ordinary of the place where is located the principal house of a religious Congregation of diocesan law which has already spread to several dioceses; or whether that right belongs rather to the Superioress General.

**Reply.** In the negative to the first part; in the affirmative to the second, according to canons 162 and 507.

II. Whether the same Ordinary mentioned in the preceding question has the right of presiding at the election of the Superioress General, and of confirming or rescinding it; or whether that right belongs rather to the Ordinary of the place where the election is held.

**Reply.** In the negative to the first part; in the affirmative to the second, according to c. 506, § 4.

**AAS 13–481**; S. C. Rel., 2 July, 1921.
*Periodica,* 10 (1922)–360 (Vermeersch); *J.P.,* 1 (1921)–9.

## Right of Ordinary to Preside Means to Preside with Jurisdiction (Cod. Com., 30 July, 1934) AAS 26–494.

The Code Commission was asked:

Whether the words "to preside," which occur in c. 506, § 2, and in the interpretation of 24 Nov., 1920,[1] are to be understood as designating a presidency of honor, or one of jurisdiction.

**Reply.** In the negative to the first part; in the affirmative to the second.

**AAS 26–494**; Cod. Com., 30 July, 1934.
*Periodica,* 23 (1934)-147 (Vermeersch); *Jus Pontificium,* 14 (1934)–223; *Amer. Eccles. Review,* 91 (1934)–498; *Irish Eccles. Record,* 44 (1934)–638; *Clergy Review,* 8 (1934)–491.

---

[1] Reported above on p. 220.

# CANON 509

## Catechetical Instruction to Be Given to All Members of Lay Religious Institutes of Men and Women (Instruction, S. C. Rel., 25 Nov., 1929) AAS 22-28.

An Instruction of the Sacred Congregation of Religious to the Superiors and Superioresses General of lay religious institutes, regarding the duty of instructing their subjects in Christian doctrine, is as follows:

How necessary to man is an accurate and serious instruction in Christian doctrine is apparent from the fact that true faith, which is necessary to live a Christian life, is nourished and strengthened by such instruction. This need is especially felt at the present time, when grave errors about God, religion, the rational soul, human society, and man's eternal destiny, are current everywhere. The duty of learning this doctrine thoroughly is incumbent especially upon those who are consecrated to God in religious Congregations: for without the knowledge of Christian doctrine they can neither nourish the spiritual life as they should in their own souls, nor labor for the salvation of others according to their vocation.

However, since especially of late years many and various religious institutes of men and women have arisen from whose works, if well done, the Church may rightly expect great fruit, this Sacred Congregation is especially solicitous in their regard, that the members of these institutes, of both sexes, be well taught in Christian doctrine, and that they may with all due diligence instruct in the same the boys and girls intrusted to their care.

To this end, the Sacred Congregation, with the approval of the Holy Father, does by these presents decree:

1. During their probationship and noviceship the young men and women shall review their Christian doctrine and learn it more thoroughly, so that each one shall not only know it by heart but also be able to explain it correctly; nor shall they be admitted to take the vows without a sufficient knowledge thereof, and a previous examination.

2. After the year of noviceship all the religious who are to be employed in teaching Christian doctrine to boys and girls in primary schools, whether public or private, must be so trained

both in the catechism itself and in the teaching of it to children, that they shall be able to pass an examination before the Ordinary or examiners delegated by him.

3. As regards the program for the preparation of this examination, the schedule which is in use by the Vicariate of Rome for determining fitness to teach catechism in the elementary schools, may be used.[1]

4. If, however, religious men or women are intrusted with the teaching of Christian doctrine to boys and girls, not in schools, but in a parish, then they must take care to procure a testimonial of their fitness from the diocesan Curia.

**AAS 22–28**; S. C. Rel., Instruction, 25 Nov., 1929.
*Periodica,* 19 (1930)–199 (Vermeersch).

## CANON 510

**Decree on the Quinquennial Report of Religious and Others, and on the Annual Prospectus** (S. C. Relig., 9 July, 1947) **AAS 40–378.**

A Decree entitled: "Concerning the quinquennial report which is to be made by religious Institutes, Societies of common life and secular Institutes," is as follows:

As more than twenty-five years have passed since the publication of the Decree, *Sancitum est,* of 8 March, 1922,[1] regulating the quinquennial report which is to be sent to the Holy See by the General Superiors of religious Institutes (c. 510), and as experience has clearly shown which of its provisions seem to merit definitive confirmation, what should be added to them, and which ones should be revoked or amended, as that Decree itself intimated, the Sacred Congregation of Religious, in the plenary session of the Eminent Fathers of 4 July, 1947, decided to provide as follows:

I. According to the Code (c. 510), the Abbot Primate, the Abbot Superior of a monastic Congregation (c. 488, 8°), the Superior General of every religious Institute, Society of common life without public vows (c. 675), and secular Institute, of

[1] This schedule may be read, in a Latin version, in the annotations of this document in *Periodica,* 19 (1930)–200.

[1] AAS 14–161; CANON LAW DIGEST, 1, p. 282.

pontifical right, and the President of any Federation of houses of religious Institutes, Societies of common life, or secular Institutes, and, in default of the above-named persons or if they are prevented from acting, their Vicars (c. 488, 8°), must send to the Holy See, that is to this Sacred Congregation of Religious, a report on the state of their religious Institute, Society, secular Institute or Federation, every five years, even if the year assigned for sending the report falls wholly or partly within the first two years from the time when they entered upon the office.

II. The five-year periods shall be fixed and common to all those mentioned above in n. I; and they shall continue to be computed from the first day of January, 1923.

III. In making the reports, the following order shall be observed:

1° From among the religious Institutes, Societies of common life, secular Institutes and Federations of pontifical right, whose members are men, the report is to be sent:

in the first year of the five-year period: by the Canons Regular, Monks, and Military Orders;

in the second year: by the Mendicants, Clerics Regular, and other Regulars;

in the third year: by the Clerical Congregations;

in the fourth year: by the lay Congregations;

in the fifth year: by the Societies of common life, secular Institutes, and Federations.

2° From among the religious Institutes, Societies of common life, secular Institutes, and Federations of pontifical right, whose members are women, the report is to be sent, according to the region in which the principal house is juridically established:

in the first year of the five-year period: by the Superioresses of religious Institutes in Italy, Spain, and Portugal;

in the second year: by the Superioresses of religious Institutes in France, Belgium, Holland, England, and Ireland;

in the third year: by the Superioresses of religious Institutes in the countries of America;

in the fifth year: by the Superioresses of religious Institutes in other parts of the world, and moreover by the Superioresses of Societies of common life, secular Institutes and Federations throughout the world.

IV. In order that the Sacred Congregation may be able to

obtain certain and authentic information regarding all those monasteries and independent houses of pontifical right, of both men and women, which are not bound by canon 510 to send the quinquennial report, and also regarding Congregations, Societies of common life and secular Institutes, of diocesan right, the following are to be observed:

1° Major Superiors of monasteries or independent houses of men which, although they are of pontifical right, neither belong to any monastic Congregation nor are federated with others, shall send to the Ordinary of the place, at the time and in the order mentioned above (n. III, 1°), a summary report of the five-year period, signed by themselves and by their proper Councillors. The Ordinary in turn shall send a copy of this report, signed by himself, with any remarks he may see fit to add, to this Sacred Congregation within the year in which the report was made.

2° Major Superioresses of monasteries of nuns, with their proper Council, according to the order above prescribed (n. III, 2°) for General Superioresses, shall send a brief and concise report of the five-year period, signed by all of them, to the Ordinary of the place if the nuns are subject to him, otherwise to the Regular Superior. The Ordinary of the place or the Regular Superior shall carefully transmit a copy of the report, signed by himself and adding any remarks he may see fit to make, to this Sacred Congregation within the year in which the report was made.

3° The General Superiors of Congregations, Societies of common life, and secular Institutes, of diocesan right, shall send a quinquennial report, signed by themselves and by their proper Council, to the Ordinary of the place where the principal house is, at the time and in the order above prescribed (n. III, 1° and 2°). The Ordinary of the place shall not fail to communicate this report to the Ordinaries of the other houses, and he shall within the year send to this Sacred Congregation a copy signed by himself and adding his own judgment and that of the other Ordinaries regarding the Congregation, Society, or secular Institute in question.

4° Independent and autonomous religious houses and houses of a Society without vows or of a secular Institute, which are not united in a Federation, whether they be of diocesan or of pontifical right, shall send a summary report of the five-year period to the Ordinary of the place, in the order above prescribed (n. III, 1° and 2°). The Ordinary in turn shall send a copy of the said report, signed by himself, with any remarks he may see fit to make, to this Sacred Congregation, likewise within the year.

V. In making out their reports, all religious Institutes, monastic Congregations, Societies of common life, secular Institutes and Federations, of pontifical right, even though they be exempt, must follow exactly the schedule of questions which will be made out by the Sacred Congregation and sent to them directly.

Monasteries of nuns, autonomous houses of religious Institutes and of Societies and secular Institutes of pontifical right, and Congregations, Societies, and secular Institutes of diocesan right, shall use shorter formulas which will be approved for them.

VI. The replies given to the questions proposed must always be sincere and as far as possible complete and based on careful inquiry; and this is an obligation in conscience according to the gravity of the matter. If the replies are deficient in necessary matters, or if they seem uncertain or not sufficiently reliable, the Sacred Congregation will *ex officio* see to it that they are completed, and if need be will even itself directly conduct the investigations.

VII. Before the report is officially signed by the Superior and by the individual Councillors or Assistants, it is to be carefully examined personally and collectively.

The General Superioress of religious Institutes of women, and of Societies of common life, secular Institutes and Federations, of pontifical right, shall send the report, signed by herself and by her Council, to the Ordinary of the place of the Generalate house, so that he, according to law (c. 510), may sign the report; she shall then in due time see that the report signed by the Ordinary of the place is sent to this Sacred Congregation.

VIII. If any of the Superiors or Councillors who have to sign the report has any objection of any consequence to make to it, which he was not able to express in giving his vote, or if he judges that anything concerning the report should in any way be communicated to the Sacred Congregation, he may do this by a private letter, and may even be in conscience bound to do so according to the case. However, let him be mindful of his own condition and remember that he will gravely burden his conscience if he dares to state in such a secret letter anything which is not true.

IX. At the end of each year, all religious Institutes, Societies of common life, secular Institutes and Federations, whether of diocesan or pontifical right, shall send directly to the Sacred Congregation of Religious the annual prospectuses according to the schedules contained in the formulas which will be made out and distributed by the Sacred Congregation, stating the principal matters which concern the state of person, works, or other things which should be of interest either to the Sacred Congregation or to Superiors.

His Holiness Pius XII, in the Audience given to the undersigned Secretary of the Sacred Congregation of Religious on 9 July, 1947, approved the text of this Decree and ordered that it be observed by all and that it be published, all things to the contrary notwithstanding.

**AAS 40–378**; S. C. Rel., Decree, 9 July, 1947.

For practical directives on the Quinquennial Report, cf. *Review for Religious,* 8 (1949)–234 (Ellis); 10 (1951)–20 (Ellis); 11 (1952)–12, 69, 151 (Gallen); *Monitor Ecclesiasticus,* 75 (1950)–188 (Pugliese).

## List of Questions for the Quinquennial Report of Papal Institutes (S. C. Rel., 9 Dec., 1948) Private.

The following is the English version of the "List of Questions" or Questionnaire, officially published by the Sacred Congregation of Religious for the Quinquennial Report of papal Institutes. It is entitled: "The List of Questions Which Are to Be Answered by Religious Institutes and Societies in the Report to Be Sent to the Holy See Every Five Years According to the Decree, *Cum Transactis.*"

### *Points to Be Noted*

A) *Regarding the drawing up and writing of the quinquennial report.*

*a*) Before the reply to each question, there should be a clear indication of the number and letter by which that question is designated in this list.

*b*) Whenever a pontifical document is brought in, its date and Protocol number should be faithfully and uniformly given.

*c*) The reply is to be developed as each case may require, and is not to be dismissed with a simple affirmation or denial.

*d*) Clerical religious Institutes and Societies are to make out the Report in Latin; others may do it either in Latin or in one of the following modern languages: English, French, German, Spanish, or Italian.

*e*) The Report should be typed and in clear characters. If for some just cause the Report is written by hand, the handwriting must be clear.

*f*) The paper to be used must not be translucent nor too thick, but durable.

*g*) The questions marked with an asterisk are to be answered only by religious Institutes of men; those marked with a cross, only by Institutes of women.

B) *Regarding things which are to be sent to the Sacred Congregation with the Report.*

1. In the first Report following the issuance of this formula, the following things are to be sent:

*a*) Two well-bound copies of the Constitutions or Statutes, revised to conform to the Code.

*b*) Two copies of existing privileges, printed or at least typed, of which one at least should be bound.

*c*) Two copies of the books in which special laws, practices, and customs are contained.

*d*) Two copies of the liturgical books and prayer books.

*e*) Two copies of the Statutes for houses of religious and clerical training, and also of the systems of piety, education, and studies.

*f*) Special Statutes for affiliated tertiaries, oblates, or other such persons.

*g*) The formularies which are in use either for appointments to offices or for making reports and visitations, and other formularies if there be any.

*h*) A historico-juridical report of the religious Institute, Society, or other Institute, in which are to be indicated: the founder, the year of foundation and of the temporary and definitive approval of the Institute and of the Constitutions, and in an accurate summary the principal events in the history of the Institute or Society. All these are to be sent neatly and stoutly bound.

*i*) If the Institute has according to law (c. 596) a distinctive habit for the professed and novices, a picture faithfully representing the same either photographically or otherwise is to be sent in duplicate; two pictures of the same size as those just mentioned should also be sent, showing the habit in colors.

*l*) As far as possible, let there be sent also the principal works, even though they be old, which show the spirit, way of life, history, and works of the Institute or Society; and collections of the documents of the Holy See which concern the Institute or Society.

2. As soon as they appear, or at least with the Report at the end of the five-year period, the General Superior shall send to the Sacred Congregation:

*a*) The official commentaries of the religious Institute or Society.

*b*) The minutes of the General Chapters.

*c*) The instructions, ordinances, and other important documents of the Superior General.

3. Religious Institutes, Societies, and other Institutes which may in the future obtain a decree of praise shall faithfully send the things which have been mentioned at least on the occasion of their first quinquennial Report to the Sacred Congregation.

*The Following Things Must Appear on the First Page of the Report*

**The name of the religious institute or society:**

(the official title in Latin, and the common name)

**Its symbols; that is, the initials or letters commonly used to designate it:**

**The seat of the generalate house:**

(complete information: post office address, telephone number, telegraphic address)

**The years which are covered by the report:**

## THE LIST OF QUESTIONS

*Concerning the Preceding Report*

1. *a*) When was the last Report sent to the Holy See.

*b*) Whether and when a reply was received from the Sacred Congregation.

*c*) Whether the observations which may have been made by the Sacred Congregation upon the Report were faithfully carried out in practice.

2. Whether the matters of information contained in the last Report can be conscientiously considered reliable and complete, or whether anything concerning them would seem to require modification.

### CHAPTER I

### *The Institute and Its Government*

ARTICLE I

### Concerning the Institute in general and its parts

§ 1. CONCERNING THE INSTITUTE IN GENERAL

3. What is the juridical nature of the Institute or Society (c. 491, § 1).

*Concerning the special end*

4. What is the special end of the Institute.

5. Was the special end authoritatively changed during the five-year period, and by what authority.

6. In practice is this end faithfully retained, or is it in part abandoned; or are any works undertaken which do not pertain to it.

7. What are the principal works through which the special end is pursued.

*Concerning Second Orders, Congregations, Societies, Institutes of Women, which are subject to the Institute or Society*

8.*[1] Whether the Institute has an Order of women (a Second

[1] Questions marked with an asterisk * concern only religious Institutes of men.

Order) subject to it by law or by privilege.

9.* How many Monasteries of this Second Order are subject to the Institute, and what are they; how many are subject to the local Ordinaries, and what are they.

10.* Whether the Institute or Society has subject to it or specially entrusted to it any, and if so what, Congregations or Societies of women, and what are the apostolic indults upon which this subjection or direction is based (c. 500, § 3).

11.* Whether the Institute has affiliated to it any, and if so how many, religious Congregations of Tertiaries of simple vows.

12.* How many sodalities of secular Tertiaries depend on the Order, and how many individual secular Tertiaries are there.

13.* Whether the Institute has as peculiar to itself any, and if so what, Associations of the faithful (c. 686, § 3), and what are the indults upon which their relationships are based.

## § 2. Concerning the Internal Organization and Division of the Institute

### *Concerning Assistancies and Congregations, etc.*

14. *a*) Whether, and if so according to what criterion (geographical, ethnological, historical, etc.), the Provinces are grouped into Parts or Assistancies, from which the general Definitors, or Consultors, Socii, etc., are chosen.

*b*) Whether any complaints or appeals have been made against the fairness of the arrangement.

15. Whether there is in the Institute any recognized internal division of the members into various Families or Congregations.

### *Concerning Provinces, Vice-Provinces, and other equivalent units*

16. Is the Institute legitimately divided into Provinces (c. 494, §1); if not, does it seem that it should be so divided.

17. Has any new Province been established since the last Report, or have any of the then existing Provinces been suppressed or modified.

18. In case of the division, new establishment, or suppression of Provinces (c. 494, § 2), by whom and how were the division and distribution of property made.

19. Are there in the Institute any other forms of union between houses: Vice-Provinces, Commissariats, regional Delegations, etc.

*Concerning the houses*

20. Which houses were modified either externally or internally during the five-year period (c. 497, §§ 1 and 4).

21. In the erection and suppression of houses, were the rules of law (cc. 497, 498) and the standards of prudence observed, among which must be numbered a written contract, clear, complete, and drawn up in accordance with Canon Law and the Constitutions, with due regard to the civil law.

22. Are all the houses provided with those things which are necessary for the common life, especially:

*a*) A separate cell for each person; or, if the dormitories are common, at least a separate bed for each person, properly set apart from the others.

*b*) A separate place fully suitable for the care and assistance of the sick.

23. Are the rooms for receiving guests sufficiently separate from the part of the house which is reserved to the community.

ARTICLE II

## Concerning the juridical government of the Institute

*Concerning the general government*

24. *a*) Is the general Council at present up to its full membership.

*b*) Do all the general Councillors reside in the Curia.

*c*) If any are elsewhere, why is this, and where do they live (the place, Province, Diocese).

25. What other general offices are there (Procurator [can. 517, § 1]; Bursar, Secretary, Prefect of studies, etc.).

*Concerning the general Chapter; its convocation and session*

26. Within the period covered by the Report, has there been a session of the General Chapter.

27. Were the norms of the common law and of the particular law (the Constitutions, etc.) which concern the General Chapter faithfully observed; i.e.:

*a*) The time of the session, the designation of the place, the letter of convocation.

*b*) The elections of delegates to the Chapter, and of Tellers and a Secretary of the Chapter.

*c*) The elections of the Superior General, Consultors or Assistants and General Officials who are elected by the Chapter (e.g., Procurator, Secretary, General Treasurer).

28. In all these matters, even in seeking information about the candidates, did all avoid procuring votes either directly or indirectly, for themselves or for others (c. 507, § 2).

29. Who presided at the Chapter:

*a*) In the election of the Superior General.

*b*) In the other elections and in the business meetings.

30. Did each of the Provinces and other equivalent units submit their own report to the Chapter.

31. Did the aforesaid reports of the Provinces faithfully represent the true state of affairs, so that they constitute authentic documents upon which general reports may safely be based.

32. Were the following reports presented to the General Chapters in due time, so that they could be conveniently examined by each of the Capitulars and by a Commission elected in the Chapter if that is prescribed:

*a*) The report on the state of persons, discipline, and works since the last General Chapter, drawn up by the Superior or Vicar General and approved by the General Council.

*b*) The report on the true and complete financial condition of the Institute, drawn up by the Bursar General and approved by the Superior General with his Council.

33. Was the decision on these reports read in Chapter and seriously weighed and discussed before the general elections.

34. Were the minutes of the General Chapter which was held within the five-year period sent to the Sacred Congregation.

*Concerning promulgation and execution*

35. When and how did the Superior General promulgate those decrees and decisions of the General Chapter which were to be communicated.

36. In the promulgation, were any of the provisions omitted or not faithfully reported; if so, why, and by what authority.

37. What measures were taken by the Superior General with his Council and by the other Superiors and Councils to see that the prescriptions of the General Chapter be faithfully reduced to practice.

*Concerning appointments to offices*

38. Were the norms of the common law and of the Constitutions observed:

*a*) Regarding the requisites and qualifications of Superiors and Officials (cc. 504, 516).

*b*) Regarding the manner of appointment (cc. 506, 507).

*c*) Regarding the duration of offices (c. 505).

39. How many and what dispensations from the provisions of the common or particular law were granted by the Holy See or by Major Superiors:

*a*) For appointments to positions or offices.

*b*) For the renewal of the same.

*c*) Were the conditions attached to these dispensations faithfully observed.

40. Did the Superiors of clerical Institutes duly fulfill, according to c. 1406, § 1, 9° and § 2, their obligation of making the profession of faith before the Chapter or Superior who appointed them, or before their delegate.

*Concerning the duties of Superiors: Residence — Making known and observing the Decrees of the Holy See — the canonical visitation — Freedom of epistolary correspondence*

41. Did the Superior General, the General Councillors, Procurator and the other Superiors, observe the law of residence according to the common law (cc. 508, 517) and the Constitutions.

42. How do Superiors see to it that the decrees of the Holy See which concern religious be known and observed by their own subjects (c. 509, § 1).

43. Is perfect freedom left to subjects, without any inspection of letters by Superiors, in their epistolary correspondence with those persons who, according to the common (c. 611) and particular law, have this right.

44. Were there any cases of secret and clandestine epistolary correspondence, either between religious or between these and secular persons, and what was done to correct these abuses.

45. *a*) Did the Superior General and other Major Superiors make at the proper time, in person, their prescribed visitations of Provinces, Missions, and houses.

*b*) Did the above-named Superiors make these visitations through delegates.

46. Were the visitations which were made according to the common law (cc. 513, 2413) and the particular law, complete so as to include:

*a*) All persons, as regards discipline, religious perfection, priestly life, religious and clerical training, and the ministries and works of the Institute.

*b*) Things and property; their conservation and administration.

*c*) Places, especially sacred places, divine worship, pious foundations, etc.

47. Were any duly appointed extraordinary delegated visitors sent at any time; what were the reasons and what were the results.

48. What was done to see that the decrees of the visitation be carried out in practice.

### *Concerning Council meetings*

49. Are Council meetings held at the prescribed times and in the required cases:

*a*) By the Superior General.

*b*) By Major Superiors.

*c*) By local Superiors.

50. *a*) Was the opinion of all the Councillors always asked.

*b*) Do absent Councillors give their opinion, and if so how.

*c*) Were any of the Councillors neglected; if so, what was the reason.

51. How often each year during the five-year period did the Superior General and Major Superiors convoke their Councils.

52. Are the matters in which, according to the common and particular law, Councillors have a deliberative or consultative vote, faithfully submitted to a meeting of the Council.

53. Is the proper liberty of all and each of the Councillors

duly recognized in the Council meetings; and in the decisions, appointments, and votes of whatever kind, were the norms of the common law (cc. 101; 105, 1°, 2°, 3°) and of the particular law always observed.

54. Are the minutes of the meetings duly drawn up and signed.

55. Are the Archives of the Institute, Provinces, and individual houses properly equipped and carefully arranged.

56. Are all the offices of the general, provincial, and local officials actually filled, or are any of them vacant.

*Concerning corrections and the abuse of power*

57. Do Superiors exercise their function of vigilance and correction either privately or publicly; by what means and in what manner do they do this.

58. Have any abuses arisen or taken root, without being corrected and without efficacious remedies being applied to prevent and remove them.

59. How often and for what reasons were canonical admonitions and penalties imposed.

60. In applying these remedies, were the sacred canons and the Constitutions of the Institute observed.

61. Were there any cases of abuse of power by Superiors, or at least were any appeals or complaints on this matter received from subjects.

62. Were Superiors guilty of any grave infringements of Canon Law or of the Constitutions, either as regards the common obligations of religious or the obligations which concern their particular office.

63. In these cases, were the penalties either common or special, which are provided for by the common law (e.g., cc. 2389, 2411, 2413, etc.) or by the Constitutions, applied.

*Concerning the exercise of authority*

64. What means are taken in order that the Superior General and his Curia be constantly, fully, and sincerely informed as to the state of the Institute.

65. Are periodical reports to be made to Major Superiors, and how often.

66. Is a faithful observance of the prescriptions in this matter insisted upon.

67. Are there in the Institute any established means by way of internal bonds which unite the members among themselves, as for example: reports on work done, published bulletins of houses, Provinces, and the whole Institute.

68. Are any other means used as necessity may require, to promote union among the Provinces and houses of the Institute; if so, what are they.

69. Is there also for each house a chronicle in which the principal events are carefully recorded.

*Concerning relations with the Ordinaries of places*

70. *a*) Are the provisions of the Code regarding the subjection of religious to the local Ordinaries faithfully observed.

*b*)* Are good and friendly relations with the Ordinaries fostered, and do the religious, without prejudice to religious discipline, exercise priestly ministrations in favor of the diocese.

*c*) Have there been in any Province or house litigation, disputes, or difficulties with the local Ordinaries; if so what were they.

71. What remedies have been or can be applied to restore harmony.

ARTICLE III

## Concerning the spiritual government of the Institute

*Concerning confessors*

72.* Are several confessors appointed for each house according to c. 518, § 1.

73.* Without prejudice to the Constitutions which may prescribe or recommend that confessions be made at stated times to fixed confessors, are the religious left free to go, in accordance with canon 519, without prejudice however to religious discipline, to a confessor approved by the local Ordinary, even though he be not among the fixed confessors.

74.†[2] Are the norms of the common law and of the Constitu-

[2] Questions marked with a cross † concern only Institutes of women.

tions faithfully observed regarding the appointment and reappointment of the ordinary, extraordinary, special, and supplementary confessors (cc. 520, §§ 1–2; 521; 524; 526; 527).

75.† Did Superioresses faithfully observe the prescriptions made for them regarding supplementary confessors (c. 521, § 3), occasional confessors (c. 522), and confessors in case of grave illness (c. 523).

76. Do Superiors take means and exercise a prudent vigilance to see that all the religious, according to law (c. 595, § 1, 3°) and the Constitutions (c. 519), approach the sacrament of penance at least once a week.

77. Have Superiors been guilty of any abuses, and if so what were they, by which the liberty of conscience of their subjects has been restricted (cc. 518, § 3; 519, 520, § 2; 521, § 3; 522; 2414).

78. Did Major Superiors and Visitors correct these abuses.

79. Has there been, under pretext of liberty of conscience, any detriment to religious discipline on the part of subjects; did any other abuses arise; were the abuses corrected by Superiors and Visitors without prejudice to liberty.

### *Concerning spiritual direction*

80.* How do Superiors provide for the solid training of spiritual Directors.

81.* Whether care is taken to see that in Novitiates (c. 566, § 2) and also in all clerical and religious residence-halls, the prescribed confessors and spiritual Directors be provided and chosen, and, in the case of clerical Institutes, that they reside there (c. 566, § 2, 2°).

82. Whether Superiors, in accordance with Canon Law (c. 530, §§ 1, 2) leave their subjects free in regard to making a strict manifestation of conscience to themselves.

83. In what ways do Superiors strive to promote spiritual direction.

### *Concerning the reception of the Most Blessed Eucharist*

84. Whether Superiors, in accordance with c. 595, §§ 2–3, promote among their subjects frequent and even daily reception

of the Most Sacred Body of Christ, always without prejudice to full liberty of conscience according to law (c. 595, § 4) and the Instructions of the Holy See.

85. Do Superiors diligently see to it that confessors be easily available before Communion, and do they allow their religious subjects a suitable time for preparation and thanksgiving.

86. Do Superiors see to it that, according to the Constitutions and the common law, there be spiritual and catechetical instructions for the entire house (c. 509, § 2, 2°), for the novices (c. 565, § 2), for the scholastics (c. 588, § 1), for the *conversi,* for the domestics and servants (c. 509, § 2, 2°).

ARTICLE IV

## Concerning the financial government of the Institute

### § 1. Concerning the Acquisition and Loss of Property

*Concerning the acquisition and registration of property*

87. *a*) What if any immovable property or precious movable property was acquired by the Institute, Provinces, and houses; what was the value of these acquisitions.

*b*) Was the aforesaid property acquired by gift or other gratuitous title, or by purchase, and in this latter case was it with the funds of the Institute, Province, or house, or with borrowed money.

88. Has the Institute, the Province, and each house an inventory of its movable property, especially of that which is classed as precious (by reason of workmanship, history, or material) (c. 1522, 2°), and of its immovable property.

89. When must these inventories be revised, and are they in fact revised.

90. In cases where works which are not the property of the house, such as clerical or religious residence-halls, hospitals, churches, etc., are entrusted to the religious houses, are these properties kept clearly distinct from those which belong to the religious house itself.

91. By what method or in whose name before the civil law is

the religious property registered; and can this registration be regarded as safe in civil law.

92. What forms of registration have been adopted as the more secure in various localities.

93. If societies have been established for this purpose, was everything done in accordance with the civil law and is everything actually being kept in good order.

94. As regards the aforesaid societies:

*a*) Were all persons to whom the administration or management of property is entrusted, chosen with due care, after making all the previous investigations which were necessary or useful.

*b*) Were the members of the Institute itself given the preference over outsiders for offices of administration, whenever this could prudently be done without loss.

*c*) What safeguards were used against dangers arising from abuses of administration.

*d*) Is a constant vigilance conscientiously exercised according to law, through the checking of accounts and through ordinary and other extraordinary and timely inspections of safety deposits and other properties.

### *Concerning expenses*

95. Were extraordinary expenses paid from ordinary or extraordinary income proper, or on the contrary with borrowed funds.

96. Did the individual houses and other units subject to the Provinces contribute toward meeting the expenses of the Provinces.

97. Did the Provinces and equivalent units and the houses which are immediately under the Superior General contribute to the common necessities of the Institute.

98. By what authority (Chapter, Council, General or Provincial Superior), on what principles and in what proportion are the contributions to the general and provincial funds determined.

99. Were these contributions paid willingly or more or less under pressure.

100. Are the Provinces and houses allowed to retain whatever is prudently foreseen to be necessary or very appropriate for their own life and growth, in view of the good of souls and the welfare of the Institute.

### *Concerning the alienation and diminution of property*

101. What capital property, whether immovable, or stable (i.e., consisting of capital funds), or precious was alienated, and by what authority.

102. In the alienation of property, were the provisions of law (cc. 534, 1531), especially regarding the previous appraisal by experts, and the norms of the Constitutions, observed.

103. Did the Institute, Provinces, and houses consume any stable or founded property or capital funds; for what reasons and by what authority.

104. Are the general, provincial, and local Superiors and Bursars making serious efforts to recover this property.

105. What properties of the Institute, Provinces, and houses have suffered loss; and what were the reasons.

### *Concerning debts and obligations*

106. *a*) What debts were contracted, and by whom.

*b*) What debts are actually outstanding.

107. In contracting debts and obligations, were the following faithfully observed:

*a*) The provisions of c. 534.

*b*) The precautions mentioned in c. 536, § 5.

*c*) The norms of the Constitutions regarding permissions, the consent of the Council, etc.

108. Was the interest on debts and obligations faithfully paid, and is diligent care taken toward the gradual payment of a debt or the amortization of the capital (c. 536, § 5).

## § 2. Concerning the Conservation and Administration of Property

109. Is the administration of property conducted, not arbitrarily, but according to the common law and the Constitutions, under the direction and vigilance of Superiors and their Councils (cc. 516, § 2; 532, § 1).

110. Are there designated Bursars (c. 516, §§ 2, 3, 4) according to the common law and the Constitutions:

*a*) For the entire Institute.

*b*) For the different Provinces and other similar units.

*c*) For the individual houses and works.

111. Does the Superior in any case act also as Bursar (c. 516, § 3).

112. Do the Councils have their part in the administration and exercise vigilance in regard to it, even when the Superiors are acting also as Bursars (c. 516, § 1); how do they do this.

*Concerning the rendering of accounts*

113. How many times a year and to what Superiors and Councils must the Bursars and other Administrators render an account of their administration.

114. Was a clear and complete rendering of account demanded of all and each of the Bursars and Administrators during the five-year period.

115. Were there presented together with the accounts the documents showing the expenditures and receipts.

116. Was there regularly an inspection and checking of the safe.

117. Are the necessary directions given to the Bursars and Administrators; if so how is this done, and what sanctions are imposed in case of necessity.

118. Have Superiors, Bursars, or Administrators, or any other religious, any money or property which they can freely use without giving a regular account of it, even though it belongs to the Institute, Province, or house.

*Concerning the investment of money and changes of investment*

119. Did Superiors, Councils, and Administrators lawfully, safely, and profitably invest (c. 533) the money which was to be invested according to law and the will of benefactors, observing the rules of law and the Constitutions.

120. Did Superiors, Bursars, and Administrators make temporary investments of surplus funds which were not required for ordinary expenses, so that they should not lie idle but might draw a reasonable interest.

*Concerning the conservation of property*

121. Are money, securities, contracts, precious articles care-

fully conserved, observing exactly the common norms and the provisions of the Constitutions.

122. On what terms, if ever:

*a*) Were money or precious articles received from outsiders on deposit.

*b*) Or conversely were such deposits made with outsiders by Superiors, Bursars, Administrators, or private religious.

123. Do Superiors, Bursars, Administrators conscientiously strive that all the property of the Institute, Province, and house be religiously conserved and providently administered (c. 532, § 1).

*Concerning foundations, pious causes, etc.*

124. What legacies and pious foundations were accepted.

125. In accepting pious foundations and legacies, were the rules of law (c. 1544, ss.) and of the Constitutions observed.

126. Was the money of foundations and pious causes, according to law and with the consent of the local Ordinary when that was required, invested (cc. 533, §§ 1, 2; 1547) and separately and faithfully administered (cc. 535, § 3, 2°; 1546, 1549).

127. Were the obligations attached to foundations faithfully and conscientiously fulfilled (cc. 1514; 1549, § 2).

128. Did Visitors demand documentary proof of their fulfillment and an account of the administration of the property.

*Concerning business and trade, etc.*

129. Did any religious, Superiors or subjects, personally or through others, engage in illicit business, that is, business not permitted to religious, in violation of cc. 142, 592.

130. In cases where for just reasons the permission of the Holy See was obtained for engaging in business (give the date and Protocol number), was every semblance, not alone of fraud but also of avarice, diligently avoided.

131. What precautions were taken that religious who are occupied in business dealings may not suffer spiritual harm.

132. Whether Superiors and Councils were attentively watchful that, according to c. 1539, § 2, in the administrative exchange of securities payable to bearer, all appearance of commerce or trading be avoided.

*Concerning actions or affairs which involve financial responsibility*

133. How did Superiors exercise vigilance over the actions and dealings of their subjects from which there might arise according to law a financial responsibility on the part of the Institute or of the Province or house (c. 536, § 2) or of the individual religious (c. 536, § 3).

134. Did Superiors clearly and effectively, according as the circumstances required, take prompt action to clear the Institute, Province, and house of all responsibility for actions and dealings done by individual religious without observing the norms of the common or particular law.

135. Do Superiors see to it that, in all matters which concern finances, or in those generally which could give occasion to litigation in the canonical or civil courts, everything be done exactly according to law, on the basis of previous written contracts and with the guarantee of perfectly valid signed agreements, etc. (c. 1529).

136. Have any lawsuits or losses resulted from failure to observe the prescribed formalities of civil law according to n. 135.

137. Have Superiors and Bursars diligently seen to it that extern workmen and all persons who work for the Institute, Province, or house receive at the agreed time a just and fair compensation according to law (c. 1524), and that the provisions of law regarding the contract of hire and other matters be faithfully observed.

138. What provision is made for the spiritual welfare of those who work in the house, especially if they also reside there.

## Chapter II

## *Concerning the Religious and the Religious Life and Discipline*

*Concerning the diversity of classes — The vows of each class*

139. What are the different classes, if any, among the members of the Institute; does harmony exist among the different classes and is fraternal charity observed among them.

140. Besides the persons who belong to the Institute or Society as members, by religious profession or lawful incorporation, are there others who are dedicated or given to it, or the like, without being members.

141. Is provision made in fairness and charity for the spiritual life of these persons and also for their material security.

142. Are there any legitimately approved statutes for them.

ARTICLE I

## Concerning the admission, formation, and profession or incorporation of members

*Concerning the postulantship in the wide sense*
(Apostolic Schools)

143. Are there in the Institute any aspirantships or postulantships in the wide sense: apostolic schools, etc.

144. For how long a time does the instruction and education in these places last.

145. In these apostolic schools and similar houses and in the residence halls, are the students of tender age habitually kept separate from the older ones.

*Concerning the postulantship in the canonical or strict sense*

146. Are the postulantships properly conducted according to law in the houses of noviceship (c. 540, § 1), or in houses where perfect religious observance exists (c. 540).

147. Was the time assigned by the common law (c. 539) or by the Constitutions for the postulantship abbreviated or prolonged; if so, for how long a time and by what authority.

*Concerning the admission of aspirants*

148. What means are used to arouse and attract vocations.

149. Are there also advertisements inserted in public bulletins and papers. If so, in what bulletins or papers did they appear.

150. Taking into account the different circumstances of various localities, what causes are regarded as having an influence on the increase or diminution of vocations.

151. What are the obstacles which aspirants most frequently have to overcome in order to follow their vocation.

*Concerning documents, testimonials, and informations*

152. Were the documents required by the common law (c. 544) and by the Constitutions demanded before admission in the case of each aspirant.

153. At least before entrance into the novitiate, were the following testimonial letters demanded and obtained:

*a*)* The common testimonial letters which are to be given by the local Ordinaries and are prescribed for all (c. 544, § 2).

*b*) The special testimonial letters which are to be given under oath by the Rector or Major Superior, for those who have been in a Seminary or a residence-hall which is equivalent to an ecclesiastical one, or in a postulantship or novitiate of a religious Institute (c. 544, § 3).

*c*) Likewise the testimonial letters which are required in the case of clerics and professed religious (c. 544, §§ 4, 5).

154. Besides the documents and testimonials which are specially prescribed by law or by the Constitutions, were further informations, which it seemed necessary or useful to know in order to judge with certainty of the vocation and fitness of the aspirants, diligently sought (c. 544, § 6).

*Concerning impediments and admission*

155. From what impediments or defects, if any, which are imposed by the common or particular law, was a dispensation granted; how often and by what authority was this done.

156. Were the admissions of aspirants always done by the competent Superiors, observing the rules of law (c. 543).

*Concerning the noviceship — The house*

157. Was every novitiate house erected or transferred after obtaining in advance the permission of the Holy See (c. 554, §§ 1, 2).

158. Does perfect religious observance flourish in the novitiate houses.

159. Did Superiors assign to them or permit to remain in

them religious who are not exemplary in their zeal for religious observance (c. 554, § 3).

*Concerning the beginning of the noviceship*

160. Did all fulfill the prescribed days of spiritual exercises before entering the noviceship (c. 541).

161. Were the rite and the rules prescribed for admission to the noviceship faithfully observed (c. 553).

*Concerning board and expenses for the postulantship and noviceship*

162. Is the right of the Institute to demand payment for the expenses of the religious habit and board during the postulantship and noviceship, given in the Constitutions or customarily recognized by express agreement.

163. Who determines the amount to be paid.

164. Was there any instance of the grave abuse of delaying the profession because the expenses of the postulantship or noviceship had not been paid.

*Concerning the discipline of the noviceship*

165. Did all the novices and each of them from the beginning of the noviceship have a complete copy of the Constitutions.

166. Are the novices, according to law and the Constitutions, kept separate from the professed, and is any undue communication between them tolerated (c. 564, §§ 1, 2).

167. Did all and each of the novices before their profession perform the canonical year of noviceship complete and continuous, without counting the first day, in a house of noviceship lawfully erected, under the care and direction of a Master (cc. 555, § 1; 556; 557).

168. Was the noviceship extended or shortened beyond the limits fixed by law (c. 571, § 2) and the Constitutions; if so, for how long a time and by what authority was this done.

*Concerning the government of the noviceship*

169. Was there always in every novitiate a Master of novices duly appointed or elected (c. 560).

170. Have the novice Master and his Socius all the qualifications and all the requisites prescribed by the common law (c. 559, §§ 1, 2) and the Constitutions, or did dispensations have to be asked for and obtained.

171. Are the Master and Socius free from all offices and ministries in or out of the house, which might interfere with their care and government of the novices (c. 559, § 3).

172. Do the Masters of novices, according to law (c. 561) and the Constitutions, under the vigilance and direction of Superiors and Visitors, have full possession of their proper authority and use it for the government and training of the novices.

173. Do all the Masters fulfill their office properly (c. 562) and remain constantly in the novitiate house.

174. Do the Master of novices and his Socius abstain from hearing sacramental confessions unless the penitents of their own accord ask them to do so according to c. 891.

*Concerning the spiritual training of the novices*

175. Were the novices, under the guidance of the Master, during the first or canonical years of the noviceship, engaged exclusively according to law (c. 565, §§ 1, 2) in exercises of piety and other exercises proper to novices; or on the contrary were they assigned to hearing confessions, preaching, and external works or ministries; or did they apply themselves expressly to the study of literature, science, or humanities (c. 565, § 3) beyond the limited measure in which this has been approved by the Sacred Congregation.

176. During the second year of noviceship or during the time which is over and above the canonical year, were the norms which were given in the Instruction of the Sacred Congregation of Religious (2 Nov., 1921) observed:

*a*) Regarding the manner of exercising the external ministries of the Institute (nn. I, II).

*b*) Regarding the conditions under which alone the novices may be sent outside the novitiate house (III).

*c*) Regarding the two months' preparation for the profession (IV).

*Concerning the documents to be drawn up before the profession*

177. Did all the novices, according to c. 569, § 1, before the first profession of simple vows, freely cede the administration and either cede or dispose of the use and usufruct of their property.

178. In case the aforesaid cession and disposition was not duly made before the profession, or in case new property was acquired thereafter, was it made or completed after the profession (c. 569, § 2).

179. Were any changes of the aforesaid cession and disposition after the profession, made always in accordance with c. 580, § 3.

180. *a*) Did the novices of the Congregation, before their first profession of temporary vows, freely make a will in due form, valid according to the civil law, regarding their present or future property (c. 569, § 3).

*b*) Did they afterward render this will valid according to the civil law (c. 569, § 3).

181. Were any changes which may have been made in this will after profession, made according to c. 583, 2°.

182. Are the aforesaid documents *a*), *b*) faithfully kept in the Archives.

*Concerning admission to profession and the act of profession*

183. Do the General Superior and General Council carefully and constantly keep a severe watchfulness as regards admissions; have they issued any special norms in this matter.

184. Does there seem to be in any Province too great facility regarding admissions, and have the prescribed norms and sound criteria been faithfully observed.

185. Has the first profession, after eight full days of spiritual exercises, always been made validly and licitly according to law and the Constitutions (cc. 572, 573, 575) in the novitiate house itself (c. 574, § 1).

186. Was the prescribed rite observed in making the profession, and was the document attesting it duly drawn up (c. 576).

### *Concerning the canonical examination*

187.† Did the Major Superioresses, or others acting in their name, two months before admission to the noviceship, to the first temporary profession, and to perpetual profession, give timely notice to the local Ordinary (c. 552, § 1), so that he or his Delegate might gratuitously conduct the canonical examination regarding the free and conscious will of the postulant or candidate (c. 552, § 2).

188.† Was the prescribed examination always made.

### *Concerning the dowry — The obligation and delivery of the dowry*

189.† According to the Constitutions, is the dowry obligatory in the Congregation, or is it left entirely or partly optional (c. 547, § 3).

190.† Was the delivery of the dowry made according to law (c. 547, § 2) and the Constitutions.

### *Concerning the investment, conservation, administration, and return of the dowry*

191.† Were the dowries, immediately after the first profession, always invested by the Major Superioresses, with the deliberative vote of her Council and the consent of the Ordinary of the place where the capital of the dowries is kept (c. 549).

192.† Were the dowries spent or encumbered in any way before the death of the religious concerned; if so, by what authority was this done. Were the dowries so spent or encumbered, even though it were done after obtaining lawful permission, afterward restored or cleared of the encumbrance; what is their condition at the present time (c. 549).

193.† Where and how are the dowries administered. Are the rules of law faithfully observed regarding their administration (cc. 550; 535, § 2).

194.† Is all property which is brought in as dowry, even though it be in excess of the sum required for a dowry in the Constitutions, or even though there be in the Congregation no obligation to bring in a dowry, accepted, invested, administered, etc., with the observance of the norms which govern dowries.

195.† In case of the departure of a professed religious, for whatever cause it occurred, and in case of transfer, were the dowry and likewise the personal belongings which the novice brought with her at her entrance, in the condition in which they were when she left, restored to the religious departing or transferring, without the income which had already accrued (cc. 551; 570, § 2).

196.† Is this done also with property freely contributed for increasing the dowry even beyond the sum required by the Constitutions.

197.† In case of the departure of a professed religious who had been received without a dowry or with an insufficient one, if she was unable to provide for herself out of her own property, did the Institute out of charity, according to law (c. 643, § 2), give her whatever was needed that she might safely and decently return home and be decently supported for a time.

*Concerning the profession and the renewal of profession*

198. What if any dispensations were necessary for the pronouncement of the vows.

199. How many and what sanations were afterward necessary.

200. Were the temporary vows which are prescribed by law and by the Constitutions (c. 574, § 1), when the time for which they were taken had elapsed (c. 577, § 1), always renewed according to law (c. 577, § 2), so that no one ever remained without vows.

201. How often was the temporary profession extended beyond the six-year period allowed by law, and by what authority was this done (c. 574, § 2).

202. Conversely, how often was the time of the temporary vows, which is prescribed by law (c. 574, § 1) or by the Constitutions, shortened.

*Concerning the solemn profession*

203. Did all the professed of simple vows in Orders, within sixty days before their profession of solemn vows, duly make the prescribed renunciation of the property which they actually possessed, in the form of a true cession but not in the form of a

will, to whomever they chose, on condition of their future profession (c. 581, § 1).

204. After the profession was made, were all things immediately done which were necessary in order that the renunciation be effective in civil law (c. 581, § 2).

205. Did the Superior who received the solemn profession give notice of it to the Pastor of baptism in accordance with cc. 470, § 2; 576, § 2.

ARTICLE II

## Concerning the religious life and discipline

### *Concerning the vows — Poverty and the common life*

206. Is a perfect common life according to c. 594, the Rule and the Constitutions, observed everywhere, but especially in novitiates and houses of studies (cc. 554, § 3; 587, § 2).

207. What has been done and is being done positively to safeguard and promote the virtue and spirit of poverty.

208. Do Superiors and officials, out of religious charity and in order to ward off for the religious occasions of sinning against poverty, provide, within the limits of poverty, what is necessary and appropriate in the way of food, clothes, and other things.

209. Do they allow the religious to ask for or receive these things from externs.

210. Are there complaints about these things; are these complaints seriously considered, and are abuses on the part of Superiors and subjects alike corrected with equal severity.

211. Are the sick and the aged religious attended to with special care and helped in both body and soul with paternal charity, so that, within the limits of religious poverty, they lack nothing which seems necessary for the recovery of their health and for their spiritual consolation.

212. Are all the above cared for in the house; and if in a case of peculiar necessity they have to be cared for out of the house, are they frequently visited.

213. Is there a suitable house for sick and aged members.

### *Concerning chastity and its safeguards*

214. Did all Superiors make it a matter of conscientious duty

to be attentively vigilant regarding those things, both in and out of the house, which may easily contain dangers against religious chastity, i.e., regarding:

*a*) Familiarities, either in the parlors or elsewhere, with persons of the other sex, young people, and children.

*b*) Epistolary correspondence.

*c*) The reading of books and papers which are unbecoming to religious.

*d*) Abuses of the telephone and uncensored listening to radio programs, etc.

215. Were any rules and regulations issued by Superiors and Chapters regarding the public and private use of the radio. (Cite the documents.)

216. If, which God forbid, religious committed any offense against the Sixth Commandment with younger students entrusted to their care, did Superiors immediately remove the culprits from the occasion and punish them, and thereafter carefully watch over their life. In the more serious cases did Superiors have recourse to the Holy See.

217. Are the provisions of the law and the Constitutions regarding cloister (cc. 598–599, 604) faithfully observed. Did any abuses creep in.

218. Did Superiors, in violation of the norms of the Constitutions, allow visits without a companion, frequent and too protracted visits and conversations with externs, especially those which are evidently useless or can become dangerous, which disturb silence, especially that which is more strictly to be observed, which interfere with exercises of piety or other community exercises, and which are in general opposed to the religious spirit.

219. *a*) Are the parlors so arranged that what goes on in them can be seen from the outside.

*b*) Is the frequency of parlor visits regulated according to the Constitutions and religious prudence.

220. Do Superiors themselves diligently observe and cause others to observe the prescriptions of the Constitutions concerning religious going out of the house and receiving visits from and making visits to externs.

221.† Except in cases of prudent necessity, do Superiors assign a companion to religious when they go out of the house, especially for the purpose of making a visit (c. 607).

222.† Do the rooms which are reserved for Chaplains and Confessors or Preachers have a separate entrance and no internal communication with the habitations of the religious.

*Concerning obedience*

223. Is religious discipline observed, and is the government of Superiors made easy by the docility of the subjects.

224. Was it often necessary to impose formal precepts in virtue of the vow of obedience.

225. Were such precepts given in due form according to the Constitutions, and never without grave reason.

*Concerning the Rule and the Constitutions*

226. Are the Rule and the Constitutions faithfully observed (c. 593).

227. Are the Rule and the Constitutions read publicly at the prescribed times (c. 509, § 2, 1°).

228. Is the private reading of the Rules and the Constitutions favored.

229. *a*) Are there any customs in effect which are contrary to the Rule and the Constitutions.

*b*) Do Superiors allow new ones to spring up, or on the contrary do they strive to prevent this and to eradicate the old ones.

230. In what places, if at all, since the last Report, did abuses spring up or become rooted.

*Concerning the religious habit*

231. Has the Institute a habit of its own (c. 596).

232. Was the habit modified or abandoned without due permission; if so, by what authority.

233. Does the habit everywhere correspond to the prescriptions of the Rule and the Constitutions, and is it uniform for all, with due allowance for the differences which may be lawfully recognized for each different class of religious.

234. Is the religious habit faithfully worn according to law (c. 596).

235. Do the excloistered religious continue to wear the habit.

### *Concerning exercises of piety*

236. Do Superiors see to it that in all the houses the exercises of piety which are prescribed for every day, every week, every month, every year, or for other fixed times, be faithfully and worthily performed according to the Constitutions.

237. Do Superiors see to it that all the religious:

*a*) Make a retreat every year.

*b*) Be present at Mass every day if not legitimately prevented.

*c*) Give themselves to mental prayer every day.

*d*) Attend earnestly to the other offices of piety which are prescribed by the Rules and Constitutions (c. 595, § 1, 1° and 2°).

238. Do Superiors see to it that all the members be able to be present at community exercises.

239. Do they give to those religious who, either because of their particular duties or for other just cause, or by way of abuse, are not present at community exercises, time in which they can conveniently and worthily make up the obligatory exercises.

240. Do they see to it that all these exercises be actually made up.

### *Concerning choir service and the divine Office*

241. If choir service is prescribed by the Constitutions, is it held exactly and worthily in each of the houses according to their Constitutions and the common law (c. 610, § 1), the religious who are bound to choir and not actually lawfully impeded being present.

242. Do Superiors see to it that priests, clerics in major orders, and the solemnly professed, who were absent from choir, recite the divine Office privately with attention and devotion (c. 610, § 3).

### *Concerning religious charity*

243. Are the relations between the different members of the Institute, between Superiors and subjects, etc., characterized by a true spirit of charity.

244. Are defects against charity severely corrected.

245. Do contentions and rivalries between Assistancies, Prov-

inces, and various localities in the Institute exist, and are they tolerated. Is there any special cause which is an obstacle to fraternal charity.

*Concerning the reading of books*

246. Are Superiors watchful that no books be used, whether in manuscript or published form, it they are not entirely safe.

247. Are the spiritual books which the religious use privately, according to law approved by the Church, conformed to the religious state and suitable for the welfare of the individual religious to whom they are permitted.

ARTICLE III

## Concerning those who have departed or been dismissed, and others who leave the Institute

*Concerning those who have gone out from the Institute*

248. *a*) How many in the Institute and in each Province, at the expiration of their vows did not renew them, either because they chose not to do so or because they were not allowed to do so.

*b*) How many of the professed of temporary vows were dispensed during their vows, and how many of the professed of perpetual vows were dispensed.

249. Were those who were dispensed from their vows at their own request or with their consent, forced, or without serious and grave reasons and precautions permitted, to leave the religious houses before the rescript was duly executed.

250. How many transfers, if any, were there to another Institute.

*Concerning apostates and fugitives*

251. *a*) How many apostates and fugitives, if any, were there during the five-year period.

*b*) Did the Society or Institute observe the provisions of law concerning apostates and fugitives, by seeking them (c. 645, § 2), and if this proved fruitless, by proceeding against them according to law, so that their juridical condition should be clearly defined.

Were the provisions of law regarding those who came back observed (cc. 2385, 2386), and is watchful provision made for their spiritual good.

*Concerning those dismissed by Superiors and those not admitted to profession*

252. *a*) Since the last Report, how many of the professed of temporary vows and how many of the professed or perpetual vows have been dismissed, according to Provinces.

*b*) In the dismissal of religious, whether of temporary or of perpetual vows, were the norms of the common law (cc. 647, § 2; 649–672) as well as those of the Constitutions observed.

*c*) Was the same done in regard to not admitting the professed of temporary vows to the renewal of their vows or to perpetual profession (c. 637).

253. Were the dismissed of temporary vows, while the recourse duly made within ten days was pending (c. 647, § 2; S. C. of Religious, 20 July, 1923, AAS 15, 1923, p. 457), and the dismissed of perpetual vows, before the decree or judgment of dismissal had been confirmed by the Sacred Congregation (cc. 652, 666), forced to leave the Institute.

254. Are the dismissed who are not in sacred orders released from their vows by the dismissal (c. 669, § 1); and if the vows remain, does the Institute show solicitude regarding their condition (c. 672, § 1).

*Concerning those dismissed by the law itself and those sent back to the world*

255. What were the cases, and the causes which led to them, for both the professed of temporary and those of perpetual vows, where they were either sent back to the world on account of grave scandal or very grave harm (cc. 653, 668) or dismissed by the law itself (c. 646).

256. Were steps immediately taken according to the Code (cc. 646, § 2; 653; 668) to determine the condition of those dismissed by the law itself and of those sent back to the world.

257. Is there any such person whose condition still remains undetermined.

258. What cases if any have occurred of the reduction to the lay state of religious who had received sacred orders; how many were voluntary and how many penal.

### *Concerning those who were excloistered*

259. How many cases of exclaustration were there, if any; are the causes carefully and conscientiously pondered in the presence of God before the petition is recommended and the rescript executed.

260. Does the Institute take care:

*a*) That if it seems necessary to ask for an extension of the indults, they be renewed in due time.

*b*) That the persons who are excloistered lead a worthy religious life and return as soon as possible to some house of the Institute.

261.* Likewise does the Institute take care regarding those who have been secularized on trial, and regarding their return to religion if at the expiration of the three-year period the indult is not renewed or they are not accepted by the Ordinary.

### *Concerning absences from the house*

262. Do Superiors see to it that subjects remain out of the house only for a just and grave reason and for the shortest possible time, according to the Constitutions (c. 606, § 2).

263. For absences which exceed six months, except for studies or ministries according to law and the Constitutions, was the permission of the Holy See always obtained (c. 606, § 2).

264. Is it allowed by reason or under color of a vacation, that time be spent with one's parents or outside a house of the Institute.

### *Concerning the deceased*

265. Were the prescribed suffrages faithfully and promptly performed for all the deceased.

ARTICLE IV

## Concerning the various classes and conditions of religious

### § 1. Concerning Clerics

(This is dealt with in the Report on formation and studies.)

### § 2. Concerning *Conversi* or Coadjutors

*Concerning their education and training*

266. Do Superiors, in accordance with c. 509, § 2, 2° give to those religious who belong to the class of *conversi,* instruction in Christian doctrine; and do Superiors, both before and after their profession but especially during the earlier years, carefully attend to their spiritual, intellectual, civil, and technical education according to the functions which they have to fulfill.

267. Are the religious allowed to engage in works which do not seem to be suitable to the religious state.

268. Do Superiors with paternal charity diligently provide also for the bodily health of the *conversi* or coadjutors.

### § 3. Concerning Those Who Are Applied to Military Service

*Concerning the profession of those who are to be called for the first time to active military service*

269.* Did Superiors regulate according to the decrees of the Holy See the temporary professions of those who are to be called for the first time to active military service or its equivalent.

270.* Were perpetual professions permitted before the first active military service or its equivalent, to which the young men are liable to be called.

*Concerning the religious during their military service*

271.* *a*) Did Superiors take care of their members in the service, watch over their life, communicate frequently with them, requiring a periodical account of their conduct, their actions and exercises of piety, etc.

*b*) What special means were used to secure their perseverance.

272.* In cases of dismissal for just and reasonable causes, or of voluntary separation from the Institute, did the Major Superior follow the prescribed procedure and faithfully conserve all the documents in the Archives.

*Concerning the renewal of temporary profession after military service and the making of perpetual profession*

273.* For admission to the renewal of temporary profession, was everything done which is prescribed by the common law and in the decrees regarding this matter.

274.* Was the prescribed time of the temporary profession completed after military service, and also the time of the temporary vows which is prescribed by law and by the Constitutions before the making of the perpetual profession.

## Chapter III

## *Concerning the Works and Ministries of the Institute*

ARTICLE I

### Concerning ministries in general

*Concerning the special end and the works of the Institute in general*

275. Were the ministries proper to the Institute abandoned or neglected.

276. Were any works engaged in which are not contained in the special end of the Institute; if so, with what permission was this done.

*Concerning abuses in the exercise of ministries*

277. Were any abuses in the exercise of ministries introduced during this time; if so, what were they.

278. Is all appearance of avarice carefully avoided on the occasion of ministries.

279. Was begging from door to door, according to law (cc. 621, 622) and the Constitutions, done with the required permissions.

280. Moreover, in begging, were the rules of law (c. 623), the instructions of the Holy See (c. 624), and the norms of the Constitutions observed.

281. By reason of or under pretext of ministries, are an excessive or too worldly communication with seculars and frequent and prolonged absences from the religious house permitted.

282. What precautions are taken in this communication in order to avoid harm to the religious and scandal to seculars.

*Concerning difficulties with the secular clergy or with other Institutes, etc., because of the ministries*

283. On the occasion of the ministries did any friction occur with ecclesiastical Superiors, with pastors and the secular clergy, with other Institutes or with Chaplains. What were the chief instances of such difficulties and where did they occur.

284. What probable reasons can be assigned for these difficulties, and what remedies can be suggested for their avoidance.

ARTICLE II

## Concerning special ministries

*Concerning Missions among infidels and heretics*

285. In the Missions, or in any one of them, did the religious life suffer any harm, and if so, what were the reasons for this.

286. What safeguards were used or should have been used so that in the apostolate the faithful observance of religious discipline and the care of one's own sanctification be better secured.

287.* In the Missions, is the internal religious Superior distinct from the ecclesiastical Superior.

288.* Did this union of offices in the same person result in advantages or rather in disadvantages.

*Concerning Parishes, Churches, and Sanctuaries*

289.* For the incorporation or union of parishes, was an indult of the Holy See obtained, according to cc. 452, § 1; 1423, § 2, so that there should be a union or incorporation properly effected.

290.* In what form were Parishes united to the Institute: *pleno iure* (absolutely, at the will of the Holy See), *in temporalibus,* etc., and from what date. (A copy of the document should be sent if there is one.)

291.* Was an agreement made with the Ordinary of the place to accept any parish. (Send copies of the agreements made during the five-year period.)

292.* How do Superiors watch over and assist those of their subjects who are pastors (c. 631, §§ 1–2), and in case of need admonish and correct them.

293.* Was the office of local Superior ever united with that of pastor, observing c. 505; did this union give rise to difficulties, or was it on the contrary attended with good results.

294.* Did the Institute obtain from local Ordinaries that Churches or Sanctuaries should be entrusted to it; if so, with what permission and on what terms and conditions was this done.

295.* How do all Superiors see to it that religious discipline suffer no harm from the ministries engaged in by the religious in parishes or in public churches which are entrusted to them.

*Concerning Colleges, Schools, and Seminaries*

296.* Has the Institute entrusted to it any Seminaries of clerics, and if so, on what terms. (Documents and agreements entered into regarding this matter during the five-year period should be attached.)

297.* In these Seminaries, are there any difficulties with the Ordinaries, concerning either the religious life and discipline or the government of the Seminary.

298.* What measures and efforts are employed toward the sound and thorough training and religious education of the students.

299. Are there houses for the residence of young people who are attending public schools.

300. In these cases is very special care taken to see that the schools are safe from the standpoint of both instruction and education; especially is a careful supervision maintained over the instruction and religious education; and if there are any deficiencies are they carefully remedied.

301.† Are there schools which are attended by both sexes; as regards fixing the age beyond which boys may not be admitted or retained, have the prescriptions made by the Ordinaries been observed.

302. Do Superiors strictly see to it that Rectors, Prefects, Teachers, and Professors receive adequate preparation for their work:

*a*) Scientifically, by acquiring knowledge which corresponds adequately to the grade of the class, and by obtaining degrees and certificates, even such as are recognized outside ecclesiastical circles.

b) Pedagogically, by the study and practice of the art of teaching.

*c*) Spiritually, so that they may exercise the office of teaching with a genuine zeal for souls and make it a means of sanctification for themselves and others.

303. Do Superiors carefully see to it that the work of teaching be properly harmonized with religious discipline.

304. Did they promptly remove from the office of teaching those who in practicing it make light of the religious life and are not a good example to the students.

*Concerning the practice of the corporal works of mercy*

305. Does the Institute practice the corporal works of mercy toward the sick, orphans, the aged, etc.

306: Are there:

*a*) Guest houses and hospitals for persons indiscriminately, even for those of the other sex.

*b*) In this case, by what authority were these institutions accepted and what precautions are used to avoid dangers and suspicions.

307. What, if any, difficulties have arisen.

308. Do superiors diligently see to it that all persons who are to be engaged in various capacities in these institutions be competently prepared:

*a*) Scientifically, by obtaining even State certificates and other equivalent credentials.

*b*) Practically, by a suitable period of trial.

309. In the assistance and care of the sick and in the exercise of corporal charity, are the provisions of the Constitutions and

the norms which have been given in this matter by the Holy See and by the Ordinaries observed.

310.† Do the religious women who attend the sick in private houses faithfully observe the special provisions of the Constitutions; do they carefully take appropriate precautions to avoid dangers.

311. Do Superiors see to it that the bodily health of the religious who are engaged in these ministries be preserved by suitable food and sleep; that moral dangers be avoided; that the religious life and the exercise of charity be properly harmonized; that zeal be kept, both in fact and in appearance, free from any form of avarice or admixture of other human affection.

*Concerning the apostolate of the press*

312. Does the Institute exercise the apostolate by writing, publishing, or editing and distributing books and papers.

313. Were the publications submitted according to law to the previous censorship of the Major Superiors and Ordinaries of places (c. 1385, § 2).

314. Was the necessary permission of Superiors and Ordinaries of places obtained for publishing books treating of profane matters, and for cooperating in the production of papers, magazines, or reviews or editing them (c. 1386, § 1).

315. In the distribution and sale of books, is the appearance of excessive profit avoided, and are proper precautions used to avoid dangers.

*Concerning Catholic Action*

316. Do the religious strive to promote Catholic Action and to collaborate in it.

317. Have any difficulties arisen in this matter, either with the directors or with the secular clergy.

318. What remedies have been used to remove these difficulties, and what further remedies can be recommended.

*Concerning priestly ministrations — The celebration of the Holy Sacrifice, and Mass stipends and obligations*

319.* Do Superiors diligently see to it that the religious priests do not fail to prepare themselves by pious prayers for the Sacrifice of the Eucharist, that they celebrate worthily and devoutly, observing the rubrics faithfully and giving the proper amount of time to it; and that after the Mass they give thanks to God for so great a gift.

320. Whether each house has, according to cc. 843, § 1; 844, a book in which are marked in due order the number of Masses received, the intention, the stipend, and who has said the Mass and when.

321. How often and by what Superiors are the books of Masses of each house examined and signed.

322. Whether all the houses as regards the manual stipend of Masses observed the decrees of the local Ordinaries and the customs of the dioceses according to cc. 831, §§ 2–3, 832.

323. Whether in each of the houses the obligations of Masses, both perpetual and manual, were faithfully satisfied in due time according to cc. 834, 1517.

324. Were any special concessions made in this matter, either as regards the reduction of the stipends or intentions, or as to deferring the celebration of the Masses; if so, what were they.

325. In accepting the obligations of Masses, in collecting and in giving up or transmitting the intentions, and in fulfilling them, did Superiors conscientiously observe the provisions of law (cc. 835–840, 842), those of the Constitutions or Statutes, and the terms of the Foundations.

### *Concerning domestic services*

326.† Do the religious women perform any services in Seminaries, ecclesiastical residence-halls, Communities of clerics or of religious men, or in other Colleges or institutions destined for male students, or in parishes. How many such Seminaries, Colleges, etc., have they, and by what permission did they accept them?

327.† Were the prescribed precautions for avoiding all danger and difficulty faithfully observed.

328.† Was there any such difficulty to be deplored during this time, and what was done about it.

CONCLUSION

## A summary comparative judgment regarding the state of the Institute

*Concerning striving toward perfection*

329. What is to be said about the desire for and the actual striving toward evangelical perfection on the part of the members (cc. 487; 488, 1°).

330. In this respect is there in the Institute progress or retrogression as compared with the preceding five-year period, and how is this manifested or proved; what are the reasons for the progress or retrogression.

331. What has been done by Superiors during the five-year period to promote the tendency toward perfection and to prevent relaxation.

*Concerning the state of discipline*

332. What is to be said summarily about the observance of the vows and of the provisions of Canon Law, the Rule, and the Constitutions, both absolutely and in comparison with the preceding five-year period.

333. What are the points of religious discipline which are more easily and frequently violated.

334. What causes may be assigned for the progress in religious observance or for its decline.

335. What difference, if any, is there between the various Provinces or localities in regard to religious observance.

336. What has been done by Superiors to secure faithful and complete regular observance in every locality, Province, and house.

337. What are the difficulties and the chief obstacles which obstruct the work of Superiors and impede its effectiveness.

*Concerning the economic condition*

338. What, in itself and in comparison with the preceding five-year period, is the condition of the Institute and of its Provinces if there are any, with regard to capital and finances.

339. To what causes is the growth or diminution of capital and income to be attributed.

340. What are the plans of Superiors and what provisions are needed for the good of the Institute and its members.

*Concerning the special end and works*

341. In comparison with the preceding five-year period, was there an increase or diminution in the activity of the Institute in regard to its specific end. What are the reasons for the increase or diminution.

342. Were there any new means or works looking toward the attainment of the specific end introduced during the five-year period, and what concrete plans are entertained for the future.

Given at Rome, from the Sacred Congregation of Religious, the 9th day of December, 1948.

**Private**; S. C. Rel., 9 Dec., 1948.

NOTE: This document is immediately followed by a "Conspectus of the Condition of the Houses," also published by the S. C. Rel. and to be filled out with the Quinquennial Report, and by a "Concordance of the Three Questionnaires," which we reproduce with due permission from the *Review for Religious*.

*Name of the Institute (Society)* ..............................

*Diocese:*[2] ..............................

*Five-year Period:*[3] ...................... CONSPECTUS OF THE

| I | II | III |
|---|---|---|
| PROVINCE[4] | DIOCESE | HOUSE |
| | | |

[1] The annex is to be made out exactly like this model.

[2] In which the generalate house is located.

[3] The years are to be indicated so as to include in the five-year period both the first and the last years, e.g., 1949–53.

[4] The individual houses are to be listed according to Provinces or similar units (Vice-Provinces, etc.), and if there are no Provinces, then according to nations; in the Province or nation, the houses are to be listed according to the Diocese in which they are located, e.g., Province of the Holy Name of Jesus, or of Italy (col. I), Diocese of Bergamo (col. II), and then let the individual houses of this Diocese be listed (col. III).

[5] If the Institute has only one class of members, all are to be listed in the first column under each title.

[6] How many priests, whether of perpetual or temporary vows, even though they are included in the foregoing classifications.

[7] The various works are to be listed as briefly as possible.

ANNEX TO THE QUINQUENNIAL REPORT[1]

## CONDITION OF THE HOUSES

| IV MEMBERS[5] | | | | | | | V |
|---|---|---|---|---|---|---|---|
| Nov. | | Temp. vows | | Perp. vows | | Priests[6] | WORKS WHICH ARE PRACTICED[7] |
| 1 class | 2 class | 1 class | 2 class | 1 class | 2 class | | |
| | | | | | | | |

TOTALS
- *Provinces* ................
- *Vice-Provinces* ............
- *Houses* ..................
- *Members* ..................
  - *Priests* ..................
  - *Perp. vows* ..............
  - *Temp. vows* ..............
  - *Novices* ..................

## A CONCORDANCE OF THE THREE QUESTIONNAIRES (from the Review for Religious)

There are three editions of the *Elenchus Quaestionum:* 1. (P) for pontifical institutes — 342 questions; 2. (D) for diocesan institutes — 322 questions; 3. (M) for independent monasteries and houses — 171 questions. However, only one English translation has been made — that for pontifical institutes. Hence, it seems advisable to publish the following correlation of numbers so that those using questionnaire 2 or 3 may be co-ordinated with the one and only translation. See note p. 273.

| D | P | M | D | P | M | D | P | M | D | P | M | D | P | M | D | P | M | D | P | M |
|---|---|---|---|---|---|---|---|---|---|---|---|---|---|---|---|---|---|---|---|---|
| 1 | 1 | 1 | 36 | 48 | | 88 | 101 | 41 | 137 | 150 | | 187 | 201 | 113 | 231 | 251 | 144 | 281 | 301 | |
| 2 | 2 | 2 | 37 | 49 | | 89 | 102 | 42 | 138 | 151 | 77 | 188 | 202 | | 232 | 252 | 145 | 282 | 302 | |
| 3 | 3 | | 38 | 50 | | 90 | 103 | 43 | 139 | 152 | 78 | | 203 | 114 | 233 | | | 283 | 303 | |
| | | 3 | 39 | 51 | | 91 | 104 | 44 | 140 | 153 | 79 | | 204 | 115 | | 253 | 146 | 284 | 304 | |
| 4 | | | 40 | 52 | 19 | 92 | 105 | | 141 | 154 | 80 | | 205 | 116 | 234 | 254 | | 285 | 305 | |
| 5 | 4 | | 41 | 53 | 20 | 93 | 106 | 45 | 142 | 155 | 81 | 189 | 206 | 117 | 235 | 255 | 147 | 286 | 306 | |
| 6 | 5 | | 42 | 54 | 21 | 94 | 107 | 46 | 143 | 156 | 82 | 190 | 207 | 118 | 236 | 256 | | 287 | 307 | |
| 7 | 6 | | 43 | 55 | 22 | 95 | 108 | 47 | 144 | 157 | | 191 | 208 | 119 | 237 | 257 | | 288 | 308 | |
| 8 | 7 | | 44 | 56 | | | | 48 | 145 | 158 | | 192 | 209 | 120 | 238 | 258 | | 289 | 309 | |
| | 8 | | 45 | 57 | | 96 | 109 | 49 | 146 | 159 | | 193 | 210 | | 239 | 259 | 148 | 290 | 310 | |
| | 9 | | 46 | 58 | | 97 | 110 | | 147 | 160 | | 194 | 211 | 121 | 240 | 260 | 149 | 291 | 311 | |
| | 10 | | 47 | 59 | | 98 | 111 | | 148 | 161 | | 195 | 212 | | 241 | 261 | | 292 | 312 | |
| | 11 | | 48 | 60 | | 99 | 112 | | 149 | 162 | 83 | 196 | 213 | | 242 | 262 | 150 | 293 | 313 | |
| | 12 | | 49 | 61 | | 100 | 113 | | 150 | 163 | 84 | 197 | 214 | 122 | 243 | 263 | | 294 | 314 | |
| | 13 | | 50 | 62 | | 101 | 114 | 50 | 151 | 164 | | 198 | 215 | | 244 | 264 | | 295 | 315 | |
| | 14 | | 51 | 63 | | 102 | 115 | 51 | | | 85 | 199 | 216 | | 245 | 265 | 151 | 296 | 316 | |
| | 15 | | 52 | 64 | | 103 | 116 | 52 | 152 | 165 | 86 | | | 123 | 246 | 266 | 152 | 297 | 317 | |
| | 16 | | 53 | 65 | | 104 | 117 | | 153 | 166 | 87 | | | 124 | 247 | 267 | | 298 | 318 | |
| | 17 | | 54 | 66 | | 105 | 118 | | 154 | 167 | 88 | | | 125 | 248 | 268 | 153 | 299 | 319 | |
| | 18 | | 55 | 67 | | 106 | 119 | 53 | 155 | 168 | 89 | 200 | 217 | | 249 | 269 | | 300 | 320 | |
| | 19 | | 56 | 68 | | 107 | 120 | | 156 | 169 | 90 | 201 | 218 | | 250 | 270 | | 301 | 321 | 158 |
| 9 | | | 57 | 69 | 23 | 108 | 121 | 54 | 157 | 170 | 91 | 202 | 219 | 126 | 251 | 271 | | 302 | 322 | 159 |
| 10 | 20 | | 58 | 70 | | 109 | 122 | | 158 | 171 | 92 | 203 | 220 | | 252 | 272 | | 303 | 323 | 160 |

| | | | | | | | | | | | | | | | | | | | | |
|---|---|---|---|---|---|---|---|---|---|---|---|---|---|---|---|---|---|---|---|---|
| 11 | 21 | | 59 | 71 | | 110 | 123 | 55 | 159 | 172 | | 204 | 221 | | 253 | 273 | | 304 | 324 | |
| 12 | | | 60 | 72 | 24 | 111 | 124 | 56 | 160 | 173 | | 205 | 222 | 127 | 254 | 274 | | 305 | 325 | |
| 13 | 22 | 4 | 61 | 73 | 25 | 112 | 125 | 57 | 161 | 174 | | 206 | 223 | 128 | 255 | 275 | | 306 | 326 | |
| 14 | 23 | 4c | 62 | 74 | 26 | 113 | 126 | 58 | 162 | 175 | | 207 | 224 | 128 | 256 | 276 | | 307 | 327 | |
| | | 5 | 63 | 75 | 27 | 114 | 127 | 59 | 163 | 176 | | 208 | 225 | 129 | | | 154 | 308 | 328 | |
| | | 6 | 64 | 76 | 28 | 115 | 128 | 60 | 164 | 177 | 93 | 209 | 226 | 130 | 257 | 277 | | | | 162 |
| 15 | 24 | 7a | 65 | 77 | 29 | 116 | 129 | 61 | 165 | 178 | 94 | 210 | 227 | 131 | 258 | 278 | | 309 | 329 | 163 |
| 16 | 25 | | 66 | 78 | | 117 | 130 | | 166 | 179 | 95 | 211 | 228 | | 259 | 279 | 155 | 310 | 330 | 164 |
| 17 | 26 | 8 | 67 | 79 | 30 | 118 | 131 | | 167 | 180 | 96 | 212 | 229 | | 260 | 280 | 156 | 311 | 331 | 165 |
| 18 | 27 | 9 | 68 | 80 | | 119 | 132 | 62 | 168 | 181 | 97 | 213 | 230 | | 261 | 281 | | 312 | 332 | 166 |
| 19 | 28 | 10 | 69 | 81 | | 120 | 133 | 63 | 169 | 182 | | 214 | 231 | | 262 | 282 | 157 | 313 | 333 | 167 |
| 20 | 29 | 11 | 70 | 82 | 31 | 121 | 134 | | 170 | 183 | 98 | 215 | 232 | | 263 | 283 | | 314 | 334 | 168 |
| | 30 | | 71 | 83 | | 122 | 135 | 64 | | 184 | | 216 | 233 | | 264 | 284 | | 315 | 335 | |
| | 31 | | | | 32 | 123 | 136 | | 171 | 185 | 99 | 217 | 234 | | 265 | 285 | | 316 | 336 | 169 |
| 21 | 32 | | 72 | 84 | 33 | | | 65 | 172 | 186 | | 218 | 235 | | 266 | 286 | | 317 | 337 | |
| 22 | 33 | | 73 | 85 | 34 | | | 66 | 173 | 187 | 100 | 219 | 236 | 132 | 267 | 287 | | 318 | 338 | 170 |
| | 34 | | 74 | 86 | 35 | 124 | 137 | | 174 | 188 | 101 | 220 | 237 | 133 | 268 | 288 | | 319 | 339 | 171 |
| 23 | 35 | | 75 | 87 | 36 | 125 | 138 | | 175 | 189 | 102 | 221 | 238 | 134 | 269 | 289 | | 320 | 340 | |
| 24 | 36 | | 76 | 88 | 37 | 126 | 139 | 67 | 176 | 190 | 103 | 222 | 239 | | 270 | 290 | | 321 | 341 | |
| 25 | 37 | | 77 | 89 | 38 | | | 68 | 177 | 191 | 104 | 223 | 240 | | 271 | 291 | | 322 | 342 | |
| 26 | 38 | 12 | 78 | 90 | | 127 | 140 | 69 | 178 | 192 | 105 | | 241 | 135 | 272 | 292 | | | | |
| 27 | 39 | 13 | 79 | 91 | 39 | 128 | 141 | 70 | 179 | 193 | 106 | | 242 | 136 | 273 | 293 | | | | |
| 28 | 40 | | 80 | 92 | | 129 | 142 | 71 | 180 | 194 | 107 | 224 | 243 | 137 | 274 | 294 | | | | |
| 29 | 41 | | 81 | 93 | | | | 72 | 181 | 195 | 108 | 225 | 244 | 138 | 275 | 295 | | | | |
| 30 | 42 | 14 | 82 | 94 | | 130 | 143 | | 182 | 196 | | | 245 | | 276 | 296 | | | | |
| 31 | 43 | 15 | 83 | 95 | 40 | 131 | 144 | | 183 | 197 | 109 | 226 | 246 | 139 | 277 | 297 | | | | |
| 32 | 44 | 16 | 84 | 96 | | 132 | 145 | | 184 | 198 | 110 | 227 | 247 | 140 | 278 | 298 | | | | |
| | | 17 | | 97 | | 133 | 146 | 73 | 185 | 199 | 111 | 228 | 248 | 141 | 279 | 299 | | | | |
| 33 | 45 | | 85 | 98 | | 134 | 147 | 74 | 186 | 200 | 112 | 229 | 249 | 142 | 280 | 300 | | | | |
| 34 | 46 | | 86 | 99 | | 135 | 148 | 75 | | | | 230 | 250 | | | | | | | |
| 35 | 47 | | 87 | 100 | | 136 | 149 | | | | | | | | | | | | | |

## Special Questions Not Included in the Questionnaire for Papal Institutes

### For Diocesan Institutes

4. Supposing all the requisite conditions, has a petition been sent to the Holy See, or is it intended to send one, to obtain the status of a Papal Congregation? Are any difficulties foreseen, or were there any actually? Enumerate them.

9. Is the Congregation perchance divided into provinces: how long ago, how many, and by what authority?

233. Same as 253 for Papal, except at the end which reads: ". . . before the decree on judgment had been *confirmed by the local Ordinary*" (c. 650, § 2, 1°; 652, § 1).

### For Independent Monasteries and Houses (Sui Iuris)

3. What is the juridical nature of the monastery or house:
*a*) To which Order does it belong, if any, and which Rule is followed?
*b*) Are the vows solemn or simple; or simple, though solemn normally (c. 488, 7°)?

5. Are there any filial houses subject to the independent monastery or house? How many?

6. Does the monastery depend on the local Ordinary or on the Regular Superior?

17. Has the canonical visitation of the local Ordinary taken place, as well as that of the Regular Superior, if the monastery is subject to him?

32. Is there an appointed chaplain, or have other provisions been made sufficient for the spiritual good by sacred functions? Are there any difficulties with regard to the spiritual good?

48. Are there any difficulties of an economic nature, and what are they?

65. How are the economic needs of the monastery provided for: by the labor of the community or by alms?

66. What, if any, activity does the community engage in for its own support?

72. Is the condition of the extern Sisters regulated according

to the statutes promulgated by the S. Congregation on July 16, 1931?

85. How many novices are there at present?

123. What kind of cloister is observed? Are the places subject to cloister clearly marked and sufficiently guarded? Are the prescriptions of the law and of the constitutions regarding cloister faithfully observed (cc. 598–604)?

124. Were the cases of dispensation from the law of cloister frequent, either for going out, or for going in? Which were the principal ones?

125. Are difficulties experienced in the observance of cloister, especially when nuns are engaged in the works of the apostolate, of education, etc.?

154. What works are carried on in the house (apostolate, education, manual labor for pay)?

162. Is the independent monastery or house fully self-sufficient: with regard to the personnel to fill the various offices of government and of personal activity? And with regard to the religious formation, as well as with regard to economic means, so that regular observance can flourish fully?

NOTE: An English translation of the complete questionnaire for diocesan institutes is published as an appendix in Creusen-Ellis: *Religious Men and Women in Church Law,* 6th English ed., pp. 296–333 (Milwaukee: Bruce, 1958), and for independent monasteries and houses in *Review for Religious,* 13 (1954)–251–269.

**How to Fill in the Annual Report** (S. C. Rel., Circular Letter, 9 Feb., 1950) **Private.**

To the Reverend Superiors General:

On the 9th of July, 1947, the Holy Father deigned to approve the Decree *Cum Transactis* of the S. C. Rel. concerning the new formula of the Questionnaire to which all the Religious of pontifical or diocesan right must answer in the *Quinquennial Report.*

This decree was published in the *Acta Apostolicae Sedis,* Vol. 40 (1948), pp. 378–381, and was annexed to the new formulary, now ready for distribution at the Archives of the Sacred Congregation.[1]

In the same decree (n. IX) an *Annual Report* for statistical

[1] The decree is reported in this volume on p. 223.

purposes was also required to be filled according to the questions which the Sacred Congregation was to send later. These questions have been printed and will be sent to every Religious Order, although those who have houses or representatives in Rome may secure them directly by applying to the Archives of the Sacred Congregation.

In order to help in preparing the answers to these questions, this Sacred Congregation thinks it opportune to give the following directions:

I. In filling the Quinquennial Report, according to the instructions prefixed to the Questionnaire, it is not necessary to include the question in the answer, but it is sufficient to put before the answer the number of the question.

The time when the Quinquennial Report must be sent back is substantially the same as that established since 1922 and reproduced in the Decree annexed at the foot of the Questionnaire.

II. The Annual Report is especially required for statistical purposes, and therefore it must be of the greatest possible precision and up to date as of the 31st of December of the year preceding the one in which the report is sent.

According to the Decree, the Annual Report is independent of the Quinquennial Report, and of the questions which it contains. It has its own questions and inquiries.

Contrary to what is done for the answers to the questions of the Quinquennial Report, the Annual Report must be made on the very forms received, and these must be returned directly to the Sacred Congregation by the Superior General of every Religious Order.

The questions do not apply to all Religious in the same way; every Religious Order must answer according to its own activities, filling in the pages which refer directly to its own scope of action.

The languages to be used may be those of the Quinquennial Report, e.g., Latin for clerical Religious; French, English, Italian, Portuguese, Spanish, and German for lay Religious.

The period of time to be included in the Annual Report must extend from the 1st of January to the 31st of December; at the top, on the right of the forms, where the year is required, the year to which the data of the Report refer must be inserted, not the year in which the Report is sent.

The partial totals of the various divisions of the statistical data, houses, personnel, works, must be added up and forwarded, showing clearly by means of a line the grand total.

The Annual Report must be sent within the first three months of the year following the one to which the data refer: for example, the data of the year 1950 must be sent during the first three months, January–March, 1951.

The obligation of sending in the reports begins in 1951 during the first three months of which year must be sent the information relating to the year 1950 brought to date as of December 31st of the said year.

In order to insure uniformity of presentation, it would be advisable to mind the following directions in filling the respective forms:

**Cover:** At the word *Dioecesis* should be written the name of the present Diocese and also that of the former if the Curia Generalizia or Mother House has been transferred of late.

**Inside Cover:** All the required information must be entered in the synoptical form.

**Question I:** At the word *fondatore* (founder), must be written in parentheses the dates of the birth and death of the founder.

**Question II:** At the words *Status domorum I,* all Religious must answer, those who are divided into provinces as well as the others. It must be noticed that it is not necessary to give the complete list of all the houses of every nation, but only the total number. This is the reason that there is only one line for each nation, and the four blanks are always filled with regard to the total number of houses of the nation.

The order of nations should be the alphabetical order of the language used in the report. Then all the nations should be arranged according to the five parts of the world in alphabetical order as follows: Africa, America, Asia, Europe, Oceania.

The word *Domus* is understood as a house canonically erected, whether it be "formed" (at least six professed members) or not; but, if in the same building there are several sections or communities, as for example the Curia, the Novitiate, and so on, such building should be considered as only one house or one *"domus."*

**Question III:** At the words *Status domorum II* should answer only the Religious Orders which are divided into provinces, meaning by provinces those parts regularly divided by the Order or

Institute according to the norms of Canon Law, even if those parts bear other names such as Inspectorate, etc., provided the Major Superiors be truly Major Superiors. The provinces should include also the quasi-provinces regularly established. The divisions which constitute a separate unit, but which have been made only by the immediate Major Superiors, are not to be included with the provinces.

Here again, in the compiling of this form, only the grand total is required.

The order of the provinces follows the alphabetical order of their denomination in the Congregation, arranging them according to the nations where are the greater number of provinces, and always in the alphabetical order of the nations and of the parts of the world.

Under the words *ambitus territorialis* must be indicated briefly the nation or part of nations or countries, etc., where every province extends.

**Questions IV and V:** In these forms also, only the aggregate number of persons in the province or nation is required. The words *primae classis* indicate a division of the community in the sense that in the clerical religious Orders, the first class is that of priests, the second that of the lay brothers or members; in the lay religious congregations, the first class is that of Religious known as such, the second that of the serving religious. The Religious who have only one class of members fill in only the space under *primae classis*.

For the registration of the members according to the various nations or provinces or houses, the norms of the Institute must be followed. The nationality does not matter if no account of it is taken in the official registration of the Institute.

The word *novices* applies only to those religious who according to the Constitutions of the Institute or Order may so be called canonically.

**Question VI:** This form is compulsory only for the Religious who are divided into provinces; it is enough for the others to have filled the foregoing papers.

**Question VII:** In this form again, only the aggregate numbers are required. The form is divided into two parts:

First part: *cura infirmorum* with four horizontal divisions: the word *quot* requires the total number of the works indicated by the horizontal divisions, while the words *religiosi addicti* require the total number of the Religious employed in such works.

Second part: *Asyla,* with three spaces, in which, under the word *quot* is asked the number of works, and under the word *degentes,* the total number of sick or assisted, while *quaenam* requires the kind of persons assisted, giving also other informations that might be useful.

In this enumeration, the alphabetical number of nations must be followed as aforesaid.

**Question VIII:** This form is only for clerical Religious. It requires the aggregate number by nations and provinces.

**Question IX:** This form deals only with Religious who have schools for outsiders, that is, those who are not aspirants to the Order itself. The word *domus* in this form means college, school, etc., and it is required to state how many colleges are owned by the Religious, and how many are not, but which are either used, directed, or employed by the members of the Order; moreover, all kinds of colleges or schools, etc., are to be counted, even though they may not be recognized by the State.

If in one building there are different types of teaching, primary, intermediate, superior, and professional, these are considered as different and as many colleges, schools, etc. Therefore in the report must enter the total number of schools or colleges of the different types, primary, intermediate, superior, or professional, of every nation, arranged in alphabetical order as said before.

The title *scholae professionales* carries under two different blanks; if there are more than two classes of schools, they must be reduced to two common divisions or classes, one being *"Arti e mestieri:* technical," and the other "Commercial, Normal, etc."

If it is difficult to classify any particular school, it must be entered into one of the above classes and after the number an explanation may be given in parentheses.

The word *media* refers to types of schools such as ginnasio liceo, baccalaureato, mittelschule Gymnasium, High School, Humanités anciennes et modernes, etc.

The word *elementaria* refers to lower studies, and *superiora* to superior studies of the university type.

**Question X:** The words *gradus interni* may refer to all the degrees of the Order itself; it is sufficient to mention them in the vertical spaces.

In the space *gradus facult. et Institut. civilium* must be inserted all the degrees obtained, even if there are degrees which are not of the university type, such as diplomas, certificates, etc.

In the mention of the members who have academic degrees, the total number of the members who obtained degrees before the 31st of December of the year for which the report is made should also be specified. The total number of the members of the Order who have obtained degrees or diplomas at any time before must be inserted in parentheses under the number during the year being reported.

**(Private)**; S. C. Rel., Circular Letter, 9 Feb., 1950. English translation made by the Sacred Congregation of Religious and officially printed and published.

For an explanation of the Annual Report, cf. *Review for Religious,* 9 (1950)–309 (Ellis).

---

**Annual Report No Longer Required.** Although no official abrogation has been or is expected to be made to this effect, we are informed by a reliable source at Rome that the fact is that the Sacred Congregation for Religious no longer requires the annual statistical report.[1] The Sacred Congregation will accept such reports but actually prefers not to receive them and is no longer giving out forms for this report. *No change* has been made regarding the prescriptions on the *quinquennial report.*[2]

## CANON 512

**Visitation of Monastic Nuns by Ordinary** (Cod. Com., 24 Nov., 1920) **AAS 12–575.**

The Code Commission was asked:

Whether according to c. 512, § 2, 1°, and 513, § 1, it is the duty of the Ordinary of the place to visit every fifth year the monasteries of nuns who are subject to regulars (even exempt) in regard to those things which concern the law of inclosure, in the manner which is provided in c. 513.

**Reply.** In the affirmative.

**AAS 12–575;** Cod. Com., 24 Nov., 1920.
*Periodica,* 10 (1922)–252 (Vermeersch); *J.P.,* 3 (1923)–117.

---

[1] See above p. 227, IX. [2] See above p. 223–273.

## CANON 514

### Canon 514 Applies to Professed and Novices Even Outside the House, But Subject to Rights of Pastor (Cod. Com., 16 June, 1931) AAS 23–353.

The Code Commission was asked:

Whether c. 514, § 1, is to be understood in the sense that, in a clerical religious institute, Superiors have the right and duty of administering to all the persons mentioned in that canon Eucharistic Viaticum and extreme unction when they are ill outside the religious house.

**Reply.** In the affirmative as regards professed religious and novices, but without prejudice to the prescription of c. 848; otherwise in the negative.

**AAS 23–353**; Cod. Com., 16 June, 1931.
*Periodica,* 21 (1932)–38 (Vermeersch).

## CANON 517

### Men's Religious Congregations of Pontifical Law to Have General Procurator at Rome (S. C. Rel., 4 June, 1920) AAS 12–301.

The Sacred Congregation of Religious gives notice to the Generals of Congregations of men of pontifical law, who have not yet named a General Procurator to conduct the business of the institute with the Holy See, that by virtue of c. 517, § 1, of the Code, every religious institute of men, of pontifical law, is obliged to depute a Procurator General to conduct the aforesaid business, and he should be chosen from the membership of the institute itself. To the end that he may be able to fulfill the duties assigned to him, the Procurator General should, in accordance with existing practice, have his habitual residence in Rome.

**AAS 12–301**; S. C. Rel., Notice, 4 June, 1920.
*Periodica,* 10 (1922)–198 (Vermeersch).

## CANON 518

**Prefects of Studies and Spiritual Directors Held by This Canon If They Are Also Quasi-Superiors** (Cod. Com., 29 Sept., 1918) **Private.**

The Code Commission declared that prefects of studies and spiritual directors, though not true superiors, if the clerical students are immediately subject to them, "must observe can. 518, § 2 if the students in any way form a section separate from the community."

(**Private**); Cod. Com., 29 Sept., 1918; reported in a book review in *Theologisch-praktische Quartalschrift* (Linz) 74 (1921)–439.

NOTE: No further information is given regarding this reply. Cf. Schaefer: *De Religiosis*, ed. 4, n. 620.

## CANON 520

**Ordinary Confessor to be Appointed** even where community numbers less than six Private replies to this effect are as follows:

10 Jan., 1920, to Archbishop of Prague. Cf. *Archiv für Katholisches Kirchenrecht,* 100 (1920)–47.

16 Jan., 1921, to Bishop of Luxemburg. Cf. *Linz Quartalschrift,* 74 (1921)–631.

18 Jan., 1921, to Bishop of Osnabruck. Cf. *Archiv K. KR.*, 101 (1921)–61.

Cf. Creusen-Ellis, *Religious Men and Women in Church Law,* n. 92 (The Bruce Publishing Company, Milwaukee).

## CANON 522

**Place Legitimately Destined for Confessions of Women** (Cod. Com., 24 Nov., 1920) **AAS 12–575.**

The Code Commission was asked:

Whether the words of c. 522: *confessio in qualibet ecclesia vel oratorio etiam semi-publico peracta, valida et licita est,* are to be understood in the sense that a confession outside of those places is not only illicit but also invalid?

**Reply.** Canon 522 is to be understood in the sense that the confessions which religious women make for their peace of conscience to a confessor approved by the Ordinary of the place for the confessions of women, are licit and valid, provided they be made in a church or in an oratory, even semipublic, or in a place which is *legitimately* destined for the confessions of women.

**AAS 12–575;** Cod. Com., 24 Nov., 1920.
*Periodica,* 10 (1922)–254 (Vermeersch); J.P., 3 (1923)–118.

NOTE: A Reply, not officially published, given by the President of the Commission to the Ordinary of Luxemburg, 16 Jan., 1921, makes it clear that the above Reply means that the confession is invalid if heard outside of the places designated. Cf. *Linz Quartalschrift,* 74 (1921)–631.

## How May a Religious Avail Herself of the Privilege of Going to Confession to Any Priest Approved for the Confessions of Women? (S. C. Rel., 1 Dec., 1921) Private.

The Sacred Congregation of Religious was asked on behalf of the Bishop of Osnabruck:

How should religious women conduct themselves when they are living in their own community and desire for their peace of conscience without the knowledge of their Superior, to go to a confessor who is approved by the Ordinary of the place for the confessions of women?

**Reply.** The Secretary of the Sacred Congregation replied:

To the question proposed, the Sacred Congregation deemed that it ought not to reply, since it involves practical cases which can be solved according to the opinions of theologians. However, I deem it proper to communicate to Your Amplitude the opinion of the Reverend Consultor who, when asked about the matter, gave it as his opinion that the reply should be as follows: Canon 522 allows a religious woman to take advantage of any opportunity she may have of going for her peace of conscience to any confessor who is approved for women, and that even without the knowledge of her Superior. The canon, however, does not in any way oblige either the Superior or the Ordinary to give the religious such an opportunity. Much less does it require any change in the discipline of the cloister or in the constitutions. As regards the question asked, I think the answer should be: let such religious women wait for an occasion which will enable them to go to the confessor without violating any rule as regards leaving the cloister: and let them bear it patiently if no such occasion is offered.

(**Private**); Letter of Secretary of S. C. Rel., 1 Dec., 1921. Cf. *Archiv. K. KR.,* 84 (1904)–102; also Creusen-Ellis, *Religious Men and Women in Church Law,* n. 121, note 40 (Bruce, Milwaukee).

## Requirements As to Place Affect Validity of Confession: Interpretation of Word *Adeat* (Cod. Com., 28 Dec., 1927) AAS 20–61.

The Code Commission was asked:

I. Whether the confession of religious women outside the places mentioned in c. 522 and the Reply of 4 Nov., 1920,[1] is only illicit or also invalid.

**Reply.** In the negative to the first part in the affirmative to the second.

II. Whether the word *adeat* of c. 522 is so to be understood that the confessor cannot be called by the religious herself to a place which is legitimately destined for the confessions of women or of religious women.

**Reply.** In the negative.

**AAS 20–61**; Cod. Com., 28 Dec., 1927, I.
*Periodica,* 17 (1928)–38 (Vermeersch); *J.P.,* 8 (1928)–3.

## Place Legitimately Destined: Interpretation (Cod. Com., 12 Feb., 1935) AAS 27–92.

The Code Commission was asked:

Whether the words, *loco legitime destinato,* which were the subject of the interpretation of canon 522 given on 24 Nov., 1920,[2] are to be understood only of a place habitually designated, or also of a place designated by way of act, or chosen in accordance with canon 910, § 1.

**Reply.** In the negative to the first part; in the affirmative to the second.

**AAS 27–92**; Cod. Com., 12 Feb., 1935.

---

[1] See above, p. 280. The date given in the present document is evidently a mistake for 24 Nov., 1920.

[2] AAS 12–575; reported above on p. 280.

*Periodica,* 24 (1935)–95; *Irish Ecclesiastical Record,* 45 (1935)–533 (Browne); *Jus Pontificium,* 15 (1935)–82; *Clergy Review,* 9 (1935)–528 (Bentley); *Amer. Eccles. Review,* 92 (1935)–506.

## CANON 526

**Ordinary Confessor:** Appointed for as many as five terms. See **c. 329,** AAS 56–5, *Motu proprio, Pastorale munus,* n. 33; reported above on p. 72.

## CANON 534

**Formalities Required for Alienation of Property or Contracting of Debt** (Apostolic Delegate, Letter, 13 Nov., 1936) **Private.**

A Letter addressed by the Apostolic Delegation at Washington to all religious Superiors in the United States, on Nov. 13, 1936, contains the following provisions.

The Sacred Congregation for Religious has considered for some time the necessity of formulating certain definite rules to assist religious Superiors in their grave and difficult obligations in the administration of temporalities.

The Sacred Congregation feels bound to recall all religious Superiors to:

1. An exact compliance with all the requirements of the Canon Law concerning the administration of temporal goods;

2. Greater prudence in every financial transaction.

To this end, the Sacred Congregation has authorized me to address a communication to all the religious Superiors in the United States in order to bring to their attention again *the obligation which they have in conscience* of fully carrying out the prescriptions of canon 534, § 1, of the Code of Canon Law. And this obligation *extends to all religious* including regulars and other exempt religious.

Canon 534, § 1, prescribes that an apostolic indult is required *under pain of nullity of the contract,* for:

1. Alienation of precious articles;

2. Alienation of goods which exceed the value of six thousand dollars;

3. For contracting debts or obligations beyond the sum of six thousand dollars.

In regard to other alienations of property which include the incurring of debts or the assuming of obligations for sums smaller than six thousand dollars, the Canon Law provides for certain formalities which should be scrupulously observed.

These required formalities are:

1. A favorable vote by secret ballot by the proper Council or Chapter, and further,

2. The written permission of the competent Superior or Superiors.

I

A proper and exact observance of canon 534, § 1, and canon 1533 requires compliance with the formalities prescribed for so-called alienations. The term *alienation* includes not only purchases or transfers of property, but includes as well any contract, debt, or obligation. The Canon Law regards all transactions, which may render the financial condition of the Institute, Province, or religious house less secure, as alienations.

The Sacred Congregation calls special attention to two systems of collecting funds or money which have become more widespread in this country in recent years. These two systems are (1) the issuance of bonds or debentures upon ecclesiastical property and the sale of such bonds or debentures in the public market or to private investors, and (2) the system of soliciting or accepting funds under the so-called annuity agreement providing for payments of an annuity to the donor for life. *Both of these systems of obtaining money fall within the provisions of canon 534.* For under both systems the moral religious person, who issues the bonds or debentures or accepts the funds under an annuity agreement, undertakes economic obligations which must be met at a certain time. Consequently both the issuance of bonds or debentures and the acceptance of annuities are governed by the provisions of canon 534. The conclusion is clear that any attempt by a religious Province, or religious house, to issue bonds or debentures or to accept annuities involving a sum exceeding six thousand dollars would be both *unlawful and invalid* if made without a papal indult. This is true in all cases where the sums of money accruing from one or both systems or from the combination of several operations either at the same time or at different times accumulate in a sum greater than the sum of six thousand dollars.

## II

The aforesaid sum of six thousand dollars should be understood, in connection with the terms of the Code, as the equivalent of "thirty thousand lire or francs" and in reference to the value of currency based upon gold in distinction to other currencies, gold coin being the true unit of value. In this connection the value is based upon such stable gold content and rate of exchange.

## III

An apostolic indult is required not only in the event of a single transaction exceeding the sum of six thousand dollars, but an apostolic indult is necessary in every case where a coalescence of the debts or obligations of every kind and nature exceeds the said sum of six thousand dollars. For example:

1. If after having contracted a loan of four thousand dollars, an occasion arises for borrowing a further sum of more than two thousand dollars before payment of the first has been made by the religious — since the total of the financial obligations will exceed six thousand dollars after the second borrowing, it is necessary to have the permission of the Holy See before incurring the second loan.

2. If a community undertakes several issues of bonds or debentures, each issue being within the limit permitted by the Canon Law, but the total of the issues aggregating a sum exceeding six thousand dollars, then an apostolic indult must be obtained.

3. In the event that a community desires to obtain money by means of *annuities* or life pensions, there will be no need of recourse to the Holy See for a sum up to six thousand dollars; but where the sums aggregate a sum exceeding six thousand dollars, then the community cannot receive any further funds through such annuities without an apostolic indult.

4. When the amount of *existing* debts or obligations totals four thousand dollars and it is proposed to increase such total indebtedness to more than six thousand dollars, then an apostolic indult is necessary. And such permission is required whether the

proposed increase in indebtedness is by contract, mortgage, bond or debenture issue, or any other form which will bring the actual or contingent obligation to a *total sum* of more than six thousand dollars.

5. When the total *present indebtedness* is over six thousand dollars, an apostolic indult is required for any contract, debt, or other obligation, even if such new indebtedness is incurred for the purpose of complete or partial payment of the pre-existing debts or obligations.

## IV

The petition which must be presented to the Holy See, according to the provision of canon 534, for permission and authorization to incur such obligations, must contain *definite and clear statements of the following facts:*

1. The *reason* for contracting the debt or assuming the obligation.

2. The *nature* of the debt or obligation. A mere general statement does not comply with the requirements for an explicit declaration of intention. For example, a mere statement that permission for a loan is required does not satisfy the requirements if an intention exists to issue bonds or debentures.

3. The *name* of the person, firm, or corporation with whom the debt or obligation is to be contracted.

*Moreover, the Sacred Congregation requires the following additional information:*

4. The proposed terms of meeting the debt or obligation. This requires a detailed and truthful statement of the arrangements for extinguishing such obligations both as to the interest requirements and the principal debt. This requirement demands a statement of the time contemplated for complete payment. In this regard, attention is called to canon 536, § 5, which warns Superiors not to allow the contracting of debts unless it be certain that the *interest* on them may be met from *current revenue* and that *within a reasonable time* the *capital* may be paid off by means of a lawful amortization fund. For example:

*a*) Loans — the plan of amortization must be presented.

*b*) Annuities — the amounts, the plan of investing the funds and interest arrangement, and plans for meeting annual payment, etc., must be stated in detail.

5. The *economic condition* of the petitioner, which must be illustrated by the following exhibits:

*a*) A balance sheet of current assets and liabilities. The value of each asset ought to be stated at the current price, not at the purchase or nominal price; e.g., bonds should be listed at the current quotation on the exchange; real estate should be listed according to the tax assessment, depreciation, income, etc.

*b*) A statement of receipts and expenditures over a sufficient period of time to give an accurate estimate of normal receipts and expenditures.

*c*) A separate list of the obligations which do not appear under (*a*); e.g., obligations as guarantor, surety, trustee, bondsman, etc. This information is required in order to estimate all the certain or contingent obligations of the petitioner, particularly with reference to the rule regarding coalescence, supra, n. III.

If the petitioner fails to declare in the petition the debts and obligations which actually encumber the Institute, Province, or religious house for which the indult or permission is sought, *canon 534, § 2, of the Code of Canon Law declares the apostolic indult or the permission of the Superior null and void.*

V

In order to avoid the serious inconveniences and evils when religious Institutes imprudently contract obligations under annuity agreements and later are not in a position to satisfy the annuity requirements, it is strictly and formally forbidden to use all or any part of the capital annuity fund which should remain intact as long as the annuitant is living.

(**Private**); Apostolic Delegation, Letter, 13 Nov., 1936.

NOTE: The publication of this important document in this form was authorized by His Excellency, the Most Reverend Amleto G. Cicognani, Archbishop of Laodicea, Apostolic Delegate to the United States, in a letter addressed to us on December 13, 1937.

**Bond Issues and Annuity Contracts** (Apostolic Delegation, U. S., 15 Feb., 1956; S. C. Rel., 1955) **Private.**

With a Circular Letter of 15 Feb., 1956, the Apostolic Delegation of the U. S. sent the local Ordinaries some replies of the

Sacred Congregation of Religious. The two documents are as follows:

I. *Letter of the Apostolic Delegation*

15 February, 1956

Your Excellency:

Occasionally inquiries have been directed to the Sacred Congregation of Religious to ascertain whether the norms set down in my circular letter of November 13, 1936 (N. 173/35), were still in effect.

The Sacred Dicastery has now graciously deigned to answer this question and certain others regarding financial transactions that have arisen.

I am enclosing a copy of the statement with the hope that, in furtherance of the desires of the Sacred Congregation for Religious, Your Excellency will bring it to the attention of the religious in your diocese.

With cordial regards and best wishes, I remain,

Sincerely yours in Christ,
Amleto G. Cicognani,
Archbishop of Laodicea,
Apostolic Delegate

II. *Replies of the Sacred Congregation of Religious*

Sacred Congregation of Religious Prot. N. 8743/55

**Questions**

1. Is the Circular Letter of the Apostolic Delegation of the United States of North America, of 13 November, 1936, N. 173/35 regarding the issuance of bonds and the establishment of permanent incomes or "annuities," still in effect?

2. If the reply to question 1 is in the affirmative, how is the amount of 30,000 francs of canon 534 to be computed? That is, should it be computed according to the equivalence stated in that Letter, namely \$6,000, or rather according to the declaration of the Sacred Consistorial Congregation of 18 October, 1952, and that of the Sacred Congregation of Religious of 29 January, 1953, that is, \$5,000?

3. Is the permission of the Holy See required whenever the

total amount which is the object of the "annuities" contract exceeds the value of 30,000 francs, or rather whenever the sum to be paid annually by the moral person to the benefactor exceeds the value of 30,000 francs?

## Replies

1. In the affirmative.

2. In the negative to the first part, in the affirmative to the second.

3. In the affirmative to the first part, in the negative to the second, *et ad mentem*. The mind is:

a. In case of the non-fulfillment of their obligation according to law on the part of the religious, the creditor or benefactor has the right, to the exclusion of any clause to the contrary, to demand the rescission of the contract and the repayment of the entire sum.

b. The obligation of the religious — in the absence of a clause to the contrary — does not extend beyond the amount received; that is to say: the sum of all the returns that are to be paid even for many years, unless there is an express agreement to the contrary, shall never exceed the amount they have received from the creditor.

**(Private)**; Letter of Apostolic Delegate, U. S., 15 Feb., 1956; and replies of the S. C. Rel., N. 8743/55.

Annotations in *The Jurist*, 22 (1962)–205–207 (Frison).

NOTE: We have reproduced the Letter and translated the Replies directly from copies which were kindly sent to us by the Most Reverend Amleto G. Cicognani, Apostolic Delegate to the United States, with permission to publish them in the CANON LAW DIGEST.

The letter of 13 Nov., 1936, immediately precedes this document. The declaration of the S. Consistorial Congregation is reported in CANON LAW DIGEST, 4, p. 391 and that of the S. C. Rel in v. 4, p. 203. However, this latter document has since been replaced by the later document which follows.

### Alienations and Debts: New Temporary Limit-Values for Religious (S. C. Rel., 30 June, 1962) Private.

Notification:

Because the value of money has frequently changed owing to

the peculiar conditions of these times, the Sacred Congregation of Religious has thought it well to bring into line with new necessities the norm according to which institutes of the states of perfection must have recourse to the Holy See in the transactions mentioned in canon 534 of the Code of Canon Law, when the value exceeds a certain definite sum.

Accordingly, after mature consideration and after having obtained the approval of His Holiness in the Audience of 22 January, 1962, this Sacred Congregation has decreed that, until a different provision is made, an Apostolic indult must always be obtained in making alienations or in contracting debts or obligations, when the amount exceeds the sums listed below, observing also the other prescriptions of the said canon 534.

| | | |
|---|---|---|
| 1. AUSTRIA | (Schillings) | 400,000 |
| 2. BELGIUM | (Belgian Francs) | 800,000 |
| 3. DENMARK | (Kroner) | 110,000 |
| 4. ENGLAND | (Pounds Sterling) | 5,500 |
| 5. FRANCE | (N.F.) | 75,000 |
| 6. GERMANY | (DM) | 60,000 |
| 7. HOLLAND | (Gulden, Florins) | 55,000 |
| 8. ITALY | (Lire) | 9,000,000 |
| 9. NORWAY | (Kroner) | 110,000 |
| 10. PORTUGAL | (Escudos) | 450,000 |
| 11. SPAIN | (Pesetas) | 900,000 |
| 12. SWEDEN | (Kroner) | 80,000 |
| 13. SWITZERLAND | (Swiss Francs) | 65,000 |
| 14. UNITED STATES, all countries of America, and all countries not mentioned in this list | (U. S. Dollars) | 15,000 |

Rome, 30 June, 1962.

**(Private)**; S. C. Rel., Notification, 30 June, 1962. Not published in the AAS, but sent to Superiors of all institutes of the states of perfection.

---

**Faculty of U. S. Apostolic Delegate to Permit Alienations,** etc., by religious in its latest renewal has been changed so that the maximum amount he now has faculties for is $300,000 in *paper* money. Therefore, the faculty as reported in CANON LAW DIGEST, 3, p. 368 and 4, p. 206, no longer obtains. Personal letter, N. 189/42, 29 March, 1960, and 8 April, 1960, kindly sent us. The above faculty has been renewed without any change of wording and is valid until 12 March, 1965. (Personal letters 184/50, 2 Oct., 1962 and 189/42, 15 Jan., 1963, kindly sent us.)

**New Limit-Values in Terms of Swiss Francs.** See below, p. 618; **c. 1532,** AAS 55–656.

**Permission of Local Ordinary** for alienations and debts. See **c. 329,** AAS 56–5, *Motu proprio, Pastorale munus,* n. 32; reported above on p. 72.

## CANON 535

### Monastery of Nuns to Give Account of Administration to Ordinary (Cod. Com., 24 Nov., 1920) AAS 12–575.

The Code Commission was asked:

Whether by virtue of c. 535, § 1, 1°, if a monastery of nuns is subject to a regular Superior (even exempt), the account of the administration is to be given to the regular Superior and also to the Ordinary of the place.

**Reply.** In the affirmative.

**AAS 12–575**; Cod. Com., 24 Nov., 1920.
*Periodica,* 10 (1922)–249 (Vermeersch); *J.P.,* 3 (1923)–119.

## CANON 538

**Careful Selection and Training of Candidates** for the state of perfection: Instruction on. See below, pp. 464–498: S. C. Rel., 2 Feb., 1961.

## CANON 542

### Words *Qui Sectae Acatholicae Adhaeserunt* Interpreted (Cod. Com., 16 Oct., 1919) AAS 11–477.

The Code Commission was asked:

Whether the words: *qui sectae acatholicae adhaeserunt,* of c. 542 are to be understood as applying to those who, moved by the grace of God, came into the Church from the heresy or schism in which they were born, or rather to those who fell away from the faith and joined a non-Catholic sect.

**Reply.** In the negative to the first part; in the affirmative to the second.

**AAS 11–477**; Cod. Com., 16 Oct., 1919, n. 7.
*Periodica,* 10 (1922)–103 (Vermeersch); *J.P.,* 3 (1923)–66.

**Admission of Orientals Into Novitiate of Latin Rite** (Cod. Com., 10 Nov., 1925) **AAS 17–583.**

The Code Commission was asked:

Whether Orientals who, without changing their rite, are being prepared to establish religious houses and provinces of the Oriental rite, may licitly be admitted to the noviceship in religious institutions of the Latin rite, without the permission mentioned in c. 542, 2°.

**Reply.** In the affirmative.

**AAS 17–583**; Cod. Com., 10 Nov., 1925, VI.
*Periodica,* 14 (1926)–184 (Vermeersch); *J.P.,* 6 (1926)–81.

**Joint Decree Does Not Concern Seminarian Who Transfers Directly from Seminary to Religious Institute** (S. C. Rel., 11 May, 1942) **Private.**

The Sacred Congregation of Religious was asked by the General of the Society of Jesus:

Whether the word *egressi* in the joint decree of the S. C. Rel. and the S. C. Sem. et Univ., of 25 July, 1941[1] includes also seminarians who wish to pass from a seminary to our Society.

**Reply:** The Decree of the Sacred Congregations of Religious and of Seminaries does not concern those who leave a seminary or college in order to embrace a life of perfection in some religious Institute, as sufficient provision is made for them in canon 544, § 3.

(**Private**); S. C. Rel., N. 5230/40, 11 May, 1942. *Periodica* 32 (1943)–172 (Creusen); *Commentarium pro Religiosis,* 23 (1942)–238.

---

**Adherence to Non-Catholic Sect:** Dispensation by local Ordinary for admission to religion. See **c. 329**, AAS 56–5, *Motu proprio, Pastorale munus,* n. 35.

**Illegitimacy:** Dispensation by local Ordinary for admission to religion. See **c. 329**, AAS 56–5, *Motu proprio, Pastorale munus,* n. 36.

**No special recourse has to be made** to the Sacred Congregation for Religious for admission of an ex-seminarian into religious life. This is brought out by a report of the Procurator General of a certain religious institute: "The decree of the two S. C. of Religious and Sem. of July

[1] AAS 33–371, reported below on p. 578.

25, 1941 [reported in CANON LAW DIGEST, 2, p. 426], *is a complete dead letter as far as entering religion is concerned.* It remains in effect as regards an ex-religious entering a seminary. I learned this incidentally while discussing a current case. . . . The young man had been refused major Orders in the seminary and left; only later did he get the idea of joining [the religious institute]. So it was clearly a case where consultation of the S. C. of Religious before admitting him was required by the decree. Accordingly we made the required consultation and were awaiting a reply. The reply will be that 'in casu' nothing more is needed than the observance of the common law (canon 544, 3). So there is and will be nothing official to show that the decree is simply inoperative; but that is the fact, as I was clearly assured. So if any cases of the kind are referred to you, you can simply tell the Provincials to forget the decree entirely."

## CANON 544

### Testimonial Letters from the Ordinary: When Not Required (Cod. Com., 28 July, 1918) Private.

For boys coming from their "minor novitiate," the Brothers of Christian Schools do not need testimonial letters from the Ordinary, for the time during which the boys were in that house.

(**Private**); Cod. Com., 28 July, 1918. Not reported in the AAS. See Vermeersch-Creusen, *Epitome Juris Canonici,* Vol. I, n. 649.

## CANON 545

### Testimonial Letter: Refusal to Swear (Reply, S. C. Rel., 21 Nov., 1919) AAS 12–17.

The Sacred Congregation of Religious was asked:

What is to be done in case the religious Superior or the rector of a college or seminary refuses to confirm by oath, as provided in c. 545, § 1, the testimonial letters requested by the Superior of another institute for the admission of a postulant in accordance with c. 544, § 3?

**Reply.** The prescription of the canons is to be observed; and the Ordinary, if there is question of institutes of diocesan law, or of lay institutes, or of colleges or seminaries; or, in clerical institutes or regular Orders, the Supreme Moderator shall proceed against such recalcitrant Superiors, compelling them, even by penalties not excluding privation from office. If, notwithstanding, sworn letters cannot be secured, the matter should be referred to the Sacred Congregation.

**AAS 12–17**; S. C. Rel., Reply, 21 Nov., 1919.
*Periodicia,* 10 (1922)–194 (Vermeersch).

## CANON 547

**Dowry**: Dispensation by local Ordinary. See **c. 329,** AAS 56–5, *Motu proprio, Pastorale munus,* n. 37; reported above on pp. 72–73.

## CANON 551

### If Dowry Insufficient, Charitable Subsidy Must Be Given to Departing Religious (S. C. Rel., 2 Mar., 1924) AAS 16–165.

The Sacred Congregation of Religious was asked:

Whether a religious institute in which the dowry does not amount to as much as the reasonably estimated charitable subsidy (cf. c. 643), is relieved of all obligation toward the departing religious by the mere restitution of the dowry, or whether, on the contrary, the institute is bound to supply the amount which is wanting to make up a fitting charitable subsidy according to c. 643, § 2.

**Reply.** In the negative to the first part; in the affirmative to the second, *facto verbo cum Sanctissimo.*

**AAS 16–165**; S. C. Rel., 2 Mar., 1924.
*Periodica,* 13 (1925)–69 (Vermeersch); *J.P.,* 4 (1924)–73.

## CANON 552

### *Exploratio Voluntatis* to Be Without Tax (S. C. Rel, 20 Mar., 1922) AAS 14–352.

The Sacred Congregation of Religious was asked:

Whether a custom which was more than one hundred years old in a certain diocese, whereby a charge was made for the work of questioning candidates for the profession in institutes of sisters, as to the freedom of their choice, could be sustained.

**Reply.** In the negative.

Approved by His Holiness, Pius XI, 20 March, 1922.

**AAS 14–352**; S. C. Rel., 20 Mar., 1922.
*Periodica*, 11 (1923)–79 (Vermeersch).

## CANON 555

**Year of Noviceship: How Computed** (Cod. Com., 12 Nov., 1922) **AAS 14–661.**

The Code Commission was asked:

1. Whether the full year of noviceship prescribed in c. 555, § 1, 2°, is to be computed according to the rule given in c. 34, § 3, 3°.

**Reply.** In the affirmative, i.e., the prescription of c. 34, § 3, 3° is to be observed.

2. Whether that way of computing the year for the noviceship is necessary for its validity or only for its licitness.

**Reply.** In the affirmative to the first part; in the negative to the second; that is, the canon is to be observed for the validity of the noviceship.

**AAS 14–661**; Cod. Com., 12 Nov., 1922.
*Periodica*, 11 (1923)–184 (Vermeersch); *J.P.*, 2 (1922)–128.

**Transfer of Canonical Year to Second Year of Noviceship: Dispensation from Second Year** (Cod. Com., 12 Feb., 1935) **AAS 27–92.**

The Code Commission was asked:

I. Whether an apostolic indult is required in order that the canonical year of noviceship mentioned in canon 555, § 1, n. 2, may be transferred to the second year of noviceship according to § 2 of the same canon.

**Reply.** In the affirmative.

II. Whether the Ordinary of the place can dispense from the second year of noviceship, if in the constitutions that year is not required for the validity of the religious profession, according to canon 555, § 2.

**Reply.** In the affirmative, provided there is question of religious institutes of diocesan law.

**AAS 27–92**; Cod. Com., 12 Feb., 1935.

*Periodica,* 24 (1935)–95; *Irish Ecclesiastical Record,* 45 (1935)–534 (Browne); *Jus Pontificium,* 15 (1935)–83; *Commentarium pro Religiosis,* 16 (1935)–371 (Maroto); *Clergy Review,* 9 (1935)–529 (Bentley); *Amer. Eccles. Review,* 92 (1935)–506.

## CANON 556

### Noviceship Interrupted by Absence of More Than Thirty Days, Even Occasioned by Transfer to Another Novitiate (Cod. Com., 13 July, 1930) AAS 22–365.

The Code Commission was asked:

Whether the words *quacumque ex causa* of c. 556, § 1, include also the transfer to another house of noviceship, which is mentioned in § 4 of the same canon.

**Reply.** In the affirmative.

**AAS 22–365;** Cod. Com., 13 July, 1930.
*Periodica,* 19 (1930)–343; *J.P.,* 10 (1930)–231.

NOTE: Vermeersch observes that since this Reply explains a law which was really doubtful, it is effective under c. 17 only from the date of its promulgation, and is not retroactive.

## CANON 559

**School for Mistresses of Novices:** Established in Rome under the name *"Mater Divinae Gratiae."* S. C. Rel., Decree, 15 March, 1957 (AAS 49–749).

## CANON 564

### Religious Training of Lay Brothers (Letter, Pius XI, 19 Mar., 1924) AAS 16–133.

In an Apostolic Letter addressed to the Superiors General of religious Orders and societies of men, His Holiness, Pius XI, speaks with great respect of the religious vocation of lay brothers, and expresses a tender solicitude that they be provided throughout their religious life with suitable spiritual helps and safeguards.

**AAS 16–133;** Pius XI, Apostolic Letter, 19 Mar., 1924.
*Periodica,* 13 (1925)–14 (Vermeersch).

# CANON 565

**Instruction on Second Year of Noviceship** (S. C. Rel., 3 Nov., 1921) **AAS 13–539.**

There are a number of religious institutes in which the constitutions prescribe a second year of noviceship, and permit Superiors to employ the novices during that time in the works of the institute. Lest the religious formation of the novices suffer from this practice, and in order to forestall abuses which might arise, this Sacred Congregation, taking advantage of the revision of the constitutions of the various religious institutes according to the Code, has studied this matter very carefully, and at the plenary session of 17 June, 1921, delivered an opinion thereon which was reported to His Holiness, Benedict XV, in the audience of 25 June, 1921.

His Holiness approved the opinion, and ordered that an Instruction be issued which all religious congregations which have by their constitutions a second year of noviceship should be bound to observe in its entirety.

I. Whenever the constitutions prescribe a second year of noviceship and allow the novices during the second year to be employed in works proper to the institute, this is allowed, without prejudice to the fundamental laws of the noviceship. It must be remembered, therefore, that the noviceship is instituted to train the souls of the novices in regard to the extirpation of evil ways, the restraint of the passions, the acquisition of virtues, and the practice of the regular life, through study of the constitutions; so that they may learn to make progress toward Christian perfection by the profession of the evangelical counsels and the vows, which progress constitutes the end of every religious. And it is quite right that a noviceship of more than one year should be prescribed in certain institutes, especially among those whose members are employed in exterior works, since these, distracted by various responsibilities and more endangered by the assaults of the world, need a more solid and firm foundation in spirit. Wherefore this Sacred Congregation orders that even during the second year of noviceship the discipline of the spiritual life be attended to above all else.

II. It is lawful, however, during the second year, that the

novice (male or female) be employed in works of the institute if the constitutions allow it. This should be done, however, with prudence and moderation, purely for the instruction of the novices; nor should they ever be so employed in these works that they perform them alone (for example, taking the place of absent teachers or instructors in schools, or ministering to the sick in hospitals), but they should be engaged in the work under the direction and supervision of an older religious man or woman, who should instruct them and show them the way.

III. If it is ever permitted by the constitutions that a novice during the second year be sent out of the house to do work of the institute, this should be only by way of exception and provided some grave reason require it. The reason should have reference to the novice; for example, that they cannot be sufficiently trained in the house, or that for some other reason they cannot remain there; but never under any pretext will the necessity or advantage of the religious institute itself be a sufficient cause, as, for example, if the novices were to be substituted for the regular members in the work of the institute, because of scarcity of workers.

IV. But whether the novices remain in the house or out of it, they must for two months before their vows be withdrawn from all exterior works, and if they have been out of the novitiate, be recalled to it, so that for two months before their profession they may prepare for it by strengthening themselves in the spirit of their vocation.

V. His Holiness, Benedict XV, in the audience of 3 Nov., 1921, approved this Instruction and ordered that it be observed by all concerned.

**AAS 13–539**; S. C. Rel., Instruction, 3 Nov., 1921.
*Periodica,* 10 (1922)–365 (Vermeersch).

## CANON 567

**Novices: Suffrages Same As for Professed** (Cod. Com., 16 Oct., 1919) **AAS 11–477.**

The Code Commission was asked:

Whether according to c. 567, § 1, and c. 578, 1°, novices and the professed of temporary vows, in case they die, have a right to the same suffrages as the professed of solemn vows or the professed of simple perpetual vows, even though the constitutions formerly approved by the Holy See provide otherwise.

**Reply.** In the affirmative, *et ad mentem:* the mind is: religious Orders and Congregations can prescribe suitable and equal suffrages for all novices, temporary professed, and professed of solemn vows or of simple perpetual vows, in their constitutions, which are to be amended and submitted to this Sacred Congregation for approval, according to the Decree of the same Sacred Congregation, of 26 June, 1918.[1]

**AAS 11–477**; Cod. Com., 16 Oct., 1919, n. 8.
*Periodica,* 10 (1922)–103 (Vermeersch); *J.P.,* 3 (1923)–67.

# CANON 569

## Will to Be Made by Novice in Congregation Even Though Invalid in Civil Law (Code Commission) Private.

The Code Commission gave the following reply to the question proposed by the Superior General of the Redemptorists:

The will mentioned in canon 569, § 3, is to be made, even though it is invalid by civil law, and also if the novice has no present property but only may acquire it in future. . . . But care should be taken that as soon as it can be done the will be made valid according to civil law, without however changing any of its dispositions except in accordance with canon 583, § 2.

**(Private)**; Code Commission. Quoted by Hannan, *The Canon Law of Wills,* p. 218. Many authors cite the document, but none whom we have found give its date, nor is the date given in *Theologisch-praktische Quartalschrift,* 73 (1920)–343, the source usually cited. Vermeersch (*Epit.* I. C., ed. 6, Vol. II, n. 716, p. 514, note 1) states that there have been several private replies of the Holy See to this effect.

## Words *Nisi Constitutiones Aliud Ferant* Interpreted (Cod. Com., 16 Oct., 1919) AAS 11–478.

The Code Commission was asked:

Whether the words of c. 569, § 1, *nisi constitutiones aliud ferant* refer to the word *libere,* so that it is allowed to deter-

[1] AAS 10–290; reported above on p. 178.

mine by the constitutions the end for which novices may dispose of the use and usufruct of their property.

**Reply.** The constitutions which were approved before the promulgation of the Code are to be observed, whether they deprive novices of the right to dispose of the use and usufruct of their property, or whether they restrict or define that right.

**AAS 11–478**; Cod. Com., 16 Oct., 1919, n. 9.
*Periodica,* 10 (1922)–103 (Vermeersch); *J.P.,* 3 (1923)–68.

## Will of Novice: Must Be Made Valid According to Civil Law (S. C. Rel., 26 March, 1957) Private.

The Sacred Congregation of Religious was asked by the General of the Congregation of the Brothers of the Sacred Heart of Jesus:

**Question:** Whether the professed who made their wills while they were of minor age are obliged to sign them again once they have attained majority.

**Reply:** *Ad mentem:* The mind is: according to the practice of this Sacred Congregation of Religious, the will mentioned in canon 569, § 3 should be made valid according to civil law, without prejudice to canon 1513. But if a will which is valid according to civil law cannot be made before profession, or if it must be deferred for some grave cause, then, after profession when civil capacity has been attained or the excusing cause has ceased, it should be made civilly valid as soon as possible, and in that case no permission of the Holy See is required and the freedom of the testator is in no way restricted.

**(Private)**; S. C. Rel., 26 March, 1957, Prot. N. 13101/56; reported in *Commentarium pro Religiosis,* 37 (1958)–56, with commentary by **Gutiérrez.**

NOTE: The entire commentary is decidedly worthy of study. Some salient points:

1. This reply, though private in form, is virtually general, expressing as it does the practice of the Sacred Congregation, which is an important formative source of ecclesiastical law. A formally public declaration in this sense seems desirable.

2. According to this reply and practice, with the exception of wills to pious causes, the will which is prescribed by canon 569, § 3 is a will *valid according to civil law,* and none other. If a novice is capable

of making such a will and is not excused by some relatively grave cause, he is obliged to do so; otherwise, he has no present obligation to make a will. But he must do so as soon as possible after he has attained civil capacity or the excusing cause has ceased.

3. Except as regards bequests to a pious cause, the will, if invalid in civil law, is equally invalid in canon law. If the testator dies leaving only such a will he dies intestate even in the eyes of the Church, except as provided in canon 1513.

4. *"Firmo canone 1513."* A will *in favor of a pious cause,* even though not valid according to civil law, is valid in canon law and binding in conscience. Hence in such a case, if a novice cannot make a civilly valid will, he is nevertheless bound to make a will. He will thus satisfy the prescription of canon 569, § 3 and will also be obliged after attaining civil capacity to make a will that is valid in civil law.

5. In making a will which is valid in civil law, "no permission of the Holy See is required and the freedom of the testator is in no way restricted." This means that without any further permission and even after his profession he can make a will freely, even though it be substantially different from the one previously made which was invalid in civil law.

6. Gutiérrez reports an *earlier private reply of* the Commission of Interpretation on this subject (23 March, 1919; given to the Congregation of the Holy Redeemer and published in *Theol. Prakt. Quartalschrift,* 73, 1920, pp. 336–347) which was as follows:

**Question:** Whether novices before their triennial profession are bound to make a will according to canon 569, § 3, even though it be invalid according to civil law because of their age.

**Reply:** In the affirmative; but when the novices attain the age which according to the respective civil laws is legitimate or valid for making a will, they must change the date stated in the will, or make it safe in a form which is valid in civil law.

This is obviously the same reply which is reported in a somewhat different form in the first document under this canon, without date because the date was not then available. Gutiérrez states that the last words of this reply as commonly reported, namely "without however changing any of the dispositions of the will except in accordance with canon 583, § 2," are not those of the Commission, but were added to the reply by reporters and commentators. In any event, these words are clearly in conflict with the reply and practice of the S. C. of Religious.

**Permission of the Holy See Not Required to Rewrite, Change, and Render Will Valid According to Civil Law** (S. C. Rel., 1 Mar., 1958) **Private.**

The Sacred Congregation for Religious was asked:

a) Without prejudice to canons 1513 and 1529, are novices obliged, at least when the constitutions of the congregation so prescribe, to make a will according to the prescription of can. 569, § 3 if said novices according to the civil law of their country lack the legal capacity to make a will?

b) Do they satisfy at least the prescription of can. 569, § 3 by such a will?

c) Are novices who make a will according to the prescription of can. 569, § 3 but whose will is civilly invalid because of defect of the age required by the laws of the country, obliged to confirm or rewrite the will later when they have attained the age required by civil law? Moreover, in the case presented, can they change the will without further permission, notwithstanding the prescription of can. 583, 2°?

The following answer was given:

In your letter to this Sacred Congregation you ask if professed religious who made their will while under age civilly, are obliged to rewrite it as soon as they have attained adult age. This Sacred Congregation replies:

*According to its mind.* Its mind is: according to the practice of the Sacred Congregation for Religious, the will mentioned in can. 569, § 3 must be valid according to the norm of civil law, without prejudice to canon 1513. However, if a will cannot be validly made according to the norm of civil law or if for a serious cause the writing of the will must be deferred, then when civil capacity is acquired or when the excusing cause ceases, a will, valid civilly, is to be drawn up as soon as possible after profession and, in the instance, no permission of the Holy See is required nor is there any restriction on the liberty of the testator.

**(Private)**; S. C. Rel., 1 Mar., 1958, Prot. No. 16710/58; reported in *Palestra del Clero,* 37 (1958)–747.

NOTE: In connection with the above questions, see first document under this canon as well as notes to document immediately preceding above document.

## CANON 572

**Rite of Profession** (Reply, S. C. Rel., 10 July, 1919) **AAS 11–323.**

The Sacred Congregation of Religious was asked:

Whether the replies of the Sacred Congregation of Bishops and Regulars, of 18 July, 1902, I, and 15 Jan., 1903, I and II, regarding the manner in which the simple and solemn profession of monastic nuns should be made after the Decree, *Perpensis,* of 2 May, 1902, are still in effect since the Code has introduced the temporary vows which must precede the solemn vows.

**Reply.** After mature consideration, the Sacred Congregation replied: In the negative, *et ad mentem:* the mind of the Sacred Congregation is that all the rites and ceremonies which relate to the perpetual nature of the religious state should be reserved to the solemn profession; for the temporary profession it is sufficient that it be received by the legitimate Superior according to the constitutions, either personally or through another, according to c. 572, § 1, 6°.

**AAS 11–323**; S. C. Rel., Reply, 10 July, 1919.
*Periodicia,* 10 (1922)–72 (Vermeersch).

NOTE: The official report refers to the canon as c. 577, § 1, 6°; but that is obviously a misprint for c. 572, as reported above.

**Religious Profession: Bishop Named in Formula of Profession is Empowered to Receive: Papal *Clausura*** (Cod. Com., 1 Mar., 1921) **AAS 13–177.**

The Code Commission was asked:

Whereas in the constitutions of certain Congregations of religious women of pontifical law, no mention is made of the Superioress but only of the Bishop or his delegate, in the formula of profession, it is asked:

1. Whether the Bishop or his delegate is to be regarded as the legitimate Superior according to the constitutions for receiving the profession, according to c. 572, § 1, 6°.

**Reply.** In the affirmative, as having a legitimate mandate.

2. Whether monastic nuns whose vows, though according to

their institute they should be solemn, are nevertheless only simple in certain places by order of the Holy See, are bound by the law of papal *clausura* under cc. 597–600.

**Reply.** In the negative, by reason of an apostolic indult which is still in effect.

AAS 13–177; Cod. Com., 1 Mar., 1921, III.
*Periodica,* 10 (1922)–325 (Vermeersch); *J.P.,* 3 (1923)–128.

**Religious Profession at the Point of Death Still Permitted to Novices** (Reply and Decree, S. C. Rel., 30 Dec., 1922) **AAS 15–156.**

Since the Code makes no mention of religious profession at the point of death, the question was asked of the S. C. Rel.: Whether the Decree of S. C. Rel. *Spirituali consolationi,* of 10 Sept., 1912, is still in effect.

**Reply.** In the affirmative, and with the approval of the Holy Father let it be announced that the faculty of receiving the profession spoken of in n. 2 of the said Decree be understood to belong not only to the Superior of the monastery or house of noviceship or probation, but also to the respective major Superiors according to the constitutions, and to persons delegated by them.

At the same time the S. C. Rel. issued a revised statement of the said Decree, of which the following is the tenor:

In every Order, Congregation, or religious society, or monastery of men or women, or even in institutes in which, although vows are not pronounced, life is common after the manner of religious, it shall hereafter be lawful to admit to the profession, or consecration, or promise, according to their own rules or constitutions, although they have not yet filled out the time of their noviceship or probation, novices or probationers who in the doctor's opinion are so gravely ill that they are considered to be at the point of death.

Nevertheless, in order that novices or probationers may be admitted to the aforesaid profession, or consecration, or promise, it is required:

1. That they shall have canonically begun their noviceship or probation.

2. That the Superior who receives the novice or probationer

to the profession, or consecration, or promise, may be not only the respective major Superior to whom this function belongs by the constitutions, but also the one who is actually Superior of the monastery or house of noviceship or probation, as well as the delegate of the aforesaid Superiors.

3. That the formula of profession, or consecration, or promise, should be the same which is in use in the institute outside the case of illness; and the vows, if they be pronounced, should be without determination of time or perpetuity.

4. That one who has made such a profession, consecration, or promise, shall share in all the indulgences, suffrages, and graces which really professed religious in the same institute receive; and also receive a plenary indulgence and forgiveness of all his sins, mercifully granted in the Lord in the jubilee form.

5. That this profession, or consecration, or promise shall have no effect other than to confer the graces mentioned in the preceding article. Hence:

A. If the novice or probationer, after such a profession, consecration, or promise, shall die intestate, the institute will not be able to claim for itself any of the property or rights which belonged to him.

B. If he recovers from his illness before the expiration of the time required for his noviceship or probation, he shall be in exactly the same condition as if he had made no profession. Accordingly: (*a*) he may freely return to the world if he wishes; (*b*) Superiors can dismiss him if they wish; (*c*) he must fill out the entire time prescribed for the noviceship or probation in each institute, even if it be more than a year; (*d*) at the expiration of this time, if he persevere, a new profession, or consecration, or promise, must be made.

Finally, the Sacred Congregation declares that there is no objection to inserting the above provisions in constitutions of Orders and Congregations, if desired.

**AAS 15–156**; S. C. Rel., Reply and Decree, 30 Dec., 1922.
*Periodica,* 12 (1924)–41 (Vermeersch).

---

**Religious Profession**: Preferably to be made within the Mass; rite to be revised. See **c. 2**; AAS 56–97, Constitution on the Sacred Liturgy, n. 80; reported above on p. 22.

## CANON 573

### These Canons Supplant Earlier Decree Even as Regards Lay Brothers Who Took Simple Vows Before the Code (S. C. Rel., 6 Oct., 1919) AAS 11–420.

The Sacred Congregation of Religious was asked:

Whether, in Orders of regulars, lay religious who already before the Code went into effect, had taken simple vows in accordance with the Decree, *Sacrosancta Dei Ecclesia,* of 1 Jan., 1911,[1] should pronounce their solemn vows in accordance with the prescriptions of that Decree, namely, six years after their simple vows and after completing thirty years of age or in accordance with canons 573 and 574 of the Code, namely, three years after their simple vows and after having completed twenty-one years of age.

**Reply.** In the negative to the first part; in the affirmative to the second.

**AAS 11–420;** S.C. Rel., Reply, 6 Oct., 1919.
*Periodica,* 10 (1922)–73 (Vermeersch).

## CANON 574

### Vows "As Long as I Live in the Congregation," Not Regarded as Perpetual (Cod. Com., 1 Mar., 1921) AAS 13–177.

The Code Commission was asked:

In certain institutes of simple vows, the vows are pronounced with the following or a similar condition: "as long as I shall live in the Congregation"; so that if the person leaves of his own accord or is dismissed by the Superior, he is *ipso facto* free from his vows. It is therefore asked:

1. In such institutes, should this profession be preceded by three years of temporary vows according to c. 574?

**Reply.** In the negative.

2. Is the dismissal of members who have made such a profession governed by canons 647–648, relating to the dismissal of religious who have made temporary vows, or by c. 649 and the

[1] See AAS 3–29.

following canons, relating to the dismissal of those who have made perpetual vows?

**Reply.** In regard to those who have already made vows under the aforesaid condition, canons 646, 647, and 648 should be observed.

**AAS 13–177**; Cod. Com., 1 Mar., 1921.
*Periodica,* 10 (1922)–325 (Vermeersch); *J.P.,* 3 (1923)–126.

## Religious Under Temporary Vows Becomes Incurably Insane: Status of Person and Duties of Institute (S. C. Rel., *Dubium,* 5 Feb., 1925) AAS 17–107.

Since it sometimes happens that a religious man or woman, during the three years of vows which, according to c. 574, must precede every perpetual or solemn profession, becomes insane, so that at the end of the three years, being still out of his mind, he cannot be admitted to the profession since he is incapable of such an act, the question has been raised what is to be done in such a case.

As the matter is of some practical importance, the Sacred Congregation, after taking counsel of several consultors, presented the following questions for decision to the Eminent Fathers:

**Questions.** I. Whether one who is professed of the simple vows in an Order or Congregation, and who during the three years loses his mind, even incurably according to the judgment of physicians, can at the end of three years be sent back to his relatives or into the world, or whether he must be kept in the religious institute. And if he must be kept:

II. What is the juridical condition of such a religious, and what are the obligations of the religious institute in the matter?

The S. C. Rel. in full session, on the 28 Nov., 1924, after mature consideration, replied:

**Reply.** I. In the negative to the first part; in the affirmative to the second.

II. The religious in question belongs to the religious institute in the state in which he was when he lost his mind, and the institute has the same obligations toward him that it had at that time.

Approved by His Holiness, Pius XI, in the audience of 30 Nov., 1924.

**AAS 17–107**; S. C. Rel., *Dubium,* 5 Feb., 1925.
*Periodica,* 14 (1926)–34; *J.P.,* 5 (1925)–5.

## Exclaustration of Religious Clerics of Solemn Vows During Military Service (S. C. Rel., 14 April, 1939) Private.

The Minister General of the Friars Minor asked the Sacred Congregation for Religious:

**Question.** Whether also in the case of clerics professed of solemn vows, who are called upon for military service, the solemn vows are suspended during their military service, as the temporary vows are suspended under these circumstances, according to the decree *Inter reliquas* and later declarations about it.

**Reply.** Major Superiors, especially in the places in question, are given the faculty to provide in individual cases of this kind, while the necessity of military service continues and during such service, by granting an indult of exclaustration, as far as possible according to canon 639.

**(Private)**; S. C. Rel., 14 April, 1939: See *Acta Ordinis Fratrum Minorum,* 1939, p. 158. Cf. *Commentarium pro Religiosis,* 20 (1939)–213.

## Obligation of Religious Order of Women to Support Sister of Perpetual Simple Vows Who Becomes Incurably Insane: Not Limited to Income of Dowry (Rota, 25 March, 1957) Private.

**The Facts:** A Sister belonging to a contemplative Order was in due course admitted to perpetual profession (of simple vows, in virtue of the apostolic indult then in effect in France). Afterward she began to show signs of mental disorder and was treated in various hospitals, until eventually becoming entirely insane, she was received in a mental hospital conducted by a Congregation of hospital Sisters. This hospital was selected by her family, with the consent of the Superiors of the contemplative Order to which she belonged. Before her mental disturbances became acute, while still in perfect possession of her faculties, she had foreseen that the treatment would be expensive, and in order to spare the expense to the Order, she arranged with the administrator of her estate (which was considerable), that these expenses should be paid from her estate. Her Superiors knew of this arrangement, but were not party to it. Accordingly for several years the administrator paid the expenses from the Sister's estate, with a slight contribution from the contemplative Order, taken from the income of her dowry. After 1940, however, the depreciation of values made it impossible to meet the expenses from the income of the Sister's estate, and the administrator, unwilling to deplete the capital, paid nothing, while the Order continued to pay the small amount from the income of the dowry.

This suit was brought by the hospital Sisters against the contemplative Order, demanding payment in full for the board and care of the Sister, which the hospital had provided for ten years (1940–1950). The defendants contended that they were not liable beyond the income of the dowry.

Neglecting the procedural steps which brought the case to the Rota, we concern ourselves only with the substance of the decision.

**The Law:** 1. The effect of religious profession, solemn or simple, perpetual or temporary, is to make the individual a true member of the religious family, with the rights and duties which pertain to that state (Wernz-Vidal, *Ius Canonicum,* III, n. 325). Fundamental among these is the right of the person to receive from the institute the necessities of life, lodging, food, clothing, care in illness. Illness, physical or mental, though it deprive the person of the capacity to render any external service, is not a reason for dismissal, nor does it deprive him of the right to receive these necessities from the institute. If he is committed by the institute or with its consent to any external agency to receive such care, the institute is still responsible. The Sacred Congregation of Religious gave a reply to this effect in the case of a religious who became insane while under temporary vows.[1] *A pari,* or *a fortiori,* it holds for perpetual profession.

2. The obligations of the institute to the subject are therefore based on religious profession, and not on the payment of a dowry. The dowry is not required in all institutes of women; it is an accessory, not an essential of religious profession. Although it is intended to provide income for the support of the

[1] 5 Feb., 1925; AAS 17–107; reported above on p. 307.

subject, the obligations of the institute are not measured by the amount of such income.

3. The defendants rely on the fact that the hospital was chosen by the Sister's relatives. That is true, but it was with the consent of the institute and therefore it does not diminish their responsibility. The defendants further contend that their consent was given because they knew of the arrangement between the Sister and her administrator that the expenses were to be paid from her estate. But this agreement cannot affect the case, because the defendant institute was not a party to it.

**Decision:** In favor of the plaintiff.

**(Private)**; Rota, 25 March, 1957; *Monitor Ecclesiasticus,* 82 (1957)–417 to 426.

---

**Religious of the Sacred Heart:** Temporary vows not required. See private reply of Code Commission mentioned by Vermeersch, *Epitome,* I, ed. 1937, p. 522, and Schaefer, *De Religiosis,* ed. 1940, p. 585. The date of this declaration is not given.

**Society of Jesus;** Temporary vows not required. See Code Com., 29 June, 1918; reported by Schaefer, *De Religiosis,* ed. 1940, p. 585, note 96, from Biederlack-Führich, *De Religiosis,* 1919, n. 94, note 4.

## CANON 576

**Profession or Renewal of Vows in Mass:** The Superioress General of a Congregation of Sisters asked the S. C. of Rites for permission to have the ceremony of profession or renewal of vows at the Offertory of the Mass, instead of before Mass as prescribed in the Ceremonial approved for the Institute. Reply, 8 July, 1950 (N. C. 112/50): *Negative* (*Monitor Ecclesiasticus,* 77 (1952)–450). The proper procedure would seem to have been to apply to the S. C. of Religious for permission to amend the Ceremonial.

## CANON 580

### Change in Cession or Disposition of Property, by a Religious (Cod. Com., 15 May, 1936) AAS 28–210.

The Code Commission was asked:

Whether the permission of the Holy See is required in order that a professed religious may, as stated in canon 580, § 3, change in favor of the religious Institute a cession or disposition, at least when it affects a notable part of his property.

**Reply.** In the affirmative.

AAS **28–210**; Cod. Com., 15 May, 1936.
*Periodica,* 25 (1936)–205 (Ellis); *Clergy Review,* 12 (1936)–76.

## CANON 582

**Concerning Money Coming to Religious in Connection With Their Military Service During the War** (S. C. Rel., 16 Mar., 1922) **AAS 14–196.**

The Sacred Congregation of Religious was asked the following questions:

I. Whether religious who are solemnly professed in accordance with the common law can rightfully retain for themselves any of the monies which came to them, or may in the future come to them, in connection with their military service during the war; or whether they are bound to turn them all over to their Order.

**Reply.** In the negative to the first part; in the affirmative to the second.

II. Whether religious who are solemnly professed, but who after their profession have by apostolic indult been made capable of acquiring property, can keep as their own any of the aforesaid monies without the express assent and permission of their major superior.

**Reply.** In the negative.

III. Whether religious who are professed of the simple vows, perpetual or temporary, whose constitutions exclude all acquisition of temporal goods after the profession, are bound to turn over all such monies to their religious society.

**Reply.** In the affirmative as regards those religious who during the time of their military service were bound by vows; in the negative as to others.

IV. Whether religious who are in any way professed of the simple vows, perpetual or temporary, in an Order or in a Congregation, if their constitutions do not forbid, can keep as their own any of the money received as pay, or whether they are bound to turn over to their respective religious societies whatever was left after their dismissal from the army.

**Reply.** In the case of those who during their military service were bound by vows, in the negative to the first part; in the affirmative to the second. In the case of those whose vows had ceased, in the affirmative to the first part; as regards the second part, they should pay a just compensation to their religious society.

V. Whether an annual pension given because of mutilation or broken health suffered in the war, to religious who are professed of the simple vows or to those referred to in c. 673, § 1, or finally to those whose vows or promises were suspended, belongs to the religious society concerned.

**Reply.** In the case of religious who during their military service were bound by vows, it belongs to the society; in the case of others, it belongs to the person, who, however, is bound to turn it over to the society as long as he remains in it.

VI. Whether pecuniary emoluments which come because of military decorations won in the war (military medals; cross of the legion of honor), belong to the ex-soldier or to the religious society.

**Reply.** In the negative to the first part; in the affirmative to the second, except in the case of those who during the war were not bound by vows.

VII. Whether money given to individual soldiers in the act of their dismissal as a token of public gratitude, belongs to the religious society.

**Reply.** In the affirmative, unless they were not bound by vows during the war.

VIII. Whether those who contrary to the above resolution have already disposed of money received in connection with the war, are bound to restitution.

**Reply.** In the affirmative, unless the religious acted according to the permission of the Superior, reasonably presumed.

AAS 14–196; S. C. Rel., 16 Mar., 1922.
*Periodica,* 11 (1923)–34 (Vermeersch); *J.P.,* 2 (1922)–58.

## CANON 584

**Capitular Entering Religion: No Right to Fruits of Benefice** (Sacred Congregation of the Council, 19 Apr., 1940) **AAS 32–374.**

**Facts.** A priest who was *mansionarius* (cf. c. 393, § 2) in a cathedral Chapter entered the religious Society of St. Francis de Sales on 8 Sept., 1936, without appointing any substitute to take his place in the Chapter, where he had the special function of leading the chant. He was thus to be absent for five years (two years of noviceship, three of religious profession) before the benefice would become vacant in accordance with c. 584. The Chapter applies to the Sacred Congregation for a definition of legal rights in the premises.

**Remarks.** Since the promulgation of the Code many such questions have been presented to this Sacred Congregation. The difficulty is that while canon 584 provides for the vacancy of parochial benefices after one year and of non-parochial benefices after three years from religious profession, it makes no provision regarding the disposal of the fruits of the benefice in the meantime. Hence this Sacred Congregation, with the consent of the Sacred Congregation of Religious, has decided to treat the general question rather thoroughly. Canon 584 safeguards the liberty of a beneficiary who enters religion, in case he afterward chooses to return to the world or is dismissed (cf. cc. 575, 637); but it does not follow that in the meantime (after his entrance into religion but before the vacancy of his benefice by religious profession) he is entitled to the fruits of the benefice. The Code is also silent on this matter in canons 613–625, where it treats of the privileges of religious. Hence, according to canon 20, we are thrown back upon "laws enacted in similar matters, the general principles of law observed with canonical equity, the style and practice of the Roman Curia, and the common and constant opinions of experts." Now the first-mentioned source, "laws passed in similar matters," does not help us, since canons 420 and 421 do not mention the present situation as a cause excusing from attendance at choir; nor does there exist any "common and constant opinion" among experts on the subject. The norm must accordingly be sought in "the general principles of law" and in "the style and practice of the Roman Curia."

1. The Code in canon 414 provides that: "Each and every one who has obtained a choral benefice is bound to perform the divine Office in choir," and in canon 419 it limits the right of substitution. Now, a beneficiary who has entered religion can neither perform the Office in choir personally nor appoint a regular substitute. It follows that he cannot receive the fruits

of his benefice, nor remunerate a substitute with a suitable stipend from the same.

2. It is true that his absence from choir is *just* and *reasonable,* since it is for the purpose of embracing a more perfect state of life; but it is not *legitimate* so as to entitle him to receive the fruits of the benefices. A *legitimate* cause is one which is expressly approved in the law (Garcia, *De beneficiis,* part III, cap. 2, n. 408). In the absence of a legitimate cause, a beneficiary has no right to the fruits, even though he have a reasonable and inculpable cause for absence from choir.

3. Since the reason for his absence is *just,* such a beneficiary does not incur the penalty mentioned in canon 2381, 2°, namely privation of the benefice, but he suffers a penalty improperly so called, that is the loss of the fruits, according to canon 2381, 1°, for being *illegitimately* absent (cf. Reiffenstuel, III, tit. 4, *De clericis non residentibus,* n. 51).

This is confirmed by the decision of this Sacred Congregation in *Toletana et aliarum* 10 July, 1920, where the question was: "Whether canon 2381 is to be applied even in case of nonresidence which is not gravely culpable or is only materially and not formally culpable and notorious"; and the reply: "In the affirmative, provided there is no excusing cause according to canons 420 and 421, nor a pontifical indult."[1] This decision also teaches us that the list of excusing causes mentioned in canons 420 and 421 is exclusive; that is *taxative* and not merely *demonstrative;* other similar causes cannot be added to it.

4. According to canon 420, § 1, 7°, attendance *once a year* at spiritual exercises as provided in canon 126 is both *a just and a legitimate cause;* hence, during such absence a capitular is entitled to receive the fruits of the benefice and the daily distributions. If however a capitular wished to absent himself for spiritual exercises *several times a year,* he would have a *just* and *holy* cause for absence from choir, and hence he could not be deprived of his benefice as provided in c. 2381, 2°; but the cause would not be *legitimate,* hence he would lose not only the daily distributions but all fruits of the benefice in proportion to his illegitimate absence.

5. It may be noted also that canon 570, § 1, provides:

---

[1] See Canon Law Digest, 1, p. 712, *ad II.*

"Nothing may be demanded for the expenses of the postulancy or noviceship."

6. Two documents from the old law may be cited against this position; namely, Boniface VIII, in VI° (cap. *Beneficium* 4, *de regularibus*), and Benedict XIV, in the Brief, *Ex quo,* of 24 Jan., 1747. Both of these authorities seem to state clearly enough that a beneficiary who enters religion retains the fruits of the benefice. However, authors of note dispute about the meaning of these texts. A more direct answer to them is that the law has simply been changed by the Code, which has completely renovated the law regarding benefices. We have here an occasion for the application of canon 6, 6°: "If, among the other disciplinary laws which have hitherto been in force, there is any which is neither explicitly nor implicitly contained in the Code, it is to be considered to have lost all force."

7. An argument to the contrary is attempted from canon 584, which leaves to the beneficiary the title to his benefice after entering religion (for according to this law it becomes vacant only three years after his religious profession), and from canon 1472, which provides: "Every beneficiary, upon taking possession of his benefice according to law, enjoys all the rights, both temporal and spiritual, which are annexed to the benefice." But these rights are correlative to the duties, of which the principal one is attendance at choir. A beneficiary who enters religion freely puts himself in a condition which makes it impossible for him to fulfill the duties; there is no reason why he should continue to enjoy the rights (cf. St. Alphonsus, *Theol. mor.*, lib. IV, n. 127).

8. Finally, appeal to the other norm of canon 20, namely "the style and practice of the Roman Curia," confirms this position. For the constant practice of this Sacred Congregation, both before and since the Code, has been to grant to a beneficiary who enters religion — and provided the Chapter agrees and the Ordinary of the place consents to it — an indult to receive the fruits of the benefice, and sometimes also the daily distributions. But such an indult would be superfluous if these rights belonged to the beneficiary by the common law.

**Decision.** At the plenary session held on the 13th of April, 1940, the Eminent Fathers of this Sacred Congregation, in reply to the question: "Whether a capitular who has entered religion has the right to the fruits of the benefice before it becomes vacant according to canon 584," replied: "In the negative, in the absence of an apostolic indult."

In the audience of 19 Apr., 1940, His Holiness Pius XII deigned to approve and confirm this decision.

**AAS 32–374**; S. C. Conc., *Dioecesis V et aliarum,* 13 and 19 Apr., 1940.

## CANON 587

**Studies of Religious** (Ap. Letter, Pius XI, 19 Mar., 1924) AAS 16–133.

A capital document on the studies of religious is the Apostolic Letter of Pius XI, 19 March, 1924, some features of which are summarily reported under canons 487, 564, 565, 589, 1364, and 1366; on pp. 86, 296, 316, 582, 583.

**AAS 16–133**; Pius XI, Apostolic Letter, 19 Mar., 1924.
*Periodica,* 13 (1925)–1 (Vermeersch).

---

**Sacred Art**: To be taught to clerics during studies. See **c. 2**; AAS 56–97, Constitution on the Sacred Liturgy, n. 129; reported above on p. 22.

**Teaching of Liturgy** in religious seminaries and houses of study. See **c. 2**; AAS 56–97, Constitution on the Sacred Liturgy, nn. 15, 16, 17, reported above on pp. 20–21.

## CANON 589

**Humanities, As a Rule, to Be Finished Before Entering Novitiate** (Ap. Letter, Pius XI, 19 Mar., 1924) AAS 16–133.

His Holiness Pius XI, in the course of an Apostolic Letter to the Superiors General of religious Orders and societies of men, citing c. 589, said:

You must see to it, therefore, that after the young candidates for the religious life have been seasonably and prudently selected, they receive, along with such training in piety as is suited to their age, instruction in the lower studies which are usually given in schools and colleges; so that they do not enter the novitiate until they shall have completed the curriculum of the so-called "humanities," unless in individual cases rather grave reasons make it advisable to provide otherwise.

**AAS 16–133**; Pius XI, Apostolic Letter, 19 Mar., 1924.
*Periodica,* 13 (1925)–14 (Vermeersch).

NOTE: Other features of this Letter are summarily reported under canons 487, 564, 565, 587, 1364, and 1366 on pp. 86, 296, 316, 582, 583.

## CANON 592

### Religious: Permission Rarely to Be Given to Go to Bathing Resorts: Precautions to Be Taken (S. C. Rel., 15 July, 1926) Private.

A letter of the Sacred Congregation of Religious to all General Superiors of religious Orders and Congregations, after calling attention to the fact that dangers and scandals can arise from the attendance of clerics and religious at bathing resorts (*stationes balneares*) and mineral springs, gives the following prescriptive norms:

*a*) Superiors are to see to it that the religious of their Institute do not easily get permission to attend such places.

*b*) When there is sufficient and reasonable cause for such permission from the standpoint of health, they are to see to it that their religious live in some religious house or at least in some respectable house suitable to their state.

*c*) The religious are to be absolutely forbidden to lay aside their religious habit for any reason, and to attend theaters, plays, cinemas, and other shows of the kind; and they are to avoid all companionship of the sort that is unbecoming to religious men.

*d*) Superiors are to exercise due supervision to see that these prescriptions are observed, and in the case of violation the subjects are to be severely punished.

Attention is called to the fact that the Sacred Congregation of the Council (in the letter of 1 July, 1926; CANON LAW DIGEST, 1, p. 138) enjoined upon Ordinaries of places to be watchful in this matter even as regards religious.

**(Private)**; S. C. Rel., 15 July, 1926. Cf. Schaefer, *De Religiosis,* 3 ed., 1940, n. 312, p. 667, note 25; *Analecta Ord. Min. Cap.,* Vol. 42, p. 244.

---

**Catholic Action in the Training and Activities of Religious of Both Sexes.** See letter of Cardinal Pacelli as Secretary of State to the Superiors General of all religious Institutes of either sex, on the promotion of Catholic Action; 15 March, 1936; Italian and Latin texts, *Periodica,* 25 (1936)–209; English translation in *The Religious and Catholic Action* by Father Anderl and Sister Ruth (St. Rose Convent, La Crosse, Wisconsin), p. 91; also in this volume, pp. 45–48.

## CANON 593

### The Use of Tobacco in the States of Perfection (S. C. Rel., 10 Jan., 1951) Private.

A Circular Letter sent by the Sacred Congregation of Religious to the Superiors General is as follows:

Prot. N. 2511/51 S. R.
Very Reverend Father:

During the past few years following the last war not a few consultations, complaints, declarations, and formal accusations have come from General Superiors and Chapters, from individuals zealous for religious observance, and even from local Ordinaries, regarding the use of tobacco by members of the states of perfection.

In those religious Institutes and Societies in which the use of tobacco is forbidden by the Constitutions or by legitimate and accepted traditions and prescriptions of Chapters or Superiors, the intervention of the Sacred Congregation, invoked in various ways, has been effectively to repress and extirpate the illicit use which had crept in here and there chiefly as a result of the war.

In religious Institutes and Societies in which the use of tobacco is not generally forbidden, it has been noted that it often gives occasion to rather grave abuses. These abuses regularly harm and impair in many ways religious poverty, the spirit of mortification, and external modesty.

On the occasion of the recent Congress on the States of Perfection the question of the use and abuse of tobacco might have been dealt with. It was not done at that time for various reasons, but the Sacred Congregation considers it a duty to take the matter up immediately in a clear and straightforward way with the Very Reverend Superiors General, in order to communicate to them the proper criteria to be observed in regard to the use of tobacco, and to stimulate their zeal in repressing the abuses of tobacco, if any such exist in their Institutes and Societies. For members of the states of perfection ought to be in this respect an example of fidelity and Christian and religious poverty, temperance, and modesty to everyone.

These then are the general norms which the Sacred Congregation considers as expressing the criteria to be observed regarding the use of tobacco.

I. In religious Institutes, Societies, and Institutes in which according to approved Constitutions or by legitimate and accepted prescriptions of Chapters and Superiors the use of tobacco is either forbidden or held within very narrow limits or subject to strict conditions, these lawful prescriptions are to be sacredly observed and enforced. The Sacred Congregation confirms and defends those provisions as rightly and for good reason forming a part of the mortification and regular religious observance in those religious Institutes, Societies, and Institutes.

II. In religious Institutes, Societies, and other Institutes in which a moderate use of tobacco is allowed and legitimate, this use is so to be regulated that religious poverty be unimpaired both as regards expense and dependence on Superiors, that the spirit of asceticism and religious mortification, which is one of the prime foundations of the states of perfection, suffer no harm, and finally that the use of tobacco as regards place, manner, and time, neither harm nor threaten in any way the good example and edification which should be given to the faithful or externs.

III. In order to avoid these dangers (n. II) and to strengthen the effectiveness of legitimate existing prescriptions of Constitutions or Chapters (n. I), Superiors with their proper Consultors may and should, if necessary, issue special norms to regulate the use of tobacco as to manner, quantity, time, and place.

IV. In general the Sacred Congregation is opposed to the introduction of tobacco, to departure from the regulations regarding its use, and to the relaxation of discipline in this matter, whether in religious Institutes, Societies, or other Institutes. For we must sincerely confess that according to actual experience these relaxations, deviations, permissions are in general not helpful and in fact can easily become seriously harmful to the religious spirit.

V. If the Ordinaries of places have made any regulations for clerics in their dioceses regarding the use of tobacco, especially in public, Superiors should strive in every way that religious and others who follow evangelical perfection shall observe them exactly, as befits their public profession of sanctity. If Ordinaries of places notify Superiors of any infraction of such regulations or of any abuses of tobacco by their religious subjects, the Superiors should deal with the matter effectively and diligently.

While I communicate these matters to Your Paternity, I beg you to present to this Sacred Congregation whatever regulations are already established in your Institute, or those which Your Paternity with your Council may have decided to establish at this time.

His Holiness by divine Providence Pope Pius XII, in the audience graciously granted to the undersigned Cardinal Prefect on the 8th of January, deigned to give his approval to this Circular Letter.

Rome, 10 January, 1951.

(**Private**); S. C. Rel., Circular Letter, 10 Jan., 1951. *Monitor Ecclesiasticus,* 76 (1951)–441; annotations, *ibid.,* p. 443 (Gutiérrez).

NOTE: In the annotations, Gutiérrez reports a private reply of the S. C. to questions proposed by a Superior General of an Institute in which the use of tobacco is forbidden (Prot. N. 10272/50):

1. Whether, everything considered, a general precept binding in conscience can be imposed or confirmed in this Congregation: (*a*) which obliges all members, Superiors and subjects, not to use tobacco for smoking either in public or in private; (*b*) which binds all Superiors not to spend any part of the money of the Congregation, even the slightest, for smoking tobacco for the use of members of the Congregation; (*c*) which forbids all, Superiors and subjects, from spending for smoking tobacco any personal money or value, no matter how it may have come to the religious in question.

**Reply.** In the affirmative to *a, b,* and *c.*

2. Whether the general precept mentioned in question 1 can, in particular cases: (*a*) be imposed *sub gravi;* (*b*) and be confirmed also under the vow of obedience.

**Reply.** To *a:* in the affirmative, provided the matter in the individual case can certainly be said to be grave *in itself* (by reason of the quantity which is illicitly used or to be used, the frequency, the habit, etc.) or *by reason of the circumstances* (the form in which it is used, scandal, etc.); to *b:* in the affirmative according to common and right doctrine.

3. Whether, in case of the certain violation of a grave particular precept which is binding also under the vow of obedience, measures may be taken against the transgressors according to law, using also admonitions and canonical sanctions.

**Reply.** In the affirmative, observing the norms of Canon Law.

**(Private)**; S. C. Rel., N. 10272/50; date not specified.

## CANON 594

**Radio and Television: Norms for Religious** (S. C. Rel., 6 Aug., 1957) **Private.**

A Letter of the S. C. of Religious "to the Superiors General of the Institutes of Perfection Regarding the Use of Radio and Television" is as follows:

As early as the first of January, 1954, the date on which the transmission of television in Italy was inaugurated, the Holy Father in an important exhortation on television,[1] communicated to the Most Reverend Ordinaries of places his anxiety over the effects which this new and powerful means of diffusing news, facts, and exhibitions from all parts of the world might have on the moral and spiritual life of the people.

This marvelous product of modern science, which within a short time has been made practically available to every one, is quite frequently to be found also in religious houses; and as we know, even in Italy where good intentions, promises, and the good will of a number of persons might have encouraged the hope that the programs would be kept within the bounds of decency and morality, these limits have not always been observed.

The Supreme Pontiff has therefore felt a still greater concern regarding the use of this instrument at once precious and dangerous, especially in Institutes of Christian perfection.

In the religious life there is question of safeguarding the discipline and holiness of that life, which is imperiled not only by things that are evidently wrong but also by the infiltration of worldliness, which destroys the relish for the things of the spirit and diminishes, often insensibly, that desire of perfection which

[1] AAS 46–18; reported in Canon Law Digest, 4, p. 129.

must always remain alive in a religious, dedicated to it as he is by his very profession.

In the aftermath of the Congress of the States of Perfection which was held at the close of the year 1950, this Sacred Congregation has taken a lively interest in the regulation of these modern inventions, the cinema, radio, and television, in their various aspects in relation to the religious life, its discipline, and its apostolate.

Especially as regards radio and television, after having drawn profit from the results of the Congress itself, it has asked for and collected the opinions of religious Superiors and of other persons from various nations and of diverse temperaments, qualified by solid learning, religious piety, and experience in the spiritual life, in order to prepare and send out an Instruction establishing some general norms from which the Superiors of the various religious Institutes might derive a more detailed and specific regulation of this matter on the basis of their particular spirit, the form of their discipline, and their internal and external aims.

Evidently, considering the good and the evil, the usefulness as well as the dangers of television, this Sacred Congregation does not see any necessity for its indiscriminate suppression in all religious Institutes; nor does it mean to approve its full and absolute admission or toleration. The former course would run the risk of alienating too completely from social life certain religious Institutes which have to live in the midst of the world and deploy a social and religious activity there; the latter would plunge the religious back into the world which he has abandoned, to be gradually tainted with that worldly spirit which is incompatible with the religious ideal.

The Church does not thereby mean to reject whatever science and progress provide for humanity, if it can be directed to a good purpose; but she cannot and does not diverge from the principle *"salus animarum suprema lex"*; to do so would be to fail in her mission. In regard to religious — that select group in the Church — she seeks to eliminate not only serious and obvious dangers but also whatever may impede or retard the progress toward perfection which is the very purpose of religious life.

With regard to radio and television some needed distinctions have to be made. The requirements of the contemplative life are different from those of the active life; in the active life itself two considerations occur: what may be allowed by way of proper relaxation and amusement, and what is demanded by the needs of the apostolate; and even in the apostolate, one question is what may be allowed for one's own instruction and experience, another, what the religious themselves can give to the faithful whom they influence and assist.

On the basis of these considerations this Sacred Congregation has thought it well to establish some fundamental norms and also to invite the Superiors of the various Institutes, together with their respective Councils, to control this matter by somewhat more concrete regulations in keeping with their own spirit and traditions, so that a thing which can be an effective aid to the apostolate may not degenerate into a cause of spiritual ruin for religious, or worse still, of a general relaxation of religious discipline.

After having considered everything this Sacred Congregation establishes the following norms and presents them to Superiors for exact observance, "*graviter onerata eorum conscientia.*"

1. There is no sufficient reason to justify introducing television apparatus in communities of contemplative life, either of men or of women. A radio apparatus can be tolerated for the sole purpose of enabling the religious to hear the words of the Pope when he speaks to the whole world and to receive his blessing, or on the occasion of some exceptional celebration of a religious character.

2. In Institutes of active life:

*a*) Never can individual radios, and much less individual television sets, be permitted, to be used freely and without the control of the Superior.

*b*) The radio and television apparatus must always be located exclusively in some community hall, in an open place, under the control of the Superior or of some one delegated by him.

*c*) Superiors must regulate the time given to television or to listening to the radio so that there be no interference with the occupations and duties of each one's state or office, the apostolate, practices of piety, exercises of the common life, and hours of rest, according to the community's daily order.

*d*) Superiors should forbid showings or broadcasts which because of their moral tone or worldliness are not suitable for religious. Aside from the daily news and transmissions of an educational or religious character, all the rest should or at least may be considered as of that type in relation to the religious life, and hence to be excluded if proposed only for the recreation of the religious.

*e*) If reasons of the apostolate clearly require, in the case of certain individual religious and in concrete cases, that some reasonable exceptions be made, the decision as to these must always be reserved to the Superior, who *"graviter onerata conscientia,"* must see to it that the danger be made as remote as possible, by making a careful choice of the religious concerned, who should be persons of solid religious spirit and sound experience of life, and well able to discern not only what might be harmful to the religious themselves but also what might harm those for whom the show is intended.

(**Private**); S. C. Rel., 6 Aug., 1957 (N. 01742/53); translated from the original Italian.

## CANON 596

**Habit, Religious:** The practice of the S. C. of Religious and the mind of the Holy See as to approving the habit chosen for new Institutes and allowing a change in the habit of existing Institutes. *"Ex Iurisprudentia S. C. de Religiosis"* (*Commentarium pro Religiosis,* 32 (1953)–93).

## CANON 598

### Wives of State Governors in U. S. May Enter Cloister of Men (Code Com., 26 March, 1952) AAS 44–496.

The Code Commission was asked:

I. Whether according to canon 598, § 2, the wives of Governors of individual States in the United States with their retinue may be admitted within the cloister of men regulars.

**Reply.** In the affirmative.

II. Whether the interpretation given in the above reply to question I is declarative or extensive.

**Reply.** In the negative to the first part, in the affirmative to the second.

Given at Rome, from Vatican City, 26 March, 1952.

**AAS 44–496**; Code Com., 26 March, 1952. Annotations, *Monitor Ecclesiasticus,* 77 (1952)–407 (Bidagor), *Commentarium pro Religiosis,* 31 (1952)–225 (Gutiérrez); *Periodica,* 42 (1953)–155 (Aguirre).

## CANON 600

**Externe Sisters Not to Reside in Cloister** (S. C. Rel., 1936) **Private.**

The Cardinal Archbishop of Genoa received the following rescript from the Sacred Congregation of Religious:

This Sacred Congregation in the meeting held on the 28th of this month considered the petition received from Your Eminence, in which you asked the following:

1. The faculty to permit monastic nuns from Italy or from foreign countries who pass through Genoa, to be received as guests in the cloister of the monastery of the same Order, during their temporary or provisional stay.

This Sacred Congregation, after carefully considering the whole matter, grants to Your Eminence the requested faculty for three years, *adhibitis cautelis ne quod oriatur inconveniens.*

2. Whether approval could be given to the *immemorial* custom or to the provisions of the *Consuetudinarium* or ancient books of a monastery of solemn vows permitting externe Sisters to reside in the cloister, notwithstanding the prescriptions of this S. C. of 16 July, 1931,[1] that they should reside in external places annexed to the monastery.

In this matter the decision of this S. C. is that all customs or provisions of ancient books or directories are abrogated by the statutes which were issued on 16 July, 1931.

Consequently, monasteries which have suitable places are obliged to observe the aforesaid statutes. To those who have no such external places, this Sacred Congregation grants the permission for five years to follow the same practice as heretofore, *provided that in the meantime they make provisions* conformable to the said statutes.

**(Private)**; S. C. Rel., 1936. See *Periodica,* 26 (1937)–81 with annotations by Ellis; and *Commentarium pro Religiosis,* 17 (1936)–209 with annotations by Larraona.

[1] CANON LAW DIGEST, 2, p. 170. For a later instruction on this subject, see p. 385.

**Monastic Nuns** (Pius XII, Apostolic Constitution, *Sponsa Christi,* and General Statutes, 21 Nov., 1950) **AAS 43–5.**

The Church, the Spouse of Christ, has from the very beginning of her history not only repeatedly manifested by action and inference but also clearly expressed in her authentic teaching the esteem and tender maternal affection which she bears toward Virgins consecrated to God.

And no wonder, for Christian Virgins, "the choice portion of the flock of Christ,"[1] impelled by charity, disdaining all the distracting preoccupations of the world and conquering the easy but perilous temptation to divide their affections, not only consecrated themselves entirely to Christ as the true Spouse of their souls, but dedicated their whole lives, resplendent with the jewels of all Christian virtues, to the Lord Jesus Christ and to His Church forever.

This mystical attachment of Virgins to the service of Christ and their dedication to the Church was, in the earliest Christian times, done spontaneously and by acts rather than words. Afterward, however, when Virgins came to constitute not merely a certain class of persons but a definite state and order recognized by the Church, the profession of virginity began to be made publicly, and to become more and more strictly binding. Later still the Church, in accepting the holy vow or resolution of virginity, inviolably consecrated the Virgin to God and to the Church by a solemn rite which is rightly counted among the more beautiful records of the ancient liturgy, and thus clearly set her apart from others who bound themselves to God by a merely private bond.

The profession of the life of virginity was protected by a watchful and severe discipline and was at the same time nourished and promoted by all the practices of piety and virtue. The early teaching of the Fathers, of the Greeks and other Orientals as well as of the Latins, gives us a faithful and very beautiful picture of the Christian Virgin. With the greatest care and affection the Fathers illustrated and vividly described in their writings

[1] St. Cyprian, *De habitu virginum,* 3 (*PL,* 4, 455). In the official text of the Constitution, this is the third of forty-five abundant and most valuable footnotes referring to the Fathers, theologians, and ecclesiastical documents. The immediate practical purpose of this Digest compels us to omit these footnotes almost entirely. Anyone making so thorough a study of the subject will surely have access to the *Acta Apostolicae Sedis* and the original text.

all the elements, whether internal or external, which could have any connection with virginal sanctity and perfection.

How well the angelic life of Christian Virgins in that first stage of its history corresponded to the exhortations and descriptions of the Fathers, and how lofty were the heroic virtues which adorned it, we know in part from the direct and certain testimony of historical documents and records, and in part we can conjecture and even deduce beyond any doubt from other reliable sources.

Especially after peace was granted to the Church, it became the more and more frequent practice, after the example of the Hermits and Cenobites, that the state of virginity consecrated to God should be completed and confirmed by an express and explicit profession of the counsels of poverty and strict obedience.

Women making profession of virginity, who, through love of solitude and for protection against the very grave dangers which threatened them on all sides in the corrupt Roman society, had already come together in a community life segregated as much as possible from ordinary human contacts, later, when circumstances became favorable, rather quickly followed the example of the great number of Cenobites, and, leaving the eremetical life mostly to men, imitated the cenobitical life, and nearly all of them entered into it.

The Church recommended to Virgins in general the common life understood in a rather wide sense, but for a long time did not wish strictly to impose the monastic life even on consecrated Virgins, but rather left them free in the world, though honored as befitted their state. It came about, however, that Virgins liturgically consecrated and living in their own homes or in a common life of a freer sort became more and more rare, until they were in many places no longer recognized in the law of the Church and were as a matter of fact extinct everywhere; they were never generally restored as a legal institution, and later still were even prohibited.

* * *

Consequently the Church turned her maternal solicitude chiefly upon those Virgins who, choosing the better part, abandoned the world entirely and embraced a life of complete Christian perfection in monasteries, professing strict poverty and full obedience as well as virginity. The Church provided an external safeguard for their profession of the common life by increasingly rigorous laws of cloister. At the same time she so regulated the internal order of their life that in her laws and religious discipline there gradually emerged as a clearly defined type the figure of the Monastic Sister or Nun entirely devoted to the contemplative life under a strict and regular regime.

About the beginning of the middle ages, when consecrated Virgins living in the world had entirely disappeared, these Monastic Nuns, who had grown tremendously in number, in fervor, and in variety, were regarded as the sole heirs and legitimate successors of the Virgins of earlier times; yet not only as their heirs and successors, but also as the faithful representatives and industrious managers of the continuing heritage, who after having received five talents had gained other five over and above. This origin and dignity of Monastic Nuns, together with their merit and holiness, are proved and vindicated by liturgical records, canonical documents, and historical testimonies of every kind, in writing, sculpture, and painting.

For several centuries up to the close of the middle ages, as clearly appears from the Decretals and from the entire *Corpus Iuris Canonici,* the state of perfection, which had already been so solemnly approved and so fully recognized that its public nature was more and more evident, had as its sole representatives among women the Monastic Nuns, side by side with the Monks and Canons Regular.

After that, though many grave difficulties had to be overcome, first all the Brothers, who were called Mendicants, or Hospitalers, or for the Redemption of Captives, or by some other name, and then about three centuries later also the Clerics who were called Regulars, were included among true religious and regulars along with the Monks and the Canons Regular; while all the Nuns, both those who clung to the old monasticism or to the life of canonesses and those who were received into second Orders of the Mendicant Brothers canonically belonged to one and the same noble and ancient institute and followed the same way of religious life.

Hence, up to the time of the first Congregations of women, which arose either in the sixteenth or in the seventeenth century, they only were considered Nuns who in fact and in law professed an acknowledged form of the religious life. And even after the Congregations were tolerated, and in the course of time recognized first in fact and then as a sort of working arrangement by the law, up to the promulgation of the Code of Canon Law, Nuns alone were strictly recognized as true religious and regulars.

And if we turn our attention to the inner elements of the monastic life, who can number and weigh the treasures of religious perfection which lay hid in monasteries? How many flowers and fruits of sanctity these enclosed gardens presented to Christ and to the Church! What efficacious prayers, what treasures of devotedness, what benefits of every sort did not the Nuns strive to bring to their Mother the Church for her embellishment, support, and strengthening!

* * *

The strict and well defined figure of the Nun, as it was engraved on the pages of Canon Law and of religious practice, was accepted readily, and in its main outlines faithfully too, by the numberless Orders, Monasteries, Convents which constantly existed in the Church, and was tenaciously retained for several centuries. From this general fidelity and constancy the sacred institution of Nuns acquired a solid consistency which always enabled it to resist innovations of any kind more vigorously than institutes of any other regulars or religious of either sex. Within certain proper limits this is certainly to its credit.

This essential unity among Nuns, which We have commended, does not mean that there were not, even from very early times, both as regards practice and interior discipline, various figures and varieties, with which God, who is wonderful in His Saints, endowed and adorned the Church of His Spouse. These variations among Nuns seem to have sprung from variations of the same sort in Orders and religious Institutes of men, to which the Orders of Nuns were in a sense accessory. In fact nearly all the Monks, Canons Regular, and especially Mendicants, sought to establish second Orders which, keeping the general character of institutes of Nuns, yet differed among themselves in much the same way as did the first Orders. Similarly in more recent times some Orders of Clerics Regular and some Congregations of men have established Nuns of their own Institutes.

These variations among Nuns are worthy of attentive consideration, both from the standpoint of the history of the institution and from that of the interior changes which were common to all its forms. They won for this ancient institution as it were a resurgence of sanctity, without changing the general character of the contemplative life or the chief norms and principles of the established discipline.

In still more recent times, especially toward the close of the sixteenth century, some new forms of Orders of Nuns were introduced and were gradually approved by the Church; as for example the Institute of Saint Ursula, of the Angelics, the Congregation of the Sisters of Notre Dame, the Order of the Visitation, the Society of Our Lady, the Sisters of Notre Dame de Charité, and many others. These new foundations, while they were, either from the start or later, induced or morally compelled to accept the common law as currently applied to Nuns — since they wished to profess a truly religious life and this was then the only form of it admissible for women — were yet in various ways paving the way for a renovation of the law itself.

These new forms of institutes of Nuns, though they professed a life which was canonically classed as contemplative, and though in deference to the opinions of that time they finally accepted sincerely if reluctantly the strict papal cloister, yet sometimes did not engage to recite the divine Office. On the other hand, they did with commendable zeal accept as their part and perform many apostolic and charitable works which were suited to their sex and to their canonical state.

* * *

As time went on, either through the example given by the new Orders or because of the growth of Congregations and Societies, which sought to combine with the life of perfection a fruitful apostolate of charity, assistance, and education, or finally because of the general trend of events and ideas, not a few monasteries of many of the Orders which according to their institute followed a purely contemplative life, accepted apostolic works in many places with the approval and under the prudent guidance of the Holy See.

From that time on, it gradually came about that the general institution of Nuns not only began to include divers Orders with their own Rules and Constitutions, but also began to admit a deeper line of demarcation between those Orders and Monasteries which followed a purely contemplative life, and those others in which, either because of their particular Constitutions or by subsequent permission of the Holy See, certain canonically approved works of the apostolate were appropriately added to the life of contemplation.

In our day the entire institution of Nuns both in those Orders and Monasteries which hitherto had practiced faithfully the pure contemplative life, and also especially in those which under the direction of the Church combined the works of the apostolate with the life of contemplation, has been not a little affected by the variations and changes of times and circumstances. Naturally, as the Orders now engage in education and other similar charitable works, which, owing either to the habit of the people or to public regulations, are now practiced in such a way that they are almost or quite incompatible with some of the classical norms of the papal cloister, these norms have had to be judiciously modified, without prejudice to the common notion of cloister, so as to be compatible with these works. This was, of course, for the good of the Church and of souls, for had it not been done the works could not have been undertaken at all or at least not in the same way. And not only the apostolic Orders but also the purely contemplative ones have been at times induced or compelled by circumstances and the grave need in which they find themselves, to modify these same norms or to interpret them more broadly.

For example, public opinion to-day will scarcely tolerate too rigorous an interpretation of canon 601, even in the case of contemplative Nuns. Hence the Holy See with maternal solicitude provides ever more liberally for many necessities and useful purposes, which according to ancient standards were not considered so serious as to justify the infraction of papal cloister or exemption from it. For that matter, the security and sanctity of residences, which though not the sole reason for papal cloister, was one among other reasons which in various ways and at various times contributed to its establishment and regulation, is to-day better protected than it used to be.

* * *

Having briefly sketched the origin and development of the

sacred institution of Nuns, We now propose to designate clearly its proper and necessary elements, those which directly concern the canonical contemplative life of Nuns, which is the first and principal end of their Institute. To these innate and principal features by which the canonical figure of Nuns is clearly defined as a matter of law, must be added certain other important ones which, though not strictly essential, are yet complementary, because they serve rather well and help to secure the public purpose for which Nuns exist. On the other hand there are some elements in the institution of Nuns which are neither necessary nor complementary, but merely external and historical, since they certainly owe their existence to the circumstances of former times which are now very much changed. These, if they are found to be no longer of any use or liable to hinder greater good, seem to have no special reason for being preserved.

Accordingly, without the least prejudice to any of the native and principal elements of the venerable institution of Nuns, as to the rest, which are found to be external and adventitious, We have decided to make with caution and prudence certain adaptations to present times, which may not only do honor to the venerable institution but at the same time enlarge its effectiveness.

We are induced or even impelled to make these moderate adjustments in the institution of Nuns, by the full information which We have on the subject from various parts of the world and the certain knowledge drawn therefrom regarding the extreme need in which Nuns often, not to say always, find themselves. Actually there are not a few Monasteries which, alas, are on the verge of extinction from hunger, misery, and want; there are many which, because of domestic difficulties, are leading a hard and almost intolerable life. Besides there are some Monasteries which, though not indigent, are so cut off and separated from any other Monasteries that they lack vitality. Frequently also the strict law of cloister easily gives rise to serious difficulties. Finally, with the ever growing necessities of the Church and of souls and the urgent need for a variety of helping hands from all classes of persons to meet them, the time seems to have come for combining the monastic life, generally even in the case of Nuns who are given to contemplation, with some moderate apostolic work.

And this judgment of Ours on this matter has been repeatedly confirmed by the testimony which has come to Us almost unanimously from local Ordinaries and religious Superiors in certain countries.

* * *

It will be useful at this point to consider some of the measures enacted below in the General Statutes of Nuns, and to draw from them some rules and conclusions which will help toward an easy, safe, and correct understanding of all the provisions.

First, as regards the contemplative life of Nuns, one thing has always been true according to the mind of the Church, and it must be kept firm and inviolate: all Monasteries of Nuns must always and everywhere canonically profess the contemplative life as their first and primary end. Therefore, the works and ministries in which Nuns may and should engage must be of such a character and must be so regulated and arranged as to place, time, manner, and method, that a truly and solidly contemplative life, both for the Community as a whole and for the individual Nuns, shall be not only preserved but constantly nourished and strengthened.

The dispositions and concessions which were formerly made under stress of circumstances for certain countries, by which the solemn vows were changed to simple ones, certainly implied an odious dispensation (canon 19); the more so as this immunity is contrary to the principal characteristic of Nuns; for the solemn vows, which imply a stricter and fuller consecration to God than other public vows, contain the principal and canonically essential characteristic of religious Orders. Consequently, since long experience in various places has clearly shown that the solemn vows both of men Regulars and of Nuns, even though the civil law makes no account of them, can easily and without difficulty be observed, and that the security of the other common goods can likewise be properly provided for by other means, even though in some places juridical personality is denied to religious Institutes and Monasteries, the legislation and practice of the Holy See for many years now have rightly tended to restrict these odious exceptions and as far as possible to remove them altogether. And surely it is not right to deprive Nuns of the honor, merit, and joy of pronouncing the solemn vows which are their proper heritage.

For the safer custody of the solemn vow of chastity and the contemplative life, and that the enclosed garden of Monasteries might be protected from the intrusion of the world, from all crafty and insidious violation, and from all disturbance through secular and profane contacts, and so become a true cloister of souls where Nuns might serve the Lord with greater freedom, the Church with wise and vigilant solicitude established strict cloister as a distinctive feature of the life of Nuns, regulated it with care, and always safeguarded it with grave pontifical sanctions. This venerable cloister of Nuns, which is called "papal" because of the supreme authority from which it emanates and the sanctions by which it is protected within and without, is, by this Constitution of Ours, not only purposely and solemnly confirmed, for the various sorts of Monasteries which have hitherto been obliged to it, but is cautiously extended also to those Monasteries which until now have not been bound to it on account of dispensations lawfully obtained.

Monasteries which profess a purely contemplative life and which do not admit within the confines of the religious house any regular works of education, charity, recollection, and so on, shall retain or accept that papal cloister which is dealt with in the Code of Canon Law (canons 600–602) and which shall be called *"major."*

As for those Monasteries which, either by their Constitutions or by lawful provision of the Holy See, harmoniously combine with the contemplative life, in the Monastery itself, certain works which are consistent with it, the papal cloister, while retaining its essential and innate elements, is modified in some points which can scarcely or not at all be observed; as to other points which are not regarded as so essential to the papal cloister as described in the Code (canons 599, 604, § *2*), it is appropriately supplemented by new provisions. This papal cloister modified and adapted to present needs, which shall be called *"minor"* to distinguish it from the stricter ancient cloister, may be allowed also to those Monasteries which, while retaining the purely contemplative life, either have not solemn vows or lack some of the conditions which are required for the major papal cloister according to the jurisprudence and practice of the Roman Curia. All these elements of the minor papal cloister will be accurately defined below in the General Statutes and in the Instructions which shall be issued by Our Authority and in Our name by the Sacred Congregation of Religious.

As to the autonomy or mutual liberty of Monasteries of Nuns, We think it appropriate to repeat here and to apply to Nuns what We said of Monks in the homily which We pronounced in the patriarchal Basilica of Saint Paul's outside the walls on the eighteenth of September, 1947, on the occasion of the fourth centenary of the death of Saint Benedict of Nursia. In view of changed circumstances there are now many considerations which make it advisable and sometimes even necessary to confederate Monasteries of Nuns. Such are, for example, an easier and better distribution of offices, the temporary transfer of individual religious from one monastery to another for a number of reasons of necessity or usefulness, mutual economic assistance, the coordination of works, the protection of common observance, and so on. That all this can be done and attained without impairing essential autonomy nor in any way weakening the observance of cloister or harming recollection and the strict discipline of monastic life, is abundantly clear not only from the ample experience of the Monastic Congregations of men, but also from the example of not a few Unions and Federations which have already been approved for Nuns. Besides, the establishment of Federations and the approval of the Statutes by which they are to be governed, will remain reserved to the Holy See.

Work, whether of the hands or of the spirit, is for all humanity, including men and women who lead a contemplative life, not only an obligation of the law of nature, but also a duty of penance and reparation. Moreover, work is a general means through which the soul is preserved from dangers and led to higher things; through which we cooperate with divine Providence in the natural and in the supernatural order; through which we practice works of charity. Finally, work is the norm and primary law of the religious life, and that from its very origin, according to the maxim, "*ora et labora*." Surely a large part of the discipline of the religious life has always consisted in the assignment, the management, and the performance of work.

The work of Nuns from the point of view of eternity, should be such that she who undertakes it do so first of all with a holy purpose, that she often think of God as present, that she accept the work through obedience and find in it a means of voluntary mortification. If work is done in this spirit, it will be a powerful and constant exercise of all the virtues and a pledge of the suave and effective union of the contemplative and the active life after the example of the Holy Family of Nazareth.

If monastic labor is considered from the standpoint of nature or of discipline, it must, according to the Rules, Constitutions, and traditional customs of the various Orders, not only be proportionate to the strength of the Nuns, but also be so managed and performed that, in the long run and according to the circumstances, it will not only produce the necessary sustenance for the Nuns themselves but also redound to the benefit of the poor, of human society in general and of the Church.

Since the perfection of Christian life consists especially in charity, and since it is really one and the same charity with which we must love God alone above all and all men in Him, Holy Mother Church demands of all Nuns who canonically profess a life of contemplation, together with a perfect love of God, also a perfect love of the neighbor; and for the sake of this charity and their state of life, religious men and women must devote themselves wholly to the needs of the Church and of all those who are in want.

Let all Nuns therefore be thoroughly convinced that theirs is a fully and totally apostolic vocation, hemmed in by no limitations of space, matter, or time, but always and everywhere extending to whatever in any way concerns the honor of the heavenly Spouse or the salvation of souls. And this universal apostolic vocation of Nuns makes it perfectly appropriate that Monasteries should consider as recommended to their prayers the needs of the Church as a whole and of all individuals and groups.

The apostolate which is common to all Nuns and by which they should work zealously for the honor of the divine Spouse and promote the good of the universal Church and of all the faithful, disposes principally of the following means:

1. The example of Christian perfection; for their life, though without words, yet speaks strongly, ever drawing the faithful to Christ and to Christian perfection, and like a standard rallies the good soldiers of Christ for battle and invites them to the crown of glory.

2. Prayer, both that which is offered publicly in the name of the Church by the solemn recital to God of the canonical hours

seven times each day, and that which is offered privately to God, continuously and in every form.

3. The generous offering of themselves, so that the hardships which come from the common life and from faithful regular observance, may be supplemented by other exercises of self-denial either prescribed by the Rules and Constitutions or undertaken entirely of their own accord, so as generously to "fill up those things that are wanting of the sufferings of Christ, for His body, which is the Church."[2]

Now that We have given a historical summary of the institution of Nuns and have accurately described the ways in which it can be adapted to the needs of present-day life, We proceed to state the general norms by which that adaptation can be made to achieve its purpose. The Sacred Congregation of Religious will attend to the administration of this entire Constitution and of the General Statutes as applied to all Federations of Monasteries already formed or to be formed in the future and to individual Monasteries; the same Sacred Congregation is empowered to do by Our Authority, through instructions, declarations, responses, and other documents of the kind, everything which concerns putting the Constitution carefully and effectively into practice and securing the faithful and prompt observance of the General Statutes.

## GENERAL STATUTES OF NUNS

### Art. I

§ 1. The name *Nuns* in this Constitution, according to law (c. 488, 7°), means, besides religious women of solemn vows, those also who have pronounced simple vows, perpetual or temporary, in Monasteries in which solemn vows are either actually taken or should be taken according to their institute; unless the contrary is certain from the context or from the nature of the case.

§ 2. The lawful use of the name of Nuns (c. 488, 7°) and the application of the law of Nuns, are in no way hindered by: 1) *simple profession* lawfully made in Monasteries (§ 1); 2) *minor*

[2] Col. 1:24.

*papal cloister* if that is prescribed for or has been duly granted to the Monasteries in question; 3) *the exercise of works of the apostolate* in conjunction with the contemplative life, either by reason of Constitutions approved and confirmed by the Holy See for certain Orders, or by reason of lawful prescription or concession of the Holy See for certain Monasteries.

§ 3. This Apostolic Constitution does not legally apply to: 1) religious Congregations (c. 488, 2°) and the Sisters who are members thereof (c. 488, 7°), who by their institute take only simple vows; 2) Societies of women living in common after the manner of religious, and their members (c. 673).

### Art. II

§ 1. The special mode of monastic religious life, which Nuns must faithfully practice under a strict regular discipline, and for which they are destined by the Church, is the canonical contemplative life.

§ 2. By the term *canonical contemplative* life is meant, not that interior and theological life to which all souls living in religion and even in the world are called, and which each one for himself can live no matter where, but rather the external profession of religious discipline which, through the observance of cloister, through practices of piety, prayer, and penance, and finally through the work to which the Nuns must devote themselves, exists for the sake of interior contemplation, so that the pursuit of this latter easily can and should effectively pervade their life as a whole and all its activity.

§ 3. If the canonical contemplative life under strict regular discipline cannot be habitually observed, the monastic character is not to be conferred, nor, if it is already conferred, to be retained.

### Art. III

§ 1. The solemn religious vows, pronounced by all the members of a Monastery or at least by one class of them, constitute the principal note by reason of which Monasteries of women are classed, not among religious Congregations, but among regular Orders (c. 488, 2°). But in these Monasteries all the professed religious come within the appellation of Regulars in law, according to canon 490, and are properly called, not Sisters, but Nuns (c. 488, 7°).

§ 2. All Monasteries in which only simple vows are taken shall be entitled to ask for the instauration of solemn vows. In fact, unless there are grave reasons to the contrary, they shall take steps to return to the solemn vows.

§ 3. The ancient solemn formulae for the consecration of Virgins, which are in the Roman Pontifical, are reserved to Nuns.

### Art. IV

§ 1. The strict cloister of Nuns which is called papal, saving always and for all Monasteries those characteristics which belong, so to speak, to its very nature, shall be hereafter of two classes: *major* and *minor*.

§ 2. 1° The *major* papal cloister, that is, the one which is described in the Code (cc. 600–602), is fully confirmed by this Our Apostolic Constitution. The Sacred Congregation of Religious, by Our Authority, shall declare for what reasons dispensation from major cloister may be granted, so that, without prejudice to its nature, the cloister may be better adapted to the conditions of our time.

2° Except as hereinafter provided in § 3, 3°, the major papal cloister must be in effect as a matter of law in all Monasteries which profess the purely contemplative life.

§ 3. 1° The *minor* papal cloister shall retain from the ancient cloister of Nuns those elements and shall be protected by those sanctions, which are expressly declared in the Instructions of the Holy See to be necessary to preserve and vindicate its natural character.

2° Subject to this minor papal cloister are Monasteries of Nuns of solemn vows which, either by their institute or by lawful permission, undertake works with externs to such an extent that many of the religious and a notable part of the house are habitually occupied in them.

3° Likewise all Monasteries, even though purely contemplative, in which only simple vows are taken, shall be subject at least to the provisions of this cloister.

§ 4. 1° Papal cloister either major or minor is to be regarded as a necessary condition, not only in order that solemn vows may be taken (§ 2), but also in order that those Monasteries in which simple vows are taken (§ 3) may hereafter be considered true Monasteries of Nuns according to canon 488, 7°.

2° If the rules of at least the minor papal cloister cannot for the most part be observed, the solemn vows which are in use shall be taken away.

§ 5. 1° The minor papal cloister, especially as regards those notes in which it differs from the cloister of Congregations or of Orders of men, is to be observed in places where Nuns do not take solemn vows.

2° If however it appears with certainty that in some Monastery even the minor cloister cannot regularly be observed, that Monastery is to be converted to a house of either a Congregation or a Society.

### Art. V

§ 1. The Church deputes Nuns alone among the women consecrated to God, for the public prayer which is offered to God in her name either in choir (c. 610, § 1) or privately (c. 610, § 3); and these she binds under grave obligation, by law according to their Constitutions, to perform this prayer by daily reciting the canonical hours.

§ 2. All Monasteries of Nuns and all individual Nuns professed of the solemn or simple vows, everywhere, are bound to recite the divine Office in choir according to canon 610, § 1 and their Constitutions.

§ 3. According to canon 610, § 3, Nuns who were absent from choir, if they have not taken solemn vows, are not strictly bound to recite the hours privately, unless the Constitutions expressly provide otherwise (c. 578, 2°); however, it is the mind of the Church, not only, as We stated above (art. IV), that solemn vows for Nuns be put in effect everywhere, but also, if this is temporarily impossible, that Nuns who in place of the solemn vows have taken perpetual simple vows, faithfully perform the divine Office.

§ 4. The conventual Mass corresponding to the Office of the day according to the Rubrics should be celebrated in all Monasteries every day if possible (c. 610, § 2).

## Art. VI

§ 1. 1° Monasteries of Nuns, unlike other houses of religious women, are, by reason of and according to the Code, *sui iuris* (c. 488, 8°).

2° The Superioresses of the individual Monasteries of Nuns are according to law Major Superiors, and have all the faculties which belong to Major Superiors (c. 488, 8°), unless as to some of them it is clear from the context or from the nature of the case that they pertain only to men (c. 490).

§ 2. 1° The extent of the condition of being *sui iuris*, or the so-called autonomy of Monasteries of Nuns, is defined by both the common and the particular law.

2° Neither this Constitution nor the Federations of Monasteries which are permitted by it (art. VII) and established by its authority, derogate in any way from the juridical supervision which the law gives either to local Ordinaries or to regular Superiors in regard to individual Monasteries.

3° The juridical relations between individual Monasteries and local Ordinaries or regular Superiors, continue to be governed by the common and particular law.

§ 3. This Constitution does not in any way determine whether individual Monasteries are under the power of the local Ordinary or are, within the limits defined by law, exempt from it and subject to the regular Superior.

## Art. VII

§ 1. Monasteries of Nuns are not only *sui iuris* (c. 488, 8°) but also juridically distinct from and independent of each other, and are not united and bound together by any other than spiritual and moral bonds, even though they be legally subject to the same first Order or religious Institute.

§ 2. 1° The mutual liberty of Monasteries, which is rather accepted as a fact than imposed by law, is in no way impaired by the formation of a Federation; neither are such Federations to be considered as forbidden by law nor as in any way inconsistent with the nature and purposes of the religious life of Nuns.

2° Federations of Monasteries, although they are not prescribed by any general rule, are nevertheless highly recommended by the Holy See, not only as a safeguard against the evils and inconveniences which can arise from complete separation, but also as a means of promoting regular observance and the life of contemplation.

§ 3. The establishment of any form of Federation of Monasteries of Nuns, or of Confederations made up of such Federations, is reserved to the Holy See.

§ 4. Every Federation or Confederation must necessarily be organized and governed according to its laws approved by the Holy See.

§ 5. 1° Without prejudice to art. VI, §§ 2, 3 or to the essential notion of autonomy as above defined (§ 1), nothing forbids that, in forming a Federation of Monasteries, after the example of certain Monastic Congregations and Orders of Canons or of Monks, certain equitable conditions and suspensions of this autonomy, which are considered necessary or advantageous, be adopted.

2° However, forms of Federation which seem contrary to the autonomy of which We have spoken (§ 1) and which approach the idea of a central government, are especially reserved to the Holy See, and cannot be set up without its express permission.

§ 6. Federations of Monasteries, in view of their source and of the Authority on which they directly depend and by which they are governed, are of pontifical right according to Canon Law.

§ 7. The Holy See may, according to need, exercise immediate vigilance and authority over a Federation through some religious Assistant, whose office it shall be not only to represent the Holy See but to see to the preservation of the genuine spirit of the Order and to give aid and counsel to the Superioress in the right and prudent government of the Federation.

§ 8. 1° The Statutes of a Federation must be conformed not only to the prescribed norms which shall be worked out with Our Authority by the Sacred Congregation of Religious, but also to the nature, laws, spirit, and traditions, ascetical, disciplinary or juridical, and apostolic, of the Order in question.

2° The principal purpose of a Federation of Monasteries is to give each other fraternal aid, not only in promoting the religious spirit and regular monastic discipline, but also in managing economic matters.

3° In approving Statutes, special norms may in a proper case be given to regulate the faculty and moral obligation of mutually asking for and granting to each other such Nuns as may be thought necessary for the government of the Monasteries, for the training of novices in a common novitiate to be established for all or several Monasteries, or finally for supplying other moral or material needs of the Monasteries or of the Nuns.

### Art. VIII

§ 1. Monastic work, to which even Nuns of the contemplative life must apply themselves, should be as far as possible in accord with the Rule, the Constitutions, and traditions of the Order in question.

§ 2. The work should be so managed that, together with the other means approved by the Church (cc. 547–551, 582), and the aid which Divine Providence will supply, it may assure the proper support of the Nuns.

§ 3. 1° The Ordinaries of places, regular Superiors, and the Superioresses of Monasteries and Federations, are bound to use all diligence to see to it that the Nuns may never lack necessary, adequate, and productive work.

2° The Nuns, on the other hand, are bound in conscience, not only to earn by the sweat of their brow the bread by which they live, as the Apostle warns (2 Thess. 3:10), but also to render themselves daily more fit for various works according to the needs of the time.

### Art. IX

All Nuns, in order to be faithful to their divine apostolic vocation, must not only use the general means of the monastic apostolate, but must moreover observe the following:

§ 1. Nuns who in their own Constitutions or lawful prescriptions have definite works of some special form of apostolate, are bound to give and consecrate themselves faithfully to those works according to their Constitutions or Statutes and prescriptions.

§ 2. Nuns who profess a purely contemplative life:

1° If they have or have had in their own traditions some accepted special form of external apostolate, shall faithfully retain the same, adapting it to the needs of the present day, always without prejudice to their life of contemplation, and if they have lost it, they shall diligently see that it is restored. As regards adaptation, if any doubt arises let them consult the Holy See.

2° On the other hand, if their life of pure contemplation has hitherto not been coupled in any permanent and constant way with the external apostolate either by the approved Constitutions of the Order or by tradition, in that case they may, and at least out of charity they should be employed, only in cases of necessity and for a limited time, especially in those individual or personal forms of the apostolate which, according to criteria to be fixed by the Holy See, seem compatible with the contemplative life as it is observed in the Order in question.

Whatever has been decreed by this Letter shall, according to Our will and command, be firmly established and valid, all things to the contrary notwithstanding, even though they be worthy of most particular mention.

And it is Our will that copies or excerpts of this Letter, even in print, provided they are subscribed by some public notary and adorned with the seal of some ecclesiastical dignitary, shall receive the same faith and credit as would be shown to the Letter itself if it were presented and shown.

Let no one, therefore, infringe or rashly impugn this page of Our declaration and will; if anyone presume to attempt it, let him know that he will incur the wrath of Almighty God and of the holy Apostles Peter and Paul.

Given at Rome, from Saint Peter's the twenty-first day of November, Feast of the Presentation of the Blessed Virgin Mary, in the Year of Jubilee, Nineteen Hundred and Fifty, the twelfth of Our Pontificate.

**AAS 43–5**; Pius XII, Apostolic Constitution and General Statutes of Nuns, 21 Nov., 1950.

Cf. *Commentarium pro Religiosis,* 31 (1952)–27 (Escudero); p. 37 (Tabera). *Monitor Ecclesiasticus,* 76 (1951)–226 (Pugliese); *Periodica,* 40 (1951)–78 (Abellán).

## Instruction on the Apostolic Constitution *Sponsa Christi* (S. C. Rel., 23 Nov., 1950) AAS 43–37.

An instruction of the Sacred Congregation of Religious "for putting into practice the Constitution *Sponsa Christi,*" is as follows:

I. Among the remarkable documents by which our Holy Father, Pius XII, by Divine Providence Pope, has willed to adorn and crown the Holy Year as with so many precious jewels, assuredly not the least is the Apostolic Constitution, *Sponsa Christi,* which deals with the renewal and advancement within God's Church of the holy and venerable institution of nuns. This Sacred Congregation, which as its appointed task, promptly and faithfully assists the Holy Father in all things pertaining to the state of perfection, has reverently and joyfully received from him the commission of putting into execution this Constitution, truly remarkable from so many points of view, and of making its application assured and easy.

II. To fulfill this honorable duty, the Sacred Congregation has assembled in this Instruction some practical norms for those points which offer greater difficulty.

III. Now, the points in the Apostolic Constitution which offer difficulty and hence require special clarification are: (1) those which refer to the major or minor cloister of nuns; (2) those which deal with the establishment of federations and the limitation of autonomy; (3) finally those which have to do with obtaining and co-ordinating productive labor for the monasteries.

## I. MAJOR AND MINOR CLOISTER FOR NUNS

IV. The Apostolic Constitution, *Sponsa Christi* (art. IV), prescribes a special cloister for monasteries of all nuns which differs from the episcopal cloister of congregations (c. 604), and which, according to the general norm of the law, is papal, as is the cloister of orders of men (c. 597, § 1). In fact, regarding a number of prescriptions dealing with both the entrance of externs into the limits of the cloister and the going out of the nuns from the same, the regulations are stricter than those which control the papal cloister of men.

V. Hereafter there will be two types of papal cloister for nuns: the one *major,* which is reserved for monasteries in which solemn vows are taken and a purely contemplative life is led, even though the number of the nuns may have decreased; the other *minor,* which, as a rule, is applied to monasteries in which a life is led which is not exclusively contemplative, or the nuns take simple vows only.

### A. Major Papal Cloister

VI. *Major* papal cloister is that which is described in the Code (cc. 600, 602) and accurately defined by the Sacred Congregation in its Instruction, *Nuper edito,* approved by the late Pope Pius XI on February 6, 1924. This cloister is fully confirmed in the Constitution, *Sponsa Christi,* safeguarding the following declarations which the Constitution empowers the Sacred Congregation to make (art. IV, § 2, 1°) so that its observance may be prudently adapted to the needs of the times and to local circumstances.

VII. Nuns bound by major papal cloister, after their profession, by reason of the profession itself and by the prescription of ecclesiastical law, contract a grave obligation:

1° of remaining always within the precincts of the monastery which have been put within the definite limits of the cloister, so that they may not leave the cloister even for a moment under any pretext or condition without a special indult of the Holy See, except in those cases only which are provided for in the canons and instructions of the Holy See, or which are envisioned in the constitutions or statutes approved by the Holy See itself.

2° of not admitting to the parts of the monastery subject to the law of cloister any person whatsoever no matter of what class, condition, sex, or age, even for a moment, without a special indult of the Holy See. Certain exceptions, however, of persons and cases are expressly made in the canons and in instructions of the Holy See, as well as in the constitutions or statutes approved by it.

VIII. 1° Indults and dispensations to leave the major cloister after profession (VII, 1°) or to enter it or to admit others (VII, 2°) are reserved exclusively to the Holy See, and can be granted by it alone or in its name and by its delegation.

2° Reasons for obtaining dispensations should be proportionately grave, due consideration being given to the circumstances of cases, times, and places, keeping in mind the practice and style of the Roman Curia.

IX. 1° The faculty to dispense may be given *ab homine,* either for a definite period of time for all cases occurring during it, or for a certain number of cases. There is nothing, however, to hinder the granting of certain permissions habitually in particular law having legitimate approval, for instance, in the constitutions, in the statutes of federations, and in similar documents.

2° Whether granted *ab homine* or by general or particular law, indults and dispensations must determine, according to the instructions of the Holy See and the practice and style of the Roman Curia, the conditions and precautions to which the dispensation is subject.

X. The penalties against those who violate the laws of cloister remain as stated in the Code (c. 2342, 1°, 3°).

### *B. Minor Papal Cloister*

XI. *Minor* papal cloister:

1° retains intact the fundamental rules of the cloister of nuns, inasmuch as it differs greatly from the cloister of congregations (c. 604) as well as from that of orders of men (cc. 598–599);

2° must safeguard and facilitate for all the observance and care of solemn chastity;

3° it must protect and efficaciously foster the contemplative life of the monastery;

4° The employments which the Church has designedly entrusted to these monasteries must be so harmonized with the contemplative life within the confines of the minor papal enclosure that the latter may by all means be preserved while these works are properly and advantageously performed.

5° In monasteries which engage in approved works, the prescription of canon 599, § 1 for the cloister of orders of men, which is likewise applied by canon 604, § 2 to the cloister of congregations, is to be strictly and faithfully observed, in such a way that a clear and complete separation be ever maintained between buildings or sections thereof set apart for the living quarters of the nuns and for the exercises of the monastic life, and those parts made over to necessary works.

XII. Minor papal cloister includes:

1° a grave prohibition against admitting into the parts of the house set aside for the community of nuns and subject to the law of cloister (c. 597) any persons whatsoever who are not members of the community, regardless of class, condition, sex, or age, according to canon 600;

2° another grave prohibition forbidding the nuns after profession to leave the precincts of the monastery, in the same way as nuns subject to major cloister (nn. VII–IX).

XIII. 1° The passage of the nuns from the parts reserved to the community to the other places within the precincts of the monastery destined for the works of the apostolate is allowed for this purpose alone, with the permission of the superior, and under proper safeguards, to those who, according to the norms of the constitutions and the prescriptions of the Holy See, are destined for the exercise of the apostolate in any way.

2° If by reason of the apostolate, dispensations from the prescriptions of n. XII, 2° become necessary, they may be given only to nuns and other religious who are lawfully assigned to the employments, under grave obligation in conscience for superioresses, for ordinaries, and for superiors regular, to whom the custody of the cloister is entrusted (c. 603).

XIV. Admittance of externs to the parts of the monastery devoted to employments of whatever kind is governed by these norms:

1° Habitual admittance is allowed to pupils, boys or girls, or to other persons in whose favor ministries are performed, and to such women only with whom necessary contact is demanded by reason and on the occasion of such ministries.

2° The local Ordinary should, by a general or habitual declaration, define as such those exceptions which must be made of necessity, for instance, those ordinarily required by the civil law for the purpose of inspections, examinations, or for other reasons.

3° Other exceptions, should such at times seem truly necessary in individual cases, are reserved to the express grant of the Ordinary, who is in conscience bound to impose prudent precautions.

XV. 1° Nuns who unlawfully leave the precincts of the monastery *ipso facto* incur excommunication reserved simply to the Holy See according to canon 2342, 3°, or by express grant reserved to the local Ordinary.

2° Nuns who illicitly leave the parts of the monastery reserved to the community and go to other places within the precincts of the monastery, are to be punished by the superior or by the local Ordinary, according to the gravity of their fault.

3° Those who illicitly enter the parts of the monastery reserved to the community and those who bring them in or allow them to enter, incur excommunication reserved simply to the Holy See.

4° Those who illegitimately enter the parts of the monastery not reserved to the community, as well as those who bring them in or permit them to enter, are to be severely punished according to the gravity of their fault by the Ordinary of the place in which the monastery is located.

XVI. Dispensations from minor papal cloister, except those admitted by law, are, as a rule, reserved to the Holy See.

Faculties more or less broad, as circumstances seem to require, can be granted to Ordinaries either *ab homine* or in the constitutions and statutes.

## II. FEDERATIONS OF MONASTERIES OF NUNS

XVII. Federations of monasteries of nuns, according to the norm of the Constitution, *Sponsa Christi* (art. VII, § 2, 2°), are earnestly recommended, both to avoid the harmful effects which both more grievously and more readily befall entirely independent monasteries, and which by union can to a great extent be avoided more effectively, as well as to foster both their spiritual and temporal interests.

Although, as a rule, federations of monasteries are not imposed (art. VIII, § 2, 2°), nevertheless, the reasons which would recommend them in general could, in particular cases, be so strong that, everything considered, they would be deemed necessary by the Sacred Congregation.

XVIII. Federations of monasteries are not to be impeded by the fact that the individual monasteries which intend to form them are subject to superiors regular. Provision will have to be made for this common subjection in the *Statutes of the Federation.*

XIX. When, because of the intention of the founder or for any other reason that may occur, there already exists some kind of beginning of a union or federation of monasteries of the same order or institute, anything already done or outlined must be taken into account in the development of the federation itself.

XX. A federation of monasteries in no way directly affects the relation, already in existence according to the common or to the particular law, of the individual monasteries to the local

Ordinaries or to the superiors regular. Hence, unless an express and lawful derogation is made to this rule, the powers of Ordinaries and superiors are neither increased nor diminished nor changed in any way.

XXI. The statutes of a federation may grant certain rights over the federation to Ordinaries and to superiors which as a rule do not belong to them, leaving intact generally the right over each individual monastery as such.

XXII. The general and principal purposes and advantages of unions and federations are the following:

1° the legally recognized faculty and the canonically sanctioned duty of a mutual fraternal assistance, both in the conservation, defense, and increase of regular observance, and of domestic economy, as well as in all other things;

2° the establishment of novitiates common to all or to a group of monasteries for cases in which, either because of a lack of personnel necessary for the directive offices, or because of other circumstances moral, economic, local, and the like, a solid and practical spiritual, disciplinary, technical, and cultural training cannot be given in the individual monasteries;

3° the faculty and the moral obligation, defined by certain norms and accepted by federated monasteries, of asking for and of mutually interchanging nuns who may be necessary for government and training;

4° the possibility of and freedom for a mutual temporary exchange or ceding of subjects, and also of a permanent assignment, because of health or other moral or material need.

XXIII. The characteristic notes of federations which are to be considered essential when taken together are enumerated as follows:

1° *From the source* from which they spring and *from the authority* from which as such they depend and which governs them directly, federations of nuns are of *pontifical right* according to the Code (c. 488, 3°). Hence not only their establishment, but also the approval of their statutes, and the enrollment of monasteries in, or their separation from, a federation, belongs to the Holy See exclusively.

Provided all the rights over individual monasteries granted by the Code to Ordinaries are safeguarded, federations are subject to the Holy See in all those matters in which pontifical institutes of women are directly subject to it, unless a lawful exception has been expressly provided for. The Holy See may commit certain items of its prerogatives, either habitually or in single instances, to its immediate assistants or delegates for federations.

2° *By reason of territory or of extension,* federations of monasteries are to be established preferably along regional lines, for easier government, unless the small number of monasteries or other just or proportionate causes demand otherwise.

3° *By reason of the moral persons* which constitute them, inasmuch as they are collegiate persons (c. 100, § 2), federations are composed of monasteries of the same order and of the same internal observance, though they need not necessarily depend on the same local Ordinary or superior regular, nor have the same kind of vows or form of cloister.

4° Confederations of regional federations can be allowed if need, or great advantage, or the traditions of the order recommend them.

5° From the standpoint of the independence of the monasteries, the bond which holds the federated monasteries together should be such that it does not interfere with their autonomy, at least in essentials (c. 488, 2°, 8°). Although derogations from autonomy are not to be presumed, they can be granted with the previous consent of each monastery, provided that grave reasons seem to recommend or demand them.

XXIV. All federations of monasteries of nuns must have their own statutes subject to the approval of the Holy See before they can be established. The statutes must accurately determine the following:

1° the aims which each federation proposes to itself;

2° the manner in which the government of the federation is to be regulated, either with regard to constitutive elements, as for example, president, visitators, council, and the like; or as to the manner of appointment to these offices; or, finally, the power of this government and the manner of conducting it;

3° the means which the federation should use that it may be able to carry out its aims pleasantly and vigorously;

4° the conditions and means to be used in putting into execution the prescriptions regarding the mutual interchange of persons laid down in art. VII, § 3, 2° of the Constitution, *Sponsa Christi;*

5° the juridical standing of nuns transferred to another monastery, whether in the monastery from which the transfer takes place, or in that to which it is made;

6° the economic help to be given by each monastery for the common enterprises of the entire federation;

7° the administration of the common novitiate or of other works common to the federation, if there be such.

XXV. 1° In order that the Holy See may be able to exercise a direct and efficacious vigilance and authority over federations, each federation can be given a religious assistant, as need or usefulness may suggest.

2° The religious assistant will be appointed by the Sacred Congregation according to the statutes, after all interested parties have been heard.

3° In each case his duties will be accurately defined in the decree of appointment. The principal ones are as follows: to take care that the genuine spirit of a profoundly contemplative life as well as the spirit proper to the order and institute be securely preserved and increased; likewise, to see that a prudent and exact government be established and preserved in the federation; to have regard for the solid religious training of the novices and of the religious themselves; to help the council in temporal matters of greater moment.

4° The Holy See will delegate or commit to the assistant such powers as may seem opportune in individual cases.

## III. MONASTIC LABOR

XXVI. 1° Since, by the disposition of Divine Providence, the temporal necessities of life are at times so pressing that nuns seem morally compelled to seek and accept labors beyond their accustomed ones, and even perhaps to extend the time given to labor, all should as true religious submit themselves promptly and humbly to the dispositions of Divine Providence, as the Christian faithful do in like circumstances.

2° They should do this, however, not anxiously or capriciously or arbitrarily, but prudently as far as may seem truly necessary or suitable, seeking with simple hearts a balance between their understanding of fidelity to the letter and to tradition, and a filial subjection to the permissive and positive dispositions of Divine Providence.

3° Keeping these directives in mind, let them submit to ecclesiastical or to religious superiors, as the case may require, whatever arrangements seem advisable.

XXVII. Ecclesiastical and religious superiors must:

1° by all means seek and obtain profitable labor for the nuns who need it, and, should the case require it, also employ committees of pious men or women, and, with due caution and prudence, even secular agencies established for such purposes;

2° maintain a careful supervision of the quality and orderly arrangement of the work, and require a just price for it;

3° to superintend diligently the coordination of the activities and the labor of individual monasteries so that they may help, supply, and complement one another, and see to it that every vestige of competition is entirely avoided.

**AAS 43–37;** S. C. Rel., Instruction, 23 Nov., 1950.

NOTE: The above translation is reproduced with the kind permission of the Editors, from the *Review for Religious,* 10 (1951)–205.

For annotations on this Instruction, cf. *Periodica,* 40 (1951)–78 (Abellán).

## Apostolic Constitution and General Statutes to Be Explained to Monasteries of Nuns (S. C. Rel., Letter, 7 March, 1951) Private.

A Letter of the Sacred Congregation of Religious:

Your Excellency:

His Holiness has entrusted to the Sacred Congregation of Religious the task of putting into effect the Apostolic Constitution *Sponsa Christi* of 23 Nov., 1950, and the General Statutes therein contained which are designed to promote the greater good of monasteries of Nuns (*Moniales*).

For the exact fulfillment of the mandate of His Holiness, the Sacred Congregation now appeals to Your Excellency, with entire confidence that Your Excellency will fully supply whatever cooperation is demanded by the interests of the monasteries in the country in which Your Excellency so worthily represents the Holy Father.

Above all the Sacred Congregation considers it very important that the Apostolic Constitution *Sponsa Christi* and the Instruction of the same Sacred Congregation, which appeared in the

*Acta Apostolicae Sedis,* Vol. 43, p. 5 sq., be made known to all monasteries of Nuns, so that they may appreciate the love which the Church bears toward them and her solicitude for them, that those timely improvements which experience and the present state of religious life suggest, may serve for the defense and advancement of their state of life.

I. Hence the Sacred Congregation asks Your Excellency to entrust to the Most Excellent Bishops the task of presenting and explaining the aforesaid pontifical documents to the monasteries of Nuns which are under their jurisdiction.

So that the explanation may be made in the manner best suited to the spirit of each Monastery, Your Excellency will kindly ask the Most Excellent Ordinaries to designate: *a*) for Monasteries of a Second Order, preferably Religious of the corresponding First Order who are qualified for this important work, whether they reside in the diocese or out of it; *b*) for the other monasteries, let the Most Excellent Ordinaries select qualified persons among the Religious or diocesan or extra-diocesan priests.

The names of the persons chosen for each Monastery should in every case be reported to Your Excellency, who will according to your prudent judgment definitely confirm the appointment.

Finally, for monasteries of Nuns which are actually under Apostolic Visitation, and for those which are subject to Regulars, this Sacred Congregation will assign the task of explaining the two pontifical documents, to the Apostolic Visitors and to the Regular Superiors respectively.

II. Your Excellency will please recommend that the persons appointed explain to the Nuns the following points especially:

1) These new documents are a new concrete proof of the solicitude of the Church for the true welfare of Monasteries of Nuns, in line with her practice throughout the centuries according to the exigencies of various times and places. It is due to this action of the Church that the monastic life of Nuns, while remaining in substance unchanged, has been enriched with new elements, profiting from the improvements and wise adaptations which the religious life has manifested in various centuries (cf. *Sponsa Christi,* AAS, Vol. 43, pp. 6–11).

2) Far from wishing to encroach upon the contemplative life of those who, "choosing the better part" (*Sponsa Christi, loc. cit.,* p. 6), have retired to Monasteries, the Apostolic Con-

stitution, after having explained the nature of the contemplative life (Statutes, Art. II), desires that, both for the Community as a whole and for the individual Nuns, "a truly and solidly contemplative life shall be not only preserved but constantly nourished and strengthened" (*Sponsa Christi, l. c.*, p. 11). To this end the Constitution emphasizes the obligation according to the Constitutions, and the public character of Choir in Monasteries of Nuns.

For the same reason, papal cloister remains substantially unchanged; however, in monasteries which have apostolic works, cloister is regulated and adapted so that the contemplative life may suffer no harm and that at the same time the works, nourished by the contemplative life, may be able to develop as need may require (Statutes, Art. IV; Instruction, nn XI–XV).

3) So that the religious life of Nuns may correspond more perfectly to their desire of complete consecration to God, the Holy See earnestly exhorts those Monasteries where — in the past — the profession of solemn vows had to be abandoned because of special circumstances, to resume them, unless there still exist grave reasons to the contrary (Statutes, Art. III).

4) The two documents also bring out the fact that the vocation of Nuns, though it be a vocation to a purely contemplative life, is in the fullest sense an apostolic vocation, seeing that the love of God cannot be separated from the love of the neighbor. It is for this reason that these documents recommend to all the apostolate of good example, prayer, and sacrifice (*Sponsa Christi, l. c.*, p. 14). The Apostolic Constitution recalls the rise of Institutes of Nuns which harmoniously combined the contemplative life with apostolic works, and recommends to these Institutes and to the monasteries which have a tradition to that effect, to dedicate themselves wholeheartedly to it (Statutes, Art. IX). For Monasteries of the purely contemplative life, on the other hand, it provides that only by reason of special necessity may or shall the external apostolate be practiced; and this must always be of such a character that the contemplative life shall suffer no harm therefrom (Statutes, Art. IX).

5) The introduction of Federations of monasteries of Nuns appears as the source of numberless advantages, spiritual, disciplinary, and even economic (*Sponsa Christi, l. c.*, p. 13).

In exhorting Monasteries to unite in Federations, the Holy

Father repeats in the Apostolic Constitution what he had already said in 1947, in his Homily to the Benedictines in the Basilica of St. Paul's.

Coming out of the complete isolation in which monasteries professing the same Rule and the same norms of life and spirituality existed for centuries, will mean: *a*) a mutual fraternal collaboration for the attainment of their proper end; *b*) the possibility of making better provision for young vocations and of finding a way out of difficult situations in which the Monasteries may be implicated; *c*) a guarantee of fidelity to the proper spirit and tradition of the Order (Instruction, nn. XVII–XXII).

All of these benefits will be furthered by the presence and activity of a religious Assistant for such Federations, appointed by the Holy See (Instruction, n. XXV).

Naturally, in order that the Federations may actually produce the benefits mentioned, it will be necessary that they be carefully prepared and wisely organized. This Sacred Congregation will not be backward in offering its own assistance and in giving all the instructions which the various cases may require.

6) Federations will also facilitate the organization of that productive monastic labor, which is presented to Nuns as a duty of penance, a way of mortification, and a means of support (Statutes, Art. VIII, Instruction, nn. XXVI–XXVII). To promote their development, ecclesiastical authorities and pious lay persons will not fail to offer their benevolent cooperation. Among other benefits, this will help to extricate the Monasteries from the serious economic difficulties in which not a few of them are entangled.

Your Excellency will kindly require of the Most Excellent Ordinaries and then transmit to this Sacred Congregation a report covering especially the following points: *a*) how the two pontifical documents have been explained to the different Monasteries; *b*) how the said explanation was received; *c*) what benefits are expected from it in the various Monasteries; *d*) what difficulties may arise from the explanation and application of the documents.

This Sacred Congregation expresses in advance its gratitude to Your Excellency and to the Most Reverend Ordinaries who will be good enough to furnish the required information and thus enable the Sacred Congregation to fulfill the task assigned to it by the Holy Father.

Thanking Your Excellency in advance . . . etc.

**(Private)**; S. C. Rel., Letter, 7 March, 1951. Translation made from the Italian text which was printed officially by the Sacred Congregation. Annotations, ***Periodica,*** 40 (1951)–298 (Abellán).

NOTE: The above Letter was sent to the Apostolic Nuncios, Internuncios, and Delegates in the various countries. Another Letter almost identical with this and bearing the same date, was sent to the Superiors General of the various Orders of Regulars which have Monasteries of Nuns dependent on them, asking them to see that the Regular Superiors explain the Apostolic Constitution and the General Statutes to the Monasteries subject to them, following the same order of points as outlined above.

## Manner of Taking Solemn Vows by Permission of the Holy See: Various Questions (S. C. Rel., 9 Aug., 1951) Private.

A private reply of the Sacred Congregation of Religious, 9 Aug., 1951:

Your Excellency:

This Sacred Congregation has received the notice of the promulgation of the Decree of 22 Feb., 1951 (N. 292/51), which provides that in future the nuns of the Monastery of D, in the city of L, must take solemn vows and observe the papal cloister. We thank you cordially for the communication.

On the same occasion Your Excellency presented some questions to this Sacred Congregation for solution. Accordingly, this S. C. after carefully considering the matter decided to reply as follows:

1. Q. Is the formula of profession necessary for the validity of solemn vows recently pronounced?

R. In the negative; that is, it is not necessary for validity, without prejudice to canon 572, § 1, 5°.

2. Q. Is a promise of obedience, made to one who is not the Superior, valid?

R. In the negative, unless the power of the Superior has been merely *suspended* by prescription of the Holy See; in which case the promise is valid *in se,* though it cannot be exercised.

3. Q. When the Mother Prioress pronounced the solemn vows in the hands of the Bishop, should she not have promised obedience to the same Bishop?

R. In the negative.

4. Q. The Master General of the Order of Preachers is not the canonical Superior of nuns who are subject to the local Ordinary. For that matter he was neither present nor represented at the promulgation of the Decree and at the taking of the vows.

R. This is provided for in 2 and 3.

**(Private)**; S. C. Rel., Replies, 9 Aug., 1951. Annotations, *Commentarium pro Religiosis,* 32 (1953)–111 (Gutiérrez).

NOTE: The *formula* for the decree by which the Holy See, at the request of particular Monasteries of nuns, grants them permission to take solemn vows, is reported above, p. 357. The same formula appears in *Commentarium pro Religiosis,* 32 (1953)–108, with a commentary by Gutiérrez, who also reports and comments on the above *private replies* on that subject.

**Permission to Take Solemn Vows and Observe Papal Cloister** (S. C. Rel., 12 Nov., 1951) **Private.**

Inasmuch as the nuns of the Monastery of the Discalced Carmelites of N.N. have petitioned from the Holy See the faculty of taking solemn vows and of observing the major papal cloister, the S. C. for the affairs of Religious, having heard the wish of the Ordinary of N.N., and having given the matter careful attention, has decreed that for the future, in the aforesaid Monastery, the nuns, having first made temporary vows according to the norm of canon 574 of the Code of Canon Law, may take solemn vows; and that the papal cloister, as prescribed by the Code of Canon Law and by the Apostolic Constitution, *Sponsa Christi* and the Instruction of the S. C. of Religious, *Inter praeclara,* of Nov. 23, 1950,[1] should be observed. All this should be done prudently, however, in such a manner that the nuns will realize the obligations of their solemn vows and with provision made for their proper sustenance.

When all these circumstances have been provided for, the Ordinary of N.N., either personally or through a delegate, can

[1] Both documents reported above in this volume on pp. 326 and 344 respectively.

in the name of the Holy See receive the solemn vows of the Superior of the Monastery; she in turn can receive the solemn profession of the other nuns, provided they have been professed for at least three years.

If any of the present members of the community wish not to oblige themselves by solemn vows, they are free to remain in simple vows, but they must realize that they are nevertheless bound to a strict observance of all the laws of the major papal cloister. Extern sisters, having completed their period of temporary vows, are to be admitted only to simple perpetual vows.

Finally it is committed to the Ordinary of N.N. to publish this Decree in the Monastery of the Carmelite nuns at N.N., once he is certain that the required conditions have been fulfilled. A document attesting to the publication and execution of this Decree is to be preserved in the archives of the Monastery, and a copy of that Document is to be sent to this Sacred Congregation.

All things to the contrary notwithstanding.

**(Private)**; S. C. Rel., 12 Nov., 1951. This Rescript (N. 11646/51) was given to an Archbishop in the United States for a Monastery of Discalced Carmelites. We reproduce it with the kind permission of the Archbishop and through the kindness of the Reverend Adam Ellis, S.J.

**External Apostolic Work of Monastic Nuns** (S. C. Rel., 19 March, 1952) **Private.**

A Letter of Father Larraona, Secretary of the Sacred Congregation of Religious, addressed to Ordinaries of places, is as follows:

As Your Excellency is aware, the venerable institution of Monastic Nuns was inspired with fresh vigor and provided for in such a way as to enable it to make continuous progress in the fulfillment of its mission in the Church and in human society, by the Apostolic Constitution, *Sponsa Christi*, of 21 November, 1950 (*AAS*, Vol. 43, p. 5).[1]

In that Constitution the Supreme Pontiff openly reminded Nuns, who are of such value for their service to the Church and to souls, that their vocation is "fully and totally apostolic" (*Sponsa Christi, loc. cit.*, p. 14),[2] since the love of the Heavenly

[1] Reported above on pp. 326–344. [2] *Ibid.*

Spouse cannot be separated from the love of souls, for whose salvation and sanctification He did not hesitate to lay down His life.

Hence in following primarily their vocation of the contemplative life, Nuns are already surely exercising the apostolate by their example of Christian and religious perfection, by their prayers and their practice of mortification.

To this form of apostolate, however, which constitutes the specific vocation of Nuns, immediate action in aid of the neighbor by works which are consistent with their peculiar way of life, may at times, and under certain circumstances should, be added as accessory.

Accordingly the Apostolic Constitution rightly declares that the exercise of apostolic works, if undertaken with due moderation and for sufficient reason, not only does no harm to the contemplative life, but may and should constitute an element which gives it a higher value and enlarges its effectiveness (*loc. cit.*, pp. 10–11).[3]

As regards Nuns "who in their own Constitutions or lawful prescriptions have definite works of some special form of apostolate," the Pontifical document renews the obligation to give and consecrate themselves faithfully to those works (General Statutes, IX).

But those who profess a purely contemplative life, "if they have or have had in their traditions some accepted special form of external apostolate" are earnestly exhorted by *Sponsa Christi* "faithfully to retain the same, adapting it to the needs of the present day, always without prejudice to their life of contemplation, and if they have lost it, to see to it diligently that it be restored" (General Statutes, IX, § 2, n. 1).

Finally for all Monasteries, even those in which "the life of contemplation has hitherto not been coupled in any permanent and constant way with the external apostolate," the Holy Father prescribes that "they may, and at least out of charity they should, be employed in cases of necessity and for a limited time, especially in those individual or personal forms of the apostolate" (General Statutes, IX, § 2, n. 2).

Consequently, the Constitution itself more than once envisages cases in which the supreme ecclesiastical authority may impose

[3] ***Ibid.***

some apostolic activity, according to criteria and norms to be fixed by the Holy See (*loc. cit.*, p. 15, art. I, § 2; p. 20, art. IX, § 2, n. 2).

Certainly Your Excellency is aware that the Supreme Pontiff, considering the present grave needs of the Church and of souls which require the cooperation of everyone without exception to meet them, has declared that "the time seems to have come for combining the monastic life, generally even in the case of Nuns who are given to contemplation, with some moderate apostolic work" (*loc. cit.*, p. 11).[4]

Accordingly the S. C. of Religious, faithfully following the august direction of the Supreme Pontiff in this matter, considers it its duty in these most critical circumstances of our times, to urge upon Monastic Nuns the obligation of collaborating appropriately and effectively in those apostolic works which can be harmoniously adapted to their peculiar way of life, such as the teaching of Christian doctrine, the preparation of boys and girls for their First Communion, and so on.

According to circumstances the Nuns may engage in these and similar works, while keeping the major papal cloister, or if necessary by obtaining appropriate adaptations or dispensations; sometimes however, at least temporarily, it will be necessary to adopt the minor papal cloister.

At all events the canonical contemplative life must always be protected and kept inviolate in its essential elements, keeping in mind also the peculiar character of each Monastery.

This Sacred Congregation kindly asks that, together with the particular needs of your diocese, Your Most Reverend Excellency make known to this Sacred Congregation also your opinion as to the cooperation in works of the apostolate, even on a temporary basis, which might possibly be expected of Nuns who are under cloister.

In case Your Excellency judges that the active cooperation of Nuns in these works is necessary, kindly indicate also how Nuns might furnish such assistance, and ask for the necessary faculties.

**(Private)**; S. C. Rel., Letter, 19 March, 1952; reported in *Commentarium pro Religiosis,* 31 (1952)–6.

---

[4] *Ibid.*

**Federation of Monasteries of Nuns: Formula for Nomination of Delegates** (S. C. Rel., 1953) **Private.**

The Sacred Congregation of Religious allowed to be published the following formula which it is accustomed to use in a decree nominating a Delegate to prepare a Confederation of Monasteries of nuns.[1]

Sacra Congregatio Negotiis Religiosorum praeposita, bonum Monasteriorum Monialium promovere cupiens, tempusque advenisse existimans Constitutionem Apostolicam, "Sponsa Christi," in iis quae ad Foederationes instituendas pertinent, ad praxim deducendi in Ordine ——, vi praesentis Decreti, Rev.mum Patrem —— pro Monasteriis —— DELEGATUM nominat ac designat.

Reverendissimi Patris Delegati munus erit de iis omnibus quae necessaria ad Foederationem constituendam visa fuerint curam gerere eaque diligenter perficere, ut puta conventibus ad hunc finem coactis praesidere, Documenta Pontificia institutum Monialium spectantia, prout opus erit, explanare, difficultates, si quae exstiterint, expedire, hisque similia.

Ut vero munus suum recte valeat exercere, Sacra Congregatio Rev.mo Patri Delegato quae sequuntur concedit facultates:

a) Permittendi —— aliisve Antistitis ut e clausura, una cum socia, ad conventus cum aliis —— vel Antistitis agendos, egrediantur;

b) Permittendi —— aliisve Monialibus egressum e clausura, ut alia Monialium —— Monasteria invisant ibique commorentur, cum ad Foederationem constituendam necessarium vel utile hoc ipsi videbitur;

c) Ingrediendi Monasteriorum clausuram si, ad eundem finem, necessarium vel utile fore censuerit.

Valeat, praeterea, Rev.mus Pater Delegatus commissam sibi potestatem alteri moderate subdelegare, sive ad actum sive etiam habitualiter, ad normam canonis 199, § 2. Moneat vero semper Exc.mos locorum Ordinarios, quorum res quomodolibet interest, de accepto mandato, et omni ope adnitatur ut cuncta prudenter et ordinate procedant, eo consilio ut bonum Monasteriorum revera promoveatur.

---

[1] Reproduced in the original Latin, since there seems to be no advantage in translating it.

In omnibus difficultatibus, quae in munere obeundo exstiterint, Rev.mus Pater Delegatus ad Sanctam Sedem recurrat, ad Quam de omnibus quae, sive a seipso sive a sui subdelegato, acta erunt, relationem transmittet. Eiusdem vero Apostolicae Sedis erit, quatenus oporteat, Foederationis erectionem decernere eiusdemque Statuta approbare.

Contrariis quibuslibet non obstantibus.

Datum Romae, ——

(**Private**); S. C. Rel., Formula, 1953. Annotations, *Commentarium pro Religiosis,* 33 (1954)–26 (Ruiz).

## Accommodation of Minor Papal Cloister (S. C. Rel.) Private.

Subsequent to the publication of the Apostolic Constitution, *Sponsa Christi,* and the Instruction on the same,[1] and prior to the recent Instruction *Inter cetera* (S. C. Rel., 25 March, 1956),[2] an accommodation of minor papal cloister was made available and use of it could be petitioned in individual cases for those communities which felt they could not fully observe the norms given in the *Sponsa Christi* and the earlier Instruction. The text of the accommodation is as follows.

### Accommodation of the Minor Papal Cloister to Orders of Nuns Who From Their Institute Engage in the Works of the Apostolate

*Criterion*

1. The minor papal cloister can be delimited in a special manner for certain Orders or Monasteries of Nuns, provided that it remains more severe than the cloister which is in force for religious Congregations of women and even for Orders of men, and that it is based on the exercise of the apostolate itself.

A full delimitation and ordering will have to be made in each one's own Constitutions or Statutes.

---

[1] Both documents reported above on pp. 326 and 344 respectively.

[2] Reported below in this same volume on p. 368.

*Subject*

2. The special minor papal cloister is applied to the Monasteries of those monastic Orders or Congregations which from their institute or from their foundation are destined by Rule and Constitution and constant tradition to works of the apostolate, especially the education of children and youth, the care of fallen or imperilled girls, and the care of the sick.

3. The same cloister can be granted for a serious reason to those monasteries which from legitimately approved tradition undertake the works of the apostolate for the same reason and in the same method as Monasteries set up for those works by their institute and in which, therefore, the whole community is habitually engaged in the works of the apostolate.

Care should be taken, however, that this manner of life be not contrary to the Constitutions or character of the Order or Monastery.

*Extent*

4. This cloister also carries with it a division of the Monastery into two parts, one of which is set aside for the community, the other for the works.

5. The parts of the Monastery set aside exclusively for the use of the nuns should be clearly defined under the authority of the local Ordinary.

6. Among the parts set aside for the works can be reckoned all those which lie within the confines of the Monastery and are not exclusively for the use of the nuns: thus, the church, parlors, quarters for guests, etc., as long as it is not otherwise provided for in particular law.

7. Places for the exercise of the works should be annexed to the Monastery itself, not, therefore, situated outside the precincts of the Monastery.

By way of exception, with the approval of the Holy See, the exercise of the works can be allowed in the proximity of the Monastery itself and, in special circumstances, e.g., in mission localities, more extensive exceptions can be made.

8. Outside the Monastery nuns may engage in works of the apostolate which are, as it were, a complement to the works habitually carried on inside the Monastery, e.g., assisting girl-

pupils in church and in processions, frequenting schools or making visitations with girl-pupils, etc.

To reduce the number of goings-out, certain works can usefully be performed by oblates regular or by affiliates.

*Protection of Cloister*

9. The parts of the Monastery set aside exclusively for the nuns should be entirely protected against entrance by externs in a stable and secure manner as is set down for major cloister.

10. The other parts of the Monastery, and so the choir in the church, the parlors, the places for the works, etc., should likewise be protected against the entrance of externs by a wall or other sufficiently safe way.

Moreover, the separation from externs who are admitted into those places and the manner of dealing with them should be well defined in each one's own Constitutions or Statutes, care always being taken, however, that in the parlors, the choir in the church, etc., everything unbecoming be avoided and the observance of chastity and recollection be safeguarded.

## Government of Cloister

*Going Out of the Monastery*

11. Minor cloister for such Monasteries forbids every kind of departure from the confines of the Monastery which is not founded on the apostolate as a basis and which is not done with the lawful permission of superiors.

12. With permission of legitimate superiors, to be granted according to the norm set down in the Constitutions or other particular law, the nuns may go out:

a. to acquire the necessary preparation for the works of the apostolate to be exercised later;
b. to exercise the works of the apostolate itself, provided that the going out is, as it were, a complement of that apostolate which is habitually carried on within the precincts of the Monastery;
c. to carry on the businesses connected with the apostolate, e.g., treating of business with religious or civil authorities,

making acquisitions of greater moment, other businesses for the good of the Monastery;

d. to take part in conventions, congresses, or sessions of studies when it appears necessary or very useful for the exercise of the works of the apostolate or for the completing or perfecting of the capability of the nuns who are engaged in them.

It is not lawful, therefore, to go out for reasons of curiosity or the satisfaction of personal interest.

13. To go out of the Monastery, provided a legitimate permission or order is given according to the Constitutions, is also lawful:

a. for superiors of Monastic Federations or Congregations for the exercise of the office committed to them;

b. for all nuns taking part in chapters, councils, and other meetings legitimately convoked, for transfer to another house in a case allowed by the Constitutions, for a new foundation, etc.

14. Special faculties can be granted to superiors because of necessity or great utility rising out of reasons not foreseen above, always excluding cases of curiosity, personal satisfaction or interest.

*Transit to Places of Works*

15. Nuns are allowed to go to places of works either occasionally or habitually by reason of assignment or with permission of Superiors according to the norm of the Constitutions or other particular law.

*Entrance of Externs into Places Reserved for the Community*

16. No extern of any condition, sex, or age is allowed to enter the parts of the Monastery reserved exclusively for the nuns and designated *Cloister,* even for a short time, without prejudice to all those provisions set down for major cloister.

*Entrance of Externs into Places for Works*

17. To enter the places set aside for the works is lawful for all persons, i.e., pupils, both boys and girls, and all others for

whom the works are destined or who are employed as collaborators or helpers in carrying on the works.

18. Entrance into the place of the works is also lawful for those who from canon or civil law have the right of vigilance over the works carried on.

19. Entrance with the permission of Superiors, granted according to the norms of the Constitutions or other particular law, is also lawful for those who come by reason or on occasion of the apostolate or who are parents of or bound by other bond to persons for whom the apostolate is directed or who, for a just cause in the judgment of superiors, are considered admissible.

20. Opportune precautions should be prescribed regarding the admission of extern persons, especially when it concerns men.

21. The scope of the apostolate with regard to permitting entrance, saving however the spirit, tradition, and character of each Monastery or Order, can be understood in a broad sense so as to include those works which are, as it were, the complement of the principal works engaged in, e.g., an affair carried on for the parents or other relatives of the pupils, boys or girls, on the occasion of a religious or scholastic celebration; likewise an affair conducted for them in special meetings destined for them; similarly an affair which continues its influence on those who formerly were the object of the apostolate, as would be former girl-pupils.

### *Custody of Cloister*

22. Statutes or Constitutions should accurately determine those things which pertain to the parlors; the manner of conduct by nuns when occupied in the works of the apostolate or with persons who come to the Monastery on occasion of the apostolate; precautions to be taken lest the entrance of externs cause inconvenience; precautions and the manner of conduct for nuns legitimately going out of the Monastery.

23. Vigilance over the observance of cloister, besides being the right and duty of the superiors of the federation and the superior of the Monastery, is the right and duty of the local Ordinary.

24. Nuns illegitimately going outside the precincts of the Monastery automatically incur excommunication which is re-

served to the local Ordinary unless in the Statutes it is said to be reserved to the Holy See.

25. Illegitimate passing from the quarters of the community to the places of the works should be punished by superiors.

26. Illegitimate entrance of externs into places reserved exclusively for the nuns is punished with excommunication reserved simply to the Holy See (perhaps it could be reserved to the local Ordinary).

Illegitimate entrance into the places set aside for the works should be punished by the local Ordinary according to the gravity of the fault.

**(Private)**; S. C. Rel. Translation made from the Latin text which was supplied to us through the kindness of the Very Reverend Albert Drexelius, O.P., Rel. Assist., S. Cong. Rel.

## Cloister of Nuns (S. C. Rel., Instruction, 25 March, 1956) AAS 48–512.

This Instruction, entitled *Circa Monialium Clausuram,* is as follows:

1. Among the motives which prompted His Holiness Pius XII to promulgate the Apostolic Constitution *Sponsa Christi,*[1] he himself attached considerable importance to the difficulties occasioned by the present rather strict laws of papal cloister. And this is not to be wondered at, since he clearly perceived the changes which time and circumstances have wrought in the entire institution of Nuns. When it came to outlining the general character of the renovation and adaptation of this institution, the Apostolic Constitution wisely provided: "Accordingly, without the least prejudice to any of the native and principal elements of the venerable institution of Nuns, as to the rest, which are found to be external and adventitious, We have decided to make, with caution and prudence, certain adaptations to present times, which may not only do honor to the venerable institution but at the same time enlarge its effectiveness." His Holiness, therefore, whereas in the General Statutes (art. IV) he paternally decreed some adaptations of the papal cloister of Nuns to the conditions of our time, in other respects confirmed and restored it everywhere.

[1] Ap. Const., 21 Nov., 1950; *AAS,* Vol. 43, p. 5 f; reported above pp. 326–344.

For one of the peculiar and most important elements of the canonical contemplative life is that strict enclosure which, based on ancient tradition and defended in the course of the centuries, is at the same time a safeguard for the solemn profession of chastity and an excellent way of disposing the soul for a more intimate union with God. And in these days, the more violently men's minds are drawn to external things, the stronger must be the observance of the cloister, which enables Nuns to be more closely united to God.

2. The Sacred Congregation of Religious, in pursuance of the task assigned to it by the Supreme Pontiff, namely, "through instructions, declarations, responses and other documents of the kind, to do everything which concerns putting the Constitution carefully and effectively into practice and securing the faithful and prompt observance of the General Statutes," as early as the 23rd of November, 1950, published an Instruction, *Inter praeclara,* the first part of which is entirely concerned with the major and minor cloister of nuns.[2]

3. And now after the fruitful experience of several years and after having repeatedly examined and carefully considered all the reports that have reached the Holy See on this matter, seeing that after the introduction of the minor papal cloister by the Apostolic Constitution *Sponsa Christi* of 21 November, 1950, the Instruction of the Sacred Congregation of Religious, *Nuper edito,* of 6 February, 1924,[3] is no longer in agreement with the present discipline, the same Sacred Congregation considers that it is now possible and appropriate to make some further provisions and to deal anew with the entire subject (cf. c. 22); and this it proposes to do in the present Instruction.

## I. Papal Cloister in General

4. Nuns of all Monasteries, even though by way of temporary exception they still profess only simple vows (Const. *Sponsa Christi,* art. III, § 2), if they wish to retain the name and juridical status of Nuns, must necessarily accept and keep at least the minor pontifical or papal cloister (art. IV, § 5, 2°).

5. Whether there is question of founding a new Monastery

---

[2] *AAS,* Vol. 43, p. 37; reported above on p. 344.

[3] *AAS,* Vol. 16, p. 96; CANON LAW DIGEST, 1, p. 314.

where cloister is established for the first time, or of a Monastery already founded where cloister is to be restored, the Nuns will be strictly bound actually to observe the pontifical or papal cloister, which shall apply to the ingress and egress of all persons, from a precise moment to be carefully fixed and defined in writing by the competent ecclesiastical authority, that is, by the Ordinary of the place.

6. The law of cloister, major or minor, affects every Monastery which is subject to one or the other, even though the number of the Nuns who live there be diminished or small (c. 597, § 2).

## II. The Major Papal Cloister

### *Character of the Major Papal Cloister*

7. The major pontifical or papal cloister is the one which is in the Code (cc. 597, 600–602) and which is clearly and solemnly confirmed and more fully described in the Apostolic Constitution *Sponsa Christi,* and more exactly defined in the Instruction *Inter praeclara* (VI–X).

8. *a*) The major pontifical or papal cloister exists by rule and is binding in all Monasteries where solemn vows are actually taken and which profess an exclusively contemplative life (Const. *Sponsa Christi,* art. IV, § 2, 2°).

*b*) In Monasteries where, although the Nuns are given to an exclusively contemplative life, yet exceptionally and by indult only simple vows are taken (Const. *Sponsa Christi,* art. III, § 2), although the cloister should be the major one if that is possible (art. IV, § 2, 2°), yet, especially as regards the sanction by the Holy See, the minor cloister may be granted and is applied prudently according to the case (Const. *Sponsa Christi,* art. IV, § 3, 3°; Instr. *Inter praeclara,* V).

9. Monasteries in which according to the Rule and the Constitutions only the contemplative life is to be followed, may retain the major cloister even though for grave reasons and for their duration certain apostolic works are assigned to or allowed them by the Holy See, provided that only some of the Nuns and a part of the Monastery, carefully distinguished and separated from the part where the community lives and practices the common life, be assigned to those works.

10. The law of cloister is binding on all Nuns (c. 601), Novices, and Postulants (c. 540, § 3). The professed of temporary vows after their vows have expired, and Novices and Postulants always, may go out of the cloister only when they intend to leave the Monastery for good.

11. *a*) The cloister necessarily includes not only the Monastery building and its annexes in which the Nuns reside, but also the yards and gardens, and whatever places they frequent.

*b*) Outside the cloister are: those parts of the parlors which are reserved for outsiders; the church and oratory *outside the choir reserved to the Nuns;* the sacristy and places adjacent to it which are open to the clergy and servers; the place where the priest hears the Nuns' confessions; the house where the extern Sisters live; and the places destined for the chaplains and guests.

12. *a*) Although the church and the sacristy and its annexes devoted to worship are not within the cloister, still if it is really necessary that the Nuns themselves occasionally perform some service there, local Ordinaries can on their own authority permit that, during such necessity and while the work continues, the cloister be actually extended to include these places, provided that all the prescriptions given below for the protection of the cloister be observed there during that time.

*b*) In the same circumstances and under the same conditions, Ordinaries can permit that the cloister be extended for the occasion to the parlors and other places annexed to the Monastery when, because of the want of extern Sisters or for some other reason, it is considered really necessary that the Nuns perform some service there also.

13. *a*) The parts of the Monastery which are subject to cloister as above must be so protected and secured that not only entrance into them be entirely prevented but also that the view inward by outsiders and outward by the Nuns be as far as possible effectively shut off.

*b*) Hence also the yards and gardens must be surrounded either by a high wall or by some other effective means, such as wooden boards, an iron grating, or a thick and strong hedge, according to the judgment of the Ordinary and the regular Superior, with due consideration especially of the site, the number of seculars, and so forth.

14. *a*) Windows looking out on the street and on neighboring houses, or which afford any opportunity for communication with outsiders, must be equipped with glass that is not transparent and with fixed shutters or lattices so as to cut off the view from either side.

*b*) If there are terraces or walks to which the Nuns have access above the roof of the Monastery, they should be surrounded with screens or in some other effective manner.

15. Unless some stricter provision exists by particular law, the Nuns, in accordance with the general spirit of the liturgy, should not be prevented by the law of cloister from seeing the altar, but in such a way that they themselves be not seen by the faithful.

16. The part of the parlor which is reserved to the Nuns must be separated from the part destined for outsiders, by two screens securely fixed some distance apart, or in some other effective way according to the judgment of the Ordinary and the regular Superior — and this is a strict conscientious obligation for them — so that the persons on one side cannot be reached from the other.

17. Near the entrance to the Monastery and also in the parlors, the sacristy, and wherever it is needed, there should be inserted in the wall a revolving wheel or box, according to usage, for passing necessary articles through from one side to the other. It is not forbidden to have small openings, so as to see what it being put into the box.

### *Egress of the Nuns*

18. The law of major cloister obliges the Nuns to remain perpetually within the precincts of the Monastery which are designated as within the cloister by ecclesiastical authority, and not to leave the same under any pretext even for a short time, outside the cases provided for by law or legitimate permission.

19. They may not leave the cloister on the occasion of their clothing, profession, Communion, or for any such reason.

20. The Nuns may not go from one Monastery to another even of the same Order, even for a short time, without the permission of the Holy See, except as provided by duly approved particular law for Federations of Monasteries of Nuns.

21. *a*) It is allowed to go out of the cloister in case of imminent danger of death or of any other very serious harm (c. 601, § 1). Such cases are: fire, flood, earthquake, dilapidation of the building or walls threatening to crumble, air raids, incursion of soldiers, urgent requisition of the Monastery by military or civil authorities.

*b*) Also, an urgent surgical operation or other urgent medical treatment to be had outside for the care of health, a disease of one person which is truly dangerous to the whole community.

*c*) Likewise, if a grave and urgent necessity of this sort occurs in the case of an extern Sister or of some one who is taking her place, who cannot otherwise receive the needed care, the Superioress in person or through another Nun, with a companion, may visit her.

*d*) These dangers (*a*), and grave and urgent necessities (*b*), (*c*), are to be acknowledged in writing by the local Ordinary if there is time (c. 601, § 2); otherwise he should be notified afterward.

22. A going out is regarded as legitimate when there is an urgent obligation to exercise some right or perform some duty of a civil nature, and the local Ordinary has previously issued a declaration to that effect.

23. Nuns who have obtained permission to go out of the cloister are bound to go directly to the place for which the permission was given, and they may not on such an occasion go elsewhere.

When Nuns are outside the Monastery they are bound to observe strictly the norms and safeguards which are prescribed for religious women in similar cases either by the Code (c. 607) or by the Holy See, or by Ordinaries (c. 607).

24. *a*) Seriously difficult circumstances or absolute or moral necessities, as well as advantages of great importance, may constitute just and canonical causes for asking appropriate dispensations or even some moderate and carefully defined habitual faculties from the Holy See.

Such circumstances are:

1) the care of health outside the Monastery;

2) to visit a doctor, particularly a specialist, e.g., for the eyes, teeth, radiotherapy, medical observation;

3) to accompany or visit a Nun who is ill outside;

4) to take the place of extern Sisters or persons similarly employed who are missing;

5) to look after fields, lands, buildings, or the house where the extern Sisters live;

6) to do important acts of administration or of economic management which otherwise could not be done at all or not be done properly;

7) monastic work, either apostolic or manual;

8) to take up an office in another Monastery — and the like.

*b*) In the use of these dispensations and faculties, the limits imposed and the precautions prescribed must be exactly observed.

25. Habitual faculties for a definite time or for a stated number of cases can be prudently granted to local or regular Ordinaries or to religious Assistants to permit brief exits from the cloister in necessities which occur frequently. These are always to be exercised in the name of the Holy See, and cannot be extended in any way, but must be held within their proper limits.

### *Ingress of Outsiders*

26. *a*) The local Ordinary or the regular Superior if the Monastery is subject to him, or a Delegate of either of them or of the Holy See, may enter the cloister on the occasion of the canonical visitation, only for the purpose of inspecting the building according to law (cc. 512 and 600), taking care that the Visitor be accompanied constantly from his entrance to his exit by at least one cleric or religious, who may be a *conversus,* of mature age, and that he do not remain beyond the time needed for the inspection, nor attend on that occasion to any other business or do any other acts which have nothing to do with the visitation.

*b*) The visitation of persons should take place in the common parlor, the Visitor remaining outside the cloister, unless there is question of interviewing a Nun who is sick and cannot come to the parlor.

*c*) For exercising other functions, for example the *exploratio voluntatis* of candidates, to preside at elections, for a visitation or profession and the like, the Prelate or Delegate may not enter the cloister, but must do all these things outside.

27. *a*) The confessor of the community or, *servatis servandis,*

any other priest, may with the proper precautions enter the cloister: to administer to the sick the Sacraments of Penance, the Most Holy Eucharist, and Extreme Unction; also to assist the dying, and where it is the custom, to bury the dead, in which case he may be accompanied by the servers according to the rubrics. The entrance of priests for other services is not permitted.

*b*) The precautions to be faithfully observed according to the case are as follows:

For administering Holy Communion, the priest should be accompanied from his entrance to his exit by at least two Nuns. But there is nothing to prevent the whole community from accompanying the Blessed Sacrament in procession, according to existing customs.

For hearing confessions, two Nuns should accompany the priest as far as the cell of the sick person, and after the confession is finished conduct him immediately to the exit. The same holds for Extreme Unction and assistance to the dying.

28. The preaching of the word of God is to be done at the screen of the choir or of the parlor; if this is not convenient, application should be made to the Holy See for the faculty to have the sermons in the choir itself or in the chapter room or, with the consent of the local Ordinary, in the church, to which in that case the cloister is extended, the doors of the church being kept closed during that time.

29. The following persons may enter the cloister:

*a*) Those, by whatever name they are called, who are actually at the time the heads of any State, even one of a Federal Union, and their wives and retinue.[4]

*b*) Cardinals of the Holy Roman Church; and these may bring with them one or two attendants, either clerical or, if they belong to the Cardinal's family, lay persons.

*c*) Physicians, surgeons, or other persons engaged in the care of the sick, architects, craftsmen, workmen, and other such persons whose services are necessary for the Monastery in the judgment of the Superioress, with the previous at least habitual approval of the local Ordinary. The Superioress may obtain this approval at the beginning of each year on presenting a list of

[4] Code Com., 26 March, 1952; *AAS*, 44–496; reported above, p. 324.

the persons to the Ordinary. In case of urgent necessity when there is not time to ask for this approval, it is rightly presumed.

30. All persons who are to be admitted frequently into the cloister must be of excellent reputation and outstanding moral character.

31. Without prejudice to Constitutions and Statutes which may prescribe stricter regulations, persons legitimately entering the cloister must, when they pass through the very house of the Community, be accompanied both coming and going by two Nuns.

32. *a*) Whatever be the reason for which entrance is permitted, those who enter may not remain in the Monastery beyond the time which is really necessary for the purpose for which the permission was given.

*b*) None of the Nuns, except those who must do so by reason of their office, should speak to persons from outside while they are in the Monastery.

33. *a*) Except as provided in the Constitution *Sponsa Christi,* it is not allowed without special permission of the Holy See to admit to the cloister girls or women to receive instruction, to try out their vocation for a short time, or for any other pious or apostolic purpose (Const. *Sponsa Christi,* art. IX, § 2, 1° and 2°).

*b*) Application must likewise be made to the Holy See for special permissions not contained in approved Statutes, in favor of extern Sisters.

34. Postulants (c. 540) may enter the cloister with only the permission of the local Ordinary.

### *The Custody of the Cloister*

35. It is the right and duty of the local Ordinary to watch over the custody of the cloister of all the Monasteries in his territory, even those which are subject to a regular Superior, although the latter also has this right and duty in Monasteries which are subject to him (c. 603, §§ 1 and 2).

36. Within the Monastery, however, the immediate custody of the cloister belongs to the Superioress. She must keep the keys to all the doors of the cloister with her day and night, giving them only to the Nuns who have charge of various offices

when they need them; without prejudice to particular law which may make further prescriptions.

37. As regards the access of the Nuns to the parlor (time, frequency, quality of persons to be admitted, and so forth) and the manner of their presence there (the veil, a companion who can hear what is said, and the like), let them observe their own Constitutions. If these seem to require some accommodation, recourse should be made to the Holy See.

38. Nuns (cfr. *Sponsa Christi,* General Statutes, art. I, § 1) (not Novices and Postulants) who unlawfully go out of the major cloister contrary to the prescription of canon 601, are *ipso facto* under excommunication simply reserved to the Holy See (c. 2342, 3°).

39. The same penalty attaches to any person of whatever class, condition, or sex, who violates the major cloister, either by illegitimately entering it or by illegitimately introducing or admitting others to it (c. 2342, 1°).

## III. The Minor Papal Cloister

### *Character of the Minor Papal Cloister*

40. The minor pontifical or papal cloister is outlined as follows:

1) Being truly pontifical no less than the major cloister, it protects and favors the observance and custody of public and solemn chastity and the contemplative life of the Monastery.

2) In as much, however, as it is minor, though far more severe than the cloister of Congregations (c. 604) or even of Orders of men (cc. 598–599), it affords the faculty and the convenient facility of duly and fruitfully practicing certain select works legitimately entrusted to Nuns (Instr. *Inter praeclara,* XI).

41. *a*) The minor cloister does not admit works of every sort, but only such as are harmoniously associated with the contemplative life of the entire Community and of the Nuns individually (Const. *Sponsa Christi, AAS,* Vol. 43, p. 11).

*b*) These works, whether they be undertaken in virtue of the Constitutions of the institute, or by legitimate permission, or by command of the Church in view of her ever increasing necessities and the needs of souls, are to be performed in such an orderly and moderate way, according to the nature and spirit of the particular Order, as not only not to disturb or affect adversely the true contemplative life, but rather to nourish and strengthen it (Const. *Sponsa Christi,* art. IX).

*c*) Such works are: teaching Christian doctrine, religious instruction, the education of boys and girls, retreats and exercises for women, preparation for first Communion, works of charity in relief of the sick, the poor, and so forth.

42. *a*) The minor cloister must necessarily be in effect where the majority or many of the Nuns and a notable part of the Monastery are habitually given to works of the apostolate (General Statutes, art. IV, § 3, 2°).

*b*) On the other hand, if only a few Nuns are assigned to these works and if the works are confined or can practically and prudently be confined to narrow limits in the Monastery, then the major cloister may be retained according to the judgment of the Holy See, with the requisite faculties and dispensations as mentioned above (n. 9).

### *The Division of the Monastery*

43. To begin with, the buildings of the Monastery which because of the works to be done are subject to minor cloister, should be divided into two parts, one of which is reserved to the Nuns and the other given over to the apostolic works (Instr. *Inter praeclara,* XI, 5°).

44. *a*) In the part which is reserved to the Nuns after the manner of the major cloister, should be: the cells, the choir, the chapter room and so forth, the refectory, the kitchen, places for recreation, walking, and community work, and that side of the parlors to which all the Nuns have access.

*b*) In this part of the house there should not be: the places inhabited by the extern Sisters, the rooms and places destined for guests; nor the church with its sacristy and annexes, except as provided in n. 12.

45. *a*) The other part of the Monastery is reserved for the apostolic works or ministries which are done by the Monastery itself. Hence this part of the building is equally open to those Religious who are legitimately engaged in the works and ministries and to other persons who direct the apostolate.

*b*) The church and public oratory, with the places annexed to them and the others mentioned in n. 12, *b*), should not be within, but as a rule outside this latter part of the Monastery.

In the church and the places annexed to it, exception may be made for the halls or rooms which are legitimately reserved for the works of the apostolate. Even the entire church, usually open to all the faithful, may, in case of urgent necessity with the consent of the local Ordinary, be counted among the places assigned to the works, during the time that the Nuns are obliged to exercise their proper ministries there, provided the following prescriptions are faithfully observed and prudent precautions are taken.

46. *a*) There must not be places which are reserved alternately, now for the Community, now for the works of the apostolate.

*b*) However, the local Ordinary can for reasonable cause permit, either by way of act or for a definite time, that some places which are habitually destined for works be given over to the Community; and in such case during that time those places are subject to all the regulations and prescriptions mentioned above for the part of the Monastery which is habitually reserved to the Community.

47. Also as regards the part of the Monastery which is reserved for works, the view in and out must be precluded. If this cannot be done with the same completeness as for the part of the Monastery reserved to the Nuns, the Ordinary should provide prudently and carefully.

48. *a*) The division between the two parts of the Monastery shall be precisely defined and openly indicated, so as to be clearly known to all.

*b*) The doors which close the part of the Monastery which is reserved to the Nuns (n. 49, *a*) are subject to all the prescriptions established for the doors of the major cloister.

*c*) If the entire Monastery has only one door on the public street, to admit outsiders, there must moreover be an inside door properly guarded through which the persons to be admitted are led to the place of the works.

49. The passage of the Nuns from the part which is for the Community to the part which is for the works:

*a*) Must be always directly through a special door.

*b*) It is permitted only at the times lawfully designated and only to those Nuns who are assigned to the works by the Superioress, either by way of act or habitually according to the Constitutions or Statutes. Among these should be included the Superioress herself or a Nun designated by her, even for the sole purpose of exercising vigilance.

*c*) For the Nuns who are legitimately engaged in the place of the works, special parlors should be provided there, not necessarily equipped with screens, but with proper safeguards, where they may speak with outsiders in regard only to the works.

### *Egress of the Nuns*

50. *a*) The minor cloister entails a grave prohibition, for all and each of those subject to it, from going outside the limits of the Monastery, just as the major cloister does for Nuns and other persons who are bound by it (Instr. *Inter praeclara,* XII, 2°).

*b*) Dispensations from this grave prescription can be given for reasons of the apostolate, if really necessary, only to those Nuns and members who are legitimately engaged in ministries as above explained (n. 49).

*c*) Permission to go out for the reasons acknowledged herein (n. 51) or in the Constitutions, for as long as such reasons certainly exist, can be granted by the Superioress upon her responsibility in conscience. In other cases not expressly mentioned in the law, even though they could clearly be considered as equivalent because of the similarity of the reasons, recourse should be made to the local Ordinary, so that he, after considering the matter before God, may grant the permission and, if he thinks well, leave the matter in future to the Superioress.

*d*) Both the local Ordinary and the regular Superior, to whom the protection of the cloister is entrusted (c. 603), have a strict obligation in conscience to watch carefully over the observance of these regulations.

51. The causes from which the required necessity from the standpoint of the works may be estimated so that a just dispensation may be given for going out (n. 50, *c*), fall under the following three heads:

*a*) *For the sake of the work itself,* which actually requires the going out so that it may be properly done, as for example if girls must necessarily be accompanied out of the cloister because of studies, health, or recreation, and there are not available teachers, oblates, or other persons who can do this.

*b*) *For the sake of preparation for the works,* namely: to acquire knowledge, culture, degrees, acknowledgments of competency, and so to attend schools, academies, universities, conferences, and congresses, as may seem necessary. In case any of these institutions are so permeated with an anticlerical and profane spirit as to create imminent danger for religious virtue or give rise to the possibility of scandal from their attendance, the local Ordinary should always be consulted in advance. In all cases the Instructions issued by the Holy See must be observed.

*c*) *By reason of business,* procedures, or questions concerning the works, which cannot be safely or conveniently transacted and finished by other persons through ecclesiastical or civil authorities or public or private offices.

### *Ingress of Outsiders*

52. The laws concerning entrance into major cloister apply equally to Monasteries of minor cloister as regards the part reserved to the Nuns (Instr. *Inter praeclara,* XII, and above, n. 26 *seq.*).

53. *a*) Women and girls or boys for whom the works are intended may enter that part of the Monastery which is assigned to those works, and may stay there day and night, according to the nature of the works.

*b*) The same holds for women who may be needed for the works, such as teachers, nurses, maids, working women.

54. *a*) By way of act or transiently, other persons may be admitted who have some special relationship with those for whom the works are conducted, e.g., parents, relatives, or benefactors who accompany the girls or boys or who wish to visit them; the persons mentioned, or others when it is called for or appropriate according to the nature of the work and the customs of the place, may be invited to certain festivities or demonstrations of a religious or scholastic nature.

*b*) All this should be appropriately defined in the legitimately approved Statutes or Ordinances.

55. All persons who have by ecclesiastical law or civil ordinance a legitimate right of inspection of any sort, should be admitted.

56. Into the part destined for works, no less than in that reserved to the Nuns (c. 600, 4°), as is reasonable, the physician, workmen, and the like, may in case of necessity be admitted with the permission, even habitual, of the local Ordinary (n. 29, *c*).

57. The permission of the local Ordinary is required and sufficient for other cases of necessity or real utility which are not provided for above (nn. 54–56, *a*) or in the Statutes of the works concerned.

58. Saving all the prescriptions concerning major cloister as to the part reserved to the Nuns, also as regards the less severe cloister which affects the part destined for works, the local Ordinary, and in a proper case the regular Superior, as well as the one who exercises authority over a Federation, have the right and duty to keep a strict vigilance and if need be to prescribe appropriate safeguards, in addition to those which are contained in the Statutes, for the custody and protection of the cloister.

### *The Custody of the Cloister*

59. *a*) The immediate custody of this cloister is entrusted to the Superioress.

*b*) She is to keep the keys for passage from one part of the Monastery to the other, or prudently entrust them to the Nuns who are assigned to the works.

*c*) She should not give the keys of other doors in the house devoted to works, except to persons who are altogether reliable.

60. Nuns who illegitimately go out of the precincts of the Monastery incur *ipso facto* an excommunication simply reserved to the Holy See according to canon 2342, 3°, or, by express grant of the Holy See, reserved to the local Ordinary (Instr. *Inter praeclara*, XV, 1°).

61. *a*) "Nuns who illicitly leave the parts of the Monastery reserved to the Community and go to other places within the precincts of the Monastery, are to be punished by the Superioress or by the local Ordinary, according to the gravity of their fault" (*ibid.*, 2°).

*b*) The transit is illegitimate whenever it is made without the permission, at least habitual or reasonably presumed, of the Superioress.

62. "Those who illicitly enter the parts of the Monastery reserved to the Community and those who bring them in or allow them to enter, incur an excommunication reserved simply to the Holy See" (*ibid.*, 3°).

63. "Those who illegitimately enter the parts of the Monastery not reserved to the Community, as well as those who bring them in or permit them to enter, are to be severely punished according to the gravity of the fault by the Ordinary of the place where the Monastery is situated" (*ibid.*, 4°).

## IV. Papal Cloister and Federations

64. The Statutes of Federations can make such regulations regarding the major or minor cloister of Federated Monasteries as are considered necessary to attain the ends of the Federation.

65. As to government, the faculty may be given to go out of one's own Monastery and go into another: for the purpose of assembling the Chapter, the Council, or some other such gathering; of timely visitations to be made by the Authority which governs the Federation or by its delegates; of summoning or, with all necessary observances, transferring the Superioress or another Nun.

66. In order to promote fraternal collaboration among the Monasteries, the same faculty may be decreed: for the purpose of assuming in another Monastery an office which has been conferred by election or appointment; of affording aid of any kind to another Monastery or of relieving its necessities; or even for the private benefit of some individual Nun, but within the limits prescribed in the Statutes.

67. For the better formation of the Nuns, when common houses have been established for this purpose, the faculty, to be clearly defined in the Statutes, may be given for Nuns who are legitimately assigned to such houses or recalled from them, to go there, to remain, and to return.

68. *a*) The Statutes may make some provisions to secure a uniform observance of the cloister in the Monasteries of a Federation.

*b*) For this same purpose, and always without prejudice to

the rights of local Ordinaries and regular Superiors, also special interventions of religious Assistants or of the Superioresses of Federations may be provided for as regards petitions which may have to be presented to the Holy See concerning the cloister, e.g., for extraordinary journeys, long absences from the Monastry, and the like.

69. With regard to the Monasteries of a Federation which engage in apostolic works and are subject to the common minor cloister, the Statutes may decree: what works can be undertaken, what persons may be admitted to the place of the works, habitually or transiently, for what reasons and with what conditions and safeguards.

## V. The Establishment of Papal Cloister

70. *a*) All Monasteries of Nuns must observe the pontifical or papal cloister either major or minor, according to the regulations above stated.

*b*) For Monasteries of Nuns which, though they profess exclusively the contemplative life, nevertheless engage legitimately in works of the apostolate in the manner above described (n. 41, *a*), unless provision has already been made by the Holy See itself since the issuance of the Apostolic Constitution, *Sponsa Christi,*[5] it shall pertain to the local Ordinary, together with the regular Superior if the Monastery is subject to him, to introduce the minor papal cloister.

*c*) In doubtful cases the matter should be referred to the Holy See.

*d*) In future, in order to change from the major to the minor papal cloister for the reasons stated above (n. 41), applications must always be made to the Holy See.

71. It pertains to the local Ordinary when the minor papal cloister is introduced, to prescribe the limits of the cloister (c. 597, § 3) and to recognize and approve the assignment of the places of the Monastery to the Community or to the works respectively, and the necessary separation between them.

72. If special difficulties, temporary or habitual, stand in the way of the establishment of the pontifical or papal cloister, the

[5] *AAS,* Vol. 43, p. 5; reported above, pp. 326–344.

matter should be referred to the Holy See with a faithful statement of the circumstances.

73. *a*) Statutes, Indults, Privileges, and Dispensations in virtue of which certain Monasteries, while keeping the juridical status of Nuns, were exempted from the pontifical or papal cloister, are revoked.[6]

Therefore the so-called "episcopal" cloister cannot in future be recognized for Nuns.

*b*) But special Statutes by which the minor papal cloister is more precisely regulated and adapted for Orders of Nuns which are dedicated to works of the apostolate by their Institute, remain unchanged.

All things to the contrary notwithstanding.

Given at Rome, the 25th day of March, 1956.

**AAS 48–512;** S. C. Rel., Instruction, 25 March, 1956.

NOTE: This is the unofficial English version authorized by the Sacred Congregation of Religious. Annotations, *Commentarium pro Religiosis,* 35 (1956)–262 (Gutiérrez); *Monitor Ecclesiasticus,* 82 (1957)–398 (Gambari).

## **Externe Sisters of Monasteries of Nuns** (S. C. Rel., Instruction and Statutes, 25 March, 1961) **AAS 53–371.**

The peculiar condition of Nuns who live in the cloister is such that, in order to safeguard their life of recollection, they need some persons to attend to the affairs and relations of the Monastery outside the cloister. Accordingly there have always been pious women, living for the most part outside the cloister and bound by no obligations of the religious life or at least by none of these in the proper sense, and going by the name of Oblates, Mandataries, Portresses, or the like.

In the course of time these pious women manifested the desire to share more intimately in the life of cloistered Nuns; and in various places they were allowed to remain in the external service of the Monastery upon pronouncing a special resolution, promise, oath, or vow. There have also been Rules, Constitutions, or special Statutes approved by the Holy See, which consecrated as it were this resolve on their part to live the religious life.

---

[6] Cf. *AAS,* 43–12; see above, p. 333; and reply of the Code Commission, 1 March, 1921; *AAS,* 13–177; reported above on p. 303.

In our times the status of such Sisters of simple vows was confirmed and duly regulated by the Decree *Conditio plurimorum Monasteriorum* of the Sacred Congregation of Religious, issued on the 16th of July 1931.[1] The Sisters were declared to be "members of the Community which they serve and to share in the same spiritual benefits as the Nuns" (cf. *Statuta a Sororibus externis Monasteriorum Monialium cuiusque Ordinis servanda,* n. 4).[2] However, lest the juridical incorporation of the Sisters with the Community might harm the contemplative life of the cloistered Nuns, it was laid down as a general rule that the Sisters should live in a part of the Monastery outside the papal cloister.

The experience of the past thirty years, however, has made it quite clear that some of those Statutes of 1931 need to be improved by adapting them to more recent pontifical documents on cloistered Nuns, by omitting some prescriptions of the common law, since they are already contained in the Constitutions of the Nuns, and finally by adjusting them more closely to the Rules and Constitutions of the Second Order to which the Sisters belong. Accordingly the Sacred Congregation of Religious has decided to produce a new and shorter but nonetheless complete edition of those Statutes, without prejudice, however, to the following points:

1. Those Monasteries of Nuns which have no Sisters applied to external service and do not need them for the reason that this external service is taken care of by trustworthy secular persons engaged with the consent of the local Ordinary and living outside the cloister, are not bound to introduce this class of Sisters.

2. In case the Rule or Constitutions of a certain Order expressly require and regulate the external service of Sisters for a Monastery of Nuns, the canonical dispositions regulating such service remain in full force, provided they are not contrary to the sacred canons nor to the Apostolic Constitution *Sponsa Christi.*[3]

3. If the Nuns of any Order, the better to observe the spirit of their own foundation and vocation, wish to insert in their

---

1 Not published in the AAS. See CANON LAW DIGEST, 2, p. 170.

2 *Ibid.*

3 AAS 43–5; reported above, pp. 326–344.

Constitutions special provisions for the external service of the Monastery, they may freely do so, subject of course to the approval of the Sacred Congregation of Religious.

Provisions of the same sort, likewise with the approval of the Sacred Congregation, may be inserted in the Statutes of those Federations erected by the Holy See, which practice regular observance within the same Order in a slightly different way. But the prescriptions which may be added to the Constitutions or to the Statutes of a Federation, according to the character of the Order, must conform to the following General Statutes.

## GENERAL STATUTES

## CHAPTER I

### Functions and Habitation of Sisters Applied to External Service

#### Article 1

§ 1. Monasteries of Nuns may, with the consent of the Chapter and the permission of the local Ordinary and of the regular Superior if they have one, provide for Sisters to be applied to external service, with the special function of serving the Monastery by attending to external business which cannot be done by cloistered Nuns.

§ 2. Included in the external service to which these Sisters are applied, may be certain moderate apostolic works connected with the Monastery but to be performed outside the cloister.

#### Article 2

Sisters applied to external service are members of the Community of their respective Monasteries, and in the order of precedence come after the choir Nuns and lay Sisters (*"conversae"*); they have the same Rule and Constitutions as the Nuns, but in virtue of their proper office they are subject to these Statutes, which derogate from some of the prescriptions of the Rule and Constitutions.

## Article 3

§ 1. Without prejudice to Article 4, the Sisters applied to external service have a dwelling annexed to the Monastery and subject to common cloister (can. 604 and Instruction *Inter cetera,* n. 73),[4] but not situated within the limits of the papal cloister of the Nuns (Instr. *Inter cetera,* nn. 11 b, 44 b).[5] Consequently they may not enter the part of the Monastery reserved to the Nuns, except as provided in these Statutes.

§ 2. Without prejudice to a stricter law for individual Monasteries, the Prioress, with the consent of her Council and the approval of the local Ordinary and of the regular Superior if there is one, can give permission for the externe Sisters to come together sometimes inside the cloister with the Nuns for purposes of devotion or instruction, as also for meals and recreation, taking care that this give rise to no inconvenience. On such occasions the Sisters, even though they be imprudently questioned, should refrain from reporting what they have seen or heard outside the Monastery, and especially should keep silence about anything that does not make for good example or that might disturb interior peace and recollection. The Prioress and her Council should watch these things carefully, and if the coming of the Sisters into the Monastery becomes an occasion of abuse, appropriate remedies must be applied.

§ 3. The Sisters living outside the cloister may, at the discretion of the Prioress and her Council, with the previous general approval also of the local Ordinary and of the regular Superior if any, sometimes be engaged in the internal functions and works of the Monastery, on condition that they be not habitually intermingled with the Nuns.

§ 4. What is said in this Article about the coming of the Sisters into the cloister applies also to postulants and second year novices.

## Article 4

§ 1. With due regard to the spirit and character of each Order and to the number of Nuns living in the Monastery, upon a

---

[4] 25 March, 1956, AAS 48–512; reported immediately before this document.

[5] *Ibid.*

previous vote of the Chapter and, in the case of Monasteries which belong to a Federation, after hearing from the Council of the Federation, Monasteries may provide, with the approval of the Holy See, that the externe Sisters stay habitually within the limits of the cloister of the Monastery without being bound by the law of papal cloister. In this case precautions must be taken that this contact of the Sisters with the Nuns who are bound to observe the cloister do no harm to the spirit of recollection; among other measures, a certain separation should be established within the cloister itself, like that which is prescribed for the noviceship (can. 564, § 1), and the Sisters should be forbidden to relate to the Nuns what happens outside the cloister.

§ 2. The Sisters who live habitually in the cloister, since they are not bound by the law of papal cloister, can go out of the cloister at the discretion of the Prioress for the service or other external work of the Monastery or for any other just and reasonable cause.

The same is true of novices even of the first year of noviceship, and for postulants if the postulancy is conducted inside the cloister according to Article 9, § 2, without prejudice, however, to the discipline and purpose of the postulancy and noviceship (can. 565).

### Article 5

The dwelling and other places outside the cloister, which are destined for the externe Sisters, are subject to the vigilance and visitation not only of the local Ordinary and of the Regular Superior, if any, according to law, but also, with due allowances, of the Superioress of the Federation in the case of federated Monasteries (Instruction, *Inter cetera,* n. 24, 5°).

### Article 6

§ 1. For practicing apostolic works regularly in Monasteries according to Article 1, § 2 with the previous permission of the local Ordinary and of the Regular Superior if any, the approval of the Holy See is required.

§ 2. In the exercise of apostolic works the Sisters shall follow the regulations laid down by the local Ordinary.

### Article 7

§ 1. The habit of the Sisters shall be the same as that of the Nuns, but judiciously adapted by the Chapter to the purposes of external service according to circumstances.

§ 2. In Monasteries of the same Federation the Sisters shall as far as possible be dressed in the same way.

## CHAPTER II

## The Reception of Externe Sisters

### Article 8

In admitting and training Sisters who are destined for external service, exactly the same conditions are to be observed as those prescribed by the Constitutions for the Nuns of the Monastery in question, giving due consideration, however, to their special function. The Prioress with her Council should take care to accept only such aspirants as have a mature judgment and more than ordinary piety, so that they may give good example especially outside the Monastery in their dealings with seculars.

### Article 9

§ 1. The postulancy lasts for one year; but the Prioress with the advice of her Council can shorten it to six months or extend it for six months beyond the year, according as the postulant seems to need a longer or shorter preparation for the noviceship.

§ 2. During the postulancy the habit of the Sisters is worn, so that the postulants may be exercised and tested in their proper functions.

However, according to the judgment of the Prioress and her Council, and with the permission of the local Ordinary and of the Regular Superior if any, the postulancy may be performed in the Monastery, that is, inside the cloister of the Nuns, without prejudice to the Statutes of the Federation if the Monastery is a federated one, and to Article 4, § 2.

## Article 10

§ 1. The noviceship shall last two years, of which the first is the strictly canonical one, and although novices of this class are not bound by the law of papal cloister, it is made inside the cloister of their own Monastery together with the novices, or if there is a Federation, in the cloister of some other Monastery of the same Federation. The noviceship in order to be valid must be entire and continuous according to law.

§ 2. In order that the novices may be exercised in external activities, the second year of noviceship is usually done in the proper dwelling of the Sisters under the vigilance of a Sister deputed for this purpose, who reports to the Mistress of Novices. But during two months before the profession the novices are to abstain entirely from external service and remain in the novitiate of the Monastery, so that they may there prepare themselves more peacefully under the direction of the Mistress of Novices for their profession.

§ 3. According to the judgment of the Prioress and her Council, and with the permission of the local Ordinary and also of the Regular Superior if there is one, also the second year of noviceship may be made in the Monastery, without the novices being bound by the law of papal cloister.

§ 4. In training the novices to the religious life, while the instructions and conferences are given in just the same way as is prescribed in the Constitutions for the noviceship of the Nuns, special care should be taken to instruct them regarding the affairs and external works for which they are destined.

## Article 11

A noviceship made for Sisters dedicated to external service is not valid for choir Nuns or those called *conversae;* nor is a noviceship made for choir Nuns or *conversae* valid for externe Sisters (can. 558).

## Article 12

§ 1. After finishing the noviceship the novice shall make profession of simple temporary vows for six years, to be renewed each year for at least the first three years; at the end of six years she is to make profession of vows which are likewise simple but perpetual, or return to the world.

§ 2. In making the profession the rite of each Monastery is to be observed, changing whatever needs to be changed. The first religious profession, which follows the noviceship, is made by the Sisters inside the cloister of the Monastery; but the renovation of the vows and also the perpetual profession are made outside the cloister, at the choir screen of the Nuns. However, according to the judgment of the Prioress and her Council, and with the permission of the local Ordinary and of the Regular Superior if any, these too can be made inside the cloister.

§ 3. The formula of profession shall be the same as that for the Nuns, with the necessary additions and changes; for every profession of Sisters must be made in the character of a Sister dedicated to the external service of the Monastery, according to the Rule and Constitutions of the Monastery and the proper Statutes for externe Sisters approved by the Holy See.

Article 13

§ 1. Without prejudice to the prescriptions regarding the cession of administration and the disposal of the use and usufruct of property according to the common law (can. 569, § 1 and can. 580, § 1), a professed of simple vows, perpetual or temporary, unless the Constitutions provide otherwise, keeps the ownership of her property and her capacity to acquire other property. However, the externe Sisters should not be anxious about their property, and should already before their profession of temporary vows, make a will which is valid in civil law concerning the property presently owned and that which may come to them later; they may not change this will without permission of the Holy See, or if the matter is urgent and there is not time for this recourse, without the permission of the Prioress of the Monastery where the Sister actually is.

§ 2. Without an indult from the Holy See the Sisters cannot renounce their property nor alienate it without compensation.

§ 3. A professed Sister can change the cession or disposal mentioned in canon 569, not indeed at her own choice, unless the Constitutions permit this, but with the permission of the Prioress and also of the local Ordinary and of the Regular Superior if any, provided the change, if it concerns a notable part of the property, be not in favor of the Monastery; upon her departure from the Monastery this cession and disposal ceases to have any effect.

§ 4. Whatever she acquires by her own industry or in consideration of the Monastery, belongs to the Monastery.

## CHAPTER III

## The Discipline of Externe Sisters

### Article 14

§ 1. The Sisters, like the Nuns, are subject to the Prioress in everything, both as to religious discipline and their service. It is for the Prioress to prescribe regularly for the Sisters the order of their exercises, and with motherly care to provide for them whatever is necessary for the common life or for their individual needs.

§ 2. The Prioress may depute one of the externe Sisters or a perpetually professed Nun who is prudent and of mature age, to see to it that what concerns the discipline and service be conducted properly according to the Prioress' directions. This Sister shall prudently report to the Prioress or to another Nun deputed for the purpose, whatever needs to be reported, and shall receive instructions from her.

### Article 15

§ 1. The Prioress shall see to it that the externe Sisters perform the exercises of piety contained in the Rule and Constitutions, excepting those that are proper to the choir Nuns.

§ 2. Likewise for Holy Communion and Confession, the prescriptions for Nuns in the Constitutions are to be observed.

§ 3. For an occasional confession the Sisters have the benefit of the same faculties as those used by religious women who are not bound by papal cloister, namely: if for her peace of conscience a Sister goes to a confessor approved for women by the local Ordinary, the confession made in any church or oratory, even a semi-public one, or in any other place legitimately destined for the confessions of women or of religious women, or even legitimately chosen for a single occasion, is valid and licit (can. 522).

§ 4. The spiritual exercises of piety mentioned above in § 1 may, with the consent of the Prioress and her Council and the approval of the local Ordinary and of the Regular Superior if any, be performed by externe Sisters in the cloister of the Nuns.

### Article 16

The exercises of piety mentioned in the above article should as far as possible be performed by the Sisters in common.

The Sisters should also take their meals and their recreation in common.

### Article 17

The Prioress should be maternal in her dealings with the externe Sisters as regards the laws of abstinence and fasting which are peculiar to each Order according to the Rule and Constitutions, and so should dispense them from these when there is real need of it. It is desirable that in the various Orders or at least in the various Federations some uniform rule regarding the observance of these particular laws be established for the Sisters.

### Article 18

§ 1. The Sisters should remain at home diligently attending to their prayer and work, and should not go out except for the business of the Monastery or for some other reasonable cause, with the express permission of the Prioress; and they should not go out alone without a just cause and the permission of the Prioress. When they go out, in dealing and speaking with seculars, they must be mindful of their condition, and in their entire conduct give edification to others by careful attention to modesty, piety, gentleness, urbanity, and great reverence.

§ 2. The Prioress may not give permission for Sisters to live outside their own house, except for just cause and for the shortest possible time; for an absence beyond a month the permission of the local Ordinary and of the Regular Superior if any, is required; for an absence beyond six months the permission of the Holy See is required.

Article 19

§ 1. A Sister who is infirm and who in the judgment of the doctor or of the Prioress cannot be properly cared for in her external dwelling, should be brought into the cloister, and her cloistered Sisters should attend upon her with the greatest charity, and give her their kindly and faithful assistance.

§ 2. So also Sisters of advanced age, who have become incapable of external service and cannot receive the proper assistance in their external dwelling, may be admitted to the Monastery with the permission of the Prioress, to be given with the consent of the Council and the approval of the local Ordinary and of the Regular Superior if there is one.

§ 3. The Prioress should, however, be watchful that on such occasions the discipline of the Nuns and especially the spirit of recollection which should be constantly preserved in the cloister, suffer no harm.

The Sacred Congregation of Religious, having made their report to His Holiness John XXIII by Divine Providence Pope in the Audience granted to His Eminence the Cardinal Prefect on the 21st of March, 1961, now, in fulfilment of the commission given it in the Apostolic Constitution *Sponsa Christi* of 21 November, 1950 (AAS 43–5)[6] and in virtue of the faculties granted to it, hereby decrees and ordains that the present Norms and Statutes for Sisters dedicated to external service in Monasteries be observed.

All things to the contrary notwithstanding.

Given at Rome, 25 March, 1961.

**AAS 53–371;** S. C. Rel., 25 March, 1961. Annotations, *Periodica,* 52 (1963)–47 (Beyer).

---

**Day School for Girls within Cloister of Nuns.** A rescript of the Sacred Congregation of Religious, in granting permission to a certain community of cloistered nuns to conduct a day school for girls within the cloister, lays down regulations to be observed under these circumstances. See rescript, S. C. Rel. (no date given) published in *Periodica,* 26 (1937)–78; *Archiv für Katholisches Kirchenrecht,* 116 (1936)–164; *Commentarium pro Religiosis,* 16 (1935)–419.

---

[6] Reported above, pp. 326–344.

**Externe Nuns and Traveling Nuns, Admission of, into Cloister.** A rescript of the Sacred Congregation of Religious permitting this was published in *Commentarium pro Religiosis,* 17 (1936)–209, and later, with annotations by Ellis, in *Periodica,* 26 (1937)–81.

**Federation of Monasteries: Naming of Delegate:** The formula in use by the Sacred Congregation of Religious for appointing a Delegate for Federations of Nuns, is given in *Commentarium pro Religiosis,* 33 (1954) at pp. 25–27, with a commentary by Ruiz. This formula, with its annotations, gives a good idea of the practice which was foreshadowed in the Ap. Const., *Sponsa Christi,* Art. VII (reported above on p. 341) and in the Instruction which accompanied it, Section II (reported above on p. 349). The formula in use is also reported above on p. 326.

**Power of Local Ordinary** as to cloister of nuns. See **c. 329**; AAS 56–5, *Motu proprio, Pastorale munus,* n. 34; reported above on p. 72.

# CANON 602

**Daughters of Mary**; Founded by Saint Joanna de Lestonnac and Father John de Bordes, S.J., for the education of girls, and approved by Paul V, 7 April, 1607, as an Order consisting of a group of independent monasteries with papal cloister. A union (Congregation) of the Monasteries was effected by papal authority (1918–1921), some of them joining the union at once, others being free to come in later. This union, "the Society of the Daughters of Mary, Our Lady" included 60 of the 92 Monasteries of the Order; it had only episcopal cloister, and no solemn vows.

Pius XII, by an Apostolic Letter of 27 December, 1956, united the two organizations, that is, the Order of independent Monasteries and the Congregation or Society, in "the Order of the Daughters of Mary, Our Lady," with a centralized government, papal cloister (minor, mitigated) and solemn vows (AAS 49–889).

This Apostolic Letter, with the annotations by Gutiérrez in *Commentarium pro Religiosis,* 37 (1958)–256, constitutes an important document on the development of religious Orders of women, particularly as regards the papal cloister combined with apostolic work.

# CANON 606

## Dispersed Religious Considered as Legitimately Absent (S. C. Rel., *Monitum,* 10 July, 1955) AAS 47–519.

A *Monitum* of the Sacred Congregation of Religious, addressed to "the members of religious Institutes in Europe, who are forced to live outside their houses," is as follows:

This Sacred Congregation, as far as circumstances permit, has always a special solicitude for religious men, especially priests, and for religious women, who in certain parts of Europe are living under very difficult conditions.

Knowing the inconveniences and annoyances which they have to suffer in their daily life, this Sacred Congregation wishes to express its sympathy for these persons who are consecrated to God, and to encourage and strengthen them to persevere in the holy vocation by which they are attached to His service.

Accordingly, these religious men and women — and there are not a few — who because of the conditions of the times are obliged against their will to live outside the religious house and to do their work under very unfavorable conditions, will surely be consoled to learn that the Church considers them, not as members separated from their Institute or excloistered, but only as legitimately absent from the religious house.

Let such religious men and women, therefore, remember that in virtue of this legitimate absence they enjoy all the rights and privileges which they acquired by their religious profession; and that in like manner they are bound by their holy vows and obliged by their rules in as far as these can be reconciled to their actual state and can be observed by them without grave inconvenience.

The Church, no less than these religious themselves, ardently hopes that they may be able to return to the practice of the common life and to the due exercise of the sacred ministry; and on behalf of these her children who have so much to suffer, she prays for peace and tranquility.

It is their responsibility, so far as may be possible in the circumstances of the times, to keep in communication with their own Institute and to show a filial subjection to the local Ordinaries.

Let them freely approach their Superiors and Bishops whenever they have an opportunity, and expose to them their difficulties and needs, trusting that they will help them as far as is possible.

This Sacred Congregation will be most grateful to Their Excellencies the local Ordinaries if in their apostolic solicitude and in response to the dictates of their conscience in so grave a situation, they present themselves to these religious, both men and women, and give them special care, especially if they are unable to go to their own Superiors.

This union of spirit, this mutual trust and Christian priestly benevolence will do much to relieve the trials with which religious are now afflicted. At the same time it will contribute not a little to give the sufferers the necessary courage to be faithful in keeping their religious vows and to continue constantly to offer themselves as victims to God. This consecration of life is the principal element of the religious state, never to be hindered by any temporal vicissitudes; and it wins for the universal Church immense treasures of heavenly gifts.

Rome, 10 July, 1955.

**AAS 47–519;** S. C. Rel., *Monitum,* 10 July, 1955.

## CANON 610

### Mass in Houses of Religious Women of Simple Vows (Cod. Com., 20 May, 1923) AAS 16–113.

The Code Commission was asked:

Whether, in virtue of c. 610, § 2, which provides: "The Mass corresponding to the office of the day according to the rubrics shall also be celebrated daily in religious institutes of men, and also, as far as possible, in those of women"; the Mass corresponding to the office of the day should be celebrated only in religious institutes of regulars and monastic nuns who have solemn vows, or also in houses of religious women who have simple vows, but who by virtue of constitutions approved by the Holy See, are bound to choir duty.

**Reply.** In the negative to the first part; in the affirmative to the second.

**AAS 16–113;** Cod. Com., 20 May, 1923, III.
*Periodica,* 13 (1925)–83 (Vermeersch); *J.P.,* 4 (1924)–5.

### Religious Not Bound to More Than One Conventual Mass (Reply, S. C. Rit., 2 May, 1924) AAS 16–248.

The Sacred Congregation of Rites was asked:

Whether the new General Rubrics of the Roman Missal, tit. I, n. 1, where there is question of several conventual Masses to be celebrated in choir or out of choir, apply to the churches of religious in which there is an obligation of attending choir.

**Reply.** In the negative; i.e., those churches are not included, and religious are not bound, according to the General Rubrics of the Roman Missal, tit. III, n. 2, and canons 413, §§ 1 and 2, and 610, § 2, and the Decrees 1331–1332, 13 Feb., 1666 ad 6; 2514, 27 March, 1779 ad 5; and general Decree 3757, 2 Dec., 1891; in the absence of lawful custom or their constitutions.

**AAS 16–248**; S. C. Rit., 2 May, 1924.
*Periodica,* 13 (1925)–119 (Pauwels); cf. *Periodica,* 13 (1925)–(20).

---

**Divine Office in Choir:** Permission to recite it in Italian refused. The nuns of a certain monastery, for the benefit of those of the community who did not know Latin, asked for permission to say the Divine Office in Italian. The reply, S. C. Rit., 29 March, 1950 (N.A. 28/50): *Negative* (*Monitor Ecclesiasticus,* 77 (1952)–448.

## CANON 611

**Correspondence of Exempt Religious With Bishop** (Code Com., 27 Nov., 1947) **AAS 40–301.**

The Code Commission was asked:

Whether exempt religious, in the cases in which they are subject to the Ordinary, can, according to canon 611, freely send to the said Ordinary and receive from him letters subject to no inspection.

**Reply.** In the affirmative.

**AAS 40–301**; Code Com., 27 Nov., 1947.
*Periodica,* 37 (1948)–286 (Cappello).

## CANON 613

**Privileges Acquired by Communication Before the Code Not Revoked** (Code Commission, 30 Dec., 1937) **AAS 30–73.**

The Commission of Interpretation was asked:

Whether the words of canon 613, § 1: *exclusa in posterum qualibet communicatione,* are to be understood in the sense that privileges which were acquired through communication and peacefully enjoyed by religious institutes before the Code of Canon Law, were revoked.

**Reply.** In the negative.

AAS 30–73; Cod. Com., 30 Dec., 1937. *Periodica,* 27 (1938)–157 (Ellis).

---

**Faculties and Privileges of Religious:** when shared by Bishop of diocese. See **c. 329**; AAS 56–5, *Motu proprio, Pastorale munus,* n. 29; reported above on p. 72.

## CANON 615

### Blessing of Benedictine Abbots: Mandate *Semel Pro Semper* to Bishops (Letter, Benedict XV, 19 June, 1921) AAS 13–416.

An Apostolic Letter of Benedict XV, 19 June, 1921, begins by recalling that two formulas exist in the Roman Pontifical for the blessing of Abbots; one to be used for blessings imparted by authority of the Holy See, the other for blessings by authority of the Ordinary. The latter is used for Abbots who are not exempt, and who are bound to promise subjection and obedience to the Ordinary of the place in the ceremony itself. The former is used for Abbots who enjoy the privilege of exemption. All Benedictine Abbots belong to this class (cf. c. 615). In their case, therefore, the practice before the Code had been, when the blessing was to be imparted outside the Roman Curia, that an apostolic mandate be directed to the Ordinary within whose territory the monastery of the future Abbot was located, except in the case of Abbots *nullius dioecesis* or of those who, by privilege, could be blessed by any Bishop.

Since the Code in this matter renews the discipline theretofore existing, apostolic mandate is still required in these cases. At the request, however, of the Abbot Primate of the Order of St. Benedict, the Holy See by these presents grants perpetually for the future, *semel pro semper,* a general or common mandate, directed to the respective diocesan Bishop, which may be read at that point in the ceremony of blessing in the *Pontifical,* where the question is asked, *Habetis mandatum Apostolicum?*[1]

[1] Cf. *Pontificale Romanum, Pars I, De Benedictione Abbatis Auctoritate Apostolica.*

Moreover, since the diocesan Bishop may at times be prevented from imparting the blessing at an opportune time, the peculiar privilege is granted, whereby not only Abbots *nullius dioecesis* who are mentioned in cc. 322, § 2, and 323, § 1, and Abbots whose monasteries are located in the territory of some prelate *nullius,* but also all other Abbots of the Order of St. Benedict, can receive the aforesaid blessing from any Bishop in communion with the Holy See, whenever the episcopal see is vacant, or whenever written proof exists that the diocesan Bishop is either legitimately impeded from giving the blessing himself, or has consented that it be given by another.

In the solemn ceremony of blessing, it is ordered that the Abbot shall bind himself by the customary oath to be forever faithful.

**AAS 13–416**; Benedict XV, Letter, 19 June, 1921.
*Periodica,* 10 (1922)–341 (Vermeersch).

## CANON 621

### Mendicant Orders: Permission of Ordinary to Beg Alms

(Cod. Com., 16 Oct., 1919) **AAS 11–478.**

The Code Commission was asked:

Whether c. 621, § 1, is to be understood as applying only to religious who are mendicants in the strict sense; or also to those who are called such in a broader sense, as for example, the Order of Preachers.

And if the reply is in the affirmative to the first part: whether the aforesaid mendicants need the permission of the Ordinary, if they wish to collect money in the diocese for the building, ornamenting, etc., of their churches.

**Reply.** In the affirmative to the first part; in the negative to the second. As regards the obtaining of permission from the Ordinary, that is provided for in the aforesaid canon 621, § 1.

**AAS 11–478**; Cod. Com., 16 Oct., 1919, n. 10.
*Periodica,* 10 (1922)–103 (Vermeersch); *J.P.,* 3 (1923)–68.

## CANON 622

**Collecting Money for the Missions** (S. C. Prop. Fid., 29 June, 1952) **AAS 44–549.**

An Instruction of the Sacred Congregation for the Propagation of the Faith on the proper way of collecting money for the missions is as follows:

For many years now the Christian people are increasingly zealous in promoting the propagation of the Catholic faith among infidels, by supplying not only preachers of the Gospel but also financial support.

According to norms laid down by the Roman Pontiffs, all the funds which are offered for the progress of the Missions are brought together both through the two Pontifical Works for the Propagation of the Faith, namely that of Saint Peter the Apostle for the Native Clergy and that of the Holy Childhood, and through the collection which is to be taken up at the time of Epiphany for the African Negroes.

Those norms, in the words of Pius XI of happy memory in his *Motu proprio, Romanorum Pontificum,* provide for "all Catholic Missions, through collections taken up in a certain way and method, from the whole Catholic world, so that even small sums collected in all nations from all the children of the Church, are put together in one fund destined to take care of the Missions in general, and all this money, which is entirely under Our control and disposal and that of the Sacred Congregation for the Propagation of the Faith, is distributed among all the Missions according to each one's needs, by men chosen by Ourselves."[1]

In order diligently to develop for the benefit of the Missions the cooperation of all the resources of the faithful in their respective countries according to the prescriptions of the sacred canons (cf. cc. 622, §§ 1 and 2; 691, §§ 3–5; 1341, § 1; 1503) and of the *Motu proprio* documents, *Romanorum Pontificum* of 3 May, 1922, *Vix ad Summi* of 24 June, 1929,[2] *Decessor Noster* of 24 June, 1929,[3] and others, this Sacred Congregation for the

---

[1] Cf. *Motu proprio* of Pius XI, 3 May, 1922; AAS 14–321; CANON LAW DIGEST, 1, p. 163. This language is quoted from AAS 14–323.

[2] AAS 21–345.

[3] *Ibid.,* 21–342.

Propagation of the Faith felt that certain norms ought to be recalled to the minds of all Directors, national or diocesan, who are in charge of Pontifical Mission Works, and also of the religious Orders and Congregations and the Societies without vows, all of which for brevity's sake will be referred to in this Instruction as Missionary Institutes; and it has accordingly decreed that the said norms be exactly observed by all the persons and organizations above mentioned.

1. Missionary Institutes are allowed to make known to the faithful through sermons and publications the needs of their schools for the training of missionaries and of the Missions entrusted to them, and to urge the faithful to generosity. They should not forget, however, to inform their hearers and readers of the particular purpose of the Pontifical works, and should persuade them to give their support to those works, especially when Mission Day comes round.

2. Missionary Institutes, in promoting any kind of missionary cooperation in their respective countries, shall obtain the permission of the Diocesan Mission Board and shall avoid using names and appearances which might create in the minds of the faithful false notions about the purpose of the Missionary Institutes and of the Pontifical works, or which might seriously interfere with the progress of those same Works.

3. Missionary Institutes shall take care to cooperate willingly in the preparation and celebration of Mission Day. They shall send to the proper Diocesan Board all the money which is collected on that day, even in parishes and churches which are entrusted to the care of religious; and in order to avoid interfering in any way with the successful celebration of that day, they shall, at least for a reasonable time before the annual recurrence of Mission Day, abstain from all profit-seeking or appearance of securing any advantage for their Missions.

4. The National Directors shall be watchful that no one, abusing the purpose of the Pontifical Mission Works, take up collections for the Missions in general in order to meet necessities existing in territories which are not dependent on this Sacred Congregation for the Propagation of the Faith.

5. The National and Diocesan Directors shall so manage the activities which they are to promote among the faithful for the benefit of the Missions, as to avoid all unnecessary expenses and

all projects which do not conduce directly to consolidate the work for the Missions.

6. Mission Day shall be celebrated in accordance with the norms established by authoritative documents and with the regulations which the various National Boards shall see fit to adopt in view of special circumstances.

7. In schools, academies, and all such institutions which are controlled by religious and sisters, the persons in charge shall consider it their duty to favor enrollment of the young people as members of the Pontifical Missionary Works and to celebrate Mission Day with special solicitude, sending to the proper Diocesan Board all the money that is collected both from the enrollments and by contributions.

Given at Rome, from the office of the Sacred Congregation for the Propagation of the Faith, the 29th day of June, Feast of the Holy Apostles Peter and Paul, in the year 1952.

**AAS 44–549**; S. C. Prop. Fid., 29 June, 1952. Annotations, *Monitor Ecclesiasticus,* 77 (1952)–399 (Paventi).

## CANON 625

### Violet Skull Cap Allowed, Where Its Use is Based on a Privilege — Private.

Private replies of the S. C. Rit. are to the effect that, although c. 625 does not confer on regular Abbots who are actually governing a community the right to wear a violet skull cap, yet it is not the intention of this canon to derogate from privileges theretofore granted which are still in effect.

(**Private**); Cf. *Periodica,* 18 (1929)–244; 20 (1931)–143 (Vermeersch).

## CANON 627

**Religious Appointed Prefect Apostolic** is subject to this canon during his office. See private reply *ex audientia Sanctissimi,* 2 Dec., 1920, reported by Vermeersch in *Epitome,* I, ed. 1937, n. 787, p. 581.

## CANON 632

**Authority of Ordinary to Permit Transfer of Nuns from One Monastery to Another** (Reply, S. C. Rel., 9 Nov., 1926) **AAS 18–490.**

The Sacred Congregation of Religious was asked:

I. Whether nuns of monasteries in which only simple vows are pronounced, in accordance with c. 488, 7° and the Decree of S. C. Rel., 23 June, 1923,[1] can go from their own monastery to another monastery of the same kind which is *sui juris* and belongs to the same Order, upon the authority merely of the Ordinary or Ordinaries.

**Reply.** In the negative; and let c. 632 be observed.

II. Whether these same nuns can be transferred by the Ordinary or Ordinaries from their own to another monastery as above, with their consent and that of both communities, at least for a time, so that in the new monastery while they remain there they may be able to enjoy the rights and perform the duties in the same way as nuns of that community.

**Reply.** In the negative without previous permission from the Holy See.

Approved and confirmed by His Holiness, Pius XI, 9 Nov., 1926.

**AAS 18–490;** S. C. Rel., Reply, 9 Nov., 1926.
*Periodica,* 15 (1926)–230 (Vermeersch).

**Religious Women of Simple Vows Transferring From One Independent House of Their Institute to Another, Are subject to This Canon** (S. C. Rel., 19 Nov., 1931) **Private.**

The following question was asked by the Bishop of Brooklyn:

**Question.** Having in mind the provisions of canon 632 and the replies of the S. C. of Religious of 9 Nov., 1926,[2] we ask whether religious women who according to their Constitutions pronounce only simple vows, are bound by the prescription of

[1] See above, p. 203; AAS 15–357.
[2] See immediately preceding document.

canon 632, if each of their houses is entirely independent of the other houses of the same Institute.

For such religious women acknowledge no Superioress other than the local one, and hence their houses seem to be as it were independent. In the Constitutions their houses are generally called monasteries. On the other hand, they can in no sense be called monastic nuns, and so they cannot be included in the terms of the above mentioned replies.

Since the canonists whom we have consulted are not of one mind on the question, it would seem that appropriate instructions in the matter would be very useful.

On 19 Nov., 1931 (N. 26/31), the Secretary of the S. C. sent the following reply:

**Reply.** After having carefully considered the question presented by Your Excellency: whether the Sisters Adorers of the Most Precious Blood, who according to their Constitutions pronounce only simple vows, are bound by the prescription of canon 632, if each of their houses is entirely independent of the other houses of the same Institute, this S. C. considering all aspects of the question, has decided to and does reply as follows: The provision of canon 632 (633, § 3) is to be observed also in the transfer of Sisters of the Most Precious Blood to another monastery of their Institute.

(**Private**); Secretary of the S. C. Rel., 19 Nov., 1931. Published in Konrad, *The Transfer of Religious to Another Community*, pp. 102, 103.

---

**Power of Local Ordinary** to permit transfer from one diocesan institute to another. See **c. 329**; AAS 56–5, *Motu proprio, Pastorale munus,* n. 38; reported above on p. 73.

## CANON 633

### Religious Transferring to New Order Wears Habit of Novice of New Order (S. C. Rel., 14 May, 1923) AAS 15–289.

The Sacred Congregation of Religious was asked:

Whether a religious who has taken his vows in a certain religious society, and has been transferred by apostolic indult to another one, is bound to receive and to wear the habit of novices in that Order to which he has been transferred, while his noviceship in that Order lasts.

**Reply.** In the affirmative.

**AAS 15–289**; S. C. Rel., Reply, 14 May, 1923.
*Periodica,* 12 (1924)–67; cf. *Periodica,* 12 (1924)–16 (Vermeersch); *J.P.,* 3 (1923)–130.

## CANON 634

**Religious Coming from Another Institute** (Cod. Com., 14 July, 1922) **AAS 14–528.**

The Code Commission was asked:

Whether the vote of the Chapter (cf. c. 575, § 2) in admitting a religious under the circumstances mentioned in c. 634 to the solemn profession or to the perpetual profession of the simple vows, is deliberative or only consultative.

**Reply.** In the affirmative to the first part; in the negative to the second.

**AAS 14–528**; Cod. Com., 14 July, 1922, VII.
*Periodica,* 11 (1923)–166 (Vermeersch); *J.P.,* 2 (1922)–123.

## CANON 638

**Proper Bishop for Exclaustration or Secularization** (Code Commission, 24 July, 1939) **AAS 31–321.**

The Commission of Interpretation was asked:

Whether the words *loci Ordinarius,* in canon 638, mean the Ordinary of the place where the religious is staying or the Ordinary of the place where the principal house is situated.

**Reply.** In the affirmative to the first part, in the negative to the second.

**AAS 31–321**; Cod. Com., 24 July, 1939. *Periodica,* 29 (1940)–145 (Bouscaren).

**Definite Acceptance of Indult of Secularization** (S. C. Rel., 19 April, 1951) **Private.**

**Facts.** A certain religious woman, having received the indult of secularization, at first refused to accept it formally. Later she declared that she wished to go back to the world; she left the religious house, laid aside the habit, accepted the return of her dowry; a suitable means of livelihood had been provided for her. But on arriving at the railroad station she changed her mind and wished to return to the religious house. She called the Superioress by telephone and spoke with her expressing this desire; but the Superioress refused to take her back. The Sacred Congregation of Religious, to which recourse was then taken, replied as follows:

**Reply.** *In Congressu,* 19 April, 1951. This matter having again been discussed in the *Congressus,* it was unanimously decided that the dispensation had been accepted according to law, and hence that according to law the lady in question is no longer a religious and cannot be admitted in religion (canons 542, 1°; 640, § 2).

(**Private**); S. C. Rel., Reply, 19 April, 1951, Prot. N. 7922/50; reported, with commentary by Gutiérrez, in *Commentarium pro Religiosis,* 32 (1953)–196.

**Definite Acceptance Given Orally Held Sufficient** (S. C. Rel., 17 Nov., 1951) **Private.**

**Facts.** A religious woman asked for an indult of secularization and received it; she was summoned to the Curia and the indult was read to her by the Vicar General before a Notary. She replied that she accepted the indult, stating that she had already laid aside the religious habit. She was then asked to sign the indult to signify her acceptance, but this she refused to do. Upon recourse to the S. C. of Religious, the decision was:

**Reply:** Nov. 17, 1951. The Sister in question is to be considered as secularized according to law from the day when the indult of secularization which she had asked for was communicated to her in the Curia and she signified *orally* that she accepted it (Prot. N. 3532/51).

(**Private**); S. C. Rel., 17 Nov., 1951. Reported in *Commentarium pro Religiosis,* 32(1953)–197.

**Indult of Secularization Expires If Not Accepted Within Ten Days: New Formula** (S. C. Rel., 1953) **Private.**

In granting an indult of secularization to religious *who are not priests,* the S. C. of Religious has introduced a change in its practice. Formerly, that is, from September or October of 1951 until 1953, the following clause was placed on the reverse side of the Rescript (where the tax is indicated and the execution of the Rescript is to be noted): "Praesens rescriptum acceptari vel reiici debet intra decem dies a communicatione exsecutionis. Quod si Orator (Oratrix) intra decem dies a communicatione exsecutionis imploratam dispensationem expresse non recusaverit, praesumitur rescriptum acceptasse."

In place of this clause, the practice was begun about 1953 of inserting in the body of the Rescript the following clause: "Post decem dies a recepta communicatione decreti exsecutorialis ex parte Oratoris (Oratricis), praesens rescriptum, si non fuerit acceptatum, nullius roboris esto."

**(Private)**; S. C. Rel., 1953. Practice explained by Gutiérrez in *Commentarium pro Religiosis,* 32 (1953)–189.

---

**Secularization:** Acceptance of the Indult. The practice of the S. C. of Religious in this matter is explained by Gutiérrez in *Commentarium pro Religiosis,* 32 (1953)–186, and illustrated by several private replies of the Sacred Congregation. These replies are reported in this volume under canon 638. The article is a semi-official and authoritative statement of the practice of the Sacred Congregation, summarizing one of the lectures given by Father Larraona and his aides in the Practical School of Canon Law for Religious, conducted by the same Sacred Congregation.

## CANON 639

### Qualified Exclaustration for Priest Religious Who Asks for Reduction to the Lay State (S. C. of Religious, Formula, 1954) Private.

The Sacred Congregation of Religious, upon adopting the practice represented by the following formula about the year 1954, allowed the formula itself to become known for the benefit of religious Superiors and others who might be interested. We present the formula of both petition and rescript in the original Latin, with an English version in the footnote.

Beatissime Pater:

N.N., Sacerdos professus in (tali Congregatione vel Ordine), ad pedes Sanctitatis Vestrae provolutus, humiliter implorat reductionem ad statum laicalem, cum solutione a votis ceterisque oneribus sacris Ordinibus adnexis, salva tamen manente lege sacri Coelibatus, cum omnino imparem se sentiat ad onera vitae religiosae et sacerdotalis sustinenda.

Et Deus,

Haec Sacra Congregatio, attentis instantibus Oratoris precibus, omnibusque quae allegata fuerunt in Domino semel iterumque ponderatis, antequam laicizationem sine spe readmissionis definitive imponat, Rev.mo P. (Praeposito Generali) benigne committit ut, pro suo arbitrio et conscientia, absolutis censuris poenisque remissis, in quas Orator forte incursus sit, *exclaustrationem qualificatam* ad annum sub his legibus concedat:

1. Praeter normas exclaustrationis communes in can. 639 statutas, Orator illico dimittat habitum etiam ecclesiasticum, quam dimissionem prohibitio ac privatio omnium ministeriorum ecclesiasticorum subsequetur atque privilegiorum et obligationum clericalium suspensio, *salva tamen semper lege sacri Coelibatus.*

2. Exclaustratione perdurante, Orator in usu ac receptione Sacramentorum laicis assimilatur.

3. Sub disciplina et adsistentia Exc.mi Ordinarii ac Religionis Orator remaneat, ut efficaciter et opportune, impositis etiam ipsi piis precibus, ad honestam et dignam rationem vivendi et crisim superandam adiuvari et caritative manuduci valeat.

4. Superiori in exeundo scriptam tradat declarationem se sibimetipsi sine onere Religionis provisurum in saeculo.

5. Transacto indulti tempore, ad hanc Sacram Congregationem recurrendum est, ut Oratori convenienter in Domino provideri possit.

Contrariis quibuslibet minime obstantibus.

(**Private**); S. C. Rel., Formula, 1954.[1]

---

[1] Most Holy Father:

N.N., priest professed in (such a Congregation or Order), prostrate at the feet of Your Holiness, humbly asks for reduction to the lay state, with release from his vows and from the other obligations attached to sacred Orders, but without prejudice to the obligation of sacred Celibacy, for the reason that he feels completely incapable of fulfilling the obligations of the religious and priestly life.

And may God,

This Sacred Congregation, in consideration of the earnest prayer of the Petitioner, and after having more than once pondered before God all the allegations adduced, before imposing laicization definitively without hope of readmission to the clerical state, graciously commits to the Very Reverend

**Qualified Exclaustration: Practice of the Sacred Congregation** (S. C. Rel., 1955) **Private.**

The practice of the Sacred Congregation of Religious in regard to this new form of exclaustration, known as *exclaustratio qualificata,* is explained by Gutiérrez in *Commentarium pro Religiosis,* 34 (1955) 374–379.

The *formula* of the petition and rescript are given precisely as reported above in this volume under this same canon 639.

*Qualified exclaustration* is a provisional remedy granted as a favor but only in proper cases and after thorough investigation, to religious priests who ask for reduction to the lay state. Sometimes the definite abandonment of the priesthood can be prevented by this means. The causes for granting it are usually temporary, or at least such as it may be hoped will pass away with time: a grave crisis of faith; decided incapacity to live the religious and priestly life due to tedium, discouragement, ill-health; psychic depression, perhaps with danger of public scandal, apostasy, or suicide; notable bad example through obstinate

---

Father (usually the Superior General of the Institute) the authority, according to his judgment and conscience, after having absolved the Petitioner from censures and penalties which he perchance incurred, to grant him *qualified exclaustration* for one year, on the following terms.

1. Besides observing the common norms of exclaustration laid down in canon 639, the Petitioner must immediately lay aside also the ecclesiastical dress, and this laying aside will have as a consequence the prohibition and privation of all ecclesiastical ministries and the suspension of all the privileges and obligations of clerics, *always however without prejudice to the law of sacred Celibacy.*

2. During the exclaustration the Petitioner is treated as a layman in the use and reception of the Sacraments.

3. The Petitioner remains under the authority and assistance of the Most Excellent Ordinary and of his Institute, so that he may be effectively and appropriately helped and charitably led, also through pious prayers which may be imposed upon him, to an honest and worthy way of life and to overcome his crisis.

4. When he leaves the Institute he is to give to the Superior a written declaration that he will provide for himself in the world, without any burden upon the Institute.

5. When the time of the indult has expired, recourse is to be made to this Sacred Congregation, so that appropriate provision in the Lord may be made for the Petitioner.

All things to the contrary notwithstanding.

abstention from Mass and the Sacraments; an invincible repugnance for the priestly ministry, and the like.

It is a true *exclaustration* and has much in common with the usual exclaustration described in canon 639: namely, it is reserved to the Holy See; it is temporary (for one or two years); the priest remains a member of the Institute, and continues to enjoy its purely spiritual privileges, but his active and passive voice and other rights as a religious are suspended; he must lay aside the religious dress; he is under the jurisdiction of the local Ordinary. The institute is not bound in justice to provide for him, but special circumstances may create an obligation in charity, and in such case number 4 of the formula of the rescript may be omitted.

It is, however, a *qualified* exclaustration, and as such differs in several respects from the ordinary exclaustration.

*The Nature of the Indult.* It is an indult but not a pure favor; it has consequences which are independent of the will of the subject or of the executor of the rescript. Some of these are in the nature of privations.

*Consequences for the Subject as a Religious.*

The *religious vows* are suspended, but the law of celibacy remains binding.

As regards *poverty,* the subject can, as long as the indult remains in effect, acquire property and freely provide for himself. Superiors, however, must exercise some vigilance to see that he does nothing which would be prejudicial to the Institute should he afterward return, for example contracting debts.

As to *obedience,* since the vow is suspended, he is not subject to the local Ordinary in virtue of the vow, but he "remains under the authority and assistance of the Most Reverend Ordinary and of his Institute" (rescript formula, n. 3).

The *common life* may not be freely resumed by the subject as in a common exclaustration; he is rather, in this respect, in the same position as one who is *exclaustratus ad nutum Sanctae Sedis,* except that Superiors *may permit* him to come back, subject to the privations which the indult imposes (see below).

*Consequences for the Subject as a Priest.*

He is bound, not merely permitted, to lay aside the *clerical dress.*

He loses the right to exercise *any priestly or clerical ministry* or function, such as preaching, saying Mass, or administering the Sacraments.

He is deprived of the *rights and privileges of clerics.*

He is dispensed from all *priestly obligations* except celibacy.

In the *reception of the Sacraments,* he is treated as a layman.

*Cessation of the Indult.*

When the time for which the indult was given has expired, the subject must return to his Institute; but until further provision is made he remains subject to the privations which the indult imposes.

Before the expiration of the time, the indult may be revoked by the Sacred Congregation either at the request of the subject or *ex officio.* Superiors have no power to revoke it.

*Reduction to the lay state* may be granted definitively by a new indult of the Sacred Congregation, or it may be imposed as a penalty in case of grave scandal. In both cases, the exclaustration comes to an end.

If the subject can find a Bishop willing to receive him in accordance with canon 641, he may obtain an indult of secularization and be restored to his ministries as a priest.

**(Private)**; S. C. Rel., practice since October, 1953, outlined by Gutiérrez in *Commentarium pro Religiosis,* 34 (1955)–374–379.

---

*Exclaustratio ad Nutum Sanctae Sedis:* The practice of the S. C. of Religious in this matter is explained by Gutiérrez in *Commentarium pro Religiosis,* 32 (1953)–336. This exclaustration differs from that mentioned in canons 638, 639, etc., in that it is not asked for by the subject but *imposed by the Holy See* — not strictly as a penalty, however, even though the causes leading up to it may have been culpable, but for the good of the Institute and sometimes also of the individual. Its duration is indefinite, yet not strictly perpetual. It does not cease by the mere cessation of the causes for which it was imposed, but a new decree of the Sacred Congregation revoking it is required. If the subject is a priest and finds no Bishop who will accept him, he may be permitted to say Mass only in a definite pious or religious house whose Superior is willing to assume some responsibility for him. If not even this can be assured, the Holy See will usually not impose *exclaustratio ad nutum.* When it does so through necessity in exceptional cases, the subject is suspended (not penally) from the exercise of any order or sacred ministry. As to obedience, he remains subject to his own Superiors.

# CANON 640

**Indult of Secularization Need Not Be Accepted** (S. C. Rel., 1 Aug., 1922) **AAS 14–501.**

The Sacred Congregation of Religious was asked:

Whether a religious who has obtained an indult of secularization or a dispensation from simple vows can refuse to accept the indult or the dispensation when he receives notice of it from the local Superior, although the General Superior has already issued in writing, in accordance with c. 56, the Decree executing the rescript.

**Reply.** In the affirmative, provided Superiors have not grave reasons to the contrary, in which case they should refer the matter to the Sacred Congregation.

AAS 14–501; S. C. Rel., Reply, 1 Aug., 1922.
*Periodica* 11 (1923)–150 (Vermeersch); *J.P.,* 2 (1922)–90.

**Canon 640 Interpreted** (Cod. Com., 12 Nov., 1922) **AAS 14–662.**

The Code Commission was asked:

1. Whether c. 640, § 1, includes all who have obtained an indult of secularization, whether from the Holy See or from the Ordinary of the place.

**Reply.** In the affirmative.

2. Whether those who have obtained an indult of *exclaustration* from the Ordinary of the place, are bound by the conditions laid down in c. 639.

**Reply.** In the affirmative, without prejudice to the power of the Ordinary to permit the person to retain the religious habit, for special reasons.

AAS 14–662; Cod. Com., 12 Nov., 1922, III.
*Periodica,* 11 (1923)–184 (Vermeersch); *J.P.,* 2 (1922)–129.

**Religious Secularized Before the Code, If Readmitted Need Not Repeat Noviceship or Profession** (S. C. Rel., 25 Jan., 1923) **Private.**

A rescript of the S. C. of Religious to the Procurator General of the Capuchins is as follows:

I am happy to inform Your Paternity that religious who were secularized before the Code came into effect, if they are allowed to reenter religion, are not bound to a new noviceship nor to a new profession, because by the terms of the indult of secularization which was usually granted before May 19, 1918, they were not released from their vows but were merely dispensed from such obligations as could not be reconciled with their new state, and so they remained religious, bound to the substantial observance of their vows.

(**Private**); S. C. Rel., 25 Jan., 1923; *Analecta Ord. Min. Capuccin.*, 1925, p. 36; *Periodica*, 14 (1926)–78.

## CANON 641

**Priest of Mission Society Not Incardinated after Six Years' Residence in Diocese** (Case, S. C. Conc., 15 July, 1933) **AAS 26–234.**

**Facts.** N entered the Lyons Society for the African Missions in 1898 and was ordained therein in 1910, taking the customary oath of perseverance. For some years thereafter he was teaching in the seminary of the said Society. During the war he was engaged as an infirmarian and chaplain. Returning in 1919, he soon afterward asked, through the Superior General of the Society and through the Sacred Congregation of Propaganda, to be released from his oath. The Sacred Congregation replied that he must first find a Bishop who was willing to receive him, and must present to the Sacred Congregation a certificate of his incardination. Since he failed to do this, he never obtained the release from his oath to the Mission Society. Nevertheless, with the permission of the Superior General, he left the Society in 1920, exercised the ministry for three years in the diocese of C, then removed to the diocese of S, where he remained from January, 1924, until July, 1933. He asked for formal incardination there in 1927, but was refused by the Bishop, who, however, permitted him to remain until 1931, when he requested him to leave the diocese.

N now applies to the Sacred Congregation of the Council,

claiming that he has become incardinated implicitly in the diocese of S by virtue of canon 641, § 2, which declares that a *religious*, after six years' trial in a diocese, becomes incardinated therein if he has not been dismissed before the expiration of that time.

The Bishop of S resists the claim of N to incardination in his diocese.

**The Law of the Case.** 1. Canon 488, 7°, defines a religious as one who has taken vows in a religious society; and canon 488, 1°, defines a religious society as one in which the members take public vows. Since the members of the Lyons Society for the African Missions do not take vows, that society is not a religious society, and its members are not religious.

2. The same conclusions are derived from canon 673, § 1, which applies to societies without vows.

3. Canon 678 declares that the members of such societies are governed in regard to studies and the reception of orders, by the same laws as are the secular clergy.

4. It follows that canon 641, which forms the basis of N's claim, has no application to the case. Hence:

**Question.** Is N incardinated in the diocese of S?

**Reply.** In the negative.

This reply was approved by His Holiness, Pius XI, in the audience of 17 July, 1933.

**AAS 26–234**; S. C. Conc., Resolution, *Sedunen.*, 15 July, 1933. *Jus Pontificium,* 14 (1934)–227.

## Time of Probation Before Incardination of Secularized Religious Can Be Extended Tacitly (Code Commission, 27 July, 1942) AAS 34–241.

The Code Commission was asked:

Whether the words of canon 641, § 2: *Episcopus potest probationis tempus prorogare,* are to be understood only of express prorogation, or also of tacit prorogation.

**Reply.** In the negative to the first part, in the affirmative to the second.

**AAS 34–241**; Code Com., 27 July, 1942. *Periodica,* 32 (1943)–110 (Aguirre).

**Formula for Exclaustration and Eventual Secularization of Religious Priest Who Is Accepted in a Diocese by Way of Trial** (S. C. Rel., 1953) **Private.**

The formula in use by the S. C. of Religious (1953) for the exclaustration of a religious priest who has been accepted *by way of trial* for a diocese, is as follows:

**The Petition:** Beatissime Pater: N.N., ad pedes Sanctitatis Vestrae provolutus, humiliter implorat indultum saecularizationis, praevio experimento ad normam canonis 641, § 2, ob causas Sacrae Congregationi de Religiosis allatas.

Et Deus, etc.

**The Rescript:** Vigore facultatum a SS.mo Domino Nostro concessarum, Sacra Congregatio Negotiis Religiosorum Sodalium praeposita, audito voto (Rev.mi Procuratoris Generalis) et attentis litteris testimonialibus Ordinarii ——, eidem Ordinario benigne commisit ut, pro suo arbitrio et conscientia, Oratori concedat indultum exclaustrationis, durante experimenti tempore, deposita exteriore forma habitus religiosi et servatis ceteris servandis ad normam canonis 639 Codicis Iuris Canonici. Si forte, perdurante experimento, ab Ordinario, praemonitis Superioribus —— dimittatur, statim ad clausura redire teneatur. Transacto vero praefato experimenti tempore, vel etiam prius si definitive recipiatur, Orator, novo titulo canonico vel, ipsius Ordinarii iudicio, alio modo, congrua sustentatione provisus, maneat saecularizatus, ideoque liberatus a votis in religione emissis, firmis oneribus Ordini maiori adnexis, ac ipso facto incardinatus —— (Dioecesi ——) ad normam canonum 640, § 1, nn. 1, 2 et 642 Codicis Iuris Canonici. Decretum autem exsecutoriale huius Rescripti communicetur cum hac Sacra Congregatione et cum Superiore Generali ——

Contrariis quibuslibet non obstantibus.

Datum Romae, die —— 19—

**(Private)**; S. C. Rel., 1953; reported and explained by Gutiérrez in *Commentarium pro Religiosis,* 32 (1953)–190.

NOTE: At times (if a Bishop has accepted the priest absolutely according to canon 641, § 2), the indult of secularization is given immediately and its execution is committed to the Ordinary. No particular time limit for its acceptance is specified, as is done in the indult of secularization of religious who are not priests.

## CANON 642

### Prohibitions of this Canon Apply Also to Those Who Returned to the World Before the Code (Cod. Com., 24 Nov., 1920) AAS 12–575.

The Code Commission was asked:

Whether the prohibitions contained in c. 642 prevent religious from obtaining offices or benefices, only in case they returned to the world after the promulgation of the Code; or whether, notwithstanding c. 10, those prohibitions apply also to those religious who, before the promulgation of the Code, were, with the permission of the Holy See, already out of the religious life.

**Reply.** In the negative to the first part; in the affirmative to the second.

**AAS 12–575**; Cod. Com., 24 Nov., 1920.
*Periodica,* 10 (1922)–252 (Vermeersch); *J.P.,* 3 (1923)–119.

### Priests, Formerly Religious, Allowed as Confessors of Religious Women (S. C. Rel., 9 July, 1962) Private.

The undersigned Ordinary, humbly prostrate at the feet of Your Holiness, requests an indult in accord with Canon 642, § 1, 3° to permit certain priests to exercise the office of confessor to religious women. All of these priests were formerly members of religious Institutes, and were duly secularized and incardinated into the Diocese according to the prescriptions of Canon 641, § 2. The reason for the indult is the shortage of priests qualified according to Canon 524 to fulfill these offices for the large number of religious communities working in the Diocese. All of these priests have shown themselves to be of good character and sound piety since their arrival in the Diocese and for this reason we deigned to incardinate them into the Diocese. None of them has displayed any attitude adverse to any religious institute and if permitted to act as confessors to religious women, there is no danger that they would influence religious to seek exclaustration or secularization under any pretexts. The priests for whom indults are sought are:

(An individual petition for each priest was sent in the following form: Beatissime Pater, Ordinarius ad pedes S. V. provolutus, humiliter implorat dispensationem super praescripto can. 642, § 1, C.J.C., favore P. N.N. ob causas S. C. de Religiosis allatas.)

**Reply.** In the virtue of faculties granted by our Holy Father, the Sacred Congregation for the Affairs of Religious, after attending to the recitals, graciously grants the favor as requested, with due observance of all requisites.

All things to the contrary notwithstanding.

(**Private**); S. C. Rel., 9 July, 1962, Prot. No. 3251/58; reported by the Rt. Rev. Msgr. Paul V. Harrington, Chairman of the Committee on Research, to the 1962 National Convention of the Canon Law Society of America; it can also be found in *The Jurist,* 23 (1963)–119–120; date and protocol number kindly given by the Rt. Rev. Msgr. Joseph P. Conway, Vice-Chancellor of Albany, N. Y.

## CANON 646

### Declaration of the Fact is Not Necessary (Cod. Com., 30 July, 1934) AAS 26–494.

The Code Commission was asked:

I. Is it necessary that the fact which is referred to in c. 646, § 2, shall have been declared, in order that the religious be considered *ipso facto* as legitimately dismissed?

**Reply.** In the negative.

**AAS 26–494**; Cod. Com., 30 July, 1934.
*Periodica,* 23 (1934)–147 (Vermeersch); *Amer. Eccles. Review,* 91 (1934)–498; *Irish Ecclesiastical Record,* 44 (1934)–638; *Clergy Review,* 8 (1934)–492 (Bentley).

### Provisions Regarding Return and Rehabilitation Do Not Apply (Cod. Com., 30 July, 1934) AAS 26–494.

The Code Commission was asked:

II. Whether the provision of c. 672, § 1, applies also to religious who are *ipso facto* dismissed according to c. 646.

**Reply.** In the negative.

**AAS 26–494**; Cod. Com., 30 July, 1934.
*Periodica,* 23 (1934)–147 (Vermeersch); *Amer. Eccles. Review,* 91 (1934)–498; *Irish Ecclesiastical Record,* 44 (1934)–638; *Clergy Review,* 8 (1934)–492 (Bentley).

# CANON 647

**Recourse to Holy See** (Replies and Declaration, S. C. Rel., 20 July, 1923) **AAS 15–457.**

The Sacred Congregation of Religious was asked:

Since c. 647, § 2, provides that a professed religious of temporary vows who receives a decree of dismissal from Superiors, shall have the right of recourse to the Apostolic See, and that pending the recourse the dismissal shall have no juridical effect, the question is:

How much time is allowed for the interposition of the recourse, as regards its suspensive effect?

The Eminent Fathers of the Sacred Congregation of Religious at the plenary session held at the Vatican, 13 July, 1923: replied:

**Reply.** The available time (*tempus utile*) for the interposition of the recourse as regards the suspensive effect mentioned in c. 647, § 2, is ten days from the notice to the dismissed religious, according to the norm established in similar cases, as in cc. 1465, § 1, and 2153, § 1.

His Holiness, Pius XI, approved this resolution in the audience of 17 July, 1923.

In order to remove all occasion of doubt, both regarding the aforesaid limit of time and regarding certain consequences from it, this Sacred Congregation observes that the following points are to be noticed and attended to:

1. The religious may interpose a recourse from the decree of dismissal, either immediately by a letter sent to this Sacred Congregation, or mediately through the person who communicated to him the decree.

2. To prove the fact that the recourse has been made, an authentic document, or at least the testimony of two trustworthy persons, is required and sufficient.

3. The available time of ten days from notice of the decree given to the religious, is to be computed according to c. 34, § 3, 3°; and according to c. 35 it does not run if the dismissed religious does not know he has a right to make the recourse, or if he is unable to do so. Hence, it is well that the Superior inform him of his right and of the limit of time for its exercise, at the same time when he notifies him of the decree of dismissal.

4. The recourse duly made has a suspensive effect; hence, until the decree of dismissal is confirmed by the S. C. Rel., and until the Superior who did the dismissing has been notified of its confirmation by an authentic document from the Sacred Congregation, the decree of dismissal is ineffective and cannot be put into execution.

5. While the recourse is pending, the person dismissed remains a religious, and hence has the same rights and obligations as other religious, in exactly the same way as before his dismissal. Hence, he has the right and obligation of dwelling in the religious house, and remains under the obedience of Superiors, without prejudice to the provision of c. 2243, § 2.

**AAS 15–457;** S. C. Rel., Reply and Declaration, 20 July, 1923.
*Periodica,* 12 (1924)–101 (Vermeersch); *J.P.,* 3 (1923)–134.

NOTE: This document was cited in a case before the S. C. Conc. Cf. **c. 2146;** AAS 16–162.

## CANON 650

**Dismissal From Religion:** Of priest who has perpetual vows and who finds no Bishop who will receive him. Under the heading, *"Ex Iurisprudentia S. C. de Religiosis,"* the practice of the S. C. of Religious is explained by Gutiérrez in *Commentarium pro Religiosis,* 32 (1953)–261. The practice is as follows: in confirming the decree of dismissal as provided by canon 650, § 2, 2°, the S. C. inserts in the rescript a clause obliging the Institute to provide for the dismissed priest until he finds a Bishop (even though, by exception to canon 669, § 1, the vows have been dispensed).

## CANON 654

**Dismissal After Perpetual Vows in Society of Jesus** (Code Com., 29 June, 1918) **Private.**

The dismissal of religious professed of perpetual vows in the Society of Jesus is regulated, as before, by the law of the Society itself, with the following reservations:

*a*) The provision of canon 647, § 2 as to the causes for dismissal must be observed.

*b*) The one to be dismissed must be given a full opportunity to reply to the charges against him (c. 650, § 3) and his replies must be faithfully reported to the Father General.

*c*) There is a recourse with suspensive effect to the Holy See.

**(Private)**; Code Commission, 29 June, 1918. Reported by Vermeersch-Creusen, *Epitome,* Vol. I, ed. 1937, n. 820, p. 606, from Biederlack-Führich, *De Religiosis,* n. 175, note. As regards dismissal of the professed of *solemn* vows, the Society of Jesus is governed by the common law.

## CANON 659

**Fugitive From Religion: Impossibility of Warnings and Citation for Trial** (Code Com.) **Private.**

**Reply.** If a fugitive from religion cannot be reached by way of warning or citation, the case is sufficiently provided for in the canons which treat of the penalties against apostates and fugitives from religion.

**(Private)**; this reply is reported, without indication of the date or source, in Vermeersch-Creusen, *Epitome,* Vol. I, ed. 1937, n. 815, p. 603. Cf. also *Antonianum,* 17 (1942)–223.

## CANON 673

**Societies of Clerics Without Vows** (Cod. Com., 3 June, 1918) **AAS 10–347.**

The Code Commission was asked:

Whether canons 2386, 2387, 2389, 2410, 2411, 2413 are applicable to societies of clerics without vows.

**Reply.** As to canons 2386, 2387, and 2389, in the affirmative in as far as the members live a common life; as to c. 2410, in the affirmative in as far as the society has the privilege of granting dismissorials to its members for orders; as to the first part of c. 2411, in the affirmative, without prejudice, as regards the rest, to the constitutions of the society; as to c. 2413, in the affirmative.

**AAS 10–347;** Cod. Com., 3 June, 1918.
*Periodica,* 9 (1921)–151 (Vermeersch); J.P., 2 (1922)–55.

---

**Careful Selection and Training of Candidates** for the states of perfection: Instruction on. See below, pp. 464–498; S. C. Rel., 2 Feb., 1961.

## CANON 681

**Societies Without Vows: Dismissal** (Cod. Com., 1 Mar., 1921) **AAS 13–177.**

The Code Commission was asked:

In canon 681 it is prescribed that in the dismissal of members of societies without vows canons 646–672 relating to the dismissal of religious are to be observed. Since these canons make different requirements according as the case is one of temporary or of perpetual vows, it is asked to which class of cases c. 681 refers, since it deals with members who have no vows at all?

**Reply.** If the bond binding members of a society without vows is temporary, the canons dealing with the dismissal of religious of temporary vows are to be observed; if the bond is perpetual, the canons dealing with the dismissal of religious of perpetual vows.

**AAS 13–177**; Code Com., 1 Mar., 1921.
*Periodica,* 10 (1922)–325 (Vermeersch).

# BOOK III

## THINGS

## Canons 726–1551

# BOOK III

## THINGS

## Canons 726–1551

### CANON 782

**Maternity Homes, Lying-in Hospitals and Orphanages: Confirmation of Infants in Danger of Death** (S. C. Sacr., 18 Nov., 1948) **Private.**

A Rescript of the S. C. of the Sacraments (N. 5869/48):

The Archbishops and Bishops of the United States of North America, prostrate at the feet of Your Holiness, humbly ask a derogation from the Decree, *Spiritus Sancti munera,* issued by the S. C. of the Sacraments on the 14th of September, 1946,[1] so that in so-called maternity homes or lying-in hospitals or infant asylums or hospitals of their dioceses the sacrament of confirmation can be validly and licitly administered by the chaplains of these institutions to the infants received therein who are found to be in the circumstances mentioned in the said Decree.

The reason for the request is the very great difficulty on the part of the local pastor, already burdened with other duties of the ministry, to confer confirmation almost without cessation because of the great number of infants found in the aforementioned institutions.

In the audience of 25 October, 1948, His Holiness, Pope Pius XII, upon receiving the report on this matter from the undersigned Pro-Prefect of this Sacred Congregation, graciously deigned to grant the petition on condition, however, that the sacrament of confirmation, in the circumstances mentioned in the aforesaid Decree, be personally administered to the infants by the chaplain who is assigned *regularly* to the institutions mentioned in the petition. Moreover, if several chaplains have

[1] AAS 38–349; CANON LAW DIGEST, 3, p. 303.

been assigned to the same institution, only the head chaplain, to the exclusion of the others, is authorized.

The chaplain, however, may use this faculty only if the Bishop of the diocese cannot be had or is legitimately prevented from administering confirmation himself; and if there is not at hand another Bishop, even a merely titular one, who is in communion with the Apostolic See and who can, without serious inconvenience, take the place of the local Ordinary; and if likewise the pastor of the place, in the same circumstances, cannot be had or is legitimately prevented from administering the sacrament. If the chaplain is absent or if it is impossible for him to confirm personally, no one else, except the Bishop or the local pastor, can validly confer this sacrament. In other respects, the terms and clauses of the aforesaid Decree must be observed. All things to the contrary notwithstanding.

The present grant to be in effect for *one year* from the date of this Rescript.

**(Private)**; S. C. Sacr., 18 Nov., 1948 (N. 5869/48); *The Jurist*, 9 (1949)–261; published with the permission of His Excellency, the Most Reverend Apostolic Delegate.

NOTE: This Rescript was renewed for one year on 6 Feb., 1950, by the same Sacred Congregation (N. 9219/49). Cf. *The Jurist*, 10 (1950)–214. It was renewed again for *three years* by Rescript N. 458/51, pursuant to the Audience of 22 Jan., 1951, with an *"Advertatur"* by the S. C. in these terms: "Ordinaries are to see to it that the renewal of the indult be applied for on time: otherwise, if Confirmation was administered in the interval between the expiration of the indult and its renewal, the sacrament would be invalid." Cf. *The Jurist*, 11 (1951)–312, 313. It was renewed again for another period of three years, by the same S. C., on 21 Jan., 1954. Cf. *The Jurist*, 14 (1954)–208, note 26. This faculty was again renewed on 19 Dec., 1956 (N. 6872/56) for three years to be computed from the *date of renewal.*

The whole matter of the extraordinary minister of Confirmation is treated in an article under that title by the Very Reverend Joseph A. M. Quigley, in *The Jurist*, 14(1954)–194.

## Confirmation in Danger of Death: *Formula Brevissima* Approved (Holy Office, 10 Apr., 1958) Private.

The following reply of the Holy Office (Prot. N. 71/58) was

sent on April 10, 1958, to the Most Reverend Bernard Joseph Flanagan, Bishop of Norwich, Connecticut:

Exc.me as Rev.me Domine,

Huic Supremae S. Congregationi propositum fuit ab Excellentia Tua Rev.ma sequens DUBIUM:

"Utrum in casu verae necessitatis in Confirmatione administranda a simplici Sacerdote iis qui ex gravi morbo in mortis periculo constituti sunt, licite et valide adhiberi possit formula brevissima:

N. Signo te signo Cru ✠ cis (quod dum dicit, imposita manu dextera super caput confirmandi, producit pollice signum crucis in fronte illius, deinde prosequitur) et confirmo te chrismate salutis. In Nomine Pa ✠ tris et Fi ✠ lii et Spiritus ✠ Sancti. Amen."

Ad praecedens Dubium Sanctum Officium respondit; Affirmative.

Quae dum Tecum communico, quo par est obsequio, me profiteor

Excellentiae Tuae Rev. mae
Addictissimum
G. Card. Pizzardo

**(Private)**; Holy Office, 10 Apr., 1958. Thanks to the Most Reverend Bishop of Norwich and the Reverend Henry J. Dziadosz, J.C.D., who kindly sent us a copy of the original Rescript for publication in the CANON LAW DIGEST.

---

**Chaplains of Hospitals, Infant Asylums, Prisons,** can obtain from the local Ordinary faculties to administer confirmation in danger of death. See **c. 329**; AAS 56–5, *Motu proprio, Pastorale munus,* n. 13; reported above on p. 71.

## CANON 815

### When Blessed Sacrament Is Reserved in an Ante-room on Holy Thursday and Good Friday, Community Religious Exercises There Are Not Forbidden (S. C. Sacr., July, 1932) Private.

We are indebted to *The Jurist* for the following private reply of the S. C. Sacr.:

**Question.** In the Instruction of the S. C. Sacr., of 26 May, 1929 (AAS 21–636),[1] it is said:

"As regards the reservation of the Blessed Sacrament on the last three days of Holy Week, it is reserved for the celebration of the Mass of the Presanctified, and to give Communion to the sick. . . . *b*) For giving Communion to the sick, in parish churches and other churches from which the Blessed Sacrament is usually taken, some consecrated particles are to be reserved in a ciborium, and as regards the reservation of this ciborium, the following should be observed. According to the mind of the Rubrics, this ciborium should be kept outside the church, that is, near the sacristy in a fitting and convenient place, where the Blessed Sacrament is to be kept with becoming reverence, not, however, exposed for the veneration of the faithful, but only kept for the purpose of giving Communion to the sick. . . ."[2]

And in n. 9 of the Instruction it is stated:

"As regards the reservation of the Sacred Hosts for the Communion of the sick on the last three days of Holy Week, Ordinaries of places should bear in mind the intention of the Rubrics and of the Decrees of the Sacred Congregation of Rites; the hosts are not reserved for public veneration; in fact, that is prohibited; yet every effort must be made that, especially as regards the place, the Sacrament of the Eucharist be not deprived of the tribute of due honor and elegance."[3]

Now the question is: Whether the above prohibition of veneration forbids also going to the place where the Sacred Particles are kept, for acts of common religious observance, such as common prayers, etc., in a religious house.

**Reply.** In the negative.

**(Private)**; S. C. Sacr., reply by the *Congressus,* July, 1932. Cf. *The Jurist,* 2 (1942)–186.

## CANON 818

### Calendar of Tertiary Sisters to Be Used by Priest Celebrating in Their Churches and Oratories (S. C. Rit., 4 June, 1920) Private.

The Procurator General of the Order of Preachers proposed

[1] See Canon Law Digest, 1, p. 353; the date of this Instruction is 26 March, 1929; AAS 21–631.

[2] See Canon Law Digest, 1, pp. 359, 360.

[3] See Canon Law Digest, 1, p. 363.

the following question to the Sacred Congregation of Rites:

Whether, by reason of the Decree of the S. C. Rit. of 28 Feb., 1914, priests who celebrate in the churches and oratories of Tertiary Sisters, are bound, when they celebrate Mass, to conform to the calendar which the Sisters use.

**Reply.** In the affirmative.

(**Private**); S. C. Rit., 4 June, 1920. Reported in *Periodicia,* 26 (1937)–38; *Amer. Eccles. Review,* 64 (1921)–272.

NOTE: The Decree of 28 Feb., 1914, referred to in the question, was as follows: "Regular Orders must absolutely have their own calendar, which is likewise to be used by the nuns and Sisters of the same Orders" (*Decr. Auth.*, n. 4312). The "calendar which the Sisters use" is therefore the calendar of the Order to which they belong as Tertiaries. Hecht, in his annotations to this reply in *Periodica,* points out that such Sisters have a right to use the calendar of the Order even though they recite only the Little Office of the Blessed Virgin, and not the Divine Office (*contra, Commentarium pro Religiosis,* 16 [1935]–160).

## Masses of Holy Founder or Foundress in Institute Which Is Not Bound to Recite Office (S. C. Rit., 23 Dec., 1932) AAS 25-41.

The Sacred Congregation of Rites was asked:

Whether Masses of a saint, founder or foundress of a Congregation or institute which is not bound to recite the divine office, have the same liturgical privileges as Masses of other saints who, in the case of a Congregation which is obliged to recite the office, are commemorated with the rite of a double of the first class with a common octave, according to the mind of the New Rubrics of the Roman Breviary.

The Sacred Congregation, having heard the opinion of the Code Commission, and having maturely considered the question, replied:

**Reply.** In the affirmative.

**AAS 25-41**; S. C. Rit., Rescript, 23 Dec., 1932.

**Calendar for Mass in Churches and Chapels of Vicariates and Prefectures Which Are Entrusted to Religious Who Have a Calendar of Their Own** (Three replies: S. C. Rit., 23 March, 1929; S. C. Prop. Fid., 18 May, 1932; S. C. Prop. Fid., 7 Nov., 1932) **Private.**

These three private replies on a rather complicated matter are grouped together for better understanding.

*I. S. C. Rit., 23 March, 1929, Prot. N. C. 41/929.*
Cf. *Periodica,* 21 (1932)–34.

Joseph Rutten, Superior General of the Congregation of the Immaculate Heart of Mary (Scheut), humbly asks the S. C. of Rites to give a solution to the following questions:

1. According to the Decree of 22 Apr., 1910 (N. 4252), *Secovien.,* if a parish is united to a monastery or religious house, or if it is entrusted perpetually or for an indefinite time to the care of such a monastery or house, the religious calendar is always used in Masses; otherwise, the diocesan calendar is used, as in the case where the church is entrusted, not to the religious family but only to some private person belonging to it, according to the Decree, *Urbis,* of 15 Dec., 1899.

But in territories of Missions which are entrusted to a particular missionary Institute, the churches which are built are quasi-parochial or belong to a mission station not yet erected as a quasi-parish, and a missionary from the same religious Institute has charge of them as rector.

The question is whether churches of quasi-parishes or of a mission station which is not yet erected as a quasi-parish, are considered as entrusted to the Congregation, or only to a private person; hence, whether in these churches the calendar of the Congregation or of the Vicariate Apostolic is to be followed.

2. On 14 Dec., 1927, Saint Thérèse of the Child Jesus was declared the special Patroness of all Missionaries of both sexes and of Missions all over the world, on a par with Saint Francis Xavier, "with all the liturgical rights and privileges which belong to this title."

The question is whether it follows from this that in territories of Missions and in Congregations of Missionaries the feast of Saint Thérèse of the Child Jesus should be celebrated as a duplex of the first class, with a common octave and the *Credo* in the Mass.

The S. C. of Rites, having heard the opinion of the special commission and duly considered everything, decided to reply:

**Replies.** 1. Let the calendar of the religious Congregation be used until the ecclesiastical hierarchy has been established in the place in question.

2. In the affirmative, in all respects for the secular clergy, but without the octave for the regular clergy. And it was so decreed and replied, March 23, 1929.

*II. S. C. Prop. Fid., 18 May, 1932, Prot. N. 1672/32.*
Cf. *Periodica,* 21 (1932)–248.

Some questions have been proposed to this Apostolic Delegation (Pekin) regarding the calendar to be used in the Missions and regarding the celebration of feasts in honor of Blessed Odoric of Pordenone, the Blessed Chinese Martyrs, and the principal Patrons of the Missions. It has therefore been thought advisable to refer the matter to the Holy See for a reply which may settle all the discussions which have arisen on the subject.

The S. C. for the Propagation of the Faith, by Rescript N. 1672/32 of 18 May, 1932, replied as follows to the following questions:

1. Whether, in Missions which are entrusted to a certain religious Order or Congregation, the (religious) Ordinary can adopt, for the secular clergy subject to him, the calendar proper to the Institute, or whether he must on the contrary conform to the Decree of the S. C. of Rites of 28 Oct., 1913 (AAS, 5–463, sect. V, 2, e) and establish a proper calendar, for example the calendar of the universal Church, in which are to be added the special feasts of the place, the feasts in honor of Blessed Odoric of Pordenone, of the Blessed Chinese Martyrs, and of those principal Patrons of the Missions, Saint Francis Xavier and Saint Thérèse of the Child Jesus.

**Reply.** In the negative to the first part, in the affirmative to the second.

2. Whether religious missionaries who for the recitation of the Office follow their own calendar, can celebrate the Mass which is assigned in the calendar of their Institute, also in churches

(of the Vicariate or Prefecture), which do not *de iure* belong to their Order or Congregation; or whether on the contrary they too must, in these churches, celebrate the Mass which is assigned in the proper calendar of the Mission in which they are staying.

**Reply.** In the negative to the first part, in the affirmative to the second.

3. Whether the religious missionaries, although they have a calendar of their own, are obliged everywhere in China to celebrate the Mass and recite the Office in honor of the Blessed Chinese Martyrs and Blessed Odoric of Pordenone according to the provisions of the Decrees of the S. C. Rit. (namely, the Decrees of 13 Nov., 1925, 13 March, 1930, 8 July, 1931, 16 Feb., 1932, etc); and whether moreover these same religious missionaries must celebrate the feasts of the principal Patrons of the Missions, Saint Francis Xavier and Saint Thérèse of the Child Jesus, as duplexes of the first class.

**Reply.** In the affirmative to all, *et ad mentem:* the mind is that religious who are endowed with the title of missionaries to pagan nations should for this very reason feel the appropriateness of celebrating the feasts in honor either of the Patrons of the Missions or of the Blessed of the people among whom they are "Ambassadors of Christ." Hence the various Orders are to be warned that they should add as a supplement to the Office of their Missions the proper feasts of the Church in China.

While I am sending these replies to Your Excellency, let me at the same time recommend that the above prescriptions of the Holy See regarding the feasts above mentioned be put into effect in your territory, in order to obtain the desired uniformity in the Missions and especially in order to implore the aid of the heavenly Patrons.

*III. S. C. Prop. Fid., 7 Nov., 1932, Prot. N. 3984/32.*
Cf. *Periodica,* 22 (1933)–194.

The Regular Superior, S.J., in the Vicariate Apostolic of Anking (Anhwei) humbly asks the Sacred Congregation to provide an answer to the following question:

**Question.** Whether there is a contradiction between the replies to the second question of the Apostolic Delegate, of 18 May, 1932, and to the first question proposed by Father Rutten,

23 March, 1929 (quoting both questions and replies as given above). In other words, there could be a doubt whether the churches of the Vicariate should be considered as belonging *de iure* to the Order, since they are entrusted to it, or as not belonging, although entrusted to the Order. We have hitherto used the calendar proper to the religious Institute, since the ecclesiastical hierarchy is not yet established and the Mission of Anking is entrusted to the Society of Jesus. I therefore ask how these churches are to be considered and which calendar is to be followed.

**Reply.** In the celebration of Masses you are to follow the calendar of the Order in churches which are adjacent to a real convent in the sense that all the functions are celebrated by the Fathers of the Convent and by the Community itself; in other churches, however, you are to follow the calendar of the Vicariate. This Sacred Congregation recently gave an answer in this same sense to the Vicar Apostolic of Bac-Ninh.

**(Private)**; S. C. Rit., 23 March, 1929; S. C. Prop. Fid., 18 May, 1932; S. C. Prop. Fid., 7 Nov., 1932.

NOTE: As Vermeersch had correctly conjectured in his commentary on the two apparently conflicting replies (*Periodica*, 22 (1933)–30*). the conflict is reconciled by considering the earlier reply of the S. C. Rit. as a particular favor rather than as a norm of law. This is confirmed by the S. C. Prop. Fid. in those parts of its latest reply (7 Nov., 1932) which are omitted from our report.

## Mass in Chapel of Sisters of Third Order of Saint Dominic: Rubrics of Mass and Little Office (S. C. Rit., 4 June, 1934) Private.

The following questions were proposed to the Sacred Congregation of Rites by the Prefect Apostolic of Bulawayo:

I. Whether the Sisters of the Third Order of Saint Dominic living in community have the privilege of using the proper Calendar of the Order of Saint Dominic.

II. Whether priests who celebrate Mass in their chapels are obliged to use the aforesaid Calendar, if the Sisters, in the recitation of the Little Office, make a commemoration only of the Saints and Blessed of their own Order, omitting the other Saints who are in their Calendar.

III. If the priests are obliged to follow the Calendar of the Sisters, which Missal is to be used, in case the proper Mass which is to be said is one which is not in the Roman Missal but only in the Missal of the Order of Saint Dominic? And which Missal is to be used, in case the Mass is in both Missals, but a commemoration is to be made which on that day is only in the Dominican Missal? Is it sufficient to make such a commemoration from the "common" of the Roman Missal?

IV. When the Sisters recite their Little Office, do they satisfy their obligation if they add commemorations of the saints of their own Order, according to their Calendar, omitting the other saints, especially in view of the words of the rescripts and the consequences in regard to celebrating according to the Calendar, and perhaps with regard to the Missal to be used?

**Reply.** The Sacred Congregation of Rites, having heard the opinion also of the Code Commission, and having maturely considered the matter, replied:

I. In the affirmative.

II. Priests celebrating Mass must follow the entire Calendar of the Order of Saint Dominic.

III. Both as regards Masses and commemorations to be made in the Masses, let the priests use the proper Missal of the Order of Preachers, but let them not follow the peculiar rites which are proper to the said Order, in accordance with the New Rubrics of the Roman Missal, tit. IV, n. 6.

IV. In the affirmative.

**(Private)**; S. C. Rit., Rescript, 4 June, 1934.
*Clergy Review,* 8 (1934)–327.

## *Missa Dialogata:* Five Replies of the Sacred Congregation of Rites (S. C. Rit., 18 Feb., 1921; 25 Feb., 1921; 27 Apr., 1921; 4 Aug., 1922; 30 Nov., 1935) Private.

We reproduce, from *Periodica,* five rescripts of the Sacred Congregation of Rites on this subject. Only one of them, that of 4 Aug., 1922, was officially published in the *Acta.* It appeared in AAS 14–505, and was summarily reported in the CANON LAW DIGEST, 1, p. 382.

(1) Rescript of 18 Feb., 1921, to the Bishop of Mantua:

**Question:** Is it allowed to introduce or to tolerate the practice which is beginning in some places, according to which the faithful or the nuns in unison make the responses to the priest who is celebrating, and also recite aloud with him the *Gloria, Credo,* etc.?

**Reply.** *Ad Rev.mum Ordinarium et ad mentem.* The mind is as follows: Things which are in themselves licit are sometimes not expedient, because of some difficulty, such as, for example, if such a practice should confuse and distract the one or several priests who are celebrating; which would seem to be the case in the question proposed, in accordance with other similar replies to like petitions. Moreover, the said practice departs from common and current usage.

(2) Rescript of 25 Feb., 1921, to the Bishop of Pesaro, Italy:

**Questions.** 1. Is it allowed to the faithful who assist at Mass to join themselves to the celebrant by giving aloud the responses to the celebrant whenever the server should give them?

2. If so, are the people allowed to recite aloud with the celebrant the *Credo, Gloria, Sanctus, Agnus Dei?*

3. Are the faithful allowed before Communion, during Mass or outside of Mass, to recite or sing the *Confiteor,* and to make the responses to the priest either with or instead of the server.

**Reply.** Send the Most Reverend Bishop this opinion (of one of the consultors): Things that are in themselves licit are sometimes not expedient, because of difficulties which may easily arise, as in the present case in numbers 1, 2, and 3; and let the common practice be retained.

(3) Rescript of 27 Apr., 1921, to the Cardinal Archbishop of Malines:
**Reply.** Send the rescript, *in Mantuana,* of 18 Feb., 1921.

(4) Rescript of 4 Aug., 1922, published in AAS 14–505:

**Questions.** 1. May the congregation, assisting at the Sacrifice of the Mass, make the responses to the celebrant in unison, instead of the server?

2. Is the practice to be approved, according to which the faithful assisting at Mass read aloud the Secrets, the Canon, and the very words of the Consecration, all of which except a very few words of the Canon should, according to the Rubrics, be said secretly by the priest himself

**Reply.** The Sacred Congregation of Rites, having heard the opinion of the Special Commission, and having duly considered everything, has decided to reply:

1. *Ad Rev.mum Ordinarium iuxta mentem.* The mind is: Things that are in themselves licit are sometimes not expedient, owing to difficulties which may easily arise, as in this case, especially on account of the disturbances which the priests who celebrate and the people who assist may experience, to the disadvantage of the sacred action and of the Rubrics. Hence it is well to retain the common usage, as we have several times replied in similar cases.

2. No; nor can the faithful who assist at the Mass be permitted something which is forbidden by the Rubrics to the priests celebrating, who say the words of the Canon secretly, for the sake of greater reverence toward the Sacred Mysteries, and to enhance the veneration, modesty, and devotion of the faithful toward these Mysteries; hence the proposed practice is to be reprobated as an abuse, and if it has been introduced anywhere it is to be entirely removed.

And it is thus replied, declared, and decreed. Aug. 4, 1922. AAS 14–505.

(5) Rescript of 30 Nov., 1935, to the Cardinal Archbishop of Genoa:

**Questions.** 1. In seminaries, religious Congregations, and in some parishes, a practice has become established whereby the people together with the server make the responses in private Masses, provided that no confusion is occasioned. It is asked whether this practice may be sustained, and even propagated.

2. In some places, in private Masses, the people recite aloud and in unison, together with the priest, the *Gloria, Credo, Sanctus, Benedictus,* and *Agnus Dei.* The promoters of this practice give this reason: a private Mass is an abbreviated *Missa decantata.* Now, in the *Missa decantata,* the people sing the *Gloria, Credo, Sanctus, Benedictus,* and *Agnus Dei.* Therefore, this can be done by way of recital also in private Masses. It is asked whether the practice and the reason assigned for it can be sustained.

**Reply.** This Sacred Congregation, having heard also the opinion of the Liturgical Commission, replies that, in accordance with decree n. 4375, it is for the Ordinary to decide whether, in individual cases, in view of all the circumstances, namely, the place, the people, the number of Masses which are being said at the same time, the proposed practice, though in itself praiseworthy, in fact causes disturbance rather than furthers devotion. This can easily happen in the case of the practice mentioned in the second question, even without passing on the reason assigned, namely, that a private Mass is an abbreviated *Missa decantata.*

According to the above standard, Your Eminence has the full right to control this form of liturgical piety according to your prudent discretion.

**(Private)**; S. C. Rit., Rescripts, 18 Feb., 1921; 25 Feb., 1921; 27 Apr., 1921; 4 Aug., 1922; 30 Nov., 1935.

*Periodica,* 25 (1936)–57*, with a full dissertation by Father Hanssens, S.J., of the Gregorian University, on the five rescripts and the principles which underlie the discussion.

## Priests of the Roman Rite Celebrating in a Chapel of the Sisters of the Third Order of Saint Dominic: Calendar and Rite (S. C. of Rites, 18 June, 1956) Private.

The Sacred Congregation of Rites was asked:

**Question:** Whether priests of the Roman rite who celebrate Mass in a chapel of the Sisters of the Third Order of Saint Dominic are obliged to follow not only the Calendar of the Sisters but also their *Ordo* for the celebration of Mass. For these Sisters, since they do not belong to the Roman rite as regards the Mass, are not bound by the recent Decree on the simplification of the Rubrics; and hence in their *Ordo* for the celebration of Mass, they retain many things which the said Decree forbids for the Roman rite, for example, regarding the orations *de tempore,* the *Credo,* the last Gospel, and so forth.

**Reply:** In a letter of last February, certain questions were asked regarding priests who celebrate Mass in churches of the Order of Preachers.

After carefully considering everything, the Sacred Congregation of Rites replied: All Calendars made for the Roman rite must conform to the new Decree of 23 March, 1955, "on reducing the Rubrics to a simpler form."[1] Moreover, all priests who celebrate in a church of a rite other than their own are obliged to follow the Calendar of that church, retaining, however, their own rite.

(**Private**); S. C. Rit., 18 June, 1956. Prot. N. S. 64/956.

## CANON 821

**Christmas Midnight Mass in Religious and Pious Houses: Ancient Restrictions No Longer in Effect** (Code Com., 5 March, 1954) **Private.**

The Code Commission was asked:

**Question:** Whether, after the promulgation of the Code of Canon Law, the declaration of the Holy Office of 26 November, 1908,[2] *ad* I, remains in effect, concerning the use of the faculty granted by canon 821, § 3; and if so, whether this implies the exclusion of strangers from assisting at the Christmas midnight Mass.

**Reply:** His Eminence Cardinal Massimo Massimi, President of the Pontifical Commission for the Interpretation of the Code of Canon Law, replied under date of 5 March, 1954 (Prot. N. 1/54):

One does not see how it can be held that in the sacred functions mentioned in the canon cited, strangers should not be admitted, and still less that the doors should not be opened;

---

[1] Reported in CANON LAW DIGEST, 4, p. 25.

[2] AAS 1–146.

since there is no trace of such a prohibition in the same canon which regulates the matter.

(**Private**); Code Com., reply by the President, 5 March, 1954. Reported in *Commentarium pro Religiosis,* 33 (1954)–329; annotations by Ochoa, *ibid.,* pp. 330–352; by Palazzini *in Apollinaris,* 28 (1955)–71–74.

## CANON 852

**Holy Communion Through a Tube** (Holy Office) **Private.**

Prot. 404/350

**Petition:** The Bishop of ——, humbly prostrate at the feet of Your Holiness, requests in behalf of ——, afflicted with an incurable illness and unable to receive either solid or liquid nourishment except through a tube fitted into his stomach, the privilege of receiving the Holy Eucharist by the following artificial means. . . .

**Reply:** His Holiness Pope John XXIII, in an Audience granted to His Eminence the Cardinal Secretary of the Holy Office, graciously allowed the privilege to be left to the prudent judgment and conscience of the Bishop of ——, who may permit —— to receive the Holy Eucharist by the artificial means described in the petition, only in danger of death and outside of this danger only for satisfying his Easter duty, provided that:

1. Reverence for the Blessed Sacrament is maintained, and therefore not only should care be taken for the cleanliness of the tube before administering Holy Communion, but also every danger is to be avoided lest the Sacred Species reach the stomach and remain there undissolved.

2. Decency and modesty are preserved, so that in performing the sacred rite nothing is done which would offend in any way the norms of decency or modesty.

3. Danger of scandal or wonderment of the faithful is eliminated, and for this reason the Holy Communion should be administered privately with the intervention only of those who may be absolutely necessary for the proper administration.

All things to the contrary notwithstanding.

(s) Sebastiano Masala

(Seal, Holy Office)

(**Private**); Holy Office, no date given; Prot. 404/350. Reported in the *Homiletic and Pastoral Review* for February 1964, volume 64, pages 442 and 444.

## Permission Granted to Receive Communion Under Species of Wine Through Tube (Holy Office, 20 Sept., 1961) Private.

In your letter of 28 August of this year, Your Excellency requested that N.N. be allowed to receive the Holy Eucharist under the species of wine through a tube inserted into the stomach.

In this regard I wish to inform you that this Supreme Sacred Congregation, after mature consideration of all the circumstances of the case, agrees that the Holy Eucharist may be administered to N.N. under the species of wine provided it is impossible for the person to receive Communion under the species of bread. However, in order that the administration of Communion under the species of wine may take place safely and becomingly, this Supreme Sacred Congregation has decided to annex the following instruction.

The wine which is to be consecrated can be placed in some container (gold or silver) such as the small container in which the oil for anointing (*oleum infirmorum*) is kept. At the upper edge of this container should be constructed a kind of spout so that the species of wine can be more easily and securely poured into the tube.

The container with the unconsecrated wine should be placed on the altar. The wine should be consecrated in this container so that after the consecration all "manipulations" can be avoided. Then the consecrated wine can be carried in the said container without danger of being spilled. It should be carried in the same way and with the same rite as in the case of a consecrated host.

When about to pour the species of wine, the priest should place a purificator at the mouth of the tube and slowly pour the wine through the spout into the tube. When the sacred species have been administered, some wine or water should be at once put into the empty container to purify it (just as the priest is accustomed to do after the reception of the Precious Blood in the celebration of Mass). This ablution should be given to the patient so that in this way there is also a purification of the tube.

Moreover, Your Excellency should notify the priest who is to administer Communion to the said patient that a few drops of wine do not suffice to administer the sacrament but that a quantity of wine is required such as is ordinarily used at Mass. Otherwise, there is danger that all the wine poured in may adhere to the inner wall of the tube and none reach the stomach.

**(Private)**; Holy Office, 20 Sept., 1961, Prot. N. 414/61. Copy of the rescript kindly sent us by the Most Reverend Loras T. Lane, Bishop of Rockford, through the Rev. David J. Rock, Tribunal Secretary.

---

**Communion under Both Species** in Mass of religious profession. See **c. 2**; AAS 56–97, Constitution on the Sacred Liturgy, n. 55; reported above on p. 21.

## CANON 856

**Reserved Instruction on Daily Communion and Precautions to Be Taken Against Abuses** (S. C. Sacr., 8 Dec., 1938) **Private.**

A reserved Instruction addressed "to the Most Excellent and Most Reverend Archbishops, Bishops, Ordinaries of places, and major Superiors of Orders and clerical religious institutes, on the daily Communion which is usual and almost general in seminaries, colleges, and communities including religious ones, and on the abuses to be guarded against in connection therewith," is *verbatim* as follows:

Since Pius X of happy memory aroused the faithful to frequent and daily Communion by the Decree of the Sacred Congregation of the Council, *Sacra Tridentina Synodus,* of 20 Dec., 1905, and invited even children to it by the Decree, *Quam singulari,* of this Sacred Congregation, 8 Aug., 1910 — which decrees the Code of Canon Law has made its own in canon 863 — the practice of frequent and daily Communion, as all are aware, has been happily spread.

This practice, a source of innumerable blessings, is not only to be commended but to be further propagated, and that, not only among the faithful in general, but also among young people and children, according to the precept imposed by the aforesaid decrees, and with due observance of the rules there laid down.

"Frequent and daily Communion . . . must be promoted as much as possible in seminaries of clerics . . . also in other Christian institutions for the young, of whatever kind" (Decree, *Sancta Tridentina Synodus,* n. 7). And "those who have charge of children must make every effort that the children, after their first Communion, may approach the Holy Table frequently, and if possible even daily, as Christ and Mother Church desire, and that they do so with all the devotion of which they are capable at their age" (Decree, *Quam singulari,* n. 6).

I. But just as frequent and daily Communion is to be commended, so too there must be insistence on the observance of the conditions which are necessary, and which consist in the state of grace and a right intention. Suitable precautions should also be taken that no one eat this Bread unworthily. For the Apostle says, "whosoever shall eat this bread, or drink the chalice of the Lord unworthily, shall be guilty of the body and of the blood of the Lord" (I Cor. xi, 27).

For the danger of receiving Communion unworthily, which is seen to be as it were inherent in the widespread practice of frequent and daily Communion, in view of human nature which tends to have little esteem for things to which it is accustomed by frequent use, is increased when the faithful, especially the young, approach the Holy Table, not singly but generally and in a body, as happens daily in seminaries and religious communities, frequently in colleges and institutions for the training and education of Christian youth, and sometimes in the gatherings which are held for the purpose of receiving the Most Blessed Eucharist at Easter time or on some other solemn occasion.

For it can happen that some one, though conscious of grave sin, may yet approach the Holy Table influenced by the example of his associates and moved by the vain fear that if he stays away he will cause astonishment in the others, especially in his Superiors, and will be suspected of having committed a grave sin.

II. Therefore in order to prevent as far as possible all abuse, it has seemed necessary to this Sacred Congregation to consider appropriate remedies and to communicate them to the Pastors of souls. These remedies are as follows:

1. Preachers and spiritual directors, when they either publicly or privately exhort the faithful, particularly young people, to frequent and daily Communion, must not be content with this

exhortation, but must at the same time inform them: (*a*) that daily Communion is not obligatory; (*b*) that it may not be practiced without the concurrence of the necessary conditions.

*a*) Frequent and daily Communion is indeed very much recommended, but it is not commanded by any law. It is, therefore, left to each one's devotion and piety. So true is this that even the obligation of Paschal Communion is modified by the clause "unless by advice of his own priest, for some reasonable cause (the person) judge that he should abstain from it for a time" (c. 859, § 1). Now it follows from this that there is no occasion for astonishment or suspicion if, where the practice of daily Communion is in use, someone occasionally abstains. And if this truth is clearly grasped, the vain fear which can be the occasion of receiving Communion unworthily will be entirely removed.

*b*) Holy Communion, which is *life to the good,* is *death to the wicked.* Hence, first of all, the *state of grace* is required. Horror of sacrilege must be thoroughly inculcated, and attention must be directed to the law according to which "no one who is conscious of mortal sin, however persuaded he be that he is also contrite, shall go to Communion without previously making a sacramental confession . . ." (c. 856).

There is further required a *right* or pious *intention,* which "consists in this, that a person approach the Holy Table, not from routine, or vanity, or human motives, but because he wishes to please God, to be more closely united to Him in charity, and to come with his infirmities and defects to that divine physician" (Decree, *Sacra Tridentina Synodus,* n. 2).

Moreover, "in order that frequent and daily Communion may be received with greater prudence and be crowned with greater merit, it is necessary that the advice of the confessor be obtained" (Decree cited, n. 5).

2. Together with frequent Communion, frequent confession also must be promoted: not that confession must precede every Communion, unless a person is conscious of mortal sin, but that the faithful who live in communities should not only go to confession on stated days but should be free to go, without any remarks from their Superiors, to a confessor of their choice, and, what is especially important, that they should have the opportunity to make a confession also shortly before the time of Communion.

*a*) Accordingly Pastors of souls must make every effort to provide in each community, according to the number of the members, one or two confessors to whom each one may freely go. They must keep in mind the rule that, where frequent and daily Communion is in vogue, frequent and daily opportunity for sacramental confession, as far as that is possible, must also be afforded. It is desirable also that other confessors, chosen from among those that are approved, be given rather frequently to all communities.

*b*) As regards seminaries we have the provisions of canons 1358, 1361, and 1367 of the Code of Canon Law, according to which there must be in every seminary at least two ordinary confessors and a spiritual director, and besides the ordinary confessors others must be designated to whom the students have free access: if these confessors live outside the seminary and a student asks that any of them be called, the rector must send for him, without in any way asking the reason for the request or showing that he takes it ill: if they live in the seminary, the student must be allowed freely to go to him, without prejudice to the discipline of the seminary. Let Superiors consider the serious opinion of Saint Alphonsus, namely that students of a seminary are in great danger of committing sacrileges if they always confess to confessors who are known to them. (Cf. S. Alphonsus, *Regolamento per i Seminari,* § 1, n. 3.) Bishops should see to it that the students go to confession at least once a week.

*c*) As regards all religious communities of men or women, the provisions of law are found in canon 518 and the following canons, and they are to be religiously observed in their letter and spirit. "In each house of a clerical institute, several duly approved confessors in proportion to the number of the members, must be deputed, with the faculty, in the case of an exempt institute, to absolve also from cases which are reserved in the institute (c. 518, § 1). "Superiors must be careful that they do not, either in person or through another, by force, fear, or importunate persuasion, nor by any other means, induce any of their subjects to go to confession to themselves" (c. 518, § 3). ". . . If a religious, even exempt, for his peace of conscience goes to a confessor who is approved by the Ordinary of the place, even though he is not among those designated, the confession is valid and licit, every privilege to the contrary being hereby revoked; and the confessor can absolve the religious also from sins and censures which are reserved in the institute" (c. 519). "Every community of religious women should be given an extraordinary confessor, who should go to the religious house at least four times a year, and to whom all the religious must present themselves, at least to receive his blessing" (c. 521, § 1). "Ordinaries of places in which there are communities of religious women, must designate a number of (*aliquot*) priests for each house, to whom the Sisters can easily go in particular cases, without the necessity of applying to the Ordinary each time" (c. 521, § 2). "If any religious woman, for her peace of conscience and greater progress in the way of God, asks for any special confessor or spiritual director, the Ordinary should easily grant the request. . . ." (c. 520, § 2). "So too if any religious woman asks for one of . . . the confessors (designated by the Ordinaries of places for each house of religious women), no Superioress may, in person or through others, directly or indirectly, ask the reason of the request, nor refuse it by word or act, nor in any way show that she takes it ill" (c. 521, § 3). Moreover, notwithstanding the above provisions, "if . . . any religious woman, for her peace of conscience, goes to a confessor who is approved for women by the Ordinary of the place, the confession made in any church or oratory even semipublic or in any other place lawfully destined for the confessions of women (Commission for the Interpretation of the Code, 24 Nov., 1920),[1] is valid and licit, every privilege to the contrary being hereby revoked; nor may the Superioress forbid it nor inquire about it even indirectly; and the religious women are not bound to give any account to the Superioress" (c. 522). Likewise: "all religious women, when they are seriously ill, although there be no danger of death, may send for any priest who is approved to hear the confessions of women, even though he is not designated for religious, and may as often as they choose, as long as the serious illness continues, make their confession to him, nor may the Superioress forbid it either directly or indirectly" (c. 523).

Nuns who are bound by the law of enclosure and who are not allowed to go out nor to go to their own church or to a semipublic oratory, have the same faculty: they may call any con-

[1] See above, p. 280.

fessor they choose who is approved for the confession of women to come to the ordinary confessional of the monastery to hear their confessions (cf. Reply of the aforesaid Commission of Interpretation, of 28 Dec., 1927),[2] and, if they are seriously ill, even to their own room, with the necessary precautions, nor may the Superioress forbid it directly or indirectly.

Ecclesiastics, therefore, who are delegated for communities of religious women should do all in their power to prevent Superioresses from inquiring even indirectly why their religious subjects sent for or went to another confessor; and they should inform the said Superioresses that they have no power to forbid this to their subjects in any way. The aforesaid delegates must know that it can easily happen that religious women fear to ask the Superioress for an extraordinary confessor, and so are not free to provide for the welfare of their conscience. Let them therefore carefully watch that in a matter of such importance the liberty which has been wisely provided by law for religious women be not diminished.

Of course, the exercise of this liberty of conscience must be appropriately combined in each community with the regular observance of discipline, which the Ordinaries of places should try to preserve intact; and they should likewise take care that no abuses arise from the use of these privileges, and that such as may have already crept in be cautiously and prudently removed, always without prejudice to liberty of conscience (c. 520, § 2).

Also in lay institutes of men an ordinary and an extraordinary confessor are to be designated; and if a religious asks for a special confessor, the Superior must allow it without in any way seeking to know the reason of the request or showing that he takes it ill.

*d*) Finally, in all communities of young people of either sex, every effort must be made that a confessor be at hand and easily accessible at the time when Communion is being distributed to the community.

3. Besides these general remedies, the Superiors of each community should employ others which are suitable to secure the same end.

*a*) The Superior should say very plainly to his subjects that he is in general much pleased with their frequent approach to

---

[2] See above, p. 282.

the Holy Table, but that he has no word of reproach for those who do not receive, but rather sees in this a sign of liberty and of a tender and delicate conscience. And let him not contradict this declaration by his conduct, nor give any indication that he seems to notice those who go to Communion frequently, and to praise them while blaming the others.

In seminaries and other institutions of the kind, where at stated times a judgment on each student is made by Superiors as regards piety, study, and discipline, the said Superiors, in giving their judgment regarding the progress of the young man in piety, must take no account of this greater or less assiduity in receiving the Most Blessed Eucharist.

*b*) In communities of boys and girls there should never be an announcement of a *general Communion* with special solemnity, and even outside communities, the very name "general Communion" should either not be used at all or its meaning should be carefully explained: namely, that all are invited to the Holy Table, but no one is obliged to approach, on the contrary each individual is entirely free to abstain from it. As regards religious communities, attention should also be paid to the provisions of the Decree *Sancta Tridentina Synodus,* n. 8: "If there are any institutes of either solemn or simple vows, in whose rules and constitutions, or calendars, Communions are attached to certain days and ordered to be received on those days, these rules are to be considered merely directive and not preceptive."

*c*) When Holy Communion is being received, all those things are to be avoided which create greater difficulty for a young person who wishes to abstain from Holy Communion, but in such a way that his abstinence will not be noticed; hence there should be no express invitation, no rigid and quasi-military order in coming up, no insignia to be worn by those who receive Communion, etc.

*d*) The Superior of the community should see to it that Holy Communion be not brought to the sick who do not expressly ask for it.

*e*) Promoters and directors of gatherings of young people which are convened, for example in public schools, for the sake of receiving Holy Communion, must take notice that in such gatherings there are dangers akin to those which exist in communities, and they must employ all the means for removing them, not only by announcing that each one is free to receive Communion or not, and by supplying sufficient opportunity for confession, but also by striving to remove all circumstances which might expose those who do not receive to astonishment from the others, as was said above.

III. These are the principal remedies which this Sacred Congregation considered should be put at the disposal of the Most Excellent Bishops, Ordinaries of places, and major religious Superiors to prevent abuses, or if they have already crept in anywhere (which God forbid), to remove them. This same Sacred Congregation earnestly exhorts the Most Excellent Prelates in the Lord to add to these such other remedies as, in their prudence and zeal for the salvation of souls, they may find more suitable in view of the circumstances of places and persons in each institute. For attentive vigilance and care must be used that the Sacrament of the Most Blessed Eucharist, which was instituted by God for the progress and spiritual welfare of souls, may not, through the malice of men and their negligence in failing to forestall or remove abuses, be turned to the detriment and eternal ruin of souls, contrary to the nature and purposes of its institution.

At the plenary session held in Vatican City on 22 July, 1938, the Eminent and Most Reverend Cardinals carefully considered this Instruction and unanimously approved it; and His Holiness Pius XI in the audience of 3 Aug., 1938, upon hearing the report of the undersigned Secretary of the Sacred Congregation, deigned to ratify and confirm the said Instruction, and ordered that it be communicated as a reserved Instruction to all Ordinaries of places and major Superiors of Orders and clerical religious institutes, to be exactly observed by them.

The Most Reverend Ordinaries of places and major religious Superiors will please inform this Sacred Congregation of the receipt of this Instruction.

Given at Rome, from the office of the Sacred Congregation of the Sacraments, on the 8th of December, the Feast of the Immaculate Conception of the Blessed Virgin Mary, 1938.

**(Private)**; S. C. Sacr., Instruction, 8 Dec., 1938.

## CANON 858

**Eucharistic Fast:** ***Per Modum Potus*** **Officially Defined** (Holy Office, 7 Sept., 1897) **Private.**

A reply of the Holy Office:

**The Petition:** N.N. states that because of a chronic illness he obtained the faculty of taking something "*per modum potus*" before Holy Communion. As the illness has grown much worse and matter taken by way of drink is no longer sufficient for him, he prays Your Holiness to permit him to take also some solid nourishment.

**The Reply:** Let the reply give the mind of the Sacred Congregation as in *Abellinen.*, 4 June, 1893: The mind is that when the expression "*per modum potus*" is used, it is understood that the person may take broth, coffee, or other liquid food, in which is mixed some substance such as wheat meal, grated bread, and the like, provided the whole mixture continues to have the nature of liquid food. His Holiness approved this reply.

**(Private)**; Holy Office, 7 Sept., 1897.

NOTE: Notwithstanding its antiquity this reply is valid and much needed today as an interpretation of the new legislation on the Eucharistic fast. It is given by Castellano in *La Nuova Disciplina del Digiuno Eucaristico e delle Messe Vespertine,* Rome, 1954, p. 103. Also published in *Acta Sanctae Sedis,* Vol. XXX, p. 629; *Collectanea S. C. Prop. Fid.* II, n. 1983; Gasparri, *Fontes,* n. 1192, Vol. IV, p. 497.

**Eucharistic Fast: Extension of the Provisions of "*Christus Dominus*"** (Pius XII, *Motu proprio,* 19 March, 1957) **AAS 49–177.**

This *Motu proprio,* entitled *Sacram Communionem,* is as follows:

In order that the faithful might be able to receive Holy Communion more frequently and to fulfill more easily the precept of hearing Mass on days of obligation, at the beginning of the year 1953 We promulgated the Apostolic Constitution *Christus Dominus,*[1] by which We mitigated the discipline of the eucharistic

[1] 6 Jan., 1953, AAS 45–15; reported in CANON LAW DIGEST, 4, p. 269, and Instruction, 6 Jan., 1953 AAS 45–47; reported in *op. cit.,* 4, p. 277.

fast; and We gave local Ordinaries the faculty to permit the celebration of Mass and the receiving of Holy Communion in the hours after noon, on certain conditions.

The time during which the fast was to be observed before Mass or Holy Communion celebrated or received in the hours after noon, We reduced to three hours for solid food and one hour for non-alcoholic drink.

Moved by the abundant benefits which have been experienced from this concession, the Bishops have thanked Us very heartily, and many of them, for the greater good of the faithful, have earnestly and repeatedly asked for the faculty to permit the celebration of Mass in the hours after noon every day. They have also asked that We establish the same time for observing the fast before Mass or Holy Communion which is celebrated or received in the morning.

In consideration of the notable changes which have taken place in the order of labor and public offices as well as in the whole tenor of social life, We have decided to grant these earnest requests of the Bishops, and We consequently decree as follows:

1. Local Ordinaries, excepting Vicars General without a special mandate, can permit the celebration of Mass in the hours after noon every day, if the spiritual good of a notable part of the faithful require it.

2. The time for the keeping of the eucharistic fast by priests before Mass and by the faithful before Holy Communion, either in the morning hours or in those after noon, is limited to three hours as to solid food and alcoholic drink, and one hour as to non-alcoholic drink; the fast is not broken by drinking water.

3. The eucharistic fast for the time stated above is to be observed also by those who celebrate Mass or receive Holy Communion at midnight or in the first hours of the day.

4. The sick, even though not confined to bed, can take non-alcoholic drink and true and proper medicines, either liquid or solid, without limitation of time, before celebrating Mass or receiving Holy Communion.

But We earnestly exhort priests and the faithful who are able to do so, to observe the ancient and venerable form of the eucharistic fast before Mass or Holy Communion.

Finally, let all who benefit from these faculties do their best to repay the favor received, by more shining examples of Christian living, especially by works of penance and charity.

The provisions of this *Motu proprio* Apostolic Letter become effective from the 25th of March, Feast of the Annunciation of the Blessed Virgin Mary.

All things to the contrary notwithstanding.

Given at Rome, from Saint Peter's, on the 19th day of March, Feast of Saint Joseph Patron of the Universal Church, in the year 1957, the nineteenth of Our Pontificate.

**AAS 49–177**; Pius XII, *Motu proprio* Apostolic Letter, 19 March, 1957. Annotations, *Periodica* 46 (1957)–220–289 (Hürth).

**Faculty of Prison Chaplains to Dispense From Eucharistic Fast** (S. C. Sacr., 13 March, 1961) **Private.**

The Bishop of Gary, adviser to the National Association of Catholic Prison Chaplains in the United States of North America, prostrate at the feet of Your Holiness, humbly petitions the faculty whereby prison chaplains can dispense from the law of the Eucharistic fast those faithful detained in prison, so that they, in view of their special circumstances and the discipline obtaining in prisons, may take something by way of solid food before Holy Communion.

In the audience with His Holiness on 13 March, 1961, after he had heard the report of the undersigned Cardinal Prefect of the Sacred Congregation of the Sacraments and attended to the recitals, our Holy Father, Pope John XXIII, graciously deigned to grant the Bishop of Gary the favor according to his petition, provided, however, that: a fast of one hour from solid food is observed; all danger of wonderment, scandal, and irreverence to the Holy Mysteries is removed; proper dispositions of body and soul are had; and the other requirements of law fulfilled.

All things to the contrary notwithstanding.

The present grant is valid *for two years* and can be used twice a week.

**(Private)**; S. C. Sacr., 13 March, 1961, Prot. N. 428/61; copy of the original kindly sent us by the Rev. Robert J. Kelly, S.J.

Another indult in identical terms, except that a fast of *two* hours is required, was granted to chaplains in Germany; issued by S. C. Sacr., 13 Nov., 1961, Prot. No. 5970/61 — 238/61; reported in *Archiv für Katholisches Kirchenrecht,* 130 (1961)–487.

## Faculty of Chaplains of Mental Hospitals to Dispense From Eucharistic Fast (S. C. Sacr., 19 Jan., 1963) Private.

**Petition.** His Eminence, Cardinal Richard Cushing, moderator of the Catholic Chaplains who are assigned the spiritual care of the faithful in mental hospitals in the United States of North America, prostrate at the feet of Your Holiness, humbly requests the faculty of permitting the aforesaid chaplains to dispense the faithful from the law of the Eucharistic fast at any time of day so that, in view of the special discipline obtaining in the above-mentioned hospitals, the patients may take something by way of solid food before Holy Communion.

**Reply.** In the audience of 19 January, 1963, our Holy Father Pope John XXIII, having heard the report of the undersigned Cardinal Prefect of the Sacred Congregation of the Sacraments and having attended to the recitals, graciously deigned to grant to the Most Eminent Petitioner the favor as requested, *once a week,* provided, however, that: a fast of one hour from solid food is observed; all danger of wonderment, scandal, and irreverence to the Holy Mysteries is removed; the other dispositions of body and soul are had; and the other requirements of law are fulfilled.

All things to the contrary notwithstanding.

The present grant is valid *for three years.*

**(Private)**; S. C. Sacr., 19 Jan., 1963, Prot. No. 46/63; copy of the original rescript kindly sent us by the Rev. Robert J. Kelly, S.J.

NOTE: An accompanying letter, dated 1 March, 1963, from the committee elected by the priest-members of the Association of Mental Hospital Chaplains, was sent to all priest-chaplains and noted that this privilege is "limited to the U. S. and [does] not include either V. A. or Military facilities."

# CANON 867

## Holy Communion to the Sick in the Afternoon (Holy Office, 21 Oct., 1961) AAS 53–735.

A question entitled: "Concerning the giving of Holy Communion to the sick in the afternoon."

This Supreme Sacred Congregation has been asked whether

those who are sick but not in danger of death nor confined to bed and yet unable to leave the house, may receive Holy Communion in the afternoon as often as they cannot receive the Holy Eucharist in the morning because of the absence of a priest or because of any other reasonable impediment.

On Thursday (instead of Wednesday) the 19th of October, the eminent and most reverend Cardinals in charge of safeguarding matters of faith and morals decided to answer the Doubt: *In the affirmative,* provided:

1) there is question of sick persons who have not been able to leave the house for a week;

2) the time and frequency for reception of Holy Communion are determined by the pastor or other priest having the spiritual care of the sick person;

3) the regulations already set down regarding the Eucharistic fast are observed.

On the following Friday, the 20th of October, 1961, in the audience granted to His Eminence, the Cardinal Secretary of the Holy Office, His Holiness, by Divine Providence, Pope John XXIII, confirmed this decision and ordered that it be made part of public law.

Given at Rome, from the Holy Office, the 21st of October, 1961.

**AAS 53–735**; Holy Office, 21 Oct., 1961. Annotations in *Nouvelle Revue Theologique,* 83 (1961)–1092–1093 (Bergh); *Periodica,* 51 (1962)–248–260 (Navarrete).

---

**Communion Outside Mass:** To a complaint by a Bishop against certain religious communities of women who insisted upon the practice of receiving Communion outside Mass without grave reason and to the serious inconvenience of their chaplains, the Sacred Congregation of Rites replied: *Let the Bishop use his right.* S. C. Rit., Rescript, 25 May, 1934. (*Documentation Catholique,* 33 [1935]–1465).

## CANON 872

### Jurisdiction for Confessions Granted in Extraordinary Manner to Dispersed Religious Behind Iron Curtain (Vatican Radio, Broadcast, 17 Sept., 1952) Private.

The Vatican Radio on 17 Sept., 1952, and for some days following, by order of the Holy See, broadcast the following notice in various languages:

To religious priests who, because of the deplorable circumstances under which the Church is to-day oppressed in certain countries, are obliged to live outside the houses of their Institute, the Supreme Pontiff grants jurisdiction for hearing the confessions of the faithful of both sexes in any territory where the aforesaid conditions exist, without regard to the boundaries of the various dioceses, provided the said priests:

1. Had the faculty to hear confessions in some place at the time when they were deported or expelled from their religious house, and were not thereafter deprived of the same faculty according to the sacred canons because of their own fault;

2. And are unable, because of the aforesaid circumstances, to obtain the said faculty from the legitimate local Ordinary.

Only for the duration of the circumstances above mentioned.

**(Private)**; Vatican Radio by order of the Holy Father Pius XII, 17 Sept., 1952.

## CANON 883

### Confessions at Sea: Ordinary Does Not Include Major Superiors of Exempt Clerical Society (Cod. Com., 30 July, 1934) AAS 26–494.

The Code Commission was asked:

Whether, under the designation "Ordinaries" in canon 883, § 1, are included also the major Superiors of an exempt clerical religious institute.

**Reply.** In the negative.

**AAS 26–494**; Cod. Com., 30 July, 1934.

*Periodica,* 23 (1934)–147 (Vermeersch); *Jus Pontificum,* 14 (1934)–224; *Clergy Review,* 8 (1934)–492 (Bentley); *Irish Ecclesiastical Record,* 44 (1934)–638; *Apollinaris,* 8 (1935)–60 (Canestri).

## CANON 888

### Norms for Confessors in Matters Pertaining to the Sixth Commandment (Holy Office, 16 May, 1943) Private.

The following Instruction was issued by the Holy Office to

Ordinaries under the title: Some Norms on the Conduct of Confessors in Dealing with the Sixth Commandment.

The Church has constantly exercised all care and solicitude lest the Sacrament of Penance "given by divine bounty as a refuge after the loss of baptismal innocence, through the wiles of the devil and the malice by which men abuse the gifts of God, become for miserable and shipwrecked sinners an occasion of eternal ruin,"[1] and lest what was established for the salvation of souls be in any way turned to their harm and to the detriment of priestly holiness and dignity through human inattention and levity.

Especially there is in this matter no slight danger if in questioning and instructing penitents on the sixth commandment — a thing which is to be done with consideration and circumspection as required by the difficulty of the matter and the dignity which is due to the Sacrament — the confessor fails to restrain himself and goes too far afield, beyond what is called for by his duty of seeing to the integrity of the confession and the welfare of the penitent; or if his whole conduct, especially in dealing with women, lacks the sanctity and gravity which it should have. For these faults easily do harm to the souls of the faithful, give occasion to suspicions, and can be the first step in the profanation of the Sacrament.

In order to provide with all its resources and energy against such a danger, this Supreme Sacred Congregation has thought it well to recall to mind those norms, to which confessors must earnestly apply their minds and hearts, and to which the attention of future confessors in seminaries and schools of theology must be drawn in good time.

I. The Code of Canon Law very appropriately warns confessors not to detain anyone with curious and useless questions, and especially not to ply young persons imprudently with questions about matters of which they are ignorant (canon 888, § 2). Useless questions are those which are clearly altogether unnecessary to supplement the penitent's self-accusation and to enlighten the confessor as to his interior dispositions. For the penitent is by divine law obliged to confess only all and each of the grave sins which, after a careful self-examination, he is conscious of having committed since his Baptism and which

[1] Const. of Benedict XIV, *Sacramentum Poenitentiae,* 1 June, 1741.

have not yet been directly forgiven through the power of the keys entrusted to the Church, and to explain in confession the circumstances which change the species of the sin;[2] provided, however, that when he committed the sin he knew the specific malice contained in it and was therefore guilty of the same. It is, therefore, only these matters on which the confessor is usually obliged to question the penitent, if he has reason to suspect that they have been omitted from the confession either in good or in bad faith; and if it occasionally happens that he has to make the entire examination of conscience for some individual penitent, he must not go beyond the bounds of reasonable conjecture, taking the circumstances of the penitent into account.

He must, therefore, omit as useless, troublesome, and in this matter very dangerous, all questions about sins of which there is no positive and firm reason to suppose the penitent to be guilty; also about kinds of sin which he is not likely to have committed; about material sins, unless the good of the penitent himself or danger to the common good make it necessary or advisable to warn the penitent about them; finally, about circumstances which are morally indifferent, and especially about the manner in which the sin was committed. Even if the penitent of his own accord, through ignorance or an account of scruples or with evil intent, should exceed the bounds of moderation or offend modesty in explaining sins or temptations of impurity, the confessor should prudently, but promptly and firmly, stop him.

Moreover the confessor must remember that the divine precept regarding the integrity of confession is not binding where it would involve a grave harm to the penitent or to the confessor, which is extrinsic to the confession; and therefore that questioning should be omitted whenever there is prudent ground to fear that it may cause scandal to the penitent or ruin to the confessor. And in doubt, let him constantly bear in mind the common warning of moralists that in this matter it is better to err on the side of caution than to expose oneself or another to ruin by going too far.

Finally, the confessor, in asking questions, should always proceed with the greatest caution, asking first rather general questions and later, if the case requires it, more definite ones; and

[2]Council of Trent, Sess. XIV, cap. 5; Code of Canon Law, c. 901.

these latter should always be brief, discreet, decent, avoiding absolutely any expressions which might excite the imagination or the senses or give offense to a pious soul.

II. The confessor needs no less prudence and gravity when in the fulfillment of his function as physician and teacher he comes to the task of warning and instructing penitents. Let him first of all be deeply conscious of the fact that it is the healing, not of bodies but of souls, which is entrusted to him. Consequently it is usually not his business to advise penitents in regard to medicine and hygiene, and he must entirely avoid whatever would cause astonishment or scandal. If any advice of this sort is regarded as necessary, even for reasons of conscience, it should be given by an expert who is upright, prudent, and acquainted with moral doctrine; to such a one therefore the penitent should be referred.

Likewise the confessor should not dare, either on his own initiative or at the request of anyone, to instruct penitents on the nature and manner of the act by which life is transmitted; and under no pretext should he ever be induced to do this.

He should, however, give his penitents moral instruction and appropriate direction according to the doctrine of approved authors, and should do this prudently, decently, and moderately, without going beyond the real needs of the penitent; and it is to be observed that a confessor who in his questions and admonitions seems to be almost exclusively concerned with sins of this kind, is acting inconsiderately and is not rightly performing his office.

III. Finally it must never be forgotten that the world is seated in wickedness,[3] and that "the priest is by daily association like one in the midst of a depraved people, so that often in the very ministering of pastoral charity, he has to be on his guard against the hidden wiles of the infernal serpent."[4]

Hence he must always conduct himself with the greatest caution, especially in dealing with women penitents, watchfully avoiding anything which might savor of familiarity or encourage dangerous affection. Let him not, therefore, be curious to learn who they are, nor dare to ask their names directly or indirectly. In speaking to them, he should never use the pronoun *"tu"* in

---

[3] I John 5:19.

[4] Pius X, Exhortation to the Catholic Clergy, *Haerent animo,* 4 Aug., 1908.

places where that denotes a familiar relationship; he should not allow their confessions to last longer than is necessary; he should not in confession speak of things which are not matters of conscience; he should not without real necessity admit mutual visits or epistolary correspondence with them, nor long conversations, either in the sacristy, halls, parlors, or anywhere else, not even under pretext of giving spiritual direction.

The confessor must use all possible vigilance to prevent merely human affections from gradually insinuating themselves and being encouraged either in himself or in his penitents; but he must constantly bend all his efforts to the end that "whatever he does for the sacred ministry be according to God and be done under the impulse and guidance of faith."[5]

IV. In order that confessors may be able the more readily and securely to perform this office, they must in good time be instructed and trained in it by their teachers, and not in the principles merely but also by trial and practice, so that they will know exactly how penitents should be questioned about the sixth commandment, whether they be children, young people or adults, especially women; what questions are necessary or useful, and what ones on the contrary are to be omitted; and what words are to be used in the language of the country.

Given at Rome, from the Holy Office, 16 May, 1943.

**(Private)**; Holy Office, 16 May, 1943; *Periodica,* 33 (1944)–130.

## CANON 924

### Cord Rosary Can Be Blessed and Enriched With Indulgences (S. Paen., 15 May, 1948) Private.

The Secretary of State to His Holiness inquired whether a cord rosary could be blessed and enriched with indulgences.

Our Office gave an affirmative answer provided that such rosaries verify the essential condition required for rosaries in general, namely, that "they be made of solid material, that is, material which cannot be easily broken or worn out."

His Holiness was asked to signify that he had nothing contrary to such a response to the Secretary of State.

[5] Pius X, Exhortation to the Catholic Clergy, *Haerent animo,* 4 Aug., 1908.

In the audience of 15 May, 1948, His Holiness replied: *In the affirmative.*

**(Private)**; S. Paen., 15 May, 1948, Prot. N. 2287/48; copy of original rescript provided by the Rt. Rev. Msgr. Henry Frank, St. Cloud, Minn., who also sent along the following notation written from Rome, Italy, 10 March, 1959, by the Rev. Dr. Jerome Gassner, O.S.B.: "This morning I went to the S. Penitenziaria and asked about the rosary. I was shown the decree of May 15, 1948, wherewith the Holy Father upon the request of Cardinal Canali has approved such rosaries (cord) forever and for anybody. The Officialis was not sure whether or not that decree has been published or not. *Anyway, it is in force.* Upon the cross can be given the papal indulgences and the indulgences of the Stations. Upon the cord rosary all the indulgences of any rosary."

On this subject see also S. de Angelis: *De Indulgentiis,* ed. 2, n. 225. De Angelis is *Substitutus* for indulgences in the Sacred Penitentiary and notes in his book that cord rosaries nearly always are more solid than those which are made from other materials and yet are blessed and enriched with indulgences.

## CANON 925

### When a Plenary Indulgence Is to Be Gained on the Usual Conditions, Some Other Prayer Must Be Added to Those for the Intentions of the Holy Father (S. Paen., 15 June, 1954) Private.

The Procurator General of the Order of Friars Minor, prostrate at the feet of Your Holiness, humbly proposes the following question:

Whether, for a plenary indulgence which is to be gained on the usual conditions, besides the prayer for the intentions of the Holy Father, some other prayer either oral or mental must be added in the very visitation of the church.

**Reply:** In the affirmative.

**(Private)**; S. Paen., 15 June, 1954; N. 5515/54; published in *Acta Ordinis Fratrum Minorum,* August, 1954, p. 212. The document was kindly sent to us for publication in the CANON LAW DIGEST, by the Reverend Walter Bedard, O.F.M., Rector of Regina Cleri Seminary, Regina, Saskatchewan.

NOTE: This additional prayer may be even a brief ejaculation. It is required in order to fulfill the definition of a "visit to a church," since, according to the Declaration of 20 Sept., 1933 (AAS 25–446; CANON LAW DIGEST, 1, p. 458), such a visit *in itself* (i.e., independently of the other "usual conditions") must include some oral or mental prayer.

However, if a plenary indulgence is to be gained, not on "the usual conditions" but on special conditions which include a visit to a church and the recital of some prescribed prayers in the visit itself, then the special prayers so recited fulfill also the requisites for the "visit to the church"; so that in that case no additional prayer is required. By its very terms, the above reply does not apply to such cases.

## Little Office of the Blessed Virgin: Indulgence Valid for New Enlarged Edition and for All Congregations of Sisters (S. Paen., 11 March, 1955) Private.

**Petition:** The Superioress General of the Congregation of Sisters of the Holy Cross, whose motherhouse is in Menzingen in the Diocese of Basle, prostrate at the feet of Your Holiness, humbly prays that the indulgences already granted for the recitation of the Little Office of the Blessed Virgin (cf. *Enchiridion Indulgentiarum,* ed. 1952, n. 318) be extended to the recitation of the same Little Office in the new and enlarged form edited by Father Augustine Bea, S.J., not only in favor of the Sisters of the aforesaid Congregation, but also of other religious Institutes who may now use or may in future use this new edition of the Little Office of the Blessed Virgin.

**Reply:** The Sacred Apostolic Penitentiary, in virtue of the faculties granted to it by His Holiness Pius XII, graciously grants the favor according to the terms of the petition. All things to the contrary notwithstanding.

**(Private)**; S. Paen., 11 March, 1955. *Commentarium pro Religiosis,* 34(1955)–26.

NOTE: See also the summary of the practice of the S. C. Rel. regarding the substitution of the Breviary for the Little Office, reported in this same volume under canon 489. The Letter of the Holy Father to these same Sisters of Menzingen, which is reported in the note, makes reference to this same edition of the Little Office.

## New Indulgences Attached to Acts in Favor of the Dying (S. Paen., 21 Oct., 1960) AAS 53–56.

A decree of the Sacred Penitentiary:

His Holiness John XXIII by Divine Providence Pope, in

order the better to provide for the salvation of souls about to leave this life, in the Audience granted to the undersigned Cardinal Major Penitentiary on the 15th of October of this year (1960), graciously deigned to grant the following Indulgences: a *partial Indulgence of ten years* to be gained with at least a contrite heart by the faithful who devoutly offer the fruits of the Sacrifice of the Mass of which they can dispose, in favor of the dying; a *plenary* Indulgence to be gained under the usual conditions by the faithful who do this every day for a whole month. The present decree is to be effective *in perpetuum* without the sending of any Apostolic Letter in the form of a brief; all things to the contrary notwithstanding.

Given at Rome from the Sacred Penitentiary, the 21st of October, 1960.

**AAS 53–56;** S. Paen., 21 Oct., 1960.

**Offering the Day's Work to God: Indulgences** (S. Paen., 25 Nov., 1961) **AAS 53–827.**

His Holiness John XXIII by Divine Providence Pope, desiring that human labor by being offered to God be ennobled and elevated, in the Audience granted to the undersigned Cardinal Major Penitentiary on the seventh of October of the present year (1961), graciously deigned to grant the following Indulgences:

1. a *plenary* Indulgence, on the usual conditions, to be gained by the faithful who, using whatever formula they choose, offer to God in the morning the manual or intellectual work of the whole day;

2. a *partial indulgence of five hundred days,* to be gained by the faithful every time they, at least with a contrite heart, likewise devoutly offer their present work, manual or intellectual, by any pious invocation.

The present provision to be valid *in perpetuum*. All things to the contrary notwithstanding.

Given at Rome from the Sacred Apostolic Penitentiary, the 25th of November, 1961.

**AAS 53–827;** S. Paen., Decree, 25 Nov., 1961.

---

**Holy Hour:** Privately, in church, public oratory, or (for those legitimately using it) semi-public oratory: besides partial indulgence (Ench. Indulg. 1952, n. 168), a plenary indulgence now granted. Conditions: confession, Communion, prayers for intentions of Pope. S. Paen., 13 Aug., 1959 (AAS 51–656).

**Religious Vocations:** Prayer for, composed by His Holiness Pius XII; ten years each time; plenary on usual conditions if recited daily for one month. S. Paen., 9 Feb., 1957 (AAS 49–100). English version: *The Pope Speaks,* 4 (1957)–29.

**Rosary:** Indulgence of fifty days once a day for kissing the Rosary one is carrying, and reciting the first part of the Hail Mary. S. Paen., 30 March, 1953 (AAS 45–311).

**Teachers' Prayer:** Composed by His Holiness Pius XII: one thousand days *each time,* with contrite heart. S. Paen., 28 Dec., 1957 (AAS 50–118). English text, *The Pope Speaks,* 4 (1957–58)–380.

## CANON 934

### Six Our Fathers, Hail Marys, and Glorias, for All *Toties Quoties* Plenary Indulgences Where Visit to Church is Prescribed (Decree, S. Poen., 5 July, 1930) AAS 22–363.

Whereas by the Reply of 13 Jan., 1930, ad II,[1] it was declared by this Sacred Penitentiary through the Office of Indulgences, that the six *Paters, Aves,* and *Glorias* mentioned in the Decree of 10 July, 1924, IX,[2] in the visitation of churches for the gaining of the plenary Portiuncula indulgence *toties quoties,* are necessary in the sense that these very prayers must be said in each of the visits; His Holiness, Pius XI, for the sake of uniformity, and in order to remove all doubt in this matter, in the audience granted to the undersigned Major Penitentiary on 4 July, 1930, graciously deigned to decree the same for the gaining of all plenary indulgences *toties quoties* for which a visit to a church is enjoined, so that in future it is necessary and sufficient to recite those prayers in each visit in all such cases.

**AAS 22–363;** S. Poen., Decree 5 July, 1930.
*Periodica,* 19 (1930)–341 (Vermeersch); *J.P.,* 10 (1930)–241.

---

[1] AAS 22–43; reported in CANON LAW DIGEST, 1, p. 456.
[2] AAS 16–345; reported in CANON LAW DIGEST, 1, p. 453.

**"Visiting a Church or Oratory" and "Praying According to the Intention of the Holy Father" Defined** (Declaration, S. Poen., 20 Sept., 1933) **AAS 25–446.**

A Declaration of the Sacred Penitentiary is as follows:

Since learned men have been discussing without coming to an agreement upon the meaning and force of the clauses "to visit a church or public oratory, or (for those legitimately using the same) a semipublic oratory," and "to pray according to the intention of the Holy Father," which clauses are frequently added to grants of indulgences, His Holiness, Pius XI, at the request of the undersigned Cardinal Major Penitentiary, in the audiences accorded to him on the 16th of June and the 8th of July, 1933, in order to remove all doubt and anxiety for the future, graciously deigned to declare: that by a visit to a church or oratory (as above) is meant "going to a church or oratory at least with some general or implicit intention of honoring God in Himself or in His saints, and making some prayer, the one prescribed if any has been imposed by the one who granted the indulgence, otherwise, any prayer, oral or even mental, according to each one's piety and devotion"; and that the clause, "to pray according to the intention of the Holy Father," is quite fulfilled by adding to the other prescribed works the recitation according to his intention, of one *Pater, Ave,* and *Gloria;* each of the faithful, however, remaining free, according to canon 934, § 1, to recite any other prayer according to his piety and devotion toward the Holy Father.

**AAS 25–446;** S. Poen., Declaration, 20 Sept., 1933.

## CANON 973

**Careful Selection and Training of Candidates for the States of Perfection and Sacred Orders** (S. C. Rel., 2 Feb., 1961).

An Instruction, *Religiosorum institutio,* to the Superiors of Religious Communities, Societies without vows, and Secular Institutes on the careful selection and training of candidates for the states of perfection and Sacred Orders is as follows:

## PURPOSE, BINDING FORCE, AND EXTENT OF THIS INSTRUCTION

### 1. *The Instruction "Quantum Religiones"*

The training of religious and of others pursuing perfection and aspiring to the ranks of the clergy in the states of perfection has always been particularly close to the heart of the Sacred Congregation for Religious. Thus, in the Instruction *Quantum Religiones,* of 1 December, 1931, the Sacred Congregation instructed the superiors general of religious communities and clerical societies on the proper religious and clerical training of their subjects, and on the investigation to be carried out before profession and the reception of Sacred Orders.[1]

The main purpose of this Instruction was, in so far as human frailty may permit, to forestall serious cases of defection not only from the religious state but likewise from the sacred ranks in which religious had been enrolled through the reception of Orders.

### 2. *The purpose of this Instruction and its binding force*

Now, however, without any change in the chief directives and criteria contained in the aforesaid Instruction, this Sacred Congregation proposes to take up this same question again and to treat it anew (can. 22), especially as regards the selection and training of candidates and the investigation to be made prior to professions and Sacred Orders in order that the aforesaid Instruction may be in complete harmony with subsequent developments and with later pertinent pontifical documents.

### 3. *The principal sources of this Instruction*

In the Jubilee Year of 1950 there was held at Rome an International Congress of the States of Perfection, in which specialists summoned from all over the world on the basis of their knowledge and experience, spoke and wrote on the selection, nurtur-

---

[1] AAS 24 (1932)–71–81; *Enchiridion de Statibus Perfectionis,* Rome, 1949, n. 363, pp. 471–479. Cf. also the Instruction *Illud saepius, De Qualitatibus recipiendorum,* 18 August, 1915, in *Enchiridion de Stat. Perf.,* n. 286, pp. 340–344. English version of *Quantum Religiones* in CANON LAW DIGEST, 1, pp. 473–482.

ing, and perfecting of religious and clerical vocations. These discussions were published in the four-volume *Acta et Documenta* of the Congress. Later, congresses were held in various nations and in them the same topics were taken up.

During this same period other documents of the utmost importance appeared. These were the encyclical letter of Pope Pius XI, of immortal memory, *Ad Catholici Sacerdotii,* of 20 December, 1935,[2] and various others published by Pope Pius XII, of venerable memory, to whom the states of perfection are so indebted, such as his Exhortation to the Clergy, *Menti Nostrae,* of 23 September, 1950,[3] his encyclical letter, *Sacra Virginitas,* of 25 March, 1954,[4] his allocution, *Sollemnis Conventus,* of 24 June, 1939, to all clerical students and their superiors,[5] his allocution, *Haud Mediocri,* of 11 February, 1958, to the superiors general of religious orders and congregations resident in Rome,[6] and especially the Apostolic Constitution, *Sedes Sapientiae,* of 31 May, 1956, on religious, clerical and apostolic training of clerics in the states of perfection.[7] Nor of any lesser value are those documents which the Sovereign Pontiff, John XXIII, happily reigning, has issued on the priesthood and priestly formation, both in his solemn allocution on the occasion of the first Roman Synod and likewise in the Synodal Constitutions.[8] There was also published a reserved *Circular Letter* of the Sacred Congregation of the Sacraments on 27 December, 1955,[8a] addressed to local Ordinaries for secu-

---

[2] AAS 28 (1936)–5–533; *Ench. de Stat. Perf.*, n. 367, 481–521.

[3] AAS 42 (1950)–657–702.

[4] AAS 46 (1954)–161–191.

[5] AAS 31 (1939)–245–251; *Ench. de Stat. Perf.*, n. 373, pp. 530–537; CANON LAW DIGEST, 2, pp. 427–433.

[6] AAS 50 (1958)–153–161; reported above, pp. 194–202.

[7] Cf. the doctrinal section in AAS 48 (1956)–354–365. The *Statuta Generalia* appended to this same Apostolic Constitution were printed and promulgated separately from the AAS. The references in the Instruction are to the second edition published under the direction of the Sacred Congregation for Religious. English version of doctrinal section given above, pp. 105–117; English version of the *Statuta* is available from the Catholic University of America Press.

[8] These documents of Pope John XXIII can be consulted in AAS 52 (1960)–179–309, and in the *Prima Romana Synodus,* A.D. 1960, Vatican Press.

[8a] English version in CANON LAW DIGEST, 4, pp. 303–315.

lar clerics, imposing an investigation of candidates before their promotion to Orders.

Certainly it was most opportune for, and even the duty of, this Sacred Congregation to incorporate the fruits of this long-standing and rich experience and evolution into a new Instruction, which would likewise serve as a particularized commentary on the Apostolic Constitution, *Sedes Sapientiae* (cf. n. 40 and the *Statuta Generalia,* art. 17).

### 4. *To whom this Instruction is addressed*

This Instruction is addressed to the superiors of religious communities, societies living the common life, and secular institutes, especially as far as the last are concerned, if their members are incorporated into the institute as clerics. Therefore, although frequently, for the sake of convenience, only religious will be mentioned, the norms and criteria set forth in this Instruction are also applicable to the members of the other states of perfection (cf. *Stat. Gen.,* art. 16, §§ 1–2).

Likewise, although the Instruction refers especially to candidates for the clerical state, nevertheless those points which by their very nature deal with the selection and training of candidates for the states of perfection are, with due adaptations, to be applied also to lay religious, including religious women (*Ibid.,* § 3, 2°).

## I. THE MORE COMMON CAUSES OF DEFECTION

### 5. *An inquiry into the causes of defections*

It is necessary at the very outset to set down the most frequent grounds alleged for defections and to lay before superiors the reasons which religious priests claim to be the causes why they lose interest in the life they have embraced and ask the Holy See for secularization or even for "laicization," i.e., reduction to the lay state. Attention must be drawn also to the pretexts under which these same religious priests presume to leave the religious life and return to the world on their own initiative, or even make so bold as to question before the Apostolic Dicasteries their clerical obligations, especially celibacy. Once the causes of defections are known, superiors will be able to exercise more experienced care and vigilance either in examining the divine vocation of candidates or in strengthening and preserving it by their devoted efforts.

In general, the aforesaid religious claim either that they entered on this way of life and continued in it without a genuine divine vocation, or that they lost the genuine divine vocation during the period of their formation or in the early years of their ministerial life.

6. *Undue family influence*

Frequently such religious claim undue influence from parents and members of their family, inasmuch as they were born into a large or poor family and thus were advised either by their parents or by other relatives to leave the paternal home and go to the seminary as a happy solution of family difficulties and were even at times pressured by request, persuasion, or even disguised threats, into embracing the life of perfection and the priestly life and continuing in it. As a result, they allege that their repugnance or reluctance to accept the religious clerical state, for which they had an aversion, was broken down.

7. *Undue influence of superiors and directors*

There were also those who lay at the door of their religious superiors and their spiritual directors the responsibility for their most difficult situation, claiming that these latter, although they had noticed in them no happiness in the religious clerical life, no spirit of piety, and no zeal as they grew older, nevertheless did not hesitate to urge them on, either because they hoped the subjects would do better in the future or because they were more interested in the number than in the quality of vocations, or because, blinded by a false sense of kindness toward the candidates, they threatened them with the danger of loss of eternal salvation if they left the religious clerical state.

8. *Ignorance of obligations and lack of liberty in accepting them*

Not infrequently religious priests plead insufficient knowledge of religious and clerical obligations, especially celibacy, or uncertain will in advancing to perpetual profession or Sacred Orders. If they entered a religious seminary as young boys or in their early adolescent years with only a confused knowledge of the religious and ecclesiastical vocation or with a very uncertain will, these unfortunate religious and priests claim that they never got over this state of mind, once they had completed their studies and their years of formation. Nevertheless, they did not withdraw from the path on which they had entered either because they heedlessly followed their companions according to custom, or because, being bashful and incapable of any serious decision, they unwillingly went along with the urgings and counsels of their superiors. Hence they affirm that in making profession or receiving Orders they were not sufficiently aware of the obligations of the priestly life or did not accept them with full freedom.

### 9. *Fear of an uncertain future*

At times such candidates, on the verge of Sacred Orders or perpetual profession and somewhat mature in age, finding themselves without academic degrees and untrained in any art or liberal profession, were afraid to leave the religious life, feeling deep down in their hearts that if they returned to the world, they could not make an upright living unless by manual labor, or would be obliged to make difficult and uncertain efforts to acquire a liberal profession. Therefore they regarded the decision to continue in the religious clerical life as a lesser evil.

### 10. *Difficulty with chastity*

Sometimes these religious priests affirm that it is now impossible for them to observe chastity, first because of bad habits contracted in youth, which were sometimes corrected but still never completely eradicated, and secondly because of sexual tendencies of a pathological nature, which they feel cannot be brought under control either by ordinary or extraordinary means, even those of a spiritual order, in such a way that they frequently fall into the solitary sin.

### 11. *Loss of the religious spirit*

Lastly, not infrequently there is adduced as a cause the loss of the religious spirit either because, under the insidious impact of present-day naturalism, these priests become incapable of discipline and religious observance, or because, living in religious houses an indolent and unproductive life, deceived by the desire of life outside and ill-regulated pseudo-apostolic activism and neglecting the interior life, they fall victims to dangers of all kinds, which they do not avoid and do not even recognize.

12. *Weakness and subjective character of such arguments*

Unfortunate religious priests bring forth these and other similar arguments, at times even attempting to make the Church responsible for their deplorable condition, as though the Church, through her ministers, had admitted them to the religious and priestly life without the necessary qualifications, or did not know how to train and protect them once they had been called unto the portion of the Lord. But, as the Sacred Congregation of the Sacraments states in the above-mentioned *Circular Letter:* "it cannot be denied that these charges made by the priests during the trials have only a shadowy appearance of truth, for often the only proof is the statement made by the plaintiff alone, a very interested party, and not by witnesses or documents proved in court."[8b] Nor is this surprising since these unfortunate religious priests not infrequently take their present state of mind and psychic crisis, which has gradually evolved over a period of years, and unconsciously transfer it to the time of their profession and ordination, being unaware of the inner change which has taken place within themselves.

13. *Removal of all appearance of justification for these claims; superiors' obligation in conscience*

And yet the honor of the Church, the welfare of religious communities and the edification of the faithful demand of superiors most accurate diligence and untiring zeal in order not to provide even a vestige of foundation for priests advancing such claims.

Superiors should see to it that they be not responsible for the mistakes or errors of those in charge of selecting and training young men. This will be the case if they are culpably uninformed of the norms laid down by the Church, or ignore them, or apply them carelessly; if, ignoring the necessary discernment of spirits, they admit into religious life and allow to remain therein those who have not been called by God, or if they neglect to give proper formation to those who are evidently

[8b] CANON LAW DIGEST, 4, p. 308.

called and to safeguard them in their divine vocation. Therefore, this Sacred Congregation regards it as its duty to exhort superiors most earnestly always to keep before their eyes the norms herein set forth, being mindful of the grave warning of this Sacred Congregation in its Instruction, *Illud Saepius,* of 18 August, 1915: "When a religious leaves his order, the superior of that same order, if he has diligently examined his conscience before God, will very frequently be well aware that he himself is not without fault and has failed in his duty. This neglect of duty is often verified either in the admission of candidates or in training them to the religious life, or, after they have made vows, in keeping watch over them."[9]

## II. THE CARE TO BE TAKEN IN THE SELECTION OF CANDIDATES FOR THE STATE OF PERFECTION AND THE CLERICAL STATE

### A) GENERAL WARNINGS

14. *Quality before quantity*

First of all, although vocations to the state of evangelical perfection and to the priesthood are to be promoted by every means (*Stat. Gen.,* art. 32), still care must be taken lest an immoderate desire to increase numbers should interfere with quality and selection.

Let all be convinced that, unless great zeal for an abundance of students is closely bound up with proper care for their formation, such zeal does not produce the desired effects, and even does just the contrary. For just as it is evident that, with the help of God's grace, nothing contributes more to inspiring vocations than the exemplary life of those who have been properly formed, in the same way nothing is more conducive to impeding the growth of vocations or to suffocating them than the example of mistakes which are unfortunately beheld in those who are without proper solid formation.

"Seek ye first the kingdom of God and His justice and all these things will be added unto you. We can say, and all superiors should repeat: Let us seek out quality first of all, because

[9] *Ench. de Stat. Perf.,* n. 286, p. 341.

then, if we may use such an expression, quantity will automatically be present by itself. This will be the concern of Divine Providence. It is not our task to look for numbers, since it is not given to us to inspire vocations in souls. In this truth there is contained the whole of the theology of a vocation: it comes from God and only God can give it. It is our task to nurture this vocation, to enrich it, and to adorn it. . . . This is the guarantee and promise of your future prosperity."[10]

As a matter of fact, experience teaches us that God favors with an abundance of vocations those religious communities which flourish with the rigor of discipline and carry out their own proper role in the Mystical Body of Christ, and that, on the contrary, those communities suffer a lack of candidates, whose members do not comply faithfully with His divine counsels.

Wherefore, those who are suffering from a shortage of vocations and anxiously devote themselves to collecting them, using at times methods and procedures which are certainly not to be recommended, would do well to exert the greatest care in training in the best way possible the candidates who spontaneously come to them or are drawn to them by prudent means and are already entrusted to them by the Church and Divine Providence.

For the rest, let us not be unmindful of the teaching of Holy Scripture, which the Sovereign Pontiff recalls to us in such timely fashion: "Gedeon, who had at his disposal an immense multitude of men apparently ready and prepared to fight all battles and conquer all difficulties, heard the voice of the Lord declaring that to accomplish hard and difficult tasks, rather than large numbers, the courage of a few was sufficient."[11]

15. *Positive signs of a vocation*

It will be helpful to recall, then, that only those candidates can be admitted who are free of any canonical impediment and

[10] Allocution of Pius XI to the General Chapter of the Oblates of Mary Immaculate, 14 September, 1932. Allocution of Pius XII to the Superiors General, 11 February, 1958, in AAS 50 (1958)–160; see above, p. 202.

[11] John XXIII, allocution of 28 January, 1960, to the clerical students of the Diocese of Rome or residing in Rome, in AAS 52 (1960)–263; English version in *The Pope Speaks,* 6 (1960)–364. *Prima Romana Synodus,* p. 436. Cf. Pius XI, encyclical *Ad Catholici Sacerdotii,* AAS 28 (1936)–44; *Ench. de Stat. Perf.,* n. 367, p. 513.

who, at the same time, show positive signs of a divine vocation, conformably to the prescriptions of the Apostolic Constitution, *Sedes Sapientiae,* and the *Statuta Generalia,* art. 31, § 2, 1°, 2°. Let this be the first and absolute principle in selecting vocations. For, as we are clearly admonished by the same Apostolic Constitution, *Sedes Sapientiae:* "A call from God to enter the religious or the sacerdotal state is so necessary that, if this is lacking, the very foundation on which the whole edifice rests is wanting. For whom God has not called, His grace does not move nor assist."[12]

The canonical fitness of the candidate for bearing the obligations of the institute (can. 538; *Stat. Gen.,* art. 31, § 1) must be evinced by *positive arguments* (can. 973, § 3), and it must consist in all the requirements and, according to differences in age, all the physical, intellectual and moral qualities, either of nature or of grace, whereby a young man is rightly prepared for the worthy acceptance and performance of religious and priestly obligations (*Stat. Gen.,* art. 33).

16. *Moral certainty of the fitness of candidates*

Candidates should not be admitted to religious seminaries except after careful investigation and the securing of detailed information on each individual. In seminaries and novitiates the necessary proofs and investigations are to be repeated with faithful observance of the General Statutes of the Apostolic Constitution *Sedes Sapientiae,* art. 31–34. Doubtful fitness is not enough but "as often as there still remains some prudent doubt as to the fitness of a candidate, it is wrong to permit him to contract obligations (can. 571, § 2), especially if they be definitive, (can. 575, § 1; 637).[13] Still greater care must be exercised in this regard if there be question of Sacred Orders.[14] The period of trial is to be continued as provided for in canon law, and all possible means must be employed which may be useful in acquiring this moral certitude" (can. 571, § 2; 574, § 2; *Stat. Gen.,* art. 34, § 2, 1°, 2°, 3°). Appropriately, therefore, all due proportion being guarded as to the different degrees of probation and selection, should superiors and all those engaged

[12] Apostolic Const. *Sedes Sapientiae,* nn. 12–13; see above p. 108.
[13] *Stat. Gen.,* art. 34, § 2, 1°.
[14] *Ibid.,* n. 2°.

in deciding vocations apply to themselves the canonical prescriptions whereby the bishop is warned "that he should confer Sacred Orders on no one unless he is morally certain, by positive arguments, of the candidate's canonical fitness; otherwise, he not only sins most grievously himself but exposes himself to the danger of sharing in the sins of others" (can. 973, § 3). For the selection and training of a religious candidate is a step toward sacred ordination and in the ordination of religious, as Pius XI wisely warns, the Bishop "always places full confidence in the judgment of their superiors."[15] Consequently, in case of doubt as to fitness, it is certainly unlawful to proceed further for there is involved something on which the welfare of the Church and the salvation of souls depend in a special manner, and in which, consequently, the safer opinion must always be followed. "This safer opinion in the question now before us, does more to protect the best interests of ecclesiastical candidates since it turns them aside from a road on which they might be led on to eternal ruin."[16]

### 17. *The responsibility of the internal and external forum; both should use the same principles*

In this most important task the chief responsibility lies with major superiors. It is their work to organize and direct this entire activity, to be acquainted thoroughly with the norms set down by the Apostolic See, and to make sure they are faithfully carried out. On them, consequently, in this matter lies the greatest burden of responsibility (*Stat. Gen.*, art. 27, § 1).

But major superiors need the helpful cooperation of all who are in charge of selecting and training candidates, whether they be superiors and directors in the external forum or confessors and spiritual prefects, each within the limits of his office. For some of the signs of a divine vocation or lack of it, by their very nature, come to the knowledge of superiors in the external forum, while others, since they belong rather to the intimate realm of mind and conscience, can oftentimes be known only by confessors and spiritual directors. All these individuals accept a burden in

---

[15] Pius XI, Encyclical *Ad Catholici Sacerdotii,* AAS 28 (1936)–44; *Ench. de Stat. Perf.,* n. 367, p. 513.

[16] Pius XI, *ibid.,* AAS 28 (1936)–41; *Ench. de Stat. Perf.,* n. 367; p. 511. Cf. also the Encyclical *Sacra Virginitas,* AAS 46 (1954)–180–181.

conscience in the choice of priests and religious and in their admission to profession and to ordination, and through their ignorance or negligence they may have a share in the sins of others.

Nevertheless, they must use different methods in discharging their duties. Directors in the external forum must do their duty exteriorly according to the norms of common and particular law. The case is different with confessors who are bound by "the inviolable sacramental seal," and with spiritual directors in the stricter sense (cf. *Stat. Gen.*, art. 28, § 2, 9°), who are likewise bound to secrecy "by virtue of the religious office they have accepted." Confessors and spiritual directors should strive, but only in the internal forum, to see that those who either are not called by God or who have become unworthy should not go farther.

But although the procedure in the internal and the external forum is different, it is of the utmost importance that "all should use the same principles in testing vocations and taking appropriate precautions to the end that young men may be prudently admitted to profession and to Orders."[17]

### 18. *The role of the confessor and the spiritual director*

Confessors have the grave duty of warning, urging, and ordering unfit subjects, privately and in conscience, with no regard for human respect, to withdraw from the religious and clerical life. Although they may appear to have all the dispositions required for sacramental absolution, they are, nevertheless, not for that reason to be regarded as worthy of profession or ordination. The principles governing the sacramental forum, especially those pertinent to the absolution of sins, are different from the criteria whereby, according to the mind of the Church, judgment is formed on fitness for the priesthood and the religious life. Consequently, penitents who are certainly unworthy of profession and ordination can be absolved if they show proof of true sorrow for their sins and seriously promise to drop the idea of going on to the religious or clerical state, but they must be effectively barred from profession and ordination.

Likewise spiritual directors are under obligation in the non-sacramental internal forum, to judge of the divine vocation of those entrusted to them and are also under the obligation to warn

[17] *Prima Romana Synodus*, 484, § 3.

and privately urge those who are unfit, to withdraw voluntarily from the life they have embraced.

19. *The careful choice of confessors and spiritual directors*

Lastly, using this occasion, this Sacred Congregation earnestly stresses for superiors both the importance and the necessity of carefully choosing as confessors and spiritual directors in religious seminaries men properly trained and gifted with great prudence and perspicacity in understanding the minds of the young (*Stat. Gen.*, art. 24, § 2). Superiors themselves must encourage a watchful and uniform policy among all those dedicated to the formation of the young lest they allow unqualified candidates to ascend to Orders.

20. *The cooperation of candidates; recommendation of sincerity and docility*

Finally, candidates should be prudently urged to cooperate in the formation of a correct judgment on their vocation, for to them this is of the utmost importance. They should understand correctly that leaving the religious life and the ranks of the clergy is not always and for everyone an evil. It is not an evil but is actually something good for those who are not called or are not properly disposed. Indeed, infidelity resulting in the loss of a divine vocation is certainly dangerous, but the situation would be still more serious if those who are not called or who are unworthy were blindly to take on religious and clerical obligations. Therefore, they are especially urged to practice simplicity and sincerity in opening their hearts, and docility and perfect obedience to the counsels and precepts of their confessors, directors, and superiors: "According as young men will be known for their integrity and sincerity, all the more effectively can they be assisted by their superiors, when the time comes to decide if they are divinely called to enter upon the way of perfection and to receive Sacred Orders."[18]

Consequently, all candidates should be well aware of the mind of the Church on the manifestation of conscience as set forth in canon 530, § 2, and as explained in the *Statuta Generalia*.[19]

---

[18] Cf. *Prima Romana Synodus*, 477.

[19] Cf. *Stat. Gen.*, art. 28, § 3, 1°.

### 21. *The time for definitive selection*

As for the time when the definitive selection is to be made, every means should be diligently employed to insure that this selection takes place within the time limits determined by law. Superiors shall bear well in mind that only rarely should a further extension of probation be requested (cf. *Stat. Gen.*, art. 34, § 3). The excellent norm laid down in the encyclical letter, *Ad Catholici Sacerdotii,* should be observed: "And although it is better not to postpone this selection unduly, since in this matter delay usually leads to error and causes harm, nevertheless, whatever may have been the motive for the delay, just as soon as it is evident that there has been a deviation from the right path, then, with no trace of human respect, the remedy must be applied."[20]

## B) THE REQUIRED FREEDOM

### 22. *Freedom: a sign of a divine vocation*

Among the requisites for a genuine divine vocation there is rightly listed the free will of the candidates or a choice free of all moral pressure along with perfect knowledge of the obligations of their state. Full freedom is prescribed by ecclesiastical law for the reception of Orders and for the validity of the novitiate and profession[21] and, in virtue of art. 32, § 3 of the *Statuta Generalia,* in the recruitment of vocations everything must be avoided which could diminish the freedom of the candidates or improperly affect it. Particularly in the free acceptance of this counsel there is discerned the special call from God or the movement of the Holy Spirit, who interiorly enlightens and inspires a person, who has the other qualifications, to pursue the evangelical counsels or to embrace the priesthood. For the divine inspiration required by St. Pius X[22] in a true vocation, or that marked attraction for sacred duties mentioned by Pius XI in his encycli-

[20] Pius XI, Encyc. *Ad Catholici Sacerdotii,* AAS 28 (1936)–39; *Ench. de Stat. Perf.*, n. 367, pp. 509–510.

[21] Cf. canons 971; 542, 1°; 572, § 1, 4°; 2352.

[22] St. Pius X, Apostolic letter, *Cum primum,* 4 Aug., 1913, in AAS, 5 (1913)–388; *Ench. de Stat. Perf.*, n. 279, p. 331.

cal letter, *Ad Catholici Sacerdotii,*[23] is discerned in their right propensity and intention of mind or the choice of their free will (cf. can. 538), rather than in an inner urging of conscience and sensible attraction which may be lacking.

23. *Superiors should seek out supernatural motives*

Since it is the task of superiors to pass judgment on the vocation of their candidates, they should the more carefully examine the spontaneous response of these candidates or the decision of their free will. Let them examine very frequently into the supernatural motives of vocations in their students, especially if they come from poor families, or are without the means of leading an upright life in the world, or are lacking academic degrees, or if they are known for narrow-mindedness, anxiety or ambivalence, worried by scruples, or completely incapable of facing up to anything important. To provide fuller knowledge of candidates, they can request of them an "historical sketch" of their vocation in so far as this may be possible. Thus they can be brought face to face with genuine personal reflection on their own vocation.

24. *Fatherly help for those who suffer interior or exterior trials*

Superiors should not fail to remind candidates in a fatherly way that if any one, as the result of undue influence from parents or relatives, or because of financial difficulties, feels himself being forced into profession or ordination against his will, he should confidently make the situation known to his superiors or confessor. These latter should show themselves ready to provide assistance to enable the candidate to escape this danger unscathed, providing ways and means, if possible, to help him conveniently obtain a respectable livelihood in the world.[24]

25. *Acquiescence to the judgment of directors of the internal forum*

When any student, on the advice of his confessor or spiritual director, informs his superiors that he does not have the qualifications for the priesthood, then the superior should accept this

---

[23] Pius XI, Encyc. *Ad Catholici Sacerdotii,* AAS 28 (1936)–39; *Ench. de Stat. Perf.,* n. 367, p. 510.

[24] *Circular Letter* of the Sacred Congregation of the Sacraments, n. 5; CANON LAW DIGEST, 4, p. 311.

statement and make no further investigation. If the candidate in question is a subdeacon or deacon, then, with his consent, the superior should take up with the Apostolic See his reduction to the lay state.[25]

### 26. *How to handle the hesitant*

In the case of candidates who are undecided and apprehensive and who cannot make up their minds either to accept or leave the religious life or to receive or decline Orders, superiors should dismiss those whom they recognize as unworthy. Those whom they deem qualified should be exhorted to make vows or to agree to be ordained. Nevertheless, they should refrain from forcing profession or ordination on them and should leave the final decision to their own free will, avoiding all undue influence which could give the impression of drawing them on to profession or ordination by coaxing or by threatening spiritual disaster and the pains of hell which they would incur if they withdrew from profession or ordination.[26]

## C) NECESSARY KNOWLEDGE OF THE OBLIGATIONS

### 27. *Candidates should be taught the obligations to be assumed*

Candidates must make vows and receive Orders deliberately; otherwise they would not be free. Superiors are seriously obliged in conscience to make sure that aspirants and novices as well as students throughout the entire period of their studies be carefully instructed on the duties and obligations of the religious and clerical life.

The duties and obligations of the religious and clerical life should be discussed frequently by novice masters and spiritual prefects, each in his own field, by means of timely warnings and the usual instructions and exhortations. Preachers should likewise take up this subject in retreats before perpetual profession and sacred ordinations. Lastly, in their explanation of the tract on Orders, professors of moral theology should provide lectures on

---

[25] *Ibid.*, n. 6; Canon Law Digest, *loc. cit.*

[26] *Stat. Gen.*, art. 32, § 3. *Cf. Prima Romana Synodus*, 467, § 2. *Circular Letter* of the Sacred Congregation of the Sacraments, n. 7; Canon Law Digest, 4, p. 311.

clerical duties and obligations, and candidates for Orders should be questioned on these points in their examinations.

### 28. *Denunciation of temerity in embracing the religious and clerical life*

It is commendable to keep the sanctity of the religious life and the dignity and excellence of the priesthood frequently placed before candidates from the very beginning and throughout the whole period of their formation, and defection from a genuine divine vocation is justly censured. But similarly, and even more severely, should rashness in embracing the religious and priestly state be denounced and its manifold dangers pointed out for those who either were not called by God or have become unworthy of a divine vocation, but who venture to make vows or to receive Sacred Orders. Superiors should form the conscience of candidates, carefully avoiding all error and confusion in their teaching on the religious and priestly vocation, and on virginity and Christian marriage. Let all be firmly convinced that the time for sounding out a vocation does not lapse completely with the first admission of the candidate, but continues on to perpetual profession and ordination to the priesthood.[27]

## D) THE REQUIRED CHASTITY

### 29. *Importance of this point; young persons are to be properly instructed and warned of its dangers*

Among the proofs and signs of a divine vocation the virtue of chastity is regarded as absolutely necessary "because it is largely for this reason that candidates for the ranks of the clergy choose this type of life for themselves and persevere in it." Consequently:

a) "Watchful and diligent care is to be taken that candidates for the clergy should have a high esteem and love for chastity, and should safeguard it in their souls.

b) "Not only, therefore, are clerics to be informed in due time on the nature of priestly celibacy, the chastity which they are to observe (cf. can. 132), and the demands of this obligation, but they are likewise to be warned of the dangers into which they can fall on this account. Consequently, candidates for Sacred

[27] Cf. *Stat. Gen.*, art. 39, § 1, 1°.

Orders are to be exhorted to protect themselves from dangers from their earliest years."[28]

c) Although virginity embraced for the kingdom of heaven is more excellent than matrimony, nevertheless, candidates for Sacred Orders should not be unaware of the nobility of married life as exemplified in Christian marriage established by the plan of God. Therefore, let them be so instructed that, with a clear understanding of the advantages of Christian matrimony, they may deliberately and freely embrace the greater good of priestly and religious chastity.

d) But should superiors find a candidate unable to observe ecclesiastical celibacy and practice priestly chastity, then, completely ignoring any other outstanding qualities, they should bar him from the religious life and the priesthood (cf. *Stat. Gen.*, art. 34, § 2, 4°), conforming to the following directives and using all prudence and discretion in the application of the same, namely:

30. *Those to be excluded; practical directives*

1. A candidate who shows himself certainly unable to observe religious and priestly chastity, either because of frequent sins against chastity or because of a sexual bent of mind or excessive weakness of will, is not to be admitted to the minor seminary and, much less, to the novitiate or to profession. If he has already been accepted but is not yet perpetually professed, then he should be sent away immediately or advised to withdraw, according to individual cases, no matter what point in his formation he has already reached. Should he be perpetually professed, he is to be barred absolutely and permanently from tonsure and the reception of any Order, especially Sacred Orders. If circumstances should so demand, he shall be dismissed from the community, with due observance of the prescriptions of canon law.

2. Consequently, any candidate who has a habit of solitary sins and who has not given well-founded hope that he can break this habit within a period of time to be determined prudently, is not to be admitted to the novitiate. Nor can a candidate be admitted to first profession or to renewal of vows unless he has really amended his ways. But if a novice or a temporarily professed religious gives evidence of a firm purpose of amendment

---

[28] Pius XII, Exhort. *Menti Nostrae,* AAS 42 (1950)–690–691; cf. Encyc. *Sacra virginitas,* AAS 46 (1954)–164, 170, 174, 179, 182.

with good grounds for hope of success, his probation can be extended as provided for in canon law (canons 571, § 2; 574, § 2; 973, § 3; *Stat. Gen.*, art. 34, § 2, 3°).

Well-grounded hope of amendment can be provided by those youths who are physically and psychically normal or endowed with good bodily and mental health, who are noted for solid piety and the other virtues intimately connected with chastity, and who sincerely desire the religious and priestly life.

3. A much stricter policy must be followed in admission to perpetual profession and advancement to Sacred Orders. No one should be admitted to perpetual vows or promoted to Sacred Orders unless he has acquired a firm habit of continency and has given in every case consistent proof of habitual chastity over a period of at least one year. If within this year prior to perpetual profession or ordination to Sacred Orders doubt should arise because of new falls, the candidate is to be barred from perpetual profession or Sacred Orders (cf. above, no. 16) unless, as far as profession is concerned, time is available either by common law or by special indult to extend the period for testing chastity and there be question of a candidate who, as was stated above (no. 30, 2), affords good prospects of amendment.

4. If a student in a minor seminary has sinned gravely against the sixth commandment with a person of the same or the other sex, or has been the occasion of grave scandal in the matter of chastity, he is to be dismissed immediately as stipulated in canon 1371, except if prudent consideration of the act and of the situation of the student by the superiors or confessors should counsel a different policy in an individual case, sc., in the case of a boy who has been seduced and who is gifted with excellent qualities and is truly penitent, or when the sin was an objectively imperfect act.

If a novice or a professed religious who has not yet made perpetual vows should be guilty of the same offense, he is to be sent away from the community or, should the circumstances so demand, he is to be dismissed with due observance of canon 647, § 2, 1°. If a perpetually professed religious is found guilty of any such sin, he is to be perpetually excluded from tonsure and the reception of any further Order. If the case belongs to the external forum, he is to receive a canonical warning unless, as provided for in canons 653 and 668, there be grounds for sending him back to the world (cf. *Stat. Gen.*, art. 34, § 2, 4°).

Lastly, should he be a subdeacon or deacon, then, without prejudice to the above-mentioned directives and if the case should so demand, the superiors should take up with the Holy See the question of his reduction to the lay state.

For these reasons, clerics who in their diocese or religious who in another community have sinned gravely against chastity with another person are not to be admitted with a view to the priesthood, even on a trial basis, unless there be clear evidence of excusing causes or of circumstances which can at least notably diminish responsibility in conscience (*Circular Letter* of S. C. of the Sacraments, n. 16; CANON LAW DIGEST, 4, p. 314).

Advancement to religious vows and ordination should be barred to those who are afflicted with evil tendencies to homosexuality or pederasty, since for them the common life and the priestly ministry would constitute serious dangers.

5. Very special investigation is needed for those students who, although they have hitherto been free of formal sins against chastity, nevertheless suffer from morbid or abnormal sexuality, especially sexual hyperesthesia or an erotic bent of nature, to whom religious celibacy would be a continual act of heroism and a trying martyrdom. For chastity, in so far as it implies abstinence from sexual pleasure, not only becomes very difficult for many people but the very state of celibacy and the consequent loneliness and separation from one's family becomes so difficult for certain individuals gifted with excessive sensitivity and tenderness, that they are not fit subjects for the religious life. This question should perhaps receive more careful attention from novice masters and superiors of scholasticates than from confessors since such natural tendencies do not come out so clearly in confession as in the common life and daily contact.

### 31. *Care of psychopathic cases*

In addition, special attention must be paid to those who give evidence of neuropsychosis and who are described by psychiatrists as neurotics or psychopaths, especially those who are scrupulous, abulic, hysterical, or who suffer from some form of mental disease (schizophrenia, paranoia, etc.). The same is true of those who have a delicate constitution or, particularly, those who suffer from weakness of the nervous system or from protracted psychic melancholia, anxiety or epilepsy (can. 984, 3°), or who are afflicted with obsessions. Similarly, precautions are needed in examining the children of alcoholics or those tainted with some hereditary weakness, especially in the mental order (cf. *Stat. Gen.*, art. 33; 34, § 1). Finally, those young men are in need of special attention who manifest exaggerated attachment to the comforts of life and worldly pleasures. Superiors should carefully examine all these types and subject them to a thorough examination by a prudent and expert Catholic psychiatrist who, after repeated examinations, will be in a position to determine whether or not they will be able to shoulder, with honor to that state, the burden of religious and priestly life, especially celibacy.

## III. CARE IN TRAINING AND STRENGTHENING VOCATIONS

32. *Experienced directors should be appointed and sought out wherever they may be*

After the accurate selection of vocations, superiors should have as their second principle the task of appointing excellent and experienced directors for the education of young religious conformably to art. 24 of the *Statuta Generalia*. "To these religious houses," advises Pius XI, "assign priests adorned with excellent virtue, and do not be afraid to take them away from other tasks which may be apparently more important but which cannot match this work of capital importance, which can be replaced by no other. Look for them also in other fields, wherever you find men capable and fit for this most noble task."[29] Only if this advice is heeded will this Instruction produce any real fruit; if this counsel is not heeded, then the entire Instruction will be to no purpose.

33. *The qualities and appointment of those in charge of formation*

Let all superiors, each one within his own jurisdiction, exactly carry out all the pertinent prescriptions of the Apostolic Constitution, *Sedes Sapientiae,* articles 24 and 25. Two points call for special emphasis in this Instruction:

[29] Pius XI, Encyc. *Ad Catholici Sacerdotii,* AAS 28 (1936)–37; *Ench. de Stat. Perf.*, n. 367, p. 508.

1. *Responsibility for formation should not be entrusted to younger religious.* It should be observed, first of all, that it is extremely dangerous to turn over to younger priests the very difficult work of religious and priestly formation and especially the task of training minds, since these younger religious have not yet fully completed their own personal formation nor achieved the maturity of age required by canon 559, § 1, nor acquired any measure of experience in the ministry.[30]

2. *Nor should they be assigned without preparation.* Secondly, superiors should beware of directors who are chosen haphazardly or who are unprepared. A natural disposition is not enough but, presupposing all the natural and supernatural gifts needed for this difficult task, they usually have a real need to study ecclesiastical pedagogy because, in this sacred discipline, those in charge of formation learn the principles, criteria, and the practical norms of clerical and religious training according to the words and the mind of the Church. On the other hand, ignorance of these principles gives rise to many lamentable evils.

### 34. *Avoiding false humanism*

The Apostolic Constitution, *Sedes Sapientiae,* with the accompanying *Statuta Generalia,* deals with religious, clerical, and apostolic formation. Nothing needs to be added to this Constitution lest we fall into unnecessary repetitions, but some points having a particular bearing on our purpose need to be mentioned.

In the first place, those charged with the training of youth should never lose sight of the warning of Pius XII, formulated in the Apostolic Constitution, *Sedes Sapientiae,* n. 23 (see above, p. 111), where he states: "Nevertheless, though all should make much of the human and natural training of the religious cleric, the supernatural sanctification of the soul undoubtedly has the first place in the entire course of his development."

Therefore, the religious life must be defended against any appearance of false humanism or naturalism, and its supernatural character and sanctity must be safeguarded by all available means. "This is necessary particularly today, if at any time, when so-called naturalism has worked its way into the minds and souls of men."[31]

---

[30] Cf. *Stat. Gen.,* art. 51.

[31] Pius XII, Exhort. *Menti Nostrae,* AAS 42 (1950)–673.

35. *Natural considerations are not to be made light of but supernatural ones are to be preferred*

Consequently, supernatural reasons for embracing religious vows and the priestly life should be stressed and they should be preferred to the natural virtues in the training of young religious. For rightly, in this matter, does Leo XIII warn: "It is truly difficult to understand how those imbued with Christian wisdom can prefer natural to supernatural virtues and attribute to the former greater efficacy and fecundity. Will nature, with the help of grace, be weaker than if left to its own powers? Did those most holy men whom the Church admires and openly honors show themselves weak and incompetent in the order of nature because they were outstanding for Christian virtue?"[32]

And Pius XII in the Apostolic Constitution, *Sedes Sapientiae,* teaches as follows: "With regard to the resources and methods of education, those which nature itself supplies and those which are offered by the human ingenuity of the present age, if they are good, are clearly not to be neglected, but to be highly esteemed and wisely employed. However, there is no more fatal mistake than to rely exclusively or excessively on these natural means and to relegate supernatural aids and resources to a secondary place or in any way to neglect them. Because in order to attain religious and clerical perfection and apostolic results, the supernatural means, the sacraments, prayer, mortification, and the like, are not merely necessary but altogether primary and essential."[33]

36. *Training in obedience and self-sacrifice*

On more than one occasion in these modern times the Roman Pontiffs have spoken on religious obedience and abnegation of the will, and they have enlightened us on their supernatural nature, the diligence and perfection with which religious should practice them, on dangerous doctrines on these subjects and, in particular, on the false concept of personality and a certain popular or democratic spirit which is making its way into men's minds

[32] Leo XIII, Letter *Testem benevolentiae,* 22 Jan., 1899, in *Acta Leonis XIII,* vol. XIX, pp. 15–16.

[33] Pius XII, Apost. Const. *Sedes Sapientiae,* n. 21; cf. also Pius XII, Alloc. *Haud Mediocri,* 11 Feb., 1958, to superiors general resident in Rome, AAS 50 (1958)–153 ff. Cf. above respectively, pp. 110–111; 194–202.

and which makes obedience as taught and practiced by Christ our Lord altogether void of meaning.

Attention should be called to the pernicious effects on the religious life of that practical "system" which, ignoring more or less the obligations of the religious life, gives in to all the inclinations and pleasures of nature, which are not only not regarded as unlawful but are even looked upon as a postulate of our times and as a perfecting of human nature and, as a result, as something owed to nature or at least altogether permitted. Whence, upon the pretext of progress, bodily comforts and pleasures of all kinds are sought out as well as freedom for the internal and external senses, the satisfaction of one's faculties, and the indiscriminate indulgence of curiosity in regard to books, newspapers, radio, movies, television,[34] profane worldly spectacles, and, lastly, a life without subjection, with ample free play for one's will and activity. All these endanger even the essential obligations of the religious life since they preclude any spirit of humility, self-sacrifice, and mortification which, on the contrary, according to the words of Christ, "If any one wishes to come after Me, let him deny himself, and take up his cross and follow me," (Matt. 16:24), must be taken as the foundation of the entire Christian life[35] and which can be achieved only through crucifixion to the world (Gal. 6:14).

"He who is half-hearted or slothful," the Sovereign Pontiff exhorts, "who wishes to loll around in the comforts of this life, who burns with excessive thirst for human things and human knowledge, and who wants to experience all that earth can give, can neither be nor be called a true soldier of the kingdom of God. Beloved sons, take careful note of this, namely, that the secret and fruitful power of your future apostolate lies particularly in the necessary right detachment of soul from the things of earth." "The man who, shying away from the austerity of religious discipline, would want to live in a religious community just as if he were a man of the world, who seeks out according to his own will whatever seems to be to his own advantage, what-

[34] Cf. Sacred Congregation for Religious, Letter to the Superiors General of the Institutes of Perfection on the use of radio and television, 6 August, 1957; see above, pp. 321–324.

[35] Cf. Alloc. of Pius XII, *Haud Mediocri,* as quoted above in note 33; Alloc. to the Superiors General, 11 Feb., 1958, in AAS 50 (1958)–156; see above, p. 196.

ever pleases and satisfies him — would that man be worthy of Christ his Head?"[36]

Consequently, superiors have a grave obligation to implant the following rule of the life of perfection in the souls of their young subjects: religious may use these comforts and pleasures of life only in so far as they contribute to the pursuit of evangelical perfection and the proper exercise of the apostolate according to one's own constitutions. This norm differs not a little from the one used as a standard for the common state of the Christian life.

However, this does not prevent the acceptance of today's fine, useful discoveries when they are regarded as aids to a fuller formation, or as helps in multiplying apostolic activities and advancing perfection, carefully shunning all the extras which please and satisfy nature but which are not at all necessary for the achieving of the scope of the religious life and the apostolate.

Wherefore, buildings intended for seminaries should be built and furnished according to the norms of religious simplicity and poverty, which demand that these houses be so organized that the minds of the students will be imbued with that spirit of austerity and self-sacrifice which, by its very nature, is required both by the state of the evangelical counsels and likewise by their future apostolic life.

### 37. *Students should be trained for the apostolate, but especially for a spiritual and deeply religious and priestly life*

Lastly, it is an all too clear fact that many young men at the present time are more interested in the external activity of the apostolate, which falls in well with their particular bent of mind, than in the religious perfection of their own souls, of which they have only vague ideas and little esteem. Because of this, after some years in the active life, they are bored by religious practices whose real value they do not understand, or which they regard as hindrances to the apostolate. Then they want to be free of these observances and wish to enter the secular clergy. In order to forestall this danger, superiors, in training their students,

[36] Quotations from John XXIII and Pius XII respectively: John XXIII, Alloc. to the ecclesiastical students in Rome, AAS 52 (1960)–264; *The Pope Speaks,* 6 (1960)–364; *Prima Romana Synodus,* p. 437; Pius XII, Alloc. to the Society of Jesus assembled in General Congregation, 10 Sept., 1957, in AAS 49 (1957)–808; *The Pope Speaks,* 4 (1957–58)–449.

should take very special care that the life of evangelical perfection is kept before them and explained in its various phases that they may be attracted to the religious life and be strengthened in perseverance therein, not merely out of the desire of engaging in the apostolate, but particularly from a sincere determination to pursue evangelical perfection unwaveringly through the observance of the evangelical counsels and their own constitutions (can. 593) out of an intense love of God in imitation of Jesus Christ and a supernatural desire of sanctifying their souls, because, as Pius XII notes, "the priest is by his very office an instrument for the sanctification of others, so much so that the salvation of souls and the growth of the Kingdom of God depend in a considerable degree upon his holiness."[37]

## IV. DECLARATIONS AND INVESTIGATIONS REQUIRED BEFORE PROFESSION OR INCORPORATION, AND BEFORE ORDERS

38. *Attestation of one's own vocation to Sacred Orders in the religious life*

Since in the acceptance of religious or clerical obligations it is most important to safeguard and foster the liberty and spontaneous freedom of the candidates and to avoid completely the weakness which may be called the "follow-the-crowd" attitude, and since it is altogether proper that in serious decisions in matters affecting their own life they form the habit of thinking for themselves, the following directives shall henceforth be observed by all superiors of clerical Religious Communities, Societies and Secular Institutes.

Before temporary profession, which absolutely must precede promotion to tonsure and Minor Orders, novices are to present to their superiors a written declaration in which they attest explicitly to their vocation to the state of perfection and the clerical state, and at the same time declare their firm intention to bind themselves forever to the ranks of the clergy in the state

[37] Pius XII, Apost. Const. *Sedes Sapientiae,* n. 23; see above, p. 112; also his Allocution to Superiors General, 11 Feb., 1958, in AAS 50 (1958)-157; see above, p. 198. Cf. *Stat. Gen.,* art. 37; 40, § 2, 1°, 2°, 3.

of perfection.[38] This declaration can again be demanded of temporarily professed candidates before perpetual profession. These petitions and attestations are to be preserved in the archives. Lest the students sign approved printed formulas mechanically, they should write out these declarations in their own hand and, before they sign their name, should carefully consider, in consultation with their spiritual director, each and every one of the points contained therein.

39. *Above all, the fitness of the candidate is to be established clearly*

Superiors should not allow any one to be advanced to Orders, even only Minor Orders, without clear evidence, secured through careful examination, regarding his conduct, piety, modesty, chastity, inclinations for the clerical state, progress in ecclesiastical studies, and religious discipline.[39] To obtain this with greater certainty, superiors should get the opinion of the spiritual prefect, if he is directly responsible for the training of the students, and that of others who, because of their special association with the students, may be in a position to have a thorough knowledge of their life and conduct.[40] These opinions should not be accepted lightly but should be carefully weighed, with all due consideration of the prudence, sincerity, and maturity of judgment of those who have given them.

An authentic report of these investigations and of the outcome of these inquiries should be drawn up and kept in the archives.

Finally, the superiors, either personally or through some other experienced and prudent priest likely to win the confidence of the students, should question them carefully in order to acquire still greater certainty that they are aspiring to Orders in the religious state freely, deliberately, and for supernatural motives.

---

[38] Cf. can. 973, § 1; Sacred Congregation for Religious, Instruction *Quantum Religiones,* 1 Dec., 1931, in AAS 24 (1932)–79; *Ench. de Stat. Perf.,* n. 363, p. 447; Canon Law Digest, 1, pp. 479–480.

[39] Cf. can. 973, § 1 and can. 1357, § 2.

[40] Cf. *Stat. Gen.,* art 28, § 2, 3°, 9°, 10°, and the Instruction *Quantum Religiones,* n. 14, as quoted above in note 38.

40. *The best time for conferring Sacred Orders; Major Orders should not be conferred before perpetual or definitive profession*

As regards ordination itself, this Sacred Congregation adopts the timely directives formulated by the Sacred Congregation of the Sacraments in no. 14 of its *Circular Letter,* namely: For the more careful and immediate preparation of candidates for Orders, especially Sacred Orders, provision should be made that sacred ordinations be had at the time more fit for them, at a date well known ahead of time and never unexpectedly. As a result, it seems very appropriate to exclude the time immediately preceding or following the end of the scholastic year. At this time, as a rule, the students, tired by work and preoccupied in mind because of the examinations recently taken in sacred studies or because of those soon to be taken, lack the necessary peace of mind for being properly able to ponder the very serious business of their ordination.

As for the reception of Major Orders, superiors of the states of perfection should bear in mind that they may not promote their students to these orders before perpetual profession or incorporation (can. 964, 3°, 4°). In those states of perfection which do not have perpetual obligations or vows, superiors are likewise forbidden to promote their candidates to Sacred Orders before these vows or obligations have become definitive.[41]

41. *New inquiry before subdeaconate*

Before candidates are admitted to the subdeaconate, superiors must make a new inquiry on the above-mentioned points (n. 39). To this end, the records of the investigation already made and preserved in the archives are to be examined anew and further testimony on the conduct and spiritual qualities of the student is to be compared with previous reports in order to see clearly what progress these young men have made since their first profession both in religious discipline and in clerical studies. After all this, if the candidates are found worthy and fit, and if there is no canonical reason for withholding them from the reception of Orders, the superiors may issue dimissorial or testimonial letters

[41] Cf. *Stat. Gen.,* art. 8 § 1, 2°; Sacred Congregation for Religious, Instruction *Quantum Religiones,* n. 15, in AAS 24 (1932)–80; *Ench. de Stat. Perf.,* n. 363, p. 478; CANON LAW DIGEST, 1, p. 480.

for their ordination, with due observance of the prescriptions of canon law and their own constitutions.[42]

### 42. *Oath to be signed before the subdeaconate*

In all the states of perfection, before presenting candidates for the subdeaconate, superiors must, in view of the sacred ordination which is to follow in proper time and in addition to the inquiry prescribed above, demand an attestation written personally by the candidates and confirmed under oath before the superior in the following terms:

"I, the undersigned, ......., a member of the (Order, Congregation, Society, Institute of ......), in presenting this petition to Superiors for the reception of the Order of the Subdeaconate, after having carefully considered the matter before God, do hereby testify under oath: 1) that in the reception of the said Sacred Order I am moved by no coercion, compulsion, or fear, but am seeking it of my own accord, and do of my own full and free will desire to embrace it together with the obligations that are attached to it. 2) I acknowledge that I am fully informed of all the obligations that flow from the aforesaid Sacred Order, and I freely embrace them, and resolve with the help of God to keep them faithfully during my entire life. 3) I declare that I clearly understand all that the vow of chastity and the law of celibacy prescribe, and I firmly resolve with the help of God to observe these obligations faithfully until the end of my life. 4) Finally, I sincerely promise that I will always, according to the sacred canons, most respectfully obey in all things which are commanded me by my Superiors according to the discipline of the Church, and am prepared to give good example both in work and in word, so that in the reception of this great office I may be worthy to receive the reward which God has promised. To all this I testify and swear upon these sacred Gospels which I touch with my hand.

This ...... day of ......, 19...[43]

(Signed) ........................

[42] Sacred Congregation for Religious, Instruction *Quantum Religiones*, n. 16; CANON LAW DIGEST, 1, pp. 480–481.

[43] *Ibid.*, n. 17; CANON LAW DIGEST, 1, p. 481.

### 43. *Before deaconate or priesthood superiors should carefully inquire into the fitness of candidates*

Although for the Order of deaconate and priesthood it is not necessary to gather such detailed information and to require new testimonials, nevertheless, superiors should be watchful and determine whether, in the interval between the conferral of one sacred ordination and the next, any new factors may have emerged which might raise doubts on their vocation to the priesthood or show they have no vocation. In this case, after a most careful investigation and after seeking the advice of prudent men, superiors should strictly forbid the reception of any new Order and should refer the case to this Sacred Congregation, which, according to the requirements of individual cases, will decide what seems most opportune in the Lord.[44]

### 44. *In general, dispensations are not to be requested*

Superiors should bear in mind the prescription of the *Statuta Generalia,* art. 34, § 3, 2°, 3°, namely: "Only in individual cases and for causes which are proportionately really serious should superiors venture to ask for dispensations concerning: ....... 2° age and the other requirements for Orders, especially Sacred Orders; 3° the organized course of studies, either as regards the individual disciplines, attendance at class, or passing examinations." Superiors of religious orders who have the faculty of anticipating sacred ordinations beyond the limits laid down by common law should, in the use of this privilege, as long as it remains in force, follow the same restrictive criterion as that formulated in art. 34. In addition, as is proper in the use of other privileges, they should comply with the practice and rules customarily observed by the S. Congregation for Religious in granting similar indults to those subject to common law.

When there is question of age, superiors should lean more toward postponing rather than anticipating ordination.

### 45. *Superiors' obligation in conscience in issuing dimissorial or testimonial letters*

As regards the ordination of religious, in virtue of canon law major superiors either issue dimissorial letters to the ordaining

[44] *Ibid.,* n. 20; Canon Law Digest, 1, p. 482.

Bishops (can. 964, 2°, 3°; 966, § 1) or at least they present their candidates for ordination with testimonial letters (can. 993, 5°). By these testimonial letters the religious superior not only testifies that the candidates belong to his community but also certifies that they have completed the prescribed studies, have taken the oath, and have complied with the other requirements of law (can. 995, § 1). Hence it is clear that the very serious obligation which binds Bishops to train, test, and choose their secular candidates who wish to receive Sacred Orders, likewise extends to religious superiors to whom it pertains to permit their subjects to advance to Sacred Orders. And although, as canon law provides (can. 997, § 2), Bishops are free to disregard the declarations of superiors and to examine religious ordinands personally, nevertheless, they are not bound to do so but, before God and the Church, they may accept the testimony of superiors and throw back on them the full responsibility in conscience for the training and the worthiness of their candidates (can. 970; 995, § 2).

## V. THE CARE OF NEWLY ORDAINED PRIESTS

### 46. *Precautions to be taken in the first years of the priesthood; the dangers of inexperience*

After they have completed their course of studies and the pastoral year and have received Sacred Orders, young priests should start their ministry with all due precautions, aware of the very special dangers confronting them in the first years of their priesthood, during which, not infrequently, as Pius XII observed in his exhortation to the clergy, the great hopes entertained for young priests have apparently faded away.[45]

At the outset of their ministry, both because of the passions besetting their youth and because of their more frequent contacts with the world, many serious difficulties usually arise along with new kinds of temptations. And since new priests experience a certain sense of independence and feel that they must do their work in their own way in the ministry entrusted to them, they easily tend to shake off all restraint and, because of their in-

[45] Pius XII, Exhort. *Menti Nostrae,* AAS 42 (1950)–692. Cf. also the Instruction *Quantum Religiones,* n. 10; CANON LAW DIGEST, 1, p. 478.

experience, can fall into numerous errors and failings which may rightly be feared to lead to deplorable defections. This is why young priests sometimes think they must act on their own and introduce many reforms, disregarding the methods and systems of older priests. Lastly, they frequently are either left without any fruitful occupation or else are overloaded with self-assigned work or work which has been given to them by their superiors, not without danger to their spiritual life.

### 47. *The danger of the "heresy of action"*

On this spiritual danger Pope Pius XII, of venerable memory, has warned us in the following most serious words: "We cannot refrain from expressing Our concern and Our anxiety for those who, because of special circumstances of our day and age, have too frequently so engulfed themselves in a whirl of external activity as to neglect the first duty of priests, that is to say, procuring their own personal sanctification. We have already publicly stated (cf. A.A.S., 36 [1944] — 239, Letter *Cum proxime exeat*) that 'those men must be recalled to the right path who rashly hold that man can be saved by what is rightly and deservedly called the "heresy of action," that kind of action, We say, which is not based on the assistance of Divine Grace and does not make constant use of the necessary means for the pursuit of sanctity provided by Jesus Christ.' "[46]

### 48. *The danger of imitating worldly conduct*

It happens that the sacred ministry, which should be an instrument for personal sanctification, at times becomes for some people, through their own fault, an occasion for relaxation of discipline and harm to their religious spirit. Not rarely in the exercise of this ministry religious priests adopt the habits of people in the world in speech, conduct, and comportment; they violate poverty through uncontrolled use of material things; they lose esteem for regular discipline and the exercises of piety through prolonged absence from their religious house. Such priests quickly go seeking outside their religious house activities which provide stable and permanent work in order to have a pretext for withdrawing from religious discipline.

---

[46] Pius XII, Exhort. *Menti Nostrae,* AAS 42 (1950)–677.

### 49. *Young priests should be introduced into the ministry gradually under the direction of an experienced guide*

Superiors will forestall these difficulties if, in the first place, they effectively put into practice the excellent advice, based on experience, of the *Statuta Generalia,* art. 51, namely: that "the young priest should not be regarded as definitively formed and put to the test in his religious and apostolic life until, after the completion of about his thirtieth year and through personal contact with the ministry," he has rounded out his formation. In the meanime, according to the directives contained in the aforementioned exhortation of Pope Pius XII,[47] young priests should be introduced gradually into the apostolic ministry, safeguarded with wise and watchful care, and paternally directed in their activities. For this reason, contact with the world should not be either abrupt, frequent, or awkward; rather it should be moderate, humble, and gracious while the young priests devote themselves to study and prayer under the direction of a skilled spiritual director and, as far as possible, the guidance of some other experienced priest assigned to assist them. For "just as long periods of time are necessary for oak trees to put down solid roots, in the same way long-standing patience is always required for the formation of a man of God. Consequently, restraints should be placed on the generous self-assurance of youth whereby they would be plunged into activity before their time, since undue haste in activity scatters rather than builds, and is both for him who indulges in it and for the apostolic ministry itself a source of harm."[48]

### 50. *Young priests should not be assigned to small houses; interest in those who are absent*

As a general rule, young priests should not be assigned to small houses but should rather be assigned where religious discipline is easily reconciled with moderate exercise of the apostolate and where the prescriptions of the preceding article can be conveniently complied with.

In addition, superiors should see to it that the aforesaid priests

---

[47] *Ibid.,* p. 692.

[48] Pius XII, Alloc. *Quamvis Inquieti,* 17 Sept., 1946, in AAS 38 (1946)–383; *Ench. de Stat. Perf.,* n. 385, p. 574.

do not spend unduly long periods away from their religious house and, in every case, that they return to the community for the monthly day of recollection and for their retreat.

Finally, they shall exercise special vigilance over those who are absent from the religious house in what concerns their life, conduct, comportment, and the use and administration of temporal goods.[49]

51. *Vacations with relatives, at spas and other worldly centers*

Superiors should not allow religious priests to spend long periods with relatives or friends for vacation or rest since this practice causes surprise to people of the world and becomes a source of criticism among their fellow-religious. Nor for purposes of health should they be permitted to make frequent visits to the homes of relatives nor given easy access to spas and other public places, which are indeed places for convalescence but are likewise centers of unrestrained and worldly satisfactions, contrary to religious decorum and spirit. If there be question of sojourns at beaches or if religious must spend time outside their house at warm springs, "they should carefully conform to the prescriptions laid down by local Ordinaries."[50] For the rest, the directives enumerated by this Sacred Congregation for Religious for superiors general[51] on the frequentation of spas are confirmed and once again it is recommended that religious houses be located in healthful climates where those in need of rest and treatment may occupy themselves and at the same time live their religious life.

## THE READING OF THIS INSTRUCTION

52. It is of the greatest importance for the Church that the criteria and directives here set down should, first of all, be known and that they should be kept in mind and constantly put into

[49] Cf. the Instruction of the Sacred Congregation for Religious on religious military chaplains, in AAS 47 (1955)–93–97, and the decree on religious in military service, especially articles IV and V, 30 July, 1957, in AAS 49 (1957)–871–874. For these documents respectively see above, pp. 74–79; 38–41.

[50] Cf. *Prima Romana Synodus,* 87.

[51] Sacred Congregation for Religious, Circular Letter of 15 July, 1926; reported above on p. 317.

practice. It is no less important that there should be a uniform policy in all the states of perfection and, especially, that within the same institute there should be concerted action on the part of all those dedicated to the training of youth.

Wherefore, let superiors see to it that at the beginning of each school year, in place of the Instruction *Quantum Religiones,* this Instruction be read or at least summarized before the superiors, masters, spiritual prefects and their assistants, confessors, and professors, as well as in monastic, general, and provincial councils.

At the same time there should be read or made known to the young candidates the prescriptions which touch them directly, such as those referring to freedom and the conditions to be complied with in embracing the religious and clerical life, the sworn declaration mentioned in n. 42, and other similar provisions.

By the faithful observance of all these directives, the task of investigating the canonical fitness of candidates for the state of perfection and Sacred Orders will meet with success; those who are not fit will be barred in time and at the very outset, and only those worthy and fit will be admitted to Sacred Orders. These, in turn, properly instructed and trained, will effectively promote the glory of God and the salvation of souls to the honor of the Church and the state of evangelical perfection.

In the audience graciously granted on 23 January, 1961, to the undersigned Cardinal Prefect of the Sacred Congregation for Religious, our Holy Father, Pope John XXIII, deigned to approve this Instruction and ordered that it be communicated to superiors of institutes of evangelical perfection.

Rome, the 2nd day of February, feast of the Purification of the Blessed Virgin Mary, in the year 1961.

S.C. Rel., 2 Feb., 1961; translated from the original Latin text; references to English versions were, of course, entered by us.

NOTE: Although this Instruction was not published in AAS or any other public form but was privately circulated, it is nevertheless, referred to by the S. C. Rel. itself as "a matter of *public law*" (cf. below: S. C. Rel., 28 April, 1961).

**New Practice of S. C. Rel. Regarding Early Ordination to the Priesthood** (S. C. Rel., 28 April, 1961) **Private.**

The following communication was sent to all superiors general of religious institutes of men by the Cardinal Prefect of the S. C. for Religious.

In the Instruction "On the Careful Selection and Training of Candidates for the States of Perfection and Sacred Orders,"[1] recently made a matter of public law by this Sacred Congregation, it is indicated in no. 44 that, in general, dispensations should not be requested from the Holy See, sc., "as regards age and the other requirements for Orders, especially Sacred Orders; the organized course of studies, either as regards the individual disciplines, . . . When there is question of age, superiors should lean more toward postponing rather than anticipating ordination."

Relative to this very important matter, the following practice will be followed by the Sacred Congregation after the end of the year 1961, that is, beginning with the first day of January, 1962:

1° Only for truly serious reasons should superiors venture to request ordination to the Sacred Order of the Priesthood at the outset of the fourth year of the theology curriculum.

2° Ordination to the Sacred Order of the Priesthood at the end of the third year of the theology curriculum will no longer be granted unless the case is very exceptional and a most serious reason is had. However, Religious Communities, Societies, or Secular Institutes which already possess such a privilege, may not use it unless the candidate has completed the twenty-sixth year of his age and a true need is had on the part of the Church or the Religious Community, Society, or Secular Institute.

3° Economic difficulties will never be considered a valid reason.

Our Holy Father, Pope John XXIII, in the audience of 23 January, 1961, deigned to confirm and approve all the above.

**(Private)**; S. C. Rel., 28 April, 1961, Prot. N. S. R. 1398/59; translated from the original notice.

## CANON 976

**Dispensation for Early Ordination of Religious: Condition as Regards Continuance of Studies and Abstinence from Ministerial Works** (S. C. Rel., 27 Oct., 1923) **AAS 15–549.**

In granting dispensations from the course of studies which

[1] Reported above, pp. 464–498.

according to c. 976, § 2, must precede sacred orders, the Sacred Congregation of Religious has made it a practice to include in the rescripts the following conditions:

"They shall continue diligently to study sacred theology at least until the prescribed four years are completed, and are forbidden in the meantime any ministry of souls; that is, they should not be employed in preaching or hearing confessions or in exterior works of the institute; and these points remain a grave responsibility in conscience upon the Superiors."

Inasmuch, however, as such dispensations have already been obtained by any religious Order or Congregation, either in general for all its members or in particular for some of them, His Holiness, Pius XI, on 23 Oct., 1923, has declared and decreed: that all faculties or dispensations which have been obtained in this matter since the promulgation of the Code, in any way whatsoever, even immediately from the Supreme Pontiff either *viva voce* or by rescript signed by his own hand, are subject to the above conditions, and those conditions are to be understood in them, unless exception from them has been made expressly.

**AAS 15–549**; S. C. Rel., *Declaratio,* 27 Oct., 1923.
*Periodica,* 12 (1924)–155 (Vermeersch); *Amer. Eccles. Review,* 70 (1924)–68.

---

**Illegitimacy in Religious Candidates** destined for the priesthood: power of local Ordinary to dispense. See **c. 329**; AAS 56–5, *Motu proprio, Pastorale munus,* n. 36.

## CANON 1044

### Ordinary Can Be Reached Only by Telephone or Telegraph (Cod. Com., 12 Nov., 1922) AAS 14–662.

The Code Commission was asked:

Whether in the cases mentioned in cc. 1044 and 1045, § 3, it is to be considered that the Ordinary cannot be reached when recourse can be had to him neither by letter nor by telegraph nor by telephone; or also when it is impossible to reach him by letter, though he can be reached by telegraph or telephone.

**Reply.** In the negative to the first part; in the affirmative to the second; that is, for the effect mentioned in cc. 1044 and 1045, § 3, it is to be considered that the Ordinary cannot be reached, if recourse to him can be had only by telegraph or telephone.

**AAS 14–662**; Cod. Com., 12 Nov., 1922, V.
*Periodica,* 11 (1923)–185 (Vermeersch); *J.P.*, 2 (1922)–130.

## CANON 1065

### Atheistic Sect: Effect of Membership as Regards Ordination and Marriage (Cod. Com., 30 July, 1934) AAS 26–494.

The Code Commission was asked:

Whether according to the Code of Canon Law, persons who belong or have belonged to an atheistic sect are to be considered, as regards all legal effects, even those which concern sacred ordination and marriage, the same as persons who belong or have belonged to a non-Catholic sect.

**Reply.** In the affirmative.

**AAS 26–494**; Cod. Com., 30 July, 1934.
*Periodica,* 23 (1934)–145 (Vermeersch); *Jus Pontificium,* 14 (1934)–222; *Clergy Review,* 8 (1934)–491 (Bentley); *Amer. Eccles. Review,* 91 (1934)–498; *Irish Ecclesiastical Record,* 44 (1934)–637; *Apollinaris,* 8 (1935)–54 (Canestri).

## CANON 1116

### Child Begotten While Parents Were Under Impediment of Age or Disparity of Cult, Not Legitimated by Subsequent Marriage (Cod. Com., 6 Dec., 1930) AAS 23–25.

The Code Commission was asked:

Whether in virtue of c. 1116 the subsequent marriage of the parents has the effect of legitimating a child begotten by them while they were under the impediment of age or disparity of cult, which impediment, however, had ceased at the time of the marriage.

**Reply.** In the negative.

**AAS 23–25**; Cod. Com., 6 Dec., 1930.
*Periodica,* 20 (1931)–149 (Vermeersch).

## CANON 1147

**Faculty to Consecrate Chalices and Patens Denied** (S. C. Rit., 14 April, 1950) **Private.**

The Superior General of a certain Congregation of priests asked for himself and his successors the faculty to consecrate chalices and patens for the churches of his Institute, whenever the Bishop was absent, either because of a notable distance separating the place from the Episcopal See, or for some other reason.

**Reply.** *Non expedire.*

(**Private**); S. C. Rit., 14 April, 1950; Prot. N. C. 53/50. *Monitor Ecclesiasticus,* 77 (1952)–453.

---

**Consecration of Virgins:** Rite to be revised. See c. 2; AAS 56–97, Constitution on the Sacred Liturgy, n. 80; reported above on p. 21.

## CANON 1169

**Electrophonic Bells for Churches May Be Permitted by the Ordinary** (S. C. Rit., 3 Feb., 1951) **Private.**

In response to a question whether electrophonic bells may be used as a substitute for church bells of bronze, the Sacred Congregation of Rites replied:

**Reply:** It is left to the prudent judgment of the Ordinary.

(**Private**); S. C. Rit., 3 Feb., 1951 (Prot. N. — R. 29/51).

## CANON 1221

**Provisions of This Canon Do Not Apply to Postulants Nor to Students of Apostolic Schools in Religious Institutes** (Cod. Com., 20 July, 1929) **AAS 21–573.**

The Code Commission was asked:

Whether the prescription of c. 1221 extends also to postulants and to students of apostolic schools in religious institutes.

**Reply.** In the negative.

**AAS 21–573**; Cod. Com., 20 July, 1929, IV.
*Periodica,* 18 (1929)–254 (Cappello); *J.P.,* 9 (1929)–195; *Amer. Eccles. Review,* 81 (1929)–511.

## CANON 1230

**Funeral of Nonexempt Nuns Pertains to Chaplain, Not to Pastor** (Code Commission, 31 Jan., 1942) **AAS 34–50.**

The Code Commission was asked:

Whether, according to canon 1230, § 5, the pastor or the chaplain has the right to conduct the funeral services of nuns who are not exempt from the jurisdiction of the Ordinary according to canon 615.

**Reply:** In the negative to the first part, in the affirmative to the second.

**AAS 34–50**; Code Commission, 31 Jan., 1942. *Clergy Review,* 22 (1942)–285 (Mahoney); *Periodica,* 31 (1942)–196 (Bidagor).

## CANON 1234

**Diocesan Schedule of Funeral Taxes Binding Also on Exempt Religious** (Cod. Com., 6 Mar., 1927) **AAS 19–161.**

The Code Commission was asked:

Whether religious, even if exempt, are bound by the schedule of funeral taxes mentioned in c. 1234.

**Reply.** In the affirmative.

**AAS 19–161**; Code Com., 6 Mar., 1927, II.
*Periodica,* 16 (1927)–59 (Vermeersch); *J.P.,* 7 (1927)–6.

## CANON 1252

**Abstinence and Fast of Christmas Eve May Be Anticipated** (S. C. Conc., Decree, 3 Dec., 1959) **AAS 51–918.**

Acceding to the wishes of a number of Bishops from many countries, His Holiness Pope John XXIII, by the present Decree of the Sacred Congregation of the Council, deigned to grant to the faithful of the entire Catholic world the favor of hereafter anticipating the obligation of abstinence and fast from the twenty-fourth, the Vigil of the Nativity of Our Lord Jesus Christ, to the twenty-third of December.

Given at Rome, the 3rd of December, 1959.

**AAS 51–918**; S. C. Conc., Decree, 3 Dec., 1959. Annotations, *Commentarium pro Religiosis,* 39 (1960)–47 (Diez).

NOTE: Differences of opinion and confusion have arisen because of news reports concerning the anticipation of the Christmas Eve fast and abstinence; cf. *The Jurist,* 20 (1960)–228–229 (texts of notices) and pp. 220–226 (article by Dziadosz).

**Explanation of the Faculty to Anticipate the Fast and Abstinence on the Vigil of Christmas** (S. C. Conc., 3 Feb., 1962) **Private.**

Following is a letter from the U. S. Apostolic Delegate.

I recently asked the Holy See whether the faithful, in observance of the law of fast and abstinence on the Vigil of Christmas according to the Decree of the Sacred Congregation of the Council of 3 December, 1959,[1] may select this year the 23rd of December which falls on Sunday and if so, are they held to observe the obligation of fast and abstinence.

The Sacred Congregation of the Council has now replied under date of 3 February, 1962 (N. 69446/D), that in the above noted Decree the Holy Father has given to each of the faithful the faculty to select either the day of the Vigil or that preceding it, i.e., December 23rd. If the day chosen falls on Sunday the observance of the law ceases by reason of Canon 1252, § 4 of the Code of Canon Law which is not abrogated by the above Decree.

**(Private)**; S. C. Conc., 3 Feb., 1962, Prot. N. 69446/D, reported in letter of the U. S. Apost. Del., 16 Feb., 1962, Prot. N. 472/41, whose contents were kindly sent us.

## CANON 1253

**Fast Days of Religious Rule Not Affected by Code** (S. C. Rel., 22 March, 1921) **Private.**

The Sacred Congregation of Religious was asked:

[1] Reported above under this same canon.

Whether the law of fast contained in the Rule of the Friars Minor ceases on feast days of obligation outside of Lent.

**Reply.** In the negative.

(**Private**); S. C. Rel., 22 March, 1921. Cf. Sartori, *Enchiridion Canonicum,* p. 328.

## CANON 1261

**Visitation of Churches of Exempt Religious** (Code Commission, 8 Apr., 1924) **Private.**

The Commission of Interpretation was asked:

I. Whether the Ordinary of the place can make a visitation every five years of the churches of the Society of Jesus which are in his diocese; and if not:

II. Whether, in a case where diocesan (i.e., synodal) laws do not contain new matter as contemplated in canon 1261, but merely urge existing ecclesiastical laws, the Ordinary can make a visitation; and if not:

III. Whether the visitation mentioned in canon 1261, § 2, is to be made in the same manner as the usual quinquennial visitation of nonexempt churches; and if not:

IV. Whether the replies given before the new Code by the Sacred Congregation of Bishops and Regulars can be extended to the visitation mentioned in canon 1261, § 2; namely, that, generally speaking, the Ordinary may use his right of visitation only in as far as he has positive information that the particular laws enacted by him are not being observed in the churches of exempt Regulars.

**Reply.** The Eminent President of the Commission replied as follows: To I, II, and III, in the negative; to IV, in the affirmative.

Rome, 8 Apr., 1924.

(**Private**); Code Commission; replies by the President, Cardinal Gasparri, 8 Apr., 1924.

NOTE: These replies, though private, have been published for some years. Cf. Wernz-Vidal, *De Religiosis,* n. 146, note 92; Schäfer, *De Religiosis,* n. 97 b, p. 165.

# CANON 1264

**Pontifical Institute of Sacred Music: General Superiors of Religious Institutes Urged to Send Select Students** (S. C. Rel., Letter, 11 April, 1951) **Private.**

The following Letter of Father Larraona, Secretary of the Sacred Congregation of Religious, was sent to the Superiors General of Religious Institutes:

Prot. N. 2545/51

Everyone knows what great services Orders and Congregations of Religious rendered in past centuries to the cultivation of sacred music, as well as to that of the other departments of culture in the arts.

This is not to be wondered at, for from the time when monasteries throughout the Catholic world seemed to be almost the only beam of light in the darkness, until now, when Congregations of men and women founded in earlier times or in our own, as well as secular Institutes, by new forms of apostolate, are bringing to an evil world, or rather injecting into it, the divine ferment of the religious spirit and the religious life, religious, dedicated to the common good of the Church, have stood as effective witnesses to the value of truly sacred music for advancing divine worship and raising the minds of the faithful to God.

However, not all religious families have in this matter followed faithfully and constantly the example of their fathers; some have even, by a sort of levity, been gradually drawn to depart here and there from the right road and from their earlier traditions.

Hence this Sacred Congregation, as a watchful guardian also of this treasure, feels obliged to recall to Major Superiors the documents of the Holy See in this regard, among which are especially noteworthy the prescriptions of the Apostolic Constitution, *Divini cultus sanctitatem,* of the Supreme Pontiff Pius XI of happy memory, of 20 Dec., 1928.[1]

The Sacred Congregation, moreover, feels bound to mention to the General Superiors of religious the exhortation of the same Supreme Pontiff in this regard and to urge compliance with it; that is, that they should send to the Pontifical Institute of Sacred Music in Rome at least some select persons among

[1] AAS 21–33; summarily reported in CANON LAW DIGEST, 1, p. 598.

their subjects, endowed with a truly liturgical spirit and a talent for music, who, after finishing the usual course of training, can exercise an "apostolate of liturgy and music" among the members of their Institute.

There is no doubt that such action will, as far as may be necessary, give to religious Institutes of men and women a growing knowledge of and participation in the genuine spirit of the Church, and rid them of new and strange notions and practices.

May God grant, through the prayers of His Servant Pope Pius X, that all religious Institutes may so comply with the exhortations of the Holy See that sacred music will retain its place of due honor among them and be the resonant voice and herald of the fervent charity which they all have toward Almighty God.

From Rome, 11 April, 1951.

**(Private)**; S. C. Rel., Letter of Secretary, 11 April, 1951. Annotations, *Monitor Ecclesiasticus,* 76 (1951)–244 (Romita).

## Popular Hymns in the Vernacular During Low Mass
(S. C. Rit., 1 June, 1956) **Private.**

Replies of the S. C. of Rites to questions presented by the Cardinal Archbishop of Paris:

His Eminence Maurice Cardinal Feltin, Archbishop of Paris, presenting the petitions of the Professors of singing in the Gregorian Institute which is attached to the Catholic Institute of Paris, humbly submits to the S. C. of Rites the following questions regarding the interpretation of certain passages of the Encyclical *"Musicae sacrae disciplina."*[1]

**Questions:** 1. Whether the words of the Encyclical concerning the prohibition of the vernacular are to be understood of a solemn Mass in the wide sense, that is, of any kind of Mass which is sung by the Celebrant, with or without sacred Ministers.

2. Whether the words of the said Encyclical concerning the permission of the vernacular are to be understood as applying to any other Mass than one which is read by the celebrant without singing.

---

[1] AAS 48–5; English text, *The Catholic Mind,* 54 (1956)–222; *The Pope Speaks,* 3 (1956)–7.

**Replies:** The Sacred Congregation of Rites, after having heard the opinion of the Special Commission, decided to reply:

1. In the affirmative.
2. In the negative.

And the S. C. so replied and declared, 1 June, 1956.

**(Private)**; S. C. Rit., 1 June, 1956; reported in *Monitor Ecclesiasticus,* 81 (1956)–629, with annotations by Romita. These annotations as well as the Encyclical itself must be read in order to get the state of the question. There is no question here on substituting the vernacular for the Latin *in the liturgical text of any Mass,* whether sung or read.

**Sacred Music and the Liturgy** (S. C. Rit., Instruction, 3 Sept., 1958) **AAS 50–630.**

An Instruction of the Sacred Congregation of Rites entitled: "Concerning Sacred Music and the Sacred Liturgy in the Light of the Encyclicals of Pope Pius XII, *Musicae Sacrae Disciplina* and *Mediator Dei,*" is as follows:

Three very important documents on sacred Music have been issued by the Supreme Pontiffs in our time, namely: the *Motu proprio* of Saint Pius X, *Tra le sollecitudini,* 22 Nov., 1903; the Apostolic Constitution of Pius XI of happy memory, *Divini cultus,* 20 Dec., 1928; finally, the Encyclical of Pius XII, happily reigning, *Musicae sacrae disciplina,* 25 Dec., 1955. There have also been other lesser pontifical documents and some decrees of this Sacred Congregation of Rites, by which various matters concerning sacred Music have been regulated.

As everyone knows, the natural connection between sacred Music and the sacred Liturgy is so close that it is scarcely possible to issue laws or regulations concerning the one, without regard to the other. And actually, in the above mentioned pontifical documents and in the decrees of the Sacred Congregation of Rites, matters concerning sacred Music and the sacred Liturgy occur together.

Moreover, since the Supreme Pontiff Pius XII, before his Encyclical on Sacred Music, had issued that other most important one, *Mediator Dei,* of 20 Nov., 1947, on the Sacred Liturgy, in which liturgical doctrine and pastoral needs are admirably coordinated, it seems very appropriate to gather from those documents the principal points concerning the sacred Liturgy and sacred Music, and to present them more precisely in a special Instruction, so that the teachings of those documents may be more readily and securely put into practice.

It is to this end therefore that experts in sacred Music and the Pontifical Commission for the General Restoration of the Liturgy have worked together in the preparation of this Instruction.

The entire Instruction is arranged as follows:

Chapter I. *General Notions* (nn. 1–10).

Chapter II. *General Norms* (nn. 11–21).

Chapter III. *Particular Norms:*

1. Concerning the principal liturgical actions in which sacred Music is used.
   - *A*) The Mass.
     - *a*) Some general principles regarding the participation of the faithful (nn. 22–23).
     - *b*) The participation of the faithful in sung Masses (nn. 24–27).
     - *c*) The participation of the faithful in low Masses (nn. 28–34).
     - *d*) The conventual Mass, also called Mass in choir (nn. 35–37).
     - *e*) The attendance of priests at the Holy Sacrifice of the Mass, and so-called synchronized Masses (nn. 38–39).
   - *B*) The divine Office (nn. 40–46).
   - *C*) Eucharistic Benediction (n. 47).

2. Concerning certain kinds of sacred Music.
   - *A*) Sacred polyphony (nn. 48–49).
   - *B*) Modern sacred Music (n. 50).
   - *C*) Popular religious singing (nn. 51–53).
   - *D*) Religious music (nn. 54–55).

3. Books of liturgical song (nn. 56–59).

4. Musical instruments and bells.
   - *A*) Some general principles (n. 60).
   - *B*) The classic organ and similar instruments (nn. 61–67).
   - *C*) Sacred instrumental music (nn. 68–69).
   - *D*) Musical instruments and automatic devices (nn. 70–73).

*E*) The diffusion of sacred actions by radio and television (nn. 74–79).
*F*) Times during which the playing of musical instruments is forbidden (nn. 80–85).
*G*) Bells (nn. 86–92).

5. Persons who have the chief part in sacred Music and the sacred Liturgy (nn. 93–103).

6. The cultivation of sacred Music and of the sacred Liturgy.
*A*) The general training of clergy and people in sacred Music and the sacred Liturgy (nn. 104–112).
*B*) Public and private institutes for the cultivation of sacred Music (nn. 113–118).

Accordingly, after certain general notions have been stated (Chapter I), the general norms governing the use of sacred Music in the Liturgy are given (Chapter II); after this foundation is laid, the whole matter is explained in Chapter III. In each paragraph of this chapter, certain more important principles are first stated, and then the special norms which naturally derive from them.

## CHAPTER I. GENERAL NOTIONS

1. "The sacred Liturgy is the entire public worship of the mystical Body of Christ, that is, of its Head and of its members."[1] Consequently, "liturgical actions" are those sacred actions which, by institution of Jesus Christ or of the Church, and in their name, according to liturgical books approved by the Holy See, are performed by persons lawfully deputed to do so, in order to pay due worship to God and to the Saints and Blessed (cf. canon 1256); other sacred actions which are performed either in or out of the church, even in the presence or under the leadership of a priest, are called "pious exercises."

2. The Holy Sacrifice of the Mass is an act of public worship which is given to God in the name of Christ and the Church, in whatever place or manner it is celebrated. Hence the term "private Masses" is to be avoided.

---

[1] Encyclical, *Mediator Dei,* 20 Nov., 1947; AAS 39-528, 529.

3. There are two kinds of Masses: the Mass that is "sung" and the Mass that is "read." A Mass is "sung" if the priest celebrant actually sings those parts which according to the rubrics should be sung by him; otherwise the Mass is "read" (a low Mass).

A "sung" Mass, if it is celebrated with the assistance of sacred ministers, is called a *solemn* Mass; if without sacred ministers, it is called a *Missa cantata.*

4. The term "sacred Music" here includes:

*a*) Gregorian chant;
*b*) Sacred polyphony;
*c*) Modern sacred Music;
*d*) Sacred Music for the organ;
*e*) Popular religious singing;
*f*) Religious music.

5. The "Gregorian" chant which is to be used in liturgical actions is the sacred chant of the Roman Church which, piously and faithfully cultivated and arranged according to an ancient and venerable tradition, or in more recent times modulated after the manner of the early tradition, is presented for liturgical use in various books duly approved by the Holy See. Gregorian chant does not by its nature require that it be accompanied by the organ or other musical instrument.

6. By "sacred polyphony" is meant the measured chant developed from the Gregorian, employing several voices together without any accompanying musical instrument, which came into use in the Latin Church during the middle ages, had as its chief exponent in the latter half of the XVI century Peter Aloysius Prenestinus (Palestrina, 1525–1594), and is still cultivated today by masters skilled in the same art.

7. "Modern sacred music" is music consisting of several voices and not excluding musical instruments, which has been composed in more recent times in the course of the progress of the art of music. Since this music is directly intended for liturgical use, it should breathe a spirit of piety and religion, and it is on this condition that it is accepted in the service of the liturgy.

8. "Sacred Music for the organ" is music composed exclusively for the organ, which, from the time when the pipe organ became better adapted to harmony, has been greatly cultivated by distinguished masters and can contribute notably to the embellish-

ment of the sacred Liturgy, provided the laws of sacred Music are exactly observed.

9. "Popular religious singing" is singing which springs as it were by nature from the sense of religion with which the human creature is endowed by the Creator, and hence it is universal and flourishes among all peoples.

And since this singing is very well suited to imbue the private and social life of the faithful with the Christian spirit, it was very much cultivated in the Church from very early times,[2] and is warmly recommended also in our days, to foster the piety of the faithful and to embellish pious exercises; and it can even be admitted at times in liturgical actions themselves.[3]

10. "Religious music," finally, is that which, in the intention of the composer and by reason of the matter and purpose of the work itself, tends to express and to arouse pious and religious sentiments, and hence "is very helpful to religion."[4] However, since it is not adapted to religious worship and is of a rather free character, it is not admitted in liturgical actions.

## CHAPTER II. GENERAL NORMS

11. This Instruction applies to all rites of the Latin Church; hence what is said of *Gregorian* chant applies also to the distinctive liturgical chant, if any, of other Latin rites.

The term "sacred Music" in this Instruction means sometimes "singing *and* instrumental music," sometimes "instrumental music" alone, which will be easily understood from the context.

The term "churches" ordinarily includes all "sacred places," that is: a church in the strict sense, a public, semi-public and private oratory (cf. canons 1154, 1161, 1188), unless it is clear from the context that only churches in the strict sense are meant.

12. Liturgical actions must be performed according to liturgical books duly approved by the Apostolic See either for the universal Church or for some particular church or religious family (cf. canon 1257); pious exercises, on the other hand,

---

[2] Cf. *Eph.,* 5:18–20; *Col.,* 3:16.

[3] Cf. Encyclical on Sacred Music, 25 Dec., 1955; AAS 48–13, 14.

[4] Encyclical on Sacred Music; AAS 48–13.

are done according to the customs and traditions of localities or groups of persons, which have been approved by the competent ecclesiastical authority (cf. canon 1259).

Liturgical actions and pious exercises may not be mingled one with the other; but in a proper case pious exercises should either precede or follow liturgical actions.

13. *a*) The language of liturgical actions is Latin, unless in the above mentioned liturgical books, general or particular, some other language is explicitly admitted for certain liturgical actions; and allowing also for the exceptions hereinafter mentioned.

*b*) In liturgical actions which are celebrated with singing, no liturgical text translated literally into the vernacular may be sung,[5] unless this is allowed by particular concessions.

*c*) Particular exceptions granted by the Holy See to the general rule of using only Latin in liturgical actions, remain in effect; but, without authority from the Holy See they may not be broadly interpreted nor transferred to other countries.

*d*) In pious exercises, any language which is more suitable for the faithful may be used.

14. *a*) In *sung* Masses the Latin language alone is to be used, not only by the priest celebrant and the ministers, but also by the choir of the faithful. "However, where there is a centenary or immemorial custom to the effect that in the solemn Eucharistic Sacrifice (that is in a sung Mass), some popular hymns in the vernacular may be inserted after the sacred liturgical words which are sung in Latin, local Ordinaries can permit this, if they judge that in the local and personal circumstances the custom cannot prudently be suppressed (canon 5); without prejudice, however, to the law forbidding that the liturgical words themselves be sung in the vernacular."[6]

*b*) In *low* Masses the priest celebrant, his server and the faithful who participate with the celebrant in the liturgical action *directly*, that is, who recite in a clear voice those parts of the Mass which pertain to them (cf. n. 31), must use only the Latin language.

But if the faithful, in addition to this *direct* participation in

[5] *Motu proprio, Tra le sollecitudini,* 22 Nov., 1903; ASS 36–334; *Decr. auth.* S.R.C. 4121.

[6] Encyclical on Sacred Music; AAS 48–16, 17.

the liturgy, wish to add certain prayers or popular singing according to local custom, this may be done even in the vernacular.

*c*) Except as provided in n. 31, it is strictly forbidden that either all the faithful or some commentator recite aloud with the priest celebrant parts of the *Proprium,* the *Ordinary,* or the *Canon* of the Mass, either in Latin or literally translated.

It is desirable that on Sundays and feast days, in low Masses, the Gospel and also the Epistle be read by some *lector* in the vernacular for the benefit of the faithful.

Moreover a sacred silence is recommended from the *Consecration* to the *Pater Noster.*

15. In the sacred processions which are described in liturgical books, let that language be used which those books prescribe or permit; in other processions, which are performed after the manner of pious exercises, the language which is most convenient for the faithful participating may be used.

16. The *Gregorian chant* is the sacred chant proper to the Roman Church and holding the first place; hence it not only may be used in all liturgical actions but, other things being equal, it is to be preferred to other kinds of sacred Music.

Consequently:

*a*) The language of the Gregorian chant, as the liturgical chant, is exclusively Latin.

*b*) Those parts of liturgical actions which according to the rubrics are to be sung by the priest celebrant and his ministers, must be sung only according to the Gregorian notation as arranged in typical editions, excluding accompaniment by any instrument.

The choir and the people, when in virtue of the rubrics they respond to the singing of the priest and ministers, must likewise use only the same Gregorian notation.

*c*) Finally, where it is permitted by particular indults that in sung Masses the priest celebrant, the deacon and subdeacon, or the *lector,* after the texts of the Epistle or Lesson, and of the Gospel, have been sung in Gregorian chant, may pronounce the same texts also in the vernacular, this must be done by reading them in a loud and clear voice, without any Gregorian chant, authentic or simulated (cf. n. 96 *e*).

17. *Sacred polyphony* may be used, in all liturgical actions,

on the sole condition that there be a choir capable of executing it artistically. This kind of sacred Music is especially appropriate in liturgical actions which are to be celebrated with solemnity and splendor.

18. *Modern sacred Music* may likewise be admitted in all liturgical actions if it is truly worthy of the dignity, gravity and sanctity of the Liturgy and if there is a choir which can execute it in a truly artistic fashion.

19. *Popular religious singing* may be freely used in pious exercises; but in liturgical actions, what has been prescribed above in nn. 13–15 must be strictly observed.

20. *Religious music* is to be entirely excluded from all liturgical actions; it may be used in pious exercises; as regards concerts in sacred places, let the norms given below in nn. 54 and 55 be observed.

21. Everything which according to liturgical books is to be sung by the priest and his ministers, or by the choir or the people, belongs wholly to the sacred Liturgy. Therefore:

*a*) It is strictly forbidden to change in any way the order of the text which is to be sung, to change or omit words, or to repeat them unbecomingly. Also in music which is composed in the style of sacred polyphony and modern sacred Music, all the words of the text must be clearly and distinctly recognized.

*b*) Similarly, in any liturgical action it is explicitly forbidden to omit entirely or in part any liturgical text which is to be sung, unless the rubrics provide for such omission.

*c*) If for some reasonable cause, for example because of an insufficient number of singers or because they are not perfectly trained, or also sometimes because of the length of the rite or of the song, some liturgical text or other which pertains to the choir cannot be sung as it is written in the liturgical books, it is permitted only to sing those texts in their entirety either *recto tono* or after the manner of psalms, with organ accompaniment if desired.

# CHAPTER III. SPECIAL NORMS

## 1. The Principal Liturgical Actions in Which Sacred Music Is Used

### *A*) The Mass

#### a) *Some General Principles regarding the Participation of the Faithful*

22. The Mass by its very nature requires that all who are present participate in it in the manner proper to them.

*a*) This participation should in the first place be *interior*, that is, consisting in pious attention of the mind and affections of the heart, through which the faithful "are intimately united to the Supreme High Priest . . . and offer (the Sacrifice) together with Him and by Him, and with Him dedicate themselves"[7]

*b*) The participation of those present becomes fuller if to the interior attention is added *exterior* participation, namely, that which is manifested by exterior acts such as the position of the body (kneeling, standing, sitting), ritualistic gestures, and especially by responses, prayers, and singing.

Of this participation the Supreme Pontiff Pius XII in the Encyclical *Mediator Dei* on the Sacred Liturgy, has these words of general commendation:

"They are to be commended who strive to make the Liturgy even externally a sacred action in which all who are present may share. This can be done in more ways than one; when for instance the whole congregation in accordance with the rules of the sacred rites either answer the priest in an orderly and fitting manner, or sing hymns suited to the different parts of the Mass, or do both, or finally in high Masses when they answer the prayers of the minister of Jesus Christ and sing together the liturgical chant."[8]

It is to this harmonious participation that pontifical documents refer when they speak of "active participation,"[9] of which the foremost example is that of the priest celebrant and his

---

[7] Encyclical *Mediator Dei,* 20 Nov., 1947; AAS 39–552.

[8] ASS 39–560.

[9] AAS 39–530 to 537.

ministers, who assist at the altar with proper interior piety and the exact observance of the rubrics and ceremonies.

*c*) Perfect active participation is reached when there is also *sacramental* participation, that namely by which "the faithful who are present communicate not only by spiritual affections but also by the sacramental reception of the Eucharist, through which they receive more abundantly the fruit of this most holy Sacrifice."[10]

*d*) But as the conscious and active participation of the faithful can be obtained only through their adequate instruction, it is good to recall that wise regulation made by the Council of Trent, which prescribes: "The sacred Synod enjoins upon pastors and all who have the care of souls, that frequently in the celebration of Mass (that is in the homily after the Gospel or when catechetical instruction is given to the people), either personally or through others, they explain some part of the text of the Mass and among other things say something about the mystery of this most holy Sacrifice, especially on Sundays and feast days."[11]

23. The various ways in which the faithful may actively participate in the most holy Sacrifice of the Mass should be controlled in such a way that all danger of abuse be removed and the chief purpose of such participation be attained, that is, more perfect worship of God and the edification of the faithful.

### b) *The Participation of the Faithful in Sung Masses*

24. The more excellent form of the Eucharistic celebration is the *solemn Mass,* in which the combined solemnity of ceremonies, ministers, and sacred Music expresses the magnificence of the divine mysteries and invites those present to pious contemplation upon them. Hence an effort should be made to the end that the faithful may have a proper appreciation of this form of celebration, taking an appropriate part in it as hereinafter explained.

---

[10] *Conc. Trid.*, Sess. 22, cap. 6. Cf. also the Encyclical *Mediator Dei;* AAS 39–565: "It is very fitting, as the Liturgy for that matter provides, that the people receive Holy Communion after the priest has partaken of the divine Repast at the altar."

[11] *Conc. Trid.*, Sess. 22, cap. 8; Encyclical on Sacred Music; AAS 48–17.

25. In the solemn Mass, the active participation of the faithful may be had in three degrees:

*a*) The first degree obtains when all the faithful sing the *liturgical responses: Amen, Et cum spiritu tuo; Gloria tibi, Domine; Habemus ad Dominum; Dignum et iustum est; Sed libera nos a malo; Deo gratias.* Every effort should be made that all the faithful, everywhere on earth, be capable of singing these liturgical responses.

*b*) The second degree is had when all the faithful sing also the parts from the *Ordinary* of the Mass, namely: *Kyrie eleison; Gloria in excelsis Deo; Credo; Sanctus-Benedictus; Agnus Dei.* Certainly measures should be taken to assure that the faithful be able to sing these parts of the Ordinary of the Mass, at least according to the simpler Gregorian notations. If they cannot sing all of them, there is no objection to selecting the easier ones, for example the *Kyrie eleison,* the *Sanctus-Benedictus,* the *Agnus Dei,* to be sung by all, whereas the *Gloria in excelsis* and the *Credo* are sung by the *"schola cantorum."*

Moreover, care should be taken that everywhere the following easy Gregorian melodies be learned by the faithful: *Kyrie eleison, Sanctus-Benedictus* and *Agnus Dei,* according to numbers I or III. In this way can be achieved the very desirable result that everywhere in the world the common faith which the Catholic people manifest by active participation in the most holy Sacrifice of the Mass may be shown also by their joyful singing together.[12]

*c*) Finally, the third degree is attained if all those present are so well trained in the Gregorian chant that they can sing also the parts from the *Proprium* of the Mass. This full participation in sacred song is to be urged especially in religious communities and in seminaries.

26. Much is to be made also of the *Missa cantata,* which, though it has no sacred ministers and lacks the full magnificence of ceremonies, is nevertheless embellished with singing and sacred Music.

It is desirable that on Sundays and feast days the parochial or principal Mass be sung.

All that was said in the preceding number about the partici-

---

[12] Encyclical on Sacred Music; AAS 48–16.

pation of the faithful in the solemn Mass, is quite applicable also to the *Missa cantata*.

27. In sung Masses the following points are moreover to be noted:

*a*) If the priest with the ministers enters the church *per viam longiorem,* it is quite permissible that, after the *antiphon at the Introit with its versicle* has been sung, several other verses of the same psalm be sung also; in which case the antiphon may be repeated after each verse or after every two verses, and when the celebrant arrives at the altar, the psalm is interrupted if need be, the *Gloria Patri* is sung, and the antiphon repeated at the end.

*b*) After the *antiphon at the Offertory,* it is allowed to sing the old Gregorian tones of those verses which used to be sung after the antiphon.

But if the antiphon at the Offertory is taken from some psalm, it is allowed to sing other verses from the same psalm; in which case, after each verse or after every two verses of the psalm, the antiphon may be repeated, and when the Offertory is finished the psalm closes with the *Gloria Patri,* and the antiphon is repeated. If the antiphon is not taken from a psalm, some other psalm suitable to the solemnity may be chosen. It is allowed, however, after the antiphon at the Offertory is finished, to sing some Latin hymn, which must be appropriate to this part of the Mass and must not be continued beyond the *Secret*.

*c*) The *antiphon at the Communion* should normally be sung while the priest celebrant is receiving the Most Blessed Sacrament. But if Communion is to be given to the people, the singing of this antiphon should begin while the priest is distributing Holy Communion. If this antiphon at the Communion is taken from a psalm, other verses from the same psalm may be sung; in which case, after every verse or every two verses, the antiphon may be repeated, and after the Communion is finished the psalm closes with the *Gloria Patri* and the antiphon is repeated. If the antiphon is not from a psalm, a psalm suitable to the solemnity and to the liturgical action may be selected.

When the antiphon at the Communion is finished, particularly if the Communion of the faithful lasts a considerable time, it is allowed to sing also another Latin hymn which is suitable to the sacred action.

Moreover the faithful who are to receive Holy Communion may recite *Domine, non sum dignus* three times together with the priest celebrant.

*d*) The *Sanctus* and *Benedictus,* if they are sung in Gregorian chant, are to be sung continuously; otherwise, the *Benedictus* is placed after the Consecration.

*e*) During the Consecration all singing must cease and, where such is the custom, also the playing of the organ and of any musical instrument.

*f*) After the Consecration, unless the *Benedictus* is still to be sung, a sacred silence is recommended until the *Pater Noster.*

*g*) While the priest celebrant is giving the blessing to the faithful at the end of the Mass, the organ should be silent; and the priest celebrant should pronounce the words of the blessing so that they can be understood by all the faithful.

### c) *The Participation of the Faithful in Low Masses*

28. Diligent care must be taken that even at low Mass the faithful be not "like strangers or mute spectators,"[13] but that they contribute the participation which is demanded by so great a mystery and which is abundantly fruitful.

29. The first way in which the faithful can take part in the low Mass is when each individual *by his own activity* takes part either interiorly, by paying attention to the principal parts of the Mass, or exteriorly, according to the approved customs of various localities.

They are especially to be commended in this regard who have a small missal suited to their capacity and say the prayers with the priest in the very same words of the Church. But since all are not equally capable of understanding correctly the rites and liturgical formulas, and since spiritual needs are not the same in all persons nor permanently unchanging in any one, there is another better and easier way for these people to take part, namely "by piously meditating on the mysteries of Jesus Christ, or performing other pious exercises and saying other prayers, which, though of a different form than the sacred rites, are still essentially in harmony with them."[14]

---

[13] Apostolic Constitution *Divini Cultus,* 20 Dec., 1928; AAS 21–40.

[14] Encyclical *Mediator Dei;* AAS 39–560, 561.

It must also be observed that if it is customary anywhere to play the organ during low Mass, without any participation of the faithful either by saying prayers in common or by singing, the practice of playing the organ, harmonium, or other instrument almost *without intermission*, is to be disapproved. These instruments therefore should be silent:

*a*) From the arrival of the priest celebrant at the altar to the *Offertory;*

*b*) From the first versicles before the Preface to the *Sanctus* inclusive;

*c*) From the Consecration to the *Pater Noster,* in places where that is the custom;

*d*) From the Lord's Prayer to the *Agnus Dei* inclusive; at the *Confiteor* before the Communion of the faithful; while the *Postcommunion* is being said and while the blessing is being given at the end of Mass.

30. The second way of participation is when the faithful take part in the Eucharistic Sacrifice by reciting prayers and singing hymns *in common.* The prayers and the singing should be perfectly appropriate to the respective parts of the Mass; observing also however, the provisions of n. 14 *c.*

31. Finally, the third and most complete method is for the faithful to respond liturgically to the priest celebrating, as it were holding a "dialog" with him, and *pronouncing in a clear voice the parts that pertain to them.*

In this fuller participation, four degrees may be distinguished:

*a*) The first degree, if the faithful give in response to the celebrant the easier liturgical responses, namely: *Amen; Et cum spiritu tuo; Deo gratias; Gloria tibi, Domine; Laus tibi, Christe; Habemus ad Dominum; Dignum et iustum est; Sed libera nos a malo;*

*b*) The second degree, if the faithful pronounce also the parts which according to the rubrics are to be said *by the server;* and, if Communion is given during the Mass, say also the *Confiteor* and three times *Domine, non sum dignus;*

*c*) The third degree, if the faithful recite with the celebrant also the parts from the *Ordinary of the Mass;* that is: *Gloria in excelsis Deo; Credo; Sanctus-Benedictus; Agnus Dei.*

*d*) Finally the fourth degree, if the faithful pronounce together with the celebrant also the parts which belong to the

*Proprium of the Mass: Introit; Gradual; Offertory; Communion.* This final degree can be practiced in a worthy and becoming manner only by select groups of people of some education and who have been well trained.

32. In low Masses the entire *Pater Noster,* since it is an appropriate and ancient prayer for Communion, may be recited by the faithful together with the priest celebrant, but only in Latin, and all saying *Amen;* no recitation of it in the vernacular is allowed.

33. In low Masses popular religious hymns may be sung by the people, on condition, however, that they be entirely in accord with the corresponding parts of the Mass (cf. n. 14 *b*).

34. The priest celebrant, particularly if the church is large and there are many people, should pronounce whatever the rubrics prescribe to be said in a clear voice, loudly enough so that all the faithful may suitably and conveniently follow the sacred action.

### d) *The Conventual Mass, also Called Mass "in Choir"*

35. Among the liturgical actions which are of special dignity is very properly included the "conventual" Mass, or Mass "in choir," namely the Mass which is to be celebrated every day in connection with the divine Office by those who are bound by ecclesiastical law to choir duty.

For the Mass together with the divine Office is the sum total of Christian worship, the fulness of the praise which is daily offered to Almighty God with external and public solemnity.

But as this full public collective offering of divine worship cannot be made every day in all churches, it is performed as it were *vicariously* by those who are designated for this duty by the law "of choir"; this is particularly true of cathedral churches representing the entire diocese.

Usually, therefore, all celebrations "in choir" should be performed with special elegance and solemnity, that is, with the embellishments of singing and sacred Music.

36. The conventual Mass therefore should *per se* be a solemn one, or at least a *Missa cantata.*

Where by particular law or special indult there exists a dispensation from the solemnity of the Mass "in choir," at least the recitation of the canonical Hours during the conventual Mass should be entirely avoided. On the contrary it is better in such case that the conventual Mass be celebrated as a low Mass in the manner proposed in n. 31, excluding however all use of the vernacular.

37. In regard to the conventual Mass the following also should be observed:

*a*) Each day there should be only one conventual Mass, which should correspond to the Office recited in choir, unless the rubrics provide otherwise (*Additiones et Variationes in Rubricis Missalis*, tit. I, n. 4). However, the obligation to celebrate other Masses in choir by reason of pious foundations or other legitimate cause, remains unaffected.

*b*) The conventual Mass follows the regulations for a sung or a low Mass.

*c*) The conventual Mass is to be said after Terce, unless the one in charge of the community decides for a grave reason that it is to be said after Sext or None.

*d*) Conventual Masses "outside of choir," which hitherto were sometimes prescribed by the rubrics, are suppressed.

### e) *The Attendance of Priests at the Holy Sacrifice of the Mass and So-called "Synchronized" Masses*

38. If it be remembered in the first place that sacramental concelebration in the Latin Church is limited to the cases defined by law; and if moreover the Reply of the Holy Office of 23 May, 1957,[15] be kept in mind, declaring invalid the concelebration of the Sacrifice of the Mass on the part of priests who, though clothed in sacred vestments, and whatever be their intention, do not pronounce the words of consecration, it is not forbidden that when a number of priests are gathered together on the occasion of Congresses, "one only performs the sacrifice, and others (all or many) are present at this one Mass and receive the Holy Eucharist during it from the hands of the celebrant," provided "this is done for a just and reasonable cause and the Bishop has not provided otherwise to prevent wonder on the part of the faithful," and provided the basis for acting in this way be not the error mentioned by the Supreme Pontiff Pius XII, namely that the celebration of one Mass at which a hundred priests assist

[15] AAS 49–370; CANON LAW DIGEST, 4, p. 256.

is the same as a hundred Masses celebrated by a hundred priests.[16]

39. So-called "synchronized Masses" are forbidden; that is, Masses celebrated in such a way that two or more priests at one or more altars celebrate Mass so simultaneously that all the actions are performed and all the words are pronounced at the same time, using also, especially if a great number of priests are celebrating in this way, certain modern instruments by which this absolute uniformity or "synchronization" may be more easily obtained.

### *B*) The Divine Office

40. The divine Office is performed either "in choir," or "in common," or individually (*"a solo"*).

It is said to be done "in choir," if the divine Office is performed by a community which is bound to choir duty by ecclesiastical law; "in common," if done by a community which is not so bound.

In whatever way it is done, whether "in choir," "in common," or *"a solo,"* if it is done by persons who are deputed by ecclesiastical law to do it, the divine Office is always to be considered an act of *public* worship paid to God in the name of the Church.

41. The divine Office is essentially so composed as to be performed by mutually alternate voices; some parts even, *per se* require to be sung.

42. In view of these postulates, the performance of the divine Office "in choir" is to be retained and encouraged; its performance "in common," and also the singing of at least certain parts of it, according to the convenience of various localities, times, and persons, is warmly recommended.

43. The recitation of the psalms "in choir" or "in common," whether it is done in Gregorian chant or without singing, should be dignified and well executed, keeping the right tone, observing the pauses and producing the words in perfect unison.

44. If the psalms which occur in a canonical Hour are to be

---

[16] Cf. the Allocutions of Pius XII to the Cardinals and Bishops, 2 Nov., 1954 (AAS 46–669, 670; Canon Law Digest, 4, p. 142); and to the International Congress on Pastoral Liturgy at Assisi, 22 Sept., 1956 (AAS 48–716, 717).

sung, they should be sung in Gregorian chant, at least in part; that is, either alternate psalms or alternate verses of the same psalm.

45. The ancient and venerable practice of singing Vespers on Sundays and feast days together with the people according to the rubrics is to be retained wherever it is in effect; where it is not, it should if possible be introduced, at least a few times during the year.

Local Ordinaries should also make an effort to prevent the singing of Vespers on Sundays and feast days from falling into desuetude on account of evening Mass. For evening Masses, which the local Ordinary can permit "if the spiritual good of a notable part of the faithful require it,"[17] should not be a detriment to the liturgical actions and pious exercises by which the Catholic people have been accustomed to sanctify feast days.

Consequently the practice of singing Vespers or celebrating other pious exercises with the Eucharistic Benediction is to be retained wherever it is in effect, even if evening Mass is celebrated.

46. In seminaries of clerics, secular or religious, at least some part of the divine Office should often be performed in common, and as far as possible with singing; and on Sundays and feast days Vespers at least should be sung (cf. c. 1367, 3°).

### *C*) Eucharistic Benediction

47. Eucharistic Benediction is a true liturgical action; hence it should be performed as described in the *Roman Ritual,* tit. X, cap. V, n. 5.

If another way of giving the Eucharistic Benediction is practiced in some locality in virtue of an immemorial tradition, it may be retained with the permission of the Ordinary; but it is recommended that the Roman way of giving the Eucharistic Benediction be prudently encouraged.

---

[17] Apostolic Constitution *Christus Dominus,* 6 Jan., 1953; AAS 45–15 to 24; Instruction of the Holy Office of the same date; AAS 45–47 to 51; *Motu proprio, Sacram Communionem,* 19 March, 1957; AAS 49–177, 178. All these documents are reported in full in Canon Law Digest, 4, pp. 269–282; 286–288. *Sacram Communionem* is also reported above in this volume, pp. 450–452.

## 2. Concerning Certain Kinds of Sacred Music

### *A*) Sacred Polyphony

48. Compositions of sacred polyphony, whether ancient or modern, should not be introduced in liturgical actions unless it is previously established with certainty that they are so written or adapted as to be really in accord with the norms given on this subject in the Encyclical *Musicae sacrae disciplina.*[18]

49. Ancient specimens of this art which may be still preserved in the archives should be carefully searched out, appropriate measures should be taken if necessary for their conservation, and competent experts should be engaged to prepare editions of them, either critical or for use in the liturgy.

### *B*) Modern Sacred Music

50. Works of modern sacred Music should not be used in liturgical actions unless they conform to liturgical laws and to those of the art of sacred Music itself, according to the Encyclical *Musicae sacrae disciplina.*[19] The decision in this matter rests with the diocesan Commission on Sacred Music.

### *C*) Popular Religious Singing

51. Popular religious singing is to be highly recommended and earnestly promoted; for by it Christian life is imbued with the religious spirit and the minds of the faithful are raised to higher things.

This popular religious singing has its proper place in all Christian public or family celebrations, and even in the activities of daily life; it attains a more excellent role in all pious exercises, whether performed in the church or outside it; and sometimes it is even admitted in liturgical actions according to the norms given above in nn. 13–15.

52. But in order that popular religious hymns may attain their purpose, "they must be in full accord with the doctrine of the Catholic faith; they must express and explain that doctrine correctly; they must use plain language and simple melody; they

[18] AAS 48–18 to 20.

[19] AAS 48–18 to 20.

must be free from pompous expressions and vain excess of words; and, even though short and easy, they should manifest a religious dignity and seriousness."[20] The observance of these prescriptions should be the object of particular care on the part of local Ordinaries.

53. It is therefore recommended to all who may have an interest in this matter, to make an appropriate collection of popular religious hymns which have been either written or handed down traditionally by ear, including the older ones, and to have them published, with the approval of the local Ordinaries, for the use of the faithful.

### *D*) Religious Music

54. That music also is to be highly esteemed and appropriately cultivated which, though by its nature inadmissible in liturgical actions, is yet well suited to arouse religious sentiments in the hearers and to foster religion itself, and hence is rightly called *religious* music.

55. The proper places for producing religious music are concert halls or auditoriums for shows and conventions, but not churches, which are dedicated to divine worship.

In places where there is no musical auditorium or other suitable hall, and yet it seems that a concert of religious music might be of spiritual benefit to the faithful, the local Ordinary can permit such a concert to be held in a church, observing however the following conditions:

*a*) For arranging any such concert, the written consent of the Ordinary is required;

*b*) To obtain this permission a petition should be made in writing, in which are stated: the time of the concert, the character of the pieces, the names of the *maestri* (organist and choir master) and of the musicians;

*c*) The local Ordinary should not grant the permission unless, after hearing the opinion of the diocesan Commission on Sacred Music and taking counsel of any others who may be competent in this field, he is quite sure that the pieces on the program are not only truly artistic but also of a sincerely pious Christian character, and moreover that the persons who are to take part

[20] Encyclical on Sacred Music; AAS 48–20.

in the program have the qualities mentioned in nn. 97 and 98;

*d*) At the proper time the Blessed Sacrament must be removed from the church and deposited in some chapel, or even, with due reverence, in the sacristy; if this cannot be done, the audience must be informed that the Most Blessed Sacrament is present in the church, and the Rector of the church must carefully see to it that there be no irreverence toward It;

*e*) If tickets are bought at the door or programs distributed, all this must be done outside the body of the church;

*f*) The behavior and dress of the musicians, the singers, and the audience, must bespeak the gravity which is due to the holiness of the sacred place;

*g*) As far as the circumstances permit, it is desirable that the concert close with some pious exercise, or better still with Eucharistic Benediction, so that the spiritual uplift which the concert aims to produce may be crowned as it were by a sacred action.

### 3. Books of Liturgical Song

56. Books of liturgical singing for the Roman Church hitherto issued in a typical edition are:

*Graduale Romanum, cum Ordinario Missae;*

*Antiphonale Romanum,* for the *Horae diurnae;*

*Officium Defunctorum, Maioris Hebdomadae* and *Nativitatis D. N. Iesu Christi.*

57. The Holy See reserves to itself all rights of ownership and use of all Gregorian hymns which are contained in liturgical books of the Roman Church approved by the Holy See.

58. The Decree of the Sacred Congregation of Rites, of 11 August, 1905, "Instruction regarding the publication and approval of books containing liturgical Gregorian chant,"[21] and also the later "Declaration regarding the publication and approval of books containing liturgical Gregorian chant," of 14 February, 1906,[22] and another Decree of 24 February, 1911 on certain particular questions regarding the approval of books of chant for the *Propria* of any diocese or religious family,[23] remain in effect.

The regulations issued by the Sacred Congregation of Rites

---

[21] *Decr. auth.,* 4166. [22] *Decr. auth.,* 4178. [23] *Decr. auth.,* 4260

on 10 August, 1946, "on permission to publish liturgical books"[24] apply also to books of liturgical chant.

59. Consequently, the *authentic* Gregorian chant is that which is given in "typical" Vatican editions, or is approved by the S.C. of Rites for some particular church or religious family, and which therefore must be reproduced exactly in all respects, that is both song and text, by publishers who have the required permission.

The so-called *"rhythmic"* notations introduced into Gregorian chant by private authority are permitted, provided the value and arrangement of the notes as found in Vatican books of liturgical chant are preserved.

## 4. Musical Instruments and Bells

### *A*) Some General Principles

60. As regards the use of musical instruments in the sacred Liturgy, the following principles are to be kept in mind:

*a*) In view of the nature, holiness, and dignity of the sacred Liturgy, the use of whatsoever musical instrument should *per se* be as perfect as possible. Hence it will be better to omit altogether the playing of instruments (the organ alone or other instruments) than to have it done in an unworthy manner; and in general it is better to do something well, though it be of limited scope, than to attempt greater projects for which adequate means are not at hand.

*b*) Also the difference between *sacred* and *profane* music must be taken into consideration. For there are some musical instruments, the classic organ for example, which by their nature and origin are directly destined for sacred music, and others which are easily adapted to use in the liturgy, for example those of strings and bow; on the other hand certain instruments are by common consent so specially suited to profane music that they can nowise be adapted to sacred use.

*c*) Finally, only such musical instruments as are played by personal manipulation can be admitted in the Liturgy, not those which are mechanical or automatic.

---

[24] AAS 38–371; Canon Law Digest, 3, p. 571.

### B) The Classic Organ and Similar Instruments

61. The principal and solemn liturgical musical instrument of the Latin Church has been and remains today the classic or pipe organ.

62. An organ destined for liturgical use, even though it be small, must be artistically constructed, and equipped with the tones which are suited to sacred use; before being put into service it ought to be duly blessed; and it is to be guarded with all diligence as a sacred object.

63. Besides the classic organ, the use of the instrument called a "harmonium" is also admitted, on condition of course that in quality of tone and volume of sound it is suitable for sacred use.

64. The similar instrument called the "electrophonic" organ may be tolerated for a time in liturgical actions when there are not sufficient funds to buy even a small pipe organ. But in each case there should be an explicit permission from the local Ordinary. And he should first consult the diocesan Commission on Sacred Music or other well informed persons, who should try to make all appropriate recommendations to render the instrument as suitable as possible for sacred use.

65. Those who play the instruments mentioned in nn. 61–64 must be sufficiently skilled in their art either to accompany the sacred singing or the concert of other instruments, or to play the organ beautifully alone; moreover, since it is often necessary in liturgical actions to extemporize by playing music which is appropriate to the various parts of the action, they should have knowledge and experience in the principles governing the organ and sacred music in general.

These players should take the greatest care of the instruments entrusted to them. When they take their place at the organ for sacred functions, they should be conscious of the active part they are taking to promote the glory of God and the edification of the faithful.

66. The playing of the organ either in liturgical actions or in pious exercises should be carefully adapted to the quality of the season or day in the liturgy, to the character of the rites or exercises themselves and to their various parts.

67. Unless there is a custom of long standing or some special reason approved by the local Ordinary to the contrary, the organ

should be placed near the main altar in a convenient position, but always so that the singers and musicians on the platform or in the gallery cannot be seen by the people who are in the body of the church.

### C) Sacred Instrumental Music

68. In liturgical actions, especially on the more solemn days, besides the organ, other musical instruments also — especially those that are played by passing a small bow over the strings — may be used, either together with the organ or without it, by way of an instrumental concert or to accompany singing, with strict attention, however, to the following regulations which flow from the principles mentioned above (n. 60):

*a*) The instruments must be of a kind which can really be adapted to sacred use;

*b*) The playing of these instruments must be done in such a way and with such gravity, and as it were with such chastened religious spirit, as to avoid all suggestions of profane music and to foster the piety of the faithful;

*c*) The director, the organist, and the players must be well trained in the use of the instruments and in the laws of sacred Music.

69. Local Ordinaries, especially through the services of the diocesan Commission on Sacred Music, should carefully watch that these prescriptions regarding the use of instruments in the sacred Liturgy be really observed; and if necessary they should issue special regulations on the matter in accordance with local conditions and approved customs.

### D) Musical Instruments and "Automatic" Devices

70. Musical instruments which according to common consent and usage are suited only to profane music, are to be entirely excluded from all liturgical actions and pious exercises.

71. The use of "automatic" instruments and machines, such as the automatic organ, the gramophone, radiophone, dictaphone, or magnetophone, and others of the same sort, is absolutely forbidden in liturgical actions and pious exercises, whether they are held in or out of the church, even though there is question only of transmitting sacred words or sacred music, or of taking the place of

the choir and the faithful, or even merely of accompanying them in the singing.

However, it is allowed to use these instruments, even in the church but outside of liturgical actions and pious exercises, in order to hear the voice of the Supreme Pontiff or of the local Ordinary or of other sacred speakers; or to instruct the faithful in Christian doctrine or in sacred or popular religious singing; finally, in processions outside the church, to direct or sustain the singing.

72. Instruments known as "amplifiers" may be used even in liturgical actions and pious exercises to amplify the living voice of the priest celebrant or of the "commentator" or of others who according to the rubrics or by order of the Rector of the church may speak.

73. The use of machines to project pictures, especially those classified as "cinema," either "silent" or "with sound," is most strictly forbidden in the church, for any reason whatever, even a pious, religious, or charitable one.

Moreover, in building or adapting halls for meetings or shows near the church or, when no other location is available, under the church, care must be taken that there be no direct access from these halls to the church itself, and that the noise from them in no way disturb the holiness and silence of the sacred place.

### *E*) The Diffusion of Sacred Actions by Radio and Television

74. In order to transmit by radio or television liturgical actions or pious exercises, which take place inside or outside a church, express permission of the local Ordinary is required; and he should not give it without being assured in advance:

*a*) That the singing and sacred Music are perfectly in accord with the laws of the Liturgy and of sacred Music;

*b*) That moreover, in the case of television, all who are to take part in the sacred function are so well prepared that the performance will be fully conformed to the rubrics and will come off with perfect dignity.

The local Ordinary can give this permission habitually for transmissions which are made regularly from the same church, if he knows that all the requirements will be carefully observed.

75. Instruments for sending television should not be brought into the sanctuary if it is possible to avoid it; and they should never be placed so near the altar as to interfere with the sacred rites.

Moreover the operators of these instruments must conduct themselves with the gravity which befits the place and the sacred rite, so as not to disturb the pious attention of those present, especially at those moments when most profound devotion is called for.

76. The provisions of the above article are to be observed also by photographers the more so in view of the facility with which they can move about with their cameras.

77. All rectors of churches must see to it that the prescriptions of nn. 75 and 76 be faithfully observed; and local Ordinaries should not fail to issue more specific regulations if the circumstances so require.

78. Since radio transmission of its nature demands that the hearers be able to follow it without interruption, when the Mass is being transmitted by radio it is better that the priest celebrant, especially if there is no "commentator," pronounce the words which according to the rubrics should be said *"submissa voce,"* in a voice slightly louder (*"voce tantisper elevata"*); and so also that he pronounce those which should be said *"clara voce"* more loudly (*"altius"*), so that those listening may be able easily to follow the whole Mass.

79. Finally, before the transmission of holy Mass by radio or television, it is well to inform those who are listening or looking on, that this is not sufficient to satisfy the precept of hearing Mass.

### *F*) The Times During Which the Playing of Musical Instruments Is Forbidden

80. Since the sound of the organ, and still more of other instruments, is an *ornament* of the sacred Liturgy, their use is to be regulated according to the degree of joy which characterizes the various liturgical days or seasons.

81. Hence in all liturgical actions, with the sole exception of Eucharistic Benediction, the playing of the organ or of other instruments is forbidden:

*a*) During Advent, that is from the first Vespers of the first Sunday of Advent to None of the vigil of the Nativity of Our Lord;

*b*) During Lent and Passiontide, that is from Matins of Ash Wednesday to the *Gloria in excelsis Deo* in the solemn Mass of the paschal Vigil;

*c*) On the Ember Days of September, if the Office and Mass of the day are celebrated;

*d*) In all Offices and Masses of the dead.

82. The playing of other instruments than the organ is moreover forbidden on the Sundays of Septuagesima, Sexagesima, and Quinquagesima, and on the ferias following these Sundays.

83. However, for the days and seasons above mentioned, the following exceptions are allowed:

*a*) The playing *of the organ and of other instruments* is permitted on feasts of obligation and holidays (except Sundays), and on the feast of the principal patron of the place, on the titular feast of the church or the anniversary of its dedication, on the titular feast of the religious family or the feast of its founder; or on the occasion of some extraordinary solemnity.

*b*) The playing *of only the organ or the harmonium* is permitted on the third Sunday of Advent and the fourth Sunday of Lent; in the Mass of the chrism on Holy Thursday, and from the beginning of the solemn evening Mass *in Cena Domini* until the end of the hymn *Gloria in Excelsis Deo.*

*c*) Likewise the playing *of only the organ or the harmonium* is permitted at Mass and Vespers, only to accompany the singing.

Local Ordinaries can further determine these prohibitions and permissions according to approved local and regional customs.

84. During the entire sacred Triduum, that is from midnight before Holy Thursday to the hymn *Gloria in excelsis Deo* in the solemn Mass of the paschal Vigil, the organ and harmonium must be absolutely mute, and must not be used even to accompany the singing, save for the exceptions provided for above in n. 83 *b*.

The playing of the organ and harmonium is forbidden during this Triduum, without any exception and notwithstanding any contrary custom, also in pious exercises.

85. Rectors of churches or other persons whose duty it may be should properly explain to the faithful the reason for this liturgical silence, and should take care that on the same days or in

the same seasons the other liturgical prescriptions as to not adorning the altars be also observed.

### *G*) Bells

86. The ancient and fully approved practice regarding the use of bells in the Latin Church should be religiously observed by all concerned.

87. Bells should not be used for churches unless they have previously been solemnly consecrated or at least blessed; and from that moment they should be duly cared for as sacred objects.

88. Approved customs and different ways of ringing bells according to the different purposes for which they are rung are to be carefully retained, and local Ordinaries should not fail to make a summary of the norms that have been given or established by usage in this matter, or, if these are lacking, to prescribe them.

89. Innovations which tend to give the bells a fuller tone or to make it easier to ring them, may be allowed by local Ordinaries after hearing the opinion of competent persons; in case of doubt the matter should be submitted to the Sacred Congregation of Rites.

90. Besides the various customary and approved ways of ringing sacred bells mentioned above in n. 88, there are in some places special apparatuses consisting of a number of bells which are hung in the belfry itself and produce various melodies or chimes. This playing of bells, which is commonly called a "carillon" (in German, "Glockenspiel") is entirely excluded from liturgical use. The bells destined for this purpose can neither be consecrated nor blessed according to the solemn rite of the Roman Pontifical, but may receive only a simple blessing.

91. Every effort should be made that all churches and public and semipublic oratories be provided with at least one or two bells, even though they be small ones; it is strictly forbidden to use instead of sacred bells any machine or instrument to imitate or amplify the sound of bells mechanically or automatically; it is allowed, however, to use machines or instruments of this sort after the manner of a "carillon," as above provided.

92. For the rest let the prescriptions of canons 1169, 1185, and 612 be exactly observed.

## 5. Persons Who Have the Principal Parts in Sacred Music and the Sacred Liturgy

93. The *priest celebrant* is in charge of the entire liturgical action. All the others take part in the liturgical action in their own way. Hence:

*a*) *Clerics* who are engaged in the liturgical action in the way and according to the form determined by the rubrics, that is as clerics, whether they act as sacred ministers or as minor attendants, or even if they have a part in the choir or the *"schola cantorum," exercise a true and direct ministerial service,* and that by virtue of their ordination or reception into the clerical state.

*b*) *Lay persons supply an active liturgical participation,* and this in virtue of their baptismal character, whereby even in the most holy Sacrifice of the Mass, they offer the divine Victim to God the Father in their own way with the priest.[25]

*c*) Lay persons of the male sex, whether they be boys, youths, or grown men, when they are deputed by competent ecclesiastical authority to serve at the altar or to execute sacred Music, if they perform that function in the way and according to the form prescribed by the rubrics, exercise a *direct but delegated ministerial service,* on condition, however, in the case of singing, that they form part of the "choir" or *"schola cantorum."*

94. The priest celebrant and the sacred ministers, besides exactly observing the rubrics, should try to perform the parts assigned to them in the singing as correctly, distinctly, and beautifully as they can.

95. Whenever there is a choice of persons for the celebration of a liturgical action, it is well to give the preference to those who are known to be quite good at singing, especially in the more solemn liturgical actions and those in which the singing is rather difficult or those which are transmitted by radio or television.

96. The active participation of the faithful, especially in holy Mass and certain more complicated liturgical actions, can be better obtained by having a "commentator" who, at the proper moment and in few words, interprets the rites themselves or the prayers and readings of the priest celebrant or of the sacred ministers, and directs the external participation of the faithful,

---

[25] Cf. the Encyclicals *Mystici Corporis Christi,* 29 June, 1943; AAS 35–232, 233; and *Mediator Dei,* 20 Nov., 1947; AAS 39–555, 556.

that is, their responses, prayers, and singing. Such a commentator may be admitted, observing the following norms:

*a*) It is fitting that the commentator be a priest or at least a cleric; if these are not available, the task may be given to a layman of good Christian character who has been well prepared for it. Women may never serve as commentators; the most that can be allowed is that in case of necessity a woman may in some way lead the singing or the prayers of the faithful.

*b*) If the commentator is a priest or a cleric, he should wear a surplice and be in the sanctuary or at the railing, or in the ambo or the pulpit; if he is a layman, he should be in front of the faithful in a suitable place but not in the sanctuary nor in the pulpit.

*c*) The explanations and directions to be given by the commentator should be prepared in writing, few, faultless in sobriety, delivered at the proper time and in a moderate voice; never overlapping with the prayers of the priest celebrant; such as to help and not impede the devotion of the faithful.

*d*) In directing the prayers of the faithful the commentator should be mindful of the prescriptions given above in n. 14, *c*.

*e*) In places where the Holy See has given permission for the Epistle and Gospel to be read in the vernacular after the singing of the Latin text, the commentator cannot take the place of the celebrant, the deacon, the subdeacon or the *lector* (cf. n. 16, *c*.).

*f*) The commentator shall take account of the priest celebrant and accompany the sacred action in such a way that it need not be retarded or interrupted, so that the entire liturgical action be well balanced, worthy, and devout.

97. All those who have any part in the sacred Music, such as the composers, the organists, choir-masters, singers, and even the players, since they take part directly or indirectly in the sacred Liturgy, should be outstanding among the faithful by the example of their Christian conduct.

98. Besides this excellence in Christian faith and morals, they should also, according to their condition and liturgical participation, be more or less instructed in the sacred Liturgy and sacred Music. In particular:

*a*) The *authors or composers of sacred Music* should have a fairly complete knowledge of the sacred Liturgy itself, in its historical, dogmatic or doctrinal, and practical or rubrical aspects;

they should also know the Latin language; finally, they should be thoroughly trained in the art of both sacred and profane Music, and in the history of music.

*b*) Also the *organists and choir-masters* should have a rather wide acquaintance with the sacred Liturgy and a sufficient knowledge of Latin; finally, they should be so well trained in their own art as to perform their work in a worthy and competent manner.

*c*) The *singers* too, whether they be boys or adults, should be given in proportion to their capacity enough instruction on the liturgical actions and on the texts which they are to sing, so that they may sing with the understanding and religious sentiment which their service reasonably demands. They should also be taught to pronounce the Latin words correctly and distinctly. Rectors of churches and others who may be in charge must carefully see to it that good order and genuine devotion be kept in that part of the church where the singers are stationed.

*d*) Finally, the *players* who are to produce the music must not only be expert in the artistic use of their instruments but must also know how to adapt them to sacred Music, and have enough knowledge of liturgical matters to flavor the exterior practice of their art with a becoming degree of piety and devotion.

99. It is very desirable that cathedral churches and also at least parochial and other important churches should have their own musical "choir" or "*schola cantorum,*" capable of rendering true ministerial service according to article 93, *a* and *c*.

100. In places where a musical choir of this sort cannot be had, it is allowed to make up a choir of the faithful, either "mixed" or consisting only of women and girls. Such a choir however, should keep its own place, outside the sanctuary or outside the railing; the men should be apart from the women or girls, and all unbecoming circumstances should be carefully avoided. And local Ordinaries should not fail to issue precise regulations on this matter, which rectors of churches shall be bound to observe.[26]

101. It is desirable and recommended that the organists, choir-masters, singers, musicians, and others in the service of the church, give their services gratis for the love of God and from pious and

[26] Cf. *Decr. auth.*, 3964, 4210, 4231, and the Encyclical on Sacred Music: AAS 48–23.

religious motives. If they are unable to do so, Christian justice as well as charity requires that ecclesiastical superiors pay them a just salary according to the approved practice of various localities, observing also the provisions of civil law.

102. It would be well also that local Ordinaries, after hearing the advice of the Commission on Sacred Music, issue a schedule fixing the salaries to be paid throughout the whole diocese to the various persons mentioned in the last article.

103. Finally, all the measures which concern so-called "social welfare" for these same persons should be carefully attended to, observing the provisions of civil law if there are such, if not, following the regulations to be made by the Ordinaries.

## 6. The Promotion of Sacred Music and the Sacred Liturgy

### *A*) The General Training of Clergy and People in Sacred Music and the Sacred Liturgy

104. Sacred Music is intimately connected with the Liturgy; sacred singing is an integral part of the Liturgy itself (n. 21); finally, popular religious singing is very widely used in pious exercises and sometimes even in liturgical actions (n. 19). Hence it is easily seen that training in sacred Music and in the sacred Liturgy cannot be separated; both belong to Christian life in a degree which varies according to the various states and orders of the clergy and faithful.

Everyone therefore should have some training in the sacred Liturgy and sacred Music, corresponding to his status.

105. The natural and original school of Christian education is the *Christian family* itself, in which children are gradually led to know and practice the Christian faith. Hence children, according to their age and mental development, should be taught to take part in pious exercises and even in liturgical actions, especially the sacrifice of the Mass, and should begin to know and to like popular religious singing, both at home and in the church (cf. nn. 9 and 51–53 above).

106. In *primary and elementary schools*, the following should be observed;

*a*) If the schools are conducted by Catholics and can follow their own order, the children should learn popular and sacred singing rather well in the school itself, and especially should be taught more fully according to their capacity, about the holy Sacrifice of the Mass and how to take part in it, and should begin to sing the more simple Gregorian hymns.

*b*) In the case of public schools which are governed by the civil law, local Ordinaries should try to issue suitable regulations to provide for the necessary training of the children in the sacred Liturgy and sacred singing.

107. What has been said of primary or elementary schools is still more to be urged in *intermediate or secondary schools,* where the boys and girls should attain the maturity required for the right conduct of social and religious life.

108. The liturgical and musical education hitherto described should be continued with greater thoroughness in the *higher institutions of letters and science* which go by the name of "universities." For it is of the highest importance that those who have finished their higher studies and entered upon the serious duties of social life, should have received also a fuller education in all aspects of Christian living. Hence all priests to whom the care of university students is in any way entrusted should strive to bring them practically as well as theoretically to a deeper knowledge of and a fuller sharing in the sacred Liturgy and, as far as circumstances permit, should use for these students also the form of Holy Mass which was mentioned in nn. 26 and 31.

109. If some knowledge of the sacred Liturgy and sacred Music is required of all the faithful, *young men aspiring to the priesthood* should have a full and solid training in the entire sacred Liturgy and in sacred singing. Hence all the provisions of Canon Law in this matter (canons 1364, 1°, 3° and 1365, § 2) and whatever more specific regulations have been made by competent authority (cf. especially the Apostolic Constitution *Divini cultus* on the ever greater advancement of the Liturgy, Gregorian chant and sacred Music, 20 Dec., 1928),[27] must be exactly observed, and this is an obligation in conscience for the persons concerned.

110. Also religious of both sexes, as well as members of secular

[27] AAS 31–33 to 41.

Institutes, from their probation and noviceship, should receive a progressive and solid training both in the sacred Liturgy and in sacred singing.

Moreover in religious communities of both sexes and in colleges dependent on them, care should be taken to provide capable teachers to teach, direct, and accompany sacred singing.

Superiors of religious men and women should see to it that in their communities not only select groups but all the members of the community receive sufficient practice in sacred singing.

111. There are certain *churches* which *by their very nature* require that the sacred Liturgy together with sacred Music be presented in them with special elegance and splendor; that is, the larger parish churches, collegiate, cathedral, abbatial or religious churches, and the more important sanctuaries. Persons connected with such churches, whether they be clerics, servers, or musicians, should work with all diligence and earnestness to make themselves fit and ready to do sacred singing and perform liturgical actions with distinction.

112. Finally, special care should be taken to introduce and develop the sacred Liturgy and sacred singing in *foreign Missions*.

First of all, the difference should be recognized between peoples with a high civilization going back perhaps a thousand years, and others who are not yet touched by higher culture.

With this as a basis, certain general rules are to be kept in mind, namely:

*a*) Priests who are sent to the foreign Missions should have a suitable training in the sacred Liturgy and sacred singing.

*b*) In the case of populations which have made some advance in cultivating their own music, the missionaries should try to bring the native music also into sacred use; they should try especially to arrange pious exercises in such a way that the native faithful may express their religious sentiments in their own language and with melodies suited to their own people. And it should not be forgotten that, as experience proves, even Gregorian hymns can sometimes be easily sung by natives, as they often bear some resemblance to the native songs.

*c*) In the case of people of lower culture, what has been said above in *b* will have to be modified and adapted to their capacity and character. Where their family and social life is deeply imbued with the religious sense, the missionaries should be very careful, far from stifling that religious spirit, rather to purge it of superstitions and make it Christian, especially through pious exercises.

### *B*) On the Promotion of Public and Private Institutes of Sacred Music

113. Pastors and rectors of churches should carefully see to it that for liturgical actions and pious exercises, "servers" be available, boys, youths or grown men, who are pious, well trained in the ceremonies and sufficiently practiced in sacred and popular religious singing.

114. Closely linked with sacred and popular singing is the institute known as the "Boy Choristers," which has several times been commended by the Holy See.[28]

It is desirable and an effort should be made that all churches have their own choir of boy singers, well trained in the sacred Liturgy and especially in the art of singing with skill and devotion.

115. It is recommended that in every diocese there be an institute or school for singing and organ music, in which organists, choir-masters, singers, and even musicians may be properly trained.

Sometimes it will be better that such an institute be established by several dioceses through their united resources. And pastors and rectors of churches should attract select young men to these schools and give appropriate encouragement to their studies.

116. Very highly esteemed, finally, should be those higher institutes or academies which are expressly designed for the more complete cultivation of sacred Music. The first among these is the Pontifical Institute of Sacred Music established in Rome by Saint Pius X.

Local Ordinaries should interest themselves in sending some priests who have special talent and inclination for this art to these institutes, especially to the Roman Pontifical Institute of Sacred Music.

117. Besides the institutes for teaching sacred Music, several societies have been founded which, under the name of Saint Gregory, Saint Cecilia, or other saints, have for their purpose to

---

28 Apostolic Constitution *Divini cultus;* AAS 21–28; Encyclical on Sacred Music: AAS 48–23.

cultivate sacred Music in various ways. Sacred Music will profit greatly from the multiplication of such societies and from their association on a national or even an international scale.

118. From the time of Saint Pius X, there should be in every diocese a Commission on Sacred Music.[29] Its members, priests or laymen, are appointed by the local Ordinary, who should choose men of learning and experience in the various kinds of sacred Music.

There is no objection to the establishment of a common Commission by several local Ordinaries together.

And since sacred Music is intimately associated with the Liturgy, and this latter with sacred Art, *Commissions* on *Sacred Art*[30] and on the *Sacred Liturgy*[31] should also be established in every diocese. It is not forbidden and may even at times be advisable that these three Commissions meet, not separately but together, and try to deal with and settle their affairs with the aid of mutual counsel.

Local Ordinaries should see that these Commissions meet rather frequently as occasion may require; and it is desirable that sometimes the Ordinaries preside at the meetings in person.

———

His Holiness Pius XII, when this Instruction on sacred Music and the sacred Liturgy was submitted to him by the undersigned Cardinal Prefect of the Sacred Congregation of Rites, deigned to give it his special approbation in all and each of its provisions and to confirm it by his authority; and he ordered that it be promulgated and attentively observed by all concerned.

All things to the contrary notwithstanding.

Rome, from the office of the Sacred Congregation of Rites, the feast of Saint Pius X, 3 September, 1958.

**AAS 50–630;** S. C. Rit., Instruction, 3 Sept., 1958. Annotations, *Periodica,* 47 (1958)–420 to 480 (Schmidt); *Monitor Ecclesiasticus,* 83 (1958)–637 (Romita).

---

[29] *Motu proprio, Tra le sollectitudini,* 22 Nov., 1903; ASS 36, n. 24; *Decre. auth.* S.R.C. 4121.

[30] Circular Letter of the Secretariate of State, 1 Sept., 1924, Prot. N. 34215.

[31] Encyclical *Mediator Dei,* 20 Nov., 1947; AAS 39–561, 562.

## Doubts Concerning the Interpretation of the Instruction on Sacred Music and the Liturgy (S. C. Rit., 10 July, 1959) Private.

Following are some doubts proposed by the Bishop of Segni concerning the interpretation of the instruction on sacred music and the liturgy.[1]

1) Notwithstanding n. 76 of this instruction, can the local Ordinary simply prohibit the taking of photographs in churches either during or outside of liturgical actions or pious exercises.

2) In view of n. 100 of the same instruction, can it be permitted that a mixed choir or one consisting only of women or girls sing the sacred music in the usual section (in common parlance, the traditional choir loft) at the back of the church or at the side of the sanctuary.

3) According to the mind of n. 18 of the instruction is it allowed that the whole of the sacred music in liturgical actions be sung by only one male singer or by only one woman.

4) Finally, during the singing of one and the same sacred musical composition by a mixed choir or by a homogeneous choir either of men only or of women, can it be permitted that a male or female soloist sing only part of it.

The Sacred Congregation of Rites, after having listened to the opinion of a special Liturgical Commission, replied:

To I. *In the affirmative.*

To II: *In the affirmative,* but in its proper place outside the sanctuary, that is, behind a grill.

To III: *In the negative.*

To IV: *In the affirmative* as regards the male soloist; *in the negative* as regards the female soloist.

(**Private**); S. C. Rit., 10 July, 1959; reported in *Ephemerides Liturgicae,* 74 (1960), 457.

---

**In Religious Novitiates and Houses of Study:** Teaching and practice of sacred music. See **c. 2**; AAS 56–97, Constitution on the Sacred Liturgy, n. 115; reported above, p. 22. **N.B.:** In the same Constitution, the entire Chapter VI (nn. 112–121) should be considered in connection with the Instruction on Sacred Music reported above under this same canon.

[1] Reported immediately before this document.

## CANON 1267

**Interpretation of Words "Only in the Church or the Principal Oratory"** (Cod. Com., 3 June, 1918) **AAS 10–346.**

The Code Commission was asked:

1. Is c. 1267, which provides that in a house of religion or piety the Blessed Sacrament may be kept only in the church or principal oratory, to be understood as forbidding that it be kept anywhere except in a public church for the convenience of the faithful, even in the principal oratory in which the members come together for religious exercises in common?

2. If not, is the same true if the church ordinarily remains closed and is not accessible to the faithful?

3. Is the same true if there are several oratories in the same house of piety, destined for several classes of members (two or three, for example, novices, lay-brothers, students, priests), so that each class can have its separate oratory with the Blessed Sacrament; or is the privilege to be limited to the church or oratory which is for the whole community?

**Reply.** The meaning of c. 1267 is this: if a house of religion or piety is connected with a public church and makes use of it for its ordinary daily exercises of piety, the Blessed Sacrament may be kept there only; otherwise it may be kept in the principal oratory of the said house of religion or piety (without prejudice to the right of the church, if any), and nowhere else, unless in the same material building there are distinct and separate families, so that formally they constitute distinct houses of religion or piety.

**AAS 10–346**; Cod. Com., 3 June, 1918.
*Periodica,* 9 (1921)–151 (Vermeersch); *J.P.,* 2 (1922)–54.

## CANON 1269

**Instruction on the Careful Custody of the Most Blessed Eucharist** (Sacred Congregation of the Sacraments, Feast of the Ascension, 26 May, 1938) **AAS 30–198.**

1. At no time has the Holy See failed to supply the Ordinaries of places with support and safeguards to the end that the Most Blessed Eucharist which either by common law or by indult is

reserved in our churches should be diligently guarded and safe from all profanation. The rules of canonical discipline, which as time went on strove to provide for the situation, are in their present form contained in canon 1269 of the Code of Canon Law, which provides as follows:

§ 1. *The Most Blessed Sacrament must be kept in an immovable tabernacle set in the middle of the altar.*

§ 2. *The tabernacle must be well built, solidly closed on all sides, properly appointed according to liturgical laws, must contain nothing else, and must be so carefully guarded that all danger of sacrilegious profanation be prevented.*

§ 3. *For some grave cause approved by the Ordinary, it is allowed to keep the Most Blessed Sacrament during the night outside the altar, but on a corporal, in a safe and becoming place, observing the prescription of canon 1271.*

§ 4. *The key of the tabernacle in which the Most Blessed Sacrament is kept must be most carefully guarded, and this is a grave obligation in conscience on the priest who has charge of the church or oratory.*

2. This Sacred Congregation, which has charge of the discipline of the seven sacraments (canon 249), and which has already issued an Instruction, on 26 May, 1929, *de quibusdam vitandis atque observandis in conficiendo Sacrificio Missae et Sanctissimae Eucharistiae Sacramento distribuendo et asservando,*[1] has deemed it opportune to call the attention of all persons, on whom rests the grave duty of caring for the Most Blessed Eucharist, to the canonical provisions on that subject, adding some brief explanations, and to decree certain safeguards and measures, in accord with present circumstances, so that the Most Blessed Eucharist may be most carefully guarded and preserved from all profanation.

3. The attainment of this noble purpose will be distinctly promoted by the faithful observance of the precepts of certain canons of the Code of Canon Law. Let it be observed to begin with that two conditions are prescribed *sub gravi* in order that the Most Blessed Eucharist may be reserved in a church: 1° *there must be someone to take care of It;* 2° *as a rule a priest must celebrate Mass in the sacred place at least once a week*

[1] See Canon Law Digest, 1, p. 353; AAS 21–631. The date is 26 *Mar.*, 1929.

(canon 1265, § 1). Although, owing to the scarcity of priests, the Holy See sometimes permits that Mass be said only every two weeks, for the renewal of the sacred species, always in the absence of actual danger of their corruption, yet it never dispenses but rather insistently urges the rule that there must always be a person charged with the custody of the Most Blessed Sacrament day and night (cf. reply of the Sacred Congregation of Rites, 17 Feb., 1881, n. 3527).

Moreover, in canon 1269 cited above, three things are to be observed: (*a*) The Most Blessed Eucharist must be kept in a tabernacle which is immovable (§ 1) and solidly closed on all sides (§ 2); (*b*) the tabernacle must be so carefully guarded that all danger of sacrilegious profanation be prevented (§ 2); (*c*) the key of the tabernacle must be most carefully guarded by a priest (§ 4). On each of these points some observations are to be made.

4. *a*) *The tabernacle must be immovable and solidly closed on all sides:* from this precept, which *per se* is grave, neither can the Bishop dispense nor can custom though centenary or immemorial derogate, except in the case mentioned in § 3, which is itself, as it were, the first precaution taken for the safe custody of the Most Blessed Eucharist. The complete enclosure of the tabernacle on all sides requires that it be built of solid and strong material. According to liturgical laws the tabernacle may be made of wood, or of marble, or of metal (*Caeremoniale parochorum iuxta novissimas A.S. sanctiones concinnatum, Art. VII, De tabernaculo, etc., n. 9 ad 4*), which last-mentioned material is stronger than the others; but, what is of more importance, the tabernacle must be made of solid material, its parts must be firmly joined together, the lock must be as secure as possible and firmly attached to the door, whose hinges must be strongly made and firmly attached, connecting the door to the tabernacle itself. In some places the Bishops have prescribed, for the greater security of the Blessed Eucharist, that the tabernacle be made entirely of metal, and this regulation, where it is in force, must absolutely be observed, as Cardinal Gasparri teaches (*De Sanctissima Eucharistia,* II, 263, n. 994). It is an excellent idea that the tabernacle be a real safe (*cassaforte, coffre-fort*) so that it cannot be pierced or broken open by the means commonly employed by thieves; this should be firmly attached with strong

iron bars to the altar at its first shelf or to the opposite wall. These iron safes must either be made in the form of a tabernacle and then covered with marble and embellished with other ornaments so as to present the appearance of a well-finished piece of work, according to canon 1269, § 2, or at least they must be so constructed that they can be put into tabernacles already made. They are called safe-tabernacles (*de securitate,* or in Italian *di sicurezza*). To remove all doubt as to the observance of liturgical laws in making tabernacles of this sort, attention is called to the reply of the Sacred Congregation of Rites, of 1 Apr., 1908, to the petition presented to it in the name of the Ordinaries of the ecclesiastical Province of Milwaukee, in North America, by a priest who submitted for approval a new form of tabernacle very solidly built, and so designed as to be in no way contrary either to the Rubrics of the Roman Ritual or to the decrees of the said Sacred Congregation. The reply was: "Send the petitioner the reply of the Sacred Congregation of Rites given in a similar case under date of 18 March, 1898: to wit, that the purpose of the inventor is praiseworthy, but that the matter in the case and for the purpose in question pertains to the local Ordinaries themselves."

Similarly, in the case *Superioren., de nova quadam custodia Sanctissimi Sacramenti,* the Most Reverend Bishop, in order to proceed more securely in approving a certain form of tabernacle, reverently inquired of the Sacred Congregation of Rites: "Whether the liturgical rules permit a tabernacle door as described, in semicircular form, set on ball bearings and revolving without hinges, so that from this standpoint there is no objection to its being recommended to priests by the Bishops, or whether the tabernacle must be equipped with a door or gates attached to hinges, and be turned in that manner"; and the Sacred Congregation of Rites, after asking the opinion of the Liturgical Commission, replied to the proposed question, on 8 May, 1908: *"Per se,* there is no objection; but for the rest the matter pertains to the Most Reverend Bishop."

When such solid tabernacles are used, an additional efficacious safeguard is provided for the custody of the Most Blessed Eucharist. This Sacred Congregation does not impose the obligation of providing these tabernacles in churches which are now equipped with ordinary ones, provided those now in use offer solid prospects of genuine security; but it does recommend that they be specified in churches to be built in future: and it very specially recommends to the Most Excellent Bishops that, in their zealous devotion toward the Blessed Sacrament, they be very vigilant and careful that even the ordinary tabernacles which are in use in the churches of their dioceses be sufficiently solid to prevent all danger of sacrilegious profanation, and that they rigorously remove those tabernacles which fail to afford complete certainty of the absence of this danger.

5. *b*) *The tabernacle must be so carefully guarded that all danger of sacrilegious profanation be prevented.* It is not enough that there be a custodian in the place; it is not enough that the tabernacle be so strong that it cannot be pierced with a drill nor dismantled with a chisel, and have such good locks that they cannot be opened with false keys; a third safeguard is prescribed by the law — *careful custody.* This vigilance, to be exercised all the time, includes several precautions both common and extraordinary, according to the circumstances of time and place.

As regards the custodian, although it is desirable that he be a cleric and even a priest, it is not forbidden that he be a layman, *provided a cleric is responsible for the key,* which locks the place where the Most Blessed Eucharist is kept. This person should remain near the place day and night, so as to be promptly on hand when there is need, that is, he should exercise constant vigilance: he should never be away from the church at times when it is open to the faithful and is little frequented. This is especially to be insisted on in city churches, where thieves, not known as such to the faithful, wander through the church in the guise of pilgrims or beggars, keenly watch for an opportunity when vigilance is relaxed, and then quickly, in the twinkling of an eye, perpetrate their sacilegious thefts; or, in passing through the places in the daytime, they carefully undermine the gates, windows, gratings, doors, especially those other than the principal ones, and then at night proceed to the execution of their wicked design. Though this rarely happens in country places, where the presence of an unknown stranger roaming around and entering the church is more readily noticed and arouses the suspicion of priests and laymen, this does not relieve the pastor or rector of the church of the obligation of guarding the Blessed

Sacrament. The method and manner of this custody is left to his prudence in view of the circumstances of the place; for example, he may either personally or through some other person visit the church from time to time in the course of the day, or entrust this vigilance for the day to reliable persons living in the neighborhood, or arrange for private visits to the Blessed Sacrament to be made by the parishioners at various hours.

There must be careful vigilance also over workmen and other persons who by reason of their work or for other reasons frequent the church, the sacristy, the adjoining house of the priest or caretaker.

Nor is the sedulous custody of the Most Blessed Sacrament as prescribed by law to be relaxed at night when the church is locked. For these nocturnal hours, according to the dictates of prudence, the following are the principal *ordinary* precautions, that is, those constantly to be employed, both for the protection of the Most Blessed Eucharist, and to guard against the theft of the sacred vessels, the records, the alms, and the furnishings of the church: 1° All the entrances to the church should be provided, as far as necessary and possible, with strong doors equipped with firm locks and bars such that they can be opened only with a key from the inside of the church, and the windows should have bars or gratings; 2° When the church is closed in the evening it must be carefully seen to that no miscreant is left inside; 3° The duty of closing the church and the custody of the keys should be entrusted to persons who are above suspicion, and especially who are not given to drink. To these precautions we wish to add another, especially recommended, which is daily being more widely used, and which when employed is sometimes very helpful in frustrating attempted thefts: namely to install in suitable places bells which ring by electricity when the doors are opened or when the bells or the tabernacle or the altar or the altar table or the candelabra are touched, and thus quickly arouse the attention of the priest or the custodian; or a special electrical apparatus which suddenly floods the church with light and immediately informs the custodian that thieves have entered. But these devices, in order to attain their purpose, must be skillfully and ingeniously concealed so as to arouse no suspicion in the malefactors, and must be daily inspected to see that they are properly functioning.

Finally, there is a special extraordinary precaution in § 3 of the canon cited: *For some grave cause approved by the Ordinary, it is allowed to keep the Most Blessed Sacrament during the night outside the altar, but on a corporal, in a safe and becoming place, observing the prescription of canon 1271.* The place in question is usually the sacristy, provided it is really a safe and suitable place, or a strong and well-locked safe (in Italian, *cassaforte*) if that is preferred, set in the wall of the church. If neither the church nor the sacristy affords the necessary security, the Blessed Eucharist may be kept in some other safer place, even though it be private: in that case the pastor must take care that the Most Blessed Sacrament be guarded with due reverence and honor, and that the faith of the people in the real presence be not impaired. In keeping the Blessed Sacrament in this way, the Sacred Species are never to be covered only with a corporal, but must always be enclosed in a vessel or ciborium (cf. the decree cited above, S.C.R. 17 Feb., 1881, n. 3527): moreover, when the Blessed Sacrament is withdrawn from the tabernacle of the church, or is being taken back to it, the priest must be vested in surplice and stole, and accompanied, at least as a rule, by a cleric carrying a lighted candle.

To prevent thefts the rectors of churches should as far as possible also see to it that ciboria and sacred vessels of great value be not left in the tabernacle, since this serves to stimulate the cupidity and boldness of thieves. When such vessels are used on the occasion of some solemnity, it is very desirable that they be purified at the last Mass and put in some place of security other than the tabernacle; the particles that remain should be placed in an ordinary ciborium. They should also refrain from decorating the altars and the statues and paintings (and leaving them so elaborately decorated exposed to public worship) with elegant votive gifts such as gold and silver rings, chains, necklaces, earrings, pearls, etc.; if this is done on the occasion of some feast, they should see to it that afterward the gifts be removed from the church and that the faithful be told the reason for their removal.

6. *c*) *The key of the tabernacle must be most carefully guarded by a priest.* All the precautions already mentioned will be useless unless attention be given to the principal one, namely, that the key of the tabernacle be carefully guarded, as provided

in canon 1269, § 4, which specifies that this is a *grave obligation in conscience* on the priest to whom its care is entrusted. In order that the rector of the church may fulfill this obligation of *most careful custody,* prescribed by the canon, he is strictly enjoined never to leave the tabernacle key on the altar table or in the lock of the tabernacle door, not even during morning hours when divine services are held at the altar of the Blessed Sacrament and Holy Communion is distributed, especially if this altar is not in a conspicuous place. Rather, after these services the key should either be kept by the rector in his house or carried about on his person, with precautions against losing it, or it should be deposited in the sacristy, but in a secure and secret place to be locked with another key which the rector should keep as above stated (cf. Encyclical, Benedict XIV, 9 Feb., 1751, published by the Sacred Congregation of Bishops and Regulars).

Let priests who have charge of the Blessed Sacrament seriously reflect that the duty of very careful custody of the key to the tabernacle is a grave one, as is perfectly clear both from the purpose and from the words of the law. The priest who ordinarily and *per se* has the right and duty to take charge of the key is the rector of the church or oratory. In case he goes away, he may and should give the charge to another priest for the duration of his absence. If he is keeping the key in the sacristy under another lock, he should give this second key to the sacristan for the time of his absence if the tabernacle key is likely to be needed — a practice which is manifestly confirmed by general usage. In the case of a parish church the key is to be kept by the pastor; if a cathedral or collegiate church is also a parish church, the custody of the Blessed Sacrament pertains to the Chapter, and a second key to the tabernacle should be kept by the pastor (c. 415, § 3, 1°). In a parish church, even if a confraternity is erected there, the exclusive right of keeping the tabernacle key belongs to the pastor. In nonparochial churches where the Blessed Sacrament is kept by virtue of an indult of the Holy See, the key is to be kept by the chaplains or rectors, never by laymen even though they are patrons: without an apostolic indult laymen *per se* can never have charge of it.

7. Some special observations are to be made about the custody of the tabernacle key in churches of nuns or religious

women and in pious or religious houses of women. First of all, in view of the provision of canon 1267, which, revoking all contrary privileges, forbids that the Blessed Sacrament be kept either in a religious or pious house elsewhere than in the church or principal oratory, or by nuns inside the choir or enclosure of the monastery, it must be deeply impressed on the minds of Ordinaries, and strictly observed, that *the key of the tabernacle is not to be kept within the walls of a monastery* (cf. reply of the Sacred Congregation of Rites, 2 May, 1878, ad VI; decr. n. 3448; and Gasparri, *De Sanctissima Eucharistia*, 266, n. 998). In future, therefore, it should be kept in the sacristy so as to be at hand when needed, and when the sacred functions in the church are finished, and especially at night, it should be deposited in a safe, strong, and secret place, and locked with two keys, of which one should be kept by the Superioress of the community, either personally or through another, and the other by one of the nuns, for example the sacristan, so that the concurrence of the two is necessary in order to open the place where the key is kept. Let the Most Excellent Bishops carefully consider this precept, and be rigorous in carrying it out, putting aside all undue consideration of persons, so as to prevent the abuses and irreverence which may otherwise affect the Most Blessed Eucharist.

8. As regards oratories of a seminary and ecclesiastical college, a school for the religious instruction and training of the young of either sex, a hospital or other such institution, which may have the faculty of keeping the Blessed Sacrament, the tabernacle key is to be kept in each case by the rector or head of the institution, if he is a priest, otherwise by the spiritual director or chaplain who has charge of the regular celebration of Mass and of sacred functions, and he must take good care that it does not fall into other hands.

9. Finally, in the case of private oratories which by apostolic indult have the faculty of reserving the Blessed Sacrament, the key is usually kept in the sacristy in the care of the family rather than in that of the chaplain (Gasparri, *op. cit.*, II, 267, n. 999); but if the Bishop deems it better that the key be not entrusted to the holder of the indult, he should entrust it either to the priest who celebrates the Mass, especially if he celebrates regularly there, or to the pastor, in which case it is to be de-

livered each time, if conveniently possible, to the priest who is to say the Mass. Laymen who have the indult of a private oratory and have custody of the key must remember, and clerics whatever their dignity must seriously consider, that they are under a grave obligation to see to it that the key does not fall into the hands of anyone even of their own family or household.

10. The Sacred Congregation well knows that the proposed precautions will not fully attain their purpose unless the Most Excellent Bishops and Ordinaries of places, in addition to seeing that these are observed by pastors, rectors of churches, heads of institutions of all kinds, and superioresses of nuns, keep in mind also the four following precepts, which the Sacred Congregation has very much at heart:

*a*) Especially when they make the visitation of their dioceses, but also at other times as occasion offers, they should, either in person or through proper and prudent ecclesiastical persons, diligently inquire and actually observe how the safe custody of the Most Blessed Eucharist is provided for by those to whom it pertains, not only in all parish churches, but in other churches and oratories, even private ones; and whenever they find that not all the provisions of the law are being observed, they should order that they be put into effect at once, assigning a brief time limit, under pain of a pecuniary fine and also of suspension *a divinis* in the case of priests, or *a munere,* according to the gravity of the fault, to be incurred by those on whom rests the duty of providing all the safeguards of secure custody. Nor should they relieve these persons of the obligation in question on the ground, which may be alleged, that no profanation or untoward incident has yet occurred; for things that have not yet happened may very well happen in the course of time through the malice of men, if the necessary precautions are neglected.

*b*) Whenever sacrilegious thefts by which the Most Blessed Sacrament is violated have occurred in his diocese (which God forbid!), whatever be the cause, the Bishop of the place shall, either in person (as is desirable) or through the Official of his Curia to be specially delegated for the task, conduct an administrative process against the pastor or other priest, whether secular or religious, even though exempt, who had charge of the Most Blessed Sacrament; and shall send the record of the trial to this Sacred Congregation together with his own opinion, in which he shall first of all carefully describe the circumstances of time and place connected with the theft, and then, especially in view of the record of the trial, name the persons to whose fault or culpable negligence the crime is to be attributed, and propose the canonical penalties which should be inflicted on the guilty parties, and then await the orders of this Sacred Congregation.

*c*) They should maturely consider the gravity of the penalties which are provided by canon 2832 against a pastor who is gravely negligent in the custody of the Most Blessed Sacrament, even though his negligence does not attain the extreme limit; these penalties go so far as the privation of the parochial office. In view of the purpose of the law, Bishops should see to it that analogous penalties be inflicted also on other rectors of churches, who are gravely delinquent in the high duty entrusted to them, adopting the provisions of the law to their case, and obtaining for the purpose the necessary and proper faculties, as far as need be, from this Sacred Congregation. The pastor or other persons charged with the care of the Blessed Sacrament cannot escape these penalties by alleging, as they may, that it was due to the negligence of some other priest that the tabernacle was left open and the keys were not kept in a secure place: for they themselves are charged with the duty of diligent and solicitous care of the sacred vessels and of the Blessed Sacrament, and with the special office of faithfully and vigilantly seeing to it that, when the divine services are finished, the place where the Blessed Sacrament is kept be not exposed to any injury or sacrilegious plundering. Such a priest, and any other who should be guilty of such negligence, should be visited with similar punishments, as one who through his own fault gave occasion to so grave a crime. In order that the Ordinaries of places may penally prosecute also delinquent religious of either sex, even exempt ones, in accordance with these apostolic prescriptions, in this matter, we hereby give them the necessary faculties cumulatively with the major religious superiors, on whom this Sacred Congregation imposes the same duty, reserving however to the Bishop alone the faculty of conducting the trial mentioned under (*b*) in the case there described.

*d*) They should diligently inquire whether the churches and oratories which have not by common law the right to keep the

Most Blessed Sacrament (cf. c. 1265, § 1, 1°, 2°) have such faculty by apostolic indult, by papal brief in perpetuity, or by rescript for a time: and whenever they find that the privilege is not founded on a legitimate right, they should endeavor to remove it as an abuse. Moreover, let them not be too easy in accepting and recommending petitions asking for the faculty of keeping the Most Blessed Sacrament in places which have not that faculty by the common law; rather let them entirely abstain from encouraging such petitions, unless there are very grave reasons in their favor, especially in the case of private oratories and churches which are situated in desert mountain places and immense tracts too remote from the homes of the faithful, and which have not all the facilities which are needed for the faithful and secure custody of the Sacred Species. Surely it is more tolerable that even a notable number of the faithful should at times be deprived of the advantage of adoring the Most Blessed Eucharist, than that the Most Holy Sacrament should be exposed to the probable danger of profanation. Moreover, the power is hereby granted to the Most Excellent Bishops and Ordinaries of places to revoke the faculty of keeping the Blessed Sacrament in churches and oratories, even private ones, which have this apostolic privilege by indult, whenever they find either that grave abuses have occurred or that not all the conditions are verified for the safe custody, the reverence, and the worship which are due to the Most Blessed Sacrament.

These are the canonical norms and principal precautions which this Sacred Congregation has seen fit to enjoin upon Ordinaries of places, that they in turn may more insistently urge their execution upon pastors and others who have the custody of the Most Blessed Sacrament, so that any abuses which may have crept in may be eradicated, and their very approach forestalled; other measures, which according to circumstances of time and place may seem suitable for the fuller attainment of the same end, are left to the zeal and intelligent initiative of the aforesaid Prelates. Fortified, therefore, with these resources, we beg and implore them in our Lord to strive with all their power efficaciously to protect the Most Blessed Sacrament, and to guard from the impious plots of wicked men that sacrament "than which the Church of God has nothing of higher dignity, nothing more holy and admirable, since in it is contained the principal and greatest gift of God, and the very source and author of all grace and sanctity, Christ our Lord" (Roman Ritual, tit. IV, cap. 1, n. 1). The same will be to them and to their priests and people the unfailing pledge of divine protection from above.

His Holiness Pius XI, in the audience granted to the Most Excellent Secretary of this Sacred Congregation on 7 May, 1938, graciously deigned by his Apostolic Authority to confirm and ratify this Instruction, which had been approved by the Eminent Fathers at the plenary meeting of 30 March, 1938, and ordered that it be published in the official Commentary, *Acta Apostolicae Sedis,* and that it be most religiously observed by all Ordinaries, whether of places or of persons, and by all others whom it concerns, all things to the contrary notwithstanding.

Given at Rome, from the Sacred Congregation of the Sacraments, on the Feast of the Ascension, 1938.

**AAS 30–198**; S. C. Sacr. Instruction, 26 May, 1938. *Periodica,* 27(1938)–386 (Pauwels).

NOTE: *The Irish Ecclesiastical Record* for October, 1940 (Vol. 56, p. 385) gives a letter of the Sacred Congregation of the Sacraments dealing with a case of sacrilegious profanation of the Blessed Sacrament committed since this Instruction was issued. After the event a report on it was sent by the Bishop to the Sacred Congregation as required by law (cf. Instruction, n. 10, b). The report showed that the tabernacle was a solid one, and that the key was kept, as prescribed, in a separate place which was closed and locked. Accordingly the letter of the S. C. exonerated the pastor of negligence, but recommended that in future even greater precautions be taken, even to the locking of the church doors during hours when it was likely to be empty of worshippers. The tabernacle key was thereafter to be kept, not in the sacristy, but in the personal custody of the pastor. Public services of reparation were to be held. The *Record* adds in a note that these were held throughout the diocese immediately after the sacrilege.

## Custody of the Most Blessed Eucharist: Observance of Instruction Urged (S. C. Sacr., 10 Feb., 1941) AAS 33–57.

This Sacred Congregation knows how earnestly the Ordinaries of places have endeavored to make known to priests, secular and religious, and to have them observe the prescriptions contained in the Instruction of this Sacred Congregation regarding careful custody of the Most Blessed Eucharist.[1]

Nevertheless, in order that this Most Sacred Bread of Life may be even more watchfully shielded from all injury, this Sacred Congregation does not hesitate to exhort the same Ordinaries to repeat their warnings to all pastors and rectors of churches, that they increase their diligence and observe fully the prescriptions of the said Instruction.

In case any sacrilegious theft nevertheless unhappily occurs, the Ordinaries must never fail to conduct at once the administrative process mentioned in the said Instruction (n. 10, *b*), and then to send all the records to this Sacred Congregation.

Rome, from the office of the Sacred Congregation of the Sacraments, 10 Feb., 1941.

**AAS 33–57**; Exhortation, S. C. Sacr., 10 Feb., 1941.

**Custody of the Blessed Sacrament: Tabernacle** (S. C. Rit., 1 June, 1957) **AAS 49–425.**

That the Most Blessed Eucharist should be reserved with the greatest honor has always been the object of earnest and watchful solicitude on the part of Holy Mother Church. This care has, however, been manifested in various ways in the course of the centuries. Hence too the ever increasing eucharistic piety of the faithful has made of the place where the Body of Christ is kept, the very center of a flourishing Christian life.

In order to prevent abuses, and that all might be properly done, the competent Authority has often issued documents, decrees, and regulations, specifying the place, the form, and the practice of reserving the Most Blessed Eucharist. And these are all resumed in the Code of Canon Law and expressed as follows:

Canon 1268, § 2: The Most Holy Eucharist shall be kept in the most distinguished and honorable place in the church, and hence as a rule at the main altar.

Canon 1269, § 1: The Most Holy Eucharist must be kept in an immovable tabernacle set in the middle of the altar.

Very recently His Holiness Pius XII, in an address delivered

[1] See Decree of S. C. Sacr., 26 May, 1938, reported above immediately before this document.

on the 22nd of September, 1956,[1] to those who attended the International Congress on Pastoral Liturgy at Assisi, explained clearly some of the principal points of the doctrine and practice of the Church regarding the real presence of Christ our Lord in the tabernacle, refuted certain modern errors, and highly commended the exercises of devotion toward the Sacrament of the Eucharist reserved in the tabernacle according to the approved tradition of the Church.

Accordingly, this Sacred Congregation of Rites, in virtue of the faculties granted to it by His Holiness by divine Providence Pope Pius XII, has decreed as follows:

1. The Norms established by the Code of Canon Law regarding the custody of the Most Blessed Eucharist (canons 1268, 1269) are to be strictly and religiously observed; and local Ordinaries must not fail to watch carefully over this matter.

2. The tabernacle must be attached to the altar so firmly as to be immovable. As a rule it should be at the main altar, unless some other be considered more convenient and suitable for the veneration and worship of so great a Sacrament, as is ordinarily the case in cathedral, collegiate, or conventual churches, where choral functions are usually performed, or sometimes at the great sanctuaries, lest the peculiar devotion of the faithful toward the object of their veneration overshadow the supreme worship of adoration which is due to the Most Blessed Sacrament.

3. At the altar where the Most Blessed Eucharist is kept, the Sacrifice of the Mass should be habitually celebrated.

4. In churches where there is only one altar, this may not be so constructed that the priest celebrate facing the people; but on the altar itself, in the middle, should be placed the tabernacle for keeping the Most Blessed Eucharist, built according to liturgical laws, in a form and dimensions altogether worthy of so great a Sacrament.

5. The tabernacle should be solidly closed on all sides, and so secure in all its parts that all danger of profanation be precluded.

6. The tabernacle, while the sacred species are kept in it, must be covered with the veil, and a perpetual light should be burning before it according to the ancient tradition of the Church.

[1] AAS 48–711; English text, *The Pope Speaks,* 3 (1956)–273.

7. The tabernacle should be of a form in harmony with the style of the altar and of the church; it should not be too different from the ones that have hitherto been in use; it should not be reduced to the form of a simple box, but should in some way represent the dwelling place of God among men; it should not be ornamented with symbols or figures which are unusual or such as to cause wonder to the faithful, or which could be erroneously interpreted, or which have no relation to the Most Blessed Sacrament.

8. Strictly forbidden are eucharistic tabernacles which are placed off the altar itself, for example in the wall, or beside or behind the altar, or in niches or columns separated from the altar.

9. A custom to the contrary as regards either the manner of keeping the Eucharist or the form of the tabernacle, cannot be presumed, unless there is question of a centenary or immemorial custom (cf. c. 63, § 2),[2] as in the case, for example, of certain tabernacles built in the form of a tower or shrine. But these forms are not to be reproduced.

All things to the contrary notwithstanding. Rome, 1 June, 1957.

**AAS 49–425**; S. C. Rit., 1 June, 1957. Annotations, *Monitor Ecclesiasticus,* 83 (1958)–33 (Balboni).

## Revolving Tabernacle: Sisters May Open Mechanically for Adoration (S. C. Prop. Fid., 29 Jan., 1960) Private.

An indult of the Sacred Congregation for the Propagation of the Faith (N. 985/60):

The Superioress of the Sisters of the Cenacle in the city of Tananarive, in the Archdiocese of the same name, prostrate at the feet of Your Holiness, humbly requests the prolongation of the concession made to her by the Rescript of 25 March, 1955 (Prot. N. 1459/55) whereby either she herself or a Sister in case of necessity delegated by her may, in the absence of a priest or other cleric, so turn the revolving tabernacle containing the ostensorium with the Sacred Species, that the osten-

[2] Obviously this is the canon which was intended in the official reference. It should be noted that a *custom* contrary to law is never directly *presumed.* When such a custom has been *proved* to be centenary or immemorial, it gives rise to a presumption of the grant of a *privilege.*

sorium — which itself is never touched — becomes visible to the faithful, and may close it after the adoration.

The Ordinary of the Archdiocese of Tananarive recommends the petition.

The Sacred Congregation for the Propagation of the Faith, in virtue of faculties granted to it by His Holiness John XXIII by Divine Providence Pope, grants the requested prolongation for another period of five years, in the form and according to the terms of the prior Rescript.

Given at Rome, from the office of the Sacred Congregation, the 29th of January, 1960.

(**Private**); S. C. Prop. Fid., 29 Jan., 1960. Translation made from the authentic rescript.

## CANON 1306

**Lay Religious:** Permission from local Ordinary to wash corporals, palls, etc. See **c. 329**; AAS 56–5, *Motu proprio, Pastorale munus,* n. 28; reported above on p. 72.

## CANON 1324

### Dangers Arising From Some Works of Father Teilhard de Chardin (Holy Office, *Monitum,* 30 June, 1962) AAS 54–526.

There are in circulation certain works of Father Pierre Teilhard de Chardin, published even after the author's death, which are winning considerable favorable recognition.

Without undertaking to pass judgment on matters which pertain to the positive sciences, it is sufficiently clear that in the field of philosophy and theology the said works contain such ambiguities and even such grave errors as to offend against Catholic doctrine.

Wherefore the Eminent and Most Reverend Fathers of the Supreme Sacred Congregation of the Holy Office exhort all Ordinaries, Superiors of religious Institutes, Rectors of Seminaries and Presidents of Universities to protect effectively the minds of young persons against the dangers of the works of Father Teilhard de Chardin and his followers.

Given at Rome, from the Holy Office, the 30th day of June, 1962.

**AAS 54–526;** Holy Office, *Monitum,* 30 June, 1962.

## CANON 1327

**Norms for Sacred Preaching** (S. C. Consist., 28 June, 1917) **AAS 9–328.**

Excerpted for their pertinence to religious are the following norms which were promulgated by the S. C. of the Consistory in pursuance of Pope Benedict XV's encyclical on Preaching the Word of God.[1]

### CHAPTER II

### *How Fitness for Preaching Is to Be Determined*

13. In general, just as in order to give to any priest the faculties for hearing confessions, Ordinaries are strictly bound to make sure of his fitness for the task, and would regard themselves as guilty if they admitted to so sacred a task anyone who was either morally unfit or wanting in the required learning; so exactly and not otherwise, are the said Ordinaries to act before admitting and destining anyone to the ministry of the word.

14. The ordinary means to determine anyone's fitness for the office of preaching, especially as regards learning and action, is an examination to be undergone by the candidate in word and writing before three examiners, who at the discretion of the Ordinary may be chosen from among the synodal examiners, or from the extra-diocesan clergy, or from the regular clergy.

After having determined the fitness of the candidate as regards learning and action, or knowing this in advance, the Ordinary shall with no less, nay even with greater, care, consider whether as regards piety, purity of life, and reputation, he be worthy to preach the word of God.

15. According to the result of this twofold examination, the Ordinary may declare the candidate qualified either in general

[1] 15 June, 1917, AAS 9–305; summarily reported in CANON LAW DIGEST, 1, p. 622.

or for only a particular kind of preaching, for a limited time, or by way of trial and under certain conditions, or absolutely and perpetually, giving him a *pagella* for preaching, exactly in the same way as a *pagella* is given for confessions, or else simply denying him the permission to preach.

16. Ordinaries are not prohibited, however, in particular cases, and by way of exception, from admitting anyone to preach without the previous examination above described, provided the candidate's fitness is certain from other sources.

17. But it is absolutely forbidden to give "preaching diplomas" even to one's own subjects merely as a token of honor and esteem.

18. As regards regulars and exempt religious, their Ordinaries retain the right to depute those of their subjects whom, according to their rules and constitutions they know to be fit and worthy, for preaching within the walls of the religious house or monastery, always, however, in accordance with the prescriptions of c. 1338; but if they wish to designate anyone for preaching in the public churches, *not excluding those of their own Order*, they are bound to present him to the diocesan Ordinary of the place, to undergo the examination according to the dispositions of Articles 13, 14, and 15 above.

AAS 9-328; S. C. Consist., 28 June, 1917.
*Periodica,* 9 (1921)-37 (Vermeersch); cf. also p. 18, n. 5. Complete English version in CANON LAW DIGEST, 1, pp. 622-630.

## CANON 1329

### Catholic Instruction League Constituted as Primary Pious Union (Pius XI, Brief, 5 Aug., 1925) Private.

A Brief of Pius XI, of 5 Aug., 1925, is as follows:

For perpetual record: In the city of Chicago, at Loyola University of the Society of Jesus, is the principal headquarters of a certain pious society for Catholic instruction which is called *Catholic Instruction League,* established in the year 1912, with the approval of the Archbishop of the aforesaid diocese, by John Lyons, a priest of the aforesaid Society of Jesus, especially for the purpose of giving religious instruction to Catholic boys and girls who are attending the public schools. This same fruitful Union has, however, other ends also in view, for it strives to prepare both young and old for receiving confession and First Communion, to establish suitable separate classes for Negroes, Chinese, and others whose religious instruction in the United States of America is often neglected, to help the parochial schools, and finally to provide a timely and useful aid to both Catholics and non-Catholics of good will who desire to be thoroughly instructed regarding the dogmas and moral principles of the Catholic Faith.

Now because of the abundant fruit which, notwithstanding great difficulties, the said Pious Union has borne in very many places from its beginnings until now, it has overflowed the boundaries of the Archdiocese of Chicago, and has spread not only to twenty dioceses of the United States of North America, but also to other dioceses in other lands, as many Bishops and pastors are eagerly desirous that the said Pious Union be established also in their territories.

Therefore, as the Procurator General of the Society of Jesus has earnestly petitioned Us that We might deign with Apostolic benignity to erect that seat of this Pious Union which is at the University already mentioned, in Chicago, to the dignity of a *Primaria,* We, pleased indeed, in accordance with the practice and precedent of the Roman Pontiffs, that fruitful associations which as auxiliary cohorts of the Militant Church help the clergy in the exercise of the sacred ministry should be rewarded with honorable titles and privileges, have heartily and freely decided to grant this petition. Accordingly, after consulting the Cardinal Prefect of the Sacred Congregation of the Council, We do by Our Apostolic authority, by this Letter, permanently elevate the Pious Union called the *Catholic Instruction League,* and which is established at the University of the Society of Jesus in Chicago, to the dignity of a Primary Union, with the usual privileges thereto attached. And to the directors of the said Pious Union which has thus been raised by Us to the dignity of a *Primaria,* We do by this Letter grant, likewise perpetually, the permission duly to aggregate to the said Primary any other Unions of the same title and institute which are canonically erected anywhere in the world, and to communicate to such newly aggregated unions all the indulgences which have been granted to the said Primary Union at Chicago, or which may hereafter be granted to it, provided that these indulgences can be communicated.

Desiring to enrich this Primary Union forever with special indulgences, after conferring with the Cardinal Major Penitentiary, relying upon the mercy of Almighty God and upon the authority of His Blessed Apostles Peter and Paul, We mercifully grant: to all and each of the faithful who shall hereafter join that Pious Union, on the day of their taking membership, on condition that being truly penitent and having confessed their sins they shall have received the Most Blessed Sacrament of the Eucharist, a plenary indulgence; also, to all members, whether already inscribed or hereafter to be inscribed in the said Union, at the hour of death, provided that being truly penitent they shall have confessed their sins and received Holy Communion, or, in as far as they were unable to do this, have devoutly invoked the Name of Jesus, orally if they are able, otherwise interiorly, and shall patiently accept death as the wages of sin, a plenary indulgence; moreover, to these same members, whether they have already joined or shall in the future join the said Union, on the same condition that they shall have made a sacramental confession of their sins and shall have received the Bread of Heaven, every year on the Feasts of the Blessed Virgin Mary Mediatrix of all Graces, of Saint Joseph Spouse of the Virgin Mother of God, of the Holy Innocents, and of Saint Agnes Virgin and Martyr, provided that once a week for at least four months they shall have taught the catechism, likewise a plenary indulgence and remission of all their sins, upon the usual conditions. And to each of the boys and girls who attend the classes of the said Union, on the day when they receive Holy Communion for the first time, and likewise to the catechists on the same day, provided they receive Communion with the children, We mercifully grant in the Lord, upon the usual conditions, also a plenary indulgence and remission of all their sins. And to all and each of the present and future members of the said Primary Pious Union, if they shall have taught Christian Doctrine to the children at least twice in a month, We grant, in the usual form, a partial indulgence of seven years, to be gained once in that month.

Such is Our will; and We decree that this Letter shall ever be and remain firm, valid, and in effect; and shall have and obtain its effects in full and unimpaired; and that it shall now and forever most fully redound to the advantage of the said Union, called the *Catholic Instruction League,* which We have hereby raised to the dignity of a *Primaria;* and that all judgment and definition must be duly in accord herewith; and that if anything is done to the contrary on this matter, by any person or by whatsoever authority, the same shall be void and of no effect. Finally, it is Our will that copies of this Letter, even in print, subscribed by any Notary Public and bearing the seal of any person who holds an ecclesiastical dignity or office, shall receive exactly the same faith and credit as would be given to the Letter itself if presented in the original draft.

Given at Rome, at Saint Peter's under the ring of the Fisherman, this 5th day of August in the year 1925, the fourth of Our Pontificate.

P. Card. Gasparri, Sec. St.

**(Private)**; Pius XI, Brief, 5 Aug., 1925.
*Catholic Instruction League Messenger,* 12 (May-July, 1953)–8.

NOTE: The canonical effect of this Brief is discussed in *Amer. Eccles. Review,* 91 (1934)–73.

**Decree on Catechetical Instruction** (S. C. Conc., 12 Jan., 1935) **AAS 27–145.**

Excerpted from this Decree is the following section which pertains to religious:

Those also should be interested in this work, who are members of other Catholic associations and sodalities, and especially the religious societies of either sex who are devoted to the education of youth, whom, in the *Motu proprio, Orbem Catholicum,*[1] His Holiness, Pius XI, addresses in these words: "Another thing which We have very much at heart is that in all the places where religious societies devoted to the education of youth have their principal establishments, classes be instituted under the guidance and leadership of the Bishops, for a chosen body of young people of both sexes, who shall thus be trained by a suitable course of studies and, after passing an examination, shall be declared qualified to teach Christian doctrine and sacred and ecclesiasti-

[1] June 29, 1923; see CANON LAW DIGEST, 1, p. 632.

cal history." This goal will surely be attained if in Catholic schools and colleges religious instruction be given the first place among the studies, as reason itself suggests and requires, and if the teaching of this subject be intrusted to priests who are skilled teachers, and be taught according to a proper method.

**AAS 27-145**; S. C. Conc., Decree, 12 Jan., 1935.
*Amer. Eccles. Review,* 93 (1935)-45 (English text); *Homiletic and Pastoral Review,* 35 (1934-35)-1073; *Periodica,* 24 (1935)-137; *Irish Eccles. Record,* 46 (1935)-650 (Browne); *Irish Eccles. Record,* 47 (1936)-561 (Brennan).

## CANON 1350

### The Government of Missions: Instruction to Vicars and Prefects Apostolic and to the Superiors of Institutes to Which the Holy See Has Intrusted Missions (S. C. Prop. Fid., 8 Dec., 1929) AAS 22-111.

This important Instruction is as follows:

Since this Sacred Congregation of the Propagation of the Faith is frequently asked questions regarding the proper and lawful authority in governing missions both by Vicars and Prefects Apostolic and by the Superiors of Institutes to which missions have been intrusted, it has been thought advisable to explain somewhat more fully the principles of law which govern this matter. For doubts, hesitancies, and uncertainties of this sort usually lead to dissensions, and are an obstacle to good government in the missions and to their due progress.

The Church, having received from her Divine Founder the mandate, "As the Father hath sent Me, I also send you. Going into the whole world, preach the Gospel to every creature," is carrying on His mission on earth, seeking no other goal than to bring the whole human race to the knowledge of Jesus Christ and, through obedience to the law of the Gospel, to the glory of heaven.

In carrying out this divine mandate the Church usually begins by taking as partners of her labors in countries that are still pagan, religious or missionary institutes, and intrusting to them a certain territory to be evangelized.

Now, an institute which receives such a share in the labors of the Church embraces and makes its very own the mission of the Church herself. Hence, in the country which it has undertaken to evangelize it should seek no other end than that which is the goal of the Church's mission, namely, to announce Jesus Christ, to lead nations to the knowledge of the truth, to teach the way to eternal beatitude, to propagate the Kingdom of God. Whoever should decline even in part from this divine purpose, seeking earthly ends and striving for any other objectives whatsoever, howsoever good in themselves, would fail to appreciate the high excellence of his mission and would be false to the sacred trust which he had received and accepted.

Whoever lends his aid in this work must be entirely and solely devoted to furthering the evangelical mission of the Church.

The Church on her part, in intrusting to some institute a certain country to be evangelized, does not mean to relinquish that territory entirely and absolutely to the care of that institute. Obedient to her divine commission to which she cannot be false, she keeps the principal part, that is, the entire government of the mission, and expects from the institute as from an assistant a generous subsidy of apostolic workers and of means for the prosecution of the work.

Hence, the Church herself names the real Superior and governor of the mission. She does indeed usually ask the institute, in accordance with the latter's duty of coöperation, to propose to her certain men of outstanding learning, virtue, and apostolic zeal; but the one among them whom she chooses and places in charge of the mission governs not in the name and by the authority of the institute but in that of the Church herself.

Therefore one who is placed by the Church in charge of a mission, whether he be a Vicar or a Prefect Apostolic, or even a simple Superior, depends in the government of the mission not upon the institute but upon the Holy See, and is responsible for it not to the institute but to the Holy See who appointed him. Likewise in the performance of his duty, it is not the wishes of the Superiors of the institute that he is bound to fulfill, but he is bound to follow the leadership and fulfill the desires of the Church.

Nevertheless, it is always of the highest importance that the person who is intrusted by the Holy See with the government of a mission remain closely united with and acceptable to his institute and its Superiors. For the more cordial are his relations with them, and the more closely he is united with them in the purpose of saving souls, the more willing and fruitful will be the labors of the missionaries, and the more generously will evangelical workers be sent to the missions, and the necessary support be provided.

Therefore, the one and only true Superior of a mission is he who is named by the Holy See, to whom, as c. 1350 declares, "the entire care of the missions . . . is reserved solely." Hence, all the activity in converting that territory to the faith belongs to him and is controlled by him. He decides and ordains what course and method are to be followed. It is his business to establish mission stations, to open primary and higher schools, to provide orphanages, hospitals, dispensaries, and other works of Christian charity, to build chapels and churches. He must determine the manner, the time, and the curriculum of the catechetical work, and judge of the sufficient knowledge and fitness of the catechists to be employed.

Without him no one, whatever be his authority, can establish, change, or discontinue any work in the mission.

From what has been said, it clearly follows that the real Superior of the mission must have control not only of the means and resources which the mission has at its disposal, but also of the missionaries who are sent into its territory to spread the Kingdom of God.

The ecclesiastical Superior has control of the means and resources of the mission. Whatever subsidies are given to the mission must be in his hands whether they come from the mission works of the Propagation of the Faith, the Holy Childhood, the work of St. Peter the Apostle for the native clergy, or from other such associations, or whether they come through some other channel from the faithful or even from the institute itself to which the mission is intrusted, or are given by the civil government or by any other work of charity or humanity. All these he administers with the aid of his Council, as he does also the property of the mission, real and personal; and of all these he has the free disposal for the necessity and advantage of the mission, without prejudice to specific intentions for which property may in certain cases be donated. For if the resources and material means of the mission were under some other person's control, he could not properly govern the mission, but would be dependent on the will of that other person. It does not, however, follow that the Superior of the mission can undertake and pursue in his mission whatever works he chooses according to his own will and choice, and that the institute is then bound to provide the expenses and shoulder the debts. No; if the mission Superior should plan to undertake some work for whose execution the necessary funds were not at hand or for which suitable evangelical workers were wanting, he should take the matter up with the Superiors of his institute, or even according to circumstances have recourse to the S. C. Prop. Fid.

As the disposal of material means, so too the disposition of missionaries pertains to the ecclesiastical Superior. He has authority not only over missionaries in the strict sense, that is, those who are directly employed in preaching the Gospel and in the conversion of souls, but also over all priests who are otherwise engaged in apostolic labors in the mission, and over laybrothers who are employed in missionary works.

There is, however, no objection to the making of special agreements between the ecclesiastical Superior and the institutes of men or of nuns by which their mutual rights are equitably specified. Such agreements, for their greater force and stability, are usually submitted to the S. C. Prop. Fid.

Nor is it forbidden to erect in mission territories religious houses, even exempt ones, or even religious provinces, observing the requirements of law. The Sacred Congregation welcomes such foundations, not only because they are entirely in accord with the wishes expressed by our Holy Father, Pius XI, in his Encyclical, *Rerum Ecclesiae,*[1] but also because they are of the highest usefulness, especially where there is question of intrusting a mission to the native clergy. In these and similar cases the Superior of the mission has the same rights, as far as they are applicable, which the Code gives to Bishops in regard to such institutes.

In the use of his authority the mission Superior should always proceed with great prudence and deliberation. He should not only make much of the mission Council which according to c. 302 he is bound to establish and to consult, but he should also make great account of the judgment and advice of his religious

[1] 28 Feb., 1926; AAS 18-65.

Superior. For the institutes to which missions have been intrusted by the Holy See have done well in establishing religious Superiors for the benefit of their members and of the mission itself. It is true that the duty of the religious Superiors, which is defined by the rules of the religious institute, is absolutely limited to the religious life of the missionaries. The Superiors are set over the missionaries as religious in order to provide for their spiritual and temporal needs and interests. They see to it in the first place that the missionaries observe faithfully the constitutions of their own institute, as far as their apostolic labors permit them to do so; that they cultivate the virtues and Christian perfection, and live according to the spirit of their religious vocation. It thus appears that there are in the missions two powers to which the missionaries are subject. And although each has its own quite distinct field of action, the one governing the missionaries as such, the other governing them in their character as religious, still, since the two powers are exercised on the same persons, it will readily be seen how important it is that they act in harmony. From their friendly coöperation results peace to the mission, and on the part of the missionaries confident, sprightly, and spirited work; whereas their discord will result in disturbances, controversies, and often lamentable difficulties. In order, therefore, to avoid as far as possible all conflict of authority among Superiors, and in order that both authorities may work in perfect harmony for the greatest good of the mission and of souls, it will be well to add a few remarks regarding their mutual relations.

Let it be a primary rule that the Superior of the mission, except in the cases provided for by law, shall not interfere in the regular discipline, nor in general in any of the matters that concern the religious life. The religious Superior, in turn, is not to meddle or concern himself in any way with matters pertaining to the government of the mission. If, however, any conflict arises in these matters, the authority of the mission Superior prevails, without prejudice to the right of recourse to the Holy See (cf. c. 296).

It is the part of the mission Superior to appoint Superiors of mission stations, to change these stations and the missionaries themselves, to move them from one place to another, to employ them in various offices and tasks according to the need and advantage of the mission. All the apostolic labors of the missionaries are under his direction. All the missionaries are subject to his jurisdiction, visitation, and correction, in those things that pertain to the government of the stations, the sacred ministry, the care of souls, religious observance on the part of the people, the observance of feasts, the administration of the sacraments, the direction of schools, the teaching in seminaries, the formation of the clergy, especially of the native clergy, and also as regards offerings made for the mission and the execution of pious legacies made in favor of the mission (cf. c. 296).

But in appointing or transferring Superiors of the mission stations and in assigning the missionaries to various posts and offices, he should coöperate with the religious Superior. For the latter is usually in a position to know his subjects more thoroughly and to be better acquainted with their characters, talents, virtues, and qualifications for various duties. Hence, the religious Superior is to propose Superiors for the various mission stations and men qualified for the various posts; and the Superior of the mission is to make the appointments as he judges best in the Lord. The religious Superior, in turn, should approve and uphold the designs and undertakings of the Vicar Apostolic before his subjects, sustain and defend his authority, and strive that all should show him at all times perfect obedience and respect.

If the religious Superior believes that the spiritual or temporal welfare of any of his subjects requires his transfer from one place to another, or that he should be relieved of any office or duty, he should respectfully and confidently make the matter known to the Superior of the mission. But in case of disagreement, the decision of the Superior of the mission must prevail.

If the Superior of the mission learns that any missionary subject to him has been gravely wanting in his duty, he can take proper measures and apply merited penalties. But the religious Superior has a cumulative right with the Superior of the mission in the same case. If, however, it happens that different decisions are reached by each of them, the decree of the Ordinary must prevail (c. 631).

Finally, for very grave reasons, either the ecclesiastical Superior or the religious Superior has an equal right, without obtaining the consent of the other, to remove someone from his post or office; nor is either bound to disclose to the other the reasons for such action, and much less to justify it, without prejudice, however, to the right of recourse *in devolutivo* to the Holy See (cf. c. 454, § 5).

These, then, are the instructions which the S. C. Prop. Fid. deemed it most useful to convey to the Superiors of missions and to religious Superiors, for the harmony and union of souls in the mission, for the peace and tranquillity of those who labor in the Lord's vineyard, and for the happy success of apostolic labors.

This Instruction having been reported to His Holiness, Pius XI, by the President of the Sacred Congregation in the audience of 21 Nov., 1929, His Holiness graciously deigned to approve it in every detail and ordered that it be observed by all whom it concerns.

Rome, on the Feast of the Immaculate Conception, 8 Dec., 1929.

**AAS 22–111**; S. C. Prop. Fid., Instruction, 8 Dec., 1929.
*Periodica,* 19 (1930)–260 (Vermeersch).

## Authority of the Ordinary of the Place Over Missionary Sisters (S. C. Prop. Fid., Rescript, 12 Dec., 1936) Private.

The following questions were asked of the Sacred Congregation of Propaganda on behalf of the Vicar Apostolic of Kimberley (Western Australia):

1. Whether among the "missionaries" whom the Instruction of the Sacred Congregation of Propaganda of 8 Dec., 1929,[1] declares to be subject to the disposal of the Ordinary of the place, are included also the sisters who are engaged in education, schools, or other work in the mission?

**Reply.** In the negative.

2. Whether it pertains to the ecclesiastical Superior, after hearing the judgment and counsel of the competent Superioress, to make the definitive decision regarding the mission work of the sisters; for example, regarding the destination of sisters to the schools or to the work of training youth in any other manner?

3. Whether the ecclesiastical Superior, after hearing from the

[1] See immediately preceding document.

competent Superioress, may transfer a sister to another station, if the person in question is specially qualified or necessary for the work that is to be done there?

4. Whether, notwithstanding canon 611 and the Instruction of the Sacred Congregation of Propaganda which has been referred to above, the Superioress can forbid that letters of the mission sisters subject to her, asking alms, be sent to benefactors through the ecclesiastical Superior himself?

5. In case of disagreement between the judgment of the Ordinary of the place and that of the Superioress regarding the above matters, does the authority of the Ordinary prevail, or not?

**Reply** to questions 2–5. The prescriptions of the Sacred canons and the Constitutions of the sisters are to be observed.

This reply of the Consultors was confirmed by the authority of the Sacred Congregation itself.

**(Private)**; S. C. Prop. Fid., Rescript, 12 Dec., 1936. See *Sylloge,* n. 206. The annotations by Ellis, in *Periodica,* 26 (1937)–479, explain the reply to questions 2–5.

## CANON 1352

**Teaching of Liturgy** in religious seminaries and houses of study. See c. 2; AAS 56–97, Constitution on the Sacred Liturgy, nn. 15, 16, 17; reported above on pp. 20–21.

## CANON 1354

### Regulations for Regional Seminaries Entrusted to Religious or Missionary Institutes by the Sacred Congregation of Propaganda (S. C. Prop. Fid., 27 Apr., 1934) Private.

#### I — THE SUPREME DIRECTION

1. The Regional Seminary belongs to the Holy See, which entrusts its government to some religious or missionary institute, but under the high direction of the Sacred Congregation of Propaganda. To the institute are committed the discipline of the Seminary, its classes, and its ordinary administration.

2. The Seminary has a course in philosophy of at least two years, and in theology of four years.

3. The institute to which the direction of the Regional Sem-

inary is entrusted shall submit to the Sacred Congregation of Propaganda for approval:

*a*) The disciplinary rules of the Seminary.

*b*) The course of studies, the arrangement of the various branches, the time schedule, and a list of the textbooks.

4. *a*) The Rector of the Seminary shall be elected by the Sacred Congregation of Propaganda upon the presentation of a candidate by the Superior General of the institute.

*b*) The other superiors and the professors shall be named by the Superior General of the institute, who shall thereafter communicate their names to the Sacred Congregation.

*c*) The Rector of the Seminary cannot be removed or changed without the previous consent of the Sacred Congregation of Propaganda; any change in the professors or other superiors is to be communicated to the same Sacred Congregation.

5. As a rule all students of philosophy and theology in the region shall go to the Regional Seminary. Ordinaries may not withdraw their students from the Regional Seminary and send them elsewhere for their education, without the express permission of the Sacred Congregation of Propaganda.

6. Students of the Seminary who persevere in their ecclesiastical vocation may not, during their studies, nor until three full years have elapsed from their priesthood, enter any religious institute, without special permission from their proper Ordinary and from the Holy See, without prejudice to the provisions of canons 981, § 1 and 542 of the Code of Canon Law.

### II — RIGHTS AND DUTIES OF THE SUPERIOR GENERAL OF THE INSTITUTE

7. The appointment and distribution of offices among all the superiors and teachers of the Seminary (without prejudice to the provision of art. 4) is committed to the care of the Superior General of the institute.

8. The Spiritual Director of the students shall never be chosen from among the superiors of the Seminary; and he shall maintain his continuous residence within the walls of the institution.[1]

[1] The word here used in the original is *Instituti,* the same word which has consistently been used to designate the religious or missionary society which has charge of the Seminary. It seems clear, however, that the meaning here intended is that the Spiritual Director must reside within the walls of the seminary.

9. The Superior General shall consult with the Ordinaries of the region regarding the administration of the Seminary.

### III — RIGHTS AND DUTIES OF THE ORDINARIES OF THE REGION

10. The Ordinaries of the region shall be allowed to speak with their students and to carry on epistolary correspondence with them. They shall also be free to come to the Seminary, to assist at times at the scholastic lectures, to attend examinations, disputations, and the distribution of premiums.

11. The admission to sacred orders is a matter within the exclusive competence of the respective Ordinaries of the students; hence the Rector shall in good time send them the necessary information regarding the piety, scholarship, and other qualities of the candidates.

12. The Ordinaries of the region shall meet every year to consider carefully matters relating to the Seminary, that is, the spirit of piety, the discipline, the studies, and the temporal administration and to examine the written report of the Rector of the Seminary on these matters. The Chairman of this meeting shall be the Bishop who is first according to the canonical rules of precedence; the Secretary shall be the Ordinary most recently consecrated. At this meeting each of the Ordinaries shall approve and sign the annual report on the moral and economic condition of the Seminary, which shall be drawn up according to the annexed plan, and shall be sent to the Sacred Congregation of Propaganda.

13. If there are any remarks to be made these will generally be communicated to the Rector through the Ordinary of the place.

### IV — RIGHTS AND DUTIES OF THE RECTOR OF THE SEMINARY

14. The Rector is the immediate superior of the Seminary, and the other superiors and teachers shall obey him.

15. Every year, without as a rule being personally present, he shall submit to the Bishops' meeting an exact report of the moral and economic condition of the Seminary.

16. The Seminary, with its appendages, is exempt from the

jurisdiction of the local pastor; those duties of the pastor which are consistent with the nature of a pious institution belong to the Rector, who in regard to the confessions of the students shall be governed by the spirit of canon 518, § 2 of the Code of Canon Law.

### SCHEMA RELATIONIS ANNUAE SEMINARII REGIONALIS[1]

(*Allegatum*)

De ..........................................................

Pro anno literario ......................................

(*Ad Sacram Congregationem de Propaganda mittendum ante diem 31 decembris singulorum annorum*)

1. Elenchus nominativus omnium Moderatorum et Magistrorum Seminarii.

2. Numerus alumnorum distinctus pro singulis Ordinariatibus et pro singulis classibus ............

Numerus alumnorum qui durante anno ingressi sunt .......

Numerus alumnorum durante anno egressorum quia ad Ordines ascenderunt .............. (*dentur breves notae circa qualitates singulorum*).

Numerus alumnorum qui durante anno egressi sunt ob alias causas ........... Expulsi sunt ........... (*indicetur causa cur singuli expulsi sint*).

3. Numerus alumnorum qui in periculis scholasticis promoti sunt ............

Numerus alumnorum qui in periculis scholasticis reiecti sunt ............ (*animadversiones eventuales*).

4. Ratio oeconomica:

*a*) Summa accepta in singulis suis capitulis divisa.

*b*) Summa expensa in singulis suis capitulis divisa.

(*Indicetur quaenam fuerit media summa expensa pro singulis alumnis*).

5. Animadversiones:

*a*) Circa statum spiritualem et disciplinam Seminarii.

*b*) Circa studia.

*c*) Circa statum hygienicum.

*d*) Circa statum oeconomicum.

---

[1] Since no purpose would seem to be served by translating this formula into English, we simply reproduce the original.

*e*) Varia.

Datum ..............

Subscriptiones singulorum Ordinariorum et Rectoris Seminarii.

**(Private)**; S. C. Prop. Fid., Norms approved 27 Apr., 1934. *Sylloge*, n. 183.

## CANON 1363

### Sons Legitimated by Subsequent Marriage of Parents Are Admissible to Seminary (Cod. Com., 13 July, 1930) AAS 22–365.

The Code Commission was asked:

Whether sons who are legitimated by the subsequent marriage of their parents (cf. c. 1116) are to be regarded as legitimate for the purpose mentioned in c. 1363, § 1.

**Reply.** In the affirmative.

**AAS 22–365**; Cod. Com., 13 July, 1930.
*Periodica*, 19 (1930)–345 (Vermeersch); *J.P.*, 10 (1930)–231.

### Admission of Ex-religious to Seminary or of Ex-seminarian to Religion: Special Recourse to Sacred Congregation (S. C. Rel., and S. C. Stud., Decree, 25 July, 1941) AAS 33–371.

A joint Decree of these two Sacred Congregations is as follows:

Before a person who has belonged by any title to a religious family, is admitted to a seminary, the Ordinary must have recourse to the Sacred Congregation of Seminaries and Universities, which, after all that the case requires has been done, will inform the Ordinary of its judgment in the case.

Likewise, before a person who has for any reason left a seminary, is ascribed to a religious family, the religious superior must have recourse to the Sacred Congregation of Religious, which, after all that the case requires has been done, will inform the superior of its judgment in the case.

His Holiness Pius XII deigned to approve and confirm this Decree, and ordered that it be published.

Given on the 25 July, 1941.

**AAS 33–371**; S. C. Rel. and S. C. Stud., Decree, 25 July, 1941. *Com. pro Rel.*, 23 (1942)–225 (La Puma); *Periodica*, 31 (1942)–71 (Creusen).

## Practice of the S. C. of Seminaries Regarding Admission of Ex-postulants and Students From Apostolic Schools

(S. C. Sem. et Univ., 12 Jan., 1950) **Private.**

A Letter from the S. C. of Seminaries and Universities in reply to some questions presented by the Vicar General of Cologne, is as follows:

N. 2748/40/20 12 January, 1950

We are replying to your inquiries of January 4, and are herewith giving the clarifications which are desired by the Most Reverend Vicar General of Cologne in regard to the Decree of 25 July, 1941.[1]

1. We quite understand the attitude of the Sacred Congregation of Religious,[2] since the case of clerics passing to a more austere life is very different as a rule from that of religious who leave their community to enter the diocesan clergy. In fact, the Code of Canon Law provides sanctions for this latter case, but not for the former.

2. This Sacred Congregation insists on the application of the aforesaid Decree as to that which concerns it, namely, the admission of ex-religious to a Seminary. But, to expedite and facilitate the practice (which in many cases can be a mere formality, implying nothing unfavorable to the candidate), it is better that the Most Excellent Ordinaries and the Most Reverend Curiae send us, together with the petition, a clear documentation of the earlier record of the aspirant to the priesthood, with testimonials (in the original or certified copy) from the religious Superiors and if possible also from other ecclesiastical persons.

3. Among those who have belonged "by any title" to a religious family, we continue to include also students of religious schools which are destined to form religious vocations ("apostolic schools") and these only. Of course the manner of handling the case of a youthful candidate for the religious life who has contracted no canonical bond, is quite different from that to be used in the case of a religious in the strict sense.

We ask Your Reverence to inform any of the Most Reverend Ordinaries who may ask you about the matter that there is a

[1] Cf. AAS 33–371; see immediately preceding document.

[2] Cf. private reply of 11 May, 1942; reported above on p. 292.

very grave reason for these dispositions. Sometimes religious Superiors, in order to get rid of subjects whose vocations are deficient, make it easier for them to get into the ranks of the secular clergy. So it happens that there may be among the clergy some ex-religious who are not very edifying. If religious Superiors are bound in conscience to present sincerely the true condition of affairs, they will conceal nothing in giving their testimonials, and thus it will be less easy for persons with deficient vocations to penetrate the ranks of the secular clergy.

**(Private)**; S. C. Sem. et Univ., Letter of Cardinal Pizzardo, 12 Jan., 1950. *Periodica,* 41 (1952)–360; annotations, *ibid.,* p. 363 (Hecht). Hecht respectfully points out that the *extensive* provisions of the above practice cannot be urged as a matter of law. For some of these declarations, in as much as they clearly go beyond the existing law, require promulgation according to canon 17, § 2; and they are not promulgated by a private document such as the above.

**Transfer Direct From Religious Institute to Seminary Not Affected by Decree of 25 July, 1941** (S. C. Sem. et Univ., 17 July, 1954) **Private.**

The Bishop of Lafayette, La., received the following rescript.

We received Your petition of the 12th of this month requesting faculties to receive for the seminary N.N., a novice in the Society N.

With regard to this matter, however, since, as is apparent from Your letter, the young man referred to is still a novice, the case should be looked into and handled by Your Excellency and the Superiors of the religious congregation which he desires to leave. The stipulations set down by this Sacred Congregation on 25 July, 1941,[1] refer to young men who had in the past belonged to some religious institute, not, however, to those here and now belonging to one.

Wherefore, Your Excellency has complete power to settle the case according to Your knowledge and conscience.

**(Private)**; S. C. Sem. et Univ., 17 July, 1954; copy of the original kindly supplied us by the Rev. Rudolph Arlanti, chancellor of the Diocese of Lafayette, La.

NOTE: For a rescript concerning the reverse type of transfer, cf. S. C. Rel., 11 May, 1942, reported above on p. 292.

[1] Reported above on p. 578.

## Questions Regarding the Decree of S. C. Sem. et Univ., 12 July, 1957 (S. C. Prop. Fid., 11 Jan., 1958) Private.

The following questions were proposed to the Sacred Congregation for the Propagation of the Faith by the Procurator General of the Maryknoll Missionaries (Catholic Foreign Mission Society of America) regarding the decree of the S. C. Sem. et Univ., 12 July, 1957.[1]

1. Does the decree mentioned above apply to institutes like Maryknoll which are under the Sacred Congregation "de Propaganda Fide"?

**Reply:** In the negative.

2. Does it mean that Maryknoll may not accept a former student of its own without the permission of the Holy See?

**Reply:** Let the Constitutions alone be observed.

3. Is permission of the Holy See required when a student transfers directly from a secular seminary to Maryknoll?

**Reply:** In the negative, and let only the prescriptions of Canon Law and the Constitutions be observed.

4. Is permission of the Holy See required for the acceptance of a student from a religious institute?

**Reply:** Let the decision be based on the Constitutions.

5. Does the rule apply to all years of the seminary inclusive of the Minor Seminary (high school and college courses of Humanities) as well as the years of Philosophy and Theology in the Major Seminary?

**Reply:** Provided for in the preceding responses.

6. If a young boy, in the first year of high school, for example, suffered a serious attack of homesickness and left the seminary on that account, might he later be reaccepted without recourse to the Holy See, on the theory that he had been ill and was now completely cured?

**Reply:** Let the decision be based on the Constitutions alone.

After attentive examination, this Sacred Congregation makes haste to inform you of the responses of His Eminence herein contained.

**(Private)**; S. C. Prop. Fid., 11 Jan., 1958, Prot. No. 105/58. Publication of the above questions and replies was kindly authorized by the Superior General of Maryknoll through the Secretary General of the same Society.

[1] Report in Canon Law Digest, 4, p. 387.

## CANON 1364

**Study of Religion and of Latin Language in Seminaries of Religious** (Apostolic Letter, Pius XI, 19 Mar., 1924) **AAS 16–133.**

In an Apostolic Letter addressed to the Superiors General of all religious Orders and societies of men, His Holiness, Pius XI, cites c. 1364, 1° and 2°, in the following way:

In the lower schools the provisions of c. 1364, 1°, should be strictly observed: The first place belongs to religious instruction, which should be given most carefully and in a manner suited to the capacity and age of the students. And in this course no books should be used which have not been approved by the Ordinaries. We may remark in passing that even those who are studying Scholastic philosophy and theology should not desist from this study of religion. They will find great profit in the use of that golden book, the *Roman Catechism,* in which one knows not whether to admire more the fullness and soundness of the doctrine or the elegance of the Latin style. If your clerics from an early age have been accustomed to draw sacred doctrine from that source, in addition to being better prepared for the study of theology, they will certainly derive from the use of that perfect book the material for intelligent instruction to the people and refutation of the common objections against revealed doctrine.

In regard to the study of Latin, what We called to the careful attention of Catholic Bishops in Our Apostolic Letter, *Officiorum omnium,*[1] that same We recommend and prescribe, Beloved Sons, for your observance in your lower seminaries or colleges. For what the Code says of the students of sacred seminaries applies also to yours, namely: "Let them learn well especially the Latin language and their own native tongue" (c. 1364, 2°).

AAS 16–133; Pius XI, Apostolic Letter, 19 Mar., 1924.
*Periodica,* 13 (1925)–14 (Vermeersch).

NOTE: Other features of this Letter are summarily reported under cc. 564, 589, and 1366 on pp. 86, 296, 316, 583.

---

[1] AAS 14–449; reported in CANON LAW DIGEST, 1, p. 643.

## CANON 1366

### Higher Seminaries of Religious: Number and Qualifications of Professors (Apostolic Letter, Pius XI, 19 Mar., 1924) AAS 16–133.

In an Apostolic Letter addressed to Superiors General of religious Orders and societies of men, His Holiness, Pius XI, says:

We recommend particularly to you to see to it that well-qualified professors be chosen to teach the higher subjects among you; men who by the ordered purpose of their lives will stand out as examples, and who are thoroughly learned in the subjects which they are required to teach. Hence, every professor or lecturer should have completed with honor the course in philosophy, theology, and the allied branches, and should have sufficient skill and talent for teaching. Be mindful, too, of that provision of the Code: "There should be separate and distinct professors at least for Sacred Scripture, dogma, moral, and Church history" (c. 1366, § 3).

**AAS 16–133**; Pius XI, Apostolic Letter, 19 Mar., 1924.
*Periodica,* 13 (1925)–14 (Vermeersch).

NOTE: Other features of this letter are reported under canons 487, 564, 587, 589, 1364 on pp. 86, 296, 316, 582.

### Qualifications of Professor of Sacred Scripture (*Motu proprio,* Pius XI, 27 Apr., 1924) AAS 16–180.

His Holiness begins by recalling the importance of Biblical studies in the Church, especially in these days, when rationalists have gone so far as to deny the inerrancy of the Scriptures. A thorough training is needed especially for those who teach Sacred Scripture in seminaries and universities, and who write on the subject. In recognition of this need, continues the Holy Father, "Our Predecessors founded the Biblical Commission and the Biblical Institute in Rome, and have more than once insisted that the professors of Sacred Scripture should be chosen with great care."

Now, in addition to the provisions already made, the Holy Father decrees:

I. Academic degrees conferred after examination by the Biblical Commission or the Biblical Institute confer the same rights and have the same canonical effects as degrees in sacred theology or in canon law granted by any pontifical school or Catholic institute.

II. No benefice to which is canonically attached the duty of explaining the Sacred Scriptures to the people shall be conferred upon anyone who has not in addition to the other qualifications also a licentiate or doctorate in Sacred Scripture.

III. Likewise no one shall be a professor of Sacred Scripture in seminaries unless he shall have completed the special course of studies in that subject and shall have duly received a degree from either the Biblical Commission or the Biblical Institute. We desire, however, that the title of the baccalaureate which is conferred by the Biblical Institute on those who have followed a two-year course there, taking the more important branches, shall be sufficient both for the teaching of Scripture and for the obtaining of a benefice according to paragraph II, without prejudice, however, to the right of giving the preference to those who have received the licentiate or the doctorate.

IV. Let the Supreme Superiors of religious Orders and other religious societies take notice that it is Our wish that of the students whom they judge best qualified among those who are engaged in studying Scripture either at Rome or elsewhere, one, if not all, be sent to the Biblical Institute after finishing the course in theology.

V. The same shall be held as a sacred duty by the Catholic Bishops of the world, who moreover will please Us very much if they establish or obtain the establishment of scholarships so that one or more priests of each diocese may be maintained in Rome while they attend the Biblical Institute in order to obtain their degrees. Those whom the Bishops send to Rome for this purpose will certainly be hospitably received there.

VI. In order to confirm by Our example the exhortation We have just made, We donate 200,000 Italian lire, the annual income of which We shall apply, through the Sacred Congregation of Seminaries and Universities, to the support of two priests while studying at the Biblical Institute as above provided. The same Sacred Congregation shall have charge of the execution of the provisions made in the foregoing five paragraphs, and shall administer the said provisions in their prudent discretion.

May the Divine Wisdom favor Our undertaking, which so clearly concerns the interests of religion.

**AAS 16–180;** Pius XI, ***Motu proprio,*** 27 Apr., 1924.
***Periodica,*** 13 (1925)–107 (Vermeersch).

## Sociology in the Philosophy Curriculum: Writings of Ortega y Gasset Forbidden in Religious Scholasticates

(S. C. Rel., 28 March, 1962) **Private.**

A letter of the S. C. of Religious, of 28 March, 1962 (Prot. N. S.R. 8/61) sent to all members of the Roman Union of Superiors General, is as follows:

Very Reverend Father: Among priests in general and especially among the younger ones, it is not infrequent in these days to observe a certain want of docility in obeying the precepts and exhortations of the Church, especially in regard to social doctrine.

This is perhaps due to the fact that the human environment from which vocations are drawn is not only thoroughly imbued with the spirit of the world — which is contrary to the love of sacrifice and voluntary mortification — but is also tainted with laicism and materialism, altogether opposed to the obedience due to ecclesiastical authority, especially as regards the sound principles of Christian sociology, which are little known and insufficiently esteemed.

In order to protect young candidates for the priesthood, lest they depart from sound doctrine, it is therefore necessary that they thoroughly understand the social doctrine of the Church; and consequently at the present time this subject is of great weight and importance in their training.

Accordingly this Sacred Congregation feels itself in duty bound to issue a warning and to repeat the exhortation which it has already given to the members of some religious institutes, namely, to reduce faithfully to practice the prescription of Article 44, paragraph 3 of the General Statutes annexed to the Apostolic Constitution, *Sedes Sapientiae: "Sociology also, in its principles, is to be solidly taught in the philosophy curriculum"*; and this is to be done in connection with the principal social teachings of the Popes which have recently appeared.

With this consideration in view, this Sacred Congregation informs you, Very Reverend Father, that after examination of the views and writings of the Spanish writer, Joseph Ortega y Gasset, who died in 1955, it has been found that his philosophical principles are far removed from Catholic doctrine. Consequently this Sacred Congregation has decided to forbid and by this letter does forbid the reading of the works of the aforesaid writer in all houses of study and colleges of Religious, Societies of the common life and Secular Institutes which are subject to it.

Entrusting the matter to your care, I remain,

Faithfully yours in Christ,
Valerius Cardinal Valeri,
Prefect

**(Private)**; S. C. Rel., 28 March, 1962. Sent by order of the Sacred Congregation, by the Very Reverend Augustine Sépinski, O.F.M., President of the Roman Union of Superiors General, to all the members, 5 Apr., 1962.

**Sex Education and Eugenics** (Holy Office, 21 Mar., 1931) **AAS 23–118.**

The Holy Office had proposed to it for solution the following questions:

I. Can the method which is called "Sex Education" or "Sex Initiation" be approved?

II. What is to be thought of the so-called "Eugenic" theory, whether "positive" or "negative," and of the means which it proposes for the improvement of human progeny, in disregard of the laws, natural, divine, or ecclesiastical, pertaining to marriage and the rights of individuals?

**Reply.** I. In the negative; and in the education of youth that method is absolutely to be observed which has hitherto been used by the Church and by holy men, and which is commended by the Holy Father in the Encyclical on the Christian Education of Youth, of 30 Dec., 1929. That is, the first care must be the full, strong, and uninterrupted religious instruction of the youth of both sexes; they are to be taught above all to be instant in prayer, regular in the sacrament of penance and in receiving the Blessed Eucharist, to have filial devotion to the Blessed Virgin, the Mother of holy purity, and to place themselves entirely under her protection; they must carefully avoid dangerous reading, immodest shows, bad company, and all occasions of sin.

Hence, the things which have been written and published even by some Catholic writers, especially of late, in defense of the new method, can in no way be approved.

II. That theory is to be absolutely disapproved, held as false, and condemned, as is declared in the Encyclical on Christian Marriage, *Casti connubii,* of 31 Dec., 1930.

The above Replies were entirely approved and confirmed by His Holiness, Pius XI, in the audience of 19 March, 1931.

AAS 23–118; Holy Office, Decree, 21 Mar., 1931.

*Periodica,* 20 (1931)–242 (Vermeersch); *Amer. Eccles. Review,* 85 (1931)–392 (Kirsch).

NOTE: The following quotation gives the substance of the teaching of the Encyclical on Christian Education, on this subject:

"Another grave danger is that naturalism which nowadays invades the field of education in that most delicate matter of purity of morals. Far too common is the error of those who with dangerous assurance and under an ugly term, propagate a so-called sex education, falsely imagining that they can forearm youth against the dangers of sensuality by means which are purely natural, such as a foolhardy initiation and precautionary instruction for all indiscriminately, even in public; and worse still, by exposing them at an early age to the occasions, in order to accustom them, so it is argued, and as it were to harden them against such dangers.

"Such persons grievously err in refusing to recognize the inborn weakness of human nature, and the law of which the Apostle speaks, fighting against the law of the mind; and also in ignoring the experience of facts, from which it is clear that, particularly in young people, evil practices are the effect not so much of ignorance of intellect as of weakness of a will exposed to dangerous occasions and unsupported by the means of grace.

"In this extremely delicate matter, if, all things considered, some private instruction is found necessary and opportune, from those who hold from God the commission to teach and who have the grace of state, every precaution is to be taken. Such precautions are well known in traditional Christian education, and are adequately described by Antoniano, cited above, when he says:

" 'Such is our misery and inclination to sin that often in the very things considered to be remedies against sin, we find occasions for and inducements to sin itself. Hence it is of the highest importance that a good father, while discussing with his son a matter so delicate, should be well on his guard and not descend to details, nor refer to the various ways in which this infernal hydra destroys with its poison so large a portion of the world; otherwise it may happen that instead of extinguishing the fire, he unwittingly stirs or kindles it in the simple and tender heart of the child. Speaking generally, during the period of childhood it suffices to employ those remedies which produce the double effect of opening the door to the virtue of purity and closing the door upon vice.' "

The teaching of the Encyclical, *Casti connubii,* in regard to Eugenics will be found clearly explained in *What Is Marriage,* Vermeersch-Bouscaren, nn. 114, 117, 129 (America Press, 1932).

## Purposes of Catholic Teaching: Ideal of the Catholic Teacher (Pius XII, Allocution, 10 April, 1950) AAS 42–395.

Excerpts from an Allocution of Pius XII, 10 April, 1950, to an audience composed of various groups representing all classes of grades of Catholic teachers and students, from France:

To open, expand, enlighten, and equip progressively the mind of the child and the youth just awakening to life; to guide youth in its curiosity, its ardor, its high ambition to discover the truth, its eagerness to pluck the fruit from all branches of the tree of knowledge! Is there a calling more beautiful, of wider scope, more varied in its marvelous unity, than this? For after all, at every age, in every field of study there is but one thing in view: the acquisition and possession of light ever purer, in order to love and enjoy it, to defend and propagate it, to give it to everyone according to each one's capacity, to multiply and spread its blessings everywhere.

We congratulate you, therefore, members of the Catholic teaching profession, with your truly heavy burden and your task which might seem an ungrateful one, were you not sustained in it by your ideal. For without an ideal, without the highest ideal, who would have the courage, or even the right, to sacrifice — apparently — the researches and creations of an intellectual life which he feels to be rich and exuberant, the brilliant conquests of an apostolic life which is throbbing within him eager to spend itself in the service of the Church and of souls, the joys of family life during the short hours of leisure in a home that is often quite modest, though secure? Who would have the courage, or the right, to sacrifice all this in order to dedicate himself without respite and without reserve to teaching other people's children, at that wild age when profit and progress are scarcely apparent at all or begin to be faintly discernible only at the moment of passing to the next grade? Concerning every child, one may well ask himself: "What a one, think ye, shall this child be?"[1] Disillusionments are so frequent, disappointments so many and so bitter! But, thanks be to God, even while you wear yourselves out in talking, and tire your eyes in deciphering and correcting papers, your hearts are lifted to God, to Christ, to Whom you wish to give these children whom He has entrusted to you. Many of them, even though they forget you, will owe to you the vigor and charity of their Christian lives, and most of those who fall away will at their last hour feel an awakening within them of the convictions and sentiments of their earlier years.

In the hope and confidence that, through the grace of the Holy Spirit, under the protection of the Immaculate Queen who is the Throne of Wisdom, you will transform yourselves daily more and more into "burning and shining lights,"[2] We impart to all of you, to your families, your colleagues, and your pupils, Our Apostolic Benediction.

**AAS 42–395**; Pius XII, Allocution, 10 April, 1950.

## CANON 1375

### Religious Schools Ought Not to Be Placed in a Worse Condition Than State Schools (Pius XII, Apostolic Exhortation, 13 Sept., 1951) AAS 43–738.

In the course of an Apostolic Exhortation to the first International Congress of Teaching Nuns, 13 Sept., 1951, His Holiness Pius XII said:

It may be added, not for Italy alone, but in general: Those who have a part in the framing of school legislation must have a sufficient intent of justice and a sufficient — so to speak — democratic sense, to meet the will of the parents in such a way that schools founded and directed by religious Institutes be not placed in a worse condition than State schools and that they be given the liberty necessary for their development.

**AAS 43–738**; Pius XII, Exhortation, 13 Sept., 1951. Complete English text in: Courtois: *The States of Perfection* (Westminster, Md.: Newman, 1961), pp. 194–202.

---

[1] Luke 1:66.
[2] Cf. John 5:35.

## CANON 1376

**Universities in Care of Secular Clergy or Religious Depend on the Sacred Congregation of Seminaries** (S. C. Sem. et Univ., 17 Nov., 1959) **AAS 51–920.**

A Declaration of the S. C. of Seminaries and Universities:

**Question:** Since the question has arisen whether a University entrusted to the secular clergy or to a religious Institute, even though it be not canonically erected, is dependent on the Sacred Congregation of Seminaries and Universities, the said Sacred Congregation decided to reply:

**Reply:** In the affirmative, to the extent that the University in question is in any way subject to the secular clergy or to a religious family.

His Holiness John XXIII by divine Providence Pope, in the Audience granted on the 16th of November to the Cardinal Prefect of the Sacred Congregation of Seminaries and Universities, deigned to approve and confirm the above reply of the said Sacred Congregation and ordered that it be published; all things to the contrary notwithstanding.

Rome, from the office of the Sacred Congregation, the 17th of November, 1959.

**AAS 51–920**; S. C. Sem. et Univ., 17 Nov., 1959.

## CANON 1377

**Non-Catholic Graduate Students in Ecclesiastical Institutions** (Holy Office, 17 July, 1961) **Private.**

The following letter was addressed by Cardinal Ottaviani to Cardinal Pizzardo, Prefect of the S. C. for Seminaries and Universities.

Your Most Reverend Eminence, under date of the 24th of May, requested of me an answer to a question proposed at the time regarding the propriety of Catholic Faculties admitting non-Catholic students at least for the attainment of academic degrees in ecclesiastical sciences.

On this subject I have the pleasure of informing You that

the Most Eminent and Reverend Fathers of this Supreme Sacred Congregation, bearing in mind the opinion of the Reverend Consultors, have, in the plenary session of Wednesday, the fifth day of the present month, set down the following criteria as norms according to which non-Catholics may be admitted to our universities:

1) A non-Catholic student may not be admitted into an *Ecclesiastical Faculty* without previous recommendation by a Catholic ecclesiastical *Authority* which testifies to the student's moral uprightness and good disposition toward the Church in such wise that moral certitude will be had that the candidate will at least not use the academic degrees to the detriment of the Church herself.

2) Other things being equal, preference is to be given to a Catholic student rather than to a Protestant and still more to a Jew.

3) With special reference to enrollment in the *Pontifical Oriental Institute,* or also in the *Institute of Christian Archeology, a Faculty of Canon Law,* or that of *Scholastic Philosophy,* a norm of greater freedom may be used.

4) In a case where a non-Catholic student, after having been admitted into an *Ecclesiastical Faculty,* shows that he no longer deserves the trust placed in him at the time of his admission, and especially if he has carried on anti-Catholic propaganda, he is to be dismissed.

5) A non-Catholic student who, after having been admitted and conducted himself in the proper manner, passes the prescribed examinations, will obtain the respective *academic degrees* which will take care to recognize the fitness of the candidate to teach but which will not confer the right to teach. In such a case there will be given a dispensation from the profession of faith mentioned in canon 1406, par. 1, n. 8 (Apostolic Constitution, "Deus scientiarum Dominus," art. 21, n. 4).

Moreover, in the doctorate diploma the name of the Roman Pontiff is not to appear.

**(Private)**; Holy Office, 17 July, 1961, No. 278/60; reported in *Archiv für Katholisches Kirchenrecht,* 130 (1961)–485, and in *Herder-Korrespondenz,* 16 (1961–62)-201.

# CANON 1381

**Coeducation: Principles, Norms, Precautions** (S. C. Rel., Instruction, 8 Dec., 1957) **AAS 50–99.**

An Instruction of the Sacred Congregation of Religious, entitled: "on the indiscriminate education of youth of both sexes," is as follows:

The Sacred Congregation of Religious, always desirous to strengthen and to help religious men and women in the performance of their various duties, has by command of the August Pontiff made a serious effort to deal rather thoroughly with the intricate question of the indiscriminate education of the youth of both sexes, which goes by the name of "coeducation."

Accordingly this Sacred Congregation, after having consulted the Legates of the Apostolic See in those countries which are most concerned with this matter, in obedience to the orders of the Supreme Pontiff, called a combined Plenary Meeting (*Plenarium mixtum*) for the thorough and careful study of the question. This Plenary Meeting, under the direction of this Sacred Congregation, was attended by chosen members of the Sacred Consistorial Congregation and of the Sacred Congregations for the Oriental Church, of the Council, for the Propagation of the Faith, and of Seminaries and Universities.

The findings, opinions, and recommendations were then gathered together and presented by the undersigned Cardinal Prefect of this Sacred Congregation to the August Pontiff in the Audience of the 5th of March, 1957, for his approval. His Holiness deigned to ratify and confirm everything, and ordered that the conclusions be published by this Sacred Congregation in the form and according to the tenor of the present Instruction, to be duly and faithfully observed not only by religious but by all concerned.

These conclusions are divided into three parts under the following heads: 1. Principles; 2. Norms; 3. Precautions.

1. Principles, or primary and as it were basic considerations, are proposed, according to which a true judgment regarding coeducation can be reached both as to theory and practice.

2. The norms, which have obligatory force, must be kept in mind and observed in all cases in which coeducation is found to be necessary because of particular circumstances.

3. The precautions which are presented here are proposed as a complement to the principles and norms; it may be considered that they are given as guides to the action to be taken in particular cases.

The subject of coeducation is here treated only as it concerns secondary schools; for it does not concern Universities, and as to elementary or grammar schools, Ordinaries are given power to determine the time during which boys and girls may be taught together in them.

## I. Principles

1. Coeducation in its proper and true sense cannot be approved in general and *per se*.

2. Although certain advantages may be derived from coeducation, which is in fact a continuation as it were of a healthy family life in which the youth of both sexes, associating together in a modest way and engaging in a sort of noble rivalry, are stimulated to excellent and distinguished work, those of one sex serving as a complement to those of the other, nevertheless, if the matter is considered squarely as it occurs in daily life, that is according to the way this manner of education is commonly practiced, the moral dangers which attend it — especially at the age of puberty — are undoubtedly far greater than the advantages that may be derived from it.

3. Accordingly the Encyclical *Divini Illius Magistri* is always to be considered the *Magna Charta* as regards education and this indiscriminate practice in teaching. That Encyclical prescribes: "the method of teaching adolescents, which is commonly called coeducation, must be considered fallacious and offensive to Christian education; for among those who defend it, many do so for the reason that they either disregard or deny the truth that man is born tainted with original sin; and most or all of them do so because they are so confused in their ideas that they think of normal human society as an indiscriminate mass of men and women who are in every respect absolutely alike,"[1]

4. However, it must be admitted that in certain cases the practical necessity of educating boys and girls together cannot be avoided, because altogether peculiar circumstances and local conditions make coeducation the lesser evil.

---

1 AAS 22 (1930)-72.

5. It cannot be denied that in some countries young people who attend the public schools are in grave danger of losing their faith.

And Catholics — who are in the minority — have not always the means to build, equip, and support separate schools for boys and for girls; to do so would double the cost, and they are sometimes scarcely able to build and support a single Catholic school.

Consequently the children are obliged:

a) either to go to the public schools, where they are taught, boys and girls together, and without any concern for religion, with great danger to faith and morals;

b) or to attend mixed Catholic schools, where there is no danger to the faith and where the danger to morals can be avoided by certain precautionary measures.

6. If there are mixed Catholic schools in line with what has been said (cf. n. 5), and if the precautions are observed, it seems that coeducation can be tolerated even according to the Encyclical *Divini Illius Magistri,* because it is clear that the teachers in those schools do not fall under the censure of those words: "that they either disregard or deny the truth that man is born tainted with original sin; and most or all of them do so (i.e., defend coeducation) because they are so confused in their ideas that they think of normal human society as an indiscriminate mass of men and women who are in every respect absolutely alike."

## II. Norms

7. Since in some places it is really necessary to tolerate coeducation, some norms must be given to forestall the dangers that might arise from this way of teaching.

8. The Holy See advises or favors the system of education which is called "co-institutional," according to which one institution or building has two schools, for the boys and the girls separately, under the same direction, with a common library and a common set of rooms for teaching the natural sciences, to which the boys and the girls can come separately at different hours. In this way the expense is greatly reduced, and there is really no longer question of "coeducation."

If a "co-institution" according to this plan cannot be had, it is prescribed that a number of questions be inserted in the quinquennial reports so as to inform the Holy See as to the manner of directing schools in which youths of both sexes are educated together.

As has been said, Their Excellencies the local Ordinaries are to see that the general principles and norms be put into practice as the various cases arising in their dioceses may require.

Moreover, in the Bishops' Meetings in each country the Ordinaries can work out certain definite norms which are to be kept in mind and observed in cases where coeducation seems to be necessary.

## III. A General Indication of Precautions to Be Used

Since it would seem to serve no purpose and would not be prudent for the Holy See to make a list of all the precautions in detail, seeing that personal and local conditions are widely different in different countries, it will be sufficient here to add to the norms already stated a few general remarks which may serve as guides to proper action in individual cases.

1. Religious Superiors of men or women should assign to coeducational schools religious subjects whose virtue and mature judgment have been tested by experience. And they should exercise a special vigilance over them so that all disorder may be avoided and that they may have the protection which comes from the faithful observance of religious discipline.

2. Every school should have a Prefect of religion or Master of piety, who shall be in charge of directing the spiritual life of the institution.

3. Religious should not be permitted to direct coeducational secondary schools except in rare instances and extreme necessity, and then only after having obtained an Apostolic indult from this Sacred Congregation.

4. When lay teachers are employed, the greatest care must be taken that the persons chosen be above suspicion and of such character as to be capable of effective work in the moral training of the boys and girls.

5. The mutual daily contacts which take place between the boys and the girls in the same school (such as social gatherings and the like) must be conducted with great moderation and modesty, and never without supervision as different temporal and local circumstances may require.

6. There should be no sports or athletic contests in which boys and girls take part together.

7. Boarding and living quarters for both sexes together should not be allowed.

8. Special care should be taken that the boys and girls be separated:

a) in the classrooms, so that they occupy different places, that is, the boys on one side, the girls on the other;

b) at the entrances and exits, in the cloak rooms, and so on;

c) for certain classes, namely: (1) where matters relating to the sixth commandment are dealt with; (2) in any series of very special instructions in biology; (3) when there are lectures or instructions on matters which concern the students of the other sex in the field of good behavior or psychology; (4) in classes of gymnastics;

d) in recreation.

9. There should always be a religious or some other tried and trustworthy person on duty as supervisor.

10. The boys and girls should be trained to treat each other with becoming dignity and respect.

11. Religious men who teach or exercise the sacred ministry among female students, also in institutions where coeducation is in effect, must exercise only the charge entrusted to them and see to it that no relationship of another sort arise between themselves and these students.

All things to the contrary notwithstanding.

Given at Rome from the Sacred Congregation of Religious, 8 Dec., 1957.

**AAS 50–99**; S. C. Rel., Instruction, 8 Dec., 1957. Annotations, *Monitor Ecclesiasticus,* 83 (1958)–241 (Huot); *Commentarium pro Religiosis,* 37 (1958)–274 (Frisón).

## Coeducation: High Schools With Communities of Sisters as Teachers (S. C. Rel., 24 Nov., 1959) Private.

The Most Reverend Bishop of Little Rock received the following letter from the Sacred Congregation of Religious (Prot. N. 11767/59), 24 Nov., 1959:

This Sacred Congregation has received your letters of November 10 and 11, in which you ask permission for a number of communities of Sisters to teach in coeducational institutions on the secondary level in your diocese.

It is the mind of this Sacred Congregation that the Instruction of December 8, 1957,[1] be interpreted to require that in those cases where coeducation is to be tolerated because of existing conditions, only Communities of men must obtain the authorization of this Sacred Congregation, to allow their members to teach in such institutions. In the case of the Sisters' Communities, the decision in this matter is left to the prudent judgment of the local Ordinary. In view of the presently existing conditions in your diocese, as explained in your letters, it is evident that Your Excellency is justified in permitting the Sisters to teach in the Institutions that you have mentioned.

**(Private)**; S. C. Rel., 24 Nov., 1959. This case was kindly sent to us by the Reverend Lawrence P. Graves, *Officialis* of the Diocese of Little Rock.

## CANON 1384

**Decree on Media of Social Communication** (Conc. Vat. II, 4 Dec., 1963) **AAS 56–145.**

Paul, Bishop, Servant of the Servants of God, together with the Fathers of the Sacred Council, for a perpetual Memorial

### DECREE ON MEDIA OF SOCIAL COMMUNICATION

### Introduction

1. Among the wonderful technological discoveries which men of talent, especially in the present era, have made with God's help, the Church welcomes and promotes with special interest those which have a most direct relation to men's minds and which have found new avenues for communicating most readily news, opinions, and teachings of every sort. The most important of these inventions are those media which, such as the press, movies, radio, television, and the like, can of their very nature reach and influence not only individuals but the very masses and the whole of human society, and thus can rightly be called the media of social communication.

---

**[1] Reported above in this volume under this same canon.**

2. The Church recognizes that these media, if properly used, can be of great service to mankind, since they greatly contribute to men's entertainment and instruction as well as to the spread and support of the Kingdom of God. The Church recognizes also that men can employ these media in a way that is contrary to the plan of the Creator and which works to their own detriment. Indeed the Church experiences maternal grief at the harm which is too often done to society by their evil use.

Hence this Sacred Synod, mindful of the watchful concern manifested by the Supreme Pontiffs and the Bishops in a matter of such grave importance, judges it to be its duty to treat of the principal questions connected with the media of social communication. It trusts, moreover, that the teaching and regulations which it thus sets forth will serve to promote not only the welfare of Christians but also the progress of all mankind.

## CHAPTER I

3. The Catholic Church, since she was founded by Christ our Lord to bring salvation to all men and thus is obliged to preach the Gospel, considers it one of her duties to announce the Good News of salvation also with the help of the media of social communication and to instruct men in their proper use.

It is therefore an inherent right of the Church to have at her disposal and to employ any of these media in so far as they are necessary or useful for the instruction of Christians and for all her efforts for the good of souls. Pastors have a duty to instruct and guide the faithful so that with the help of these media they may further their own salvation and that of the entire human family.

Moreover, the laity especially must strive to instill a human and Christian spirit into these media, so that they may fully measure up to the great expectations of mankind and to the designs of God.

4. For the proper employment of these media it is most necessary that all who employ them be acquainted with the norms of morality and that they conscientiously put them into practice in this area. They must therefore look to the nature of what is communicated, given the special character of each of these media. At the same time they must take into consideration the entire

situation and all the circumstances, namely, the persons, place, time, and other conditions under which communication takes place and which can affect or totally change its propriety. Among these circumstances to be considered is the precise manner in which a given medium achieves its effect. For its influence can be so great that men, especially if they are unprepared, can scarcely become aware of it, govern its impact, or if necessary reject it.

5. But it is especially necessary that all parties concerned should adopt for themselves a proper moral outlook on the use of these media, especially with regard to certain questions which have been vigorously discussed in our day.

The first question has to do with information, or the search for and reporting of the news. Certainly this has become most useful and very often necessary for the progress of contemporary society and for achieving closer links among men. The prompt publication of affairs and events provides every individual with a fuller and continuous acquaintance with them; and thus all can contribute more effectively to the common good and more readily promote and advance the well-being of all civil society. Innate in human society is the right to be informed regarding things which are of interest to men either as individuals or as members of society, according to the circumstances of each case. The proper exercise of this right, however, demands that the news which is communicated be true and, within the bounds of justice and charity, complete. Moreover, the manner in which the news is communicated must be proper and decent. This means that both in the search for news and in reporting it, there must be full respect for the laws of morality and for the legitimate rights and dignity of the individual. For not all knowledge is helpful, but "it is charity that edifies" (1 Corinthians 8:1).

6. The second question concerns the relationship between the so-called rights of art and the norms of morality. Since the mounting controversies in this field often grow out of false teachings about ethics and aesthetics, the Council proclaims that all must hold to the absolute primacy of the objective moral order, since this order alone surpasses and fittingly coordinates all other spheres of human affairs, even though they be of outstanding dignity — the arts not excepted. For man, who is en-

dowed by God with the gift of reason and called to a supernatural destiny, is affected in his whole nature by the moral order alone; and if he faithfully observes it in its entirety, he will be brought to the attainment of complete perfection and happiness.

7. Finally, the narration, description, or portrayal of moral evil, even through the media of social communication, can serve to bring about a deeper knowledge and study of humanity and, with the aid of appropriately heightened dramatic effects, can reveal and glorify the magnificence of truth and goodness. Nevertheless, such presentations must always be subject to the laws of morality lest they work to the harm rather than to the benefit of souls, particularly when there is question of subjects which demand that they be treated with reverence, or which, given the baneful effect of original sin in men, might easily arouse base desires.

8. Since public opinion exerts the greatest power and authority today in every sphere of life both public and private, every member of society must fulfill the requirements of justice and charity also in this province. Consequently all should strive through these media of social communication to form and spread sound public opinion.

9. All who of their own free choice make use of these media of communication as readers, viewers, or listeners have special obligations. For a proper choice demands that they fully favor those presentations that are outstanding for their moral goodness, their knowledge, and their artistic or technical merit; but on the other hand that they avoid those which may be a cause or occasion of spiritual harm to themselves, or which may lead others into danger through bad example, or which hinder desirable presentations and promote those that are evil; to patronize such presentations would as a rule merely reward exhibitors who use these media only for profit.

In order that those who make use of these media may fulfill the moral law, they ought not neglect to inform themselves in time about judgments passed by authorities that are competent in these matters, and they ought to follow such judgments according to the norms of an upright conscience. In order the more easily to resist improper inducements and to encourage those that are desirable, they should take care to instruct their conscience with suitable aids.

10. Those who make use of these media, especially the young, should take steps to accustom themselves to moderation and self-control in their regard; they should moreover try to deepen their understanding of what they see, hear, or read; they should discuss these matters with educators and experts, and learn to pass sound judgments on them. Parents must remember that it is their duty to watch carefully that shows, publications, and other things of this sort, which may be offensive to faith or morals be not allowed to enter their homes nor to reach their children through other channels.

11. The principal moral responsibility for the proper use of the media of social communication rests on newsmen, writers, actors, designers, producers, displayers, distributors, operators and sellers, critics, and others who have any part in the production and transmission of mass presentations. It is perfectly evident how very important are the functions which all of these exercise in the present day when they are in a position, by informing and arousing the people, to lead the human race for good or for evil.

Hence they must so adjust their economic, political, or artistic and technical arrangements, that they will never be contrary to the common good. In order the more readily to achieve this purpose, they are to be commended when they join professional associations which oblige their members — even if necessary under an agreed code of ethics — to respect the moral law in the business and activities of their craft.

They must always remember that a large part of their readers and spectators consists of young people, who need a press and entertainment that offer them decent amusement and draw their hearts to higher things. They must also see to it that presentations concerning religious matters be entrusted to persons who are worthy and capable, and that they be performed with due reverence.

12. In this matter the civil authority has special responsibilities in view of the common good which these media are designed to serve. For this same authority in virtue of its office has the duty to protect and safeguard true and just freedom of informa-

tion, which the society of today absolutely needs for its due progress, especially with regard to the press. It ought also to encourage religion, culture, and the better aspects of professional and social life, and to guarantee the rights of those who use the media. Moreover, the civil authority has the duty of helping those projects which, though they are most beneficial especially for young people, cannot otherwise be undertaken.

Finally, the same public authority, which legitimately concerns itself with the health of the citizenry, is obliged, through the promulgation and careful enforcement of laws, to exercise a just vigilance lest, through an evil use of these media, serious harm be done to public morals and the progress of human society. Such vigilance is not by any means a restriction of the liberty of individuals or groups, especially where those who are professionally engaged in using these media have failed to take adequate precautions themselves.

Special care should be taken to safeguard young people from publications and performances which may be harmful to them at their age.

## CHAPTER II

13. All the children of the Church should by common consent unite in a prompt and most earnest effort to make effective use of the media of social communication in various apostolic works, as circumstances and conditions demand; they should prevent harmful developments, especially in regions where more urgent efforts are needed to advance religion and morality.

Pastors should therefore hasten to fulfill their duty in this respect, a duty which is intimately connected with their ordinary preaching responsibility. Also the laity who have some part in the use of these media should endeavor to bear witness to Christ, first of all by performing their respective functions with skill and in an apostolic spirit, and further, by being to the best of their ability, through their technical, economic, cultural, and artistic talents, directly helpful in the pastoral activity of the Church.

14. A good press should be fostered, first of all. In order thoroughly to imbue readers with a Christian spirit, there should be established and promoted a truly Catholic press, that is, one

which — whether immediately promoted and directed by ecclesiastical authorities or by individual Catholics — should be edited with the clear purpose of forming, supporting, and advancing public opinion in accord with the natural law and with Catholic doctrine and precepts, and should disseminate and correctly explain news which concerns the life of the Church. And the faithful should be reminded of the necessity of reading and spreading the Catholic press, so as to form Christian judgments on all current events.

The production and showing of films which have value for decent entertainment or for human culture and art, especially when they are designed for young people, should be encouraged and assured by every effective means. This can be done chiefly by supporting and bringing together the projects of decent producers and distributors, by encouraging worthwhile films through critical approval and awards, by patronizing or jointly sponsoring theaters operated by Catholics and by responsible managers.

Similarly, effective support should be given to good radio and television programs, especially those that are suitable for families. Catholic programs should be promoted, in which listeners and viewers may be brought to share in the life of the Church and learn religious truths. An earnest effort should also be made, where it may be necessary, to set up Catholic stations. In this case, however, care should be taken that their offerings be distinguished for technical perfection and effectiveness.

Also there should be an effort to see that the noble and ancient art of the drama, which is now diffused everywhere by the media of social communication, serves the cultural and moral betterment of audiences.

15. In order to provide for these needs, priests, religious, and laymen who are equipped with the proper qualifications for adapting these media to the purposes of the apostolate, should be appointed in due time.

In the first place, laymen should be given technical, doctrinal, and moral training. For this purpose the number of schools, faculties, and institutes should be increased, where newsmen, writers for the screen, radio, and television, and other interested parties, can receive a complete formation, instinct with the Christian spirit, especially with regard to the social teaching of the Church. Finally, care must be taken to prepare literary, film, radio, television, and other critics, who will be masters of their own crafts and will be trained and encouraged to render judgments which always put moral issues in their proper light.

16. Since the right use of the media of social communication which are available to audiences of different ages and cultural backgrounds calls for instruction and practice suited to their needs, programs which are suitable for this purpose — especially if they are intended for young people — should be encouraged, increased in number, and organized according to Christian moral principles, in Catholic schools of every grade, in seminaries, and in groups of the lay apostolate. In order that this may be accomplished more promptly, catechetical manuals should present and explain the Catholic doctrine and discipline in this matter.

17. Since it is entirely unbecoming for the children of the Church idly to let the message of salvation be thwarted or impeded by the technical delays or expenses, however vast, which are characteristic of these media, this Sacred Synod warns them of the obligation they have to maintain and assist Catholic newspapers, periodicals, and film projects, radio and television stations and programs, which have as their principal purpose to spread and defend the truth and to foster Christian influence in human society. At the same time the Synod earnestly invites those organizations and individuals who have great financial and technical capabilities to support these media willingly and generously with their resources and their skills, inasmuch as they contribute to genuine culture and to the apostolate.

18. In order that the various forms of the apostolate of the Church with regard to the media of social communication may be more effectively strengthened, each year in every diocese of the world, according to the determination of the Bishops, there should be celebrated a day on which the faithful are to be instructed on their responsibilities in this regard, and invited to pray and to contribute funds for this cause. Such funds are to be expended exclusively on the promotion, maintenance and development of institutes and projects of the Church in this field, according to the needs of the whole Catholic world.

19. In fulfilling his supreme pastoral charge with regard to the media of social communication, the Supreme Pontiff has a special Office of the Holy See.[1]

---

[1] **The Fathers of the Council, freely acceding to the wish of the "Secre-**

20. It will be the task of the Bishops, however, to watch over such works and projects in their own dioceses, to promote them and, as far as the public apostolate is concerned, to guide them, not excepting those that are under the direction of exempt religious.

21. Since an effective apostolate on a national scale calls for unity of planning and resources, this Sacred Synod decrees and orders that national offices for affairs of the press, films, radio, and television be established everywhere and given every aid. It will be the special task of these offices to see that the consciences of the faithful be properly instructed with regard to these media, and to foster and guide whatever is done by Catholics in this field.

In each country the direction of such offices should be entrusted to a special committee of Bishops or to a single Bishop as their delegate; laymen also, who are well instructed in Catholic doctrine and experts in these crafts, should have a part in these offices.

22. Since the effectiveness of these media extends beyond national boundaries and makes of every individual as it were a citizen of the human family as a whole, national offices should cooperate among themselves on an international plane. The offices mentioned in n. 21 should work assiduously in conjunction with their own international Catholic associations. These Catholic international associations are legitimately approved by the Holy See alone, and depend on it.

## ADDITIONAL CLAUSES

23. In order that all the principles and norms of this Sacred Synod regarding the media of social communication may be put into practice, by the express mandate of the Council a pastoral Instruction should be issued by the Office of the Holy See mentioned in n. 19, with the help of experts from various nations.

24. For the rest, this Sacred Synod is confident that its issuance of these instructions and norms will be gladly accepted

---

tariate for the Supervision of Publications and Entertainment," reverently request the Sovereign Pontiff to extend the duties and competence of this Office to all media of social communication including the press, and that experts from various countries, including laymen, be appointed to it.

and religiously observed by all the children of the Church, and that, by using these aids, far from experiencing any harm, they will, like salt and light, give savor to the earth and enlighten the world. Moreover the Synod invites all men of good will, particularly those who have charge of these media, to strive to turn them solely to the good of society, whose fate depends more and more on their proper use. Thus, as was the case with ancient monuments of man's ingenuity, these new inventions also may glorify the Name of the Lord, according to those words of the Apostle: "Jesus Christ, yesterday and today, and the same forever" (Hebr. 13:8).

Paul VI, Supreme Pontiff, in the public session of 4 December 1963, approved this decree and ordered its promulgation in these words:

In the Name of the Most Holy and Individual Trinity, the Father and the Son and the Holy Spirit. The decrees which have just been read in this Second Holy and Universal Vatican Synod legitimately assembled, have pleased the Fathers.

And We, by the Apostolic authority conferred on Us by Christ, together with the Venerable Fathers, do approve, decree, and establish them, and what has been thus synodally established, We order to be promulgated to the glory of God.

**AAS 56–145;** II Vatican Council, 4 Dec., 1963, Decree on The Media of Social Communication.

---

**Cinema:** Shows presented by religious cannot be forbidden or absolutely controlled by local Ordinaries. In a case decided by the S. C. of Religious, a Bishop wished to close or suppress all moving picture shows presented by religious, reserving all such shows to the parish halls. The Sacred Congregation decided: 1. This is beyond the power of the Bishop, since it would restrict unreasonably a means of apostolate which the law leaves religious free to employ; such a restriction would be especially odious if made for the financial benefit of the parish halls. 2. In case of proven abuses the Bishop can use the power given him by canon 1382, and proceed even to imposing penalties, which might include the temporary suspension of some particular house or show (canon 619). This case is reported in *Commentarium pro Religiosis,* 32 (1953)–163 under the title, *"Ex Iurisprudentia S. C. de Religiosis."*

## CANON 1385

### Writings of Catholic Theologians in Collaboration With Protestants (Holy Office, 28 Feb., 1962) Private.

The Holy Office has frequently had need to examine works of a religious character written by Catholic theologians in collaboration with Protestants. This Sacred Congregation has been especially asked if and under what conditions Catholic theologians may participate in similar editorial endeavors.

After considering the various aspects of the question, this same Congregation believes that participation by Catholic authors in works of a mixed theological character can be authorized by Ordinaries only under the following conditions:

1. The works must be exclusively of a scientific character.
2. The articles, signed by each author, must be accompanied by a written notation of their nature as Catholic or Protestant.
3. In as far as possible, the publishing firm should be one which is very serious and, preferably, non-Catholic.
4. Finally, the Ordinary should also be informed by the Catholic authors about the writings of the non-Catholics or, at least, be made acquainted with their content so that he can form a judgment as to the appropriateness of collaboration on the part of the Catholics.

I have the pleasure of communicating these norms to Your Excellency so that they may be brought to the attention of the President of the Bishops' Conference and, through his mediation, to all the Ordinaries of the country.

**(Private)**; Holy Office, 28 Feb., 1962, Prot. N. 327/58; reported in *Annales Congregationis Missionariorum Filiorum Cordis B. Mariae Virginis,* Maio-Iunio, 1962, pp. 344–345; use of the said issue of *Annales* kindly granted us by the local superior of the Claretian Novitiate at Terre Haute, Indiana.

## CANON 1393

### Diocesan and Religious Censors of Books Must Be Really Qualified and Learned: Superiors Must Be Careful (Holy Office, 29 Mar., 1941) AAS 33–121.

Decree of the Holy Office:

Since it has frequently happened that books, which had been

published with the requisite permission of the Ordinaries, later had to be forbidden or withdrawn from circulation by decree of the Holy Office, the same Sacred Congregation of the Holy Office earnestly exhorts the Ordinaries of places and religious superiors to proceed with the greatest caution in attending to the previous recension of books, and not to grant permission for publication unless they have a favorable judgment on the books from censors deputed to examine them, who are *really qualified and truly learned in the subject* in question.

Given at Rome, from the Holy Office, 29 Mar., 1941.

**AAS 33–121**; Holy Office, 29 Mar., 1941.

## CANON 1395

**Sister Faustina Kowalska: Writings** (Holy Office, 6 March, 1959) **AAS 51–271.**

A Notification by the Holy Office:

The Supreme Sacred Congregation of the Holy Office, having examined the alleged visions and revelations of Sister Faustina Kowalska of the Institute of Our Lady of Mercy, who died in 1938 near Cracow, has decreed as follows:

1. The distribution of pictures and writings which present the devotion to the Divine Mercy *in the forms proposed by this Sister Faustina,* should be forbidden;
2. It is left to the prudent discretion of the Bishops to remove such pictures which may have been already exposed for worship.

From the Holy Office, 6 March, 1959.

**AAS 51–271**; Holy Office, Notification, 6 March, 1959.

## CANON 1399

**Instruction on Sensual and Sensual-Mystic Literature** (Holy Office, 3 May, 1927) **AAS 19–186.**

An Instruction of the Holy Office to Archbishops, Bishops, and other Ordinaries of places on sensual and sensual-mystic literature, is as follows:

Among the most terrible of the evils which in our age are utterly undermining the moral teaching of Christ, and doing so much harm to the souls redeemed by His precious Blood, a prominent place belongs to that type of literature which exploits sensuality and lust, or even a certain lascivious mysticism. To this class belong especially certain romances, fanciful tales, plays, and comedies — types of literature of which our age is remarkably prolific, and which are daily being produced in increasing quantities.

Such works of literary art, which exert so great an influence upon many persons, especially among young people, if only they kept within the bounds of decency, which certainly are not too narrow, would be able not only to afford innocent pleasure, but even to elevate the morals of the reader.

But the fact is, alas, that this abundance of books which combine a frivolous fascination with immorality, is the cause of a very great loss of souls. For many of these writers depict immodesties in flaming imagery; relate the most obscene details, sometimes guardedly, sometimes openly and shamelessly, without the least regard for the requirements of modesty; they describe even the worst carnal vices with subtle analysis, and adorn them with all the brilliancy and allurements of style, to such a degree that nothing in the field of morals is left inviolate. It is easy to see how harmful all this is, especially to young people, in whom the fire of youth makes chastity more difficult. These books, often small in size, are sold at low prices in bookstores, on the streets and squares of cities, at railroad stations; they come very quickly into everybody's hands, and bring great and often fateful dangers to Catholic families. For it is well known that writing of that sort violently excites the imagination, wildly inflames the passions, and drags the heart into the mire of impurity.

There is a kind of love story worse than the rest, being written by authors who, to their shame, do not hesitate to give to their sensuality the appearance of rectitude by blending it with sacred things. Into their stories of impure love they weave a sort of piety toward God and a very false religious mysticism; as if faith could be consistent with the neglect, or rather the impudent denial of a right moral standard; or the virtue of religion be found associated with immorality! On the contrary the teaching of the Church is that no one can attain eternal life, no matter how firmly he may believe the truths of revelation, unless he keeps the commandments of God; for one who professes faith in Christ and does not follow the footsteps of Christ is not deserving even of the name of Christian. "Faith without works is dead" (James ii, 26). And our Saviour warns us: "Not everyone that saith to Me, Lord, Lord, shall enter into the Kingdom of Heaven: but he that doth the will of My Father who is in heaven, he shall enter into the Kingdom of Heaven" (Matt. vii, 21).

Let no one make these excuses: that many of those books have a truly admirable brilliance and elegance of style; that they are remarkable for inculcating a psychology in accord with modern discoveries; that the lascivious bodily pleasures are reprobated in as much as they are represented in their true light as most foul, or are sometimes shown to be connected with qualms of conscience, or in as much as it is shown how often the basest pleasures give way at last to the sorrow of a sort of repentance. For neither elegance of style nor medical or philosophic lore — if indeed these things are to be found in that sort of writing — nor the intention of the authors, whatever it may be, can prevent the readers, who owing to the corruption of nature are usually very weak and much inclined to impurity, from being gradually enmeshed in the allurements of those unclean pages, from becoming depraved in mind and heart, and finally from throwing away the reins that curb their passions, falling into all kinds of sins, and at times, grown weary of a life full of squalor, even committing suicide.

It is not to be wondered at that the world, which seeks its own even to the contempt of God, should be delighted with such books and should spread them; but it is very deplorable that writers who call themselves Christian should give their time and talent to such deadly literature. Can one who contradicts the ethical principles of the Gospel, yet be a follower of the Blessed Jesus who commanded all men to crucify their flesh with its vices and concupiscences? "If any man will come after Me," said He, "let him deny himself and take up his cross, and follow Me" (Matt. xvi, 24).

And we find some writers who have gone to such lengths of boldness and impudence as to propagate in their books those very vices which the Apostle forbade to be so much as mentioned by Christians. "But fornication, and all uncleanness . . . let it not so much as be named among you, as becometh saints" (Eph. v, 3). O that such men might learn at last that they cannot serve two masters, God and lust, religion and impurity! "He that is not with Me is against Me," said the Lord Jesus (Matt. xii, 30), and certainly those writers are not with Christ who by their filthy descriptions poison morality, which is the true basis of civil and domestic society.

In consideration, therefore, of the deluge of filthy literature which is pouring in a rising flood upon practically all nations, this Supreme Sacred Congregation of the Holy Office, which is intrusted with the guardianship of faith and morals, does by apostolic authority and in the name of His Holiness, by Divine Providence Pope, Pius XI, command all Ordinaries of places to strive by all means in their power to remedy so great and so urgent an evil.

Certainly it is the part of those who have been placed by the Holy Ghost to rule the Church of God to exercise an alert and diligent watchfulness over everything that is printed and published in their dioceses. Everyone knows that the books which nowadays are current all over the world are too numerous to be all examined by the Holy See. Hence, Pius X of happy memory declared in his *Motu proprio, Sacrorum Antistitum:* "Whatever books are current in your dioceses of such a nature as to be harmful to readers, make earnest efforts to get rid of them, even by solemn proscription. For although the Holy See is making every effort to get rid of such books, they have already grown so numerous that it is scarcely possible to examine them all. And so the remedy often comes too late, after the evil through long delays has grown inveterate."

And yet the greater part of those volumes and booklets, although most pernicious, cannot be condemned by a special censure of this Supreme Congregation. Hence, the Ordinaries, according to c. 1397, § 4, must, either by themselves or through the Council of Vigilance which the same Supreme Pontiff established by his Encyclical, *Pascendi dominici gregis,* constantly and earnestly strive to fulfill this most important duty; and they should not fail to denounce those books, as occasion offers, in their diocesan papers, as condemned and extremely harmful.

Moreover, as everyone knows, the Church has already provided by general law that all books which are tainted with immorality, and which of set purpose or openly attack the integrity of morals, be regarded as forbidden just as if they had actually been placed on the Index of forbidden books. It follows that persons who without due permission read a book that is undoubtedly salacious, even though it is not condemned by name by the ecclesiastical authorities, commit a mortal sin. And since in this most important matter false and disastrous opinions are current among the faithful, Ordinaries of places must see to it that especially pastors and their assistants give attention to this matter and give the needed instruction to the people.

Besides, the Ordinaries must not fail to declare openly according to the needs of their respective dioceses, what books by name are forbidden by the law itself. And if they think that they can more effectively or speedily protect the faithful from any particular book by condemning it by special decree, they must by all means make use of this power, just as the Holy See commonly does when grave reasons require it, according to c. 1395, § 1: "The right and duty of forbidding books for grave cause belongs not only to the supreme ecclesiastical authority for the universal Church, but also to particular Councils and Ordinaries of places, for their subjects."

Finally, this Supreme Sacred Congregation orders all Archbishops, Bishops, and other Ordinaries of places, on the occasion of their diocesan report, to make known to the Holy See what measures they have taken and put into execution against lascivious books.

**AAS 19–186**; Holy Office, Instruction, 3 May, 1927.
*Periodica,* 16 (1927)–20.

## Examples of Books Which the Holy Office Has Declared to Be Condemned *Ipso Jure* Under Canon 1399

*Sainte Thérèse, by Cazal.* AAS 13–222.

All works of Anatole France, declared forbidden *ipso jure* under c. 1399, nn. 2, 3, 6, 8, 9. AAS 14–379.

*L'Esperienza etica dell' Evangelico,* by Omodeo. AAS 16–368.

*Padre Pio da Pietrelcina.* AAS 18–186.

Giuseppe Cavaciocchi: *Padre Pio da Pietrelcina.* AAS 18–308.

*Le voyage de Shakespeare;* by Leon Daudet. AAS 19–446.

*Der historische Jesus,* and *Der geschichtliche Jesus;* by Ditlef Nielsen, translated by H. Hommel. AAS 21–489.

*Date a Cesare,* by Missuoli; *Stato Fascista, Chiesa e Scuola,* by Ignotus. AAS 22–24.

Twelve books of the condemned priest, Joseph Turmel, who wrote Modernistic dogma under assumed names. AAS 22–517.

*La Iglesia Católica ante la crítica en el pensamiento y en el arte,* by Dellhora. AAS 23–13.

*Padre Pio da Pietrelcina, l'Araldo del Signore;* condemned as *ipso jure* forbidden under c. 1398, § 1 and 1399, 5°. AAS 23–233.

Four books of Edward Le Roy: *L'Exigence idéaliste et le fait de l'évolution; Le problème de Dieu; La pensée intuitive; Les origines humaines et l'évolution de l'intelligence;* condemned as forbidden *ipso jure* under c. 1399, 2° and 6°. AAS 23–330.

*Les Bacchantes,* by Leon Daudet; condemned as *ipso jure* forbidden under c. 1399, 9°. AAS 24–71.

NOTE: The above books are given merely as examples. They do not constitute a complete list of the books that have been forbidden by name by the Holy Office.

## CANON 1402

**Power of Local Ordinary** to permit reading of forbidden books. See **c. 329**; AAS 56–5, *Motu proprio, Pastorale munus,* n. 40; reported above on p. 73.

## CANON 1406

### Profession of Faith: Superiors in Clerical-Religious Societies Without Vows (Cod. Com., 25 July, 1926) AAS 18–393.

The Code Commission was asked:

Whether Superiors in clerical-religious societies without vows, which are dealt with in canons 673–681, are obliged to make a profession of faith according to c. 1406, § 1, 9°.

**Reply.** In the Affirmative.

**AAS 18–393**; Cod. Com., 25 July, 1926, III.
*Periodica,* 15 (1926)–171 (Vermeersch); *J.P.,* 6 (1926)–133.

## CANON 1423

### Parish Entrusted to Religious Order: Conditions Imposed (S. C. Conc., 30 Oct., 1947) Private.

The following is a Rescript of the S. C. of the Council, 30 Oct., 1947 (N. 6037/47):

Archbishop N.N., most humbly prostrate at the feet of Your Holiness, asks the permission of the Holy See, so that, upon the relinquishment of parish A.A. in the metropolitan city by the Order N.N., he may entrust to the same Order another parish, N.N., in accordance with an agreement entered into between the Archbishop and the Order on the 31st of January, 1937.

The Sacred Congregation of the Council, in view of the representations made by Archbishop N.N., graciously grants him the faculty according to his request, with the understanding however that, in addition to what is provided in the particular agreement: 1) the minimum number of religious who shall be attached to the parish be specified; 2) the new parish and benefice be governed and administered in the same manner as the other parishes and benefices of the diocese; 3) the parish and benefice be understood to be entrusted to the said religious *ad nutum Sanctae Sedis,* and subject to the observance of the other provisions of law.

Given at Rome, the 30th of October, 1947.

**(Private)**; S. C. Conc., 30 Oct., 1947; reported in *The Jurist,* 9 (1949)–85.

NOTE: This private Rescript is reported because of its value in showing the conditions that are regularly imposed in such cases according to the practice of the S. C. of the Council. In this case, a supplementary agreement embodying the new conditions was executed between the Archbishop and the religious Order.

## CANON 1425

### Full Religious Parish: Administration of Funds and Legacies (Cod. Com., 25 July, 1926) AAS 18–393.

The Code Commission was asked:

Whether in virtue of cc. 631, § 3; 535, § 3, 2°; 533, § 1, 3° and 4°, the Ordinary of the place has the right to demand an account of the administration of funds and legacies of a religious parish such as is mentioned in c. 1425, § 2.

**Reply.** In the affirmative, without prejudice to the prescriptions of c. 630, § 4, and c. 1550.

**AAS 18–393**; Cod. Com., 25 July, 1926, IV.
*Periodica,* 15 (1926)–172 (Vermeersch); *J.P.,* 6 (1926)–135.

---

*Unio Paroeciae Pleno Iure* **to a Religious Order:** An example. Bull of Pius XI, 1 Apr., 1932 (AAS 24–105). Cf. *Periodica,* 21 (1932)–173.

## CANON 1513

**"Pious Cause" and "Pious Foundation": Fiduciary Gift for Pious Cause: Terms of Trust Obligatory and Not Subject to Change by Ordinary** (Case, S. C. Conc., 23 Apr., 1927) **AAS 20–362.**

**Facts.** A, a priest of diocese P, started and endowed a "patronage," or sort of social center for the religious and moral training of boys of three parishes of that diocese. It was not, however, erected as a moral person by ecclesiastical authority. For a time it was incorporated under the civil law; but the society so formed was later dissolved, and thereafter A continued to operate the center, holding all the property in his own name. In order to perpetuate the work after his death, A, in 1918, willed everything absolutely to B, a priest belonging to a different diocese, V. In a letter to B written at the same time, A explained the purpose of the trust and stated that the property was being willed to B in order to carry on, as far as possible, the work already begun. Before accepting the bequest, B obtained the permissions of the Bishops of both the dioceses concerned, P and V, and their consent that the money should be used "for the benefit of Christian youth." After A's death, B began to extend the benefits of the patronage to boys outside the parishes and the diocese of P for which it had originally been intended. This being objected to by the residents of the place, the question was presented to the Sacred Congregation of the Council.

**Question.** Whether the will of A in favor of B contains a fiduciary gift for the purpose of preserving the property for the use of the "patronage," or whether it is an independent bequest.

**Animadversiones.** 1. A "pious will" includes all gifts made for a "pious cause," whether *inter vivos* or *mortis causa* (cf. cc. 1513, 1515). By c. 1513, § 2, the fulfillment of "pious wills" is obligatory on the grantee even if legal formalities which would be required to make the obligation binding in civil law, are omitted. It is clear by c. 1516 that "fiduciary gifts" may be made not only by last will and testament but also by acts *inter vivos.*

2. Property so dedicated to a "pious cause" becomes strictly ecclesiastical property and is called a "pious foundation," *only* in case it is given to some *moral person* in the Church (cf. cc. 1497, § 1, 1544).

3. It follows that the property in this case constitutes a pious cause but not a pious foundation; the property therefore remains lay property, but has attached to it the obligation binding in conscience, that it be used for the pious cause.

4. Even lay property belonging to a pious cause is subject to the vigilance of Ordinaries according to cc. 336, 344, 1515–1517. But the Ordinaries could not change the terms of the trust, since c. 1517, § 1, reserves such changes to the Holy See, unless authority to make them has been expressly committed to the Ordinary. Hence:

**Reply.** In the affirmative to the first part; in the negative to the second; and let cc. 1515, 1516, and if necessary c. 1517 be applied.

**AAS 20–362**; S. C. Conc., *Resolutio, Diocesis* P, 23 Apr., 1927.
*Periodica,* 18 (1929)–44 (Mostaza); *J.P.,* 8 (1928)–145.

## CANON 1532

**Value of Money: Coalescence of Partial Sales** (S. C. Prop. Fid., 10 July, 1920) **Private.**

A declaration of the Sacred Congregation of Propaganda is as follows:

As regards canon 1532, the value of the franc is to be judged according to the normal value of the currency, and not according to the fluctuations of exchange. If a piece of real estate is sold by parts, the various partial sales, for the purposes of canon 1532, coalesce if the partial sales (whether simultaneous or separated by some interval of time) are made with the intention of selling the entire piece; on the contrary they do not coalesce if one part is sold without the intention of selling the remainder.

**(Private)**; S. C. Prop. Fid., 10 July, 1920; *Sylloge,* n. 80.

## *Pretium* Here Means Appraised Value, Not Offered Price (Cod. Com., 24 Nov., 1920) AAS 12–577.

The Code Commission was asked:

1. Whether the value referred to in c. 1532, § 3 (*pretium*), means the value of the thing according to the appraisal made in writing by trustworthy experts under c. 1530, § 1, 1°; or the higher priced offered in the public auction referred to in c. 1531, § 2.

**Reply.** In the affirmative to the first part; in the negative to the second.

2. Is the *beneplacitum* of the Holy See required for the sale, if a thing which has been legitimately appraised by experts under 30,000 francs, is bid upon at the auction for a price higher than 30,000 francs?

**Reply.** This case is provided for in the reply to 1.

**AAS 12–577;** Cod. Com., Reply by the Eminent President of the Commission, 24 Nov., 1920.
*Periodica,* 10 (1922)–249 (Vermeersch) ; *J.P.,* 3 (1923)–125.

## Various Articles of Ecclesiastical Property Belonging to The Same Person, Sold at the Same Time: Value in Excess of 30,000 Francs: Permission of Holy See Required (Cod. Com., 20 July, 1929) AAS 21–574.

The Code Commission was asked:

Whether in virtue of c. 1532, § 1, 2°, the permission of the Holy See is required in order to alienate at one transaction several articles of ecclesiastical property belonging to the same person when the value of the articles taken together is in excess of 30,000 francs.

**Reply.** In the affirmative.

**AAS 21–574;** Cod. Com., 20 July, 1929, V.
*Periodica,* 18 (1929)–256 (Cappello) ; *J.P.,* 9 (1929)–196.

## Faculty of Apostolic Delegate for Alienations: New Formula (S. C. Consist., 27 Apr., 1953) Private.

The Sacred Consistorial Congregation issued the following formula "to be substituted in place of the faculty reported in

N. 20 of the Index of Faculties for Nuncios, Internuncios and Apostolic Delegates, Formula I" (Prot. N. 347/12):

20. In all cases where there is an urgent necessity, evident utility, and danger in delay, the faculty is granted to permit persons interested, according to canons 534, § 1 and 1532, § 1, 2°, alienations of ecclesiastical property or property of pious causes whose price does not exceed double the increased amount fixed by the Sacred Consistorial Congregation in various countries by the Notification of 18 Oct., 1952.

The competent Sacred Congregation should be notified within a year of the alienation made.

Given from the Office of Sacred Consistorial Congregation, 27 April, 1953.

**(Private)**; S. C. Consist., 27 April, 1953. Published, with annotations by Gutiérrez, in *Commentarium pro Religiosis,* 32 (1953)–251.

NOTE: The text of n. 20 of the earlier formula, which this replaces, was as follows:

"In all cases where there is urgent necessity, evident utility and danger in delay, the faculty is granted to permit alienations of ecclesiastical property or property belonging to pious causes, up to the value of 60,000 lire or francs for the countries of Europe and 100,000 outside of Europe; with the obligation to notify the Sacred Congregation of the Council within a year of the alienation made."

We are informed on absolutely reliable authority that in the latest pagella of Apostolic Nuncios and Delegates, this faculty has been again enlarged. They now have the faculty to permit alienations, etc., where the amount does not exceed *triple* the sum mentioned in the Notification of the S. C. Consist. of 18 October, 1952.

## Limit-Values for Alienations and Debts Defined Anew in Terms of Swiss Francs (S. C. Consist., 13 July, 1963) AAS 55–656.

A decree of the Sacred Consistorial Congregation:

Because the course of events and the conditions of commerce were constantly changing, the Holy See has more than once been obliged to employ new decrees in regard to the prescriptions of canons 534 and 1532.

Consequently the Sacred Consistorial Congregation, taking account of present conditions, so that one uniform standard may be followed, by order of His Holiness Paul VI, through this new decree prescribes the following regulations:

1. The thirty thousand francs mentioned in canons 534 and 1532 shall be understood as 66.000 Swiss francs (Franken, Francs, Franchi).

2. One thousand francs shall be understood as one thirtieth part of 66.000, therefore as 2.200 Swiss francs.

3. All administrators of ecclesiastical property who are concerned in this matter are bound to observe these norms.

4. Bishops' Conferences in the various countries shall determine the amount in local currency which is equivalent there to the number of Swiss francs above mentioned, and shall give notice of their decision to the Holy See.

All previous regulations are abrogated.

Given at Rome from the Sacred Consistorial Congregation, 13 July, 1963.

**AAS 55–656**; S. C. Consist., 13 July, 1963. Annotations, *Periodica,* 52 (1963)–531 (Buijs); *Laurentianum,* 4 (1963)–492 (Di Iorio).

# BOOK IV

## PROCEDURE

Canons 1552–2194

# BOOK IV

## PROCEDURE

## Canons 1552–2194

### CANON 1657

**Religious Priests as Advocates in Matrimonial Cases** (S. C. Sacr., 7 May, 1958) **Private.**

A request from the Archdiocese of New Orleans for the faculty to appoint religious priests to the roster of advocates for help in matrimonial cases received the following reply from the Cardinal Prefect of the S. C. of the Sacraments (Office of Vigilance over Tribunals concerning Marriage Cases):

Upon receipt of Your Excellency's official letter of April 21st, this Sacred Congregation has decreed to send the following communication:

1. It is probable that no special faculty is required in order that the Ordinary, in formal cases concerning the nullity of marriage which are to be tried in his tribunal may assign to the parties as procurators and advocates, *ex officio,* a religious man, provided he exercises his office without compensation.

2. The prohibition of canon 1657 § 3 seems to refer rather to procurators or attorneys who have been hired by the parties for pay, especially in contentious, non-spiritual cases, and not to procurators and advocates assigned *ex officio* by the Ordinary in spiritual cases.

3. In any event, in as far as this faculty from the S. C. may be required at least *ad cautelam,* this S. C. by these presents freely grants the faculty to Your Excellency *for ten years,* to be used whenever in your prudent judgment it seems expedient to depute a religious priest for the said offices, either for a single case or for a certain number of cases, always however with the permission of his Superior.

**(Private)**; S. C. Sacr., 7 May, 1958; reported in *The Jurist,* 20 (1960)–82.

## CANON 1905

***Restitutio in Integrum:* Evident Injustice** (Case, Signatura, 6 Apr., 1920) **AAS 12–252.**

According to c. 1905, § 2, 4°, the evident injustice of the judgment may appear from the fact that "some prescription of law was evidently neglected." In granting a *restitutio in integrum* the Supreme Signatura pointed out that this provision applies not only to the neglect of some general prescription of the Code, but also to the neglect of any particular law or statute which is obligatory in the case, for example, any provision of a foundation, a will, or a contract, which was binding on the parties. This is the settled rule in the Signatura, and it is expressed, not changed by the provision of c. 1905, § 2, 4°.

In the present instance the lower court had entirely neglected to inquire whether the legacy which was in dispute had been left to a religious house *for divine worship* in the sense of c. 533, § 1, 3°, and whether it had been left to religious *in consideration of the parish or mission* in the sense of c. 533, § 1, 4°. The lower court had also neglected to consider the presumption of law which arises from c. 1536, that whatever is given to the rector of a church (even a church of religious), is given to the church.

The *restitutio in integrum* was therefore granted, on the ground that the judgment was manifestly proved to be evidently unjust.

**AAS 12–252**; Supreme Signatura, 6 Apr., 1920.

# BOOK V

## CRIMES AND PENALTIES

Canons 2195–2414

# BOOK V

# CRIMES AND PENALTIES

## Canons 2195–2414

## CANON 2313

### Decree Governing Pilgrimages to the Famous Shrines

(S. C. Conc., 11 Feb., 1936) **AAS 28–167.**

Among the common public manifestations of Christian piety in the Catholic Church from the earliest times, a distinguished place is held by pious pilgrimages to the more famous sanctuaries dedicated to God, to the Blessed Virgin Mary, or to the Saints; for they are very suitable as works of penance, and serve admirably to manifest and strengthen faith, and as means of thanksgiving for divine favors received.

Hence, it is natural that, with the present facility and conveniences of travel, these pilgrimages have become more frequent, owing chiefly to the active zeal of a number of societies which have been established in almost all countries for the purpose of promoting and managing them.

It is also evident that this same facility and convenience of travel has also had the effect of multiplying journeys which are undertaken chiefly or entirely for other reasons, for example, for recreation, sightseeing, study, business, and so on.

This condition of affairs may, as is evident, have some unfavorable effects upon the pious pilgrimages unless the controlling authority of the Church, which has entire charge of regulating acts of religion and piety, establishes appropriate and, as far as possible, uniform regulations.

Accordingly, this Sacred Congregation of the Council, with the approval of His Holiness, Pius XI, instructs the Ordinaries of places to observe the following regulations in the preparation and conduct of these pilgrimages:

5. As regards the secular or religious clerics who attend to the so-called technical preparation of these pilgrimages, let them not concern themselves with this function, since it is not becoming to ecclesiastical dignity. This work shall, therefore, be intrusted to honest and expert laymen, and these shall be absolutely held responsible, under the vigilance of ecclesiastical authority, that in the conduct of the pilgrimages, not only there be nothing inconsistent with their religious purpose, but that everything be in harmony with, and favorable to Christian piety.

**AAS 28–167**; S. C. Conc., Decree, 11 Feb., 1936.

*Irish Ecclesiastical Record,* 48 (1936)–426; *Apollinaris,* 9 (1936)–189 (Barbieri).

# CHRONOLOGICAL INDEX

In the column next to the last, the reference is to the volume and page of the *Acta Apostolicae Sedis;* in the last column, it is to the volume and page of this **Digest** where the document appears.

| *Year* | *Day* | *Mon.* | *Document and Source* | *AAS* | *C. L. D.* |
|---|---|---|---|---|---|
| 1921 | 18 | Jan. | Reply, S. C. Rel. | ...... | I. 280 |
| 1921 | 18 | Feb. | Reply, S. C. Rit. | ...... | I. 436 |
| 1921 | 25 | Feb. | Reply, S. C. Rit. | ...... | I. 437 |
| 1921 | 1 | Mar. | Replies, Code Com. | 13–177 | I. 303, 306, 423 |
| 1921 | 6 | Mar. | Norms, S. C. Rel. | 13–312 | I. 185 |
| 1921 | 22 | Mar. | Reply, S. C. Rel. | ...... | I. 504 |
| 1921 | 27 | Apr. | Reply, S. C. Rit. | ...... | I. 437 |
| 1921 | 19 | June | Letter, Benedict XV | 13–416 | I. 400 |
| 1921 | 2 | July | Reply, S. C. Rel. | 13–481 | I. 221 |
| 1921 | 26 | Oct. | Declaration, S. C. Rel. | 13–538 | I. 179 |
| 1921 | 3 | Nov. | Instruction, S. C. Rel. | 13–539 | I. 297 |
| 1921 | 12 | Nov. | Resolution, S. C. Conc. | 14–459 | I. 35 |
| 1921 | 1 | Dec. | Letter, S. C. Rel. | ...... | I. 281 |
| 1922 | 6 | Mar. | Reply, S. C. Rel. | 14–163 | I. 206 |
| 1922 | 16 | Mar. | Reply, S. C. Rel. | 14–196 | I. 311 |
| 1922 | 20 | Mar. | Reply, S. C. Rel. | 14–352 | I. 294 |
| 1922 | 16 | Apr. | Letter, S. C. Prop. Fid. | 14–287 | I. 70 |
| 1922 | 10 | June | Resolution, S. C. Conc. | 14–459 | I. 35 |
| 1922 | 1 | July | Reply, Code Com. | 14–406 | I. 50 |
| 1922 | 14 | July | Reply, Code Com. | 14–526 | I. 43 |
| 1922 | 14 | July | Replies, Code Com. | 14–528 | I. 407 |
| 1922 | 1 | Aug. | Reply, S. C. Rel. | 14–501 | I. 414 |
| 1922 | 4 | Aug. | Reply, S. C. Rit. | 14–505 | I. 437 |
| 1922 | 11 | Oct. | Reply, S. C. Rel. | 14–554 | I. 139 |
| 1922 | 12 | Nov. | Replies, Code Com. | 14–661 | I. 295 |
| 1922 | 12 | Nov. | Replies, Code Com. | 14–662 | I. 414, 500 |
| 1922 | 30 | Nov. | Decree, S. C. Rel. | 14–644 | I. 140 |
| 1922 | 7 | Dec. | Replies, Special Com. | 15–39 | I. 58, 59 |
| 1922 | 30 | Dec. | Reply, S. C. Rel. | 15–156 | I. 304 |
| 1923 | 25 | Jan. | Rescript, S. C. Rel. | ...... | I. 414 |
| 1923 | 14 | May | Reply, S. C. Rel. | 15–289 | I. 406 |
| 1923 | 20 | May | Reply, Code Com. | 16–113 | I. 398 |
| 1923 | 23 | June | Decree, S. C. Rel. | 15–357 | I. 203 |
| 1923 | 20 | July | Reply, S. C. Rel. | 15–457 | I. 420 |
| 1923 | 27 | Oct. | Declaration, S. C. Rel. | 15–549 | I. 499 |
| 1924 | 1 | Feb. | Reply, S. C. Rel. | 16–95 | I. 218 |
| 1924 | 2 | Mar. | Reply, S. C. Rel. | 16–165 | I. 294 |
| 1924 | 19 | Mar. | Letter, Pius XI | 16–133 | I. 85, 296, 316, 582, 583 |
| 1924 | 8 | Apr. | Reply, Code Com. | ...... | I. 505 |
| 1924 | 27 | Apr. | *Motu proprio,* Pius XI | 16–180 | I. 583 |
| 1924 | 2 | May | Reply, S. C. Rit. | 16–248 | I. 24, 398 |
| 1925 | 5 | Feb. | Reply, S. C. Rel. | 17–107 | I. 307 |
| 1925 | 5 | Aug. | Brief, Pius XI | ...... | I. 563 |
| 1925 | 10 | Nov. | Replies, Code Com. | 17–582 | I. 25, 79 |
| 1925 | 10 | Nov. | Replies, Code Com. | 17–583 | I. 292 |
| 1925 | 24 | Nov. | Declaration, S. C. Rel. | 18–14 | I. 142 |
| 1926 | 15 | July | Letter, S. C. Rel. | ...... | I. 317 |
| 1926 | 25 | July | Replies, Code Com. | 18–393 | I. 219, 613, 614 |
| 1926 | 9 | Nov. | Reply, S. C. Rel. | 18–490 | I. 405 |
| 1927 | 6 | Mar. | Reply, Code Com. | 19–161 | I. 503 |
| 1927 | 25 | Mar. | Reply, S. C. Rel. | 19–138 | I. 86 |
| 1927 | 23 | Apr. | Resolution, S. C. Conc. | 20–362 | I. 615 |
| 1927 | 3 | May | Instruction, Holy Office | 19–186 | I. 608 |

| *Year* | *Day* | *Mon.* | *Document and Source* | *AAS* | *C. L. D.* |
|---|---|---|---|---|---|
| 1927 | 28 | Dec. | Reply, Code Com. | 20–61 | I. 282 |
| 1928 | 9 | July | Declaration, S. C. Prop. Fid. | 20–266 | I. 64 |
| 1928 | 13 | July | Decree, Com. Russia | 20–260 | I. 85 |
| 1929 | 23 | Mar. | Reply, S. C. Rit. | ...... | I. 432 |
| 1929 | 20 | July | Replies, Code Com. | 21–573 | I. 502 |
| 1929 | 20 | July | Reply, Code Com. | 21–574 | I. 617 |
| 1929 | 25 | Nov. | Instruction, S. C. Rel. | 22–28 | I. 222 |
| 1929 | 8 | Dec. | Instruction, S. C. Prop. Fid. | 22–111 | I. 567 |
| 1930 | 5 | July | Decree, S. Paen. | 22–363 | I. 463 |
| 1930 | 13 | July | Replies, Code Com. | 22–365 | I. 296, 578 |
| 1930 | 5 | Dec. | Decree, S. Paen. | 23–23 | I. 44 |
| 1930 | 6 | Dec. | Replies, Code Com. | 23–25 | I. 74, 501 |
| 1931 | 29 | Jan. | Reply, Code Com. | 23–110 | I. 74 |
| 1931 | 21 | Mar. | Decree, Holy Office | 23–118 | I. 586 |
| 1931 | 16 | June | Reply, Code Com. | 23–353 | I. 279 |
| 1931 | 19 | Nov. | Reply, S. C. Rel. | ...... | I. 405 |
| 1932 | 1 | Apr. | Bull, Pius XI | 24–105 | I. 615 |
| 1932 | 18 | May | Reply, S. C. Prop. Fid. | ...... | I. 433 |
| 1932 | .. | July | Reply, S. C. Sacr. | ...... | I. 429 |
| 1932 | 25 | July | S. C. Rel. | ...... | I. 64 |
| 1932 | 28 | July | Reply, S. C. Prop. Fid. | ...... | I. 69 |
| 1932 | 7 | Nov. | Reply, S. C. Prop. Fid. | ...... | I. 434 |
| 1932 | 23 | Dec. | Reply, S. C. Rit. | 25–41 | I. 431 |
| 1933 | 15 | July | Resolution, S. C. Conc. | 26–234 | I. 415 |
| 1933 | 20 | Sept. | Declaration, S. Paen. | 25–446 | I. 460, 464 |
| 1934 | 27 | Apr. | Norms, S. C. Prop. Fid. | ...... | I. 574 |
| 1934 | 25 | May | Reply, S. C. Rit. | ...... | I. 454 |
| 1934 | 4 | June | Reply, S. C. Rit. | ...... | I. 435 |
| 1934 | 30 | July | Replies, Code Com. | 26–494 | I. 221, 419, 455, 501 |
| 1935 | 12 | Jan. | Decree, S. C. Conc. | 27–145 | I. 566 |
| 1935 | 12 | Feb. | Reply, Code Com. | 27–92 | I. 44, 282, 295 |
| 1935 | 20 | Nov. | Letter, Pius XI | 27–482 | I. 189 |
| 1935 | 30 | Nov. | Reply, S. C. Rit. | ...... | I. 438 |
| 1935 | 8 | Dec. | Instruction, Ap. Del. Japan | ...... | I. 185 |
| 1936 | .. | ... | Reply, S. C. Rel. | ...... | I. 325 |
| 1936 | 11 | Feb. | Decree, S. C. Conc. | 28–167 | I. 627 |
| 1936 | 11 | Feb. | Instruction, S. C. Prop. Fid. | 28–208 | I. 180 |
| 1936 | 15 | Mar. | Letter, Sec. State | ...... | I. 45, 318 |
| 1936 | 15 | May | Reply, Code Com. | 28–210 | I. 310 |
| 1936 | 13 | July | Reply, Spec. Com. | 28–306 | I. 183 |
| 1936 | 19 | Sept. | Decree, S. C. Rel. | 28–405 | I. 184 |
| 1936 | 13 | Nov. | Letter, Ap. Del. U. S. | ...... | I. 283 |
| 1936 | 12 | Dec. | Reply, S. C. Prop. Fid. | ...... | I. 573 |
| 1937 | 19 | Mar. | Instruction, S. C. Prop. Fid. | 29–275 | I. 185 |
| 1937 | 3 | July | Declaration, Holy Office | ...... | I. 185 |
| 1937 | 30 | Dec. | Reply, Code Com. | 30–73 | I. 399 |
| 1938 | 26 | May | Instruction, S. C. Sacr. | 30–198 | I. 545 |
| 1938 | 8 | Dec. | Instruction, S. C. Sacr. | ...... | I. 442 |
| 1939 | 14 | Apr. | Reply, S. C. Rel. | ...... | I. 308 |
| 1939 | 24 | July. | Reply, Code Com. | 31–321 | I. 407 |
| 1940 | 20 | Jan. | Norm, S. C. Prop. Fid. | ...... | I. 190 |
| 1940 | 19 | Apr. | Resolution, S. C. Conc. | 32–374 | I. 312 |
| 1940 | 12 | Sept. | Letter, S. C. Rel. | ...... | I. 64 |

| *Year* | *Day* | *Mon.* | *Document and Source* | *AAS* | *C. L. D.* |
|---|---|---|---|---|---|
| 1941 | 10 | Feb. | Exhortation, S. C. Sacr. | 33–57 | I. 557 |
| 1941 | 29 | Mar. | Decree, Holy Office | 33–121 | I. 607 |
| 1941 | 25 | July | Decree, S. C. Rel. and Stud. | 33–371 | I. 578 |
| 1942 | 31 | Jan. | Reply, Code Com. | 34–50 | I. 503 |
| 1942 | 26 | Mar. | Decree, Holy Office | 34–148 | I. 54 |
| 1942 | 11 | May | Reply, S. C. Rel. | ...... | I. 292 |
| 1942 | 27 | July | Reply, Code Com. | 34–241 | I. 416 |
| 1942 | 2 | Dec. | Declaration, S. C. Prop. Fid. | 35–26 | I. 65 |
| 1943 | 16 | May | Instruction, Holy Office | ...... | I. 455 |
| 1944 | 24 | Jan. | Decree, S. C. Rel. | 36–213 | I. 59 |
| 1944 | 10 | June | Letter, S. C. Rel. | ...... | I. 60 |
| 1947 | 2 | Feb. | Const., Pius XII | 39–114 | I. 143 |
| 1947 | 21 | Mar. | Encyclical, Pius XII | 39–137 | I. 176 |
| 1947 | 25 | Mar. | Decree, S. C. Rel. | 39–131 | I. 155 |
| 1947 | 29 | May | Reply, Code Com. | 39–373 | I. 25 |
| 1947 | 26 | June | Reply, Code Com. | 39–374 | I. 31 |
| 1947 | 9 | July | Decree, S. C. Rel. | 40–378 | I. 223 |
| 1947 | 24 | July | Reply, S. C. Rel. | ...... | I. 156 |
| 1947 | 17 | Sept. | Homily, Pius XII | 39–452 | I. 176 |
| 1947 | 30 | Oct. | Rescript, S. C. Conc. | ...... | I. 613 |
| 1947 | 27 | Nov. | Reply, Code Com. | 40–301 | I. 399 |
| 1948 | 1 | Feb. | Formula, S. C. Rel. | ...... | I. 156 |
| 1948 | 12 | Mar. | *Motu proprio,* Pius XII | 40–283 | I. 157 |
| 1948 | 19 | Mar. | Instruction, S. C. Rel. | 40–293 | I. 161 |
| 1948 | 15 | May | Reply, S. Paen. | ...... | I. 459 |
| 1948 | 18 | Nov. | Rescript, S. C. Sacr. | ...... | I. 427 |
| 1948 | 9 | Dec. | Questionnaire, S. C. Rel. | ...... | I. 227 |
| 1949 | 26 | Jan. | Reply, Code Com. | 41–158 | I. 32 |
| 1949 | 19 | May | Reply, S. C. Rel. | ...... | I. 167 |
| 1949 | 1 | Aug. | Reply, S. C. Rel. | ...... | I. 168 |
| 1949 | 8 | Aug. | Reply, S. C. Rel. | ...... | I. 169 |
| 1950 | 12 | Jan. | Letter, S. C. Sem. | ...... | I. 579 |
| 1950 | 9 | Feb. | Letter, S. C. Rel. | ...... | I. 273 |
| 1950 | 22 | Mar. | Decree, S. C. Conc. | 42–330 | I. 48 |
| 1950 | 29 | Mar. | Reply, S. C. Rit. | ...... | I. 399 |
| 1950 | 10 | Apr. | Allocution, Pius XII | 42–395 | I. 588 |
| 1950 | 14 | Apr. | Reply, S. C. Rit. | ...... | I. 502 |
| 1950 | 8 | July | Reply, S. C. Rit. | ...... | I. 310 |
| 1950 | 24 | Oct. | Indult, S. C. Rel. | ...... | I. 102 |
| 1950 | 21 | Nov. | Const., Pius XII | 43–5 | I. 326 |
| 1950 | 23 | Nov. | Instruction, S. C. Rel. | 43–37 | I. 344 |
| 1950 | 8 | Dec. | Allocution, Pius XII | 43–26 | I. 86 |
| 1951 | 10 | Jan. | Letter, S. C. Rel. | ...... | I. 318 |
| 1951 | 3 | Feb. | Reply, S. C. Rit. | ...... | I. 502 |
| 1951 | 7 | Mar. | Letter, S. C. Rel. | ...... | I. 353 |
| 1951 | 11 | Apr. | Letter, S. C. Rel. | ...... | I. 506 |
| 1951 | 19 | Apr. | Reply, S. C. Rel. | ...... | I. 407 |
| 1951 | 9 | Aug. | Reply, S. C. Rel. | ...... | I. 357 |
| 1951 | 13 | Sept. | Exhortation, Pius XII | 43–738 | I. 178, 589 |
| 1951 | 2 | Oct. | Indult, S. C. Rel. | ...... | I. 189 |
| 1951 | 23 | Oct. | Decree, S. C. Rel. | 43–806 | I. 64 |
| 1951 | 12 | Nov. | Formula, S. C. Rel. | ...... | I. 358 |
| 1951 | 17 | Nov. | Reply, S. C. Rel. | ...... | I. 408 |
| 1952 | .. | ... | Practice, S. C. Rel. | ...... | I. 52 |

| *Year* | *Day* | *Mon.* | *Document and Source* | *AAS* | *C. L. D.* |
|---|---|---|---|---|---|
| 1956 | 18 | June | Reply, S. C. Rit. | ...... | I. 438 |
| 1956 | 2 | July | Reply, S. C. Prop. Fid. | ...... | I. 191 |
| 1956 | 7 | July | Decree, S. C. Rel. | ...... | I. 118 |
| 1956 | 27 | Dec. | Letter, Pius XII | 49–889 | I. 396 |
| 1957 | 9 | Feb. | Indulgence, S. Paen. | 49–100 | I. 463 |
| 1957 | 16 | Feb. | Reply, S. C. Rel. | ...... | I. 118 |
| 1957 | 12 | Mar. | Letter, S. C. Rel. | ...... | I. 119 |
| 1957 | 12 | Mar. | Norms, S. C. Rel. | ...... | I. 120 |
| 1957 | 12 | Mar. | Norms, S. C. Rel. | 49–869 | I. 178 |
| 1957 | 15 | Mar. | Decree, S. C. Rel. | 49–749 | I. 177, 296 |
| 1957 | 19 | Mar. | *Motu proprio,* Pius XII | 49–177 | I. 450 |
| 1957 | 25 | Mar. | Letter, S. C. Rel. | ...... | I. 138 |
| 1957 | 25 | Mar. | Decision, Rota | ...... | I. 308 |
| 1957 | 26 | Mar. | Reply, S. C. Rel. | ...... | I. 300 |
| 1957 | 24 | Apr. | Allocution, Pius XII | 49–291 | I. 53, 139 |
| 1957 | 1 | June | Decree, S. C. Rit. | 49–425 | I. 558 |
| 1957 | 2 | June | *Motu proprio,* Pius XII | 49–433 | I. 3 |
| 1957 | 1 | July | Decree, S. C. Rel. | 49–751 | I. 178 |
| 1957 | 11 | July | Letter, Pius XII | 49–726 | I. 178 |
| 1957 | 30 | July | Decree, S. C. Rel. | 49–871 | I. 38 |
| 1957 | 30 | July | Reply, S. C. Rel. | 50–103 | I. 124 |
| 1957 | 6 | Aug. | Letter, S. C. Rel. | ...... | I. 321 |
| 1957 | 10 | Sept. | Allocution, Pius XII | 49–806 | I. 178 |
| 1957 | 12 | Sept. | Faculties, S. C. Consist. | ...... | I. 27 |
| 1957 | 8 | Dec. | Instruction, S. C. Rel. | 50–99 | I. 592 |
| 1957 | 9 | Dec. | Allocution, Pius XII | 50–34 | I. 125 |
| 1957 | 28 | Dec. | Decree, S. Paen. | 50–118 | I. 463 |
| 1958 | .. | .... | Practice, S. C. Rel. | ...... | I. 219 |
| 1958 | 11 | Jan. | Reply, S. C. Prop. Fid. | ...... | I. 581 |
| 1958 | 11 | Feb. | Allocution, Pius XII | 50–153 | I. 194 |
| 1958 | 1 | Mar. | Reply, S. C. Rel. | ...... | I. 302 |
| 1958 | 1 | Apr | Reply, S. C. Rit. | ...... | I. 3 |
| 1958 | 10 | Apr. | Reply, Holy Office | ...... | I. 428 |
| 1958 | 7 | May | Indult, S. C. Sacr. | ...... | I. 623 |
| 1958 | 19 | July | Radio Address, Pius XII | 50–563 | I. 139 |
| 1958 | 25 | July | Radio Address, Pius XII | 50–570 | I. 139 |
| 1958 | 2 | Aug. | Radio Address, Pius XII | 50–579 | I. 139 |
| 1958 | 25 | Aug. | Allocution, Pius XII | 50–674 | I. 178 |
| 1958 | 3 | Sept. | Instruction, S. C. Rit. | 50–630 | I. 508 |
| 1958 | 14 | Sept. | Allocution, Pius XII | 50–696 | I. 53 |
| 1959 | .. | .... | Faculties, S. C. Consist. | ...... | I. 29 |
| 1959 | 26 | Jan. | Letter, S. C. Rel. | ...... | I. 191 |
| 1959 | 6 | Mar. | Notification, Holy Office | 51–271 | I. 608 |
| 1959 | 19 | Mar. | Allocution, John XXIII | ...... | I. 53 |
| 1959 | 4 | Apr. | Letter, John XXIII | 51–296 | I. 177 |
| 1959 | 16 | Apr. | Allocution, John XXIII | 51–307 | I. 177 |
| 1959 | 4 | May | Letter, John XXIII | 51–630 | I. 176 |
| 1959 | 1 | July | Letter, John XXIII | 51–634 | I. 178 |
| 1959 | 10 | July | Reply, S. C. Rit. | ...... | I. 544 |
| 1959 | 13 | Aug. | Decree, S. Paen. | 51–656 | I. 463 |
| 1959 | 17 | Nov. | Declaration, S. C. Sem. | 51–920 | I. 590 |
| 1959 | 24 | Nov. | Reply, S. C. Rel. | ...... | I. 596 |
| 1959 | 3 | Dec. | Decree, S. C. Conc. | 51–918 | I. 503 |
| 1960 | .. | .... | Faculties, S. C. Prop. Fid. | ...... | I. 30 |

| *Year* | *Day* | *Mon.* | *Document and Source* | *AAS* | *C. L. D.* |
|---|---|---|---|---|---|
| 1960 | 29 | Jan. | Indult, S. C. Prop. Fid. | ...... | I. 560 |
| 1960 | 13 | Feb. | Decree, S. C. Consist. | 52–420 | I. 55 |
| 1960 | 20 | Feb. | Letter, John XXIII | 52–147 | I. 178 |
| 1960 | 29 | Mar. | Letter, Ap. Del. U. S. | ...... | I. 290 |
| 1960 | 8 | Apr. | Letter, Ap. Del. U. S. | ...... | I. 290 |
| 1960 | 26 | July | Declaration, S. C. Rit. | 52–730 | I. 4 |
| 1960 | 27 | July | Letter, Holy Office | ...... | I. 205 |
| 1960 | 21 | Oct. | Decree, S. Paen. | 53–56 | I. 461 |
| 1961 | 2 | Feb. | Instruction, S. C. Rel. | ...... | I. 464 |
| 1961 | 14 | Feb. | Instruction, S. C. Rit. | 53–168 | I. 5 |
| 1961 | 28 | Feb. | Faculties, S. C. Prop. Fid. | ...... | I. 66 |
| 1961 | 13 | Mar. | Indult, S. C. Sacr. | ...... | I. 452 |
| 1961 | 14 | Mar. | Faculties, Ap. Nuncio | ...... | I. 66 |
| 1961 | 25 | Mar. | Instruction S. C. Rel. | 53–371 | I. 385 |
| 1961 | 28 | Apr. | Communication, S. C. Rel. | ...... | I. 498 |
| 1961 | 15 | July | *Monitum,* Holy Office | 53–571 | I. 43 |
| 1961 | 17 | July | Letter, Holy Office | ...... | I. 590 |
| 1961 | 20 | July | Reply, S. C. Rit. | ...... | I. 18 |
| 1961 | 31 | July | Letter, S. C. Rel. | ...... | I. 134 |
| 1961 | 20 | Sept. | Rescript, Holy Office | ...... | I. 441 |
| 1961 | 6 | Oct. | Letter, S. C. Rel. | ...... | I. 136 |
| 1961 | 21 | Oct. | Reply, Holy Office | 53–735 | I. 453 |
| 1961 | 13 | Nov. | Indult, S. C. Sacr. | ...... | I. 452 |
| 1961 | 25 | Nov. | Decree, S. Paen. | 53–827 | I. 462 |
| 1961 | 1 | Dec. | Indult, S. C. Conc. | ...... | I. 56 |
| 1961 | 7 | Dec. | Allocution, John XXIII | 53–815 | I. 53 |
| 1961 | 16 | Dec. | Reply, S. C. Prop. Fid. | ...... | I. 18 |
| 1961 | 16 | Dec. | Allocution, John XXIII | 54–32 | I. 139 |
| 1962 | 3 | Feb. | Reply, S. C. Conc. | ...... | I. 504 |
| 1962 | 16 | Feb. | Letter, Ap. Del. U. S. | ...... | I. 504 |
| 1962 | 28 | Feb. | Reply, S. C. Rit. | ...... | I. 19 |
| 1962 | 28 | Feb. | Norms, Holy Office | ...... | I. 607 |
| 1962 | 27 | Mar. | Letter, John XXIII | 54–385 | I. 177 |
| 1962 | 28 | Mar. | Letter, S. C. Rel. | ...... | I. 585 |
| 1962 | 30 | June | Notification, S. C. Rel. | ...... | I. 289 |
| 1962 | 30 | June | *Monitum,* Holy Office | 54–526 | I. 561 |
| 1962 | 9 | July | Reply, S. C. Rel. | ...... | I. 418 |
| 1962 | 16 | July | Letter, John XXIII | 54–566 | I. 177 |
| 1962 | 1 | Sept. | Allocution, John XXIII | 54–661 | I. 178 |
| 1962 | 2 | Oct. | Letter, Ap. Del. U. S. | ...... | I. 291 |
| 1962 | 15 | Nov. | Letter, S. C. Rel. | ...... | I. 137 |
| 1962 | 8 | Dec. | Letter, John XXIII | 55–444 | I. 177 |
| 1963 | 15 | Jan. | Letter, Ap. Del. U. S. | ...... | I. 291 |
| 1963 | 19 | Jan. | Indult, S. C. Sacr. | ...... | I. 453 |
| 1963 | 1 | Feb. | Rescript, S. C. Rit. | ...... | I. 19 |
| 1963 | 8 | Feb. | Allocution, John XXIII | 55–229 | I. 178 |
| 1963 | 27 | June | Letter, Paul VI | 55–736 | I. 177 |
| 1963 | 13 | July | Decree, S. C. Consist. | 55–656 | I. 618 |
| 1963 | 30 | Aug. | Allocution, Paul VI | 55–744 | I. 178 |
| 1963 | 24 | Sept. | Decree, S. C. Rit. | 55–838 | I. 53 |
| 1963 | 30 | Nov. | *Motu proprio,* Paul VI | 56–5 | I. 71 |
| 1963 | 4 | Dec. | Constitution, C. Vat. II | 56–97 | I. 20 |
| 1963 | 4 | Dec. | Decree, C. Vat. II | ...... | I. 597 |
| 1964 | 25 | Jan. | *Motu proprio,* Paul VI | 56–139 | I. 23 |

# GENERAL INDEX